NYE BEVAN

and the Mirage of British Socialism

NYE BEVAN
and the Mirage of British Socialism

John Campbell

WEIDENFELD AND NICOLSON · LONDON

TO PATRICK

© 1987 John Campbell

All rights reserved. No part of this
publication may be reproduced, stored in
a retrieval system, or transmitted, in
any form or by any means, electronic,
mechanical, photocopying, recording or
otherwise, without the prior permission
of the copyright owner.

First published in Great Britain by
Weidenfeld and Nicolson Ltd
91 Clapham High Street, London SW4 7TA

ISBN 0 297 78998 8

Printed in Great Britain at The Bath Press, Avon

268947

Contents

Contents

List of Illustrations

Acknowledgements

This is not an 'authorised' biography. The idea of taking a fresh look at Nye Bevan was entirely my own, and the book has been written without the material assistance of either his widow, Jennie Lee, or his literary executor, Michael Foot. I make no complaint about this. Jennie Lee was unwell when I approached her in 1983, and is anyway committed to a second volume of her memoirs; while Mr Foot told me at the outset of my work that he was already helping Dr David Smith of University College, Cardiff, with a similar project. In any case, since they have both already written at length about Bevan and the main purpose of my book was to attempt an alternative to their view of his career, I was not unduly worried. I must emphasise that they put no obstacles in my way; on the contrary, Mr Foot has been generous in allowing me to quote freely from Bevan's writings. Meanwhile there are advantages to a biographer in being under no obligation to his subject's family and friends.

On the other hand I am very grateful to those who have given of their time to talk to me about Bevan and about the politics of his time. In particular I should like to thank for their hospitality and kindness Lord Brockway; the Rt Hon Lord Strauss; Ian Mikardo, MP; the Rt Hon Roy Jenkins, MP; Mr John Pater; Miss Constance Cummings; and Mrs Anne Swingler.

Among historians I am grateful to Dr Kenneth Morgan for sharing with me some of his unequalled knowledge both of Welsh politics and of the 1945–51 Labour Government; to Dr Ben Pimlott likewise for numerous helpful conversations and invaluable hints; to Dr Charles Webster of the Wellcome Institute for two most illuminating seminars on the early years of the National Health Service; to Dr Philip Williamson for information and references on the period 1929–31; to Dr Kathleen Burk for the long-term loan of a number of books; and to Simon Burgess for sending me a chapter of his unfinished thesis. Above all I am grateful, as always, to Dr Paul Addison for his interest and encouragement throughout the project, for offering many suggestive insights, and for finding the time to read through the entire typescript at the end, saving me from many errors and some infelicities. Needless to say I am myself entirely responsible for any errors of fact or of judgement that remain.

I am grateful to the following for permission to quote from copyright material: Earl Attlee, for the Attlee papers; the British Library, for the Chuter Ede diary; the British Library of Political and Economic Science, for Hugh Dalton's diary and papers; the Rt Hon Michael Foot, MP, for a number of letters of Nye Bevan; the Rt Hon John Freeman, for a letter to

Acknowledgements

Hugh Dalton; Nuffield College, Oxford, for the Herbert Morrison papers and two interviews in the Nuffield Oral History project; the Rt Hon Lord Strauss for his Nuffield interview.

At Weidenfeld, it was Robert Baldock who commissioned the book. I am sorry that he had moved on before it was delivered, but correspondingly grateful to Juliet Gardiner for taking it over with such understanding, and also to Benjamin Buchan for his help with the pictures. I must also record once again my gratitude to my agent, Bruce Hunter, of David Higham Associates, for his continuing faith and encouragement.

I also gratefully acknowledge assistance from the Arts Council of Great Britain, whose timely bursary in 1985 kept me going when the book outran its contracted timetable.

As always, however, my greatest debt is to my wife Alison for her unfailing love and support, for keeping the children at bay and for her usual eagle-eyed scrutiny of the proofs. With this book completed, I am happy to pass back to her at least half of the burden of keeping us in gin.

JOHN CAMPBELL
August 1986

Introduction

It is more than a quarter of a century since Nye Bevan died. In his lifetime, right up to the onset of his final illness in 1959, he was the most colourful and controversial, the most loved and the most loathed political personality in Britain. By the time of his death in July 1960 he was widely recognised, by opponents as well as by his long-time supporters, as one of the most gifted and creative political leaders to have graced British politics this century – the equal in potential, if not in achievement, of David Lloyd George and Winston Churchill. And yet in the twenty-five years since his death no one has written directly about him except his adopted political son and faithful disciple, Michael Foot, and his fiercely loyal widow, Jennie Lee. Both have movingly recalled his abundant humanity and have eloquently described and refought the political battles which they shared with him. But no independent historian has tried to reassess him or attempted seriously to measure his impact on his times.*

Michael Foot's book has had the effect – possibly intentional – of warning off other writers who might have been drawn to the subject. It is a very big book, published in two fat volumes with a gap of eleven years between them; in its way it is authoritative and in its way it is brilliant. Inevitably it encouraged the idea that Bevan, as a subject for a biography, had been 'done'. And yet Foot's volumes are very far from being the last word on Bevan. They suffer very severely from the defects of their considerable qualities. All biographers necessarily wear a form of blinkers; they must narrate events to a great extent through their subject's eyes. But making every allowance for this natural sympathy, Foot's view of Bevan is quite exceptionally partisan. In the interests of drama and advocacy his account of complex political arguments is so slanted that his portrait, though wonderfully vivid, frequently tips over into hagiography. In his determination to vindicate Bevan he distorts and systematically misrepresents practically everyone else. As a result, his book, particularly his second volume, is best read as an episode in the eternal civil war within the Labour Party. This places a severe limitation on its usefulness as history. Even more seriously perhaps, from the narrower perspective of biography, Foot's view of Bevan substantially distorts and misrepresents

---

* There was one biography published during Bevan's life – a somewhat highly coloured study by Vincent Brome written at the height of the Bevanite crisis (*Aneurin Bevan*, Longman, 1953); and very soon after his death an American, Mark Krug, published a valiant attempt, little-noticed in this country, to explain the phenomenon of a British socialist to the Americans (*Aneurin Bevan: Cautious Rebel*, T. Yosseloff, New York, 1961). But that is all.

Bevan himself. The reason is that Foot's book is not merely an idealised biography, but a transferred autobiography.

It is not the intention of the present work to compete with Michael Foot in what his close association with his subject has enabled him to do uniquely well. I have not attempted to portray at any length Bevan the man, Bevan the dazzling conversationalist, Bevan the generous friend or Bevan the loving husband; still less am I out to expose private peccadilloes or – except where Jennie had a clear and direct influence on Nye's actions – probe the nature of his rare and remarkable marriage. To that extent it could be said that I have written less a fully rounded biography in the manner of – to cite the supreme recent example – Ben Pimlott's *Hugh Dalton* than a political study, couched in biographical form. What I have tried to do is to complement Michael Foot, not replace him. Whereas Foot wrote to a very great extent from his own knowledge and private information, I have relied predominantly on the written sources – not only *Hansard*, *Tribune* and other newspapers but the Cabinet papers for 1945–51 which were not available to Foot, and the diaries of Hugh Gaitskell (which Foot did not have), Hugh Dalton and Richard Crossman (which he used very selectively). I have tried to take a detached historian's look at the limitations as well as the strengths of Bevan as a politician; to trace the development of his political ideals and see how far they were realised and how they stood up to reality when put to the test; to judge Bevan, in other words, not emotionally but objectively as the principal exponent of a view of socialism which signally failed to recommend itself to the British Labour Party – not, I suggest, because of the folly, feebleness and treachery of Bevan's colleagues, as Foot contends, but quite simply because the party and the electorate, including his own class, could not be persuaded, even by his superb oratory, to share his vision. The sad, even tragic, fact which the biographer has to face is that Bevan's life – the immense achievement of the National Health Service notwithstanding – was essentially a failure, not because of the machinations of his pygmy rivals but because his great gifts were all his life in thrall to an erroneous dogma, with the result that he utterly misread what he most passionately believed himself to understand, the trend of history.

Michael Foot cannot face this, any more than Bevan could himself. So what he does is to evade it. This is where I believe he misrepresents his hero. For he chooses to present Bevan throughout his two volumes as a romantic rebel, heroically alone, but relishing the wilderness, battling for truth against the big battalions of wicked capital and craven labour: Bevan *contra mundum*, everyone out of step except our Nye. Clearly there were periods in his career when Bevan did cast himself in this light and there was a side of his character which responded to this role. But Foot plays up this aspect disproportionately, at the expense both of the strongly practical and realistic side of Bevan's nature and, I believe, of the dogmatic side.

Much of Bevan's potency as a politician derived from the unusual combination of these two characteristics.

It was his realism and practicality which first made his name as a union negotiator and local councillor in Tredegar; which kept him in the Labour Party in the thirties when others (including Jennie) were splitting off; which made him, to general amazement, a successful Minister after 1945; and which, in agonised conflict with his more impulsive instincts – played on, significantly, by Michael Foot and Jennie – held him back from leading a serious left-wing faction against Morrison and Gaitskell in the fifties. Though often in revolt, Bevan was never a happy rebel. His purpose in politics was the winning and using of power.

At the same time, underpinning both the realist and the rebel was an unwavering confidence, at once fierce and serene, in the inevitability of the supersession of a primitive, irrational and inefficient order of society – capitalism – by a superior, rational and efficient order – socialism. The foundation of Bevan's political thought was Marxist; he saw himself not as an inspired individual but as a scientific socialist, in step with history. He was not, of course, an orthodox Marxist; most of the superstructure of his thinking was highly unorthodox, not to say eccentric. In practice his humanity kept modifying his faith in the iron laws of historical determinism; in particular he was convinced that in Britain at least the class struggle could be won through the agency of Parliament. But Marx was the one intellectual mentor whom he unashamedly and frequently acknowledged, and it is not unfair to suggest that his theoretical education never got very far beyond Marx. Early on he evolved his personal mélange of democratic neo-Marxism, and for better or worse it served him throughout his whole career. It was the source both of his strength up to about 1950 and of his loss of direction thereafter when he began to realise that history was not working out according to plan.

Foot underplays Bevan's primitive Marxism, partly perhaps because he thought it tactful but more likely because it was his purpose – consciously or unconsciously – to annex Bevan to his own political tradition: the tradition of English Radical nonconformity. Foot's socialism is in fact another curious hybrid, in this case the bookish Asquithian Liberalism of his father Isaac overlaid with a romantic idealisation of revolt. His imagination thrills to the dates of the great European revolutions – 1789, 1848, 1917. His view of the English working class is derived from E.P. Thompson's celebration of brave but futile popular radicalism – millenarians, levellers and Chartists. Like his friend A.J.P. Taylor, but much more crudely, his sympathies are always with those whom Taylor dubbed the 'troublemakers' of English history – the insular dissenting tradition culminating in CND. Another characteristic hero of his (and Taylor's) personal pantheon is the sinister sprite of political irresponsibility, Lord Beaverbrook. Bevan, of course, as a young MP, also came under Beaverbrook's spell for a time. But he broke away. The point is that Foot is essentially opposition-minded, suspicious of power, happiest – as his ill-advised spell as Leader of the Opposition showed – as an irresponsible polemicist. As a result he underestimates that side of Bevan which was practical, constructive and government-minded. All his life Bevan was fascinated by the idea of Power – not primarily for himself, but for his class. In the pursuit of it he could be compromising; in the exercise of it he could be dictatorial. At other times the dazzling abstraction could blind him to the tiresome necessity of programme-making. But never did he doubt that power was something to be wrenched from those who had it and then used. Foot, on the contrary, instinctively prefers the righteous impotence of opposition. As a loyal disciple he found it hard at the time – in 1951 and still more in 1957 – to understand or (in the latter case) to forgive Bevan's susceptibility to the responsibilities of power; and as biographer he still found it hard in 1973. It is in projecting on to Bevan his own instinct to avoid the contamination of power that I believe that Foot to an important extent misrepresents his hero.

Yet it is just because Bevan was a more serious politician than Foot allows that his life must be written down finally as a failure. For twenty years after his death Foot's romantic rebel – his cult assiduously tended by his biographer, his widow and his self-appointed heirs – was regularly invoked as an inspiring and legitimising icon in the speeches of successive Labour leaders. As former Bevanites – Harold Wilson, Richard Crossman, Barbara Castle, eventually Foot himself – moved into positions of power in the party, dropping Bevan's name at every opportunity, it was possible to pretend that the spirit of Nye lived on and to believe that the principles he had fought for would now triumph. In fact, of course, all the Bevanite rhetoric was spurious. His former associates quoted Bevan and boasted their left-wing credentials to legitimise policies and courses of action directly opposed to everything he had stood for. But what they were recalling was his rare and unforgettable personality which, now that he was safely dead, could be represented in a woolly way as embodying the generous conscience of the party. They were invoking Bevan the man, not Bevan the socialist. His memory was in fact adopted as a sort of mascot to disguise the abandonment, by professed left-wingers, of practically everything he had meant by socialism.

Bevan had already lost the battle to make the Labour Party socialist long before he died. Indeed there had never really been a battle. In his whole life there were only two or three years, between 1931 and 1933, when the party leadership was in step with his ideas or the party could be said to have been moving his way. During the later thirties, when there was a substantial though fragmented left in British politics, led by Cripps within the Labour Party in shaky alliance with the Communists and the ILP outside it, the combination of Attlee, Dalton and Morrison in Parliament with the big trade unions under the thumb of Ernest Bevin still kept the party firmly on moderate lines while Bevan poured furious anathemas on them from the columns of *Tribune*. Throughout the war he was convinced, correctly but almost alone, that Labour's hour was about to strike; history was on the march and he was confident that the moment of transition to socialism was at hand. Yet when Labour's hour did strike, the transition was not to socialism but to a form of welfare capitalism. He welcomed this initially as a first instalment. Indeed as Minister of Health he was allowed to play a leading role in inaugurating the new consensus. As the creator of the National Health Service his name actually became indissolubly linked with its most characteristic achievement. But he knew that it was not socialism, and increasingly, even before Labour lost office in 1951, he knew that socialism was not going to come. And there was nothing he could do about it.

As the Conservatives consolidated their hold on power through the fifties and the Labour Party turned its face more and more firmly against any commitment to the fundamental transformation of society, Bevan became by turns angry, frustrated, bewildered and ultimately disillusioned. He tried to restate his philosophy for the 1950s, but only demonstrated that while the world had moved on since the thirties he had stood still. He continued to fight his corner within the party. Sometimes he was elected, on the sheer strength of his personality, to the Shadow Cabinet, and eventually he reached the Deputy Leadership; the party could not ignore him or afford to reject his oratorical gifts. But it steadily rejected his ideas. The party Conference loved him; the activists in the constituencies regularly voted him top of the popularity contest for the National Executive. He clung to the belief that if the party could only be released from the dominance of the trade unions it might yet be won, or won back, for socialism. But this was an irony, too. For it was part of his realism to know that Labour could only succeed as a mass party, the party of the organised working class, which meant a trade union party. Socialism meant nothing unless it was the triumph of the working class. And yet it was the organised workers who most consistently and vehemently rejected socialism. Practically the only followers he could find to back the cause of socialism were middle-class intellectuals – like Michael Foot. Thus the so-called 'Bevanite' movement which he found himself leading in the early fifties gave him little pleasure. Increasingly towards the end of his life he despaired of the British working class itself in which he had placed such faith. 'History gave them the chance,' he reflected in 1959. 'They didn't take it. Now it is probably too late.'[1] Sickened by Macmillan's 'affluent society', he believed that the British people had sold their socialist destiny in return for the short-term gratifications of fridges, cars and television sets. Even ten years earlier he had begun to fear that 'Our people have achieved material prosperity in excess of their moral stature'.[2] He died knowing that the idea for which he had lived had failed utterly to win the adherence of the class it was supposed to benefit.

It may be that this is why he has been so little written about, other than by Michael Foot. In Foot's 1,150 pages old socialists have been able to warm their memories of his eloquence, his brilliant phrasemaking and the rows with Gaitskell. But younger socialists have not wanted to know about his ideas. I think this is a pity, for his ideas have uncommon interest, if only as a vision of a road that Britain did not take. The reason that Bevan has not received more scholarly attention may be that he is seen as historically irrelevant. He is certainly very much a figure of his time: even in the fifties he was becoming an anachronism, and socialism of his sort today seems extraordinarily dated. This is despite the fact that in the last few years the Labour Party has come close to transforming itself, for the first time in its existence, into a truly socialist party. Since 1983 Neil Kinnock, while mouthing, like all his predecessors, pieties to Bevan, has been doing his best to reverse this process; but as a result of changes both in the composition of the party and in the constitution, the time when the parliamentary party could dictate to the constituency activists may now be passed. Whether Kinnock likes it or not, fundamentalist socialism is now back on the Labour Party's agenda.

But the new left-wingers are of a very different type from Bevan. Bevan was to the very core of his being a *democratic* socialist. The new socialists are not. He was philosophically a Marxist; but he believed passionately in Parliament. They on the contrary are essentially Leninists; they believe in the party. The difference is vital, for it illuminates the essential quality of Bevan's socialism which his successors do not share: his optimism. It was because he believed in the inevitability of socialism that he could confidently expect it to be achieved democratically. The working class was the majority of the country; therefore when the working class saw its interest correctly Parliament would provide the means for its conquest of power. The capitalist class would of course resist; but it could only do so by suspending democracy, which Bevan believed was a force too strong to be suppressed. Democracy in his view must inevitably lead to socialism. Very different are the views of today's left, who start from the recognition that socialism will not be achieved in the foreseeable future by the majority vote of the electorate and who therefore set themselves to acquire the power to impose it by controlling a party which, under a distorting electoral system, has a chance of winning power without a majority. (Even so good a democrat as Foot has explicitly opposed proportional representation on this ground.) The idea of socialism does not die, though it has been in such retreat for the past thirty years that it has practically been driven underground. What did die with Bevan was the self-confidence that could combine socialism with the humanity, individualism and faith in democracy for which his memory can still be cherished even by those who are not and never have been socialists.

Bevan has not been well served by his iconographers. Though he has been dead for only twenty-seven years, he seems already to belong more to mythology than to history. Yet the struggles, successes and ultimate disappointment of his career highlight with exceptional clarity the rise and fall of the idea of democratic socialism in this country. From the syndicalism of the early years of the century through the anti-fascism of the thirties to the false dawn of 1945 and the inexorable fading of the dream thereafter, no single life encapsulates the whole cycle so graphically. Bevan was in the thick of the struggle at every stage, arguing, protesting, prophesying and recriminating with unequalled articulacy and vigour. If any individual could have sold socialism to the British it was surely Bevan. He failed, yet for this very reason he remains an exceptionally potent, because symbolic, figure. The present book is an attempt to reclaim him for history.

1

The South Wales Coalfield, 1897–1929

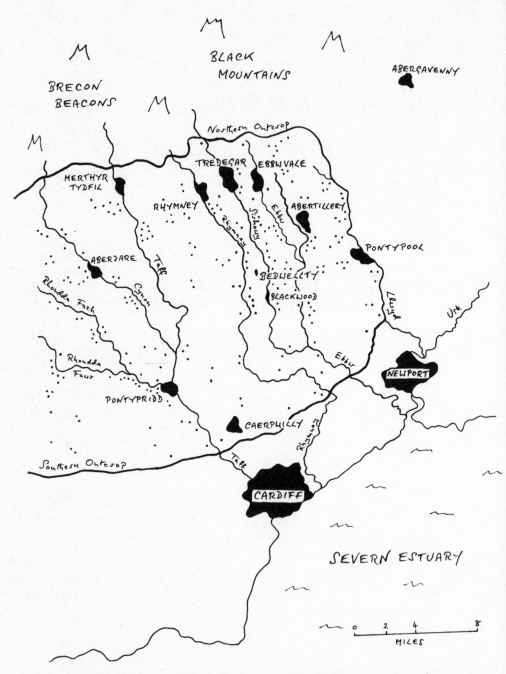

BRECON
BEACONS

BLACK
MOUNTAINS

ABERGAVENNY

Northern Outcrop

MERTHYR
TYDFIL

RHYMNEY

TREDEGAR

EBBW VALE

ABERTILLERY

Taff

Rhymney

Sirhowy

Ebbw

PONTYPOOL

ABERDARE

Cynon

BEDWELLTY

BLACKWOOD

Rhondda Fach

Llwyd

Usk

Rhondda
Fawr

Ebbw

NEWPORT

PONTYPRIDD

CAERPHILLY

Rhymney

Southern Outcrop

Taff

CARDIFF

SEVERN ESTUARY

0   2   4   8
MILES

MONMOUTHSHIRE AND EAST GLAMORGAN
showing the number of working collieries in 1913.

J.C.

Chapter 1

The Education of a Socialist

Tredegar is a typical small South Wales colliery town, situated at the head of the Sirhowy valley in western Monmouthshire, the middle one of a group of three parallel valleys running from the foothills of the Black Mountains in the north down towards Newport, twenty miles to the south. To the west is the Rhymney valley, dominated by Rhymney; beyond that lies Merthyr Tydfil, the Rhondda and the rest of the South Wales coalfield stretching another forty miles to Llanelli. To the east, divided from Tredegar by the bare Waunpond, is the Ebbw valley with Ebbw Vale at its head, and Abertillery; beyond there is only Pontypool, the easternmost valley of the coalfield, and then England.

The importance of this singular geography is twofold. On the one hand, the South Wales coalfield is the largest concentrated industrial region in Britain, an area of nearly a thousand square miles built upon just two industries, coal mining and iron and steel production. In the first two decades of this century the coalfield was at its zenith, producing about 50 million tons a year (mainly for export) and directly employing (in 1913) 230,000 men. Yet at the same time, within this densely concentrated area, mining is the most dispersed of industries, the individual valleys physically separated from one another, each pit with its own isolated and proudly independent community huddled around the workings; before the telephone and the motor car quite small towns like Tredegar (population around 20,000) acted as local centres; Cardiff and Newport, let alone London, were a world away.

The industrial geography dictated the political economy. In South Wales in 1900 there were only two classes that mattered. On one hand were the coal owners and their managers, once individual entrepreneurs but now increasingly grouped into large combines, who owned the pits, very often the nearby steel works, and most of the surrounding land and the houses in which the miners lived – thus, through their placemen on the local councils, extending their economic power into every corner of their employees' lives; on the other were the miners, organised from 1898 into the South Wales Miners' Federation, a workforce at once united and scattered, torn by the conflicting claims

3

of solidarity and local chauvinism. Here was, on paper, despite this frag-mentation, an almost perfect Marxist situation, ripe for class conflict, without the complicating ambiguities, social gradations and inter-union rivalries of other, industrially more mixed, regions. In South Wales, the SWMF *was* the labour movement. Far more than a trade union, the 'Fed' not only negotiated wages and working conditions but operated a sophisticated network of social services, covering health, education, recreation and welfare, for the whole working population. Above all it provided political leadership, at first in the local community, then on the wider national stage. From 1906, as the influence of Liberalism waned, it sent its leaders in increasing numbers to Westminster, where the miners' representatives easily predominated over all other groups in the emerging Labour Party. Coal was King, and the miners – nearly a tenth of the whole working population – were the acknowledged aristocrats of labour. In 1918, when Labour returned sixty-three Members to the House of Commons, twenty-three were miners and eight of those Welsh miners; even in 1945 the victorious Labour army still included forty-five miners, thirteen of them from the valleys of South Wales.

Aneurin Bevan was first elected an MP in 1929. The son of a miner, for nine years a miner himself, then a miners' agent, his career is at first sight indistinguishable from that of dozens of other SWMF MPs. His mining pedi-gree was unimpeachable; from that background, it is easy to say, he could only have been a socialist. Clearly his coalfield origins explain a lot, determined particularly the courses into which his life inevitably flowed and framed his perspective on the world beyond South Wales. Yet the more one looks at Bevan, the less does he seem to be explained by his background alone, the more he seems an entirely different sort of animal from all the others who followed the same road from the valleys to Westminster and Whitehall. Taken as a whole, with notable exceptions, the miners' MPs have been the solid ballast of the Parliamentary Labour Party, not its stars or leaders; they have been marked by moderation, loyalty and a certain dullness. In their company – and once he got to Westminster he was not in it more than he could help – Bevan stands out as an exotic, and not only in the extravagance of his personal lifestyle, pronounced though that was. Throughout his life, Bevan was characterised by two outstanding qualities, somewhat unusually combined: a remarkably sustained level of primitive *anger* at the capitalist system and all its consequences in human misery and degradation, and a rare and sophisticated self-taught *intellectualism* which took the form both of an unshakeable commitment to socialist theory and – paradoxically again – a philosopher's love of ideas for their own sake. These two qualities – though their roots can certainly be traced in the experience of the coalfield – place Bevan entirely outside the mainstream of the SWMF and indeed frequently threatened to carry him outside the Labour Party itself. He was, perhaps, more like a continental than a British socialist. To measure the difference one has only to compare Bevan with the only other Cabinet

Minister in the 1945 Government to share the South Wales mining background – James Griffiths from Llanelli, a few years older admittedly, but all his life the soul of gentleness, moderation and conciliation, a chapel-going, Welsh-speaking Welshman whose socialism was ethical and compassionate, not angry and theoretical. A few years older again, Arthur Jenkins, miners' agent, Monmouthshire County Councillor and MP for Pontypool, was another gentle soul; a decade younger than Bevan, George Thomas from Tonypandy, Speaker of the House of Commons in the 1970s, is yet a third, a devoutly Christian socialist. All these men – Griffiths, Jenkins, Thomas – in their different generations represented the Labour tradition of the valleys far more accurately than Bevan; for the Marxist class struggle did not after all take fire even in Wales, where the social conditions for it seemed in many ways so conducive.

So the question poses itself: where did Bevan spring from? He was at pains himself, in his only full-length book, *In Place of Fear*, to play down the role of personality. As a good socialist, he believed in historical forces, not in individuals. In the South Wales of his youth, he wrote, spurning autobiography, 'Individual ambition was overlaid by the social imperative. The streams of individual initiative therefore flowed along collective channels already formed for us by our environment.'[1] True enough: for a miner the 'Fed' represented the only ladder of advancement. But the passionate collectivist was an exceptional individual, touched with an awkward streak of genius. A compulsive rebel, he was all his life unwilling to subordinate his judgement to anyone else's, class enemy or comrade. For the deepest values of the labour movement – loyalty, unity, submission to majority decisions – he had a temperamental impatience bordering on contempt. The outstanding British socialist of his generation was personally, politically and intellectually the most ungovernable individualist. That conflict is the story of his life.

There was little enough in his family background to differentiate him from the crowd of miners' sons. Aneurin Bevan was born on 15 November 1897 at 32 Charles Street, Tredegar, one of a long row of typical four-roomed miners' cottages on the northern edge of the town. He was the sixth of ten children born to Phoebe and David Bevan, of whom only eight survived infancy and only six to adulthood – not an unusual ratio in those days, nor was it an unusually large family. He grew up, in practice, as the fourth child, preceded by Blodwen, William and Myfanwy and followed by Margaret May (who was to die in 1917), Iorwerth and Arianwen. Today such a size of family crammed into a four-roomed cottage seems intolerable, and it was certainly hard; but in South Wales at the turn of the century it was quite normal. The historian of the Tredegar Workmen's Institute is indignant at any suggestion that Bevan can be explained by childhood deprivation.

It is sheer legend that his surroundings were those of extreme poverty. His father was a mine worker, his mother a typical housewife of the mining valleys, keen, careful and persevering. The family was reared in circumstances similar to those in thousands of good-class working homes.[2]

David Bevan was in work; that was the main thing. And of course by the time the younger children were growing up, the elder ones were earning too. These were good years in the coalfield, relatively speaking. Phoebe, too, used to supplement the family income by dress-making, at one time employing six apprentices in her small front room. In 1906, when Aneurin was eight, they moved up the road to 7 Charles Street, a slightly larger house from which David Bevan built out another room at the back. He also installed a gas stove and an organ. This house boasted a bathroom, hot water and an inside toilet. There was room for not one but two uncles to come to stay. Most *bourgeois* of all, they bought the house with £130 of their own money.* So it was not a childhood of grinding poverty.

David Bevan, like so many of the Welsh miners of those days, seems to have been a gentle soul. He loved music and hymn-singing round the organ, wrote poetry and won prizes at *eisteddfodau*. Surprisingly, he failed to teach his children Welsh, and Aneurin at least could never sing. But the streak of poetry was certainly in him; and it was from his father that Aneurin learned his devouring love of books which, even in that extraordinarily literate self-educated community, typified by Tredegar's pride, the Workmen's Institute, first marked him out as something special. It was through his father, too, that he was first made aware of politics. David Bevan himself aspired no further than to be treasurer of his lodge; but he was a loyal union man who, when the miners first put up their own candidate in West Monmouthshire in 1906, naturally transferred his allegiance from Liberal to Labour and, under the influence of Robert Blatchford's weekly *Clarion*, became – in the warm-hearted and utopian fashion of the time – a socialist. When his son began to take up a more theoretical and aggressive socialism, he gave his quiet encouragement.

His wife was not so sure. Again like so many mothers, Phoebe Bevan nursed ambitions for her children, when they showed some sign of talent, that reached beyond the pit and union politics. Some accounts even see her as a staunch Conservative. Whatever she was, she was undoubtedly the dominating personality in the home, a strict disciplinarian and a formidably efficient housekeeper, skilled at making a little money go a long way (for instance by buying in bulk, whole sides of bacon or big tubs of butter). Of

---

* In 1937 Bevan remembered the sum as £40. Whatever they actually paid he did not consider it a good bargain. The pit workings underneath, he told the House of Commons, caused subsidence. 'We had to spend our spare evenings in putting up timber to keep up the roof.... The landlord, having taken out the kernel [i.e. the coal] wanted to sell the shell, that is to say the land' (House of Commons, 14 December 1937). The landlord was the coalowner, the second Lord Tredegar.

English stock – the daughter of a Radnorshire blacksmith who had found work in the Tredegar mines – she was a strongly built woman with an imposing manner: photographs leave no doubt that it was from his mother, not his slight and modest father, that Aneurin derived both his powerful physique and the proud thrust of the chin that characterised him throughout his life. Though his love of books was his father's – Phoebe had long ago 'lost the knack' of reading, if she ever had it – the determination, energy and practicality that drove Aneurin to try putting dreams and theories into effect was clearly inherited from his mother. These two sides of his personality could hardly be more obviously attributable.

And yet the bitterness is not explained; neither parent possessed Aneurin's explosive anger. It might be said that this came later, when the boy was old enough to learn to hate those whom he held responsible for the poverty and inequality he saw around him. But many others had the identical experience; and Bevan's anger was too deeply rooted in his personality to be explained solely by extraneous circumstances. It cannot be accounted for by his family life, which was warm and loving, nor by actual physical deprivation. He had enough to eat, and though the house was crowded, there was plenty of space outside in which to play: open country lay just across the road. Remembering the adult Bevan's loathing of big cities, it is important to emphasise that he was, in a real sense, a country boy. The mining communities are not truly urban, but *valleys*, with open hillsides between them. (The popular novel *How Green Was My Valley* makes the point.) Moreover Tredegar is at the very head of the Sirhowy valley, and Charles Street is at the top of the town. The mountain – more accurately, the bare heathery moors – came almost literally to his doorstep. From an early age they were his favourite escape: many years later he could recall in the House of Commons learning to swim in the moorland pools and tarns (though for the purposes of his argument he remembered it as a question of swimming from one decomposing sheep's carcase to another).[3] His was not a slum childhood, miserably eked out amid satanic mills, but quite normally healthy, active and happy – except for one thing: he suffered from a serious stammer.

Why he stammered it is impossible to say. A popular theory, which in Bevan's case has more plausibility than usual in view of his extreme clumsiness with his hands, is that he was naturally left-handed but was forced, as was common in those days, to write and throw with his right. But this his mother strenuously denied. Her explanation is that he developed it by imitating one of his uncles who came to stay; but this is utterly unconvincing. A deeper explanation, which his mother could not be expected to recognise, might be sought in her loss of two elder boys – Herbert, who died in infancy, and the eldest, David, who (though dates are hard to come by) died aged eight when Aneurin was either on the way or very small. Was she perhaps over-protective to the young Nye? (She lost yet another boy, Idris, before he was four.) Whatever the reason the handicap was crippling, particularly when he went to Sirhowy school, where an insensitive and bullying school-master made his life a misery (and doubtless encouraged the other boys to do the same). School cannot have caused the problem; but it undoubtedly made it worse. For an intelligent boy to be tongue-tied by inability to get his words out is a galling experience; to be treated as an idiot and barred from the fellowship of the playground leaves deep scars. What is extraordinary about Bevan is the way he overcame his difficulty. Though it made him hate school – and perhaps, by extension, all forms of authority for the rest of his life – it did not make him hate himself or in the least degree diminish his self-confidence. Instead it drove him not only to voracious reading – the normal recourse of the lonely or persecuted child – but, more unusually, to public speaking, first at Sunday school, later at lodge meetings, as a technique of mastering the demon by meeting it head on. On long walks with a friend or one of his sisters he used to practise declaiming large chunks of poetry; he became adept at the stammerer's device of using an alternative word when he might stick on the obvious one, and combed Roget's *Thesaurus* for grandiloquent synonyms – the more tongue-twisting, for purposes of practice, the better. Here, plainly, is the origin of the later Bevan's immense vocabulary, not always appropriate and often apparently pretentious. Here, too, in the need to escape the treacherous rhythms of everyday speech, is the explanation of his expansive rhetorical style. His great antagonist in later battles, Winston Churchill, developed his rather similar style by similar techniques for a similar reason. A handicap overcome became a source of strength. Whatever caused Bevan to stammer, and whatever scars his stammer left, the determination and ultimate success with which he faced, harnessed and practically eradicated it was the first revelation, and the first exertion, of an exceptional will.

It is tempting to link the frustration of his stammer to his taste for the favourite author of his boyhood, Jack London. Though he was as easily transported as any other young reader of the period by the patriotic adventure yarns of Henty, Rider Haggard and the rest, his imagination was fired particularly by London's nature-red-in-tooth-and-claw animal stories (*White Fang, The Call of the Wild*, etc.) and above all by his explicitly political novel of socialist revolution *The Iron Heel*, published in 1907 when Bevan was ten. In teaching himself to speak, he had always before him the model of London's idealised revolutionary hero Ernest Everhard. ('I wanted to see him mastering men in discussion, the war-note in his voice,' writes Everhard's adoring wife; 'to see him in all his certitude and strength shattering their complacency, shaking them out of the ruts of their thinking. What if he did swashbuckle? To use his own phrase, "it worked," it produced effects'.)[4] London's neo-Darwinian world of evolutionary struggle – animals fighting for survival, classes contending for hegemony in 'the organised wolf-pack of society'[5] – made an appeal to something very deep in Bevan; his assimilation of it was the foundation of his political thought. London's socialism led

Bevan on to Marx; but his work contains equally the seeds of fascism, and in London one can see the origin of Bevan's lifelong fascination with the concept of Power, a Promethean flame at present held by one class but there to be grasped by his own class if it only dared. 'There is the word,' gloats one of the capitalist oligarchs in *The Iron Heel*. 'It is the King of words – Power. Not God, not Mammon, but Power. Pour it over your tongue until it tingles with it. Power.' 'I agree with all that you have said,' Everhard replies. 'Power will be the arbiter, as it always has been the arbiter .... It does not matter whether it is in one year, ten or a thousand – your class shall be dragged down. We of the labor hosts have conned that word over till our minds are all a-tingle with it. Power. It is a kingly word.'[6] To most boys London's books were just good stories; but to Bevan they were the beginning of a philosophy – to the extent that, for much of his career, he seemed to be almost self-consciously acting out the life of Everhard.

For all his wide reading, Sirhowy school detected no conventional academic promise in the stuttering boy. It was his elder sister Myfanwy who won the prizes and a scholarship to the grammar school. There was, it seems, no doubt that Aneurin should follow his father and brother William down the pit. For two years from the age of eleven he worked after school as a butcher's boy, earning 2s 6d a week for long hours which involved staying open until midnight on Saturdays and one o'clock on Sundays. Then, on his thirteenth birthday, in November 1910, his childhood abruptly ended: he went to work in the Ty-Tryst colliery of the Tredegar Iron and Coal Company* for 1s 4½d a day.

Though Bevan worked as a miner, underground, for only nine years, they were the years in which he grew to manhood, and he never forgot them. He never forgot the darkness, vividly recalling in 1954 'the experience of a boy aged thirteen stumbling back in the dark to get his lamp relit' – an oil lamp, of course.[7] He never forgot the physical exhaustion: 'There is a tiredness which leads to stupor,' he wrote in 1932, 'which forms a dull persistent background to your consciousness. This is the tiredness of the miner, particularly of the boy of fourteen or fifteen who falls asleep over his meals and wakes up hours later to find that his evening has gone and there is nothing before him but bed and another day's wrestling with inert matter.' He claimed not to remember a meal at this time when he did not fall asleep at the table. He never forgot the danger: the 'runaway trams hurtling down the lines; frightened ponies kicking and mauling in the dark, explosions, fire, drowning'.[8]

> In our mine we had what we called a mane and tail, that is to say a steel rope attached to the journey of tubs or trams. This journey usually of 16 trams had to be let down a steep incline very quickly indeed in order to carry over the swamps down below, and the steel rope at the end used to flog the roof and sides

---

* The iron works had closed in 1898.

like a monster in the darkness. If it hit one, one was either mutilated or killed, and to hear the thuds of that rope in a narrow dark roadway was a very frightening experience.[9]

He recalled other experiences – like getting his foot stuck between the rails as a loaded tram approached – which, when he was nearly sixty, he claimed still gave him nightmares.

Nevertheless he was a good miner – strong, skilful and proud of his skill. From the point of view of his future, it was immensely important that he had done his stint at the coal face, sharing in close and equal companionship the hardships of those he came, in increasing personal comfort, to represent. These nine years gave him credentials which no critic could take away from him. More important, this was the narrow stage on which he first engaged with his lifelong enemy, taking on the coal owners on their own ground. Even as a boy, he quickly became known to the management as a trouble-maker, disputing with authority on the least pretext and defending his own, and others', rights with stubborn ingenuity. 'Never treat those people as if they are our superiors,' he told one friend. 'His impudence, his cheek, his brass was colossal', recalled another.[10] He studied the Mines Act and learned to use its small print to infuriate pit managers who expected their word to be law – particularly to insist on the observance of safety regulations more often ignored. At least twice he moved pits, first to the Bedwellty New Pits where he worked alongside his brother William, then to Pochin, a difficult pit where he was sent by the Company management after a characteristic incident: he was dismissed for refusing to unload a tram of rubbish, but appealed to the lodge and eventually proved victimisation, obliging the Company to find him another job. In this and other ways Bevan got himself known in all the pits around Tredegar, so that by 1916 he was already the chairman of his lodge – at nineteen, the youngest chairman in South Wales.

It was a good time to be a pit militant, a time of industrial and intellectual ferment in the coalfield. The old, moderate, politically 'Lib–Lab' leadership of the SWMF, epitomised by the redoubtable old patriarch 'Mabon' (William Abraham), was under challenge from a younger generation committed not merely to the Labour Party but increasingly to achieving socialism by indus-trial struggle. In 1910–11 – just at the time that Bevan started work – there was a long and bitter unofficial strike, as much against the timid official leader-ship as against the owners, in the Rhondda pits of the Cambrian Combine. (This was the occasion of the notorious Tonypandy riot.) The men's demand was for a minimum wage, so that those working difficult seams should not be unfairly penalised for their lower production. The Cambrian strike was defeated, but the following year the Miners' Federation of Great Britain reluctantly took the issue up nationally, and after a strike of only four weeks the Government rushed through the 1912 Minimum Wages Act, which did not establish a national minimum but did provide for regional minima. This the leaders accepted. A national ballot actually rejected it, but by less than the two-thirds majority needed to prolong the strike. The militants were disgusted. Their wholesale rejection of the leadership's philosophy of accommodation and conciliation was embodied in a famous pamphlet, *The Miners' Next Step*, which had originated in the Rhondda in 1911 but sold in thousands throughout the coalfields of the whole country in 1912. Its inspirer and principal author, Noah Ablett, the leader of South Wales syndicalism, was the hero and first intellectual mentor of Bevan's youth.

Ablett was an evangelist of aggressive Marxism, a Rhondda miner who had attended Ruskin College, in Oxford, but while there (in 1909) had led a protest strike against the insidious takeover of the working-men's college by the University; this resulted in the establishment of the Central Labour College (funded jointly by the SWMF and the NUR) as a properly class-conscious training-ground for the socialist vanguard, and the formation of the Plebs League to spread the word through the country. The message which Ablett and his followers preached was class war – 'the recognition of the war of interest between workers and employers':[11] a war that could only be waged and won by the workers themselves, industry by industry, at their place of work – not in Parliament. To those already engaged in industrial conflict on the ground, particularly in South Wales, where all that seemed to be needed for victory was solidarity, and to whom Parliament seemed infinitely distant and fatally corrupting of the principles of those who went there as representatives of the working class, this was an enticing doctrine. Socialism was in the workers' own reach. 'Why cross the river to fill the pail?' Ablett asked rhetorically.[12] The only obstacles holding the workers back were their leaders' cosy relationship with the employers and the federal structure of the union which divided the different regions and individual lodges from one another and prevented united action. *The Miners' Next Step* – and the strategy of the Unofficial Reform Committee which published it – was therefore addressed to reforming the structure of the MFGB by devolving power both upwards and downwards: downwards to the lodges, shifting the decision-making power from the centralised executive (in Wales, the SWMF) to the rank and file; and upwards to a national union (such as was finally achieved in 1945) which could link local strikes together, for maximum effect, as part of a unified national strategy to win control of the industry.

This was syndicalism, at least in its South Wales manifestation. In those heady days before 1914 and after, when the war seemed to offer a revolutionary opportunity and the Russian Revolution a model, Aneurin Bevan steeped himself in the writings not only of Ablett but of James Connolly, the Irish socialist; the American labour leaders Daniel de Leon and Eugene Debs; such continental syndicalists as were translated; and of Marx himself. All these he could borrow from the Workmen's Institute library in Tredegar. He was also a keen attender at Plebs League classes given fortnightly at Blackwood, seven miles down the valley, by Sydney Jones, chairman of the Abernant and Llanover joint lodge and one of the first graduates of the

Central Labour College, 'the first local theoretical Marxist'.[13] These classes were not all Marxism. Harold Finch (later MP for Bedwellty), for instance, remembers Jones setting them to summarise *Jane Eyre* – though doubtless from the appropriate slant. He remembers Bevan, not surprisingly, as 'the star of the class',[14] despite his stammer. Not content with the classes, the two of them used to go frequently to Jones's home for further discussions before Bevan had to catch the last train back to Tredegar. According to a correspondent who wrote indignantly to Michael Foot after the publication of his biography, Sydney Jones was the most direct influence upon the shaping of Bevan's mind, giving him the opportunity to test his ideas in argument – ideas in the widest sense, including philosophy, theories of creation, and religion. Under Jones's influence he went beyond the cautious agnosticism of most of those who were rejecting their chapel upbringing, to embrace the daring certainty of outright atheism. Above all, Jones's teaching supplied what Bevan, already an instinctive rebel, was seeking: 'a realistic doctrine of revolt', with the emphasis equally on all three words. The combination, when he found it, was what distinguished Bevan all his life from every other leading figure on the British left. He believed as firmly as any Communist in the importance of correct doctrine, but always as the foundation of effective action; at the same time, unlike so many members of the Labour Party, he never let realism choke the primal instinct to revolt; while unlike the ILP he had no time for righteous but impotent opposition as its own reward. Bevan's unique mixture of philosopher/politician/rebel took shape very early, in these Blackwood sessions with Sydney Jones.

Bevan opposed the 1914–18 war, but not actively; there was little active opposition in the valleys, though little enthusiasm either. He concentrated instead on union activity. Though Ablett and others had got themselves elected to the Executive, the SWMF Conference in 1912 had defeated the Unofficial Reform Committee's restructuring proposals: the tradition of local autonomy died hard. Bevan devoted himself instead to building up the scattered pits around Tredegar into a single Tredegar Combine Lodge, the biggest in South Wales, the better to be able to bargain with the single employer. The needs of war increased the nation's demand for coal and strengthened the militants' hand commensurately. In 1917, nineteen and unmarried, he was called up under the Government's conscription Act; but he managed both to get out of it and to make his defiance a useful platform for anti-war views. He was away on union business when his papers arrived; his sister Blodwen, so the story goes, threw them on the fire. The police came for him just as his younger sister Margaret May was dying; he went quietly and spent the night in a police cell – the only basis for his later boast that he had been to prison. When he eventually came before the magistrate he was able to prove that he was ineligible anyway because he suffered from the miners' eye disease, nystagmus; thus safe, he was able boldly to declare that he was not a conscientious objector but would choose his own enemy and his own battlefield and would not let the Government do it for him. The incident helped to spread his growing fame beyond his immediate valley.

By 1919 he was prominent enough to stand as one of Labour's sixteen candidates for the Tredegar District Council, against the still entrenched majority of 'Independents' – the Tredegar Coal and Iron Company's nominees. Like most of the others he lost – even in South Wales, Labour was still a fledgling upstart: the Tredegar branch was only founded in that year. But in his first election he polled a respectable 500 votes. Soon afterwards he sat the examination, held at Blackwood, for the SWMF scholarships to the Central Labour College. When the news came through that he had won one, he excitedly sought out his friend Harold Finch and they celebrated in a local café. For all his later disparagement of personal ambition, and indeed of the College, he was delighted at the prospect of continuing his education that now opened up. In the autumn of 1919 he left Wales for a two-year spell in London.

The Central Labour College occupied two large houses in Earl's Court, 11 and 13 Penywern Road, where it had moved from Oxford in 1912. It was reopened after the war by Noah Ablett himself (Chairman of the Board of Governors) with a full-time staff of about half a dozen and a fresh intake of twenty-nine students, of whom the great majority were South Wales miners: there were also two or three miners from other areas, six railwaymen sponsored by the NUR and one lone soul from the Dyers' and Bleachers' Federation. Many of them went on to prominent positions in the Labour Party or the trade unions: among the Welsh miners who came up that autumn, in addition to Bevan, was Jim Griffiths from Llanelli, Ness Edwards from Abertillery and Bryn Roberts from Rhymney. Under the new principal, W.W.Craik, the curriculum consisted of a series of lecture courses on the history of socialism, economics and finance (given by W.H.Mainwaring of the Rhondda, one of the authors of *The Miners' Next Step*), economic geography, philosophy and literature. Marxism was not a separate subject: rather the Marxist theory of knowledge and 'scientific method' as developed by Joseph Dietzgen permeated all the others. In addition there were lectures by notable visiting speakers like H.N.Brailsford, Frederick Pethick-Lawrence and J.T.Walton Newbold (in 1922 briefly the first Communist MP). The regime was intensive, the prevailing ethos dour and the life spartan. Bevan did not enjoy it.

He brought to the College, Principal Craik thought many years later, 'something of a hangover' from his dislike of school. In that whole generation of students he was the only 'problem child'. 'He found it difficult to conform with some of the College rules, like the time to get out of bed in the morning and down to breakfast; but then he was always late getting to bed!'[15] It was scarcely that he was not used to getting up early; but College breakfast and lectures had not the same imperative as the pithead hooter. Released from that tyranny, his instinct was to suit himself. He was equally slack about writing the required essays. His method of self-education was to talk far into the night, picking up from his fellow-students what they had learned from the lectures which he had very often cut, and testing it against his own ideas. He came to the College, a fellow student reminded Michael Foot, 'very young and raw, though with much debating verve and ability'.[16] He took to discipline reluctantly. Undoubtedly, however, the experience was good for him. For one thing, it brought him into contact for the first time (if only to a limited extent) with workers from other industries and other parts of the country, where the issues did not look so clear-cut as they could easily do in Wales. More specifically the teaching of the College confronted his romantic syndicalism with orthodox Marxist doctrine on the central role of the State; his passionate faith in the efficacy of direct action came up against the less sanguine belief of others, equally strongly argued, that the only sure road to socialism lay through Parliament. Bevan did not allow himself to be converted by these late-night debates at the time; but after two years he knew the arguments inside out when grim events in the coalfield began to change his mind.

His period at the Labour College cannot have been the waste of time he liked afterwards to make out. It had a number of side benefits. However much or little he derived from the lectures, he had for the first time in his life the luxury of time (and in his second year a room to himself) for serious reading, and a wider range of books than was available in Tredegar. He had also the opportunity to explore London, though he hated the size and anonymity of it and was frustrated by lack of money from enjoying its pleasures as he would have wished: he nevertheless managed – particularly when one of his sisters came up from Tredegar – to get to a number of theatres (including the famous Playfair revival of *The Beggar's Opera* and a visit to Covent Garden to see Pavlova) and lay the foundation of his later knowledge of music and painting. London gave him another new experience. The College expected its students in their second year to pass on what they had learned by giving evening classes in other parts of the city: this was a form of public speaking rather different from making speeches, and Bevan was initially nervous of it. He was helped, however, by the College's visiting elocution teacher, Miss Clara Bunn, who is credited by his contemporaries with helping him finally to overcome his stammer. In all these ways the College equipped him to return to Wales a more mature and rounded personality.

He certainly returned with the 'realistic doctrine of revolt' that he had sought in Blackwood greatly clarified. A talker rather than a writer, he contributed only once to *Plebs*, the magazine of the Labour college movement; and the article he did write, in his second year – an appreciation of the *Communist Manifesto* – was more in the nature of a student essay, possibly compulsory, than a piece of journalism. (The next issue featured Jim

Griffiths on *The 18th Brumaire of Louis Napoleon*.) It is nevertheless the only written record of his ideas at this age, and it well displays his self-confidence in taking what he wanted from a hallowed text and discarding the rest. 'The largeness of its conception,' he enthused conventionally enough, 'its profound philosophy and sure grasp of history, its aphorisms and its satire, all these make it a classic of literature, while the note of passionate revolt which pulses through it, no less than its critical appraisement of the forces of revolt, make it for all rebels an inspiration and a weapon.'

'The first portion,' he continued more specifically, 'treating of the development of the modern capitalist class and its counterpart the proletariat, is still the best and most convincing exposition of the Marxian point of view.'

> Here, for the first time the world learned of that conception of history by which the study of social development matured into a definite science. The Materialist Conception of History runs through the historical part of the *Manifesto* like a golden thread. The transient nature of capitalist society is emphasised, and in contradistinction to Utopian Socialism – the *rights* of the workers are shown to be in accord with their social *responsibilities*.

There follows an admirable paraphrase of Marx and Engels ('Marx points out that the means to end capitalism have been supplied by modern industrial development, and that this development has been the historic purpose of the capitalist epoch') culminating in the 'proof' that while 'previous revolutions in human history were essentially "minority" revolutions', property is now so concentrated 'that the subject class is able to see in the ruling class simply a personification of private property .... Consequently, the next revolution, the Social Revolution, will have for its main object the destruction of "all private property relations", and with this, the "division of society into classes will come to an end".'

From this fundamental analysis of the movement of history, Bevan never departed. The second and third sections of the *Manifesto*, however, he threw out right away. 'Because tactics must always be sought in the conditions immediately at hand,' he warned,

> the *Manifesto* is today tactically valueless, except in so far as a persistent stress upon first principles is of tactical importance .... We should be misunderstanding the spirit of its authors if we attempted for one moment to give its findings the rigidity of a dogma or to make it anything like a touchstone for all time.[17]

Assuming that Bevan did not take this straight from one of his lectures, there is remarkable maturity in the historical perspective here displayed. In its insistence simultaneously on the spirit of revolt, the importance of first principles and the necessity for flexibility in changing circumstances, this article expressed a set of views from which Bevan never deviated all his life. It shows that by the time he left the Labour College in 1921 his anger and his intellect had come together. His innate sense of working-class grievance and

15

working-class pride was now supported by a 'scientific' belief in the historical inevitability of progress towards the socialist organisation of society. Bevan's idea of socialism was already neither mere rebellion nor mere sentimental aspiration, but defiant, impatient, confident and contemptuous: *confident* in the march of history, but *impatient* to speed it up; *defiant* in the meantime towards the class that still ruled; *contemptuous* equally of those who sought to postpone their destined fate and of those of his own class too timid to put their shoulders to the wheel. Above all, as the *Plebs* article perfectly exemplifies, Bevan always saw his socialism as practical; what distinguished him was the boldness of his vision of what *was* practical.

The really great difference between Bevan and the other graduates of the Labour College who went on to careers in politics is that he, little as he liked the place, actually believed, and continued to believe, what he was taught there. Most of them, like Jim Griffiths, were just doing their homework for two years before going back into the real world and forgetting it; it is doubtful if Griffiths gave another thought to Marx or Louis Napoleon in all his life. Bevan, already predisposed by the influence of Ablett and Sydney Jones, accepted Marxism – on his own terms – as the foundation of all his thought (and was never embarrassed to proclaim it). He was in the strictest sense of the word a socialist. By his definition of first principles, he had good reason towards the end of his life to feel that most other leading members of the Labour Party were not and never had been.

Chapter 2

The Miners' Struggle

While Bevan was arguing strategy in London, the situation in the coalfield was changed utterly. Just before he left Tredegar in 1919, the outlook for the miners had looked bright. Demand for coal was enjoying a post-war boom and the MFGB had high hopes of converting wartime Government control of the industry into full nationalisation. When the Government proposed to hand the mines back to the owners, the Federation called a national strike; Lloyd George backed down and appointed instead a Royal Commission, headed by Mr Justice Sankey, to examine the industry, undertaking without qualification to implement its recommendations. The Commission divided along predictable lines, but the majority, including Sankey himself, recommended nationalisation. The miners thought their hour had come and celebrated – prematurely. The Government pleaded the lack of agreement as an excuse to go back on its pledge. Almost immediately the short-lived boom burst and the unemployment which was to blight the next twenty years descended over the old industrial heartlands of the country. The former aristocrats of labour were suddenly the poor relations, looking vainly to other unions for support. From its wartime zenith of prosperity and confidence, South Wales plunged in a few years to a nadir of poverty and despair. Defeated politically, the miners were now squeezed materially as the owners, competing for dwindling markets, used the discipline of unemployment to force down wages. The once powerful 'Fed' was crippled, as a futile strike in 1921 all too clearly showed. Membership declined from a high point of 200,000 to below 100,000; average daily wages fell from 21s 6¾d in February 1921 to 9s 5½d in October 1922 and continued to fall. Over the next fifteen years 241 pits were closed: this was in South Wales alone. The employed workforce was halved from 271,000 to 126,000, while the annual wages bill fell disproportionately from £65 million to £14 million.[1] In other words, while half the miners lost their jobs, the other half had their wages more than halved. These stark figures are not merely the background but the foreground, the all-enveloping inescapable reality against which the next, bitter, period of Bevan's struggle was waged.

Bevan never forgot or forgave the 1919–21 betrayal. In his 1944 pamphlet *Why Not Trust the Tories?* he held it up as a classic example of capitalist chicanery, a supposedly neutral Government blatantly taking the side of property in breach of its pledged word and the acknowledged national interest. 'It is by way of being a model of the working of the Tory mind in politics.... The Gentlemen's Party has never found itself to be too squeamish to lie, twist, deceive and betray in defending its property and privileges.' As a Marxist he could not be surprised: this was how capitalism under threat was bound to behave. By contrast, he maintained, 'the poor, under-educated miners were inspired by an idea' – not higher wages alone but 'the application of new social principles to coal mining'. They represented the future. 'But the products of the Public Schools, of our Universities, the "cream" of society, buried their snouts in the swill of the trough. And they won.'[2]

According to his own account in *In Place of Fear*, it was this defeat which convinced Bevan that syndicalism was dead. He tells the famous story of Lloyd George facing down the leaders of the Triple Alliance (miners, transport workers and railwaymen) by telling them that if they defeated the Government they must be prepared to take over the functions of the State themselves: 'Gentlemen .... Have you considered, and if you have, are you ready?'[3] In fact, the evidence of his contemporaries at the Labour College is that he was still arguing for direct action all the time he was there. It was only when he got back to Wales that he saw for himself that the industrial weapon had broken in the workers' hands. 'Mass unemployment was a grim school,' he wrote. 'Industrial power was just what the unemployed did not possess. To render industry idle as a means of achieving political victory was hardly an effective weapon in such circumstances. Capitalism had already done it for us.'[4] The analysis was irrefutable: political victory would have to be achieved the hard way after all, through Parliament. Even so, Bevan was slow to accept it: it took the failure of the 1926 strike to complete his conversion.

In the meantime his personal circumstances were as grim as those around him. He had gone to London a skilled miner, with no thought that he might not be able to get work again on his return. But he came back to Tredegar as just one more recruit to the army of the unemployed. It is probably true that his record told against him: the Company was naturally in no hurry to employ a prominent trouble-maker if it did not have to. But Bevan insisted on rejoining the union and remaining a registered miner, despite his nystagmus, which would have been a perfectly good reason for trying another trade. The 'Fed' was his only possible power base; and indeed, after more than two years of idleness broken only by periods of digging gas mains to qualify for insurance benefit ('Never in the history of mankind', he recalled many years later, 'did so many people lay so few pipes'),[5] his former comrades elected him checkweighman at Bedwellty New Pits. (The checkweighman was a key official at every pit, elected by the men to check the employers' production figures.) After only ten months, however, the Bedwellty pits closed, and he found himself back on the dole.

This paid about ten shillings a week, a poor enough contribution to the family budget; but even this was stopped when his sister Arianwen got a job as a typist earning £2 a week, from which eleven shillings each was supposed to be deducted to keep her mother and unemployed brother. (Aneurin was now the only one left at home, and David Bevan had been forced to give up work by the pneumoconiosis which was soon to kill him.) This was one of the sharpest experiences of Bevan's life. He always insisted that it caused no bitterness between himself and Arianwen, but he was acutely conscious of the humiliation which fathers and brothers felt at having to live on the earnings of their daughters or sisters, or their luckier sons or brothers, and in all his denunciations of the more elaborate family means test of the thirties he never failed to describe his own experience; unquestionably it left a painful scar.

He considered the option of emigration which was tempting so many who saw no future in the coalfield to try making a fresh start in Australia or Canada. Though he decided in the end, as he recalled in *In Place of Fear*, to stay and fight ('I can't bear the thought of seeing them win over us'),[6] he was not at the time so positive about it as he later became; for in speeches in the House of Commons in the thirties attacking assisted emigration as a confidence trick which tore unemployed men from their roots only to cast them still unemployed and worse off than ever on the other side of the world, he confessed that he had, in the twenties, chaired meetings at which young men were encouraged by various Government agencies to take the risk, and regretted that he had ever lent the emigration movement his support.[7] He must have thought seriously about going himself.

Having decided to stay, however, he lost no time in getting into the thick of the fight, using his own experience of unemployment skilfully as a weapon on behalf of others. From arguments about his own entitlement to benefit he moved on to a successful fight to win sickness benefit for his father, and by extension became a sort of local ombudsman taking up and arguing with the Board of Guardians or the Company the benefit or the compensation to which they were entitled. It is at this time that his mother is supposed to have wondered if he could not have made a career in the law. But he was always too political for the Bar. His great skill lay in demanding a claimant's rights by expert legal argument while using the opportunity simultaneously to agitate against the injustice of the system: a difficult trick to bring off.

There seems to be no doubt, despite his own recollection that he was one of the leaders, that Bevan did not take part in the most dramatic local demonstration against the Poor Law system, when a large crowd besieged the Guardians for eighteen hours in the Tredegar workhouse in January 1923; but only because he was away at a union conference at the time. He very quickly established himself as a leader in every other sphere. Immediately on

19

his return from London in 1921 he formed, with his great friend Archie Lush and others, a political discussion group called the Query Club whose members formed a semi-secret cell on the trades council, in the Combine Lodge and in the Labour Party to ginger up the older men on all the principal representative bodies in the town. In April 1922, three years after his first attempt, Bevan succeeded in being elected to the District Council, fourth of four members elected for the West ward, behind three 'Independents' but ahead of three other Labour candidates including two councillors, in what was generally, despite the slump, a bad year for Labour: its representation on the Council fell to only two – the new boy Bevan and one older man.[8]

As a councillor, Bevan was most energetic in those fields for which in 1945–51 he would have national responsibility – housing and public health. These years were therefore a valuable training for the later peak of his career. Those who in 1945 thought him an ignorant ranter forgot this limited but relevant experience. He had, of course, no administrative responsibility; but he learned at first hand what could and what could not be done, and he was particularly active in pressing the Council to make maximum use of the 1924 Wheatley Act (the principal legislative achievement of the first Labour Government) by which central government for the first time subsidised local authority house-building as a social service. He anticipated one of his most characteristic concerns as Minister by insisting that the Council should build, not so-called 'workmen's houses', but houses of a decent size and quality. 'Rabbit-warren accommodation', he urged (exactly as he argued in Cabinet twenty years later), 'leads to a rabbit-warren mind.'[9] He always believed, as a matter of principle, that only the best was good enough for working people: to accept anything less was to concede the battle.

On the public health side, it was easy to lay everything at the door of the Tredegar Iron and Coal Company. Since the Company owned most of the existing housing, it was responsible for the insanitary living conditions; since it owned most of the land, it was responsible for the purity of the water supply; since it was the principal local employer, it was responsible for the high local rate of tuberculosis, nystagmus and other miners' diseases. In the Council Chamber, in the persons of the thirteen 'Independents' who formed the majority, Bevan had the Company permanently in his sights. Being unemployed, he was able to operate practically as a full-time politician, pursuing the hydra-headed enemy at every turn. After three years, in April 1925, he was re-elected top of the poll, with more than double his previous vote and another Labour colleague in second place (though the party's representation overall rose only to five), and won the usually grudging praise of the *South Wales Argus* which conceded that the youngest member of the Council 'has done valuable work' and tipped him for 'a great future'.[10]

But the Council was only one arena among many. That was where he practised the arts of opposition; but within the union's embryo Welfare State Bevan learned administration. He had been a member of the committee of the

Workmen's Institute even before he went to London: he took, naturally, a special interest in the library and in 1924 became chairman of the Book Committee and nursed it as his own. In a sense it was his own, since in recognition of his knowledge and his increasingly extensive travelling on union business, he was given unprecedented authority to buy for the library, on his own judgement, any book he thought of educational value.[11] Soon he was spending £300 a year. By 1930 the library had 70,000 volumes;[12] borrowing was at a rate of about 60,000 a year (that is an average of nearly three a year for every man, woman and child in the population). The subscription was 2d a week; but the unemployed paid nothing. In 1926 Bevan proudly opened a second branch Institute, claiming Tredegar's as the best library of any mining town in South Wales. Despite the depression, indeed to help alleviate it, the Institute continued to expand throughout the inter-war years, though after he became MP it was necessarily under Bevan's close patronage rather than his direction. In 1931 a new book room was added, with open access, and a bigger billiard room, with seven tables instead of two; in 1934 two more branches were opened; and in 1937 the old Temperance Hall was entirely rebuilt with an 800-seat cinema (also used for meetings and shows). Offering more and more varied activities, the Institute was the focus of town life and to Bevan an ideal of community socialism.

The pushy young members of the Query Club had to fight to take over the Workmen's Institute (Archie Lush became Chairman in 1927), and still more to win control of the Tredegar Medical Aid Society, where the Company not only had its nominee among the miners but was formally represented on the committee. Here again the anticipation, on a local scale, of the principle of the National Health Service is striking. Miners and steelworkers paid 3d in the £, deducted from their earnings, while other workers, teachers, shopkeepers and the like, paid a larger subscription direct to the Society, which entitled them to free medical treatment and hospital facilities. The Society employed its own doctors, six of them – to the extreme annoyance of the BMA, which disapproved of the inversion of the normally dependent relationship of patient to doctor and, as Bevan discovered in 1946, strongly objected to doctors being employed by anyone.[13] Once again, in his membership of both the committee of the Medical Aid Society and the local Hospitals Committee, he gained a valuable apprenticeship in both medical administration and medical politics, as well as the opportunity to work for better standards of treatment for working people.*

Finally there was the union itself. Bevan took a leading part in reconstituting the Tredegar Combine Lodge, which he had helped to form during the war, and became Chairman of the Executive, as well as Chairman of the Tredegar Valley Miners' Welfare Committee. The latter position

* Many years later Bevan claimed in the House of Commons that the Tredegar Medical Aid Society was the model for the similar society portrayed in A.J.Cronin's popular novel *The Citadel* (House of Commons, 30 July 1958: *Hansard*, vol. 592, cols 1382–98).

thrust on him a major responsibility in the great lock-out of 1926. At the beginning of that year, however, before the General Strike, his years of unemployment came to an end when he was elected to a specially created paid job as Disputes Agent for the lodge, at a salary of £5 a week raised by a penny-a-week levy on members. Simultaneously he moved, with his mother and sister Arianwen – his father had died in his arms in February 1925 – from Charles Street to Beaufort House in Commercial Street in the centre of Tredegar, where Aneurin was able to have the front room as an office, complete with telephone: Arianwen acted as his secretary. He was now, in addition to everything else he had been doing voluntarily, a fully-fledged trade union official.

Nineteen twenty-six saw the climax – a desperate and ultimately bitter climax – of the miners' fight against the inexorable decline of their industry. Since the war, the world markets that had once supported more than a million British miners had been lost; shipping was increasingly oil- instead of coal-fired; and British coal, mined in increasingly difficult pits by increasingly old-fashioned methods, was becoming too expensive to sell. Resisting the sort of amalgamation and rationalisation recommended by the Sankey Commission, and lacking or begrudging the capital or the will to invest in new equipment, the coal owners' only answer was to try once again to reduce costs by squeezing wages. In 1925 the Baldwin Government wilfully exacerbated the situation by returning the pound to the international gold standard at its pre-war parity against the dollar, thus further raising export prices, including that of coal. The miners dug in to defend what was left of their standard of living, with the support of the TUC, and won a temporary respite: unprepared for a General Strike, the Government retreated, appointed another Royal Commission under Herbert Samuel and in the meantime maintained wages by a nine-month subsidy while it looked to its emergency powers. In May 1926 the subsidy ran out. The owners moved at once, both to cut wages and at the same time to increase hours. The MFGB struck; and for nine days that have passed into national and labour folklore, the TUC called other key workers out in their support.

To Bevan, writing many years later, the General Strike was 'like watching a film unfold that I had already seen made'. The events of 1919–21 had already shown that the cautious bureaucrats of the TUC 'were theoretically unprepared for the implications' of a political strike. 'They had forged a revolutionary weapon without having a revolutionary intention'.[14] Their action in 1926 was indeed nothing more than a gesture of sympathy, quickly called off as soon as the Government stood firmly on its constitutional authority. But in South Wales, at the time, it was possible to believe that the labour movement really had nerved itself to a trial of its industrial strength; for in the coalfield the strike was virtually total. Such was the simplified class structure and the social predominance of the miners' union that the whole middle class of shopkeepers and tradesmen, teachers and ministers, identified downwards, with the strikers, more solidly than in any other part of the country.[15] The Government's emergency provisions – the Organisation for the Maintenance of Supplies – simply were not applied: the miners ran their communities themselves through their strike committees. And in Tredegar, who should have been the chairman of the Council of Action but the twenty-eight-year-old Aneurin Bevan? For nine days not a lorry moved in the town without his permission, sitting with the colleagues in virtually permanent session in the Institute. The police stood by to intervene, but there was no trouble. For a brief syndicalist moment, the 'Fed''s writ was unchallenged. Then, in London, the TUC gave in and the miners, betrayed again, were on their own.

Now Bevan's Council of Action was turned into a relief committee. Its principal tasks were the distribution of strike pay and the organisation of soup kitchens. Belatedly, some members of the 'Independent' majority on the Town Council protested that Bevan had pre-empted functions which should have belonged to the Council. But they could not pretend that they could have discharged them better. 'The system of feeding', the *Argus* commented, 'is admirable and ideal.' 'The fact is', a councillor admitted, 'Aneurin Bevan has been too smart for us. We are absolutely whacked.'[16] In addition to feeding the miners and their families, Bevan's committee raised both money and morale by organising concerts and other entertainments in the Institute and by sending male voice choirs around the country; he even – much as he abhorred charity – solicited gifts of clothes from the Quakers. This was the stiffest test so far of his administrative capacity; once again he passed it with tributes from all sides, so that Tredegar survived the seven-month ordeal of the lock-out better than many towns.

At the same time he was just as deeply involved with the political side of the dispute, both locally and nationally. In Tredegar he was strong in upholding the authority of the union and ruthless in suppressing the least sign of blacklegging – miners scouring the hillsides or working exposed outcrops of coal to sell on their own initiative, for instance – by force when necessary. Nationally, he attended all but one of the almost continuous delegate conferences and – though South Wales alone sent some forty delegates – spoke at every one he attended, taking an uncompromising line against any weakening of the strike. Already by midsummer there was a drift back to work in some of the less militant areas (notably, as always, Nottinghamshire). In July the churches intervened with a compromise plan which the Miners' Executive initially accepted. South Wales and Durham, however, insisted that it be put to a ballot (which subsequently rejected it). Bevan, in his first intervention, was vehement in condemning the leadership's 'defeatism'. 'Many of us remember 1921,' he told the Conference. 'Some of the younger ones remember even more than the older men.... It would be better for our men to be defeated as a conse-

23

quence of their own physical exhaustion than ... as a consequence of any moves we are taking.' Surrender now, he maintained, would shatter the union for years to come.[17]

The result of the ballot confirmed Bevan's faith in the ordinary miners. 'At the limit of their material exhaustion,' he argued in August, 'there is sufficient spirit in the rank and file to reject the advice of the leaders and conduct a policy in advance of what has been seen here.... It is the duty of the conference to try as hard as possible to find ways and means to give effect to the instructions of the rank and file to continue this struggle further.' By even debating publicly whether to 'throw up the sponge' the leaders weakened their own hand. An attitude of strength was 'more likely to elicit overtures from the other side than an attitude of panic.... I suggest if there is nothing else left a good deal of bluff can be put up yet. There are still possibilities of bluff, and not negotiations which are conducted in the spirit of a funeral march to the cemetery.'[18]

Bluff or substance, the militant South Wales delegation took the lead in early October in raising the stakes by carrying a resolution calling for a more fighting policy including – the miners' last card – withdrawal of the safety men who maintained the pits. District negotiations, Bevan declared, gave away the whole case. 'Once you start negotiating', he warned A.J.Cook, the militant leader whom he suspected of weakening, 'you are not going to be worth the snap of a finger.' If the 800,000 men still out had not succeeded, 'then what hope have the 150,000 in South Wales?... I suggest to you, you public men and leaders of long standing, if 800,000 have no power to obtain far better terms than we have got, then I suggest we ought to go back to the districts and tell them that Trade Unionism is no longer able to accomplish anything.' He admitted that 'the outlook is by no means bright'. He blamed 'the obduracy and cynical disregard of the other unions'. But he still defiantly insisted: 'If we are going to go down, at least in going down let us inflict the maximum damage on the enemy inside as well as outside.... To negotiate now is to throw away what power we have.' He still believed that if the other unions and the Labour Party would only help, the owners and the Government could yet be persuaded that 'the price they have to pay for bringing out the Miners' Federation is too heavy and in the end they will be forced to give to us more reasonable terms'.[19]

Between this conference and the next Bevan went on a speaking tour of the Nottinghamshire coalfield, where he saw for himself that not all districts were as solid as South Wales. As a result, with some personal courage, he reversed his position. 'I believe a man ought not to slavishly follow a policy merely because he has said it before,' he explained. He still thought the South Wales resolution had been right; but he now held that, 'due entirely to the militancy of the attitude adopted at the last Conference ... we have reached the meridian of our negotiating power'.

Dramatically, he distanced himself from his friend and former ally, the Rhondda Communist Arthur Horner. 'Even our friend Horner would not claim at the end of the month to be in any stronger position than we are now.' 'I do claim it,' interjected Horner. 'Well – you might claim it but nobody would give you what you claim,' Bevan retorted. The federal structure of the union was cracking. 'I come from strong men: my own men could stand until Christmas, but what is the use of arguing like that when this organisation, as a whole, is hopeless and will smash our weak areas?... What is the use of talking about an army when it is a paper one?' That being so, Bevan argued, the leadership should now negotiate; but – and here he gave the argument his own distinctive twist – it should *not* go back to the districts to seek authority to negotiate.

> I say that we ought not to broadcast our weakness in that way. If we are leading an army, that army must be led on the basis of military principles and not on the basis of democratic principles, because the time taken in going back to the men and telling your men we must enter into negotiations, the act of doing that destroys the act of negotiating.

The time had come for delegates to face up to, and not abdicate, their responsibility.[20]

This was at once too brutal and too subtle for the Conference; but it showed a sound appreciation of the realities. While the Executive consulted the men, the unofficial drift back to work gathered pace as men saw the writing on the wall and feared that there would be fewer jobs to go back to; the unions' negotiating position was crumbling day by day.* At yet another conference the following week (13 November) Bevan condemned the decision to ballot as 'moral and mental cowardice' and despairingly proposed 'massed demonstrations against the Government' which might end in 'some going to gaol for a few months' ('I would rather be there,' he added) but offered more hope of 'arousing the imagination of the workers of the country to our help' – a vain hope at this stage – than a policy of piecemeal surrender.[21] At the very last Conference before the final capitulation he had come round to arguing, in what the Vice-President rightly called 'a very complicated speech', that district negotiations were, after all, the level at which the rank and file could best be mobilised in defence of district practices and customs; but district negotiations within a national framework, with no return to work until the district agreements had been nationally approved.[22]

---

* As in 1926, so in 1984–5. Just as in both strikes Nottinghamshire was the weakest area, with the breakaway 'Spencer' union of 1926 reborn in the Union of Democratic Miners in 1985, so in both struggles South Wales was both the most solidly militant area and the first to call for a disciplined return to work when defeat was certain. Tradition in the coalfields dies hard.

District agreements it was in the end, but with only the barest national guidelines. Even in South Wales, the return to work became unstoppable and the local ballot eventually showed a majority of 50,000 to 27,000 in favour of accepting terms worse than had been available in May. The SWMF, in the words of its historian, Ness Edwards, 'had become a ghost'.

> The new South Wales agreement was dictated by the owners and was signed on 13 December. The SWMF entered the fight as an army and ended it as a rabble. This was not fighting, but a massacre.[23]

The terms, in South Wales as over the whole country, involved lower wages, longer hours and worse conditions. The national average rate per man shift – 10s 5d in May – was cut immediately only to 10s 0¾d; but so exhausted was the union by its defeat that it could not prevent a further steep fall in 1928 to 9s 3½d. The long struggle thus ended in unmitigated disaster for the miners and their families. The refusal of Baldwin's Government to impose any compromise on the owners in respect of either wages and hours or amalgamations bears a heavy share of the blame; but some also belongs to the intransigence of the miners themselves, who could have made it more difficult for the Government, and perhaps saved something from the wreck, by showing more flexibility when they still had some strength to bargain with. Bevan, misled by the exceptional solidarity of South Wales and by his own lingering romantic faith in syndicalism, preached intransigence almost to the very end. The miners' negotiating power had actually passed its meridian about four months before he recognised it. His swift reversal when he did recognise it, however, exemplified the agility of his mind. Within his fixed long-term view of historical development he was always ready to be flexible about short-term operational tactics, and his speeches throughout the long strike – both before and after his switch – demonstrate a sophisticated concern with how to maximise and concentrate the persuasive power he passionately believed the miners to possess, but which he always feared the leaders, by their reluctance to lead, were dissipating. Even in his extremism, he showed a realism which was lacking in, for instance, Arthur Horner.

Nevertheless that realism told him that the industrial struggle was over. 'The defeat ended a phase,' he wrote in *In Place of Fear*, 'and from then on the pendulum swung sharply to political action. It seemed to us that we must try to regain in Parliament what we had lost on the industrial battlefield.'[24] For the remainder of his life – often to the bewilderment of friends and foes who found a parliamentary Marxist hard to understand – Bevan's dedication to the parliamentary road was unswerving. But it was not only the failure of the General Strike which drove home at this time the lesson that it was in Parliament that power lay. In 1927 the long arm of Westminster reached out to take from Tredegar the power to look after its own poor. Seen from the Ministry of Health in London, Neville Chamberlain's Board of Guardians (Default) Act was an overdue assertion of elementary financial discipline. In the five years since 1921 the Bedwellty Union (which included Tredegar, Rhymney and Ebbw Vale) had paid out to the unemployed who had exhausted their covenanted benefit over £1 million in Poor Relief. The Board was in debt for no less than £976,000.[25] London decided that the scales paid had been too generous, suspended the elected Guardians who had been guilty of this extravagance and, under the new Act, sent in civil service commissioners who both tightened the criteria for eligibility (so that nine-tenths of those previously receiving benefit now got none) and slashed the rates of benefit (to an average of just 2s 9d a week).[26] The cruel logic was that it was the poorest areas of the country, suffering the heaviest unemployment, which had not the resources from the rates to be able to pay adequate relief without borrowing; in these poorest areas – the Act was also applied to West Ham in London and Chester-le-Street in County Durham – the Government intervened, not to ease the disproportionate burden of misery and degradation by sharing it with other areas that were less hard-hit, but to aggravate it.

Nothing in the whole bitter experience of the inter-war years enraged Bevan more than this deliberate punishment of communities that were already nearly starving. Neville Chamberlain, the author of this bureaucratic inhumanity, was marked down as the object of his special hatred. Not that the Poor Law was perfect – quite the contrary. Bevan was naturally all in favour of central government taking over the responsibility for protecting the helpless victims of the country's economic difficulties and placing the burden on the national Exchequer where it belonged. Depressed areas like the South Wales and Durham coalfields could not be expected to protect themselves. But at least the Poor Law placed the responsibility for administering benefit on locally elected people who knew the conditions they were trying to relieve and were to some degree accountable – if only to the extent that they could be locked in their workhouse by an angry mob. Chamberlain replaced them with the faceless rule of unelected officials ('a new race of robbers', Bevan called them)[27] accountable to no one but himself. It became one of Bevan's most insistent themes over the next ten years that the Tories were trying to take unemployment out of politics by denying the unemployed their democratic voice. Democracy began to loom as large as socialism in his vocabulary.

His conversion to the parliamentary road was despite the fact that the present parliamentary leadership was, from a socialist point of view, so feeble. Ramsay MacDonald's 1924 experiment of taking office without a majority in order to establish Labour's 'fitness to govern' may have been electorally astute, but it was too apologetic for those, like Bevan, who had never doubted it and already suspected MacDonald of blunting Labour's socialist purpose in an attempt to win Liberal votes and Establishment approval. The Government had only been in office a few weeks before Bevan was urging, at a knife-and-fork tea to celebrate the return of Evan

Davies as MP for Ebbw Vale, that it should either get on or get out. 'A disastrous blow would be struck at the heart of the movement', he maintained, 'if the Government remains in office longer than is necessary for immediate requirements.... If the Government cannot put a policy into effect for dealing with the country's economic problems, the sooner it gives up the better. The Government must not cling to office for the sake of office.'[28] At the 1925 Labour Party Conference, Ernest Bevin tried to commit the party never again to take office without a majority. There is every reason to believe that Bevan supported this view. He cannot, however, have argued it, as Harold Finch relates in his memoirs, in voluble discussions within the SWMF delegation – 'Who is that loquacious youth with you?', Stephen Walsh is supposed to have asked. 'Aneurin Bevan from Tredegar.' 'Well, he's a smart boy'[29] – for the simple reason that he was not a member of the delegation on that occasion. The conversation may, of course, have taken place at a Miners' Federation conference, perhaps at one of the special conferences of 1926. But Bevan did not attend his first Labour Party Conference until 1930; and then it was as an MP.

When did he first aspire to go to Parliament? It is quite possible to believe that up to 1926 he saw his role on the industrial front, within the union. Many years later he wrote in the introduction to a biography of Bryn Roberts, one of the rivals he defeated for the Ebbw Vale seat, that it was largely accident that it was he who went to Westminster while Roberts remained a trade unionist (eventually becoming President of NUPE).[30] There is some truth in this, if only because there was only one seat – Ebbw Vale, which included Tredegar and Rhymney – for which he could plausibly have applied; had Ebbw Vale had a popular sitting member Bevan might never have got in at all. On the other hand, his emerging talent was so clearly parliamentary – he was a talker who needed as large an audience as possible, wasted as a mere organiser – that one feels that Parliament must somehow have claimed him before long. Even before 1926 he was diverting more of his energies into the parliamentary field; so much so that when his father died in 1925 the *Argus*, in an obituary tribute, could describe Aneurin not merely as Chairman of the Tredegar Combine Lodge Executive and a member of Tredegar Council but as 'leader of the Labour movement in the Ebbw Vale division'.[31] In 1927 his friend Archie Lush became secretary/agent for the division. The obstacle was that the constituency already had an MP, Evan Davies, aged only fifty-two and in good health.

So Bevan had to be satisfied with climbing the next rung of the local government ladder. In 1928 he did not stand again for the Town Council (on which Labour at last won a 10–6 majority) but ran instead for the Monmouthshire County Council. Here Labour already had a majority, but one that Bevan regarded as pathetically tame. At the height of the 1926 strike he violently attacked the Council's 'ultra-constitutional' posture of neutrality, declaring extravagantly that he would be willing to 'sacrifice the prestige of the county council and wreck the whole of the local government machinery in order to win the struggle of the miners'.[32] He was answered with characteristic moderation by Councillor Arthur Jenkins of Pontypool. Now, winning a close fight with a local jeweller for one of the two Tredegar wards that Labour did not already hold – a tribute, the *Argus* commented, to his 'personality' and 'platform genius'[33] – Bevan joined Jenkins and his colleagues in Newport. 'Mr Aneurin Bevan Arrives!', trumpeted the *Western Mail*. 'Socialist Critic of Socialists. Monmouthshire Wonders What Will Happen'. 'With Mr Bevan now a member of the council', it quoted a sitting member, 'there may be "plenty of fun".'[34]

In fact, Bevan was a county councillor for only a year. This was too little time for a newcomer, even such a one as he was, to make much of an impact on a sixty-five-member body with a comfortable Labour majority of nearly 2–1. Some years later, in a famous passage, Bevan recounted semi-humorously how he had pursued power from Tredegar to Newport to Westminster, arriving at each just in time to learn that power had been there but had moved on.[35] This was a simplification: what had really happened was that the problems – principally, in the twenties, unemployment – were too big for local authorities, without help from central government, to do much about. Looking for nothing less than the economic and social reordering of society, Bevan was bound to be dissatisfied with a large provincial county council in which the executive responsibility, such as it was, was firmly in the hands of an inner-ring of senior men and party loyalty inhibited the indulgence of unfettered opposition. He was to find his first two years in the House of Commons similarly frustrating. But no one would have guessed, in the spring of 1928, how soon he would be exchanging the frustrations of Newport for the greater frustration of Westminster.

By all the normal canons of Labour Party practice it should never have happened. Evan Davies had been MP for Ebbw Vale since July 1920 when he was returned unopposed at a by-election on the retirement of the long-serving General Secretary of the MFGB, Tom Richards. He was, naturally, a miner and had been miners' agent for the Ebbw Vale district. Once elected for such a seat as Ebbw Vale, a Labour MP was normally secure for life: until the 1970s the possibility of having to face reselection was practically unknown. This security was something for which even Bevan had reason to be grateful in the years to come. But Davies threw it all away. By 1928 there was serious dissatisfaction in the three valleys with the performance of their MP. One is bound to wonder whether it was not deliberately fomented by Archie Lush in Bevan's interest; it is hard to believe that Archie, in taking on the job of agent in 1927, did not already have in mind the idea that his friend would make a better member than Evan Davies. In fact the trouble went back further than that. As early as 1923 there was apprehension in the party organisation that the seat might actually be lost 'owing to Evan Davies's shameful neglect of duties both at the House and in the constituency'.[36] It was not merely that he rarely spoke; there were plenty of silent men among the miners' MPS – though not many could have refrained from making a single intervention during the passage of the Board of Guardians (Default) Bill, so closely affecting his own constituency. He also regularly missed engagements and was slack in answering correspondence.[37] As constituency secretary, Archie Lush had much to complain of. Davies's slackness furnished the pretext his opponents needed to persuade the SWMF Executive to agree to hold a reselection. Even so the real reason for his unprecedented displacement can surely be read in the angry letters Davies wrote to the local papers afterwards, blaming 'the temporary artificial gerrymandering of a loose mob psychology' – particularly, he alleged significantly, in Tredegar. 'The body of our own people are so easily led by glib tongues and flamboyant nonsense that one despairs of any ultimate good coming out of democracy itself.'[38] 'I am rather glad I am out of my position,' he told the *Weekly Argus*, 'when I realise what the nature of the "crowd-mind" is now in this area.'[39] Though he was only fifty-three and actually outlived his successor, Davies was an old-style moderate miners' leader out of touch and out of sympathy with the sort of uncompromising socialism being successfully propagated in his back yard by the members of the Tredegar Query Club while he was away in London. Clearly he thought he was the victim of a putsch by the Militant Tendency of his time. Perhaps he was: but when his future was put to the vote of the miners' lodges in March 1929 he was comprehensively defeated, and not only by Bevan. He had sufficiently lost the confidence of his own people that another Ebbw Vale man, George Davies, took a thousand of what should have been 'his' votes, and Bryn Roberts of Rhymney (the smallest of the three valleys) beat him into third place. The voting went to three ballots: but the outcome was in no doubt from the first.[40]

	First ballot	Second ballot	Third ballot
Aneurin Bevan	3,066	3,809	5,097
Bryn Roberts	1,816	2,208	2,626
Evan Davies	1,533	1,859	1,710
George Davies	1,061	730	
T.Rowley Jones	328		
W.G.H.Bull	225		

Such a victory was not the result merely of wire-pulling by Archie Lush. The miners of the Sirhowy, the Rhymney and the Ebbw valleys realised that they had found a champion. The rest was formality. As the miners' nominee, Bevan was adopted by the divisional party on 8 April. When Baldwin called the General Election for 30 May, he was opposed by a local retired schoolmaster for the Liberals and by the nephew of the late SWMF President William Brace, a renegade now standing for the Tories. Bevan easily defeated both together:[41]

Aneurin Bevan (Labour)	20,088
William Griffiths (Liberal)	8,924
Mark Brace (Conservative)	4,287

This was the first of eight times over the next thirty years that Bevan fought Ebbw Vale, and his narrowest margin. Through all the battles he engaged in with his own party leaders, one actual expulsion and several near-expulsions, Ebbw Vale stayed faithful to him, piling up ever larger majorities. The fact remains that he was extraordinarily lucky to get the seat in the first place. Miners (and other trade unionists) were and still are more usually sent to Parliament near the end of their careers than at the beginning – in their fifties rather than their early thirties. Everything that Bevan later accomplished, the niche that he was to carve for himself in the pantheon of British socialism, was made possible by the chance that made him 'the youngest coal miner ever sent to Parliament by his fellows'.[42] Evan Davies's negligence was the determining accident of Bevan's life.

So Bevan, aged thirty-one, less than eight years after returning from the Labour College, went back to London to support Ramsay MacDonald's second, ill-fated, minority Labour Government. The first, parochial phase of his life was over. From now on, though he remained ineradicably a South Wales miner by origin, he embraced with enthusiasm the wider world to which his tastes and cultural interests drew him, taking the whole country and later the world as his parish, preaching class struggle and the inevitable victory of socialism – but always, too, the supremacy of Parliament. It was a question whether he would – it is still a question how far he did – lose touch with his roots, as so many from the pits and workshops both before and since have been accused of doing. There was, it can be argued, little in his philosophy that had not been learned in the valleys; yet less and less did he resemble a typical miners' MP. The percipience of the *Daily Herald*'s reporter in June 1929 was fully vindicated; 'There are about fifty miners' Members in the new Parliament, but I do not think Aneurin Bevan will be exactly lost in the crowd.'[43]

2

The Class War in Parliament, 1929–1939

Chapter 3

MacDonald, Mosley and the Débâcle of 1931

The Parliament to which Bevan was elected in 1929 was the first in which Labour was the largest party, with 288 seats against 260 for the defeated Tories. The Liberals, after making most of the running in the campaign with Lloyd George's proto-Keynesian plan to 'conquer' unemployment, own a quarter of the vote but were rewarded with just fifty-nine seats. With this result, MacDonald's long-term strategy of replacing the Liberals as the leftward-leaning party in a restored two-party system was well on the way to success; in the short term, however, the Liberals held the balance of power and his second Government was dependent, as his first had been, on their support. This dependence provided a useful alibi for the Government's failure, in its unhappy two-year life, to introduce any distinctively socialist measures. The fact is, however, that MacDonald and his senior colleagues had no idea of doing anything much different had they won a majority. MacDonald himself was a utopian dreamer, easily overwhelmed by the diffi-culties of the real world; Philip Snowden (Chancellor of the Exchequer), a rigid Gladstonian Liberal; Arthur Henderson (Foreign Secretary), a solidly moderate trade unionist; Jimmy Thomas, the railwaymen's leader (Lord Privy Seal, given the job of finding a cure for unemployment), a cocky working-class Tory. These were the Labour Party's tried and trusted leaders who had brought it from the margin of politics to the seats of power; but not one of them was what Bevan would have called a socialist. John Wheatley, the sole left-winger (and almost the sole success) in the 1924 Government, was significantly left out in 1929. To Bevan and those new Labour Members who thought like him – who included the twenty-four-year-old Member for North Lanark, elected at a by-election in March, Jennie Lee – disillusion was almost guaranteed from the day that Parliament met.

In view of this, it is striking how supportive and optimistic Bevan's earliest interventions were. He first tested the parliamentary water with a question on 10 July, pressing MacDonald strongly on the need for legislation to amend the 'iniquities' of the unemployment insurance system: MacDonald replied with a characteristic evasion that was ominous for the future.[1] But a week later his maiden speech expressed the fullest confidence in Jimmy Thomas. Remarkably, it appears to have been made impromptu; thus early – though nobody noticed – he announced his rare ability as a *debater*. 'I would not have intervened in this debate, as this is my first effort,' he began, 'were it not for the fact that we have listened to some very extraordinary speeches from the benches opposite. .... I think it is necessary to point out that this is the first example of what we are to expect in the form of collusion between the Tories and the Liberals in obstructionist tactics.' Unhesitatingly Bevan went straight for the biggest figures in the Chamber, Churchill and Lloyd George, and knocked their heads together for criticising Thomas's (very modest) employment schemes, for contradictory reasons – Churchill saying they did not go far enough, Lloyd George that they demanded a blank cheque.* He admitted that the Government was merely buttressing private enterprise. What else could it do, the Liberals having threatened to turn it out the moment it tried anything socialist? The opposition parties had better support the Government, he warned, or it would be forced to go back to the country to secure a majority for socialism. Meanwhile, he concluded, 'the only steps which can be taken are being taken to meet this very difficult problem'.[2]

Bevan's maiden speech could hardly have been more loyal. At this stage he accepted entirely that the Government's hands were tied by the parliamentary arithmetic, and was ready to throw all the blame for its shortcomings on the tactical 'acrobatics' of the opposition. In the meantime, even without a majority, there were things the Government could do to alleviate the conditions of its working-class supporters. Bevan was content, during the Government's first year, to cast himself in the limited role of spokesman for his own people. In his second speech he welcomed the replacement of Neville Chamberlain's special Poor Law Commissioners in Bedwellty, and took the chance for a bitter attack on Chamberlain himself: 'The worst thing I can say about democracy is that it has tolerated the right hon. Gentleman for two and half years.'[3] His third, when the House resumed in November, was a powerfully reasoned plea for legislation to remove from local authorities the necessity for private Bills in order to carry out obligations which Parliament itself had placed on them.

> We on these benches who have had some experience of local administration believe that local authorities are, to a very large extent, the most important part of our constitution, and larger and wider powers are being imposed on them every day. ...
> It appears to me, to put it in the most humble terms, to be stupid in the extreme that Parliament should impose obligations upon local authorities, and

---

* The speech also contained the first of many personal tilts over the next thirty years at Churchill, whose 'chameleon-like character in politics', Bevan suggested, 'is founded upon a temperamental disability. He fills all the roles with such exceeding facility that his lack of political stability is at once explained' (House of Commons, 16 July 1929 [*Hansard*, vol. 230, cols 338–43]).

should ask the local authorities to accelerate their schemes, and that local authorities should find it necessary to come to Parliament to ask for powers to do what Parliament has asked them to do.[4]

A Tory complimented him on this intervention: 'It was remarkable for its fluency, its choice of language, its knowledge of the situation and for the flamboyancy of youth . . . and also perhaps for a somewhat brief experience of procedure in this House.' He was beginning to make his mark.

He made a very definite mark in February 1930 with a direct attack on Lloyd George, who was visibly shaken as though by the ghost of his own radical youth when he had similarly assailed Joseph Chamberlain. The occasion was the Second Reading of the Government's Coal Mines Bill – a muddled attempt, by fixing production quotas, to reduce miners' hours without reducing wages. Again Bevan spoke purely as a miners' representative; but he spoke with passion and devastating effect, the words tumbling out of him as he faced Lloyd George across the gangway:

> We have a right to say that, if it means slightly dearer coal, it is better to have slightly dearer coal than cheaper colliers. Hon. Gentlemen here must face the issue that when they vote against this Bill, they are voting for lower wages for the colliers, and they are voting at the same time for an increase in the number of accidents in the collieries, for it follows, as night follows day, that whenever you make it more difficult for the piece-worker underground to earn a decent wage, you ask him to devote himself to output at the expense of safety in the colliery. It is always characteristic of Liberal hypocrisy to pay lip-service to these things, and refuse to face the consequences that follow from them. We say that you cannot get from the already dry veins of the miners new blood to revivify the industry. Their veins are shrunken white, and we are asking you to be, for once, decent to the miners – not to pay lip-service, not to say that you are very sorry for them, not to say that you are very sorry these accidents occur, not to say that you are very sorry for the low level of wages and for the conditions of famine that have existed in the mining districts since the War, and then to use all your Parliamentary skill, all your rhetoric, in an act of pure demagogy to expose the mining community of this country to another few years of misery.[5]

The answer to this frankly sectional appeal was that raising the price of coal raised the costs of the nation's other industries. Almost meekly, Lloyd George countered that others too were entitled to speak for their constituents. It was certainly a fair criticism of Bevan's early speeches that they looked at the country exclusively from the standpoint of Ebbw Vale. He had shown his constructive quality, however, in December, when he took a leading part (in alliance with the Clydeside members) in getting the Ministry of Labour to revise the hated 'genuinely seeking work' qualification for entitlement to unemployment benefit, demolishing the Attorney-General's legal intricacies in what the Minister herself, Margaret Bondfield, called 'a very admirable speech'. 'The whole incident', another Labour Member commented, 'shows the importance of having in the Labour Party men who can tackle even the best legal talent that can be secured.'[6] Bevan himself was invited to help hammer out, with Miss Bondfield and Horace Wilson of the Treasury, a new clause which placed on the officials the onus of proving that an applicant for benefit was not genuinely seeking work, instead of the applicant having to walk miles, as previously, to prove that he was.[7] Bevan's experience of his first year in Parliament was that the Government had to be pushed and badgered to do anything, but its heart was in the right place: it was a great deal better than a Tory Government.

Very quickly, however, his patience began to run out. As the whole world plunged into depression following the Wall Street crash, and unemployment, far from yielding to Thomas's tinkering, soared over the two million mark, the Government was plainly helpless. Snowden's only solution was to batten down the economic hatches and wait for the storm to blow over. Thomas's native ebullience lapsed into alcoholic self-pity. Only one Minister appeared to have either the will to tackle the crisis or any idea how to go about it – the dashing thirty-three-year-old baronet, the Labour Party's most sensational capture from the Tories, its rising star and widely predicted future leader, incongruously appointed by MacDonald to be Thomas's number two in the search for an unemployment policy: Sir Oswald Mosley. For all their enormous differences of background, Bevan was immediately attracted to Mosley's programme. Their brief association – the short-lived congruence of two men who within a few years would embody almost the opposite ends of the British ideological spectrum – is one of the most important and revealing episodes in Bevan's career.

His susceptibility to Mosley is in part a measure of his isolation within the Parliamentary Labour Party. The 288 members of the PLP in this Parliament can be divided into four groups: Ministers and their PPSs; the usual band of ambitious loyalists hoping to be Ministers; the trade union block, mainly elderly; and about fifty others, who comprised the organised left – the ILP – and sundry mavericks and oddballs. Even the ILP was disintegrating as people like Frank Wise and Fenner Brockway distanced themselves from the 'Red Clydeside' group led, after the death of John Wheatley in 1930, by the romantic but ineffectual Jimmy Maxton. Bevan, though nominally a trade union member, was numbered among the mavericks. He frequently combined with the Clydesiders in the lobbies but he was not a member of the ILP and never had much time for it. He kept his own company and made his own friends – few, but selected with discrimination from all three parties. One was the brilliant young Tory, the stepson of Lord Hailsham, Edward Marjoribanks, with whom he was observed to leave the Chamber arm-in-arm after his onslaught on Lloyd George. It was Marjoribanks, soon after this, who introduced him to Lord Beaverbrook, though that relationship, which opened more doors to Bevan than any other, did not take off just yet. In 1931 Marjoribanks, in a fit of depression, shot himself in his stepfather's gun-room – one more entry in the catalogue of human waste which Bevan blamed bitterly on the Tory Party. Another early friend was the youngest member of the House, the Liberal Frank Owen, a great talker later known as a swash-buckling Beaverbrook journalist and (with Michael Foot) polemical pamphleteer. He was just beginning, too, to make friends with Jennie Lee, then a striking political figure in her own right – a slip of a girl, with dark hair and flashing eyes and a passionate tongue to voice the grievances of the Scottish coalfield. Comparing their experiences, in Tredegar and Cowdenbeath, of 1921 and 1926, Bevan and she found that they had a lot in common. They could almost be brother and sister, Jennie remembers telling him after a long talk on the terrace of the House of Commons, overlooking the river. 'Yes,' Nye is said to have agreed, 'with a tendency to incest.'[8] But this may well have been later. In 1929–30 Jennie's romantic interest was centred on Frank Wise; while politically she was a protégée of Maxton and associated with the Clydeside group.

Jennie was Bevan's future. Unquestionably his closest and politically most important friend in this Parliament was John Strachey – a maverick if ever there was one. A tall, ungainly but oddly engaging Old Etonian, son of the editor of the *Spectator*, Strachey was a classic example of the type of public-school intellectual desperate to be on the side of the idealised workers: his mind was brilliant but extraordinarily pliable, as the wild swings of his career from Mosley to Communism and back to middle-of-the-road Labourism showed. To the young Bevan he was a most attractive companion, another wide-ranging talker after his own heart and a useful guide to a world which was still strange to him. 'You are very good to me John,' he wrote in a rare and remarkable baring of his soul in October 1930.

> It hurts me a little that you give so much and I can give nothing in return. So few people have given me anything that I feel a little strange and bewildered. I count our friendship as the one thing of value that membership of parliament has given me. And yet, as this friendship grows, and becomes more and more a part of me, I find myself becoming fearful. I am so conscious of bringing to our relationship nothing of value, and, therefore, am frightened of trusting so much of my affection in so ill balanced a vessel. Please forgive me for exposing so shy a feeling to the peril of words. It is your generous nature that moves me to speak, even though I know that speech would bruise where it would caress.[9]

Here is a side of the young Bevan very different from the truculent face he usually presented to the world.

Strachey's political importance was that he had been since 1925 Mosley's right-hand man and collaborator, and was now his PPS. It was through Strachey that Bevan came into Mosley's orbit. He was never personally close to Mosley; psychologically Strachey needed a leader, but Bevan could not have lived long in Mosley's shadow. Three things drew him to Mosley in 1930. The first and simplest was an overwhelming desire, in a situation where textbook socialism was ruled out, to do something or anything to tackle the nearly 50 per cent unemployment that was now affecting his constituents.

Mosley was the only man in the Labour Party who seemed to offer action of any sort. A second, related, characteristic of Mosley that appealed to Bevan was his fighting quality, quite unlike the crippling respectability of Mac-Donald. Having joined the Labour Party, he had embraced the cause of the workers' – and specifically the miners' – struggle wholeheartedly and without apology. After 1926 he enjoyed a strong base of support among the miners, was invited to speak regularly at miners' galas and was elected, principally as a result of the miners' backing, to the National Executive. He consistently used the language of class confrontation ('This is not a kissing match, but a stand-up fight'),[10] accused Baldwin of trying to make 'working class bees without a sting ... to gather honey for the rich',[11] and spoke uncompromisingly of 'breaking' and 'crushing' the Tory enemy.[12] Above all, already in the twenties he was denouncing the complacency of the House of Commons in just the same apocalyptic terms which Bevan was to use, endlessly and without effect, throughout the thirties:

> Unemployment, wages, rents, suffering, squalor and starvation; the struggle for existence in our streets, the threat of world catastrophe in another war; these are the realities of the present age. These are the problems which require the exertion of the best brains of our time for a vast constructive effort. ... But these are precisely the problems which send Parliament to sleep. ... Hush! Do not wake the dreamers. Facts will awaken them in time with a vengeance.[13]

Most important, however, Bevan found in Mosley's ideas a view of the world which, though derived from a very different starting point, closely paralleled his own. The essence of Mosley's socialism was the belief that men could control their own destiny, and a consequent rejection of liberal economics and the nineteenth-century assumption of a benevolent 'hidden hand'. In the book *Revolution by Reason*, on which Mosley collaborated with Strachey in 1925, socialism was defined as 'the conscious control and direction of human resources for human needs'.[14] Philosophically, he simply could not accept the despairing orthodoxy that unemployment was a phenomenon beyond human control. Having fought in the war, Mosley despised the older generation whose bungling had caused it. Self-consciously a modern, his vision of society was rational, 'scientific', even futuristic. Bevan's thinking had been moulded by his working experience and by Marxism into a form in which class struggle should be the motor of progress; Mosley's approach was more technocratic, more (in the Greek sense of the word) *aristocratic*. But their goals were very similar; both felt themselves in step with history – as indeed to an extent they were. What Bevan responded to in Mosley was the recognition, for which he looked in vain from his 'socialist' leaders but which Keynes, Lloyd George, Harold Macmillan and others in both the bourgeois parties were beginning to grasp, that the age of *laissez-faire* was dead, the age of collectivism and the at least semi-planned economy at hand.

By 1930 the facts of which Mosley had warned were doing their best to wake the dreamers; but the Labour Cabinet was still looking helplessly to the hidden hand to lift the curse of depression in its own good time. At the beginning of the year, without reference to Thomas, Mosley prepared a memorandum setting out his own solutions, all of which chimed closely with Bevan's emerging views. The essential themes were (1) that the regeneration of industry could not be left to the banks, operating on normal commercial criteria, but needed a programme of public investment; (2) an emphasis on restoring the *home* market, by means of protective tariffs, not, as Treasury orthodoxy insisted, on exports; (3) an end to the export of capital for investment overseas instead of at home (this was a particularly sore point with Bevan, who had been with a miners' delegation to Poland in 1927 and had been incensed to see British capital being used to sink new pits in Silesia to compete directly with South Wales); (4) a major public works programme of the sort that Lloyd George had campaigned for in 1929 and which Bevan had believed Thomas to have taken office to implement.[15] For three months, from February to May 1930, the Cabinet sat on this memorandum; finally, predictably, the Treasury turned it down. Mosley immediately resigned and took the issue to the parliamentary party.

He found support only among the mavericks. The loyalists took their lead from the Government, while the ILP, though equally critical of the Government's inaction, looked askance at Mosley's doctrinal heterodoxy.* In the vote immediately following his resignation, Mosley was defeated by 210 to 29. Bevan took the lead in gathering signatures for a motion, worded to maximise support, calling for a more vigorous policy, and mustered sixty; but in July a meeting which less than half the party bothered to attend merely referred it back to the consultative committee. There was no sense of urgency, only in most of the PLP the same sense of helplessness that pervaded the Cabinet. Mosley's firm supporters, apart from his wife Cynthia, were only five: Strachey, Bevan, W.J.Brown, Dr Robert Forgan and Oliver Baldwin, renegade son of the Conservative leader.

That summer Bevan paid his first visit to the Soviet Union, in company with Strachey, George Strauss (another of the still small band of public-school socialist MPs to whom Bevan was already paradoxically drawn), Jennie Lee and two other women, ardent fellow-travellers in both senses of the word. Strachey, characteristically, was more impressed than Bevan by what they saw. Ideologically predisposed as he was in favour of the first workers' state, Bevan was nevertheless not blind to the hardships that the transition to socialism imposed: he encapsulated his ambivalence neatly with the conclusion that 'while Britain was a slave to the past, in Russia they were slaves to the future'.[16] He recognised that eggs were being broken, but he was

---

* At the trade union group meeting before the full PLP, Ebby Edwards, the miners' MP for Morpeth 'went for' Bevan and threatened to report him to the MFGB. 'Our Loyal Lump in action', Hugh Dalton commented (Dalton diary, 22 May 1930).

Marxist enough to be confident that an historical omelette was in the making.*

Soon after their return, Mosley took his cause to the party Conference at Llandudno; and there, after an electrifying speech, he very nearly won with an astonishing 1,046,000 votes against 1,251,000 – despite the fact that he was already visibly making overtures towards the right. Rebuffed by Labour, he had spent the summer talking to dissident younger Conservatives like Oliver Stanley and Robert Boothby, emphasising the tariff reform and Empire development side of his proposals at the expense of public works. In the House of Commons on 4 November Bevan sought to redress the balance. Without mentioning Mosley, he demanded to know why the Government had not taken up Lloyd George's offer of Liberal support for a public works programme. 'This is the first time that I have spoken critically of the Government on the floor of this House,' he claimed – justly – 'but I submit that there is a case to answer, and that Parliament has a right to expect an answer from the Government.' MacDonald had said at Llandudno that the money was there:

> Being a mere tyro in politics, I would ask the Government ... if there is nothing intrinsically wrong with the schemes, if they are themselves practicable, if they add to the general economic equipment of the country, and if the Government will be given a longer life in which to realise their more ambitious proposals – if that be the condition for prolonged power, why do not the Government accept it? We are not asked from the Liberal benches to accept any proposals which are in themselves anti-Socialist. I have always thought that for a local authority to spend more and more money on public works was good Socialism. Here, from the point of view of the immediate political situation, is the chance for the Government to get a Parliamentary majority at the moment and a continuation of power.

This speech demonstrated a willingness, very characteristic of Bevan's ideological self-confidence, to compromise for tangible short-term advantage with no fear that he thereby betrayed his socialism. He scorned the ILP's purist doctrine of 'socialism or nothing'. He sincerely hoped the Government would accept the Liberal terms,

> not because I believe that schemes such as we have here will do permanent good, for I do not think they will, but because I know that they are in themselves intrinsically desirable, and because I believe that, if the Government adopts them, we shall have some hope of keeping an umbrella over the heads of the working class during the time of industrial reorganisation, since we shall be able to keep our Government in power.

---

* There was serious hardship in Britain and America, too, the three MPs pointed out in their obligatory pamphlet *What We Saw in Russia*; and that, more culpably, was being inflicted in defiance of history.

Equally characteristic was Bevan's warning that failure to do anything serious about unemployment would threaten parliamentary democracy itself: 'This matter can either be treated as an orthodox, conventional, constitutional matter, in the way in which it is, unfortunately, being treated now; or it may be treated as a means of mobilising national energy and national enthusiasm for the purpose of a broad attack on the whole problem.' He concluded on a non-party note:

> I hope this House will realise that outside people are prepared to give it a chance if it is prepared to find new unconventional expedients and will try to get rid of the cynicism that comes over people in the House, try to destroy the atmosphere of enervation and tackle the problem in the spirit that the country expects from the House of Commons.[17]

Despite the olive branch to Lloyd George, it was still with Mosley that Bevan was actually combining. At the beginning of December he, Strachey and Brown collaborated with Mosley in publishing a manifesto described by Mosley's biographer as 'a collective enterprise in the truest sense of the word'.[18] Encouraged by Llandudno, Mosley was making one more effort to get his ideas accepted within the Labour Party. The Manifesto proposed a national plan to modernise British industry within a protected home market, with a short-term programme of public works, particularly housing, financed by borrowing; most controversially, it proposed to give executive power for the duration of the emergency to five 'dictators' under the general control of the House of Commons. 'We surrender nothing of our socialist faith,' the authors asserted. 'The immediate question is not a question of the ownership but of the survival of British industry.' The Manifesto was an *emergency* programme: 'afterwards debate on fundamental principle can be resumed'.[19]

It was signed by seventeen Labour MPs (plus the left-wing miners' leader, A.J.Cook). Most were young, all but three were new MPs; eight, including Mosley himself, sat for seats in the West Midlands, six for mining seats. These were Labour heartlands, certainly; but the bulk of the party resolutely refused to have anything to do with it. The more it was praised by 'middle opinion' – by Boothby and Macmillan and the Tory left, by J.L.Garvin in the *Observer*, and by the churches – still worse by Empire protectionists on the Tory right, the more the Labour Party distrusted it. When one of the signatories, Henry Muggeridge, described it as 'applied socialism', the *Manchester Guardian* wondered why then it had been so warmly praised by Leo Amery.[20] Labour's own *Daily Herald* saw in it the spectre of coalition, involving 'the defeat of everything for which Labour stands';[21] while Herbert Morrison (overlooking Bevan) expressed a widely held suspicion of 'swell-heads not of working-class origin' with 'Tory blue blood running in their veins'.[22] This was indeed strange company for the avowed class warrior Bevan to be keeping; but he would not have called the Manifesto 'applied socialism'. He pretended no such thing, only that in the dire emergency, with socialism ('everything for which Labour stands') not an option, state action to stimulate employment and restore a degree of prosperity to the stricken areas of the country was better than doing nothing and the least the labour movement owed to its people. It had no right to insist on its socialist purity at their expense. Hence his support for Mosley – within the Labour Party.

His breach with Mosley came the moment Mosley broke with Labour and struck out to form his own, doomed New Party. It was the one absolute and unshakeable fundamental of Bevan's philosophy, however much on occasion he despaired of it, that there was no hope of socialism or salvation for the British working class except through the Labour Party and the organised labour movement. He had already, after 1926, refused to join the Communist Party when several of his friends in South Wales were doing so; he had only contempt for the ILP's self-righteous decision to disaffiliate from Labour in 1932; and all his life, while ready to face expulsion for arguing his minority view and criticising both parliamentary and union leaders, he declined to consider for a moment the possibility of joining or leading any sort of breakaway. It was Mosley's defection which put this resolution to its stiffest test. He had only just, after all, helped to write the manifesto on which the New Party was launched; his best friend, Strachey, swallowed his doubts and joined (albeit briefly). But Bevan refused. It was not simply loyalty – personal loyalty might have pulled him either way. It was rather his Marxist training which told him that a party not rooted in a class interest was mere froth on the surface of politics. 'Where is the money coming from?' he is supposed to have demanded of Mosley, adding, if the prophecy is not too good to be believed: 'You will end up as a fascist party'.[23] As a matter of fact the money was coming from Sir William Morris and a few other big industrialists; and the New Party metamorphosed into the British Union of Fascists in 1932.

Bevan never recanted his support for Mosley's ideas. In July 1931 he still defended in the House the proposals with which he had 'had the honour to be associated';[24] and the following year he good-humouredly rebuked a Tory who accused him of deserting Mosley in his adversity. Mosley's adversity, he contended, 'started when he deserted me. He was quite prosperous till then, but afterwards his adversity came.'[25] There is a touch of arrogance here, in Bevan's identification of himself with the party; but there was humility too in his recognition that the individual without the party was nothing at all. To Strachey, in July 1931, he wrote critically of the tendency of intellectuals (like Mosley and Strachey) to want to 'dominate and shape' events instead of submitting to them. 'They can influence these events', he now argued, 'only by being moulded by them. Thus the profound difference between the typical intellectual and persons who, like myself, have the security of metaphysics on a social struggle upon which to rely in moments of doubt and uncertainty.' ('I am putting these words together very incoherently and inadequately,' he added, 'but I know that, as usual, your mind will come three parts of the way to meet mine'.) He was delighted that Strachey too had now decided to break with Mosley, and looked forward to their being able to work together again, in what circumstances he could not tell. 'It seems to me', he wrote presciently, 'looking at the political situation in this country, that the cards are not yet dealt with which the final game will have to be played. It would be a profound error for us to judge the pace and direction of these social and political collusions which exist independently of us, and with which we have to deal.'[26]

A month later the Labour Government collapsed under the impact of a financial crisis with which it was not equipped to deal. A majority of the Cabinet, though they had no alternative solution, refused to be responsible for implementing the bankers' insistence on cutting unemployment benefit as part of a package of economies. In a spectacular example of 'political collusion', MacDonald, Snowden and Thomas formed a 'National' Government with the Conservatives and Liberals, initially to protect the pound, later – when the pound was forced off the gold standard anyway – to wage general war on everything they had previously been supposed to stand for. This was Labour's 'great betrayal': the three leading traitors became the convenient scapegoats for the failure of the party as a whole. Bevan's immediate reaction was ambivalent. 'Although some of us on this side of the House', he admitted on 18 September, 'must feel much happier that at last we have the opportunity of opposing policies in which we do not believe and to which for some time we have not subscribed, nevertheless the proposal which is now before the House of Commons fills many of us with great apprehension.' He feared for the impact on the unemployed, and in one characteristically torrential sentence gave the first of many dire warnings of the consequences of trying to screw down their living standards any further:

> When I think what these proposals would mean, reducing the standard benefit to 26 weeks, passing into the transitional benefit class all these men, applying a means test at a time when the greatest possible poverty exists, putting these men into the hands of the public assistance committees, curtailing the revenues coming into the distressed areas to the lowest possible point – when I consider 3,000,000 people living in conditions like that in the coming winter, and hundreds of thousands of people living in these conditions in the mining districts, I want to try to convey to the Committee some apprehension of what that situation will be and to warn the Committee and the Ministry of Labour that, if the regulations he issues for the guidance of the public assistance committees are in any way harsh in their incidence, if he is going to apply in those regulations any Poor Law tests, if he is going to curtail the income coming into those districts substantially, in other words if he makes any serious attempt, at the expense of those areas, to save that £10,000,000, he had better look to it that there is a far better temper among the marines.*

From the purely political point of view, however, Bevan welcomed the events of August as the clarification of the situation that he had looked for when he wrote to Strachey. 'In the guise and cloak of patriotism', he alleged, the new

* A reference to the naval mutiny at Invergordon three days earlier.

Government was 'making war upon the poorest members of the community'. 'As far as we are concerned, there is one thing about which we are pleased in the present crisis, and that is that the changeover of this party from there to here has clearly exposed the class issue. We shall carry it through to a final conclusion, be the circumstances what they may.'[27]

Briefly, Bevan believed that the change of Government gave Labour a strong bargaining position, if it would only use it. Snowden had appealed to the Opposition to be 'responsible' in order to help save the pound.

> I would like to impress upon my own Front Bench, as well as upon the Front Bench opposite, that this is an occasion when we have them by the throat. . . . It appears to me that the Opposition is in a position of great strategic importance, and that if we are going to win concessions from private enterprise, now is the time to win them. . . .
> If it is true that, in demanding these things for our own people, we are laying down conditions which are inconsistent with the financial structure of the country, if the maintenance of private enterprise, of unfettered finance, of property, is inconsistent with the maintenance of democratic powers in the House of Commons, it is you who have said it and not we.*[28]

The next month, however, whatever bargaining position Labour might have enjoyed by being still the largest party in the House was destroyed when MacDonald, under pressure from the Conservatives, dissolved the 1929 Parliament. Despite having failed in its central purpose of saving the pound, and despite being openly divided over tariffs, the National Government sought and obtained a 'doctor's mandate', winning an overwhelming 554 seats. Labour, though its vote in the country actually held up well (30 per cent), was reduced at Westminster to an impotent rump of fifty-two members. Secure in Ebbw Vale, Bevan was not even opposed and spent the election in North Lanark trying in vain to save Jennie Lee's seat from the general débâcle. Now the new hand of which he had written to Strachey had been dealt, and the Government held all the cards. The parliamentary road, like the industrial road five years earlier, seemed to have run into the sand. What was left?

---

* This was Bevan's first, unacknowledged, use of Colonel Thomas Rainsborough's retort to Cromwell in the Putney debate of 1647, which became in later years one of his favourite – not to say stock – quotations. (See *Why Not Trust the Tories?*, p. 88.)

Chapter 4

The Aftermath of 1931: Unemployment, the Means Test and the Impossibility of Gradualism

1931 was a traumatic setback to the whole labour movement. It was two or three years before the party began to recover its equilibrium, the end of the decade before it could be said to have succeeded. The psychological scar left by the failure of the 1929 Government, the circumstances of its collapse and the desertion of its leaders has never fully healed to this day. During the thirties, faced by persisting mass unemployment, the rise of fascism and growing international tension, different elements within the movement came to terms with the débâcle in different ways and with different degrees of success. In the immediate aftermath, the whole party suffered a spasm of overreaction in which even such level-headed leaders as Clement Attlee were persuaded that the next Labour Government would have to take emergency powers as soon as it took office to control the flight of capital and make sure that it could impose its socialist policies on the City: the 1933 Conference approved several drastic resolutions, including the abolition of the House of Lords and the curtailing of the power of the Commons – measures similar to those which Mosley, supported by Bevan, had proposed in 1930. By 1934, however, the party was beginning to get over this first, out-of-character reaction; under the growing influence of Herbert Morrison, Ernest Bevin and Hugh Dalton its traditional moderation was steadily reasserted. At Conference that year a further series of resolutions proposed by Stafford Cripps's Socialist League was heavily defeated, and little more was heard of emergency powers. Labour fought the 1935 election on a solidly constitutional programme and regained about half the ground lost in 1931, winning 154 seats; and though Attlee, to general surprise, held off the challenge of the returning Morrison and Arthur Greenwood to remain Leader (he had taken over from the veteran Lansbury the year before), he had put his aberrations of 1931–3 behind him and proved henceforth – for the next twenty years – the studiously moderate Leader of a determinedly responsible party. Dalton, with his younger protégés Douglas Jay, Evan Durbin and Hugh Gaitskell, recast the economic policy of the party in a revisionist mould, aimed less at abolishing capitalism than at controlling it; while Bevin and Walter Citrine kept the trade unions solid against all forms of left-wing infiltration. Long before 1939 the left had been thoroughly frozen out of all influence.

Labour's progress back towards the centre left Bevan once again isolated as a maverick, a sidekick now of Cripps as he had previously been of Mosley. During 1931–3 he had been, for once in his life, in broad agreement with his leaders; in 1935 he almost certainly voted for Attlee's continuation as leader. But thereafter he was disillusioned and increasingly critical of the party's tameness, respectability and lack of socialist commitment. His views scarcely counted for anything at all: in 1937 when he stood in the annual PLP elections for the Shadow Cabinet he was humiliated. Nevertheless they were distinctive, challenging and (on their own premises) intellectually coherent. They make a powerful case for an alternative road which the British Labour Party might have taken – if it had been a different sort of party. They also illustrate very clearly Bevan's characteristic mixture of intellectualism and anger, his rare combination of theorist, rebel and energetically practical politician.

From the events of 1931 he drew two lessons which to many eyes might seem mutually contradictory. First, the banker-inspired cuts in unemployment benefit which followed the formation of the National Government fully confirmed his belief in the ineluctable reality of class war: the interests of the working class and the capitalist class were clearly shown to be irreconcilable, the physical welfare of the one dependent on the material expropriation of the other. At the same time, however, 1931 also confirmed his conviction that, in Britain, the class war could be won through Parliament. It was not Parliament that had failed in 1931, but the Labour Party's willingness to *use* Parliament. Throughout his life Bevan believed that Parliament was a weapon ('the most formidable weapon of all', he called it in *In Place of Fear*) to be used both offensively and defensively by the working class. It was during a speech in the House of Commons in December 1933 that he first stumbled on the formula which was to be his watchword for the next twenty-five years. 'Democracy, poverty and property', he suggested, 'can live quite amicably side by side, in circumstances of alleviating poverty, and, so long as progress is made, property is not in serious danger.' Now, however, the House was being asked to choose 'whether it will make inroads on the rights of Property or of Democracy'. It had chosen, he alleged, 'to destroy Democracy'.[1] Very soon Bevan had polished this theory into the elegant equation finally contained in *In Place of Fear*: 'Either poverty will use democracy to win the struggle against property, or property, in fear of poverty, will destroy democracy.'[2] Parliament, on this analysis, was the weapon by which the working class would prevail. All the Labour Party had to do – descending from theory to practice – was, first, to unite the working class so as to be able to translate the majority of the population in the country into a majority in the House of Commons; and, secondly, having once won a majority, to use it resolutely.

The primary practical lesson which the party had to learn from 1931 was that achieving socialism by gradualism had been shown to be impossible.

Bevan's 'proof' of the impossibility of gradualism was contained in a long and subtle analysis included anonymously (it was said to be by 'one of the most gifted of Labour's younger supporters') in John Strachey's *The Coming Struggle for Power*, published in November 1931. It was generally agreed on the left, Bevan argued – particularly by those who sought excuses for the Labour Government's helplessness – that the 1931 Government had been brought down by a 'Bankers' Ramp'. But this was a damaging admission. 'If capitalism ... can conspire against a Government and bring it down by moving its international financial forces against it, what hope is there for a gradual and peaceful expropriation of the bankers?' There could be no half-way house between capitalism and socialism, because capitalism – quite correctly in its own self-defence – would not tolerate it.

> It must never be forgotten that the mainspring of capitalist production is the individual investor. ... We may rail against him, but while we allow him to be the prime motivator of the productive process the sensitiveness of his psychology is always a factor to be reckoned with. It is just this psychology that a Labour Party, climbing to power in circumstances of economic difficulty, not only cannot reassure but must of necessity offend.

Gradualism, Bevan argued, 'requires that private enterprise shall continue reasonably successful whilst it is being slowly and painlessly eliminated'. This 'involves the assumption that capitalism can be carried on more effectively by socialists than by capitalists'. But this was fundamentally untrue, since capitalism depends on confidence and capitalists do not have confidence in socialists. Therefore, Bevan concluded, socialism could only be achieved by a swift and sudden transfer, at one fell swoop, of the whole mechanism of economic power.[3]

Until the day when this should be possible, however, Bevan had an equally well-argued case for using Parliament as a defensive weapon to protect the working class from the attacks of the dying social order. First, despite the Government's enormous majority, he believed that it was possible for those who knew the conditions in the most distressed constituencies to bring their knowledge to bear in committee to soften some of the harshest aspects of the assistance regulations and other legislation of whose practical effect on individuals Ministers often had no idea. Secondly, he believed in using Parliament as a platform from which Labour, even though a minority, could shout to the country the conditions endured by its people, thus helping to create a popular consciousness of injustice which would eventually be translated into a majority. Accordingly, and surprisingly, in the course of the thirties, Bevan turned himself into a superb parliamentarian, both a powerful, persuasive and on occasion devastating speaker and a brilliant exponent of the intricacies of parliamentary procedure.

As a speaker he commanded a remarkable range of moods and styles, often within the same speech: one moment bitter and accusing, the next sweetly pleading; persuasive or threatening; provocative or teasingly humorous; always with a startling fertility and freshness of phrase. Probably at this period he was too many-sided to be consistently effective; the House of Commons likes to know what to expect of its Members, and Bevan was difficult to pigeon-hole except as a bolshie young know-all too fond of the sound of his own voice. ('Aneurin Bevan, the red-nosed publicity-seeker' was 'Chips' Channon's typical dismissal of him.)[4] Brief quotation cannot do justice to the variety of his interventions; nevertheless it is the only way to give an idea of their quality and of his principal themes. Rather than keep strictly to the narrative it will be better at this point to draw some characteristic examples of his various styles from different parts of the decade. The bleak landscape of unemployment, after all – at least as seen from South Wales – did not change much in these years.

Sometimes, in the conventional style of an Opposition member, he launched wholesale attacks on the monstrously bloated Tory majority and the incompetence and fraudulence of the 'National' Government. As early as December 1931, in a speech remarkable for its lack of any mention of socialism, he was pouring out his scorn for a Government so formed that it was incapable of conceiving *any* clear policy, even a Tory one, to meet the economic crisis.

> Do not let us 'kid' ourselves that anything is going to come from this National Government. Let us make an end of it as soon as possible. It may drag along its miserable carcase for a few more months. It may still seek to persuade the country that we have a real National Government, but in fact it is only cumbering the ground and preventing this House from grappling with the problems which face the country. We in this party are anxious, if any plans can be produced, if any solutions of our difficulties are forthcoming, to see those plans and those solutions as early as possible, but they are not to be expected from this Government. The Government is not a collection of Heaven-inspired statesmen. They have come together, not for the purpose of rescuing this country from the evils which afflict it, but because they themselves are the authors of our troubles and they desire to conceal their own responsibility. For a time they concealed their deformities behind the ample folds of the Union Jack and a glittering façade of generalities such as the Prime Minister is a master at constructing. But the time is soon coming when the country will see this Government for what it is – a collection of political gangsters using the sacred emblems of patriotism in furtherance of the 'racket' of protecting profits.[5]

Bevan was here striking an essentially Mosleyite note, calling for some action, any action, to acknowledge the existence of nearly three million unemployed. He continued to despise MacDonald even more than he hated the Tories. Far from the Prime Minister having been 'captured' by the Tories, he suggested in 1934 that it was MacDonald who had 'succeeded in enveloping the Cabinet in the misty, murky twilight in which he usually moves'.[6] When the Government was not activated by open class vindictiveness in cutting benefits to the poor, its attempts to be seen as trying to be constructive he dismissed as a hollow sham: most notably the 1934 Depressed Areas Bill, appointing a single Commissioner for England and Wales and another for Scotland to examine and encourage local development schemes that might stimulate employment, was 'an idle and empty farce'.[7]

> I will prophesy that in six months' time the commissioner who has been appointed will be one of the most disillusioned, cynical and soured persons that the Government has ever used as a decoy to do a shabby job of work. He will be compelled to turn down scheme after scheme. He will be frustrated by Government Department after Government Department, and he will realise that he is merely being used as a cats-paw for a Government already advanced in the stages of senile decay.[8]

Bevan repeatedly condemned the 'humbug and cant'[9] of Tory (and still more of Liberal) Members who professed sympathy for the plight of the unemployed but never voted to do anything practical to relieve it. Some of his most powerful passages were simply descriptions of the conditions in his and other distressed constituencies in an effort to bring the Government's supporters to see the problem in terms of individuals instead of statistical abstractions. In one speech in 1934 he effectively contrasted the unemployment assistance level for children – 2/- a week – with the rates of a well-known dogs' home which charged 1/3 *a day* for the smallest breed of dog, 2/- for the biggest.[10] He continually attacked the whole principle, not of the means test as such, but of the *family* means test, by which members of a household who were lucky enough to be in work were obliged to keep their fathers, sons or brothers who were unemployed. 'There is no more effective instrument', he insisted, 'for breaking up the homes of industrial workers.'[11] It was not that working people wished to evade their proper family responsibilities (though he could scarcely contain his anger when Tories like Lord Dunglass – Sir Alec Douglas-Home – got up to prate about the 'family instinct and pride of the working people of this country');[12] it was rather the shame and humiliation of the unemployed man obliged to be a burden on his family (as Bevan had been for a time supported by his sister) that drove people to leave home to throw themselves instead on the scrap heap in London or abroad. He was scathing about the ignorance of most Tories, raised by nannies and sent away to boarding schools, of the realities of ordinary family life. The dependent member of the family, he asserted, 'becomes hypersensitive ... and sees offence in every domestic relationship where no offence is intended. Working class homes are being made veritable hells of quarrelling in consequence.'[13] Instead of unemployment being recognised as a social problem which it was society's responsibility to cushion while it sought a cure, both the suffering and the cost were piled on to the working class, the victims and their families. The whole purpose of the means test, Bevan alleged, was 'to compel a large number of working class people to keep idle working class people' in order to save the taxpayer and depress wages.[14]

This was what he meant by a class policy, and he was frequently bitter, not to say abusive, in his denunciation of it. ('I do not want to threaten the Noble Lord,' he lashed out at one Tory who dared to laugh at his experience of the means test, 'but had he been nearer to me at that time I should have wiped the grin off his face. We know that the Noble Lord has no need to pass a Means Test. He and his family have thrived off the proceeds of banditry for centuries'.)[15] At the same time he would as often appeal to the humanity of the House, using all his rhetorical skill to arouse a sense of pity or social conscience in Members opposite, begging them as honourable men simply to show (a favourite word) a little *decency* to the less fortunate. For instance, after a detailed summary of a recent report on the medical condition of children in his constituency in 1932 he commented bitterly that 'The Ministry of Health and the Ministry of Labour are declaring to the Monmouthshire County Council that under their interpretation of the means test a child in Blaenavon, Nantyglo-Blaina and Rhymney-Abertwssyg is too fat, that it must sacrifice another few pounds' weight to keep the National Government in office.' But he ended passionately: 'I plead with Parliament not to try to build Great Britain on the basis of under-nourished babies. *Try to do the decent thing.*'[16] In this mood he transcended party politics.

In other speeches, however, Bevan would make a reasoned case for an explicitly *socialist* solution to whatever problem was under discussion, treating the House to a theoretical – though always vivid – lecture on why the Government's half-hearted attempts to smooth the rough edges of capitalism could not work. Though not, of course, a free trader, he scorned the Government's tariff policy which protected but did not attempt to plan the output of selected industries. 'All that the Safeguarder wants to do', he argued in November 1931, 'is to build a wall around chaos. He does not control or direct the chaos. He does not scientifically organise it. He builds a wall around the jungle and imagines that that is control. We want to clear the jungle.'[17] Welcoming, in 1933, the fact that planning was now in fashion ('The Russians have won their first victory over the West') he dismissed the Government's characteristically fraudulent attempt, in the Agricultural Marketing Bill, to apply it first to the least suitable industry, in order to prop up the landlords. This was not 'State planning as State planning has been understood'. It was merely 'the substitution of organised plunder for disorganised theft'.[18] Similarly, the subsidising of the Building Societies was no way to solve the housing shortage.

You are, in fact, pumping the oxygen of State security into a tottering industry, instead of coming forward openly and saying that this industry for the last ten years has not been able to do its job, but has been kept artificially alive by money provided by the State, and that if the job is to be done intelligently at all, it must be done on the basis of a State plan and a State drive behind it, with the State able to take a survey of the whole population and to build houses in those districts where houses will be required, not merely where they are required. The State plan should be before, not after, the fact.[19]

The area in which planning was most desperately needed was the location of industry. This Bevan made his special theme; for he had a crying example of the effects of the unplanned development of industry in his own constituency. The long-established steel works in Ebbw Vale had been idle since 1929. It was now (in 1934) sentenced to closure by GKN building a new plant at Cardiff, which was more accessible to road, rail and sea transport. But in defence of the Ebbw Vale community Bevan argued that in modern conditions 'industry is more mobile than man'.[20]

If you are going to argue that the cost of production at the new plant in Cardiff is lower than the cost of producing steel in Ebbw Vale, you must add to the cost of production certain social costs which have not yet entered into the calculation, the cost of transplanting your population, the cost of building houses, laying sewers, building schools and so on. That is an item that never appears on the balance sheet but society has to pay it; these new steel works, ultimately, will have to carry it, its products will have to carry it.[21]

At least, he maintained in 1935, the workpeople whom society 'for its own purposes and for efficiency, has specialised ... in their particular place of living' were entitled to be compensated for being thus either uprooted or made redundant.[22] In 1936 he played some part in getting Ebbw Vale reopened (no thanks, he insisted, to the Government). But in the meantime he had broadened the scope of his argument. In a tremendous speech in July 1935 he drew attention to the absurdity of spending £40 million on the electrification of railways in north London to cope with the vast influx of population while millions more were being poured out in unemployment benefit in South Wales and other areas which depopulation was leaving derelict. In the past, he argued, the location of industry was dictated by physical requirements – at the mouths of rivers or where coal was found – and centres of population were established accordingly. Now that state of affairs had ended:

The development of electrical power, the ability to create atmospheres inside factories and the transport system, all combined, have made industry infinitely mobile, and although man has developed on the old sites of industry a complicated social apparatus, the economic foundations of that apparatus have been sapped by the movements of industry in obeying the caprice of seeking a very uncertain margin of profit.

In an island the size of Britain, Bevan maintained, it made little economic difference where industry was sited. It was 'a monstrous proposition that a large community must be shifted from one spot to another, sometimes only twenty miles away . . . because the works will then be more favourably situated from a competitive point of view'. Moreover it was not just a question of preserving old communities. 'If London goes on swelling much more, it will become completely intolerable.'[23] As the new light industries multiplied in hideous ribbon developments along the arterial roads out of London, the need for controlling their location was becoming as urgent for London as for South Wales. Had the Government only discharged its responsibility, Bevan asserted in March 1936, 'the shocking excrescences, the aesthetic barbarities of the vulgarised belt around London would have been prevented'. As it was, he regarded the jerry-builder as 'a worse enemy of Great Britain than the Germans could ever be' and – anticipating John Betjemen's famous poem 'Come, friendly bombs, and fall on Slough' – positively looked forward to some air raids, so long as the population could be evacuated![24] Without deliberate planning, he warned, 'you will have the complete destruction of all the rural parts of the South and South-East of England while you leave the North and North-West an industrial graveyard'.[25]

Without compulsory powers, Bevan maintained, the Government's distressed areas legislation was useless. The new industries would continue to concentrate in the south-east because that was where the money was. The Chancellor of the Exchequer must cut into the vicious circle by increasing the purchasing power of the poor. Though he went out of his way to scorn Keynes as a Liberal concerned only to palliate the worst excesses of capitalism in order essentially to preserve it, Bevan was a strong supporter of the underconsumptionist explanation of unemployment first developed by J.A.Hobson and elaborated in the twenties by the ILP and by Mosley. 'What this country and the whole civilised world are looking for at the present time are spenders,' he remarked during a taxation debate in 1932, 'not savers.'[26] In 1934 he rebuked the Chancellor (Neville Chamberlain) for boasting of a £31 million Budget surplus. 'He had no right to boast that he had a surplus. If the Chancellor of the Exchequer has had such a surplus he has either miscalculated or has cheated people for a year.'[27] He should have used it to stimulate the home market. Unemployment, Bevan asserted in 1933, was nothing to do with the failure of the gold standard, but with 'the failure of modern industry to distribute purchasing power in the places where goods may be consumed. Until you devise a financial and economic system that bridges the gulf between modern production and consumption you are not going to solve the difficulty.'[28] 'Devising a system' meant for Bevan imposing a rational and ordered pattern upon economic life, instead of leaving it to the chances of the market place. That for him was socialism, and it was his great gift in these thirties debates to make it sound like the simplest common sense.

Finally, he threatened: not merely long-term political defeat for the Tories but, repeatedly, short-term social disorder if they remained deaf to the cries from the distressed areas. 'The demonstrations you have had this winter', he warned in November 1932, 'will be a pup compared with what you will have next winter. ... Unless the Government comes to our relief in a much more substantial way than in this Resolution, it will create such vengeance in these districts as this society will not be able to survive.'[29] Their penny-pinching, he predicted the following April, 'will cost them more in the maintenance of police and soldiers than they will save in relief'.[30] As time went on and his lurid prophecies went obstinately unfulfilled, provoking only ribaldry from the Tory benches, Bevan became more strident, not merely predicting but positively encouraging violence, as for instance in June 1936:

> I ask hon. Members opposite to tell me what they think these people can do. You have deprived them of any voice anywhere. You have established 7000 officials without the slightest responsibility to the people, and we cannot control them here. What do hon. Members opposite suggest they should do? Vote every four or five years? I am not going to use exaggerated language, but I hope that if the Regulations which are brought in worsen the condition of people in my district they will behave in such a manner that you will require to send a regular army to keep order. ['Shame'.] I say that without the slightest hesitation.
>
> I say quite frankly – I am weighing my words carefully – that there is only one way in which hon. Members opposite can be brought to reason, and that is by trouble outside, because argument inside the House has failed to move them. If Income Tax is under consideration, those benches are packed. If electricity is under consideration those benches are packed. If there is some opposition to a little municipal Bill for which hon. Members have been subsidised by private concerns, those benches are packed. If it is a sugar subsidy they are packed. If it is a swab the benches are packed, but if it is the poor, they are empty. There is only one way in which the poor can make their voice heard here and that is by making trouble outside.[31]

Always, in his despair of the present, Bevan retained his absolute confidence that the future lay with Labour. 'Small though we are,' he told the jeering Tories in 1933, 'the time will come when we shall occupy the seats of power, and you will not be here to jeer.'*[32] The inexplicable docility of the unemployed could not last for ever. The more dreadful the conditions in South Wales and elsewhere, the more palpable became the breakdown of capitalism and the more certain, therefore, its ultimate collapse and supersession by socialism. The only thing that could postpone this eventual victory was the Tories, as their system foundered, abolishing democracy, as his Marxist training assured him they were bound to do. As fascism spread over

---

* Did he, in such speeches, recall Jack London's Ernest Everhard battling to be heard in Congress (before the Iron Heel closed it down)? '"I know nothing I can say can influence you," he said. "You have no souls to be influenced. ... You are lick-spittles and panderers, the creatures of the Plutocracy. You talk verbosely in antiquated terminology of your love of liberty, and all the while you wear the scarlet livery of the Iron Heel". ... "Remember", he said, in a voice that made itself heard above the din, "that as you show mercy now to the proletariat, some day will that same proletariat show mercy to you"' (Jack London, *The Iron Heel*, pp. 160–1).

the continent, he convinced himself that this was the inevitable accompaniment of collapsing capitalism (this was the orthodox Communist view) and that Baldwinism was merely a mild British form of fascism. 'If we are allowed at this moment a large measure of liberty in this country,' he argued in April 1933, three months after the rise of Hitler, 'it is simply that we are not frightening you enough. When we frighten you sufficiently you will put us in gaol with exactly the same brutality. . . . Political toleration is a by-product of the complacency of the ruling class. When that complacency is disturbed there never was a more bloody-minded set of thugs than the British ruling class.'[33] 'As your system declines,' he solemnly prophesied a few weeks later, 'your attacks upon democracy will become more and more bitter. As you take away the workers' standard of life, you will take away the liberties about which you boast, and your moral and economic decline will be accompanied by bloody-mindedness and thuggism, because you will have nothing at all left to defend it.'[34] The implausibility of likening Baldwin and Chamberlain to Hitler and Goering sometimes drove him to paradoxical lengths. 'There is something to be said for Fascism,' he announced in March 1934. 'At any rate it is open; they bring their Fascists and their hooligans; they do not do it in evening-dress, or bring up smug-faced, mealy-mouthed lawyers to defend them. You are taking away from the working classes any means they might have had of making their voices heard in the councils of the people.'[35]

This was his chief complaint, that the Government was continually taking the most urgent interests of the unemployed away from the direct control of the House of Commons and making them the responsibility of non-elected bodies like the Unemployment Assistance Board and the Special Areas Commissioners, who were not answerable to MPs. The 1933 Unemployment Bill he condemned on this ground as 'an attempt to take poverty out of politics. . . . A Bill to make the poor dumb.'[36] 'In the past', he argued, 'the buffer between you and the people has been this Chamber.' Democracy required that the House should be 'exposed, day by day, to the aggregate pressure of public opinion'; if that access was blocked, 'then the working classes of this country had better make up their minds at once that they have to meet their enemies somewhere else than on the Floor of this Chamber. . . . If you want to take away from the ordinary man', he warned, 'the tongue with which he speaks, the voice with which he protests, the institutions through which he has for centuries given articulation to his aspirations, you do so at your own peril and you, and not we, will regret it.'[37]

With this somewhat idealised view of the historic function of Parliament, Bevan became paradoxically from his Marxist starting-point the staunchest champion of the rights of the House of Commons. It became a central tenet of his political philosophy that Ministers should be able to be questioned on every detail of public administration, even on individual cases, not able to hide behind remote bodies. In Government a decade later he insisted that he, as Minister of Health, should be accountable for every dropped bedpan in the National Health Service; conversely he regretted the Morrisonian system of autonomous corporations under which Labour fulfilled (but from the point of view of popular control betrayed) its long-standing commitment to nationalise the coal mines, railways and power industries. As a backbencher in the thirties, he developed an acute sensitivity to the most trifling instance of the National Government failing to show proper respect for the House or short-cutting – as Governments, particularly Governments with large majorities, are always inclined to do – established procedures. This was a blatantly self-contradictory posture for one who, with Mosley in 1930, had proposed far more radical measures than the National Government ever contemplated to speed up legislation; and there were younger Conservatives like Robert Boothby, themselves impatient for more action, who were unimpressed by his new-found reverence for hallowed forms.[38] On occasion, Bevan himself was frank about this inconsistency. 'The duty of a democratic party', he declared in 1931, 'is to expose the rich to the attack of the poor. ... It is the duty of a working class party ... to surrender no democratic privilege or political articulation until power has been accomplished.'[39] The implication was clear that a working-class party once in power might be entitled to act differently; and during the thirties he regularly cautioned the Government's supporters that one day it might be they who would have need of the protection of the constitution to save their skins. Through the mastery of procedure for the purposes of opposition, however, Bevan grew into an appreciation, even love, of the House of Commons for its own sake which transcended his more ruthless professions that Parliament was simply a weapon in the class war.

This did not mean that he always deferred to the Speaker. Going right back to his early days in the pits, he had always been a barrack-room lawyer; in the Tredegar Town Council and in miners' delegate conferences he was constantly in dispute with the chair; and in the Commons he was repeatedly called to order and regularly contested the Speaker's rulings. He was frequently out of order because he insisted on elevating debate from the detailed matter under discussion in order to display the opposed principles of society which he always believed lay behind it; he became highly skilled at anticipating this objection by jumping in, as soon as the Minister in his opening statement made some hackneyed generalisation, to claim that if this was in order it must equally be in order for himself, later, to refute it. There often followed lengthy wrangles over the rules of order which so tired the Speaker and the House that he frequently got away with language which would not have been tolerated from anyone else, as when in 1936 he called Neville Chamberlain 'a cynical assassin' and refused to withdraw.[40] Only once, in 1937, did he get himself suspended from the House: this was after an incident (at four o'clock in the morning on the Special Areas Bill) when he called on the chairman to 'leave the chair' and told him repeatedly that his conduct in granting the Tories the closure over Labour objections was 'abominable'.[41] Usually he was cleverer at skating on thin ice without falling in. He was a master of the sweetly veiled insult. 'The Noble Lord the Member for Hastings smiles with his customary courtesy and vacuity,' he purred in 1933;[42] alternatively (in 1936), 'If the hyena opposite would give me his attention . . .' (though this he was forced to withdraw).[43] Such childish gibes apart, however, what stands out is the deliberation and resourcefulness with which Bevan, as an individual backbencher, set out to exploit the rules of the parliamentary game to the limit, serving both the short-term end of harassing the Government at every turn and the long-term one of forcing it to pay attention to the arena where, he believed, Labour's victory must eventually be won.

Nevertheless he did not think the class war could be fought *only* in Parliament or even, given the National Government's huge impervious majority, primarily in Parliament. Working-class consciousness and unity must be promoted in the country – partly by normal electoral means to restore Labour's interrupted momentum towards winning a House of Commons majority in the future, but also by marches, demonstrations and strikes as the only means of fighting back *now* against the threat of fascism, in which he really believed. At the TUC in September 1933 the General Secretary, Walter Citrine, introduced a General Council report on events in Germany, attacking the Communist Party as the mirror-image of the Nazis and repudiating the resort to force in defence of democracy. Bevan, attending as an individual delegate, condemned Citrine's as 'the most dangerous speech' he had ever heard; the idea that the choice was between democracy and dictatorship, he argued, assumed that capitalism could recover. Instead Bevan insisted on his Marxist analysis that 'Hitlerism is the defence of capitalism by violence when democracy threatens capitalism' and sombrely predicted that 'democracy may have to be defended by the bodies of its supporters'. He urged as well an industrial offensive in pursuit of higher wages. 'Then there will be no fear of Fascism.' Congress, however, was unmoved by this sort of alarmist talk and his amendment was overwhelmingly rejected.[44]

In South Wales, Bevan was already organising physical resistance to the 'thuggism' he anticipated. Following an anti-fascist meeting at Cardiff in May which broke up in disorder after he had had a row with the chairman over the Labour Party's embargo on co-operating with Communists, he set up in Tredegar a Workers' Freedom Group which was intended to be the model for others all over the country. Its aims, as set out in the manifesto which Bevan drew up, were ambitious and a little chilling:

1. To defend liberty in every form in the certain belief that capitalism is the enemy of liberty and that as the workers learn to use the instruments of democracy more effectively, capitalism will use force against democracy and that the workers will be called upon to defend it by force.
2. To make war on the second enemy of democracy, corruption and negligence, and to cleanse and keep clean all those democratic organisations by means of which the workers hope to achieve the New Society.

3. To keep a vigilant watch on the liberties and rights won by a century long struggle for the workers and to defend them against the encroachments which are already taking place.

4. To promote all forms of working-class resistance to a lower standard of life. ...

5. To encourage and organise physical training among the workers in readiness to meet any demands that may be made upon them.

6. To form First Aid Units in every group. ...

9. To encourage the dignity and self-reliance of all workers in the conviction that they, and they alone, can redeem human society.[45]

In pursuit of the redemption of human society and the 'cleansing' of working-class organisations, Bevan led his band of former members of the Query Club on route marches over the Brecon Beacons; they had no weapons and 'physical training' only meant long walks. The reality was much less Orwellian than the sort of paramilitary vigilante force conjured up by the manifesto, little more in fact than a harmless local variant of the thirties' fitness craze. Nevertheless it is a striking indication of Bevan's frame of mind in 1933 that he could write such heady nonsense.*

Of much more real importance was his strong support for the famous Hunger Marches organised by the Communist-led National Unemployed Workers' Movement, particularly those of 1934 and 1936. On both occasions, with a handful of other Labour MPs like Edith Summerskill and Ellen Wilkinson, Bevan was one of the reception committee which met the marchers on their arrival in London, despite the official disapproval of the Labour Party and the TUC, whose timidity shocked him. 'Why should a first-class piece of work like the Hunger March have been left to the initiative of unofficial members of the Party, and to the Communists and the ILP?' he demanded in 1936. 'Consider what a mighty response the workers would have made if the whole machinery of the Labour Movement had been mobilised for the Hunger March and its attendant activities.'[46] The participation of the Communists, from whose embrace the leadership recoiled, was for Bevan the most important thing about the marches. 'The Hunger Marchers have achieved one thing,' he told a welcoming rally in Hyde Park (at which Attlee put in a somewhat sheepish appearance):

They have for the first time in the history of the national Labour Movement achieved a united platform. Communists, ILP-ers, Socialists, members of the Labour Party and Co-operators for the first time have joined hands together, and we are not going to unclasp them. This demonstration proves to the country that Labour needs a united leadership.[47]

---

* Was there yet another echo of Ernest Everhard, whose revolutionary vanguard, the 'Fighting Groups', is said in *The Iron Heel* to have been his 'greatest achievement' (Jack London, *The Iron Heel*, p. 157)?

But drawing this moral was where he clashed most bitterly with the party leadership, and in particular with Ernest Bevin, who knew all about Communists in the TGWU and wanted nothing to do with them. Bevin and Bevan could not have been more starkly opposed types of socialist. Over the next ten years each came to loathe everything that the other stood for. Bevin was the trade union block vote made flesh, a massive man with a steamroller of a mind, a proletarian contempt for intellectuals and a brutal disregard for minorities of all sorts, whom he equated with troublemakers: what was good for the Transport and General Workers, he believed, was good for all, and that was socialism. Bevan, on the contrary, regarded such an attitude as the antithesis of socialism: in their preoccupation with the short-term sectional interest of their members, the big unions neglected the higher historic claims of the working class as a whole, while their increasing preference for cosy deals with the Government behind closed doors, instead of class confrontation, reeked to him of fascist corporatism, not democracy. In his support for the NUWM, and in other more detailed ways in the House of Commons, Bevan appointed himself, to the fury of Bevin, the champion of the un-unionised – the unemployed and those whose employers did not recognise unions – against the arrogant dominion of the big bureaucracies. The fact that he was himself sponsored by the SWMF did not deter him in the slightest. For the rest of his life Bevan's battle within the Labour Party was principally against the stranglehold over its democratic processes exercised by the bosses of a few big unions, most specifically Bevin and his equally tough but less gifted successor in the early fifties, Arthur Deakin.

In the thirties the issue was unity. To Bevan, the first principle of good trade unionism dictated that the working class, under attack as he believed it to be, should be united in self-defence. Instead, the effect of 1931 was to split the labour movement into three or four mutually suspicious fragments, each claiming to show the workers the true road to socialism. Bevan had no use for splinter parties. He had never been tempted to join the Communist Party when several of his old associates in South Wales – and now his friend John Strachey, too – had done so; nor had he joined the ILP. Emotionally, he had every sympathy with the frustration with the official Labour Party which drove the ILP, under the wayward leadership of Jimmy Maxton, to disaffiliate from the party in 1932 in order to try to outflank it on the left. But, more soberly, he saw clearly that it would be a disastrous strategic error: by cutting themselves off from Labour, the ILP cut themselves off from the unions and consigned themselves instantly to irrelevance. 'You will not influence the course of British politics by as much as a hair's breadth,' he told Jennie Lee who, as a Scottish member, went loyally with Maxton against her better judgement.

> Why don't you get into a nunnery and be done with it? Lock yourself up in a separate cell away from the world and its wickedness. My Salvation Army lassie. Poor little Casabianca. That was a hell of an intelligent performance now, wasn't it? I tell you, it is the Labour Party or nothing. I know all its faults, all its dangers.

But it is the party that we have taught millions of working people to look to and regard as their own. We can't undo what we have done. And I am by no means convinced that something cannot yet be made of it.[48]

That was Bevan's essential realism, and the source of his essential, ultimately unshakeable, loyalty to Labour: 'It is the Labour Party or nothing.' In the same spirit he refused to join the Socialist League, set up by Frank Wise and other ILPers who declined to follow Maxton, which began as a left-wing research bureau but quickly became a second ILP, virtually a party within the party, politically and financially dominated by Cripps. 'I feel it in my bones', he wrote prophetically to Wise, 'that the "great days" of the Labour Party are yet to come. . . . I want to be as free as possible from personal entanglements and those obligations arising out of associations which tend to obscure one's vision and limit one's freedom of decision.'[49] Was he still scarred by his association with Mosley? Given that they existed, however, he wanted to co-operate with the League, and with the ILP, and with the Communist Party too, and throughout the decade he fought for his right to do so against the determination of the party establishment to distance Labour as far as possible from any taint of contact, particularly with the Communists. No more than the others, Bevan argued, should Labour insist on its exclusiveness: as by far the largest party it should have the self-confidence to lead all the working-class groups in a single alliance against the Government and against international fascism. The row provoked by his insistence on this view came to a head at the 1934 Conference, when the National Executive proscribed association with the Relief Committee for the Victims of German Fascism – on whose behalf he and Jennie had been on a fund-raising tour of the United States over the summer – as being a Communist front organisation. Bevan denounced not only this ruling but the principle behind it as intolerable. 'We are informed', he said, 'that in the future it is not membership of an organisation which is wrong, but *association* with members of proscribed organisations.' Yet he had frequently shared platforms with members of other parties. 'Where an organisation has invited me to go on the platform for a special job in which I have believed, I have felt it my duty to co-operate with them. In the future, however, if I speak on the platform with a member of the Communist Party, then I am immediately associating with a proscribed organisation; but' – and this was the double standard which Bevan found it hardest to bear – 'if I speak on a platform with a Tory I am not.' Co-operation with establishment bodies like the League of Nations Union was all right. Bevan always believed as a matter of principle that there were 'no enemies on the left'. He blamed 'the inertia, lack of enterprise and insipidity of the Executive' for the fact that the Communist Party was so often left to take the lead in organising marches and demonstrations which Labour should be organising for itself. In these circumstances, he declared, a Labour Member who wanted a more active policy was bound to associate with anyone who gave a lead.[50]

Bevin's reply for the Executive was characteristically brutal. The Communists, he asserted, were as much the enemy of the labour movement as were the fascists: there was nothing to choose between them. He accused Bevan of trying to 'let the Fascists in' when he had voted in the House of Commons for a Liberal amendment 'to the detriment of the trade union movement'. (The amendment was actually to give non-union workers the same right as union members to appeal against the decisions of the Unemployment Assistance Board.) Violently, Bevin denounced Bevan's disloyalty at a time when the unions 'had fought their damnedest to try and deal with this unemployment problem'. When Bevan tried to protest, he taunted him that he was too thin-skinned to take back the medicine he dished out to others. 'No, in this conference, Aneurin Bevan, you are not going to get the flattery of the gossip columns that you get in London. . . . You are going to get the facts.'[51]

Bevin's language, as well as the block votes which he commanded, demonstrated the extent to which his near-namesake remained an isolated maverick within the Labour Party.

Chapter 5

'Bollinger Bolshevik, Lounge-Lizard Lenin'

Bevin's rough treatment of Bevan at the 1934 Conference, and particularly his reference to 'the flattery of the gossip columns', is a startling indication of how Bevan, the stern class warrior, had come to be regarded in the Labour Party. Despite a record of frequent and effective speaking in the House, he was coming to be seen by many as a social-climbing dilettante who was leaving his mining origins far behind him: a hollow pot who made a lot of noise about the unemployed to cover the fact that he spent most of his time, not with them in his constituency or drinking beer with his colleagues in the trade union group in the PLP, but hobnobbing with the rich and fashionable in the West End. ('I hear', wrote one old friend to him in 1934, 'that you are now the Playboy of the Westend World.')[1] There is nothing more calculated to offend the collective class-instinct of the Labour Party. Bevan's playboy reputation did him immense harm over the next twenty years. It was both well founded in fact and politically quite irrelevant.

Bevan as a young man in Tredegar had been a bit of a puritan, dedicated exclusively to politics and self-education. He read voraciously; he walked over the hills and he talked while walking; his only social relaxation was an occasional game of billiards. He did not drink much: he was not an habitué of the pub or the workingmen's club. When he went on holiday to Blackpool he spent it speaking and handing out leaflets at street corners. London, and the luxury of a small parliamentary salary, liberated him, releasing a side of his personality hitherto submerged. He discovered art and architecture, good food and wine and the company of a far wider circle than he had previously known of clever people who stimulated and challenged his love of argument. Greedily, once he had found his feet, he threw himself into all these pleasures, hungry to make up for his lost youth and refusing to be confined within the narrow world of Westminster. Within the House, he made his friends across party boundaries; outside it he frequented the Café Royal and the company of artists like Jacob Epstein, Matthew Smith and Michael Ayrton, discovering a bohemian lifestyle and the exhilaration of speculative talk beyond the ken of his staider colleagues. Here he could spin words to his heart's – and his hearers' – content with no Speaker to call him to order.

He was also drawn into the web of that most sinister collector of conspicuous young talents, Lord Beaverbrook, the millionaire proprietor of the *Daily Express* and the last person it was wise for an ambitious Labour MP to be seen dining with. But Beaverbrook was a most unconventional Conservative and an entrepreneur of good talk: his protégés were the rebels and iconoclasts in all parties, the more provocative the better. Bevan was at this period his ideal dinner-table socialist; he in turn responded warmly to the hospitality and stimulation Beaverbrook offered, the opportunity to cross swords in a relaxed atmosphere with eminent writers like H.G.Wells and Arnold Bennett, young friends from the 1929 Parliament like Edward Marjoribanks and Frank Owen, or new sparring partners like Brendan Bracken or the journalist and society wit Lord Castlerosse. His presence in this company excited the jealousy of those who were not so favoured. Tom Clarke of the *News Chronicle*, for example, bidden to Cherkley, Beaverbrook's house near Leatherhead, in September 1932, wrote tartly in his diary that 'One very cocksure little person who seemed to be enjoying himself was Aneurin Bevan the Socialist. He addressed Beaverbrook familiarly as Max.'[2] Among Beaverbrook's regular cronies, on the other hand, Bevan's luxurious tastes were merely a matter for extravagant leg-pulling. Randolph Churchill recalled a memorable outburst by Brendan Bracken:

> 'You Bollinger Bolshevik, you ritzy Robespierre, you lounge-lizard Lenin,' he roared at Bevan one night, gesturing, as he went on, somewhat in the manner of a domesticated orang-outang. 'Look at you, swilling Max's champagne and calling yourself a socialist.'[3]

But Bevan habitually gave as good as he got. 'Why shouldn't I like good wine?' he once answered Bracken. 'The best I've ever had from you, by the way, Brendan, I'd call bottom lower-class Bolshevik Bollinger.'[4]

Unquestionably Beaverbrook liked to put his favourites in his debt. Quite soon after he adopted Bevan, in February 1932, Bevan had some medical trouble which Beaverbrook pressed him to have treated – at his expense. Bevan's reply is a model of tactful refusal, ending with a bold candour which shows that Bevan understood very clearly the risk he was running in accepting Beaverbrook's patronage and knew exactly how much he could take without compromising his independence.

> My Lord,
> I have just received your very kind and thoughtful letter.
> The delay was caused by my having run away from everything, letters included, in order to cure me of my illness.
> This I have almost succeeded in doing and I hope after the Recess to resume my public duties.

There is therefore no need for me to avail myself of your kind offer to consult your medical advisers.

Nevertheless a warmth remains with me because of your offer and the kindness which prompted it.

The circumstances in which this letter is written tempts me to say what otherwise I should lack courage to say.

You hold a position of great power and consequence and this tends to falsify your personal relationships with people. It is, therefore, difficult to speak to you as one would speak to those differently situated. But as one who hates the power you hold, and the order of life which enables you to wield it, and furthermore, because I know I shall never seek that power for myself, I feel emboldened to tell you that I hold you in the most affectionate regard, and confess to a great admiration for those qualities of heart and mind which, unfortunately, do not appear to inspire your public policy.

And now, having been as impudent as I know how, will you please take my most affectionate greetings for yourself, and convey my respectful regards to Mrs Campbell.*

Yours,
Aneurin Bevan[5]

Three years later, after his marriage to Jennie Lee, Bevan had further occasion to keep Beaverbrook's patronage at arm's length. Again he did so firmly, though with evident regret, in a letter whose beginning and ending show how much closer their relationship had become in the intervening period.

Dear Max,

This morning I talked over with Jennie the suggestion which you were kind enough to make last night about the cottage on your Cherkley estate.

As you know Jennie springs from the same Covenanter stock as yourself, only she has sprung further, or not quite as far, according to the point of view. She takes the view, for which there is of course much to be said, that it would be improper for us to live within the shadow of your castle walls. Like Lobengula,† you cast a long shadow, and it is difficult to grow under it.

In plain English, we think it would be politically indiscreet for us to take the cottage on your estate. We feel it is extremely kind of you to have offered to have us, and we are exceedingly sorry that our views of political expediency compel us to go elsewhere, in less congenial surroundings.

Yours affectionately
Aneurin[6]

Though tongues wagged, few people handled Beaverbrook more skilfully or came out of his dangerous embrace less scathed.

Bevan and Jennie Lee married in October 1934. They had then been good friends for five years, but until the previous November Jennie had been deeply in love with Frank Wise; she was prevented from marrying him only

* Beaverbrook's daughter Janet, married to Ian Campbell, later 11th Duke of Argyll.
† The King of the Zulus who defeated the British at Isandhlwana in 1879.

by the obstacle of a divorce which would have been political suicide for both of them. When Wise suddenly died, Bevan was her support; but she was doubtful about marrying him, as she wrote to a friend:

> Frank was solid gold. Ni is quicksilver. He is as unreliable as Frank was reliable. He is moody, self-indulgent, but in a curious way he is a brother to me. Our mining background, our outlooks, hopes and despairs are most similar. If I do decide to share with him it will be an emotionally and financially rocky business, and perhaps I am merely seeking another kind of pain to kill the one that is with me.[7]

'How little I knew Nye,' she commented on this letter in her autobiography. 'How blind I was to his true character.'

They got married because neither could afford gossip that they were living in sin. For Jennie in particular, trying to regain her North Lanark seat for the ILP, any scandal would have been fatal. Bevan's seat in Ebbw Vale was practically invulnerable, but his lifestyle was irregular enough already without adding a further provocation to respectable opinion. He took her for a lavish dinner in the Café Royal, the food and wine carefully ordered in advance ('You can always live like a millionaire for five minutes,' he told her) and persuaded her that they had no choice.[8] Even so the marriage was one to raise eyebrows. As a member of a party which had disaffiliated from Labour two years earlier, Jennie was a political opponent: in the 1935 election the Labour Party in North Lanark put up a candidate against her who took just enough votes to cost her victory. Cross-party friendships within the House were one thing, but to marry across party boundaries was another. Then there was Jennie's determination to keep her name – no 'Mrs Bevan' for her – and pursue her own career as a lecturer and journalist: there were to be no babies. In every way the marriage defied convention – and intrigued the gossip columnists. It took place at Holborn Registry Office before three witnesses; both bride and groom, the *Express* gasped, were hatless and gloveless, and there was no ring and no cake![9] 'We live in a kind of embattled toleration,' Nye told the *Sunday Chronicle* after two years. 'But our domestic felicity survives our political antagonism. ... Marriage is excellent if only because it gives life a rhythm, which is essential to a man in my position. In this instance, of course, the rhythm is syncopated ... which is most stimulating.'[10]

Marriage did indeed give Bevan's life a secure centre: but, as a further oddity, the security was provided by his mother-in-law. After a year in Jennie's tiny London flat, Nye hankered for the country and they eventually found a dilapidated Tudor cottage, not on Beaverbrook's estate but at Brimpton Common, near Reading, where, after they had knocked it into habitable shape, they brought Jennie's retired miner father and her redoubtable mother, 'Ma' Lee, down from Scotland to live with them. Henceforth, while Nye and Jennie came and went in their separate careers, 'Ma' Lee kept house for them and was beloved by all their visitors. Jennie's memoirs make it clear that she was the light of their lives: Nye used to say that he had only married Jennie to get Ma.*

With so unconventional a life, on top of uncomfortable opinions, it is not surprising that Bevan should have been viewed askance, with a mixture of suspicion and jealousy, by some of his less brilliant and less newsworthy colleagues, particularly among the trade union members. Envy apart, it is easy to sympathise with their bewilderment. Politically, there was a *prima facie* inconsistency between Bevan's bitter denunciations of the capitalist class in the Commons and his fondness for the company of an unscrupulous press lord such as Beaverbrook; while personally, the confidence with which he appropriated to himself the language of art and ideas, littering his speeches with high-flown and sometimes far-fetched historical parallels, was bound to strike more earth-bound members of his party as pretentious and intended to make them feel inferior. The first suspicion was unfair: his colleagues were not to know how uncompromisingly he carried his arguments for socialism into circles where they were not normally heard. The second, however, contained a good deal of substance. For the truth was that Bevan increasingly was coming to see himself as superior to the common herd: he had conceived an image of himself, in the hierarchy not of class but of intellect and imagination, as a patrician, a natural aristocrat in the original Greek sense of the word, a member of the cultivated elite. He derived this idea, and supported it, from the writings of the Uruguayan philosopher José Enrique Rodo, whose major works, *Ariel* and *The Motives of Proteus*, were published in this country during the 1920s. From about this time onward, Bevan adopted Rodo as his favourite thinker, often reading selected passages to his guests after dinner as the text for a vaulting disquisition of his own. There was undoubtedly a touch of pretentiousness here. It is perhaps significant that he very rarely risked quoting Rodo in a public speech: no one in his audience would have heard of him. Reading Rodo today, it is windy stuff: very over-written (at least in translation), impossibly idealistic and reeking of cultural snobbery. It illuminates something important about Bevan that he should have taken him as his personal prophet.

The main theme of *Ariel* is the need to elevate the lofty idealism of the spirit above the sordid reality of the workaday world (represented by Caliban). A characteristically wordy injunction which Bevan certainly took to heart is the following (one has to imagine him reading it aloud):

> Try, then, to develop so far as possible not any single aspect, but the plenitude of your being. Shrug not your shoulders before any noble and fecund manifestation of human nature, under the pretext that your own individuality ties you

* In the 1950 General Election, the young Conservative candidate for Bexley, Edward Heath, incautiously suggested that the nation's housing crisis might have been solved 'if Aneurin Bevan and Jennie Lee had had to live with their in-laws'. To which a voice from the audience replied: 'They do!'. (Andrew Roth, *Heath and the Heathmen* [Routledge & Kegan Paul, 1972], p. 69.)

of preference to a different one. Be attentive spectators where you may not be actors. When that false and vulgarised idea of education, which thinks it subordinate wholly to utilitarian ends, takes upon itself to mutilate by such materialism the natural fulness of our minds, and by a premature specialisation to proscribe the teaching of anything that is disinterested or ideal, it fails to avoid the danger of training for the future minds that have become narrow, incapable of seeing more than one aspect of a thing which immediately touches them, separated as by a frozen desert from other minds that in the same society have chosen other aspects of our life. ...

I demand of you that in the battle of life you defend your souls against that mutilation of them by the tyranny of a single and self-interested object. Never give, to either passion or self-interest, but a small part of what is *you*. For even in material servitude there is a way to keep free one's inner self, the self of reason and of feeling. So never do you try to justify, by your absorption in labour, in conflict, the enslaving of your soul.[11]

Such a passage, applied to politics, was a trumpet call against the constraints of party discipline and the narrow-minded spirits who enforced it.

More importantly, the heart of *Ariel* is a warning against the risk of vulgarisation inherent in democracy. 'The clash between the democratic rule and the higher life', Rodo writes, 'becomes a fatal reality when that rule imparts the disregard of even legitimate superiorities and the substitution of mechanical government for a faith in heroism (in Carlyle's sense). All in civilisation that is more than material excellence, economic prosperity, is a height that will be levelled when moral authority is given to the average mind.'[12] 'The true and worthy notion of equality', he asserts a little further on,

rests on the assumption that all reasonable beings are endowed by nature with faculties capable of a noble development. The duty of a State consists in seeing that all its members are so placed as to be able to seek without favour their own *best*; in so arranging things as to bring to light each human superiority, wherever it exists. In such wise, after the initial equality, inequality, when it comes, will be justified; for it will be sanctioned either by the mysterious powers of nature or the deserving merit of volition.[13]

The example that Rodo fears is that of the United States, where the praiseworthy extension of popular education has only resulted in 'a sort of universal semi-culture and a profound indifference to the higher. ... The levelling by the middle classes tends ... to plane down what little remains of *intelligentsia*: the flowers are mown by the machine when the weeds remain.'[14] 'A democracy not subject to a superior instruction,' Rodo asserts, 'not trained in liberal schools to the understanding of true human excellence, tends always to that abominable brutality of the majority which despises the greater moral benefits of liberty and annuls in public opinion all respect for the dignity of the individual.'[15]

Bevan's devotion to Rodo sheds a new light on his socialism. Marx explained for him the struggles of the past and present, the historical process which had brought forth a structure of society stratified by the possession of economic power which it was the destiny of the disinherited working class to overthrow. But Rodo provided a vision of the classless future, when the problems of production should have been solved and man should have nothing left to do but cultivate his soul; a future, that is, classless in the Marxist sense that no class or individual should any more be disadvantaged by economic circumstance, but by no means flattened to a boring sameness; a future, on the contrary, in which native talent should enjoy full scope to realise its highest potential and full recognition for doing so; a society of 'heroes' exercising their 'legitimate superiority' over the 'average mind', of 'flowers' flourishing above the 'weeds'; a democracy 'subject to superior instruction' to civilise 'the abominable brutality of the majority'. Taken in its ideal sense, this vision merely recalls the precious fairyland of Oscar Wilde's *The Soul of Man under Socialism*, or the pre-industrial utopia of William Morris. If taken literally, however, it more alarmingly recalls Plato's Guardians, leading on, as we now know, to Big Brother and the Thought Police. It would be wrong to press such sinister interpretations too hard on to Bevan's taste for Rodo. He was, by instinct and theory alike, a democrat through and through. What appealed to him in Rodo was essentially the sense that there was a higher plane beyond the material (for which as a convinced atheist he had no theological explanation). Rodo gave lofty expression to his own deeply felt loathing of twentieth-century commercialism and particularly of modern cities. ('An organised society which limits its idea of civilisation to the accumulation of material abundance ... will never make of its great cities anything that differs essentially from the heaping-up of ant-hills.')[16] Rodo was his ready rebuke to narrow-mindedness and philistinism, the inspiration for a humane socialism concerned not with levelling but with elevating, not merely materially but morally – a lofty vision which by the end of his life he was terribly afraid had been lost for ever. Nevertheless Rodo's seductive democratic elitism can only have flattered and stimulated his sense that he, Nye Bevan, was one of the democratic elite. Of course, he *was*: he had every right to be proud of his self-acquired culture. But this pride bred in him a didactic, sometimes dictatorial, arrogance which could exasperate even his friends and made sworn enemies of men like Herbert Morrison and Ernie Bevin who thought him a posturing snob.

The suggestion was wide of the mark, however, that by indulging his expensive tastes Bevan betrayed his class. On the contrary, he saw himself blazing a trail for his class. He utterly rejected the belief that champagne was for 'them' and beer was good enough for the representatives of the workers. He had always believed that only the best was good enough for the workers and was determined to smash open the great houses, their libraries and wine cellars, to their assault. He cast himself as a truculent ambassador, out to show the boss class that an ordinary miner was in every respect a match for any of them. Of course, this was a highly convenient rationalisation of his own pleasures; but it was sincere. He despaired of the timidity and deference of so many Labour Members who 'knew their place' and stayed true to their roots. That, he believed, was no way to advance socialism.

Of Bevan least of all men could it be alleged that he was tamed by the company he kept. After 1931, and the defection of MacDonald and Thomas, the Labour Party was hypersensitive to the danger of its leaders succumbing to the aristocratic embrace. And it is true that the sort of socialist whose socialism was principally a function of his class could very readily change his political complexion as he took on the governmental perspective of Westminster and Whitehall. Had Bevan been of that sort, the company of Mosley and Marjoribanks, Beaverbrook and Bracken might well have quenched the fire in his belly. But this was where his critics did not see that Bevan was different from themselves: his socialism was not merely a function of his class but rooted in his intellect, in the ineradicable Marxism of his fundamental assumptions about society. Thus his conviction that capitalism was historically doomed was not altered by the enjoyment he got from the company of individual capitalists: indeed it was the knowledge that capitalism was doomed that enabled him to enjoy their company, since he could not – at least in his more generous moods – blame them for playing out the role ordained for them.* The truth is that Bevan was intellectually inoculated against the aristocratic, or bourgeois, embrace. The British Labour Party in general, however, lacking any such fundamentalist commitment, has been for most of its history wide open to the temptations of moderation and creeping revisionism, of which Bevan, with a handful of largely middle-class allies, was all his life the most principled opponent.

Essentially, then, it was not his personal habits but his politics which isolated him in the thirties. There were few in the Labour Party who, whatever they thought of his private character, were not impressed by his ability; the trouble was that he kept on taking up impossible positions in opposition to the party line which obliged the loyalists to shun him, and seemed positively to insist on being always out of step with the majority. The sense of a great talent wasting itself in righteous irresponsibility was well caught in a perceptive profile by the Tory MP Vyvyan Adams (writing under the pseudonym 'Watchman') published in 1939:

> If he were a little less quarrelsome, if he were not so much the *enfant terrible* that Members of his own Front Bench have been known to turn round after a disorderly interjection and say 'Behave yourself, Bevan!', if he were slightly more industrious, he might be the future leader whom Labour must discover unless half our democratic organisation is to be atrophied.

* Once again, Bevan's view was taken straight from Ernest Everhard, the hero of *The Iron Heel*: 'We foment no hatred. We say that the class struggle is a law of social development. We are not responsible for it. We do not make the class struggle. We merely explain it, as Newton explained gravitation. We explain the nature of the conflict of interest that produces the class struggle' (Jack London, *The Iron Heel*, pp. 21–2).

But, while he is genuinely indignant about social injustices and has the full-blooded courage that would brave prison or the firing squad, he is in danger of growing into the dilettante observer of others' efforts and others' follies. With the equilibrium and the self-discipline which often keep a man silent when he is tempted to talk he should long ago have moved forward on to the Front Opposition Bench. Between 1931 and 1935 he debated so cogently that he was occasionally assigned an important task by the poverty-stricken leaders of the Opposition. But now he is always kicking against the pricks and that is fatal in the one army which fears above all that its privates may be out of step or breaking the ranks. What confidence can Transport House ... feel in one who was associated with Mosley in the New Party and Cripps in the Popular Front?[17]

Chapter 6

Fascism and the Approach of War: Spain, Cripps and the Popular Front

Of course Bevan never joined the New Party. Even so, as 'Watchman''s error illustrates, the Mosley connection stuck to him like pitch thoughout the thirties. And during the last years of the decade he *was* closely identified with Sir Stafford Cripps, which was nearly as damning. In 1932, when the Socialist League was founded, he had deliberately kept aloof from it; but as his exasperation with official Labour grew and he began to look for alliances with any group, within the party or beyond it, which might project a more active policy, he found himself co-operating increasingly with the League and coming strongly under the influence of its austere yet charismatic leader. Rich, religious, intense and ascetic, Cripps was an unlikely hero for the low-born, high-living atheistic Bevan; yet in his whole career this High Church Tory lawyer turned extreme socialist was the one senior figure in the Labour Party to whose judgement he was consistently willing to defer. In Cripps Bevan saw Labour's Robespierre: a leader whose commitment to socialism was beyond question, while his towering intellect made pygmies of his more cautious colleagues: a leader, most specifically, who shared Bevan's perception of the threat of international fascism leading inevitably to war and his view of the only means to combat it.

In the second half of the thirties the central preoccupation of politics switched from domestic to foreign affairs. Unemployment, though still nearer two million than one, had fallen from its peak and was continuing to decline, as the new light industries took off in the south-east. Though the plight of the distressed areas had not eased, resignation had set in and the civil disorder that Bevan had predicted was clearly not going to happen. Increasingly the external challenge of Hitler, Mussolini and Franco formed the context, and soon most of the content, of political controversy. In his first years in the House of Commons, Bevan had not once spoken on foreign affairs. When he did so for the first time in November 1934, however, he had no difficulty in extending his class-war analysis to the international scene, equating fascism with Toryism and arguing that it could be met only by concerted working-class action. The choice, he claimed, was between socialism and war, and the Government naturally, in his view, preferred war.[1] Though his expression of it became more sophisticated, this simplistic dichotomy blinkered his approach to the international situation for the next five years.

The testing ground seemed to be Spain, where civil war broke out in July 1936 following General Franco's army revolt against the elected republican Government, with Mussolini and Hitler actively backing Franco and the Soviet Union appointing itself the champion of democracy. To Bevan, as to the whole of the left, the issue was clear. Spain was where the battle between fascism and democracy was joined. But the British Government, hiding behind the sham even-handedness of 'non-intervention', which Hitler and Mussolini blatantly ignored, threw its weight effectively behind the fascists. Arms flowed in to one side but not to the other: the Republic was soon fighting for its life. This was no surprise: Bevan always took it for granted that the Government's professed neutrality was only a cover for an instinctive class sympathy for Franco which several backbench Tories from Churchill downwards openly admitted. What shocked him and Cripps and the whole of the left of the party was that the Labour leadership swallowed the pious fiction of 'non-intervention' and lined up tamely behind the Government. The 1936 Conference, at Edinburgh, was a bitter affair, with the platform battered by urgent calls for 'Arms for Spain'. 'Is it not obvious to everyone', Bevan demanded in a passionate speech in the course of which he dealt as roughly with Bevin as Bevin had done with him two years before, 'that if the arms continue to pour into the rebels in Spain, our Spanish comrades will be slaughtered by hundreds of thousands?' Like others, he ridiculed the National Executive's pretence that there was no proof that arms were getting through. If Spain fell, then the Popular Front Government in France would soon follow, he argued: 'then the Franco-Soviet pact will soon be denounced, and democracy in Europe will soon be in ruins. That is the consequence of this policy.'[2] The Executive, however, had the trade union vote tied up, and held off the hotheads by more than 3–1.

The left's defeat at Edinburgh had two tangible results – the 'United Front' campaign and the foundation of *Tribune*. The former was a misconceived attempt – futile without the participation of Labour – to construct the sort of alliance of working-class parties which Bevan had long advocated. On 1 January 1937, by a precarious conjuring trick, Cripps persuaded the mistrustful leaders of the Communist Party (Harry Pollitt, Palme Dutt and Willie Gallagher) and the ILP (Maxton and Fenner Brockway) to join with the Socialist League in a 'Unity Manifesto' which was also signed by several other members of both the Communist and Labour Parties, among them Bevan, George Strauss, Harold Laski, John Strachey and the Communist leader of the South Wales miners, Arthur Horner. Several stirring meetings were held around the country, but the fragile unity of the Communists and the ILP quickly fell apart (mirroring the internecine war of their respective counterparts in Spain, the Communists and the POUM) and under the threat of mass expulsion from the Labour Party the Socialist League was obliged to dissolve itself. Individuals like Cripps and Bevan continued to call hopefully for united action, but in reality the United Front was a blind alley. The Communists and the ILP were insignificant (and mutually antagonistic) splinters whose adherence could bring no electoral advantage, only damage, to Labour which, as Bevan himself had recognised in 1932, for better or worse *was* the working-class movement. Attlee, Bevin and Morrison, whatever their mistakes in these years, were correct in seeing that the Communists could contribute less than nothing to Labour's eventual victory.

The second outcome of Edinburgh, however, was of more lasting importance. *Tribune* was to be Bevan's platform, later his mouthpiece and loyal supporter, for the rest of his life – apart from one traumatic breach towards the end. Until it was outflanked by *Militant* in the 1970s, it remained unchallenged as the organ of the Labour left. It was founded as an attempt to rally the constituencies against the heavy-handed domination of the party by the right-wing unions, with money originally put up by Cripps and Strauss. The first editor was William Mellor of the Socialist League; Bevan was a member of the Board, along with Cripps, Strauss, Laski, Ellen Wilkinson and H.N.Brailsford. He also wrote, from the start, a weekly column, 'Inside Westminster', under the by-line 'M.P.', though the style and preoccupations must soon have given away his identity. Bevan is not normally thought of as much of a writer; but these weekly articles reveal a surprisingly good journalist. Though strictly political, their variety expresses the richness of his mind, always able to focus a general argument on a telling detail or extrapolate an historical theory from a trivial episode. As well as major polemics there are a host of throwaway epigrams, satirical squibs, some very accomplished sketch-writing* and – undoubtedly most irritating to the leaders and loyalists of the PLP – a continuous commentary, usually critical, sometimes merely patronising, on Labour's parliamentary performance.

The first four give a good taste of the variety of his subjects. The very first, on 1 January 1937, condemned with characteristic impatience Labour's failure to expose the mediaeval mumbo-jumbo of the Abdication crisis ('The Labour Party has too much reverence') and went on to expound the role of the monarchy in capitalist society.[3] The second spotlit Baldwin's pious claptrap in the case of five dockers dismissed, without trial, for alleged subversion, as an instance of Tory 'fascism'.[4] The third ridiculed assisted emigration schemes as 'Deportation – The Old Tory Cure for Un-

---

* Two inspired characterisations of his *bête noire* Neville Chamberlain must suffice as examples. On 2 April 1937: 'Listening to a speech by him is like paying a visit to Woolworth's: everything in its place and nothing above sixpence.' And on 4 June 1937, when Chamberlain succeeded Baldwin as Prime Minister: 'In the funeral service of capitalism, the honeyed and soothing platitudes of the clergyman are finished, and the cortège is now under the sombre and impressive guidance of the undertaker.' See also the appendix to this chapter.

employment';[5] while the fourth ('Government Offers Dumb-Bells to Children Who Want Food') made a powerful case for social, rather than individual, medicine, arguing bluntly that the cause of malnutrition was poverty: 'If low wages are admitted to be a cause of ill-health, then a good trade union is a better doctor than the half-trained mystic at the surgery.'[6] And so, shrewd and provocative, the column continued throughout 1937 – clearly a success, since at the start of the autumn session it was resumed under Bevan's own name, and soon his picture too. In November 1938 the paper was obliged to put itself rather too closely for its independence under the wing of Victor Gollancz's Communist-inclined Left Book Club. Under a new editor, H.J.Hartshorn, Bevan's articles were pushed to a less prominent position towards the back, and in 1939 they almost stopped altogether. The sixty-seven articles published between 1937 and the outbreak of war nevertheless constitute a vivid record of his responses as the crisis of capitalism unfolded.

Tribune's great cause, week after week, was that Labour must refuse to support the Government's rearmament programme. Today this seems an absurd posture, above all for the fire-breathing anti-fascist left. The Labour Party was in fact, at just this time, under the threat of Hitler and the influence of Dalton and Bevin, in the process of reversing its traditional pacifist objection to armaments – not a moment too soon in the eyes of most of those who saw war as unavoidable. Cripps, however, and those who followed him, including Bevan, held that for Labour to vote arms to the National Government was a betrayal of socialism since the Government, not being a working-class or even a democratic government but a proto-fascist one, would not use its arms in the cause of the workers, against fascism, but either in another purely destructive imperialist war like 1914–18 or actively against the workers' state, the Soviet Union. The Government, most notably in Abyssinia, had abandoned even lip-service to the League of Nations; it was openly taking the side of fascism in Spain and bending over backwards to secure a treaty with fascist Italy. Meanwhile it rejected as ideologically inadmissible any possibility of co-operation with the Soviet Union which geography dictated was the only way of opposing Hitler, had it been serious about doing so. Baldwin and Chamberlain, the argument concluded, would never fight Hitler: therefore to vote them arms was little better than giving them to Hitler. Britain would not lift a finger against fascism until the National Government was chased out of office: thus the zealots who a year before had been preaching the exclusive unity of the working-class parties against the rest came round in 1938 to the opposite strategy of promoting a Popular Front including the Liberals and dissident Conservatives to get rid of Chamberlain and the appeasers of Munich.

The mad logic of the *Tribune* view proceeded paradoxically from the contention, graphically set out by Bevan in a special signed centre-page spread on 19 February 1937, that the Government was constructing 'the greatest war machine ever built by the British Empire in times of peace' – not to oppose Hitler but in response to its own economic imperative.

> By this means capitalism finds employment for its millions of idle workers – they are put to dig their own graves. The whole industry of the country will be geared to the production of munitions; the one voracious and insatiable consumer for the output of modern scientific industry is found where capitalism was finally bound to find it, in preparations for war on a vast scale. ...
>
> In these circumstances it would be a crime of the first magnitude if the Labour Party helped to deceive the workers into believing that the war machine now being built either guaranteed the peace or may be used to defend the interest of the workers. ...

On the contrary:

> The people of this country must be made to realise that the danger of war arises from this Government's refusal to mobilise the peace forces of the world. It is prevented by its own class bias from entering into building alliances with countries like Soviet Russia and it permits the fabric of collective peace to be destroyed by the gangster methods of Hitler and Mussolini.[7]

'The position has arisen against which the party was warned,' Bevan wrote after the Estimates debate a month later. Labour spokesmen had made excellent speeches, but nobody paid any attention because they knew that the party would not carry its criticism of the Government to a vote. 'Our failure to oppose the whole arms plan means that our case on foreign policy goes by default.'[8] The point of voting against rearmament, he repeatedly insisted, was not to prevent the Government arming – since Labour's vote had no practical effect – but to express opposition to the Government's policy, just as Labour regularly voted against the education and other estimates. No one took that to mean that they wanted the schools closed, and he denied that defence was any different. At Conference in the autumn he ingeniously sidestepped the charge that the left would leave the country defenceless:

> We have heard in the constituencies and here that it is foolish for us to oppose armaments and yet ourselves to adopt a policy for the furtherance of which armaments are necessary, and that if we succeeded in preventing the Government from having arms we should be helpless in the face of possible Fascist aggression. When this Movement is strong enough to deny arms to the Capitalist Government, it ceases to be a Government and we become the Government. You cannot deny arms to any Government until those who are able to deny them are themselves strong enough to form a Government; and when that happens the Movement has declared – and I support it and my friends support it – that we are prepared to provide whatever support is necessary to carry out a Socialist international policy. But what we are not prepared to do is to tie the Movement behind a National Government which will betray our policy. ... We are not going to put a sword in the hands of our enemies that may be used to cut off our own heads.

Accepting rearmament, he argued, was the start of a slippery slope for Labour.

> If the immediate international situation is used as an excuse to get us to drop our opposition to the rearmament programme of the Government, the next phase must be that we must desist from any industrial or political action that may disturb national unity in the face of Fascist aggression. Along that road is endless retreat, and at the end of it a voluntary totalitarian State with ourselves erecting the barbed wire around. You cannot collaborate, you cannot accept the logic of collaboration on a first class issue like rearmament, and at the same time evade the implications of collaboration all along the line when the occasion demands it. Therefore, the Conference is not merely discussing foreign policy: it is discussing the spiritual and physical independence of the Working-Class Movement in this country.[9]

Bevan's casuistry got short shrift from James Walker of the Iron and Steel Trades Association, who bluntly put the common-sense view of the Conference:

> Mr Bevan says that if we were to carry that vote, the vote would not matter because at 4 o'clock we would vote to have no Army, no Navy and no Air Force; we would defeat the Government and at 5 o'clock we would bring the Army, the Navy and the Air Force in again. But we could not bring the Army, the Navy and the Air Force in again if it was not there, and if those people got their way there would be no defence at all.[10]

In the subsequent vote, the National Executive won its usual massive endorsement by 2,167,000 to 228,000.

'Along this road', wrote Bevan, 'lies death for the Labour Party.'[11] When Parliament met, he rejected Churchill's 'sinister' argument that Labour should not give Hitler the impression that Britain was divided.

> The Opposition must refrain from opposing because if it does so Hitler will hear of it and be encouraged thereby. The fear of Hitler is to be used to frighten the workers of Britain into silence. In short Hitler is to rule Britain by proxy. If we accept the contention that the common enemy is Hitler and not the British capitalist class, then certainly Churchill is right. But it means abandonment of the class struggle and the subservience of the British workers to their own employers.[12]

Even Bevan rarely ordered his priorities quite so candidly. What gave a stridency to his statements at this period was his conviction that capitalism was moving inescapably to its crisis and his fear that Labour, by 'patriotically' helping to shore it up, might miss its historic moment. 'All through the debate on the King's Speech', he wrote in November, 'the refrain has recurred, with what must be maddening frequency for the members of the Government – War or Slump. Slump or War. Capitalism moves to its final consummation, and as it does so the political initiative passes to the Labour Movement. It is a tremendous responsibility, and a great opportunity.'[13] His concern was that when the crisis came Labour should not shrink from demanding its price. In one of his bitterest speeches in the House against the means test in 1936 he specifically saw it as an opportunity for *revenge*:

> It is no use going on. I cannot move hon. Members to pity; it is impossible. There is only one thing left, and that is hate. I believe in hate more than pity, myself. Thousands of young men in England, and particularly young men from the North-East coast, South Wales and parts of Scotland, are now joining the Army and the Air Force, learning to defend the country which has given them these conditions. I hope that they will remember them. It will be my duty, at any rate, as I conceive it, to ask them to remember. Let hon. Members not be so complacent. Difficulties are growing up all around them now, and they will want these young men. When they want them, I hope these young men will remember what they are doing now, and I hope that when the time comes that you are in difficulties and your backs are turned, you will remember that that is their opportunity.
>
> Now they are helpless and can do nothing to defend themselves. It may be that you will be helpless and can do nothing to defend yourselves. ... I hope that when the opportunity comes they will take advantage of it, and I hope I shall be there to see your faces at the time they do so.[14]

Thus, politically, Bevan positively looked forward to the coming of war. But he despaired of Labour's readiness to take advantage of it when it came. 'Sheep in sheep's clothing', he called the parliamentary leadership in March 1937, borrowing Beachcomber's phrase about MacDonald;[15] while the industrial leadership was 'spineless'.[16] In July he elaborated his criticism of the Front Bench:

> It is the whole spirit of the leadership that is at fault. It refuses to fight desperately and heroically on matters of big principle. It refuses to arouse the electorate on burning day-to-day issues, such as the Means Test, the 40-hour week, and Spain.
>
> It is too ready to compromise with existing conditions. It is too respectable and too statesmanlike: too frightened of offending the middle class.[17]

In November, for the first time, he stood for the Shadow Cabinet himself but, unsurprisingly, came nowhere near election. He vented his anger in *Tribune*. 'Some of those the Party thought fit to elect to Front Bench positions are too old', he wrote, 'and some of them obviously too ill to perform their duties. ... Those who voted for them acted with frivolous irresponsibility and it is a pity that the secrecy of the ballot prevents them from being called to account. It is difficult to believe that the Parliamentary Labour Party seriously intends to fight for Socialism when it selects leaders whose battles are obviously behind them.'

Attlee, Morrison, Greenwood and Cripps alone were excepted from Bevan's blanket condemnation. Cripps he naturally praised as pre-eminent, while voicing the suspicion that he was being deliberately confined to legal matters and kept off the big questions where he might be disruptive. For Attlee he still expressed considerable respect:

> He has a clear and subtle mind and it has always been a pity that a certain lack of horse power has prevented him from 'getting across' as he should. ... His position in the party is much stronger than I am afraid he thinks it is. To make him realise this would be of itself a considerable contribution to the success of the Party.

Greenwood he thought charitably was exhausted by too much speaking in the country. ('A man must have time to think. ... It is undoubtedly true that too many propaganda meetings have the effect of reducing one's thoughts to the tepid consistency of stale straw.') His praise of Morrison, however, though outwardly generous, was distinctly condescending: 'He is a daring and formidable debater. As a general rule he is distrustful of political abstractions and his speeches smell more of blue books than of wide liberal reading. He is more a first-class political craftsman than a philosopher statesman.'[18]

Bevan could hardly have described the personal basis of his twenty-year duel with Morrison more clearly, or more accurately. But such candour, and such immodesty (if the party wanted a philosopher statesman it knew whom to turn to), was not calculated to make a friend of Morrison. Bevan's column as a whole, however, was rarely aimed at making friends; perhaps for that reason his articles, for all their eloquence, did not influence anyone much either. Week by week, *Tribune* merely emphasised the gulf that had opened up between the party at Westminster and the activists in the constituencies – a gulf which has existed ever since. In 1937, as a result of a successful grass-roots campaign which wisely distanced itself from the left, the constituency parties won the right to elect seven members of the NEC: in third, fifth and seventh place they promptly elected three left-wingers, Laski, Cripps and D.N.Pritt. This was a portent for the future, though of little consequence at the time.

During 1938 the left abruptly changed its tune. Recognising the futility of the 'United Front', Cripps suddenly and with an undiminished assumption of righteousness embraced the opposite idea of a 'Popular Front' against fascism to include all the anti-Government parties from Communists to Liberals, on the model of Blum's Government in France. The idea had been gaining ground for some time in the middle ground of politics that Labour on its own could not offer an effective alternative to the Government. In addition to the official Liberals now led by Sir Archibald Sinclair, the aged Lloyd George (who had always loathed Chamberlain as fiercely as Bevan did) was now powerfully attacking the Government's appeasement of the dictators and refusal to ally with Russia; while murmurings of Conservative discontent were greatly stimulated by Anthony Eden's resignation from the Foreign Office over Chamberlain's determination to pursue an alliance with Mussolini. And all the time, as Hitler swallowed up Austria and threatened

Czechoslovakia, there were the sombre warnings of Churchill, gathering force in what Bevan called, by contrast with Chamberlain's 'thin, listless trickle', 'a diapason of majestic harmony'.[19] In March, following the *Anschluss*, the Co-op paper *Reynolds' News*, quickly backed by the Liberal *News Chronicle*, the *New Statesman* and other papers, caught the mood and called for a 'United Peace Alliance'. Disillusioned with Labour's impotence, Cripps and his followers somewhat belatedly subordinated the domestic class war to the priority of defeating Hitler and jumped at this new possibility of making a start by defeating Chamberlain. The country had a straight choice, Bevan told a May Day rally in South Wales: a continuing 'drift to disaster under the National Government' or 'the establishment of a Popular Front . . . under the leadership of the Labour Party'.[20]

The qualification was important. Bevan took it for granted that Labour must predominate in any new Government, and the new spirit of unity was at this stage definitely not intended to embrace Conservatives. He admired Churchill's resolution against Hitler, but still regarded him as an unrepentant imperialist and supporter of Franco. He had never had any use for Eden ('Beneath the sophistication of his appearance and manner he has all the unplumbable stupidities and unawareness of his class and type,' he wrote in 1937)[21] and was contemptuous of his gentlemanly resignation: 'He narrowed the issue when he should have widened it. . . . If Eden had been big enough he could have ruined Chamberlain.'[22] In the House, when Eden congratulated himself that he at least could not be called a yes-man, Bevan allowed him that but added scornfully: 'He wears the same tie.'[23] Not until after Munich did Bevan see any likelihood of the Tory rebels ever doing more than talk about defeating Chamberlain. But the emergence of Tory anti-fascists changed his view of the Government. They were not, he now acknowledged, actively in league with fascism after all. 'Their instinct is to support the enemies of socialism, but their dilemma lies in the fact that these are also the enemies of British imperialism.' As a result, they were 'paralysed by indecision'.[24] Their solution to the realisation that Hitler posed a threat to themselves, he wrote in April, was to try to turn him east.

> They are striving to satisfy Germany's ambitions at the expense of her near-neighbours, in the hope that she will be gorged to repletion in the process.
>
> To accomplish this every scrap of international organisation must be destroyed, and the last remaining vestige of international security thrown to the wolves of Fascism.
>
> When that time comes let the people of this country beware, for we shall stand face to face with a giant of our own creation, fostered by our own hand, made strong by our own weakness, and made triumphant by our own blind selfishness.[25]

Churchill himself could not have put it better. But still, while Churchill and every other critic of appeasement urged the Government to prepare for war, Bevan and Cripps sought to deny it arms or any sort of co-operation.

The Popular Front idea was fatally blighted by this intransigence: it still seemed to be directed more against Chamberlain than against Hitler, and this continuing wrong-headedness gave the Labour leadership the excuse it needed to reject it. In truth Labour would not touch it anyway. On the one hand, Bevin and Dalton detected the influence of the Left Book Club and assumed that anything the Communists had a hand in must be a Communist front. On the other, the party was still haunted by the spectre of 1931: the left itself had taught it to beware of any collaboration with non-socialists and for Cripps of all people now to turn round and propose collaboration was too much to take. Besides, no Opposition likes to be told that it cannot win by itself: the NEC's formal rejection of the Popular Front juggled the electoral arithmetic to affirm that Labour could win the next election on its own and should therefore not be distracted from its aim of doing so. To Bevan's new realism, however, such irrelevant optimism – the next election might not be for two years – simply underlined the leadership's lack of urgency. Munich, he argued, marked a watershed:

> Lenin says somewhere that the first prerequisite for the victory of the workers is the demoralisation of the ruling class. Well, we have witnessed that demoralisation during this week to an extent that would have appeared incredible a few months ago.
> The initiative is passing to the Labour Party and it has only to be grasped with courage and energy to transform the present apparently hopeless situation.[26]

Instead, in another unflattering dissection of the parliamentary party ('You Will Want To Attack Me For This'), he saw only 'a softness ... which is frightening in its portents for the future'.[27] He feared that Labour would be too short-sighted to take advantage of its historic opportunity. There was mounting evidence of anti-Government feeling in the country. In November a Popular Front candidate, backed by the local Labour Party in defiance of the NEC, actually won a by-election at Bridgwater. Rebel Tories like Harold Macmillan and Robert Boothby were openly making overtures to Labour: now, sensing a real chance of splitting the Government party, Bevan wanted Labour to respond. 'It seems to me', he wrote in December, 'that the early spring will see a profound change in the political situation'.

> We are approaching a time similar to that of 1931. New political alignments are bound to arise. It is not easy to see at the moment what shape these will take, but what is certain is that the profound feelings of defeatism which are spreading throughout the ranks of the Tory party are bound to result in the disintegration of the Parliamentary Tory Party.
> THE LABOUR PARTY SHOULD PLACE ITSELF IN A POSITION TO BENEFIT BY THESE LIKELY CHANGES. FOR IT IS NOT LIKELY THAT ANOTHER SIMILAR OPPORTUNITY WILL OCCUR THIS SIDE OF ARMAGEDDON.[28]

Labour's opportunity, Bevan believed, consisted in the fact that the Government, as he had predicted all along, now needed not merely the

Opposition's vote for rearmament but its active help in mobilisation for war. Munich had not checked Hitler's ambitions: he had no sooner been ceded the Sudetenland than he was threatening the rest of Czechoslovakia, and then Poland. In December the Government announced a voluntary scheme of national service. In *Tribune*, Bevan insisted that Labour should exact policy concessions in return for its agreement. 'Supporting the normal defence services of the country is one thing. Incorporating the machinery of the labour movement into the recruiting mechanism of the State is another.' He demanded first that trade union rights be guaranteed, and three further conditions: that the Government should support Republican Spain; sign an Anglo-Soviet pact; and nationalise the arms industry.[29] In the Commons he furiously denounced Greenwood's promise of Labour co-operation in the scheme with no such conditions:

> There can have been few examples in history of an Opposition which so effectually abandoned its obligations, and which so misled the people, as to ask for the opportunity of appearing on platforms with generals and colonels and majors and lieutenants of counties in order to implore the people to put themselves under the leadership of its opponents.

'We are on test,' he declared. 'If we are not good recruiting sergeants, the Government will threaten us with conscription; if we are good recruiting sergeants, it will not be necessary for them to lead our people up the garden, because we shall have done it for them.' The Government, he concluded, should do its own recruiting. 'We ought to preserve our rights of independence and keep ourselves detached and aloof, so that we can discharge our proper functions to our own people and not bind them hand and foot and hand them over to their enemies.'[30]

This was extreme stuff, which sat strangely with the all-party campaign for a Popular Front. There was a logic in denying co-operation to the Government in order to replace it with one more broadly based; but at a time of impending national emergency it made no sense to most ordinary patriotic Labour people. Undeterred, Cripps pressed on with his campaign. In January 1939 he prepared a long memorandum for the NEC setting out the case – including the electoral case – for the Popular Front. Anticipating its inevitable rejection – it found only three supporters – Cripps circulated it to the constituencies; for this breach of discipline, when he refused to retract it, he was expelled from the party. Immediately Bevan sprang to his support. He was not alone. Cripps's expulsion gave a great boost to the Popular Front cause: his memorandum was endorsed by Lloyd George, Keynes, Bernard Shaw, among others, and a National Petition campaign was organised with well-attended meetings all round the country addressed by such non-party figures as J.B.Priestley and A.D.Lindsay, the Master of Balliol, as well as by a handful of Labour MPs and other party members willing to share Cripps's fate. 'If Sir Stafford Cripps is expelled for wanting to unite the forces of freedom and democracy, they can go on expelling others,' Bevan proclaimed. 'They can expel me. His crime is my crime.'[31] But characteristically his concern became concentrated on the point of principle, not so much the Popular Front itself as the right to argue for it. 'Cripps was expelled', he wrote in *Tribune*, 'because he claimed the right to tell the Party what he had already told the Executive. Cripps represented the Divisional Parties on the Executive. He insisted that his constituents should be informed of his views. ... The Executive insisted that only their views should be heard. ... This is tantamount to a complete suppression of any opinion in the Party which does not agree with that held by the Executive.' This was tyranny, and death to the Labour Party. 'If every organised effort to change Party policy is to be described as an organised attack on the Party itself, then the rigidity imposed by Party discipline will soon change into *rigor mortis*.'[32] 'In what manner', he demanded in a speech at Welwyn Garden City – and repeatedly elsewhere – 'do they suggest that the minority inside the Labour Party should be allowed to express itself in order to try to convert the majority?'[33] 'Not at public meetings' was the Executive's answer, and those who continued to share platforms with members of non-affiliated organisations would be liable to expulsion too. On 31 March Bevan, George Strauss, Sir Charles Trevelyan and two less prominent candidates were duly expelled.

This was the only time in his life that Bevan was actually expelled from the Labour Party, though he came close to it on several subsequent occasions. Labour has seldom made itself look more foolish to posterity than in expelling, five months before the outbreak of war, two members who were to become senior Ministers in the Government elected at its conclusion. Great as was the provocation of Cripps's and Bevan's ceaseless denunciation of party policy and denigration of those who directed it, the procedural grounds on which the Executive chose to base its action were so petty, and at the same time so vague, that the victims had no difficulty presenting themselves as martyrs to an exasperated bureaucracy that simply wanted to shut them up. ('Gad, sir,' exclaimed Low's Colonel Blimp in a cartoon joyously reprinted by *Tribune*. 'Citrine is right. The Labour Party is quite right to expel all but sound Conservatives.')[34] Repeatedly Bevan asked the Executive to spell out to them how, holding the views they did, they were entitled to express them, but he never received a satisfactory answer. He indignantly denied any disloyalty to the party.

> A particularly vicious and irresponsible argument has been used against us to the effect that we are setting up another party from which to launch an attack on the Labour Party. Nothing could be further from the truth. We do not ourselves wish to form the Popular Front. We wish the Labour Party to lead it. We have not allied ourselves with other political parties, for our purpose has simply been to persuade the Labour Party to adopt the Popular Front strategy.[35]

He won the backing of his constituency party and also of the SWMF Conference which not only demanded reinstatement of the rebels but overwhelmingly supported the Popular Front as well, confirming his conviction that the 'janissaries' of the party were out of touch with the rank and file. But the miners were untypical; appeal to Conference, held that year in May, was in vain. The fact that only Cripps was allowed to speak and that he made a poor speech can have made little difference: the block votes endorsed the expulsions by more than 5–1. Immediately the six applied for readmission on the basis that they accepted the party's decision on the Popular Front and wound up the Petition; they still insisted, however, on their unfettered freedom 'to impress upon the Party the necessity for making effective the opposition to the National Government, and to oppose every tendency to co-operate with that Government which we regard as the gravest menace to the working classes of Great Britain'.[36] There was no penitence here. Not until three months after the outbreak of war was Bevan readmitted, at the strong urging of the MFGB, whereupon Strauss was pardoned too. Cripps remained outside the party until 1945.

Meanwhile in February the Spanish Republic had fallen and Chamberlain had moved with 'obscene haste' to recognise Franco ('This surely must be the blackest page in the history of Great Britain,' wrote Bevan);[37] Hitler had occupied Prague; and at the end of March Chamberlain – still without the pact with the Soviet Union which alone could have made his pledge effective – had guaranteed Poland. In April the Government introduced the conscription of twenty-year-olds. Labour leaders were angry that their agreement to a voluntary system the previous December had been betrayed, and withheld their support; but Bevan, in the Commons, grimly reminded them that this was exactly what he had predicted. The Government, he alleged, had drawn Labour into its war preparations on the basis that 'we would defend your wealth and you would help us to defend our liberties. That is putting it in its most sordid way. ... But it seems to me that the bringing in of conscription has ruptured finally the assumption on which co-operation has been based.'

Looking back over the whole inter-war period, Bevan listed the sacrifices Labour had made for national unity. There had been no big strike since 1926, no big wages offensive by the TUC, no expansion of the social services, no help for the unemployed, and all the while Labour had supported the Government's rearmament programme and endorsed its scrapping of collective security, tying itself inextricably to the Government's war machine – all of which, of course, he had opposed. But Labour had gained nothing by its acquiescence.

> Quite wantonly, this understanding and co-operation have been violated. We have lost, and Hitler has won. ... It seems to me that the war against democracy is succeeding along the whole front. The government and their supporters remain in undisturbed possession of their wealth and their Colonial

possessions, but we surrender one stronghold after another and one institution after another.

What did conscription mean? he asked.

To you it means that there is a vast army ready to defend your Colonial possessions whenever it is necessary. To us, it means the complete abandonment of any hope of a successful struggle against the weight of wealth in Great Britain.

Strikes would be outlawed: soon elections would be suspended. 'The democratic façade remains, democratic institutions remain, but the reality is taken from them.' If people were denied any means of expressing themselves, Bevan demanded, 'where is the democracy which they are asking our people to defend?'

What arguments have they to persuade the young men to fight, except merely in another squalid attempt to defend themselves against the redistribution of international swag? Hon. Members opposite have taken away, piece by piece, everything in which we believe, and all that is left are the things which they hold precious. I say to my hon. Friends on these benches that they ought to offer this Measure stubborn, ruthless and sustained resistance here and in the country; that they should say to the country that the national unity which has been built up has been destroyed by the Conservative Party, pursuing its own narrow, selfish class aims; that hon. Members opposite are exploiting the privileges of the Left in the interests of the Right; that nothing will satisfy us except that the Government should resign and give way to a Government in which people could believe and to which the defence of democracy could be safely entrusted.[38]

On this occasion Bevan was in step with his leaders as Attlee, feeling personally cheated by Chamberlain, led the Opposition into the division lobby. But Labour could only watch helplessly as war came nearer. At the beginning of August Parliament adjourned: Bevan opposed the adjournment with the characteristic argument that it meant that for the next two months the issue of peace or war would be solely in the hands of the Government.[39] But on 23 August came the Nazi–Soviet Pact: the bitter vindication of all those who had been pressing for so long the urgency of Britain and France securing an alliance with the Soviet Union. In the last few weeks Britain had opened tentative talks with the Russians, but so reluctantly that Stalin had felt driven to secure himself by a compact with Hitler instead. Hitler now had a free hand to invade Poland, and war was only days away. Parliament was recalled for a short, grave debate. Bevan got his word in last. 'I must say', he began, 'that it is a little hard for some of us who for many years, in this House and outside, have been engaged in prophesying the moment to hear one of the chief architects of it say that he wishes to shorten the discussion.' It might still be possible even now, he maintained, to avert war by talking to the Russians. Above all though, at this sombre moment, he outraged the Tories by not moderating but intensifying his personal attack on Chamberlain, denying that he bore the heaviest burden.

His is the easiest job in the House of Commons. The more blunders he makes, the more necessity there is for unity and for no criticism to be heard. The bigger the catastrophe of which he is the architect, the safer he is. This is the same Government, its personnel is the same, as that which was the architect of Munich. The suggestion is that the people of my constituency, the colliers, steelworkers and railwaymen, should offer their bodies as a deterrent to German aggression. There is one man over there whom you could offer – offer him. Let the Conservative Party, if it wants to convince us that it is in earnest, call a Carlton Club meeting and get rid of the Prime Minister. He is the man upon whom Hitler relies; he is the man responsible for this situation.

At this point a Tory interjected: 'Be British'. Bevan exploded.

Yes, talk to us about being British, you Franco-philes. There is a Brigadier-General sitting there who, in this House, got up to defend over and over again the Government's policy in Spain, which will throw away hundreds of thousands of British lives; and you people over there dare ask for unity. It is monstrous. ...

'That is why I say that no job is easier than that of the Prime Minister,' he concluded when the House had calmed down.

No Opposition could be kinder. It has prophesied this every month for four or five years. It has fought against it at every stage of the journey and, at the end of it, abstains even from saying to the Prime Minister, 'I told you so.' It is not for the sake of saying 'I told you so' that I am making this statement this afternoon, but because I believe that the most effective way in which Germany and Italy can be persuaded that the resolution of this country is united behind its obligations is to get rid of the assassins of democracy in so many parts of Europe.[40]

Nevertheless, at this hour of destiny, even Bevan voted for the first time with the Government against four lone pacifists (six including tellers). For he was emphatically not a pacifist. Now that war had come, he wanted Britain to prosecute it with the utmost vigour – but as a war not only *against* fascism, but *for* socialism. The war against Hitler must be made to encompass what he had long and ardently predicted – the final nemesis of capitalism. From the moment of its outbreak, Bevan saw the war as Labour's great opportunity. In a solemn front-page statement in *Tribune*, he and Cripps set out the left's agenda. First, even now, there could be no question of rallying behind the Government:

A very heavy responsibility lies upon the British Government and upon those who have allowed that Government to remain in office during the last vital months. ... Mistakes that have been made so often in the past will find their counterpart in even more tragic mistakes in the future if we allow ourselves to be governed and controlled by the same incompetent and wrong-headed people. The need for a change of Government is as urgent, or more urgent, than ever it was.

In the meantime, so long as the avowed purpose of the war was arresting fascist aggression, 'every good Socialist will do his utmost to assist the anti-Fascist forces'. That was the 'immediate objective'. In the longer run, however, 'there will be other struggles in which the workers will become involved in the course of the war, which may last much longer than many now seem to think'.

> Out of the war, whatever else comes, will come an opportunity for the working class of the world to do something effective to save themselves from fresh tragedies and suffering. That opportunity they must seize and it is already time to start preparing for the moment when it arrives. War will accomplish less than nothing unless it marks the end for ever of Fascism and its aggressive brutality.

There must be no compromise, no early peace when capitalism wished to call a halt; 'nor must we permit the war to degenerate into a simple struggle between rival imperialisms'. At the moment, Cripps and Bevan conceded rather grudgingly, 'it is impossible to deny that – in part at least – the objective of the war is to stop Fascist aggression; but objectives may change and we must be alert to see that a war started with that avowed objective does not end with the purpose of defeating working-class power'. A capitalist peace would be no victory for the workers and only lead to 'another and greater war'. Labour's objectives must be clear from the outset if they were to be realised. 'It is already time to formulate the essentials of any future peace in the world, and the greatest of those is power for the working class to decide their own destiny in every country.'[41] In September 1939 Cripps and Bevan were already looking forward confidently to July 1945.

Appendix to Chapter Six

Week after week between 1937 and 1939 Bevan expounded his highly individual philosophy of socialism in *Tribune*. It has not been possible, within the context of the main narrative, to convey adequately the sheer brilliance of the best of these articles. Even here it can only be hinted at by quoting three characteristic passages exhibiting his extraordinary ability to discover support for his interpretation of history in the most mundane ministerial statement or the least obviously political of facts. For instance, in November 1937 he derived a complete condemnation of capitalism from a routine call by the President of the Board of Trade, Oliver Stanley, for 'confidence':

The position of the Government is, therefore, that it is not the coming depression which causes fear of it, but the fear of it that causes the depression. The assumption apparently is that the more ignorant one is of the future the better it is likely to be.

Economics, said Mr Stanley, is fifty per cent psychology. . . . What we need, apparently, is not statesmen but hypnotists, not scientists but witchdoctors, not confidence born of scientific prediction of the future, but confidence created by a political Confidence Trick.

There is nothing surprising in this. It is the kind of mystic Mumbo-Jumbo to which capitalism is driven when austere reason pronounces sentence of death upon it. It is the primitive recoil from reality and the burdens of reality which lies at the root of Fascist psychology. [*Tribune*, 5 November 1937.]

The next month the Government was concerned about the falling birthrate. For this phenomenon, too, Bevan had his own vividly fantastic explanation (for which the post-war baby boom provided triumphant retrospective support):

The fact is that the women of Britain in refusing to bear as many children as formerly are exercising a silent vote against the sort of world which capitalism is creating. . . . It may well be that this is the Nemesis that nature is preparing for capitalist society. In denying the progress of mankind capitalism denies the existence of mankind. Judged from this angle capitalism is a vast contraceptive condemning the old world to death by refusing the birth of the new. [*Tribune*, 3 December 1937.]

Finally, another of these articles contains the clearest statement Bevan ever put on paper of his simple, optimistic identification of socialism with science. It occurs, typically, in his description of a Coal debate:

The earlier Socialists put their case on moral grounds. The modern Socialist reinforces this by pointing out that private enterprise is now an active deterrent to improved technical and scientific changes.

The knowledge of this seeps through into the Conservative mentality and so deprives it of its main source of self-confidence. It does not conduce to assurance in one's own case to know that it is opposed to the demands of science.

It is the consciousness of this that lies at the root of Fascist reaction. Science condemns capitalism and capitalism in the form of Fascism retorts by condemning science. . . .

The coal industry is a classic example of this. . . . [*Tribune*, 10 December 1937.]

It is a measure of the failure of the socialist idea, as Bevan understood it, and of socialism's – not capitalism's – loss of confidence over the past fifty years that such arguments are habitually used today not *for* socialism, but *against* it.

3
War on Two Fronts, 1939–1945

Chapter 7

Backs to the Wall: the Phoney War, the Crisis of 1940 and the Entry of Russia

The Second World War was the decisive period of Bevan's life, in two distinct respects. In the first place, judging solely by the advancement of his career, it was in these six years that he rose unquestionably to public notice. The little-regarded backbencher of 1939 grew into the Cabinet Minister of August 1945; from being one shrill socialist agitator among many in the thirties he emerged by 1942 as the most conspicuous, outspoken and effective critic of the war-winning Government, recognised as one of the most electrifying speakers in the House of Commons. In particular Bevan attracted a mixture of furious indignation, derision and grudging admiration as Churchill's one unequal but dauntless antagonist. By the end of the war he was probably the best-hated – not least by Churchill himself – as well as one of the best-known figures in public life.

At a deeper level, however, the war years also put Bevan's political thinking to the proof. During the war, events seemed to be working out just as he had predicted. The mould of the capitalist order seemed to have been broken: revolutionary change was in the air. Bevan, just as surely as Churchill in 1940, felt himself to be walking with destiny; more confidently than Churchill in these years he felt in tune with history. Much of his criticism and many of his expectations now seem wildly extravagant or simply wrong. Yet in his conviction throughout the war that Labour's hour had come he was more clear-sighted than most of the party's leaders – though wrong, as it turned out, about the nature of that hour. Labour's victory in the 1945 election was in one sense Bevan's moment of triumph, the vindication of sixteen years' fruitless prophesying and the opportunity of his life. At the same time, however, it was the climax – the high tide of socialism in the Labour Party, Labour's high-water mark in the country – after which the tide of history began to flow against Bevan's philosophy. He was to look back on 1945 as an historic opportunity missed.

Bevan was clear from the start that the war was to be a social revolution – a war for socialism, or socialism realised through war – both at home and in Europe. The actual fighting was in this view secondary to the political revolution of which it was both the weapon and an expression. Thus Bevan conceived of the war as being fought simultaneously on two fronts: first, against Hitler and fascism abroad and, second, against Toryism at home. But he saw these as the two sides of a single coin, believing that the best way to win the external war was by the vigorous prosecution of the internal. He still believed, as throughout the thirties, that the Tories were incapable of fighting fascism vigorously and had no real wish at all to do so.

Hence Bevan's rejection of the political truce, his strong attacks on Churchill for trying to fight the war by Tory means and for Tory ends (even his criticism of the military conduct of the war invariably alleged political grounds for Churchill's strategic errors) and his excoriation of Labour's leaders for tamely subordinating themselves to Churchill instead of vigorously asserting Labour's distinctive war aims and methods. For this sweeping and persistent criticism he was accused by Conservatives and Labour equally of undermining national unity and of virtual treason, playing party politics at the expense of the war effort. Bevan's answer was that he was trying to step up the war effort; he believed that national unity could only truly be achieved on Labour principles, and that only a Labour-led coalition, in place of the superficial unity achieved on Tory terms, could really rouse the people. This view was romantic but honourable; Bevan was not unpatriotic and could on no possible interpretation of his conduct be called a traitor. Right or wrong, moreover, there is a strong case for arguing that someone had to provide some opposition to Churchill's personal ascendancy. There was a lot of fine talk about democracy during the war and a good deal of national self-congratulation that the forms of parliamentary government were maintained; but after the formation of the Coalition in May 1940 there was no regular opposition in the House of Commons except that offered by a few maverick malcontents of whom Bevan was increasingly the most prominent and by far the most consistent. (Shinwell was perhaps more prominent in the early stages, but his attacks never had Bevan's philosophical coherence.) One of Bevan's most persistent themes – as always throughout his career – was the respect due to the House of Commons even in time of war (particularly in time of war) as the guardian of individual liberties.

In Bevan, finally, Churchill – the great war leader at the height of his power – found an opponent worthy of his mettle, in many respects indeed curiously like himself, though few would have dared such a comparison at the time. It might even be said that Churchill needed Bevan. The war years were Bevan's 'Finest Hour' too.

Unlike many on the left, on whom the Nazi–Soviet Pact had a demoralising effect, Bevan never had the slightest doubt that the war against Hitler must be fought. He had no faith in the Chamberlain Government's ability to fight it successfully; and he would greatly have preferred to have been fighting alongside the Soviet Union. But in September 1939 he let neither of these considerations weaken his resolution. He was confident that the war would release forces in British society which would quickly sweep Chamberlain aside; and he held firmly to the belief that the Soviet Union would be drawn into the war against fascism sooner or later. He therefore indulged neither in the tortured apologetics for the Soviet Union into which his associates on *Tribune*, including Cripps, fell at the outbreak of war; nor in the spasm of righteous indignation which seized most of the rest of the Labour Party when Stalin invaded Finland. He too felt only contempt for the cynical about-face of the British Communists; but he thought it lunatic to divert to Finland resources which would shortly be needed in the fight against the real enemy, Hitler. He was equally unmoved by the defeatism which affected many hitherto ardent anti-fascists like Kingsley Martin and even Lloyd George when they faced the implications of opposing Hitler without the Eastern ally on whom they had counted.[1] In the hesitations and moral confusions of the 'phoney war' Bevan – in common with the great majority of the British people – desired only to get on with it, though with no very clear calculation of the odds or idea of how victory might be won.

From the first, however, he asserted that the war was a moral as much as a military confrontation. By definition he believed that such a struggle could not be won by a discredited Tory Government which had been cornered into fighting fascism only reluctantly. 'If this war is to be won by a collapse in Germany', he wrote in *Tribune* at the end of November – and this view was widespread well beyond the left–'it can only be done by first breaking down the moral authority of the National Government.... If we have no confidence in the Chamberlain Government why should the German worker?'[2] To Bevan it was axiomatic that Chamberlain and his colleagues were not essentially different from fascists themselves. In these circumstances, he argued, the labour movement must seize the opportunity which the war presented to press its case. If, as the Government claimed, it really was a war for democracy, then democracy should first be conceded on the home front. If, on the other hand, it was an imperialist war, then this was 'a situation which Labour should be able to exploit to the utmost. It should take every advantage of the difficulties in which British capitalism is enmeshed and raise the price of labour to the highest possible level.' Either way, Labour's policy should be one of 'sustained attack' in order to secure 'supreme power'.[3] Only when that had been achieved would Britain be morally armed to defeat fascism.

War presented Labour with more than a merely industrial opportunity. Despite what he called the 'mental blackout' which closed the normal channels of political expression, Bevan perceived acutely that the shock of war could jolt people into a new political awareness and accelerate the political evolution of decades into a few years, or even months. 'War', he wrote at the beginning of 1940, 'is a great mental forcing-house.'

> War opens minds that were sealed, stimulates dormant intelligences and re-
> cruits into political controversy thousands who otherwise would remain in the
> political hinterland.
>   It is with these new, eager virgin minds that Labour must concern itself if it
> is to breast the tides of war and emerge from it holding the leadership of the
> nation.

Even as he held out this historic opportunity, however, Bevan feared that Labour's traditional caution would inhibit the party from grasping it. 'If Labour does not harvest the mental stimulus of war,' he warned, 'it will die. And it will deserve to die.' This was to be his refrain throughout the entire war, sounded alternately in tones of hope, exasperation and despair.

To give full expression to these latent forces Bevan opposed the electoral truce to which Labour had agreed at the outbreak of war. He accepted that there could not be a General Election during the war, but argued that that left Labour in Parliament the prisoners of the Tories' 1935 majority, elected in entirely different circumstances. Labour should be free to campaign in the country for its view of the war and to fight by-elections as the only means by which public opinion could express itself.[4] Similarly he maintained that since the electorate had been disfranchised, Parliament must become the electorate. There should be more free votes. 'We should be able to have divisions in this House the result of which will not involve the fate of the whole Administration.... We ought to be able to dismiss incompetent Ministers without bringing the fate of the Government into question. Only in that way can the House of Commons discharge its duties in wartime'.[5] Far from muting criticism of the Government, Bevan believed that parliamentary scrutiny should be stepped up. There was no one else to do the job. 'The Children's Hour has been extended to cover the whole of British broadcast- ing and the editors of the national dailies use treacle instead of ink.' The public mind, instead of being roused for a great effort, was being rendered 'sodden and limp with the ceaseless drip of adolescent propaganda'.[6] More- over it was Tory propaganda. The Tories were using the emergency of the war to push through controls on wage bargaining and the movement of labour which cancelled 'rights won by centuries of political struggle'. 'The first major casualty of the war', he asserted on 3 November, 'was the liberty of the British people.'[7] The Government took powers to limit wages but not profits, and was screwing down social provision like pensions and workmen's compensation, deliberately using the war, he alleged in February, 'to remodel the social services in accordance with Tory principles'.[8] He blamed Labour for meekly submitting to this ruse. Attlee made the right noises, stating that the country would have to travel 'far down the road to socialism' if the war was to be won; but Bevan was scornful. 'The Labour Party is more likely to reach extinction than the Tories are to reach socialism.... The war against Hitler is on,' he complained on 26 January, 'but the war against Chamberlain has not started yet. When is it going to start?'[9]

Attlee, more concerned with the effective prosecution of the war than with using the war to promote socialism, believed that the revolt against Chamberlain could only come from the Conservative side. Labour had made its position clear by refusing to join Chamberlain's Government; it could only wait for events to displace him. During the phoney war public dissatisfaction with Chamberlain's lack of urgency, inept appointments and failure to co-ordinate production for war purposes rumbled continuously but had nothing to focus on until Hitler invaded Norway on 8 April and the Government hurriedly launched an ill-prepared and disastrous expedition to try to re-cover Narvik and Trondheim. On 25 April, before the extent of the débâcle had become clear, Bevan made his first major speech of the war in the House of Commons, a forthright attack on Chamberlain and his Government which voiced the fears of the whole Labour Party and a growing number of Tories too. The occasion was Sir John Simon's astonishingly complacent Budget, which merely raised a few taxes.

> What are they waiting for? Are they waiting for some terrible calamity at sea or on land or in the air before we can shake them out of this mood? Have thousands, it may be hundreds of thousands, of our people to lose their lives or be mutilated before these stupid Tories can be moved? Is that what they are waiting for? Tonight we have empty benches here. We have a Prime Minister whose name is anathema in every country in the world. We have a Chancellor of the Exchequer ... whose name is despised throughout the world.
>
> Is it necessary to have a terrible calamity before we can get these benches filled and hon. Members doing the job they ought to do? ... The job has to be done and it can only be done by hon. Members opposite throwing aside many of their cherished notions. It can only be done by a supreme national effort, and that effort can only be made under the inspiration of principles that take no account of orthodox profit-making such as hon. Members opposite are protecting all the while....
>
> It is a bad business ... that we should have a Budget after eight months of war which discloses so appalling a failure to organise the whole of the resources of the country.[10]

Yet Bevan was taken by surprise by Chamberlain's fall just two weeks later. Only a few days before the Norway debate on which nearly a hundred Conservatives either abstained or voted against the Government he told George Orwell that there was 'not a hope' of Chamberlain being beaten.[11] He was never able to believe that Tories might be moved by patriotic motives ahead of the 'profit-making' to which he was convinced they were dedicated. As it was, while welcoming Churchill's succession, he held that Labour had been 'outwitted' into joining a Tory-dominated coalition from which Chamberlain and his associates had not yet been excluded. A statement in *Tribune* by the Editorial Board (Bevan, Strauss, Gollancz and the new editor Raymond Postgate, who had replaced the pro-Communist H.J.Hartshorn, sacked in March) deplored Churchill's retention in senior positions of

Chamberlain, Simon, Halifax and Kingsley Wood and alleged that Bevin and Morrison had been cunningly appointed to what were bound to be the most unpopular jobs, Labour and Supply. These were the key Ministries for the waging of total war, and Bevin and Morrison were the right men for the task. Yet Labour was only being allowed to put the petrol in the car: the Tories still held the steering wheel. Or to put it another way: 'The waging of the ideological war is left to the Tories. The material war is to be waged by Labour.' With the German army overrunning the Low Countries and driving the British Expeditionary Force back in headlong retreat to Dunkirk, *Tribune* was happy to welcome the new Government as an emergency stopgap and an improvement on Chamberlain; but Bevan still insisted that a further reconstruction must come soon. The door was open, but Labour must keep on pushing. 'The working class, the true productive force of the country, at last sees the possibility of using its strength in the struggle against Nazism.'[12]

Bevan was unstinting in his admiration of Churchill's great speeches of defiance in May and June 1940, when the fall of France left Britain alone facing the imminent, unthinkable prospect of invasion. 'We shall fight them on the beaches' excited his unqualified praise, though he always insisted that Churchill did not create, but only expressed, the determination of the British people. (So, to be fair, did Churchill.) But, even at this moment, his view of Churchill's limitations was unblinking. For all the magnificence of his oratory, he wrote on 21 June, Churchill could not change his Tory spots.

> What he did not do [in his 'Finest Hour' speech] and what he could not do, was to summon the future, for Mr Churchill is the spokesman of his order and of his class, and that class and that order is dying. That is why Mr Churchill ennobles retreat and can rally the nation to make its stand here in this island, but he cannot unfold for us the plans for victory, because there is not another victory left in the order to which he belongs, and of which he is the last distinguished representative.[13]

It was up to Labour, Bevan argued, to take the moral and military offensive by forcing 'a revolutionary change in the higher strategy of the war'.[14] What he meant by this he spelled out over the next few weeks. First, 'a radical reconstruction of the Government' to remove all the proven failures of the appeasement years.[15] Second, in joining the Government, Labour must insist on 'bringing its programme with it, not leaving it outside':[16] that meant the immediate nationalisation of basic industries, not for party reasons but so as to conscript property equally with men and place the economic resources of the country wholly at the disposal of the State. Third, the Government should trust the people both with arms to defend themselves against invasion (creating a 'people's army') and with much greater freedom of information and freedom of expression. Finally the war must become a 'war of liberation' not only at home but in Europe and the Empire: to symbolise this intent India should be given her freedom immediately. In this connection Bevan had never given up hope of winning the Soviet Union back to the democratic side; he now called for greater diplomatic efforts to draw her into the war.[17] By all these means, and to achieve these ends, Bevan called on Britain to shake off the bankrupt order represented by Churchill, 'assume the moral leadership of the world and lead the way, not only to final victory over the forces of Fascism but to wider vistas of expanding liberty'.[18] The language seemed to echo Churchill's talk of 'sunlit uplands'; but the programme enshrined in Bevan's vision could hardly have been more different.

His preoccupation in 1940 was protecting the domestic liberties in whose name the war was being fought. Briefly, during the crisis of imminent invasion in May, he had accepted the need for the workers to throw all restrictive practices and trade union rights to the winds. In a fierce article principally directed at the Communists and headed 'Are You A Traitor? – Answer Now' he had asserted: 'We must be prepared to set aside every consideration except the paramount one of exerting ourselves to the utmost first to hold the Nazis and then hurl them back in defeat. If we all have to work harder and longer for a short time what of it? If the Nazis win we shall work harder and longer not for a short time but forever.'[19] But this mood did not long survive Dunkirk. By the time the Battle of Britain was under way, Bevan was again denouncing the Tories' failure to make equal sacrifices from their side and offering strenuous opposition, with a handful of other left-wingers, to the emergency powers being taken by the Government for the administration of the country in the event of partial occupation. The Government had already abused the power it had been given since September, he alleged on 23 July: 'We are now slowly degenerating into a police state.' It was high time that the House of Commons 'reasserted its control over the Executive'.[20] He was particularly severe on the Home Secretary, Sir John Anderson – a career civil servant, not a politician – who, he claimed in October, had had to be saved four times by the House from major infringements of civil liberty;[21] and contemptuous of those Tory MPs who objected to his tireless probing of matters Ministers did not want probed. ('It is time that certain hon. Members should cease to act as pimps of the Government,' he told one bluntly.)[22] But the greatest danger to democracy he saw in the unhealthy personal ascendancy of the Prime Minister.

'In the short space of a few months', Bevan conceded on 30 August, 'he has grown from being a unique parliamentary debater into the unchallenged leader and spokesman of the British people.' He had achieved a position far stronger than Lloyd George in 1917–18. But here was the danger. 'In a democracy', Bevan wrote, 'idolatry is the first sin. Not even the supreme emergency of war justifies the abandonment of critical judgement.... To surrender all to one man is to risk being destroyed by him.'[23] Bevan had no intention of abandoning his critical judgement. It soon became his mission, since no one else seemed willing to take on the job, to cut Churchill down to size – at first in the interest of democracy, then more controversially by direct criticism of his conduct of the war, finally in the electoral interest of Labour. It was an unequal contest and a role which earned Bevan no thanks, even from his own side, only misrepresentation and abuse. Yet he was careful always to found his criticism of Churchill in principle, whether democratic or socialist. Unlike Shinwell, for instance, whose attacks, though often sharp, were all over the place and widely put down to personal disgruntlement, Bevan at his most venomous never uttered a word which could be construed as betraying personal ambition. He was essentially a backbench critic, pricking Churchill's vanity, forcing him to justify himself in the House of Commons; never a potential rival. Nevertheless, as he increasingly emerged as the champion of Labour's – or what he fervently hoped was Labour's – socialist vision of the future, in explicit opposition to Churchill's backward-looking imperial vision, he could not but begin to see himself engaged in something like a duel. Bevan normally had no time for historical biographies; but during the war he read, and studied closely, Sir George Trevelyan's life of Charles James Fox.[24] It is clear that as well as feeling a warm affinity for Fox – a tempestuous, impulsive radical orator very like himself – he drew consciously on the example of Fox's pursuit of Pitt in his own assaults on Churchill. For all the ideological theorising which shaped his view of history, Bevan was a romantic too. In this sense, he and Churchill, though utterly unequal, mirrored one another. No one in the summer of 1940 would have dreamed of mentioning Bevan in the same breath as the great war leader. Yet already David was beginning to take Goliath's measure.

He ventured his first criticism, almost timidly, in the debate on 8 October following the failure of the Dakar expedition. 'I yield to no one in my personal admiration of the Prime Minister's qualities,' he began; but if one examined the content rather than the manner of Churchill's opening speech, 'I think it was profoundly disappointing.' What it lacked was any hint of the future the country was fighting for. To maintain morale, Bevan asserted, something more was needed than 'a negative ideal of resurrecting some of those ancient frontiers again'.

> The people of this country and Europe are not prepared to lose their lives in order to reassemble a ramshackle Europe. They are looking to higher ideals than that.... It is not enough to offer to the people of Belgium, France and this country merely the defence of the institutions of democracy against the threats of Nazi dictatorship, because they recognise that, after all, it is that sort of democracy that brought Europe to war. If we are to persuade them, to enthuse them and inspire them with the defence of democracy, the conception of democracy has to be fitted into modern needs. We have to fill it up with a greater social content.

Churchill, Bevan admitted, was 'a formidable personality, and it is not very easy to confront him with an unpleasant speech'. Nevertheless he went on to point out that the structure of the War Cabinet, containing five heads of great departments, was 'the very opposite of ... the kind of War Cabinet he led us to believe he would construct', complaining that Churchill owed the House some explanation of his change of mind; and mounted a lengthy attack on Anderson – 'I have decided to make a very unpleasant speech' – before turning back to the Prime Minister's responsibility for offering the people a future worth fighting for.

> Sometimes the Prime Minister's ear is too sensitively attuned to the bugle notes of Blenheim for him to hear the whisperings in the streets .... In many respects the Prime Minister is not being well advised .... We on this side of the House are deeply anxious that the Government should adopt a policy bold, visionary and inspiring to try and associate ordinary men and women spiritually and not merely formally with the war effort. If that can be done, we shall get a response which will amaze even the Prime Minister with his faith.[25]

A week later, Churchill had himself elected leader of the Conservative Party in place of the dying Chamberlain. Bevan was outraged, though not surprised. (In his August article he had shrewdly assessed the lesson Churchill had learned from his years in the wilderness.)[26] 'Once more', he stormed in Tribune, 'the Tory caucus drapes itself in the national flag. Once more the skull and crossbones of private brigandage conceals itself in the decent garments of patriotic effort.' By this partisan act Churchill had deprived himself of the title of national leader.

> It is ten thousand pities that Mr Churchill should have chosen to take a step which must agitate dormant suspicions and awaken to life rivalries which are best forgotten when the enemy's knife is at our throat. It is a million pities that he should have chosen to give new vigour to elements in our national life which must be progressively weakened if we are to gather sufficient strength to win through.[27]

Hitherto Bevan had given Churchill the benefit of the doubt. From now on he regarded the Prime Minister exclusively as a party leader.

The winter of 1940–1 was the winter of the Blitz. The Battle of Britain had been won and the threat of German invasion beaten off for the moment, though Bevan like everyone else expected Hitler to try again in 1941. In the meantime Britain still stood alone and on the defensive. Germany commanded the whole continent of Europe and clearly was not going to collapse from within. In these circumstances Churchill looked West to the United States and succeeded in negotiating with Roosevelt the Lend–Lease agreement by which America gave Britain all aid consistent with neutrality, and rather more. Bevan welcomed this assistance, but without enthusiasm.[28] He preferred to look East. In a second wide-ranging survey of the war in November 1940 he repeated his faith that Russia was bound to be drawn in very soon. Curiously, he predicted that Hitler would be obliged to adopt a new ideology of Catholicism, in place of his 'Aryan myth', through which to rule his new European empire, and for this purpose would have once again to build up the Soviet Union as his enemy. Of course, Hitler needed no such rationale to attack Russia. But if Bevan was wrong in detail, his strategic appreciation was correct. 'It seems to me', he told a hostile House, 'that we have to have a great, powerful Ally like Russia if we are to bring this war to a speedy and success-ful conclusion.... Powerful though the help of America may be, the Soviet Union could bring this war to a conclusion in one week.' Yet instead of a diplomatic offensive to bring Stalin into the war as soon as possible, the Foreign Office still seemed to miss no opportunity to snub him.[29]

For all his faith in Russia, Bevan held absolutely no brief for the British Communist Party or its Moscow-dictated policy of 'revolutionary de-featism'. In September he denounced the party newspaper, the *Daily Worker*, in *Tribune* as 'now among the ranks of those helping Hitler to win. It is doing so as openly and deliberately as it dares'.[30] This was precisely the view of the Government. Herbert Morrison, who had replaced Anderson as Home Secretary in October, could have cited Bevan's article in justification when, in January 1941, after a warning, he closed the paper under the emergency powers taken in July. It is the more remarkable, therefore, that Bevan chose to make this issue the occasion of his first explicit criticism of Labour Ministers. Morrison's action, he contended, showed 'an extraordinary deterioration in democratic standards in Great Britain'. The *Worker* was detestable but harmless: the country could afford the degree of liberty it enjoyed. The real reason for its suppression, he alleged, was that it was 'intended to serve as an instrument of intimidation against the Press as a whole'. Morrison might never take action against any other newspaper, but the power to do so would hang 'over every editorial chair in Fleet Street' – including, obviously, *Tribune*. 'So long as the Home Secretary can behave in that dictatorial manner ... he can do almost as much by intimidation and terrorism as by taking action'. The implications were alarming. 'The Government are winning the war against us, and are making Labour Ministers the catspaws of reactionary policy.' The war, Bevan concluded, had entered a third phase:

> The first phase was when the late Mr Neville Chamberlain ruled over the country disastrously. The second phase was when the right hon. Gentleman the Member for Epping took charge and inspired the country, and the third phase was when Ministers of whom we had the right to expect something greater lost their faith in democracy, lost their confidence in ordinary people and tried to lead the country to victory by methods which have proven disas-trous in other countries in Europe.[31]

Bevan won just six votes for his motion of censure on Morrison; but the division marks a watershed in his attitude not merely to the Tories but to the Coalition as a whole. For eight months he had been urging Labour to sell its co-operation dearly, to insist on land nationalisation, coal nationalisation, railway nationalisation and the abolition of the hated means test as the price of true national unity.[32] 'To talk of a new social order in any other sense', he wrote in October, 'is merely a play with words.... War aims begin at home.... If the Tory members of the Government carry their defence of private property rights to the extent of refusing the public ownership of the industries I mentioned last week, then we shall lose the war.'[33] 'Blind Men Are Leading Us',[34] he warned week after week in *Tribune*: 'It's Time Labour Kicked'.[35] In November he hailed with relief Churchill's indication that the household means test would be abolished for old age pensioners. 'At last ... the first important fruit of Labour's participation in the Government.'[36] But in February it transpired that the test was not to be abolished after all. In the Commons Bevan led a furious attack on the majority of Labour Members not in the Government who acquiesced tamely in the Determination of Needs Bill in violation of the party's most specific pledges over the past ten years. But only nineteen supported him.[37] Already the week before, following the *Daily Worker* episode, he had written bitterly that the Labour Party, by surrendering to Tory policies all down the line, had betrayed its responsibility to lift the war effort on to a higher plane. 'It is dying, and soon it may be dead.'[38] From now on he was fighting the war on *three* fronts: against the Germans, against the Tories and against his own leaders. Even though Harold Laski, the leading figure among those outside Parliament who had been calling for a declaration of socialist war aims, was elected in top place to the constituency section of the NEC, Bevan found the party Conference in May deeply depressing. Not for the first time he almost despaired of the party altogether. 'In the guise of loyalty', he wrote, 'and in the name of discipline the Labour Party has poisoned its own vitals.'[39] Under its present leadership and constitution he did not see that it could *ever* be a vehicle for socialism. As he had always done before, however, he rejected the alternative of abandoning the party and trying to begin again. The only course open to individual socialists was to campaign vigorously in the factories and within the party to create a swell of opinion which would revitalise it from below. On 6 June *Tribune* offered its columns for the purpose.

Two weeks later, Hitler attacked Russia and the war was transformed.

Churchill's response is famous: 'If Hitler invaded Hell, I would make at least a favourable reference to the Devil in the House of Commons.'[40] He welcomed the Soviet Union as an ally and promised Stalin all possible economic and technical assistance. Recognition that Hitler's action offered Britain for the first time a realistic hope of eventual victory overrode his detestation of Communism. For Bevan, however, there was no such conflict. Russia's entry into the war both ended Britain's precarious isolation and reinforced the progressive aims for which he believed the war was being fought. He rejoiced in the dilemma in which the old appeasers who had opposed an alliance with Soviet Russia in 1938–9 now found themselves, believing that now they would be flushed out and swept aside. It was part of

Hitler's calculation, he suggested, that by turning east he would weaken the will of the British ruling class to continue to fight. If he succeeded, Bevan warned, and at the same time seized the wheat of the Ukraine and the oil of the Caucasus, 'we should be within sight of losing the war. On the other hand if we get together with the Russians promptly and co-ordinate our military and political action we shall be far nearer winning both the war and the peace than seemed possible a week ago.'[41]

'Military *and political* action': Bevan welcomed the Soviet Union as a political ally in the destruction of fascism. He was not blind to the horrors that had been committed in the name of Communism since 1917. But he had always blamed the excesses of Stalinism on Russia's isolation following the Western attempt to strangle the Soviet experiment at birth. Now, he believed, 'the Soviet Union has been brought into the main stream of Western democratic history'.[42]

> Now that the Soviet Government are engaged in a life and death struggle where they must secure the maximum goodwill of the Western democracies and of their own workers and peasants, and must do their best to stir the oppressed peoples of Europe to revolt, the Stalin regime is well-nigh bound to make a reality of the promises of more democracy and social justice that are enshrined in the Soviet Constitution but have remained a dead letter since its adoption.[43]

The British and Soviet forms of democracy, he asserted, were complementary. Britain would contribute the tradition of personal liberty and civil rights: Russia's experience of economic planning would serve as a model to the West. Together they could create the society of the future, 'in which it is safe to be free'.[44] 'We should negotiate an agreement' with the Soviet Union, Bevan urged, 'on the principle of the democratic New Order, based on anti-Fascist revolution throughout Europe and a union of free peoples which we propose to put in place of Hitler's continental system.'[45]

The idealisation of Soviet Russia as Britain's great democratic ally, of course, swept much of the Labour Party, indeed a large proportion of the population, between 1941 and 1945. From E.H.Carr in *The Times* to the influential classes run by the Army Bureau of Current Affairs, fellow-travelling had never been so widespread or so respectable. Even Churchill lent it some support with his picturesque invocations of the toiling Russian masses, whose cause had suddenly become 'the cause of free men and free peoples in every quarter of the globe'.[46] Few, however, even on the left, took the fantasy so far as Bevan. Ordinary patriotic Britons, taking for granted the righteousness of their own struggle, had no difficulty in imagining that Russia had enlisted on the side of democracy. Primarily, however, their emotion was one of gratitude to the Russians for relieving, however temporarily – and not voluntarily at that – the German pressure on themselves. As the heroism of Russia's resistance and the scale of her losses became clear during 1942 they were moved increasingly by admiration and by a degree of guilt for Britain's relatively puny effort. These were the generous feelings which fed the popular agitation for a second front in France, of which Bevan was to be one of the most outspoken advocates. This sympathy was primarily human, not political. Bevan was way ahead of the public in his belief that Britain's cause was made *better* by the Soviet alliance, that Britain was now fully on the side of democracy and progress as she had not been before. He was right in that he saw immediately that Russia gave Britain fresh hope of winning the war; he was cock-eyed in imagining that Britain and Russia would be fighting together for a new world order.

The main public campaign for a 'Second Front Now' did not take off until 1942. But Bevan began demanding the opening of a second front in his very first speech on Russia's entry into the war in June 1941.[47] The argument had two aspects. The military one, at this stage when there was little confidence in Russia's ability to resist, was that it was imperative to help her by drawing off some of Hitler's strength, thus forcing him to fight what the Germans had always feared, a war on two fronts. As the German Panzer divisions sliced rapidly through the Ukraine there was a real fear that Russia would be beaten before Britain could give her any aid; and then Hitler would be free to turn again to the invasion of Britain.[48] This argument, however, took no account of the simple military unpreparedness, just a year after Dunkirk, of the British army to mount an opposed landing that would have any chance of establishing itself in France. If Russia was going to be beaten anyway, there were good military reasons for Britain to conserve her slender resources. But Bevan and most of those who supported the Second Front did not believe that military calculations were the true grounds for the Government's reluctance. The left was convinced that the Tory-dominated Government shrank from embracing Russia as an ally for political reasons.[49] More subtly Bevan also believed that the Tories were reluctant to take the offensive out of a generalised fear of the future. He developed the surprising theory that Churchill and other Ministers were 'defeatist'. If they could not invade Europe when Hitler was preoccupied in the east, when did they ever expect to be able to do it? One reason they gave was that there was still a danger of Hitler invading Britain. This possibility, at a time when he was fully engaged in Russia, Bevan scornfully discounted. This was the moment to strike Hitler in the rear. 'The Government cry "Wolf, Wolf" at the very moment when people can see the wolf engaged in a life and death struggle with a bear at the other end of the field,' he wrote in September. 'The general view is that the best way to deal with the danger from the wolf is to give the bear a hand.'[50]

'People are beginning to say', Bevan wrote of Churchill in October, 'that he is undoubtedly a superb defence Prime Minister, but he shows no signs of being a victory Prime Minister.'[51] Two weeks later, in the House of Commons he unleashed his strongest attack so far, not yet on Churchill personally but on the timid Government of which he was the over-cautious head. 'The people', he alleged, 'do not trust the Government. The people do

not trust many of the people who are in the Government. The people believe
that the Government are ratting.' If there was to be no Second Front, he
demanded, what *was* the Government's strategy for winning the war? If it was
true, as Halifax – now shuffled off to the Washington embassy – had kindly
informed Hitler, that Britain was physically unable at present to launch a
second front (a disgraceful statement which Bevan denounced as very close
to treason), then the fault was the Government's half-hearted production
policy which the trade unions and MPs of all parties had been criticising as
inadequate for months. (The responsibility for this failure Bevan fastened
directly on Churchill – 'a Prime Minister who is completely illiterate in all
matters connected with industry and who has come to think in terms of
perorations and rounded verbiage'.[52] 'Even the most exalted expressions of
the human spirit', he complained in August, 'cannot be a permanent
substitute for a sound economic organisation.')[53] Both the personnel and the
machinery of Churchill's 'one-man Government', he concluded, needed to
be overhauled. 'I believe that the time has arrived when we should do the
second half of the job which we left undone last year.'

> I believe it is time for there to be a War Cabinet of Ministers, without depart-
> mental responsibilities, who can talk back to the Prime Minister. I believe it is
> time to throw out of their office all those old, jaded, tired Ministers who have
> been associated with disastrous policies. I am convinced that this is the desire
> of the country and that this House is falling into progressive disrepute because
> it is not forcing the Government to face these realities. I am convinced that the
> last few weeks and months have shown that there exist in this country inex-
> haustible reservoirs of talent and energy if the Government could only tap
> them, but this Government cannot do it. It is suffering from nostalgia, nos-
> talgia for the days that are dead, nostalgia producing nothing at all but inertia
> and self-pity. If you cannot do the job, get out. The country demands the
> change, and it is the duty of the House of Commons to see that the will of the
> country is made known to the Government.[54]

The duty of the House of Commons was one of Bevan's most persistent
themes. Partly it was a matter of democratic principle: 'Social institutions,
like muscles, depend upon their use. If they are not used, they become
atrophied. No one wants to make any sacrifices for something which is
dead.'[55] Partly it was a matter of relaying to the Government the mood and
apprehensions of the people. Equally, however, it was the right of individual
MPs to make constructive contributions. Bevan rejected utterly the view that
military strategy should be left to the professionals. 'Strategy', he affirmed,
'is merely applied common sense, and it may be assumed that I have at least as
much common sense as other hon. Members who have discussed the
matter.'[56] This self-confidence was unusual in a Labour MP with absolutely
no military experience. Labour critics of the Government tended to stick to
the industrial, social and civil liberties aspects of the war, leaving strategy to
often uniformed Tories. But Bevan would have none of that. Jeered at as an

'amateur strategist', he refused to acknowledge that even Churchill had more relevant credentials. In 1942 he pointed out that Stalin and Roosevelt too were amateurs – and all the better for it. 'These gibes are silly. .... It is the obligation of this House to discuss major strategy and for hon. Members to say otherwise means that they are undermining the very foundation of representative government. .... Representative government is government of the experts by the amateurs and always has been.'[57] He regularly blamed the faults of the Government on the tameness of the House of Commons – as well as the muzzled and fawning press and the BBC, which trumpeted Churchill's speeches at length but rarely gave any time or space to his critics at all. The Government, Bevan alleged at the end of 1941, had become 'a little caucus communicating between themselves against the public interest'.

> We have allowed Ministers for the last two years to have an exaggerated sense of their own importance. We have allowed them to get away with things they ought not to have been allowed to get away with .... The right hon. Gentleman [Churchill] has become irresponsible, because he has not been sufficiently kicked in this House.[58]

And, of course, those above all who should have been doing the kicking, in Bevan's view, were the Labour Party, representing the mass of ordinary people in the country.

Chapter 8

Bevan at War: *Tribune*'s Finest Hour; Nye and Jennie

At the end of 1941 Bevan quarrelled with Raymond Postgate and took over himself, on behalf of the three-man Board, as acting editor of *Tribune*. Under Postgate the paper had shaken off the fellow-travelling associations which had caused its circulation to drop sharply in 1939–40: it was now back to around 10,000 copies a week. Nevertheless it was in increasing financial difficulty. Mounting costs were given as the reason for the decision to do without a full-time editor, and the price was doubled from 3d to 6d.[1] Otherwise Bevan, with his two assistants Jon Kimche and Evelyn Anderson, made relatively few changes. His own editorials became longer and weightier, often extending to 3000 words and filling the first two pages of the paper – substantial essays on the progress of the war, the evolution of democracy and the future of mankind. But he retained most of the same contributors: in particular he maintained the high level to which Postgate had raised the books and arts pages at the back of the paper, giving a regular platform to most of the left-inclined writers and intellectuals of the day – Stephen Spender and Arthur Koestler, Naomi Mitchison and J.B.Priestley, E.M.Forster, Stevie Smith and many more. '*Tribune* is not perfect,' George Orwell wrote fairly in 1945. 'But I do think it is the only existing weekly paper that makes a genuine effort to be both progressive and humane – that is, to combine a radical Socialist policy with a respect for freedom of speech and a civilised attitude towards literature and the arts'.[2] The combination was very characteristic of Bevan: though he was a tolerant editor and inevitably left much of the detailed work to Kimche and Anderson, *Tribune* during the second half of the war – at once combative, outspoken and high-principled – was a perfect expression of his personality and interests.

Bevan's greatest coup was to induce Orwell, when he threw up his job with the BBC World Service at the end of 1943, to become literary editor, writing a wide-ranging, provocative weekly column headed 'As I Please'. Orwell's name brought added lustre to a paper which, as he recalled in 1947, had already been transformed since 1939 from a somewhat lowbrow polemic-sheet aimed at politically-conscious workers into a relatively expensive, well-laid-out and well-informed journal aimed at what Orwell characteristically termed 'the out-at-elbow middle class'.

Its prestige among the BBC personnel was very striking. In the libraries where commentators went to prime themselves it was one of the most sought-after periodicals, not only because it was largely written by people who knew something at first hand about Europe, but because it was then the only paper of any standing which criticised the Government.[3]

Orwell respected Bevan. 'Those who have worked with him in a journalistic capacity', he wrote in an anonymous *Observer* profile in 1945, 'have remarked with pleasure and astonishment that here at last is a politician who knows that literature exists and will even hold up work for five minutes to discuss a point of style.'[4] Bevan equally respected Orwell. Nevertheless Kimche told Orwell's successor, Tosco Fyvel, that 'they had never really communicated.... By and large, Bevan's and Orwell's minds ran on parallel lines without meeting.'[5] Their association, which lasted only fourteen months, was a lucky accident. But then, as Fyvel himself remembered, 'The attacking, independent wartime *Tribune*' – sailing always close to the censorial wind but feeling itself buoyantly in step with history, repeating and amplifying the strictures of the Government's principal critic in the House of Commons – was itself 'a fluke that had come off'.[6] Between *Tribune* and the House, Bevan had built himself a remarkably secure platform from which to sustain his challenge to Churchill's ascendancy.

He was an irritatingly effective critic partly because, though politically isolated for voicing unpopular views, he remained excellent company. While the respectable in both parties shunned him, he retained his social contacts across the parties with the most convivial and indiscreet elements in the House of Commons and even in the Government, who would feed him information they dared not use themselves. In particular Beaverbrook, though Minister of Aircraft Production in 1940–1 and Minister of Supply 1941–2 – the one energising appointment of which Bevan warmly approved – did not cease to encourage his left-wing friends. In June 1941, for example, Dalton complained to Attlee that Bevan was getting to know from Beaverbrook 'too much of what went on inside'.[7] In 1942 Beaverbrook resigned from the Government to throw himself publicly into the Second Front campaign: for once in their lives he and Bevan were on the same side. After 1943, however, when Beaverbrook rejoined the Government and post-war party politics increasingly cast their shadow, they saw little of one another and their relations cooled.

Bevan also resumed for a time his association with Cripps – still formally outside the Labour Party – whom Churchill had sent as Ambassador to Moscow in 1940. He returned in early 1942 trailing clouds of undeserved glory as the man who had brought Russia into the war and an authoritative advocate of the Soviet alliance and the Second Front. Bevan encouraged

Cripps to demand a high price for joining the War Cabinet and hoped that his appointment as Leader of the House of Commons would mark a fresh injection of Labour ideas into the Coalition.[8] Within a few months, however, he was lamenting that Cripps had missed his opportunity.[9]

A third independent figure, though less influential, with whom Bevan remained on friendly terms throughout the war was Harold Nicolson, who characteristically worshipped Churchill but found it – in September 1942 – 'very difficult to answer' Bevan's criticism of him.[10] Nicolson, Robert Boothby and others were typical of the sort of semi-dissident opinion in the House which could never bring itself to vote or speak against Churchill but provided a background of muttering against which Bevan could act as their fearless spokesman. In December 1941 Nicolson recorded a revealing conversation with Bevan, who dilated sympathetically on the dilemma of progressive upper-class intellectuals facing the imminent loss of their privileged way of life: 'Their reason tells them that the future is right, but it is agony for them to lose the past.'[11] This, and the sort of easy friendship Bevan was nevertheless able to enjoy with 'class enemies' like Nicolson, recalls a remark he made to 'Rab' Butler before the war, when he cheerfully told Butler that his (Butler's) class was on the way down while his own was on the way up.[12] Such shafts give glimpses of the supreme self-confidence and social optimism which sustained Bevan during the war, however dismal the news or feeble, in his view, the Labour leadership. He had no doubt at all that Britain was on the brink of the revolution which he had been predicting for the past twenty years. He had therefore no need to fear Churchill or other Tories and could readily condole with Nicolson and other congenial ornaments of the old order whose time was almost up.

Another characteristic glimpse of Bevan at this time is provided by the well-connected journalist Jean Nicol, who used to meet him with other left-wing scribblers – Claud Cockburn, Frank Owen, the young Michael Foot – happily frequenting the fleshpots of the Savoy during the blackout. From the *Tribune* office just up the Strand, she wrote later, 'Aneurin Bevan brought his diatribes against Mr Churchill wet from the printing press into the comfort of the American Bar. How violently I disagreed with all he said, and yet I was no more immune to his friendly charm than his disciples.'[13] There can be no doubt that during the darkest moments of the war in 1941 and 1942 Bevan was enjoying the time of his life.

Jennie was working as a journalist too for most of the war. After a short hectic period working for Beaverbrook at the Ministry of Aircraft Production, she got a job as a columnist on the *Daily Mirror*. In the autumn of 1941 she was sent by Brendan Bracken on a propaganda tour of the United States – she was in California when the Japanese attacked Pearl Harbor – and in 1942 she made her own contribution to the Second Front campaign by writing a quick, starry-eyed book, *Russia, Our Ally*. In these years, as before the war, she and Bevan pursued their separate activities, meeting when they could at the home Ma Lee continued to keep for them at Brimpton Common. Very often, of course, particularly during the Blitz, they could not get back there. Then they would stay with friends in London. On one such evening Bevan was caught in an air-raid, but walked on unscathed to George Strauss's house in Kensington. 'I could have loved London tonight,' he told Jennie. Loathing the place as he did, he nevertheless found himself sharing the pride of Londoners that their city could 'take' everything the Luftwaffe could throw at it; he responded with excitement to the unprecedented sense of comradeship and communal spirit that was forged under the weight of bombing.[14] War had broken down at least some of the barriers of class and rank, creating out of hideous destruction a sort of model of what socialism might be.

With the end of the Blitz in May 1941, the bombing ceased; but Nye and Jennie still found it difficult to get home every night. Towards the end of the war, as Labour began to prepare for the trial of political strength that would follow the peace, they reluctantly felt the need to have a base of their own in London. Accordingly, in June 1944, they sold Lane End Cottage and bought an eleven-year lease on 23 Cliveden Place, an elegant Georgian terraced house, large enough to provide separate accommodation for Jennie's parents, just off Sloane Square, a little over a mile from the House of Commons. (London property prices were conveniently depressed by the war.) Unluckily they moved just in time for the start of Hitler's last throw, the flying-bomb campaign: Cliveden Place suffered serious damage and for some weeks they had to live in the cellar. For the next ten years, though – throughout the years of the Labour Government and the bitter Bevanite quarrels, until Bevan grew sick of London and pined for the country again – Cliveden Place was their home, the scene of their increasingly lavish political and non-political entertaining. Still presided over by Ma Lee, and decorated by Jennie, it was nevertheless quintessentially Nye – luxurious yet bohemian, more Chelsea than Westminster: a paradoxically stylish home for the proudly proletarian scourge of the bourgeoisie.

It was towards the end of the war, too, that Jennie came to the decision that shaped the rest of their life together. When they had first met in 1929, even when they had married in 1934, she had been the more prominent political figure. As a very young and vital woman in the House of Commons she could not but be conspicuous; as a fiery left-wing rebel in the 1929 Parliament she attracted plenty of publicity, while in the grim days after 1931 she was still in great demand as a rousing speaker and hard-hitting journalist. During her years out of Parliament, however, she inevitably slipped out of the limelight. Meanwhile Nye was steadily making his name, until by the middle of the war his celebrity, or notoriety, eclipsed hers. Privately she had come to recognise that he not only had the capacity, but might get the opportunity, to do great things; at the same time he needed her, as an emotional refuge but also as a practical helpmeet. Like many another Welshman of his class and generation raised in a matriarchal home with several sisters, he had not been brought up to do much for himself. Ma Lee ran a wonderful home, but she would not live for ever and if he was to fight the political battles they both wanted to see fought and won he needed a wife, not merely a mother-in-law to come home to. Accordingly, from about 1944 or 1945, Jennie determined to subordinate her career to Nye's. The sacrifice was a real one, and for an independent-minded woman who had been one of the first to break through into the male club and had entered into marriage very much in the spirit of equal part-nership, it must have been peculiarly hard to make. But it was a political decision and, considered politically, a rational one. 'I was not such a fool', she wrote, 'as not to see it was worthwhile.... He was doing what I wanted done infinitely better than I could have done it.'[15] Married to an exceptional man, she realised that she could do more to advance the cause of socialism as Nye Bevan's wife than as Jennie Lee.

She has always insisted that she had no regrets. 'I reconciled myself to the strains because he was my alter ego. We were never at any time conflicting egos.'[16] It may be that she protests too much. It would be remarkable if she had never resented having had to give up her career to nourish his, and there are signs that at times she did. In the 1950s, during the Bevanite years, when her advice to him at critical moments was generally bad, it is difficult to escape the impression that her judgement was influenced by her sacrifice and a feeling that by it she had earned the right to hold him to her somewhat narrow view of the proper course that he should follow. The loss of her own career possibly made her more emotional about his. Not that she wholly abandoned her own career, of course. In 1945 she rejoined the Labour Party and was selected to fight the Staffordshire mining seat of Cannock, which she won and held until 1970. Between 1945 and 1951, while Nye was in the Cabinet, she maintained a surprisingly independent existence as a backbencher; but for the last eight years of his life she did largely confine herself to the role of loyal and supportive wife. She achieved some compensation after 1964, when Harold Wilson made her Minister for the Arts and she was able, for the first time in thirty years, to make a notable success in her own right. But this was after Nye's death. During his lifetime she chose deliberately not to compete with him. Theirs was one of the most remarkable of political marriages, for which Jennie deserves the principal credit.

Chapter 9

'Squalid Nuisance': the Pursuit of Churchill

The war could not have gone much worse in the early part of 1942. The only bright spot was that on 7 December 1941 the Japanese had attacked Pearl Harbor and brought the United States into the war. But there was no certainty that Britain would last long enough to benefit from America's strength. On 10 December the Japanese sank the *Prince of Wales* and the *Repulse* and asserted their naval ascendancy in the Far East. In North Africa, in January, Auchinleck was driven back by Rommel to Tobruk. Then, in February, the Japanese overran Singapore. Bevan was not too worried about Singapore, except as further evidence of military incompetence. The British Empire, he believed, was already finished, and only Tories mourned it.[1] The loss of Singapore might even force them to give India her freedom before it was too late.[2] The real war, he maintained, was nearer home. 'The war will be won or lost this year,' he wrote on 13 March, 'and it will be won or lost in Europe.'[3]

The campaign for a Second Front now really got under way. The Russians had so far withstood the German assault better than anyone had expected, halting the invader on the outskirts of Moscow on 4 December 1941. But it was still touch and go. If Hitler broke through in 1942 to the oilfields of the Caucasus, Russia would be beaten. A second front in Europe, drawing away twenty or thirty German divisions from the east, could make the difference that might give Russia victory. For Bevan, the urgency of doing something to take the pressure off Russia was more important than any calculations of practicability. If Britain did not help Russia at once, he argued, with whatever forces were available, it would be too late. 'If we are not now in a position to meet the one-tenth of German forces that are left in the west, what conceivable hope is there that the time will ever come when Great Britain can engage the land forces of Germany in the event of Russia being subdued?'[4] Quite simply, it was a matter of political will. 'It can be done,' he persuaded himself. 'The people of Great Britain want it done. They want to see us setting about it now, and the politicians who refuse to do it will themselves not survive 1942.'[5]

There was some evidence to support this view. On 25 March the Government suffered its first by-election defeat of the war, at Grantham, and this was followed by further losses at Rugby and Wallasey in April and at Maldon in June. The victors were all Independents, taking advantage of the electoral truce between the major parties to voice mounting anxiety about the progress of the war. Significantly, however, all were broadly on the left and their victories were gained in Conservative-held seats. None of them made a prominent feature of the Second Front. Their themes were rather the need for greater efficiency in war production (including nationalisation where necessary), real equality of sacrifice, the democratisation of the war effort and a variety of servicemen's grievances.[6] Nevertheless their success indicated a general mood of uneasiness in the country to which the Second Front agitation gave a specific focus. Bevan was delighted, particularly with the victories of W.J.Brown (an old associate from the days of his flirtation with Mosley in 1930) at Rugby and of Tom Driberg at Maldon. These results – achieved, as he pointed out, on an old register with a disproportionately elderly electorate – were the proof of his conviction that the country was swinging leftwards under the impact of war. They confirmed what he had maintained from the beginning, that the Government was out of touch with the will of the people. At the same time he feared that Labour was too enfeebled by its adherence to the Coalition to reap the harvest that was waiting to be gathered. 'Having spent half a century in educating the people of Britain to Socialism,' he wrote, 'the Labour Party has maladroitly manoeuvred itself into a state in which it cannot take advantage of it.'[7] At the party Conference at the end of May, he powerfully backed a motion criticising the truce: despite a stern lecture from Morrison on the importance of national unity, it was only very narrowly defeated.[8] The country, and the party, were unquestionably stirring.

The same month *Tribute* published three articles by 'Thomas Rainsboro'' more outspokenly critical of Churchill than anything previously printed in the press or spoken in the House of Commons. The pseudonymous author was actually Frank Owen, but the articles expressed Bevan's views. The first two raked over the Prime Minister's blunders in Norway, North Africa, Greece and Malaya.[9] The third bluntly condemned the Government's dilatoriness over aid for Russia and its refusal to contemplate a second front until Britain and the United States together had achieved 'overwhelming strength'. 'If we could go on piling up arms and men until 1943 and then crack Hitler on the snout, it would be admirable,' Owen conceded. 'But what is Hitler going to be engaged in till 1943? War is not an addition sum but an equation in time. *Have we time to afford Churchill's strategy?*[10] *Tribune*'s answer was an emphatic 'No'.

Bevan defended the Rainsboro' articles in an editorial on 15 May. With the rest of the press and Parliament muzzled and sycophantic, he argued, it was *Tribune*'s duty to print what others would not. There was no possible danger to national unity, which was solid. Churchill was the symbol of national unity.

> But he is not the sole residue [sic] of wisdom and knowledge as to how that unity should be directed. The building up of this man's reputation has gone as far as the safety of the country warrants. The concentration of hero-worship on one individual is always full of sinister consequences for the nation which indulges in it. It is all the more dangerous when that statesman has made himself the leader of one Party in the State; exposed himself wholly to the pressure of vested interests; and speaks only the voice of tradition and not the hope and aspirations for the future which are stirring in every breast.

Other papers, Bevan continued, tried to deflect all criticism away from the person of the Prime Minister. *Tribune* would have no part in such 'cowardly obscurantism'. 'If the Prime Minister insists upon making himself responsible for all questions of higher military strategy, then he must be ready to face accusations directed against that strategy.' Churchill had just made another of his wonderful radio broadcasts. But, Bevan asked, 'How long can we afford a succession of oratorical successes accompanied by a series of military disasters?' The people of Great Britain were living in a 'dream land' of empty rhetoric.

> The lesson of the war is surely this, that military decisions have been made by a hand to mouth process, in which the individual initiative of the Prime Minister appears as a series of brilliant illuminations which are only afterwards revealed as more or less unfortunate improvisations. This kind of war cannot be fought that way. The higher direction needs planning and thinking out ahead. No one man can do this. The need, therefore, is for a central civic Directory of the war. And by civic we mean civic, not a synthetic military glamour boy. Until this is done we shall fail to make that contribution to victory which is still latent in the British people.[11]

Five weeks later, on 20 June, Rommel recaptured Tobruk, despite repeated Government assurances that the British position was unassailable. On 1–2 July the House of Commons debated the second 'No Confidence' motion of the war. (The first had been in January: Bevan had then abstained and the motion received only one vote.) This time the challenge to Churchill's authority was much more serious. A senior Conservative backbencher, Sir John Wardlaw-Milne, moved that 'this House ... has no confidence in the central direction of the war'. Unfortunately for the Government's critics, he ruined his own case by the ludicrous suggestion that the Duke of Gloucester be appointed Commander-in-Chief. Then, where Wardlaw-Milne had argued that Churchill tried to do too much and needed another strong man beside him as Minister of Defence, his seconder, Admiral Sir Roger Keyes, made precisely the opposite criticism that Churchill interfered too little with the tardy military machine and should assert himself more![12] The threat to Churchill thus collapsed before the debate had properly begun. By general consent it was left to Bevan, opening the second allotted day, to rescue the occasion from bathos. He did so with his greatest speech of the war.

He began by defending the right of the House to debate such motions, denying that criticism of the Government undermined the morale of the troops: 'It is not the speeches we make here that bring home to the soldiers the defects in the direction of the war; it is what they experience themselves in battle. It would be a serious thing if the soldiers in the field could not hear any voices raised in their behalf in the House of Commons.' He attacked Churchill for treating the debate as a vote to be won, rather than an opportunity to reassure the nation. He should have opened the debate, not reserved himself to the end.

> I know that it is better debating tactics for the Prime Minister to wind up the Debate. In that way he will win the Debate. But the country is now more concerned with the Prime Minister winning the war than with his winning a Debate in the House of Commons. The Prime Minister wins Debate after Debate and loses battle after battle.

Then Bevan summed up his indictment of the Government. 'First, the main strategy of the war has been wrong; second, the wrong weapons have been produced; and third, those weapons are being managed by men who are not trained in the use of them and who have not studied the use of modern weapons.' On the first count, Bevan charged that the Government had 'conceived the war wrongly from the very beginning, and no one has more misconceived it than the Prime Minister himself'. Churchill, as 'Maginot-minded' as the French, had not understood that this was going to be a war of movement. From that 'primary misconception' had stemmed the wrong strategy and the production of the wrong weapons, specifically – Bevan moved on to his second count – the lack of dive bombers and transport planes needed to support the desert war in Libya. The lack of dive bombers after three years of war, he charged, 'reveals that the Prime Minister and his Government have not gone to the heart of this modern war making, and I say that it is disgraceful that the lives of British soldiers should be lost because of the absence of this elementary knowledge at the top'.

Wisdom after the event is never popular. Bevan's strictures aroused resentment and a justified reminder of his own record in voting against rearmament before the war. But the House recognised an uncomfortable degree of truth in what he said. He pressed on to criticise the structure of the Government: the War Cabinet was still composed of Departmental Ministers with too much on their hands to leave them any time for the conduct of the war. Churchill, Bevan did not deny, had 'qualities of greatness – everybody knows that – but the trouble is that he has too much to do'. He could not delegate the running of the war to someone else – Bevan scouted Wardlaw-Milne's idea – but he should surround himself with a proper non-departmental War Cabinet to share fully in the key decisions with the Chiefs of Staff.

Briefly Bevan rehearsed the failures of the Government's production policy and in passing attacked the production of long-range bombing planes which could never be a decisive weapon of war. Then he turned to the use of weapons in the field, confessing that he had never fought in a battle 'so I have to speak with diffidence in this'. His charge here was that British staff officers were not trained in the co-ordination of land and air forces – the German *Blitzkrieg* technique. He actually proposed that it would be better to put British troops temporarily under the command of *emigré* Czech, Polish and French generals who were trained in modern methods. He repeated the taunt that was 'on everyone's lips' that if Rommel had been in the British army he would still be a sergeant, and called for a purge of the War Office, beginning at the top. 'The fact of the matter is that the British Army is ridden by class prejudice. You have got to change it, and you will have to change it. If the House of Commons has not the guts to make the Government change it, events will. . . . It is events which are criticising the Government. All that we are doing is giving them a voice, inadequately perhaps, but we are trying to do it.'

'If this Debate resulted in causing demoralisation in the country in the slightest degree,' Bevan concluded, 'I would have preferred to cut my tongue out.' But he did not believe it. There was no dismay in the country. 'There is anger in the country. This is a proud and brave race, and it is feeling humiliated. It cannot stand the holding out of Sebastopol for months, and the collapse of Tobruk in 26 hours. It cannot stand the comparison between these lost battles, not lost by lack of courage, but by lack of vision at the top.' It wanted not words, but leadership. In particular it expected that in the very near future 'we shall launch an attack upon the enemy in a theatre of war nearer to this country. . . . We have to do it. We cannot postpone it until next year. Stalin expects it. . . . For heaven's sake, do not let us make the mistake of betraying those lion-hearted Russians. . . . Get at the enemy where he really is – 21 miles away, not 14,000 miles away. Get him by the throat.'

> Let us get rid of this defeatist complex. This nation can win; but it must be properly led, it must be properly inspired, and it must have confidence in its military leadership. Give us that, and we can win the war, in a fashion which will surprise Hitler, and at the same time hearten our friends.[13]

'We have at last heard the authentic voice of a Vote of Censure,' the next speaker, Walter Elliot, began, 'the voice in which a Vote of Censure ought to be moved in such a Debate.' Bevan's, he conceded, was 'a powerful speech, a well-informed speech, and, especially at the end, a cogently argued speech'. Though he did not accept Bevan's arguments, he was happy to acknowledge 'an adversary against whom anybody will be proud to tilt in the House of Commons'.[14] This, it is clear, was the debate which really made Bevan's name. If before it had been possible to regard him as one discontented sniper among several, overshadowed to some extent by the greater seniority and experience of Shinwell, Winterton, Hore-Belisha and one or two others, he now emerged as the one critic both capable and unafraid of mounting a coherent attack on the Government with a passion and a power to wound worthy of the level of events. Churchill was certainly wounded. When he eventually came to reply to the debate he made no detailed attempt to answer his critics. Instead he took a grim credit for the 'unbridled freedom of our parliamentary institutions' which the debate at such a time disclosed, singling out 'the bitter animosity of the diatribe of Mr Aneurin Bevan, with all its careful and calculated hostility'; appealed for sympathy over the fall of Tobruk – his statement, wrote Harold Nicolson, who had thought Bevan's indictment 'brilliant', 'really amounts to the fact that we have more men and more tanks and more guns than Rommel, and that he cannot understand why we were so badly beaten';[15] and threw himself on the prerogative of the House to back him or sack him.[16] He won his vote of confidence by 475 to 25, 'plus a great ovation afterwards'.[17] Nevertheless, 'Rab' Butler remembered, many Tories who had listened to Bevan with 'muted anger' confessed, 'as we trooped through the lobbies ... that they had been shaken and many of them were disquieted. ... Churchill had had his day, but ... Aneurin Bevan had made his mark.'[18] One gibe in particular of Bevan's hung in the air. Churchill had been served notice that he must soon start winning some battles.

During the autumn of 1942 the Second Front campaign reached its climax, with enthusiastic meetings up and down the country demanding that the Allies do what the British had in fact already persuaded the Americans it would not be possible to attempt before 1943. *Tribune* increasingly revived the allegation that the Tories would be happy to see the Russians beaten by Hitler. If this suspicion gained ground, Bevan warned on 7 August, the Government might face something like a general strike. 'Make no mistake about it, the USSR occupies a unique place in the affections of the workers of Britain. ... They saved it against the conspiracy of Churchill in 1920. They will not stand idly by now and see it murdered. ... If the British Government does nothing in the next two months to save Russia then we shall reach a situation in this country verging on civil war.'[19] This of course was nonsense. The strand of working-class identification with the Soviet Union was genuine and strong, particularly in the mining areas which Bevan knew best. But, as so often, he deceived himself in extrapolating from this politically conscious minority to the working class and the British people as a whole. The titanic struggle on the eastern front fanned a strong flame of sympathy with the Russian people. At the same time there was an equally deep-seated tradition in the labour movement of hostility to Communism, which remained warily unconvinced by the sudden popular adulation of all things Soviet. In this respect Bevin and Morrison – who as members of the War Cabinet had no quarrel with the military judgement against the Second Front – were probably more representative of the movement than Bevan. The degree of public support which the Second Front campaign attracted sprang from simple impatience – admirably expressed by Bevan himself in the House of Commons – to get at the enemy at the nearest possible point. His proposal in *Tribune* that the Russian general Timoshenko should be put in command of it was not calculated to recommend itself widely to patriotic British opinion in any class.[20] Nor was *Tribune*'s open letter to 'Dear Comrade Stalin' in October, appealing to the Soviet leader to grasp the lead, to which the heroism of the Red Army entitled him, in setting the strategy for the United Nations and 'the upward march of all humanity'.[21] In such effusions, Bevan risked seeming to have transferred his loyalty to another country. In imagining that popular enthusiasm for relieving Russia threatened serious civil disorder, it was he who was living in a dream world. What the public wanted was victories; when it got them, the Second Front agitation died away.

Until they came, however, Bevan continued to assail the Government fiercely in the House of Commons, casting all previous restraint aside. On 9 September he made his most direct attack of the whole war on the Prime Minister's person. He criticised his now 'turgid, wordy, dull, prosaic and almost invariably empty' speeches. He objected to his wearing of uniforms: 'I wish he would recognise that he is the civilian head of a civilian government, and not go parading around in ridiculous uniforms.' He deplored his excessive resort to Secret Sessions. And he castigated Churchill's complaint that the press gave too much space to his critics: 'I say that this amounts to political intimidation without precedent in the history of this country and is evidence of the increasing paranoia of the Prime Minister's psychology, for which the docility of the House of Commons is responsible. The time has come when we should make this man realise that the House of Commons is his master.' With that off his chest he sarcastically reminded Churchill that 'the absence of continued disaster is not itself a victory' and launched into another sweeping condemnation of the whole strategy of the war. He ridiculed the Government's reliance on the long-distance bombing of Germany: 'I have found no reason at all why the German population should be more ready to succumb to night bombing than the British public. ... The idea of sending out thousands of bombers every night to bomb Germany just will not work.' The argument may still rage over the Second Front; but in this Bevan was unquestionably right – outspokenly right at a time when few other voices were raised against 'strategic' bombing. Secondly, he derided the Government's other alternative to the Second Front. The North African campaign was drawing off no more than 150,000 Axis troops. 'All that Germany has to do is to use 150,000 men in order to immobilise 1,000,000 British soldiers who have been for over two years in the Middle East. ... So ineffective has our war organisation been that the Italians can afford to send more troops to Russia than they have in Egypt. ... Hitler is luckier in his allies', he charged, 'than Stalin is in his. Hitler's allies are fighting, Stalin's are not.'

Meanwhile, Bevan concluded this indictment, Churchill kept 80,000 men in uniform kicking their heels while production was disrupted by a severe coal shortage – 'all because the Prime Minister is absolutely ignorant of the elementary facts of industrial life'. The people would lack fuel this winter: they would not be warmed by any vision of what they were supposed to be fighting for. 'We must recognise that a change in Government . . . is necessary if our people are to sustain a fourth winter of war with the same courage and buoyancy as they did the first, second and third winters.' And not just a change in the structure of the Government. For the first time, Bevan called explicitly for Churchill to go. He could no longer inspire the British people, because they no longer trusted him; he offered neither moral leadership nor the sensible use of the nation's material resources. 'I do not conceal from the Committee', Bevan announced squarely, 'that the Prime Minister's continuation in office is a major national disaster.'[22]

The question must be asked: whom would he have proposed to replace Churchill? It is not credible, nor is there any suggestion, that he ever saw himself in the role. Who then? He invariably ducked the question by arguing that the personality of the Prime Minister was irrelevant: that Churchill's dominating personality was precisely the problem and that what really mattered were the right democratic policies and the right bold strategy to release the energies of the people to win the war. 'If no other name springs to the lips', he wrote, 'it is because nothing can grow in the blighting shade of his oppressive ego.'[23] Once the Churchill tree was cut down, he suggested, other leaders would emerge perfectly capable of embodying and mobilising the national will. It was rumoured in the summer of 1942 that Bevan was trying to promote Beaverbrook as Prime Minister.[24] On grounds of friendship, belief in Beaverbrook's energising ability and his advocacy of the Second Front, this is plausible. On the other hand Bevan abhorred Beaverbrook's politics as much as he did Churchill's, and he could not seriously have imagined Beaverbrook leading the sort of social revolution he believed to be necessary. All Bevan's urgings throughout the war were for Labour to assert itself, Labour to take control. He could only have envisaged a Labour-led Government to replace Churchill. He had little time for Attlee, though he might have welcomed his unassuming personality if he had seen him as the medium through which the labour movement could make its influence felt. On the same basis Bevin or Morrison might have served, despite his harsh criticism of both of them. Bevan's best bet would appear to have been Cripps, who for a brief moment in early 1942 did seem to have the makings of a possible alternative. But after Churchill brought him into the War Cabinet in February, Cripps failed to make the impact Bevan had hoped, and faded from public view until Churchill, as soon as he felt strong enough after Alamein, unceremoniously demoted him. The truth is that Bevan was never seriously in the business of displacing Churchill. He concentrated on Churchill as the symbol of everything he thought was wrong with the direction of the war and with capitalist society. The lack of any real likelihood of defeating him actually made it easier to attack him. Bevan's uninhibited assault was unsullied by any calculations of political intrigue: it was essentially romantic, opposing to Churchill not an alternative individual but an idealised picture of the socialist future which he confidently expected to emerge at the end of the war, or as a result of the war. Bevan's denunciations of Churchill were intended to prepare the ground for Labour's revolution. And they did. Bevan did not depose Churchill in the House of Commons during the war; but he was deposed, as Bevan had predicted, by the country after the war.

In November, at last, Churchill gave the House a victory. Montgomery, newly appointed in August to replace Auchinleck, inflicted a decisive defeat on Rommel at El Alamein. This was the turning of the tide. Churchill characteristically ordered the church bells to be rung in celebration – a gesture which Bevan equally characteristically denounced as premature and foolish. In the Commons on 12 November he could not fail to welcome Montgomery's success. But to the fury of the Tories he insisted both on putting it in perspective – Montgomery had beaten fifteen Axis divisions, eleven of them Italian, while the Russians for the past eighteen months had been facing 176 divisions – and on claiming a share of the credit for the Government's 'amateur' critics, who the press now declared had been 'defeated'. 'All that I can say is that I welcome these defeats,' Bevan purred. 'I shall be delighted if they can beat me ceaselessly with such sweet chastisement.' The fact was that Alamein had been achieved precisely by the correction of those faults – of weaponry, of leadership in the field and of co-ordination (though not of political leadership) – to which the critics had drawn attention in July. 'The Prime Minister', Bevan mocked, 'always refers to a defeat as a disaster as though it came from God, but to a victory as though it came from himself.'[25] Even in Churchill's hour of success, it seemed, Bevan could not refrain from carping.

Nevertheless Churchill's ascendancy was henceforth secure, at least at home: within the triumvirate of Allied leaders he became increasingly the junior partner to Roosevelt and Stalin. Within days of Alamein, Anglo-American forces landed in French North Africa; within a few weeks the Red Army achieved at Stalingrad the decisive victory of the whole war and began throwing the Germans back out of Russia. With these developments the ultimate defeat of Germany became certain. Politically, therefore, the war now entered its fourth and final stage. The demand for an early second front faded: Russia had saved herself by her own exertions, and the British–American strategy of clearing North Africa and beating Italy before invading northern France, if unduly cautious, made slow but steady progress during 1943. Arguments over military strategy, though not wholly resolved, henceforth took second place to, or rather were subsumed in, wider questions of what sort of victory it was intended to achieve. For the last two and a half years of fighting, Bevan's criticism of the Government concentrated once again on the war aims it was pursuing, both abroad and at home.

As the military war in Europe was won, Bevan saw the ideological war being given away. He had never believed that the Tories were fighting fascism, but merely the German threat to their own Empire. Now, at the first glimmer of victory, Churchill announced at the Mansion House that he had 'not become the King's First Minister in order to preside over the liquidation of the British Empire', and had guaranteed the Spanish, Portuguese and Dutch Empires into the bargain.[26] He did not dare suggest such a thing in 1940, Bevan protested. 'We can see the Conservatives coming out of their holes now. . . . If hon. Members opposite think we are going through this in order to keep their Malayan swamps, they are making a mistake.'[27] His suspicions were confirmed when, to facilitate their landing in Algeria, the British and Americans did a deal with the Vichy collaborator Admiral Darlan rather than with the symbol of the French resistance, General de Gaulle. 'Do not', Bevan begged in the House of Commons, 'try to put these traitorous quislings, these rats now leaving the sinking ship, in place of the men who have stood staunchly by our side in our most difficult days.'[28] 'What kind of Europe have we in mind?' he demanded in *Tribune*. 'One built by rats for rats?'[29] Such cynicism, he believed, was 'worth a whole string of victories to Hitler',[30] demoralising the popular resistance movements the Allies were trying to encourage all over Europe. *Tribune* rejoiced openly when Darlan was assassinated on 24 December: 'The news of the Admiral's timely death enlivened the festivity in every Christmas home in Britain.'[31] But Bevan's conviction that the Allies, instead of spreading revolution in Europe, were bent on restoring reaction did not die with Darlan. It was revived successively in Italy, Yugoslavia and Greece, where 'royal rodents' were crawling out of their holes to welcome the Allied liberators.[32]

Bevan still thought the Mediterranean strategy misconceived. 'When we come – if we ever do' – he wrote in January 1943, 'to the main attack on Italy we shall find that the "soft under-belly" of the Axis powers will have acquired formidable armour. It will then be left for the Government and the military "experts" to explain how it will be more practicable to invade Europe at the end of a three-thousand-mile supply line across eighty miles of water than it is to do so from our bases in this country.'[33] He was right about the formidable armour with which the Germans were able to reinforce what turned out to be highly defensible terrain. The Allies did not land in Sicily until July, on the Italian mainland until September, and then found it heavy going. 'Has not the right hon. Gentleman's secret service department told him that it sometimes rains in Italy in the autumn and winter?' he asked satirically at the end of the year. The Eighth Army appeared unprepared for the discovery that 'The whole country is hills. Up you go: up one bloody hill and then down another.'

The whole of this country wants to know what strategical conception behind the war put the British and American Armies to fight their way right up the whole peninsula in the autumn and winter. . . . Does anybody suggest to me that that is a wise strategy? It is nonsense. Is that the "soft under-belly of the Axis?" We are climbing up his backbone.

With the sole exception of the Alamein campaign, Bevan alleged, 'the Government's military handling of the war has been one grievous blunder after another'. 'Had our position depended upon our own military disposi-tions alone and been unassisted by the totally unexpected victories of the Red Army, we should have been in a very dire position.'[34]

Once again there was an uncomfortable amount of truth in what Bevan was saying. Until the invasion of France was finally launched in 1944, there was growing public frustration with the slow rate of progress in Italy. Bevan's question 'What are we doing in Italy? ... What are we doing there at all?' echoed a good deal of muttering in the country, not least in the army, and it has continued to exercise historians up to the present. It was at least well worth asking. The answer had more to do with caution, the fact of one thing having led to another, compromise between British and American proposals and the slow pace of preparations for landing in France than with politics. Bevan, however, could only see the most sinister intent behind the Italian campaign. When Mussolini was toppled in July, he was appalled that the Allies should be ready to treat with the royalist government of Marshal Badoglio. In the Commons he quoted Churchill's embarrassing praise of Mussolini in 1927 and refused to trust the future of Italy to 'a Parliamentary majority who ... secretly sympathise with the principles of the Fascist enemy'. If the Allies recognised Badoglio and Victor Emanuel, he predicted, 'we shall find that we have to shoot Italians in order to support our own puppet Government. We shall find ourselves on the side of the anti-revolutionary forces in the country.' Moreover, by betraying the Italian revolution, Britain would throw away 'millions of potential allies in Europe'.[35]

Bevan saw the overthrow of fascism as the historic opportunity for a Europe-wide popular uprising against monarchism, clericalism and reaction of every sort, an opportunity which the British Tories and their American capitalist allies were determined to abort. Roosevelt and Churchill, he charged, promised democracy. But 'They don't mean the same thing by democracy that we do.'[36] *Tribune* romantically invoked the heroic tradition of 1789, 1848 and 1917. 'Our Ally – The Mob' proclaimed an editorial in September 1943 which ingeniously cited the best possible authority for according Britain a special responsibility:

In the great moments of history it is not the political Canutes that stem the floodtide of popular resurgence. The mobs of Europe ... are presenting the Allies [with] the chance to spread the end of the war. They need only one thing. With great perspicuity the prophet in Karl Marx foresaw it: 'The revolution in Europe will reach fruition', he wrote, 'only when it reaches Europe's heart and proceeds under the leadership of Britain.'[37]

It was in this connection that Bevan deplored the announcement at Casab-lanca in January 1943 that the Allies would accept nothing less than the 'unconditional surrender' of the Axis powers. 'Unconditional surrender', he wrote scornfully, was not a policy but a slogan.[38] By July 1944, when Germany was still fighting strongly long after the end had seemed inevitable, there was a very widespread belief that it was the promulgation of 'unconditional surrender' which was prolonging her resistance. It was 'a schoolboy's phrase', Bevan alleged in the House of Commons: 'a general's phrase, a tactical phrase, the phrase of a man dealing with troops immediately in front of him, but not the phrase of a statesman'.[39] Instead of threatening the Germans with unlimited and unspecified vengence which could only stiffen their will to fight on, the correct course would have been to make clear to the oppressed German people the better future the Allies offered them. It came back to the sort of Europe the Allies were intending to create. Instead of entering Germany as conquerors, they would advance much faster if they came as liberators carrying with them not a new oppression but democracy. With this encouragement, Bevan believed, the Germans would abandon Hitler in droves; faced only with the demand for 'unconditional surrender', he and others argued (and have continued to argue), they had little incentive to desert the devil they knew. 'Unconditional surrender' was 'a gift to Goebbels'.[40]

From the beginning, Bevan had set his face against the Tory idea – entirely opposed to Labour's internationalist traditions, but accepted during the war by most of the party leadership, including Attlee – that the enemy was the German nation. The enemy, he insisted, was fascism, from which the British people had gone to war to set the German people, Europe and by the same endeavour themselves, free. As the war ended he was strongly opposed to all proposals to dismember, subjugate, pastoralise or even permanently to occupy Germany.[41] While most British opinion reacted with a surge of renewed anti-German feeling to the revelation of the concentration camps, *Tribune* sounded a reminder that Buchenwald had been a camp for *Germans*, political opponents of Hitler's regime.[42] Germany should be disarmed, certainly, but this could be done without repeating the mistake of 1919 and turning her into a resentful leper in the heart of Europe, requiring the Allies to maintain great armaments to hold her down. It could be done quite simply, Bevan suggested, by means of factory inspection.[43] More fundamentally, it could be done by eradicating the forces in German society which made for fascism. These views, at a time of violent hatred of all things German, were both far-sighted and humane.

Particularly, as the war ended, Bevan pleaded the folly of trying to create a lasting peace by the old methods of great power politics. 'There can be no peace', he asserted in December 1943, 'that merely rests upon the armed might of Russia, Britain and America.' In part this was just traditional Labour hostility to the arms race. 'Is America to base her sense of security on a war machine possessed by Russia, or Russia upon the war machine possessed by America?' he asked. 'Will not each of them once more try to get a war machine equal to all the others that can be brought against it? Is not that the whole problem?' But Bevan's argument was also founded in his belief in a revived democratic Europe.

Fortunately neither Russia, America nor Britain will have as much to say in the future of Europe as they think they will. Fortunately the people of Yugoslavia, of Bulgaria, France, Greece and Italy are getting a renaissance. During the past three years under the heel of Fascism, those people have learned the lessons of personal liberty. In the experience of the pre-war years they have learned the lessons of organised society. You have in that part of Europe a number of precipitates of the most promising kind, a love of personal liberty and of economic order. Out of that combination may come people, not in Britain, nor in Russia nor in America but from a combination of these oppressed peoples, who have been learning their lessons, who are going to save mankind from a repetition of these horrors.[44]

It is significant that Bevan was now pinning his hope on the European nations, because he was beginning to lose his faith in Russia. Though in April 1944 he defended the Soviet Union's right to protect its own interests – 'It is quite natural and inevitable that Russia should influence preponderantly the life of the nations immediately on her borders, and that she should seek to prevent them from combinations that may be aimed at her'[45] – he was becoming alarmed at the evidence that Stalin took no less cynical a view of great-power politics than the Americans. 'It is painful beyond expression', he wrote in February 1945, 'that the Soviet Union is not following up the success of the Red Army by assuming the moral leadership of the world' – left vacant, he believed, by Britain.[46] He still thought Soviet behaviour attributable to the hostility of the Allies, and sought to reassure Russia by urging the creation of a non-threatening confederation of European democracies to act as a buffer between the powers.[47] His solution may have been idealistic, but Bevan saw clearly the developing confrontation of the Cold War. He also appreciated very early, and insisted on pointing out, that Britain would not be able to keep up with the two emerging Superpowers and would be mad to try. Churchill's vanity and nostalgic imperialism, he alleged, led him to 'sit down to a game in which his opponents [Roosevelt and Stalin] hold all the winning cards'. 'Even in terms of old-fashioned power politics', he wrote, Churchill was making a mistake and Britain would 'pay for it by a declining influence in world affairs'.[48] Instead of trying to compete, an enlightened Britain would accept the leadership of the Western European nations. An 'organic confederation' comprising France, Holland, Belgium, Italy, Spain and the Scandinavian nations 'along with a sane Germany and Austria, and a progressive Britain' offered 'the only solution likely to lay the foundation for peace and prosperity in Europe'.[49] Britain was in a position to make a virtue of her relative military weakness, he tried vainly to persuade the House of Commons in August 1944. 'The British Empire will have a third-class position among the big lions', he predicted, 'if we allow the world to become a jungle again.'

We can win the war militarily but lose it morally unless we succeed in raising before the eyes of mankind ... a vision of world organisation which sets aside all this talk of big armies, navies and air forces, and tries to establish co-operative principles among the nations of the world so that we can keep our national pride and patriotism and weave it into a pattern of world organisation.[50]

Such wishful thinking was typical of many on the left towards the end of the war who dreamed that a new world must somehow emerge from the ruins. That it was shared by Bevan, who was at the same time so perceptive about the inability of the great powers to establish anything more stable than a balance of insecurity (soon to be of terror), exemplifies the dichotomy that ran through all his thinking between reason and idealism, and his persistent willingness to transform what he had decided should happen into a law of social evolution whose fulfilment was historically inevitable. Bevan believed that progress towards the more rational ordering of international, as of national, society depended solely on the vision of leaders unafraid, in a favourite phrase, to 'allow the future to be born'. Toryism was by definition afraid of the future, fascism merely a more violent attempt to reverse the historical process. Churchill and the Tories were bound to try to obstruct the European revolution; Bevan mocked Churchill's 'extraordinary royalism' ('Whenever he sees a king he wants to put him on his throne and if he sees one tottering he wants to prop him up'),[51] but he expected nothing else. Those he really thought were betraying the future were the Labour leaders who were allowing Churchill to get away with it, conniving, as he wrote in August 1943, in aborting the very movement of liberation which it was supposed to be their business, as socialists, to promote.[52] Accordingly, in the last three years of the war, it was increasingly on his own leaders that he turned his fire.

Chapter 10

Labour's Reckoning: the Road to 1945

Bevan always believed that Labour had sold itself too cheaply in May 1940. At that moment of national reckoning for the failed policies of the previous decade, no Tory-led Government could have stood without Labour's participation. The fact that the Conservatives and their 'National' allies had a majority of over 200 seats in the House of Commons counted for nothing. Throughout the war Bevan proceeded on the assumption, increasingly supported by by-election results, that the House no longer represented the country. The people, he believed, demanded both the more active and the more democratic prosecution of the war, both as regards military strategy (the Second Front, support for Russia, support for European resistance movements) and the home front (nationalisation to increase production, conscription of property as well as manpower, freedom of expression). The war could only be won, would only be worth winning, by the active mobilisation of popular enthusiasm. Labour's participation in the Government was the symbol of this mobilisation; but increasingly he believed that it was a hollow symbol – that Labour was becoming less and less representative of the people for whom it was supposed to speak, that under the cloak of 'national unity' the Tories were being allowed to get their own way in all essentials and that Labour's parliamentary leaders, instead of seizing the opportunity which the war gave the party, betrayed the historic trust placed in them by subordinating themselves so meekly to Churchill. He was not suggesting, Bevan insisted, that Labour should apply crude blackmail merely to gain party advantage; he believed passionately that the war could only be won, or would be won more quickly, by the immediate implementation of Labour policies. National unity was indeed paramount; but he held that the only principles on which the nation could properly be united were Labour principles.

In the crisis years 1940 and 1941 he believed that labour, in the sense of the organised working class and the ordinary people of the country, at least as much as Churchill, had 'saved the nation'. From 1942 he believed that the Tories were reluctant to pay the debt, but were increasingly intent, as they recovered their self-confidence, on preserving or reconstructing as much as possible of the pre-war social order. As he put it after Alamein, the Tories were 'crawling out of their holes again'. Accordingly, he wrote in *Tribune*, if the Coalition had been necessary hitherto, despite the Tories' abuse of it, it was now time for Labour to reconsider its attitude. The party would have more influence, he argued, and would conduce more to genuine national unity, as an active opposition than in a Coalition dominated by the over-whelming personality of Churchill. 'A sequence of military disasters', he cautioned, 'may revive the need for elementary unity once more. ... When, however, survival is assured, then the break must come.'[1] He had never approved of the electoral truce; he did not believe that the Tories had ever stopped playing party politics (the truce itself was a crystallisation of the Tory-dominated status quo); now as national survival gave way in the public mind to the shaping of the post-war world, he called persistently for the restoration of party politics to reflect the choice facing the country. The choice between the future and the past could not, by definition, be made by a Coalition.

The event which threw the issue into sharpest focus was the publication of the Beveridge Report in December 1942 – providentially just six weeks after Alamein. An unprecedented bestseller, Beveridge was regarded almost universally as the blueprint of the new world. For the Labour Party it was the test of the Government's intentions. Even before it was published, there were rumours that the Tories were trying to scotch it. If Labour Ministers allowed publication to be postponed, warned *Tribune*, the party would 'lose any title it possesses to be regarded as a champion of the common people'. The prompt adoption of the Report, on the other hand, would give British troops 'an immediate moral rearmament' and would 'put Britain once more in the forefront of civilised mankind'.[2] Beveridge was, in domestic terms at least, the statement of progressive war aims which Bevan believed the war had so far lacked. His enthusiasm, given that the Report was explicitly non-socialist, is perhaps surprising. But he believed that Beveridge was more revolutionary than he knew. 'With Liberal fervour', he wrote, 'and even a trace of Liberal innocence ... Sir William has described the conditions in which the tears might be taken out of capitalism. We should not be surprised, therefore, if all unconsciously by so doing he threatens capitalism itself.' By the simple act of putting social security first, he put the claims of property second. The implications were enormous. The Tories, Bevan predicted, would not concede the Report. But Beveridge had given Labour a weapon. 'And if it be asked how it happens that a reformer so sedate has been able to fashion a weapon so sharp, and how a Government so timid should have presented materials for its fashioning, we must answer in the famous words of Karl Marx, "that war is the locomotive of history".'[3]

'A strictly Socialist approach', Bevan wrote in January 1943, 'would condemn the whole idea of contributory insurance.' He had never believed that the poor should be required to support the poor; the responsibility fell properly on the community as a whole and should be met, in his view, wholly from taxation. (There was no question of the community not being able to afford it: it was simply a matter of redistribution of the national income between classes, not of real expenditure.) 'But in existing circumstances wise tactics suggest that we should go for the Report in its entirety.' Any quibbling would give the Government the excuse to shelve it. Beveridge was as much a symbol as a programme. 'If Britain shows that she has the courage, imagination and resilience to embark on a social experiment of such a magnitude in the midst of a war, then she may once more assert a moral leadership which will have consequences in every sphere of her activities.'[4]

For once, Bevan expressed the general feeling of the Labour Party. The Government, while professing to welcome Beveridge, refused to give any commitment to implement it. Churchill regarded it not as moral reinforcement but as a diversion from fighting the war; Attlee, Bevin and Morrison, outnumbered in the War Cabinet, acquiesced and loyally enjoined their followers to do likewise. When the Report was finally debated in February, however, virtually the whole of the Parliamentary Labour Party not in the Government – ninety-seven members – defied their leaders to vote for a resolution calling for early legislation. This was the biggest backbench revolt of the whole war. But there were other signs that the Coalition was under growing strain. A few weeks later Bevan mustered sixty-one votes against the Government for an immediate increase in old age pensions. In the country by-elections and Gallup polls – confirmed by Home Intelligence – showed mounting dissatisfaction and a reawakening of party attitudes.[5] By July 1943 Gallup gave Labour a twelve-point lead. Yet so long as the electoral truce was in force the party was debarred from gathering in this harvest of support. Sir Richard Acland's Common Wealth Party stepped into the vacuum and won its first by-election in April, at Eddisbury. Government candidates were armed with letters of endorsement from all four party leaders, and Labour activists who worked openly against them risked expulsion. Bevan believed that Labour was allowing itself to be manoeuvred out of its inheritance. The evidence was clear that Labour would win a post-war election if it fought alone; therefore the Tories were already beginning to talk of continuing the Coalition into the peace, and by maintaining the electoral truce Labour risked binding itself so closely that it could not escape. In an exceptionally bitter article just before the party Conference in June he accused the leadership directly of planning to stay in the Government after the war had ended. They talked socialism, but betrayed it repeatedly – by accepting a hybrid compromise for the control of the mines, by backing the Darlan deal, by refusing higher pensions. They were now being drawn into Tory plans for post-war reconstruction. Labour had surrendered the initiative: 'Nowhere in the dreary expanses of wasted paper produced by the Executive for the bemusement of Conference is there the tiniest evidence of even an approach to the problem of how Labour is to get the power to put into practice what it preaches.' Delegates might imagine that they could simply end the Coalition when the war ended, but they would find that they could not. He acknowledged that Labour could not pull out immediately without its action being misrepresented. But he urged that it should announce *now* that it would come out at the end of the war, recover its liberty immediately to fight by-elections, and 'take our stand on some principle of fundamental importance and, if necessary, leave the Government on it. Anything less vigorous will not give us back the initiative we have lost.'[6]

Bevan repeated his argument at the Conference but this year, after his narrow defeat in 1942, was crushed by 2,243,000 votes to 374,000. His next article in *Tribune* was even more bitter than the last. Contemptuously he dismissed the large body of mainly trade union delegates who 'might just as well have been attending a darts club or a Wings For Victory Week demonstration for all the Socialist intelligence they have displayed', and the smaller body of unreflective party apparatchiks. 'No,' he wrote, 'I speak to you, the aware and concerned Socialist ... whose spirit must have been depressed by the monstrous farce of the Conference.' Every decision had been a foregone conclusion, due to the 'bovine, inert and irresponsible' block votes of the major unions. 'The trade unions are no longer paying affiliation fees to the Labour Party. They are paying its burial expenses.' In a situation in which the Labour Party – '*even* the Labour Party', he had written in January – could not fail to win if it stood up for itself, the unions were tying both its hands behind its back. The answer was still not to abandon the Labour Party, but for socialists to look beyond Labour, calling in, as the Socialist League and the Popular and United Fronts had attempted to do in the thirties, other progressive groupings to stimulate and widen the party's appeal from the outside, creating with the Communists, the ILP and Common Wealth 'a federation of like-minded groups' around the nucleus of the Labour Party.[7]

He returned to this theme at the end of 1943 and repeatedly throughout 1944, arguing that the alternative to a Tory-dominated Coalition of the right should be a Labour-dominated Coalition of the left. 'The people of Great Britain', he wrote on 17 December, 'are Left-minded but not Labour Party-minded. Rather they are in a state of political suspense with strong dispositions to a vigorously progressive social policy.' The by-election success of Independent and Common Wealth candidates was evidence of the disintegration of the old social order which Labour should welcome: to demand that the politically uprooted members of the newly-radicalised middle-class should simply join the Labour Party was not leadership, he scoffed, but 'arid, pedantic formalism', rejecting 'just those loyalties, diversifications and significances which would bring fresh streams of energy and idealism to progressive thought and action'. For an old class warrior and socialist fundamentalist, Bevan now took a remarkably inclusive view of the allies Labour should be ready to embrace from beyond its traditional class base: no longer socialists only, but former Liberals, the new technocracy and the whole disenchanted petty bourgeoisie should be drawn into Labour's crusade.

> They do not belong to the broad river of social change, for this rises naturally in the gathering ground of the wage earning classes. But they are invaluable feeders and freshets of the main flow if political stupidity does not dam them up, or if ruling class sophistication is not allowed to divert them to drive its own mill as in Hitler's Germany. Nor should we complain if they show at first the colouration of the social strata of their origin, nor be frightened if they appear to discolour the waters of the main stream itself when they join it. Every tributary does that at first. But ere long the mother waters assert themselves and once more sweep along mightier than ever, bearing no trace of their varied sources except the added force of the current.[8]

There was a paradox, not to say a contradiction, in Bevan's repeated assertions that Labour was 'certain' to win, 'certain' to be the next Government after the war, yet could not win by itself but must make common cause, involving an agreed programme and constituency pacts, with a medley of fringe parties. The fact was that while notably clear-sighted about the country's reaction against the Conservatives and particularly the insufficiency of Churchill's name to save them, he greatly underestimated the electorate's capacity to distinguish between the two parties to the Coalition and overestimated the ability of the minor parties to hold on to the anti-Tory vote once Labour was back in the fray. It has often been remarked that Labour derived enormous advantage during the war from being in the Government but not wholly identified with it: while its leaders acquired the experience and authority of Ministers, the party as a whole, even without fighting by-elections, was perceived as providing the Opposition. Bevan could not see this 'double dividend'.[9] By sticking with the Coalition and appearing to endorse the widely held assumption that the prestige of victory would make Churchill invincible at the end of the war, it seemed to him that Labour's leaders were aligning the party on the side of reaction, for which the increasingly leftward-looking electorate would not vote. Nevertheless Bevan saw with remarkable clarity that Churchill's war-winning qualities were not what the electorate would be looking for to win the peace: his popularity was 'a wasting asset'.

> Victory will puff it into a brief blaze, and, no doubt, he and the Tories associated with him will use it to try to light their way to victory at the polls before it dies down in diminishing smoulderings. But those who do not belong to his personal and political entourage would be foolish to imagine they can warm themselves at that fire for long.

Typically, Bevan developed his correct anticipation into a law:

> This is merely the immortal tragedy of all public life that the *hero's* need of the people outlasts *their* need of him. *They* obey the pressures of contemporary conditions whilst *he* strives to perpetuate the situation where he stood supreme. *He* is

therefore overwhelmed by a nostalgia for past glory, whereas *they* are pushed on by new needs, impelled by other hopes and led by other nascent heroes.[10]

Labour clung to Churchill, Bevan alleged, when it should be determinedly shaking off the taint of a Coalitionism whose whole purpose was to block the transformation to socialism for which Labour stood. Bevan's fundamentalist rejection of the Coalition's reconstruction plans emerged most clearly over the famous White Paper of June 1944 pledging the Government to maintain full employment after the war by Keynesian techniques of demand management. Like the Beveridge Report, the White Paper was a reflection of the revolution in Whitehall wrought by academic economists drafted into the Treasury during the war. It was accepted without difficulty by the War Cabinet and warmly recommended to the House of Commons on its behalf by Bevin. Bevan, however, in common with a good many other Labour speakers in the debate, refused to be impressed. Not only was it not socialism, but it threatened to be the negation of socialism. The Coalition was formed to win the war, he asserted: it had no mandate to pre-empt the planning of the post-war settlement.

> The questions of how the work of society is to be organised, how the income of society is to be distributed, to what extent the State is to intervene in the direction of economic affairs – all these are questions which first called this party into existence. They represent in themselves the main bone of contention between the main parties in the State. How on earth, therefore, can a Coalition Government pretend to approach these problems without the gravest sacrifice of principles? It is an impracticable proposition. Indeed, I will go so far as to say that if the implications of the White Paper are sound, there is no longer any justification for this Party existing at all.

This was a dangerous argument, but Bevan persisted with it.

> If a progressive society and an expanding standard of life can be achieved by this document and unemployment can be avoided, then there is no justification for public ownership and there is no argument for it. Nobody believes in public ownership for its own sake. This party did not come into existence demanding Socialism, demanding the State ownership of property, simply because there was some special merit in it. This party believes in public ownership of industry because it thinks that only in that way can society be progressively and intelligently organised. If private enterprise can deliver all these goods, there will not be any argument for Socialism and no reason for it.

Of course, Bevan took it for granted that private enterprise could not deliver the goods – or could do so only by means of a 'thermostatic operation to occur every five or six years by which [the workers] are taken forcibly away from their normal occupation and put to do some job of public works in order to pump spending power into the system which has caused unemployment'. He viewed the Keynesian 'revolution' as a means of propping up capitalism by means of forced-labour camps. As such it was no advance on the proposals of Mosley and Lloyd George which he had been prepared to subscribe to as an emergency programme in 1930 but which, in the conditions of 1944, he regarded as a betrayal of the much greater possibilities now beckoning. He was scathing about the Treasury's belated discovery – following the example of Roosevelt, Mussolini and Hitler – that it was not necessary to balance the budget every year, and dismissive of the 'great advance' by which the Government admitted responsibility for maintaining full employment. 'No Government', he asserted, 'would live for a minute after the war which did not admit it. Do you think that the young men and women who come back from the war would listen to a lot of doddering old gentlemen saying that the Government would have no responsibility whether they worked or not? ... The fact of the matter is', he concluded, 'that the White Paper is shallow, empty and superficial and bears all the stigmata of its Coalition origin. It runs away from every major social problem. It takes refuge in tricks, strategies and devices because it has not the honesty to face up to the implications of the social problems involved.'[11]

For thirty years Bevan's scorn seemed misplaced. For thirty years Keynesianism did seem to deliver the goods, did seem able to ensure full employment and to distribute the benefits of capitalism without extensive nationalisation and did face the Labour Party with the need to dilute its definition of socialism or go out of business. During the fifties and sixties Bevan's fundamentalism appeared increasingly antediluvian and doctrinaire. While his 1944 expectation that private enterprise could prevent unemployment only by means of labour camps proved alarmist, his apprehension that Labour's acceptance of the White Paper spelled the abandonment of true socialism proved well founded. From the perspective of the 1980s the balance of the argument looks rather different. Keynesianism has not after all proved adequate to keeping unemployment at bay indefinitely. Whether socialism could have done so is another matter. But the 1944 White Paper no longer has the authority of unchallengeable success. And it can now be seen that the Labour Party's adoption of the consensual techniques of Keynes was indeed, as Bevan feared, the moment when the possibility of the sort of thoroughgoing socialisation of society of which he dreamed was lost for good.

Bevan's own blueprint for the post-war organisation of society was set out with unusual precision in a Fabian pamphlet by several hands, including G.D.H. Cole, Jim Griffiths, Beveridge and Laski, entitled *Plan for Britain*, published in 1943. In his contribution Bevan envisaged the immediate nationalisation of all the basic industries of the country and their administration by a Supreme Economic Council of 'able men' (in an earlier *Tribune* version he had written of 'a small number of highly trained executives')[12] under the general but not the detailed control of the House of Commons; distribution of certain goods like milk and public transport should be free, the price of all other economic essentials fixed (breaking right away from

131

capitalist supply-and-demand costing), and the free market left to operate only in minor areas of economic activity. Two things stand out about this scheme; first its extreme economic centralism, but secondly the importance Bevan always attached to the ultimate control of the House of Commons and the total control by the House of Commons of matters of law and order, personal freedom and education. 'In the very foreground of any plan for a Socialist society must be a status for and a sovereignty of popular control,' he insisted. 'It is the right of the ordinary man or woman to pull at the coat-tails of those in power to exert their influence over them, for this is the guarantee that the resources of the community will be used for welfare and not for warfare.' The economic expert was to be kept firmly in his place: 'When the expert gets to work on political objectives, mankind is in danger of damnation.' He had always deplored the taking of important decisions out of political control; he had denounced as 'economic Fascism' the Government's 1942 compromise plan for the State control of the still privately owned coal mines and consistently condemned all forms of price-fixing by Government, industry and unions behind the back of Parliament as anti-social syndicalism (a youthful heresy he had long grown out of). As strong a libertarian as he was a socialist, Bevan insisted on a clear demarcation of the political from the economic, recognising that otherwise 'a new economic oligarchy will become the supreme power in the State and you get merely a species of Fascism'.[13] This comes back to his belief that the Allied victory in Europe would offer the opportunity of an historic synthesis between Western liberalism and Soviet planning – 'that is', as he expressed it in the Commons in September 1944, 'an integrated economic organisation . . . based upon libertarian democratic institutions'.[14] It was this combination that he believed during 1944 that the Labour leaders, and Ernest Bevin in particular, were attacking from both sides at once: not only were they funking the establishment of full democratic control of the economy, but in April Bevin issued new regulations to limit the individual's liberty to strike. It was on this issue that Bevan came close to getting himself expelled for a second time from the Labour Party.

The background was simmering unrest and a wave of unofficial strikes in the mines. Throughout the war Bevan, still a miners' representative before everything else, had made it his business to voice the miners' grievances in the House: the root cause, he believed, was simply the Government's – specifically Churchill's – refusal of nationalisation which for twenty years now all enquiries into the coal industry had recommended. The Government's coal policy had been a series of makeshift evasions, culminating in the insulting draft into the pits of conscripts – 'Bevin boys' – chosen by ballot because no one would volunteer for the job. In April 1944, striking, as Bevan believed, at the inevitable results of Government policy instead of at the policy which caused the trouble, Bevin introduced a new regulation imposing penalties of up to five years' imprisonment for taking part in or instigating unofficial strikes. Bevan was outraged and moved a prayer in the

House to annul the Order. Once again he condemned Bevin's high-handed action as a slap in the face for the House of Commons. Bitterly he protested at the Government-inspired press campaign of vilification of the striking miners, instead of any attempt to understand *why* they struck. 'Are we seriously asked to believe', he demanded, 'that the stolid Yorkshire miners came out on strike because of a number of evilly disposed Trotskyites?' They struck because 'the incompetence of the Minister of Fuel and the Minister of Labour' left them no other means to get anomalies redressed; when the grievance was met, the strikes had quickly ended. 'Do not people realise', he asked, citing the example of a recent stoppage on the London buses, 'that exactly the same purpose, exactly the same capacity for generous indignation, exactly the same stalwart courage that our men display on the battlefields they also display in bus garages? Do we expect men to be lions on the battlefield and sheep at home?'

'Small strikes, small disputes', Bevan went on, 'are the vent valves of society, they do not hold up the war. These minor adjustments in industrial relations are the means by which the whole apparatus is kept smoothly functioning. To make these minor disturbances major offences under the law is lunacy.' If Bevin tried to operate his Order, he would 'create more strikes than the Trotskyites have been able to do in five years'. Moreover, Bevan concluded, after five years of heroic effort by the British people it was deplorable to 'give the impression all over the world that most extraordinary measures are now necessary in Great Britain in order to keep people working for the war effort. Is not that a slander against the working people of this country?'

This, however, was not the part of his speech which caused the trouble. The furore in the Labour Party arose over a passage in the middle in which Bevan latched on to the distinction which the Order drew between official and unofficial strikes, between union officials and shop stewards, and between unionised and non-unionised labour. It was permissible to argue for a strike only in a union meeting. But there were over thirteen million workers in the country who were not in trade unions; these would have no rights under the new regulation. 'It may be said that they can all go into the unions. Of course they can, but are we now setting out to recruit trade union membership by five years' penal servitude?' Bevin's Order, Bevan claimed, was a case of 'trade union officials ... invoking the laws against their own members'.

> Do not let anybody on this side of the House think that he is defending the trade unions; he is defending the trade union official, who has arteriosclerosis, and who cannot adjust himself to his membership. He is defending an official who has become so unpopular among his own membership that the only way he can keep them in order is to threaten them with five years in gaol. Whenever you get the rank and file at trade union meetings this Regulation will be opposed.... The further you get away from the trade union official to the rank and file, the less support the Regulation gets. The more you move away from

reality, from the robust, dignified, normal worker, to the jaded, cynical, irresponsible trade union official the more support the Regulation gets. That is the situation. ...

Well, I do not represent the big bosses at the top; I represent the people at the bottom, the individual men and women, and I say that this Regulation is the enfranchisement of the Corporate Society and the disfranchisement of the individual.[15]

From a union-sponsored Labour MP this was unforgivable. Later in the debate the acting party leader, Arthur Greenwood, sternly condemned 'a speech ... of an anti-trade union character the like of which I have never heard from the most diehard Tory in this House or outside this House', and warned that 'the hon. Member for Ebbw Vale is going to risk a fall on this'.[16] But Bevan's fault lay not only in his words. He had also led a substantial revolt. Fifteen Labour MPs voted with him against the Regulation. More important, only just over half of the remaining 150 (twenty-three of them Ministers) voted with the Government: seventy-three abstained or were otherwise absent.[17] This set a problem for the leadership, which was determined, after suffering Bevan's onslaughts for years, to take the opportunity to discipline him. They decided that Bevan's record and his extreme language gave ground for proceeding against him alone; but on 10 May the PLP, reflecting the weight of the abstainers, voted 71–60, against Greenwood, for a motion proposed by Shinwell to refer the matter to a joint committee of the Shadow Cabinet and the NEC. This was generally expected to be the end of it. There was an uncomfortable feeling in the party that Bevan had indeed, as he claimed, lost the vote but won the argument. Why was Bevin so angry? he asked in his constituency. 'I suspect the reason is that he knows that my twenty-three [votes in the House of Commons] represent more trade unionists in the country than his three hundred and fourteen' (which were of course mostly Tory). He promised that if he was expelled he would still fight to retain Ebbw Vale 'for Socialism'; and the Ebbw Vale party and the SWMF backed him.[18] With the General Election likely within the year, this was no time to split the movement. Nevertheless the NEC did vote by 20–8 to require Bevan to give a written promise to toe the party line in future. Bevan interpreted the determined attempt to crush him as proving the leadership's intention to continue the Coalition after the end of the war. 'It is the precursor of a grand post-war surrender modelled on present surrender,' he wrote. 'Either we restore the healthy vigour of Parliament which comes with independence, discussion and criticism, or we submit to the corporate rule of Big Business and collaborationist Labour leaders.'[19] This analysis, however, dictated that he swallow his pride and sign the required 'vindictive and malignant' undertaking. 'It is because I believe there are elements in the Party which wish to continue the association with the Tories when the war is over', he announced, 'that I refuse to allow myself to be manoeuvred out of the party and thus leave them with a clear field to accomplish the ruin of the Labour movement.'[20] So he signed and lived to resume the fight another day.

One practical reason for not letting himself be made a martyr was that this year, for the first time, Bevan was a candidate for the National Executive. Despite or because of his parliamentary effectiveness, he had repeatedly failed to come anywhere near election to the Shadow Cabinet, to which the PLP regularly returned a slate of solid loyalists; but the seven constituency representatives on the NEC were elected by the party activists in the country whose aspirations he closely reflected. Laski and Shinwell, the two other most prominent socialist critics of the Government, already occupied the top two places. It was with evident relief that the leadership seized on the excuse of the Normandy landings to postpone the 1944 Conference from June to December. When it eventually met, Bevan was elected in fifth place, behind Laski, Shinwell, Griffiths and Morrison, ahead of Dalton and Noel-Baker. The NEC was to be his power-base for the rest of his life. In 1945 he moved up to fourth place and thereafter he was top every year until his withdrawal to fight Gaitskell for the Treasurership in 1954, the darling of Conference and the acknowledged leader of the left. With his election to the NEC in 1944 Bevan had arrived, by sheer force of personality and vigour of argument, on Labour's highest decision-making body. A most unwelcome newcomer, he could no longer be ignored. No longer a lone extremist, his claim to speak for at least a substantial body of the party was established. Among other things, he had staked his claim to office if his predictions that Labour would win the General Election were to be fulfilled.

The 1944 Conference was remarkable in other respects as well. It was dominated by the emotive issue of Greece where, for the first time, the instincts of the Labour Party as a whole recoiled from Churchill's idea of restoring democracy in Europe by backing the right-wing monarchist forces against the Communist-based EAM–ELAS resistance movement which had borne the brunt of the fighting against the Germans. In truth, there was little to choose – in terms either of democratic credentials or of brutal methods – between the two sides in what was to be a very bloody civil war. But it was one of those symbolic foreign conflicts, like the Spanish war, on which the British left and right polarised in emotional identification. For Bevan, the Greek Communists epitomised the European revolution which he thought the British Tories were determined to crush. EAM–ELAS, he believed unquestioningly, represented 'the vast majority of the Greek people'.[21] Without necessarily going so far, most of the party and much liberal opinion beyond the Labour Party, including even *The Times*, were alarmed at the sight of Churchill using British troops, as he had in Russia in 1919, to intervene militarily on the reactionary side in a foreign quarrel. 'Where we landed as liberators', Bevan alleged in the House of Commons, 'we look like staying as tyrants.' British servicemen, he warned, might have 'a very painful choice to make, either to disobey orders or to carry on a war that they did not enlist to fight'.[22] Even Labour's parliamentary loyalists were embarrassed by their leaders' association with this Government policy, and in a vote on 8 December the party officially abstained. (Bevan and twenty-nine others voted against.) At Conference Bevin stoutly presented the Government's purpose as an even-handed attempt to preserve the peace. But the NEC did not dare ask Conference to approve it; the feeling of the assembly was too obviously with Bevan's demand that the party should condemn the Government and insist that Labour's representatives 'exert a more decisive Socialist influence' against the Greek intervention 'or else leave the Tories to do their own dirty work themselves'. Otherwise, he warned, 'we may be so hopelessly compromised that the same leaders will not be able to represent us when the Election occurs'.[23]

The Greek row seemed to provide the proof of Bevan's contention, which he had maintained from the very beginning of the war, that the Tories were concerned solely to fight for their own class interest, at home and abroad. ('The Tory', he told the House of Commons, 'is a friend of the City at home and the friend of Hambros in Athens. He is the friend of the landlord here, as he is there; the friend of the rich and powerful there, as he is here. The Tories want to use our people, whom we have allowed them to put in uniform to fight the Nazis, to protect the rich and powerful vested interests wherever they are.'[24] The significant thing about December 1944 was that at last the Labour Party seemed to be coming to agree with him: suddenly other speakers, by no means all on the far left, were making a similar analysis.[25] The Greek imbroglio, with its sharp reminder of the old Churchill beneath the lofty rhetoric, dented the party's acquiescence in continued coalition more seriously than any previous incident. The second major event of the 1944 Conference was the unexpected passage, against the platform, of a fundamentalist resolution introduced by Ian Mikardo committing the party to the nationalisation of 'the land, large-scale building, heavy industry and all forms of banking', as well as transport, fuel and power. This was a programme far more sweeping than was included in the 1945 manifesto or carried out by the 1945–50 Labour Government; but it gave notice of the strongly leftward mood of the party – of which Bevan's election to the NEC was an accurate reflection – and was instrumental in ensuring the clear commitments to nationalise coal, gas, electricity, steel, the railways, road haulage and the Bank of England that were included in *Let Us Face the Future*.

Bevan welcomed this victory; but he was still unhappy with Conference's rejection of his proposal for left unity going into the General Election – a decision he described as 'little short of tragic'.[26] For all his conviction that the country was ready to swing left, he was still obsessed with the fear that Attlee and Bevin were going to blow Labour's opportunity by continuing to fawn on Churchill. As late as April 1945 he found support for his apprehension in the

Scottish Nationalists' by-election victory at Motherwell.[27] Increasingly he focused his criticism on Attlee, whom hitherto – except for one searing denunciation in 1942 ('He remains a gentleman, but only in his relations with the monopolies. He remains loyal, but only to Mr Churchill. ... By his actions and his inactions, by his speeches and by his silences, he has forfeited the right to represent [the common people] any longer in the supreme councils of the nation')[28] – he had regarded as too insignificant to deserve attention. But in January 1945 he specifically blamed Attlee for not dissociating Labour from the Greek intervention,[29] and in March he was outraged by the symbolism of Attlee attending the San Francisco Conference as deputy to Anthony Eden. 'We did not expect', Bevan wrote in *Tribune*,

> that he would affront his own followers and demean the status of the whole Labour movement by agreeing to serve as lieutenant to Anthony Eden. ... Mr Attlee has consistently underplayed his position and his opportunities. ... He brings to the fierce struggle of politics the tepid enthusiasm of a lazy summer afternoon at a cricket match. ... The whole affair is painful, humiliating and hurtful to the Labour Party. At no time has Mr Attlee stood so low in the estimate of his followers.[30]

Attlee, Bevan complained, 'seems determined to make a trumpet sound like a tin whistle'. He himself was determined to blow Labour's trumpet. As the moment of trial approached and the clearly expressed view of the party obliged even Attlee and Bevin – reluctantly – to decline Churchill's blandishments to prolong the Coalition beyond the defeat of Germany, he repeatedly emphasised the naked class issue of the election. During 1944 he had rehearsed his whole political philosophy in a short, passionate book entitled *Why Not Trust the Tories?* which sold – a sign of the times – 80,000 copies. Its purpose was to remind the electorate of what had happened after the last war, when Lloyd George, with his lieutenant Churchill, had duped them with fine talk of 'homes for heroes' and promises of coal and railway nationalisation in order to secure the re-election of a brutal Tory-dominated Coalition which systematically betrayed all their hopes. Churchill, he warned, was out to repeat the trick in 1945 if Labour failed to stop him.

> For today, as then, the Tories are faced with a crisis. Once more the expectations of the people are awakened. Once more their hopes are built up for a fundamental and equitable reconstruction of society. Once more the soldiers, sailors and airmen are coming home eager to enjoy the reward of their valour, their sufferings and their sacrifices. And once more the problem of the Tories is the same – how to ride the crisis, how to lie, deceive, cajole and buy time so as once more to snatch a reprieve for wealth and privilege.[31]

The apparent gains, Bevan argued, which had been won for working people during the war – the Beveridge scheme, the Full Employment White Paper, the promise of better housing – would turn out to be empty words if the Tories got back into power. Having served their purpose of postponing any legislation until after the General Election, they would then be cynically discarded. Beveridge was a case in point. 'Socialists allowed themselves to be persuaded to support it on the ground that it represented an agreed measure and therefore one with a better prospect of getting passed quickly into law. . . . It is obvious now that even this modest proposal is too much for the Tories to swallow.' Bevan now wanted Labour to withdraw its agreement and go back to a fully non-contributory scheme.[32] He repeated his criticism that the Employment White Paper promised nothing but public works.

> Thermostatic principles may be all very well for mechanical things like motor cars, but it is an entirely different matter when they are practised on the living flesh of men, women and children. When you are being taken to some labour camp to work on a dam or a power station, or put to dig trenches for gas or water mains, you will be pleased to know that you are a 'thermostat' helping to keep the capitalist system in equilibrium.[33]

Thirdly, Bevan warned that the Tories *wanted* a housing shortage to keep rents high, just as they needed unemployment to keep wages low.

> Politics . . . is a conflict of interest. The interests represented by the Tories are not primarily concerned with building you a house. Their primary concern is to make a profit out of building it, and then afterwards to exploit you as a tenant. If you vote Tory at the next election, you are in fact voting against your chances of obtaining the home you want in the place you want it, and at reasonable cost.[34]

Though he had no idea that he himself would be the Minister charged with housing after the election, Bevan here set out clearly the policy he would follow in office: the overwhelming direction of resources into public house-building, with stringent limits on private building.

In his conclusion Bevan explained why it was, in his view of history, 'impossible for Tories to carry out the promises they make so lavishly'.[35] It was not, he conceded – an important admission, in view of his notorious description of Tories a few years later as 'lower than vermin' – that they were individually less honest or personally less honourable than other people. It was that they did not fundamentally believe in democracy. Toryism predated democracy. It had had to adapt itself to the outward forms, but Tories still believed that Parliament was a place for settling differences among the ruling class; not, as socialists understood it, as the place where the people should take power. ('The most popular Labour Members of Parliament with the Tories', he noted, 'have always been those who plead for mercy for the poor. They have never shown anything but bare-fanged hatred for those Labour Members who want political power for the masses.'[36] Nowhere does Bevan more explicitly point up the difference, as he saw it, between himself and the majority of his parliamentary colleagues. He was not a supplicant for power.) On this understanding, 1945 represented – potentially – the end of an era, democracy's coming of age.

In the past the ordinary man was a compulsory helot. Under our political democracy he is a voluntary one. The change is profoundly important; but it is a transitory stage. He either steps back into the shadows of history once more or into the light of full social maturity. Property now rules with his permission. At any moment he can withhold it. But he must be brought to realise that he must either make the threat good or withdraw it altogether. ... The people must be brought to see that social affairs are in a bad state, because the people themselves have not clothed the bones of political democracy with the flesh of economic power.[37]

If they failed to do so, democracy would be discredited and the only alternative would be a relapse into fascism – on Bevan's definition 'the future refusing to be born'.

Bevan ended *Why Not Trust the Tories?* with his favourite historical quotation, from the 1647 debate at Putney between Cromwell and the Leveller, Colonel Thomas Rainsborough (the same in whose name Frank Owen had assailed Churchill in *Tribune* in 1942). Rainsborough was arguing for manhood suffrage, irrespective of property. 'If they who have no goods and chattels', Cromwell objected, 'make the laws equally with them that hath, they will make laws to take away the property of them that hath.' To which Rainsborough replied: 'If it be that all Englishmen cannot be free, and some Englishmen have property, then you have said it, my Lord General, and not me.' From this Bevan moved to articulate again his favourite theorem of political struggle:

It has taken almost three centuries for the situation feared by Oliver Cromwell to unfold itself fully upon the British political stage. The three elements are now present: Democracy, property and poverty. ... Cromwell saw, with clear vision, what is still hidden from so many even now. The Tories have seen it. That is why they fight democracy whenever and wherever they can. There is no compromise possible between these three discordant forces. They are the solvent of the nations and societies which refuse to yield to their logic. They pronounce the death of Coalition Governments even before these are born. They are the imperative of politics, and those who ignore them have neither a sense of direction nor an abiding purpose to fulfil. They speak across the centuries the wisdom of Thomas Rainsboro': 'Either poverty must use democracy to destroy the power of property, or property in fear of poverty will destroy democracy.'[38]

1945 was the historic moment when the power of property must be broken.

Germany surrendered on 7 May. Two weeks later Attlee finally rejected Churchill's proposal to extend the Coalition to the defeat of Japan (which was expected to take another year or more). Labour then left the Government to prepare for battle; Churchill formed a 'caretaker' Conservative administration and called the election for 5 July. 'At last', wrote Bevan in *Tribune*, 'the deadly political frustration is ended; at last the unnatural alliance is broken between left and right, between Socialism and Reaction, in other words between forces which on every single issue (bar only the defeat of Nazi Germany) proceed from opposite principles and stand for opposite policies. ... The sooner the election is held, the sooner we shall be able to get rid of the Tories and begin in earnest with the solution of the tremendous tasks before us'.[39] With excellent timing, another Labour Conference was then meeting in Blackpool. For the first time, Bevan spoke from the platform, replying – in his own way – to a debate on full employment. Only a year earlier he had been close to being expelled. Now he took the opportunity to bury the differences of the past five years, at the same time rallying the party powerfully to his own view of its task and opportunity.

> It is for us a question of where power is going to lie. There is no absence of knowledge, there is no lack of wisdom, as to what to do in Great Britain. What is lacking is that the power lies in the wrong hands and the will to do it is not there.
>
> We want to tell our friends on the other side that the men in the Services are not going to allow a repetition of what happened between the wars. We are not going to allow our financial resources to be sent all over the world, and idleness and starvation to exist in Great Britain. And we warn them that we are entering this fight with this in our hearts. We were brought up between the two wars in the distressed areas of this country, and we have such biting and bitter memories as will never be erased until the Tories are destroyed on every political platform in this country. ...
>
> It is in no pure Party spirit that we are going into this election. We know that in us, and in us alone, lies the economic salvation of this country and the opportunity of providing a great example to the world. Therefore, remember, in the elections that lie immediately ahead, we are the memories of those bitter years; we are the voice of the British people; we are the natural custodians of the interests of those young men and women in the Services abroad. We have been the dreamers, we have been the sufferers, and we are the builders. We enter this campaign at this general election, not merely to get rid of the Tory majority – that will not be enough for our task. It will not be sufficient to get a parliamentary majority. We want the complete political extinction of the Tory Party, and twenty-five years of Labour Government. We cannot do in five years what requires to be done. It needs a new industrial revolution. We require that modern industrial science be applied to our heavy industry. It can only be done by men with modern minds, by men of a new age. It can only be done by the fine young men and women that we have seen in this Conference this week.[40]

Bevan was confident that Labour would win. His belief in progress, his Marxist sense of the unfolding of history and his consciousness, particularly as editor of *Tribune*, of the shift that had occurred in public expectations over the past five years, reflected in the enthusiasm reported by Labour activists all round the country, all told him that Labour *must* win. He believed that the party had got out of the Coalition just in time, and had after all sufficiently united the left to face no threat from Common Wealth or the Communists;

he was satisfied that *Let Us Face the Future* provided an adequate programme for the first five years. ('At last we are facing in the right direction even if the pace of advance is not so quick as some of us would like.')[41] This confidence set Bevan apart from most other Labour leaders. Fully occupied with the problems of Government, Attlee and Morrison, Bevin and Dalton had been largely cut off from what was happening in the country and simply could not believe that the electorate could reject Churchill in the hour of victory. This was why they considered for so long that it would be to Labour's advantage to stay with the Coalition. Chuter Ede, junior Education Minister since 1940, was typical. In his diary for the election period, he noted the general optimism of his party workers, but did not share it. After the polls had closed, but before the count – which was delayed for three weeks to allow the Service votes to come in – Ede recorded that George Strauss was predicting a Labour victory (significantly based on *Tribune* newsgathering), 'but I know of no one else who takes so optimistic a view'.[42] The leaders' doubts, on the eve of what turned out to be one of the two great electoral landslides of modern British history, seemed to confirm Bevan's past criticism of their timidity; conversely the vindication of his own unwavering confidence throughout the war that Labour's hour of destiny was at hand gave Bevan, when the results came in, a new authority as the man who got it right. Though in no sense the architect of Labour's victory, he more than anyone else had articulated the change of mood which brought it about.

For it was he, above all, who had set himself to topple Churchill from his pedestal and insist that the election was *not* a vote of thanks for his leadership in 1940. Even after the crisis of the war had passed at the end of 1942, he had continued to harry the Prime Minister relentlessly in the House of Commons, condemning his blatant use of his 'national' prestige for Conservative Party purposes, his contempt for Parliament – notably his scandalous insistence that the House reverse, as a matter of confidence, its narrow vote in favour of equal pay for women teachers in March 1944 – and his intolerance of criticism. In the very last exchanges of the expiring Parliament in June 1945, when Churchill was attempting to make a dignified valedictory address, even thanking Bevan (ironically?) for 'the unfailing courtesy with which he has marked this long ten years' Parliament which is now departing', Bevan interrupted to object that his statement was out of order.[43] He missed not even this opportunity to puncture Churchill's pride. On 6 July, the day after polling day, he brought his sustained personal campaign to a climax in an astonishing *Tribune* article headlined 'The Menace of Churchill'. 'If democracy survives in this country', he wrote – at the end of a war in which the Prime Minister was widely thought to have saved it – 'it will be in spite of Winston Churchill.' There had been no election so dominated by the personality of a single individual since Hitler's coming to power in 1933. Churchill's voice and features had been everywhere, while the press lashed itself into 'a frenzy of glorification'.* For five years democratic values had been buried beneath a deliberately cultivated *Fuehrerprinzip*.

> The point is that the Tories have been trying finally to erase these values. It is a monstrous thing that Churchill, in order to secure party and personal advantage, should ape the tactics of the man who plunged this world into war. It is a criminal thing that a statesman who never tires of paying lip-service to democracy should lend himself to a manoeuvre which, whether successful or not, can only breed ultimate disillusionment and a corresponding decline in democratic authority.[44]

For Churchill, Bevan continued the following week, 'democracy is a state in which the people acquiesce in the rule of property. Democracy is an admirable institution so long as the poor continue to carry the rich on their backs. When the poor decide to change places, democracy falls into disrepute. That is why, whenever you scratch a Tory, you find a Fascist.'[45] For Bevan, the war against fascism had not been won until Churchill too had been defeated.

In a parliamentary exchange at the end of 1945, Churchill famously described Bevan during the war as having been 'a squalid nuisance'.[46] There can be no doubt that most Conservatives, many Labour MPs and probably the great majority of ordinary people would have agreed with that assessment. It was common currency to regard his attacks on Churchill and on his own leaders as motivated by nothing but envy, spite, hatred and thwarted ambition – malice and mischief mixed in equal parts. Churchill was not alone in believing that Bevan was actively unpatriotic, taking pleasure in military disaster.[47]† Many others feared that his unbridled criticism could only undermine national morale and help the enemy, an attitude encapsulated by A.A.Milne in the jingle:

> Goebbels, though not religious, must thank Heaven
> For dropping in his lap Aneurin Bevan.[48]

In the heightened political atmosphere of a nation fighting for its life, such a persistent, bitter and effective critic was bound to provoke violent resentment – even more when he was right than when he was wrong. And the fact is that most of Bevan's criticisms of the conduct of the war had a good deal of

---

* Bevan's old friend Beaverbrook was the chief offender. Their friendship, still close up to 1943, was now ended.

† An incident recorded by John Colville illustrates how bitterly Churchill loathed Bevan. In January 1945 Bevan was one of a four-man delegation from the NEC who went to Downing Street to register Labour's opposition to events in Greece. Churchill got his staff to ensure that the delegation was already seated behind the Cabinet table before he came in, in order that he should not have to shake hands with Bevan. (John Colville, *The Fringes of Power: Downing Street Diaries, 1939–55* [Hodder & Stoughton 1985], p. 552.) (This, incidentally, was a trick Churchill learned from Lloyd George, who took a similar precaution, with more excuse, before the talks with the Sinn Fein leaders which led to the Irish Treaty in 1921.)

truth mixed up in the often wild allegations of blame. There remain serious question marks over the North African campaign and the Italian strategy ('What are we doing in Italy at all?'), and the military uselessness of 'strategic' bombing is now established. While it was manifestly absurd to start demanding a second front a few weeks after Hitler invaded Russia, and the practical arguments against it were always a great deal stronger than Bevan's political blinkers allowed, it remains very much a live argument whether the invasion of Europe could not and should not have been launched a year earlier than it was. In a sense, though, whether Bevan was right or wrong is beside the point. He was often wrong. He was still more often unfair. Nevertheless he played an important and honourable role in the war which deserved to be acknowledged with more grace, at least when it was all over, than Churchill allowed. In a war for democracy, it was healthy that not merely democratic forms but a real clash of argument should be maintained. There was something heroic, in the face of continuous denigration, in the persistence with which Bevan – and others, but Bevan was the most persistent and principled – insisted on providing critical opposition at a time when the official Opposition interpreted their function principally as to give loyal support to their colleagues in the Government. Naturally, hard-pressed Ministers did not appreciate it; but right or wrong, day in, day out, and on minor domestic issues and matters of personal liberty as much as on the large strategic questions, Bevan by relentless questioning and his skill as a debater strove – successfully – to keep parliamentary government a reality.

It was healthy, too, that Bevan should have tried to keep alive before the country – at least after the moment of national danger had passed in 1942 – the idea of a clear political choice at the end of the war. That there had occurred a major shift in public attitudes during the war was incontestable; there was also a real danger, from a Labour point of view, of this historic opportunity being lost in a khaki election and an outpouring of national gratitude to Churchill. If it was right for Labour Ministers to join in a Government of national salvation in 1940 – and Bevan believed as strongly as anyone that it was essential – it was surely equally legitimate, particularly as the Government began to look beyond the war to the problems and opportunities of peace, that members of the Labour Party outside the Government should seek to exert pressure on their Ministers to keep Labour's end up within the Coalition and to preserve the party's goals and principles intact for the moment when the Coalition should end. Once again, Attlee, Bevin and Morrison were entitled to resent the perhaps unnecessarily offensive way Bevan sometimes went about it, yet it was still good for them and for the Labour Party and the democratic vitality of the country that he kept at them.

Where Bevan was wrong was in consistently underestimating the extent to which Labour *was* keeping its end up in the Coalition, the real influence Attlee, Bevin, Morrison and Dalton *were* having particularly on the domestic policy of the Government and the real change that was taking place in

Government attitudes to the problems of the future, reflecting the changed attitudes in the country. Bevan underestimated the former, but overestimated the latter. There *was* a major shift in the country, yet it was not the revolutionary ferment that Bevan imagined, not a demand for socialism as he understood it, rather a pragmatic adaptation to the possibilities and responsibilities of a mildly interventionist social democracy: an adaptation of which Beveridge and Keynes, not Marx, were the true prophets. From Bevan's point of view this quiet revolution within Whitehall, which shaped the assumptions and the limits within which the Labour Government would operate after 1945, was indeed a betrayal: Labour's leaders had already adopted a view of the proper extension of State power which was not thoroughly socialist. What Bevan never understood, or at any rate did not accept, however, was that the Labour Party had never been in his sense truly socialist. The reality was that Attlee, between 1940 and 1945, and then again after 1945, was not betraying but fulfilling the historically cautious purposes of the British labour movement.

Bevan the socialist philosopher railed and called for a more sweeping assault upon Tory privilege and Tory power; but Bevan the practical politician, though he was not satisfied, recognised and welcomed the reality of the change that had been wrought during the war. The final question to ask is how far he, with others, over the previous five years, helped to create the electoral mood of 1945. The answer must be that, though he was far ahead of most Labour voters, the leftward swing could not have occurred without some pull from the far left, of which he was the most prominent and articulate representative. Thus, though the demand of the electorate was not, as he afterwards discovered, for the irreversible transfer of power to a socialist state, Bevan's advocacy of such a transfer was an important component of the electoral mood. He misunderstood the nature of that mood precisely through being a part of it.

Thus 1940–45 was the key testing period for Bevan's political philosophy. In so far as he correctly gauged the leftward shift of the country and confidently predicted the result of the 1945 election, he was proved right where other Labour leaders were wrong. In so far, however, as he exaggerated the revolutionary potential of the shift which he correctly observed, he deceived himself. But disillusion lay in the future. At the time, 1945 appeared to show history working itself out inexorably according to plan. The future lay with Labour. The war and its climax left Bevan exhilarated and vindicated; feared, loathed, traduced but also respected as never before; bursting with the sense of being in step with history; ready for the supreme challenge of his life.

The election results declared on 26 July gave Labour 393 seats from nearly twelve million votes, the Conservatives only 213 from nearly ten million: an overall majority, taking in a few Liberals and others, of 146. A revolution, surely, had taken place. Why should not Labour now govern for the twenty-five years of which Bevan had spoken at Blackpool? Just one fact might have given him pause. For the first time the working men on the Labour benches were outnumbered by the middle class – lawyers, teachers and journalists. Ideologically this might constitute a shift to the left: fewer trade unionists meant more socialists. But one thing the 1945 Parliament did not herald was the seizure of power by the working class. The growing divergence between socialism and class was to cause Bevan increasing difficulty in the years ahead.

No matter: the same afternoon Attlee kissed hands and began to form his Government.

4

The Promised Land, 1945–1950

Chapter 11

Minister of Health: the Housing Crisis

The years 1945 to 1951 form the high plateau of Bevan's career, with 1948 perhaps representing the peak. For nearly six years – the only six years in his life – he held Cabinet office, first as Minister of Health, briefly as Minister of Labour, in the first majority Labour Government Britain had ever seen. For the first time in its existence Labour had won the power to put into effect – or to begin to put into effect – its programme for the transformation of British society. This was the historic opportunity which he, like all the others whose faith in the party had remained undimmed by the traumas of the 1930s, had been dreaming of since he was a boy fighting the coal owners and reading his Marx in the Workmen's Institute in Tredegar. Now, he believed, he had the chance to help direct Britain's democratic revolution. More than that, as Minister of Health he personally was given the responsibility of framing what, forty years later, still remains for many the most socialist and for most of the British people certainly the most popular achievement of that path-breaking Government. The introduction of the National Health Service in 1948 was the pinnacle of Bevan's life, as it would be of any man's. It is still widely thought of and referred to as Bevan's Health Service. Not many Ministers have the opportunity to engrave themselves so enduringly in the nation's grateful memory.

Nevertheless, from the point of view of what he really believed in – the transformation of Britain into a socialist society – the National Health Service was a sideshow. In this respect the years of the Labour Government were for Bevan years of progressive and painful disillusion. After the heady beginning in July 1945, the Cabinet was quickly forced to grapple with overwhelming economic difficulties; in doing so it shed most of its commitment to what he understood by socialism. Once it had accomplished its programme of nationalisation of basic industries – most of which in the new conditions of the post-war world aroused little controversy – the Government rapidly retreated from whatever ambition it had ever had to direct the whole economy. From 1948 the physical controls on investment and the use of raw materials, originally imposed during the war and necessarily maintained for

149

some time afterwards, were steadily dismantled and the concept of planning, so dear to Bevan's heart, reduced to little more than the setting of hopeful targets. 'Consolidation', rather than further advance towards socialism, became the Government's avowed priority. In these circumstances – for lack of anything else worthy of the name – the free Health Service became elevated into the touchstone of socialism; and socialism itself was weakly redefined as welfare capitalism.

Thus, towards the end of the six years, the pressures on Bevan mounted unbearably. The once-for-all replacement of one order of society by another to which he had spent all his life confidently looking forward was not coming about. He found himself the last unrepentant exponent in the Cabinet of Labour's philosophical commitment to thoroughgoing socialism. Then, almost before it had been fully launched, the one unquestionable domestic achievement of the Labour Government, which also happened to be his own particular achievement, came under threat from the Treasury's eternal search for economy. Bevan's generalised disillusion was now subsumed in a specific grievance personal to himself. In 1950 the Korean War brought the issue to a head, dramatising the choice before a tired Government in the classic form: guns or butter. Bevan took his stand on the narrow issue of the integrity of the free Health Service; but by extension on the wider case for socialism, in Britain and in the world at large. He took his stand on Gaitskell's Budget in April 1951, and lost. And so the six years ended, sadly but symbolically and perhaps inevitably, with the disintegration of the Government highlighted by Bevan's own embittered resignation. Britain's socialist experiment was over. Somewhere between 1948 and 1951, in Bevan's view, the historic opportunity had been lost.

On the morrow of Labour's victory which he, practically alone, had consistently predicted, Bevan had no particular reason to expect office. Both during the war and before it, he had seemed to place himself so deliberately on the outside left of the party that he could not be surprised if he were passed over, left to fret in what might be thought his natural element of opposition or at most offered some junior job to bridle him and test his capacity for regular work. This, according to Jennie, he was determined to refuse.[1] It was, therefore, a remarkable appointment for Attlee to bring Bevan straight into the Cabinet as Minister of Health – by far the boldest stroke in a generally cautious exercise in rewarding the long-serving party faithful. At forty-seven Bevan was by some years the youngest member of a Cabinet whose average age was over sixty. With the sole exception of Cripps – and Cripps was now a reformed character – he was also the one with the most unruly past. His sustained opposition to Churchill during the war, and his attacks on the Labour leaders for subordinating themselves to Churchill, were not calculated to recommend him to Attlee. But Attlee had, it may be guessed, three reasons for appointing him. First, like any Labour leader, he needed to balance both wings of the party. Neither Manny Shinwell nor Ellen Wilkinson, the other accredited left-wingers included in the Cabinet, as Minister of Fuel and Power and Minister of Education respectively, carried the weight with the constituency parties that Bevan did: his elevation was partly a recognition of his election to the National Executive in 1944. In the wake of such a victory as Labour had just won, the left was entitled to its share of the spoils. Second, Attlee was always concerned to hold a balance between the middle-class and trade union components of the party; though not a typical trade unionist, Bevan was clearly one of the ablest of the workng-class members available for office, and that was an important factor in his favour. Third, as Attlee himself characteristically expressed it some years later, 'I felt that he had it in him to do good service.'[2] Shrewdly, thinking back perhaps to the Parliament of 1931–5, Attlee recognised the subtlety, the thoughtfulness, the essential seriousness beneath the often crude and provocative irresponsibility of Bevan's public conduct. It was a perceptive appointment as well as a bold one.

Surprisingly, in view of their long-standing antagonism, Ernest Bevin liked to claim the credit for Bevan's appointment. He recalled an occasion during the war when Bevan had led a delegation to him to protest at some aspect of his manpower policy, cutting through his colleagues' woolly rhetoric to put to Bevin 'a case that I could meet and had to meet'. 'I said to myself: "There's some stuffing in that fellow. He's got sense as well as blarney. Me and him can do business."' 'He may be awkward sometimes,' Bevan claimed to have told Attlee, 'but he's got his head screwed on. He'll not let our people down.'[3] It is possible that Attlee was influenced in this matter by Bevin; certainly he would have been glad to have Bevin's approval and might well not have appointed Bevan without it. But it was Attlee's decision and Attlee deserves the credit for it.

The Ministry of Health was a good job for a troublesome left-winger, too. More than most it was a department where there was urgent work to be done which would keep him busy, test his practical ability and quickly expose him if he failed. For the Ministry of Health was responsible not only for health but for housing; and in July 1945, after five years of war, bombing, neglect and raised expectations, the housing shortage was the most urgent social priority the Government faced. With memories of the Lloyd George Government's failure to build 'homes for heroes' after 1918 still vivid, housing was just about the most politically sensitive portfolio in the Cabinet. By comparison health, though it was to offer Bevan his most lasting opportunity to leave his mark on history, was a less pressing consideration. Bevan, however, was better equipped for both parts of his new responsibilities than critics of his appointment at first sight realised. He had had experience of responsibility for housing as a councillor in Tredegar in the twenties; he also had experience of the miners' medical welfare schemes in South Wales and in the thirties had taken a close interest in health matters, particularly in the Clement Davies report on tuberculosis in Wales. Ever since Neville Chamberlain, successive Tory Ministers of Health had been his particular *bêtes noires* in the Commons (rivalled only by Ministers of Labour). Here again, in appointing Bevan to fill the shoes of those he had so bitterly criticised, Attlee knew what he was doing. Health was a job for a man who combined detailed understanding with radical fire. 'The real significance of his appointment', Attlee's press adviser Francis Williams wrote in 1948,

> was that it indicated and was meant to indicate that in dealing with the urgent and practical problem of post-war housing the Government meant to follow a clearly defined socialist policy integrated with the general pattern of social change. It meant to administer a revolution as well as carry through a health and housing programme, and that is why Bevan was chosen for these particular jobs.[4]

Even so, to leave one Minister, whoever he was, responsible for both health and housing at a time when both were going to be in the forefront of the political battle was a serious mistake. In this sense Bevan's was a bad appointment. Before the election, Labour had declared that it would split the two portfolios, merging housing with the Ministry of Town and Country Planning. Quite why Attlee went back on this sensible intention is not certain; it seems that he simply thought the reallocation of functions too complicated an operation to be undertaken at that moment. Paradoxically it may also have been just because they were going to be so important that he wanted both functions represented in the Cabinet, but did not think he had room for two Cabinet Ministers. It was a case of one Minister inside the Cabinet or two outside. This is supported by the fact that when Bevan moved on in 1951, his empire was divided and the new Minister of Health, Hilary Marquand, was not in the Cabinet. But by then the National Health Service had been launched and the housing situation was less desperate. In 1945–6 each needed the attention of a full-time senior Minister. It was not Bevan's fault that for all the pent-up administrative energy he hurled into his new job he was not able to give his whole attention to either.

There is no question that Bevan was an energetic and effective Minister. To the surprise of many, he turned out to be an excellent administrator. He established an exceptionally good relationship with his advisers – once he had decided whom he wanted. Having to appoint a new Permanent Secretary, he deliberately by-passed the Deputy Secretary, Sir Arthur Rucker, who had been Neville Chamberlain's Private Secretary both in the Ministry of Health and in Downing Street, and chose Sir William Douglas from the Ministry of Supply instead. Initially reluctant, Douglas was soon saying that Bevan was the best Minister he had ever served.[5] Bevan quickly formed equally close bonds of mutual trust and appreciation with Sir John Hawton, who was promoted to Deputy Secretary in 1947 on Rucker's disgruntled departure, and with the Chief Medical Officer, Sir Wilson Jameson. Hawton and Jameson were, with Bevan himself, the principal architects of the National Health Service. A further step down the hierarchy was John Pater, then a Principal Assistant Secretary, later Under Secretary until his retirement in 1973, when he used his inside knowledge to write the most authoritative history of the creation of the NHS. Pater too still rates Bevan the best Minister he ever served.[6]

What all these men appreciated in Bevan was the clarity of political purpose – not to mention the political limelight – which he brought to a Department more often filled by somewhat grey functionaries. He had the precious gift of being able to concentrate upon essentials and leave the detail to his civil servants: he would expound to them the principles under which he wanted them to operate and then trust them to get on with it. In other words he understood the proper roles of Minister and civil servant. Like Lloyd George, he preferred to master the work of the Department by listening, questioning and arguing rather than by reading. He was extraordinarily quick to pick up points in discussion, and never forgot anything he was told. Like Lloyd George, he was not orthodox in his methods, but he inspired and stimulated his staff and got things done. When he had taken a decision he stuck to it. He was above all a creative Minister, who believed in *using* power. The converse, it was soon being said, was that he was careless of cost and failed to control the expenditure of his Department. Temperamentally, it is true, Bevan was impatient of pecuniary restraints on the implementation of his social vision, and politically he believed that the blocking power of the Treasury needed to be curbed: even so, the extravagance of his Department was more apparent than real and much of the criticism of lack of financial control unfair. Argument, of course, continues over certain of his decisions. But both the solid record of his achievement on two fronts – not only the NHS but a million new homes of an unprecedented and subsequently unsurpassed size and quality – and the testimony of those who worked with him most closely entitle him to be regarded as a Minister of the highest calibre. In fact he was one of the successes of the Government, though he did not get the recognition he deserved.

One reason for this was that his success on the housing front looked for a long time uncomfortably like failure. There was in truth no way that any Minister, in the economic conditions prevailing after 1945, could have met in full either the real housing need which the war had left behind or the inflated expectations which Labour had aroused during the General Election. Opinion polls showed that housing was far and away the most pressing domestic issue in the minds of the electorate (41 per cent placed it first, compared with only 15 per cent who gave priority to full employment);[7] and Labour had not hesitated to create the impression that nothing more was needed to solve the problem than political will. Bevin had promised 'five million houses in quick time', while Cripps was supposed to have said that

153

the problem could be solved in a fortnight.[8] In this climate whatever miracles Bevan might have wrought were bound to appear inadequate. Sympathy must be muted, however, since none of his colleagues had done more to raise unrealistic hopes than Bevan himself. In *Why Not Trust The Tories?* he had savagely derided the Coalition Government's promise to build 100,000 houses in the first year after the war and 'put in hand' 200,000 in the second. 'Not much of a blitzkrieg, is it? It has taken five years of governmental labour to give birth to that mouse.' He quoted the General Secretary of the Building Trades Operatives to the effect that with proper planning of manpower and materials 'we could produce, with the same amount of labour as in pre-war days ... half a million houses per year'.[9] Could Bevan only have foreseen how grateful he would have been to have achieved much above half even of the Coalition target for 1946–7 he might have been more cautious. Seldom can a Minister have been more starkly confronted with the fantasy of his own election promises. Doubtless Attlee remembered the rod Bevan had made for his own back when he sent him to the Ministry of Health. 'If he now builds the houses,' commented Hannen Swaffer in the *Daily Herald*, 'he is in direct line to the Premiership. If he does not, he is for the high jump.'[10] From the moment the Government confronted reality, the latter was always the more likely. Housing was a poisoned chalice.

The dimensions of the problem were formidable. The population of the United Kingdom had increased by more than a million during the war. (In addition, the birthrate leaped as soon as the war was over.) But bombing had destroyed some 200,000 houses and damaged another three and a half million. Little new building and few repairs had been carried out for six years. The result was that the enlarged population was crowded into 700,000 fewer households than before the war. The Conservative caretaker Government estimated in May 1945 that 750,000 new houses were required immediately to clear the shortage and provide a separate home for every family, plus another 500,000 to complete the replacement of uninhabitable slums; it calculated that three to four million new homes would need to be built by the mid-fifties.[11] In the meantime, however, the pre-war building labour force was scattered to the four winds, either with the forces in Germany, the Mediterranean and all round the world, or diverted into war-related industry at home. The supply industries were not geared to producing components for the building trade, and there was a shortage of most of the necessary materials. Whatever Labour candidates might have promised on the platform, there was no quick way of switching resources to start building millions of houses overnight. The only thing that was in the pipeline was an order for 164,000 temporary houses to be built by war production methods.

Bevan also faced the problem of divided political control. It was not merely that the prime responsibility for housing was combined with responsibility for health, but that the Ministry of Health, in its housing function, was substantially dependent on and obliged to co-operate with no less than five other Ministries – Supply, Works, Town and Country Planning, Labour (for manpower) and the Scottish Office, which had parallel responsibility for housing north of the border. Having decided against merging housing with Town and Country Planning as envisaged before the election, Attlee's first device for co-ordinating the six Departments was a Cabinet Committee chaired by the Lord Privy Seal, Arthur Greenwood. But this committee met only once, on 8 August, and was quickly scrapped in favour of one chaired by the Minister of Health on whom, Attlee explicitly stated in a memor- andum explaining that there was no time for a reallocation of functions, the ultimate responsibility for the housing programme in England and Wales rested: the four other Ministers principally concerned, plus the Minister of Agriculture, one of the two Under-Secretaries for Scotland and Parlia- mentary Secretaries from the Department of Transport and the Board of Trade, would sit on this committee under Bevan's chairmanship. Their separate roles were further clarified. The Ministry of Town and Country Planning, it was stated, was 'not really directly concerned with housing', but with betterment and compensation; the Ministry of Works was not responsible for design or housing policy but for building techniques and the efficiency of the building industry; the Ministry of Supply was exactly that, responsible for supplying what the Ministry of Health ordered. 'The complaint that to give housing to the Minister of Health will overburden him', Attlee concluded, 'does not seem to be well founded.' He would be allotted an extra Under-Secretary to be responsible specifically for hous- ing.[12] But this never happened. In all his time at the Ministry of Health Bevan had just one Parliamentary Secretary (initially a sixty-two-year-old trade unionist, Charles Key) who had to divide his time, like Bevan himself, between health and housing. Nor was the arrangement satisfactory in other ways. Bevan might bear the ultimate responsibility for housing, charged with reporting direct to the Prime Minister and pursuing a building programme with 'the utmost drive and vigour';[13] but he remained wholly dependent on colleagues for labour and materials. In public – notably at the Labour Party Conference where every year he faced critical resolutions calling for a single Ministry of Housing – he stoutly insisted that no administrative reorganisation would get a single house built any faster; and once production got going that may well have been true. (In 1950, even so, he did submit to Attlee a proposal for the separation of hous- ing from health.)[14] But both within the Government and among the public at large there was widespread disbelief that the structure of responsibility was as efficient as it should be.

Faced with all these difficulties, Bevan is said to have remarked privately that it would have been better to have built no houses at all for the first year or two after the war until the machinery had been properly set up.[15] Of course, with the press and public demanding houses at once, any such delay was out of the question; but there were those even in Whitehall who, as early as October, began to complain that that might as well be his policy for all the progress that was being made. In fact Bevan had his hands full. Quite apart from the fact that it was in these first months that he had to take the critical decisions about the shape of the National Health Service, the housing side of his Department had to prepare no fewer than four essential Bills for the 1945–6 session (on rents, land acquisition, building materials and financial provisions); and he himself was continually having to fight his colleagues, in Cabinet and out, to release more manpower and materials for housing in competition with other claims, repeatedly pressing for the priority demobilisation of this or that vital category of craftsmen without whom no houses could be built.[16] He had also to draw up the *policy* on which he proposed to proceed, which he presented to the Cabinet on 6 October.[17]

First of all, Bevan accepted the caretaker Government's estimate of the number of houses required to meet the immediate need (though he very soon realised that it was far too low). Nevertheless, having seen the extent of the difficulties in the way of rapid building, he refused to announce any targets. Instead he set three principles: first, that he would concentrate on building permanent, not temporary, houses; second, that he would give priority to the building by local authorities of houses for letting to the lower-income groups, by deliberately restricting private building for sale to no more than one in five licences granted; third, he would build houses of a larger size, with more amenities (such as second lavatories) than had ever been built for working people before. All three were highly characteristic of his personal philosophy, particularly his lifelong insistence that only the best was good enough for the workers; all were to differing degrees controversial, and all reflected his new conviction that meeting the urgency of public demand could not be the most important consideration. He put it most clearly at the Party Conference in May 1947, replying to criticism of his too slow progress:

> At this moment, and for a few years to come, we are going to be judged by the *number* of houses that we build. In ten years' time we shall be judged by the *kind* of houses that we build and where we are building them, and I am not going to be panicked into doing a bad job.[18]

He realised only too well that the 'temporary' houses being thrown up at the end of the war would still be in occupation years later, and he ordered no more of them than he inherited. Similarly he was determined to build big houses; as a working man himself, brought up in a tiny cottage, he knew the importance of space and privacy to human dignity. The three-bedroomed council houses built between 1945 and 1950 accordingly averaged over 1,000 square feet of floor space, compared with 800 square feet before the war. He could have built more if he had built smaller, as both Hugh Dalton in the last months of the Labour Government and Harold Macmillan, under the Tory Government, chose to do. (Dalton, ironically, thought Bevan 'a tremendous Tory' for having insisted on the larger size.)[19] They reduced the average to just over 900 square feet, and Macmillan made great political capital by achieving 300,000 houses a year in 1954. But Bevan's remain to this day not only the biggest but the best-quality council houses, the most popular with tenants and the least trouble to the local authorities.

The decision to build houses primarily for letting is at first sight an obvious one for a Labour Government intent on redressing in favour of its own people a pre-war housing boom heavily directed towards the middle class. It was a priority agreed at the only meeting of the Greenwood committee on 8 August. But that was stated to be only for the period of the immediate housing shortage, and 'entirely without prejudice to the ultimate principle of the owner–occupier'.[20] Bevan, once given overall control, took a much more ideological line positively in favour of council letting. He believed strongly in the superiority of council housing from a socialist point of view, and he believed that good-quality council housing would be better from every other point of view than private building. 'You have only to look at the fretful fronts stretching along the great roads leading from London,' he told the House of Commons in his first major housing speech, 'to see the monstrous crimes committed against aesthetics by a long list of private speculators in house building.'[21] 'If I go down in history for nothing else', he claimed in one of his last speeches on the subject five years later, 'I will go down at least as a barrier between the beauty of Great Britain and the speculative builder who has done so much to destroy it.'[22] In the conditions of 1945, however, some of his more pragmatic senior colleagues, notably Herbert Morrison and Ernest Bevin, thought Bevan's principled determination to lay the main burden of the housing programme on the local authorities a doctrinaire luxury. Morrison urged that greater freedom for private builders, Bevin that more building undertaken directly by the Ministry of Works (on the model of wartime factories) would get more houses built more quickly and more cheaply. At Cabinet on 9 October Bevan was told to take his paper away and sharpen it up:[23] there was particular criticism of his refusal to set targets, criticism which was pressed still more strongly on Attlee by his Press Secretary, Francis Williams, and his temporary special adviser, Douglas Jay, who argued that targets were essential for both publicity and planning purposes.[24] On 11 October Attlee personally instructed that Bevan must publish targets.[25] Yet at Cabinet four days later he somehow won approval for his revised paper, still refusing to set targets and still refusing to countenance any dilution of his intention to rely primarily on the local authorities to build the necessary houses at sufficient speed.[26] With this doubtful backing he went down to the House of Commons and smote the Tories hip and thigh, blaming their neglect for the housing crisis and dismissing calls for targets as pure 'demagogy'.[27]

Bevan had won the right to tackle the problem in his own way. But he was still under heavy criticism from Jay, who continued to bombard the Prime Minister with memos castigating his performance. Jay's special nostrum was the use of housing associations, directly financed by the Government, to supplement the local authorities, on the model of the Scottish Special Housing Association to which he attributed the fact that Scotland was making faster progress than England and Wales: he was enraged that Bevan rejected such alternatives on grounds which he thought 'sweeping and doctrinal'.[28] Jay was also critical of a paper put up to Cabinet jointly by Bevan and George Buchanan (Under-Secretary for Scotland) drawing attention to the shortage of vital materials – specifically, to illustrate the range of items they were dealing with, asbestos cement, gypsum, gypsum plaster and plasterboard, glass, clay, tiles, slates, stock and facing bricks, cookers and gas meters.[29] 'This paper is reminiscent of the very early munition days', wrote Jay, drawing on his wartime experience; 'and experience shows that these difficulties are not overcome by Cabinet papers'.[30] On 2 November Jay turned his attack on the structure of the Ministry of Health itself: it appeared to have no figures whatever of houses started or completed, 'not yet even a confidential programme clearly laid down for the number of permanent houses to be built over the forthcoming period', no officer in charge of supply and no regional staff. 'I think we must accept the fact that, without much greater exertions, only a few thousand permanent houses will be started even in the first half of next year. ... It cannot be denied that the picture is gloomy, and that the building of permanent houses is likely to remain a weak point in the Government's record for many months.'[31]

This was a powerful indictment. Attlee passed it to the Secretary to the Cabinet, Sir Edward Bridges, asking him to investigate. His report confirmed that the organisational structure of the Ministry had indeed been weak ('their idea of action has been too much confined to sending out circulars'). But, he concluded, 'My private enquiries show that all this is being tackled and pretty energetically.' A new statistical section and a new supply structure were being set up.

> I think we can rely on the Ministry of Health to get their new organisation for statistics and programming in good running order by the time the permanent housing programme is well under way.
>
> It is a comfort to me that the new Permanent Secretary ... has come from a Supply Department and really understands what programming and progressing means.[32]

Such an endorsement reflects a lot of credit on Bevan, who had only been at the Ministry for three months and was clearly having just the effect a dynamic Minister is supposed to have. (It was, moreover, he who had chosen Sir William Douglas from the Ministry of Supply.) Bridges' report silenced one barrel of Jay's attack, but he still thought progress was too slow. In his first monthly report to the Cabinet on 8 November Bevan offered not so much progress as projected progress: 15,000 permanent houses to be completed by the end of June 1946 (that is after nearly a year of Labour Government) and 150,000 by the end of June 1947. He pointed out that he still had at his disposal only half the pre-war labour force – some 330,000 men of whom nearly 200,000 were dealing with war damage, another 100,000 on repairs and conversions and only 4,400 engaged on new houses, all but 500 of them in Scotland![33] Jay minuted Attlee that Bevan's targets were at once modest and optimistic, and advised that his protestations blaming lack of labour and materials 'should be received with a grain of salt'.[34] Labour, Jay insisted, was not the bottleneck, and it was up to Bevan to stimulate the Ministry of Supply by placing definite orders, not wait for it to see what it could provide.[35]

Attlee now decided to take charge himself, giving his Prime Ministerial authority to the task of sorting out these inter-departmental difficulties. On 11 December he took the chair for the first time at a new committee comprising not only all the Ministers concerned but Morrison and Greenwood and sometimes the Chancellor of the Exchequer, Dalton, as well. At the first meeting he compared it to similar committees in the war to oversee major undertakings like the Battle of the Atlantic. 'It was essential that housing should be regarded as having the same sort of urgency as military operations in the war years.' The committee immediately obliged Bevan to concede the main practical change for which Jay had been pressing: he agreed that 'there should be a Government building organisation, provided that it was made clear to local authorities that any such organisation was intended to supplement local authority building', not replace it.[36] The following April, on Attlee's initiative, a further wheel was added to speed up the administrative machine in the form of a Housing Production Executive, to be set up within and under the control of the Ministry of Health but comprising officials from the other Ministries involved, under a chief executive.[37]

Attlee's heavyweight committee undoubtedly gave more impetus to the drive to overcome shortages, though it must also have convinced the Prime Minister of the reality of Bevan's difficulties. Over the next few months it wrestled unsuccessfully with the timber shortage which was to remain Bevan's greatest headache throughout the life of the Government (at this stage because of unavailability; later because too much of it had to come from the dollar area at a time when the Government had no dollars), and rather more effectively with the fact that brick production was in January 1946 still only one-fifth of its pre-war level. All sorts of expedients were considered to attract, force or bribe labour into the brickworks, including the use of German prisoners of war and granting brick workers an extra cheese ration. In March Attlee again exerted his authority to insist that the Ministries of Works and Labour increase brick production by every possible means: by the end of the year it was back to 80 per cent of the pre-war figure. In the meantime attempts were made to save bricks by using concrete wherever possible for factories and other non-residential building. By the same token prefabricated houses were ordered from the firms that had made the Mulberry Harbours in the war, and the ordnance factories were turned over to making baths and cookers.[38] (Bevan was particularly proud of his mass-produced iron bath:[39] he was a great believer in bulk purchase and economies of scale which he thought exemplified socialist planning. He pursued the same policy with regard to artificial limbs and dental fixtures for the National Health Service.)

Eventually all these measures began to show results. By the end of 1945 there had been provided in England and Wales only 100,916 new homes, and only 229 of these were new houses – the rest were achieved by conversion and repair of existing buildings and requisitioning.[40] But during 1946 the local authority programme got under way, with 163,518 houses started around the country, justly described by one housing historian as 'an unprecedented historical achievement'.[41] In August Bevan felt confident enough to scrap the proposed National Building Corporation which had been forced on him by Attlee's committee: the Minister of Works, George Tomlinson, had got so far as to appoint a chairman and board when Bevan wrote to him to say that he had changed his mind.[42] By the end of the year he had a workforce of 250,000 engaged on new housing,[43] and in the Government's *Economic Survey for 1947* felt able for the first time to set a public target of 240,000 permanent houses to be completed in the coming year (120,000 traditional, 80,000 'prefabs' and 40,000 under private licence).[44] Even so, no more than 60,000 were completed by the end of 1946, barely more than half what Bevan had hoped for.[45] (He was still at this stage adamantly refusing to announce public targets, and had protested furiously to Cabinet in July when Tomlinson made the 'extremely embarrassing' disclosure that the Government was aiming at 100,000.)[46] That autumn saw a rising tide of public criticism embodied most dramatically in an outbreak of squatting, first in disused army camps and then in a number of empty mansion blocks in London.[47] This set an awkward problem for the Government, which felt obliged to protect property but could not be seen to expel the squatters too violently.[48] In November Herbert Morrison took up Jay's cudgels (Jay had entered Parliament at a by-election in July) and sent Attlee a wide-ranging attack on Bevan's programme, arguing that his 240,000 target for 1947 was far too ambitious in the light of his failure in 1946; alleging a reluctance to inject more efficiency into the building industry ('It will need a strong hand and ruthless methods. The Minister of Health is unhappy about this aspect of the matter'); and raising again the need for a unified Ministry of Housing.[49] Morrison was worried about the rising cost of Bevan's houses and still thought that a relaxation of controls on private building might be desirable. But at the beginning of

January he was taken ill and was out of action for several months. In his absence, on 17 January, the Cabinet approved Bevan's 1947 target – timber supplies permitting.[50]

At this point, however, just as the programme was getting into its stride, it was tripped up by factors outside Bevan's, or indeed the Government's, control. First, the severe winter of early 1947 made housebuilding practically impossible for two months, while the fuel crisis hit industry and stopped the production of essential components – particularly, once again, bricks. Then the convertibility crisis and the shortage of dollars seriously affected timber supplies, leaving thousands of half-built houses unable to be finished. Finally, the economic situation dictated that exports be given priority over domestic consumption (what timber there was, for instance, was said to be need for crating cars).[51] The housing programme was accordingly cut back to 200,000 in 1947 and 140,000 in 1948. Between August and December Bevan fought desperately for his programme, first trying to get away with a redirection towards miners and agricultural workers (particularly vital for exports and saving imports), then cancelling all private licences and all the while trying to make a special social case for sparing housing, only to be firmly told by Cripps (who replaced Dalton as Chancellor in November) that 'control of capital investment was meaningless without some reduction in the housing programme'.[52] The result was that the number of local authority completions in 1947 was only 97,340 – which meant, adding the 1946 and 1947 figures together, that only 122,353 (75 per cent) of the 163,518 houses started by the local authorities in 1946 were finished by the end of 1947. Private builders were scoring considerably better, managing to fulfil their allocation of 40,000 in the year despite all the problems.[53] The unfinished council house was becoming a depressing symbol of Labour Britain.

Bevan, however, was still characteristically defiant. 'We will build in 1949,' he told the House of Commons, 'if we get the timber, more houses than are in the projected programme and between now and 1949 we shall finish the 350,000 houses that are under construction and in contracts. Even with the limitations imposed upon housing, even with the dollar difficulties, we shall still have reached before 1950 the target set by the last Government for houses in this country.'[54] This was in the event an unnecessarily cautious estimate. Still concerned to counter-attack the Tories, however, he went on to claim that in the first two and a half years after 1945 Labour had built more houses than were built in the ten years after 1918. This was nonsense, though it was eight months before Ernest Marples refuted it, and even then Bevan was able to show that he had only exaggerated.[55] Given the difficulties of starting up after a great war, Labour's record was actually very good. In 1919–21 the Lloyd George Coalition had built only 89,000 houses: in 1946–8 Labour eventually built 440,000.[56] After the reverses of 1947, 1948 was a very good year. In

February Bevan told the Cabinet that the cuts of the previous autumn were liable to cause unemployment in the building industry;[57] the following week Cripps conceded him an extra allocation of timber sufficient for 30,000 houses in the year.[58] The completion of houses begun in 1946 and 1947 now proceeded rapidly, and houses started in 1948 were finished much more quickly: in the first nine months of the year 169,556 were completed (the final total was 223,119) and in September 1948, with a flourish of trumpets, the target of 750,000 new homes provided since the war was passed. New *homes*, that is – only 367,000 of these were new permanent houses: 156,000 were provided by temporary housing, 135,000 by repairs (mainly local authority) and 106,000 by conversions (mainly private). The Ministry also pointed out that 774,000 *occupied* houses had been repaired, using labour which could have been used to build another 100,000 new houses. Nevertheless the magic figure had been reached, well before 1950: some two and a half million people had been housed, even if it was now recognised that the target had been set far too low and a vast impatient demand for housing was still unmet.[59] (Bevan explained this by arguing that, as with every other social service which Labour had expanded, public expectation had risen: those who before the war had expected to live with their parents or their children now wanted or were able to remain in homes of their own.)[60] The effort went on. In September 1948 another 198,000 houses were in construction with a further 52,000 in contract but not yet started. By 1951 a round million had been completed (houses, not homes), 82 per cent of them, in accordance with the ratio set by Bevan in 1945, built by the local authorities.[61] Bevan had achieved, in the end, what he had set out to achieve, and by his own methods, building council houses of a size and quality which has never been surpassed. They, as well as the National Health Service, are his memorial.*

He had, as he had promised, 'broken the back' of the housing shortage by 1948. Housing was not after all, as had seemed likely in 1946–7, a serious liability for Labour at the 1950 General Election. In the last three years of the Labour Government, as it happened, the annual total of houses built never again topped 200,000; but the figure was now dictated by economic necessity and political choice, no longer by physical or administrative problems. (Attlee's emergency committee had been wound up in 1947.) Devaluation in September 1949 necessitated cutting that year's programme back to 170,000. Bevan protested with his usual vehemence to Attlee, pleading that 'housing makes its own peculiar and essential contribution to national revival' by facilitating mobility of labour;[62] but he was by then simultaneously fighting a battle even closer to his heart to preserve the National Health Service, so he had no choice but to accept. Even so, following the disappointing result of

* One child who was brought up in one of Bevan's new bungalows in Bevan's own town of Tredegar was the present Labour leader, Neil Kinnock, who remembers it in the context of the housing of the time as 'like moving to Beverly Hills. . . . People used to come just to look at it' (Robert Harris, *The Making of Neil Kinnock* [Faber 1984], p. 25).

the General Election, in which Labour's majority was practically wiped out, he was able to persuade the Cabinet in April 1950 to reverse itself and restore the housing target to 200,000 a year, to be stabilised at that level for three years – until the Korean War caused another cutback.[63] As late as December 1950, only weeks before he left the Ministry of Health and at a time when rearmament was requiring sacrifices from every other department, Bevan was successfully appealing to the new Chancellor, Hugh Gaitskell, to allow him the flexibility to build more than 200,000 a year if by bonus schemes and more effective use of resources he could manage it within his budget.[64] Though naturally he did not always get his way, Bevan emerges from the record of these latter years as a singularly effective advocate of his Department's case for priority treatment by successive Chancellors – at least so far as housing was concerned; he was ultimately less successful on the health side.*

In the exceptionally difficult conditions after 1945, then, Bevan achieved a very considerable success. He built a million houses, and he built good houses. By contrast Harold Macmillan's later success in 1951–5, with which Bevan's record was unfairly compared, was achieved in very different circumstances. He had Bevan's groundwork to build on; he was operating in a much easier economic climate, with no serious shortages, and able to give far larger Government subsidies; he also, as one would expect, made much more use of private builders. Above all, however, judged by Bevan's maxim that in ten years' time the number of houses built would matter less than their quality, Macmillan built smaller, cheaper, meaner houses and began to build more flats. Measured merely by columns of figures, there is really no valid comparison to be drawn.

The lasting criticism that can be made of Bevan is that his socialist preference for public over private housing was not shared, indeed has been decisively rejected by the British public. His council houses were better than most, but after the first urgency of the immediate post-war shortage, as living standards began to rise, even they were not sufficiently attractive to overcome the deep-seated aspiration of the ordinary English family to own their own home. Whatever horrors were perpetrated by speculative builders between the wars, few people would consider much public housing erected since the war to be more desirable, either architecturally or socially. Bevan himself had an idealistic hope, expressed in his very first housing speech to the House of Commons, that council estates should not become working-class ghettoes. Segregation by social class, he declared grandly, was 'a wholly evil thing ...

* Sir Alec Cairncross has recently shed a new light on Bevan's performance with the suggestion that for several years after the war the official figures seriously understated the number of houses completed. This, if true, would help to explain why Bevan did not get the political credit he deserved for the number of houses he was building. Sir Alec's view is that, because the figures seemed more disappointing than they really were, Bevan was allowed to claim a disproportionate share of resources for housing which seriously unbalanced the Government's investment programme as a whole. (Alec Cairncross, *Years of Recovery: British Economic Policy, 1945–51* [Methuen 1985], pp. 451–2.)

condemned by anyone who has paid the slightest attention to civics and eugenics. It is a monstrous affliction on the essential psychological and biological one-ness of the community.'[65] He hoped that council houses would be built in a range of sizes to suit every income, so as to encourage a healthy social mix and dispel the stigma of living in council accommodation. His vision was that council housing should become a universally provided social service like the National Health Service, and equally widely accepted. It did not happen. Council estates have, with some exceptions (notably in Scotland), remained working-class ghettoes from which it has been the ambition of every upwardly mobile family to escape as soon as possible. The sort of lively community pride which Bevan hoped to foster never developed: today the popular image of local authority housing (made worse by the high-rise building of the sixties) is one of vandalism and decay. It is possible to blame the architects and planners who designed the estates, too often without shops or other amenities; it is possible to blame unimaginative administration by many local authorities. The basic failure, though, has been the failure of the socialist idea. It is the emblematic failure of Bevan's career. He succeeded, against great odds, in building 800,000 excellent council houses. He believed that he was thereby helping to build for Britain a socialist future. But he was wrong. The future failed him.

Chapter 12

Minister of Health: the Creation of the National Health Service

It was the other side of his Department that gave Bevan the chance to earn the lasting gratitude of the British people. It was his difficulties with housing which occupied the attention of the public, at least in 1945–7. But nearly forty years later Bevan's one indelible claim on the notice of history is that he was the founder of the National Health Service. This was probably – certainly by popular acclaim – the Attlee Government's greatest achievement; it has some claim to be the Labour Party's greatest achievement in all its eighty-five-year life; and Bevan was the Minister who carried it through. That credit can never be taken away from him. At the same time it must be said that too much can be claimed for him, and in Labour mythology often is. As a result of subsequent events between 1948 and 1951, culminating in his resignation from the Government, Bevan and his most ardent disciples tended increasingly to represent the Health Service as his personal creation. This was both politically and psychologically understandable at a time when he seemed alone to be defending the pure principle of a free service against attack from all sides. Nevertheless it was a distortion of the long and cumulative process by which the Service came into existence in 1948. No Minister is ever the sole author of his legislation. The problem for the historian is to identify and try to evaluate Bevan's distinctive contribution to the NHS. In what precise ways might it have been different had the Tories won the 1945 General Election? Or if another Labour Minister had been responsible for introducing it? How much of the overall shape, and how many of the structural or conceptual flaws, can be specifically attributed to him? Of course there can be no certain answer to such questions. But it is essential to keep them in mind when examining the genesis of what is still often thought of as 'Bevan's NHS'.

There can be no doubt that some form of National Health Service would have come into being after 1945 whoever had won the General Election. It was one of the central assumptions ('Assumption B') of the Beveridge Report that there would be such a service alongside the comprehensive system of social security which he envisaged; and it was not one from which the

Conservatives were disposed to differ. Even before Beveridge, discussions had been going on within the Ministry of Health – under two non-Labour Ministers, the Liberal National Ernest Brown followed by the Conservative Henry Willink – to plan the expected service: it was initially hoped to introduce legislation in 1943. The Ministry's thinking at this stage, influenced on the one hand by the left-wing pressure group, the Socialist Medical Association, but also by the Medical Planning Commission of the BMA, was surprisingly radical, taking for granted many of the features to which the BMA was soon to take violent exception: a universal service, with the doctors grouped into health centres run by the local authorities and paid at least partly by salary. A salaried service was the principal objective of the SMA; it was also official Labour policy, but this was more by default than by conviction, for health was not a high priority in Labour thinking between the wars and the few but dedicated activists of the SMA had been able to fasten their somewhat doctrinaire prescriptions on to the party with little opposition. In practice, the party was more pragmatic and was happy to go along with Willink's 1944 White Paper even though it already contained a number of concessions to medical opinion, which was beginning to take fright. What had happened was that the BMA, seeing vague aspirations suddenly becoming imminent reality and fearing in particular the loss of private practice in a universal service, had ceased to function as an expert sounding board and taken on instead the role of a trade union acting for its members' often frankly commercial interests. Over the next year, 1944–5, Willink encountered determined opposition on several fronts from a profession which now wanted little more than an extension to wives and dependants of the existing National Health Insurance scheme; and in a series of public negotiations he gave way on most of them. By the time of the election the caretaker Government was left with a draft Bill so diluted that Lord Woolton decided that it would be more of a liability than an asset to the Conservatives to publish it. It would, even so, have provided free treatment for all who needed it.

Bevan, when he took over in August 1945, was not bound by Willink's Bill, which Morrison and Greenwood, Coalition Ministers closely involved with previous schemes, specifically disowned. Nor did he consider himself bound to the SMA's ideas, for all that the 1943 commitment to a 'national, full-time, salaried, pensionable service'[1] was repeated in *Let Us Face the Future*. But he was effectively committed by much of the ground which Willink had conceded to the BMA. The doctors had marshalled their forces to defeat Willink and now regarded many of the points he had given away – on salaries, health centres, the sale of practices – as settled. Naturally Bevan did not accept this; but in practice he found his room for manoeuvre limited by the positions the BMA had taken up. Four years had already been spent on the preliminaries: now he was expected to produce a Bill quickly to tie in with the National Insurance scheme being simultaneously developed by Jim Griffiths.

From this dilemma he found a diversion in the question of what to do about the hospitals. The one matter on which there was general agreement was that there was no possibility of going back to the dual system which had existed before the war: on one side the voluntary hospitals, supported by private endowments and local charity, on the other the municipal (often former Poor Law) hospitals run by the local authorities, the two in rivalry and open competition with one another. The war had enforced some co-ordination through the Emergency Hospital Scheme; it also revealed an intolerable degree of overlapping and inefficiency between the two services. The planners in the Ministry of Health wrestled with the problem of how to combine and rationalise them on a permanent basis after the war. Their instincts and the tradition of the Department favoured the municipal hospitals. But the voluntary hospitals enjoyed an immense fund of goodwill, particularly in the local Conservative Associations with whom they were often closely identified; also the greater medical prestige and the support of the doctors, who hated the bureaucratic structure and lack of professional control of the local authority hospitals. Not even the SMA believed that the voluntary hospitals could be abolished overnight, though many in the Labour Party expected to absorb them into the municipal system in due course. Though many of them had been in financial difficulties before the war, State control under the EHS had given them a new security; they now counted on continued subsidy to keep them going and while reluctantly accepting the need for some sort of co-operation with the local authority hospitals were ready, with Tory support, to fight hard for their 'independence'. The most that either the Ministry, the Labour Party or even the SMA could propose was some form of 'partnership' between the two sectors, to be controlled by joint boards. After numerous concessions to mutual suspicion, Willink's draft Bill came up with a scheme described by John Pater as 'a planning and administrative system of almost unworkable complexity'.[2]

Bevan's greatest achievement at the Ministry of Health was to cut this Gordian knot. The apparently insoluble problem of the hospitals gave him the opportunity for his one real initiative, a daring piece of lateral thinking: within two months of taking office he proposed to *nationalise* the hospitals, both municipal and voluntary. The suggestion had first been canvassed as a possible option by the then Chief Medical Officer in 1939;[3] but it had formed no part of Ministry thinking during the war. The credit for reviving it is ascribed by Pater to Sir John Hawton, who in the early weeks of the new Government's life spent several long evenings with Bevan at Cliveden Place talking all round the problem.[4] But wherever it originated, it chimed perfectly with Bevan's own instinct and he seized on it immediately. Politically, it had the beauty that it upset both the Tory-backed voluntary hospitals and the Labour local authorities equally. On the other hand it pleased the hospital doctors, whose principal fear was of being placed under the local authorities, and ensured their willingness to participate in a universal

167

service, thus dividing the profession by cutting them off from their more obstructive colleagues in the BMA (which spoke predominantly for the GPs). Above all, of course, it unified the hospitals. But with this single stroke Bevan determined, for better or worse, the whole shape of the NHS; and there were disadvantages as well as gains. First, by uniting the hospitals directly under the Minister he was obliged to give up any idea of uniting the Service as a whole, which could only have been done under the local authorities: the result was a tripartite structure, or effectively three separate services – hospitals, GPs and home nursing (maternity, chiropody, etc.) – which attracted increasing criticism leading eventually to a wholesale restructuring in 1974. Secondly, by centralising the hospitals and making their whole cost a charge on the Exchequer, he destroyed both local autonomy and local funding, leaving them in the future directly at the mercy of cutbacks in national expenditure. Third, by concentrating his energies on the hospitals he left the general practitioner services essentially unreformed. Finally, Bevan arguably paid too high a price for the consultants' support. Not only were they not required to work for the local authorities, they were allowed to retain the right to private practice and pay beds in NHS hospitals and they were given substantial representation on the new Management Committees and Regional Boards (something which even Willink had firmly denied them). Since they were now to be paid for the work they had previously done (in the voluntary hospitals) for nothing, they achieved the best of both worlds – the regular pay of the municipal hospitals with the prestige of the voluntary, plus private fees. No wonder Bevan was reported to have said 'I stuffed their mouths with gold.'[5] And as well as gold he gave them power, the predominant power to shape the new service.

Politically, this was Bevan's crucial choice. It may be argued, as both his Labour critics and the BMA alleged, that he fell too much under the influence of the subtle Lord Moran, President of the Royal College of Physicians, who persuaded him to pay the price needed to gain the consultants' support. He certainly was persuaded that he must, one way or another, induce the top doctors to join the NHS if it was to be anything more than a safety net. To do this he was prepared to reject the previous assumption of Labour leaders that doctors would have to be either inside the Service or outside it. Moran convinced him that if the doctors were not allowed to combine NHS work with private practice, a significant number of them would choose the latter, leading to the mushrooming of private nursing homes and a second-class service in the public hospitals. If he was to have a universal health service – making the *best* available to *all* – he needed the top doctors (and their patients) at least partly inside it. If he could only have this by leaving them the option of private practice in addition, so be it: he believed that, once all were inside, the superiority of the NHS would become evident and private practice would wither away. Properly understood, his decision was not a betrayal of socialism but a choice between conflicting goals of socialism. A doctrinaire attempt to impose the SMA's integrated service based on the local authority hospitals and health centres, with the doctors employed by the local authorities, might have been the 'correct' solution on paper, but it would have meant a two-tier system in practice because so many of the top doctors and their patients would have opted out. By buying the top doctors in on their own terms, Bevan secured an alternative socialist objective much more in tune with the instinct of the Labour Party and the mood of the time, a universal NHS to which all were equally entitled and of which even the wealthiest were happy to make use for everyday complaints. His decision was thus both bold, in that no one had seriously considered it before, and pragmatic, showing a shrewd preference for the substance of a national service rather than the theory. By this decision, and the determination with which, having taken it, he pushed it through the Cabinet against considerable and weighty opposition, he settled the shape of the Service. The other parts of the jigsaw now fell relatively easily into place. After this, the long-drawn-out tussle with the BMA was an unseemly irrelevance.

Bevan unveiled his plan to the Cabinet in a paper dated 5 October 1945 (that is practically simultaneous with his initial paper on housing policy). He promised the outline of the NHS as a whole soon; but first 'I need a decision on one big question of principle.' The voluntary hospitals, he asserted, were 'nowadays a complete anachronism': too small (70 per cent of them had less than thirty beds), usually of 'mediocre' quality, and already at least 70 per cent and sometimes 90 per cent dependent on the Exchequer. The patchwork of local authorities, on the other hand, was too uneven in both size and resources to support a national service: 'the first fundamental from now on is to picture, plan and provide a hospital service on a broad national scale, and get rid once and for all of any purely historical impediments to doing so'.[6] Such language was bound to raise hackles: the major local authorities like the London County Council did not see themselves as 'historical impediments'. After an indeterminate Cabinet discussion on 11 October, Herbert Morrison put up an alternative paper complimenting the Minister of Health on his 'brilliant and imaginative' scheme but denouncing it severely as an attack on local government for which the Government had no mandate. This might very well have been enough to sink it there and then. Bevan was, after all, the most junior member of the Cabinet, with no experience of office and personally distrusted by many of his colleagues as an unscrupulous windbag; he was already running into criticism over the delays in housing. Morrison was Deputy Prime Minister, in some ways a more powerful figure in the labour movement than Attlee himself: having made his name before the war as leader of the LCC – an authority particularly proud of its hospital service – he was the party's most prominent champion of local government, which he now defended passionately as 'a school of political and democratic education as well as a method of administration'. He warned of the 'potentially serious consequences ... of slicing off one of its most cherished functions' and of the delay, which might prejudice the NHS itself, which would be involved in arousing such unnecessary opposition.[7] But Bevan held his ground. In reply he noted shrewdly that Morrison did not deny the greater efficiency of a clean sweep but raised only political objections, which he endeavoured to minimise. It was nonsense, he repeated, to keep the voluntary hospitals going any longer by subsidy, but giving them to the local authorities 'would raise a tornado compared with any passing thunderstorm my scheme may provoke'; he insisted that any local authority scheme would be 'unequal in its operation' and thus 'unjust to the public, who will pay equal contributions'. He denied weakening local government, which was already overloaded; but admitted, 'Of delay I am indeed afraid'. That, he said, was why he wanted a quick decision. The NHS could be 'the admiration of the world. It is a chance which, in any one field of administration, comes but once, perhaps, in a generation.' He appealed to Morrison to back it. 'The thing can be done now. If it is not done now, it will not be done in our time.'[8]

At a second Cabinet on 18 October, Morrison switched his attack to the administrative structure of Bevan's scheme, by which Regional Boards would plan and administer the hospitals under the general control of the Ministry of Health. The Boards, he argued, 'would either be mere creatures of the Ministry or they would have to be given a dangerous freedom to pursue policies of their own at the expense of the Exchequer'. Here he put his finger on a lack of financial control which was indeed to cause problems for Bevan himself within a few years; but Bevan successfully skated over the difficulty for the moment with some vague talk about 'room for development in the techniques of government' and urged his colleagues to go boldly for the most efficient immediate solution. Morrison still maintained that the voluntary hospitals 'would in time decline and fall under public control' and on that expectation preferred 'a solution which admittedly would not be perfect but which would not range all the interests against the Government and create serious divisions among Government supporters both in Parliament and in the country, at a time when local elections were pending'. This seemed perhaps too short-sighted. Several Ministers suggested compromises to salve the local authorities' injured pride, but more responded to Bevan's appeal for boldness, and Attlee summed up in his favour, subject to some clarification of detail.[9] Morrison did not give up easily, but this was essentially the moment of his defeat. It was a considerable victory for an untried Minister.

After this Bevan had little more trouble with his colleagues. When in December and January he brought to Cabinet his plans for the remainder of the NHS, followed in March by the draft Bill, there were some misgivings about private practice but no substantial opposition; the only doubt, raised once again by Morrison and Greenwood, was whether in view of the anticipated outcry from the hospital interests the Bill could be put through in the current Session.[10] Bevan was determined that it could be and must be: he believed, rightly, that the opposition of the local authorities had been exaggerated – the LCC in fact accepted the Government's decision loyally and the other authorities quickly followed suit – and though some prominent Tories made a fuss about the 'mass murder of the voluntary hospitals'[11] he knew he had knocked the heart out of their case by making special provision in his scheme for the teaching hospitals. From now on the only opposition came from the BMA: and Bevan was resolved, as a matter of constitutional principle, to brook no delay from that quarter.

As a backbencher before the General Election, before he had any idea that he would be Minister of Health, he had made a thoroughly characteristic protest against Willink's private negotiations with the doctors behind the back of Parliament.[12] Now – though it did not stop him having substantive discussions with Lord Moran – he made great play with the announcement that he would 'consult' but would not 'negotiate' with any outside body. He accordingly declined even to meet the BMA until after he had got the major question of the hospitals settled, and then made a point of stressing that the members of their grandly named Negotiating Committee were being 'asked for their considered views as experts, not as delegates entitled to commit their principals'.[13] This blunt rejection of their claim to help shape legislation as they had done under his predecessors set the BMA's relations with the new Minister off on the wrong foot straight away: they were bitterly aggrieved to read in the newspapers rumours of the nationalisation of the hospitals without their having been even informed. Bevan's first informal meeting with leaders of both sides of the profession – the BMA and the Royal Colleges – over dinner at the Café Royal on 25 October actually went surprisingly well. On his own favourite stamping ground he delighted his hosts with his wit, his exuberant enthusiasm and his willingness to learn; socially, at least, this was not the ranting demagogue they had been led to expect.[14] Quickly, however, the BMA Committee discovered that he meant what he said about not negotiating. They were soon complaining that their meetings 'consisted of the Minister telling the doctors what he intended to do, pledging them to secrecy and showing them on their way'.[15] He received them, it was alleged in the *British Medical Journal*, 'with the silent disdain of a nineteenth-century capitalist meeting a deputation of his employees': he listened to their views, but 'withheld his response'.[16] Almost certainly these accounts are exaggerated; yet Bevan was at some pains to convey to the party and to the world that he was not negotiating, partly indeed because he had no time to do so if he was to get his Bill in 1946, but partly also to cover the fact that it was he who was not reopening most of the questions which Willink had conceded since 1943. His proposals actually posed very little threat at all to what the doctors perceived as their professional interest. He did not, despite Labour's stated policy before the election, propose to turn doctors into full-time salaried servants of the State, nor even of the local authorities. They would be in contract, on the contrary, with specially formed Executive Councils on which the medical professions (doctors, dentists, pharmacists, etc.) would have a majority of the members; and though Bevan insisted that a basic salary should form a part of their remuneration, the bulk of it would come, as it did at present under the National Health Insurance committees, from capitation fees. On the other side, admittedly, the aspiration to develop health centres was accorded a more central place in the scheme of things than Willink had latterly allowed it; the sale of practices was to be abolished (with £66 million set aside for compensation); and Bevan proposed to set up a Medical Practices Committee to control the distribution of doctors so that they should no longer concentrate disproportionally in the prosperous and already 'over-doctored' areas. But none of this interfered with professional integrity, the doctor–patient relationship or the freedom of the patient to choose his own doctor, the cardinal principles which the BMA solemnly claimed to be defending. (As Bevan justifiably pointed out, the buying and selling of practices, to which they attached such importance, exposed the third at least of these concerns as cant.)[17] In adopting from the outset a hostile attitude to his proposals, the BMA was partly reacting in pique against his refusal to treat them with the deference they thought they deserved, partly throwing up a smokescreen of simulated outrage behind which to chip a few more concessions from even this Minister's intentions.

The National Health Service Bill was published on 20 March 1946 and received its Second Reading on 2 May after a three-day debate which Bevan opened with a well-received exposition which demonstrated both his command of the subject and his concern to conciliate his critics on both right and left. It was from the latter that he rightly anticipated most difficulty in Parliament. The Tories put up a half-hearted amendment which prudently supported the principle while attempting opportunistically to marry the grievances of the voluntary hospitals and local authorities with the fears of the BMA; but Bevan swept that aside with ease. He devoted a lengthy section of his speech, on the other hand, to justifying to his own side his concession – 'which I know will be repugnant in some quarters' – on private practice. It was not possible, he explained, to prevent patients from seeking a second opinion. 'To do so would be to create a black market.' But the fact that a patient could transfer from one doctor to another, he believed, 'ought to keep paying within reasonable proportions'. Pay beds in hospitals were similarly unavoidable if there was not to spring up 'a rash of nursing homes all over the country' drawing off many of the best specialists; but he also argued that it would actually be wrong to prevent people paying for extra facilities which the NHS was not yet, through lack of resources, able to provide. 'If the State owned a theatre,' he suggested, provoking interruptions from his own side, 'it would not charge the same prices for the different seats.' A better analogy was the dental service. 'The State will provide a certain standard of dentistry free, but if a person wants to have his teeth filled with gold, the State will not provide that.' Here the need to put the best face on expediency was drawing him dangerously far from the principle that the best should be available to all.* But he got away with it.

Emphasising how much he had conceded to the doctors without antagonising his own supporters was a delicate balancing act. He defended allowing them such a big hand in the direction of the service by presenting it as participatory democracy—though he stressed that they would be subordinate to ultimate lay control ('We do not want the opposite danger of syndicalism'). Likewise he was at pains to reassure the BMA by telling his Labour friends firmly that he did not accept their case for full-time salaries: 'I do not believe that the medical profession is ripe for it, and I cannot dispense with the principle that the payment of a doctor must in some degree be a reward for zeal.' There would be a small basic salary for practical reasons, he insisted, but most doctors' main remuneration would be by capitation fees.[18] Later in the debate, however, a Tory Member picked up his phrase that the profession was not 'ripe' for a salaried service and drew from Bevan an unguarded and damaging riposte: 'There is all the difference in the world', he said, 'between plucking fruit when it is ripe and plucking it when it is green.'[19]

Was this just a neat debating reply, or did it, as the BMA immediately alleged, give away Bevan's long-term intention that the basic salary should be the thin end of the wedge, leading on when the time was ripe to full-time salaries? Whichever it was, he was never allowed to forget it; the remark deepened the doctors' suspicions that he was just waiting to 'pluck' them and stiffened their determination to resist even the basic salary. The Cabinet minutes do in fact lend some support to their suspicion: introducing his draft proposed on 20 December 1945, Bevan had told his colleagues that 'the proposed basis of remuneration for doctors should eliminate the worst features of the capitation rate system, *and lead eventually to a full-time salaried service*'.[20] Conclusive evidence? Against this it has to be said that, both in Cabinet and in the Commons, Bevan was covering himself against the charge that he had betrayed Labour's long-agreed policy. It was an obvious gesture to his party critics to suggest that he was not closing the door to a salaried service for all time. But he committed himself unequivocally to the importance of retaining capitation fees as the predominant mode of payment for the foreseeable future: there was no question of full-time salaries in the present Bill. That perhaps should have been enough for the BMA. But that single off-the-cuff remark gave them the pretext they needed to keep up a strident campaign, even after the Act had

---

* His assumption was of course that the State service, once it got into its stride, would naturally provide a *better* standard of service than private enterprise could hope to offer, leaving private medicine to cater only for a small and eccentric fringe. His failure to foresee the survival and steady expansion of private practice was due to inability to imagine the financial constraints under which the NHS would increasingly have to operate. This in turn reflected the confidence which lay at the heart of Bevan's socialism that in all spheres – in health and housing as in industry – collective organisation must inevitably by the natural process of evolution come to predominate over individualism.

passed through both Houses of Parliament and received the Royal Assent in November 1946, to whittle away even Bevan's 'basic salary' to almost nothing.

This final stage of the battle lasted eighteen months, through the whole of 1947 right up to within a few weeks of the 'Appointed Day' – 5 July 1948 – on which the NHS was due to come into being. During this period it was Bevan who was obliged to make concession after concession to the doctors while the BMA boasted that it was giving not an inch. Now that he had got his Act on the statute book Bevan had no objection to negotiating matters of administrative detail – which was all the points in contention amounted to. His need now was to persuade the doctors to work the Act: it was his turn to complain that the BMA would not negotiate.[21] They niggled about such matters as the precise legal standing of partnerships (which Bevan agreed to clear up); the right to appeal from the proposed disciplinary tribunal to the High Court (which Bevan insisted was constitutionally impossible, pointing out that the new tribunal gave dismissed doctors far more safeguards than they enjoyed at present under NHI); and the claim of all GPs, whether obstetrically qualified or not, to attend their own midwifery cases in hospital (which was conceded). They successfully squeezed the basic salary step by step until eventually it was to be paid only to new doctors in their first three years if it was specifically approved in cases of exceptional need by the local (doctor-dominated) Executive Council.[22] Yet with all this they continued to claim that the freedom of the profession was under frontal attack and refused to moderate in the slightest degree their opposition to an Act 'so grossly at variance with the essential principles of our profession'.[23] In its strenuous propaganda the BMA did not scruple to employ blatant untruths. To the Cabinet in January 1948, reporting what he called 'an attempt not merely to seek detailed improvements of the Act but completely to sabotage it and prevent it coming into operation', Bevan quoted Dr Charles Hill, the BMA's Secretary and leading campaigner, on a newsreel film being shown at meetings around the country, describing the position of a doctor under the Act as 'a salaried officer of the State' and playing shamelessly on the baseless suggestion that patients would not be able to choose – or trust – their own doctor. 'There is something personal in medicine,' Hill intoned, 'something in the doctor –patient relationship, something private and confidential, which is essential to good medicine. Break into that, make the doctor not your doctor but the State's doctor; no longer your friend, your advocate, and you will have done something to medicine that it will be impossible to repair.'[24] Coming from the spokesman of a profession which was still insisting on its freedom to buy and sell practices, this was rich. More important it was nonsense, and it would still have been nonsense if the salaried element of doctors' pay had been much larger. Yet it was effective. By the beginning of 1948 there seemed to be a serious danger that the doctors might succeed in delaying the 'Appointed Day'.

In Cabinet, Bevan was firm. A majority of doctors might vote in the BMA's plebiscite against taking part in the service. But he gave his colleagues a shrewd assessment of the realities behind the smokescreen:

> That does not mean that they will not, as individuals, take part in it. If we keep firmly to our appointed day, those who do not take part will
> (a) lose their present panel income
> (b) lose their right to share in the £66,000,000 compensation when they later come in
> (c) lose all right to have any private patient in any pay-bed in any hospital.

'They could only succeed', Bevan wrote, 'if they were to push us off our "appointed day" and delay the whole service'; and that was something the Cabinet could not consider – 'unless we want it to be known that a sectional group have succeeded, in their own words, in "rejecting" an Act of the present Parliament'.[25] Though Morrison and one or two other Ministers were privately critical of Bevan's handling of the doctors and not unhappy to see him in difficulties, this was an appeal which the Cabinet could not fail to back.

At the beginning of February, therefore, the Government took the unusual step of tabling a motion in the House of Commons noting the 'Appointed Day', welcoming the NHS and expressing satisfaction that the conditions offered to all professions were generous and fair. This was an aggressive gesture clearly intended to assert the will of the country, expose the BMA and force the Tories off the fence. After months of discretion Bevan, opening the debate, went straight on to the offensive. It was clearly not that he was provoked in the course of debate into using language he had not intended. In his very first sentences he attacked the 'small body of spokesmen who have consistently misled the great profession to which they are supposed to belong' and distinguished between 'the hard-working doctors who have little or no time to give to these matters and the small body of raucous-voiced people who are alleged to represent the profession as a whole'. 'From the very beginning,' he asserted, 'this small body of politically poisoned people have decided to fight the Health Act itself and to stir up as much emotion as they can in the profession.' And he cited as another 'modest' example a letter to the *Scotsman* which claimed that the 'State Medical Service Act' had vested 'totalitarian' powers in the Minister:

> Stripped of the goodwill of his practice, subjected to 'negative' direction,* denied the right of appeal to a court of law against dismissal from service and salaried from Whitehall – such is the lot of the physician in the Socialist future. In brigand-like fashion this would-be Fuehrer points an economic pistol at the doctor's head and blandly explains 'Yours is a free choice – to enter the service or not to enter it.'

* This was a particularly artful piece of propaganda. 'Negative direction' meant that doctors could be refused – by a professional committee – permission to set up practice in an already over-doctored area. Had there been any suggestion of 'positive direction' into areas not of the doctor's own choice, they might have had something to complain of. But 'negative direction' *sounds* worse.

Cleverly Bevan deflected criticism of himself by recalling that the BMA leaders had found Brown and Willink no more acceptable: they had set themselves successively against every Minister and all proposals. It was in fact Brown, in 1943, who had proposed full-time salaries: 'And I rejected it,' Bevan recalled. 'I thought it contained too much of the element of regimentation.' One by one he dealt with the BMA's remaining demands, and demonstrated how much had already been conceded them (in the process admitting for the first time the 'very grave danger' of a two-tier service inherent in pay beds 'unless properly controlled'). He taunted the Tories with their uncertainty whether to support or oppose the Bill; and after another denunciation of a 'squalid political conspiracy' he repeated his constitutional objection to the 'organised sabotage of an Act of Parliament'. 'We have not yet made BMA House into another revising Chamber. We have never accepted the position that this House can be dictated to by any section of the Community.'[26]

Intentionally or not, this speech only raised the temperature. It played into the hands of 'Rab' Butler's reply, which criticised Bevan's 'inept' handling of the dispute, contrasted his 'thunder and lightning' method with his own dealings with the teachers over the 1944 Education Act (though in fact the teachers as a profession were never consulted with the deference accorded to the doctors between 1942 and 1948), and claimed that all that was needed was for the Government to show a little goodwill and sensitivity to the doctors' reasonable fears.[27] Bevan's truculence on this occasion was widely held to have been both unhelpful and characteristic. *The Lancet*, which had in the past shown more sympathy with him than with the BMA, now criticised his 'preference for strife';[28] and his apparent attempt to bully the doctors in the middle of their plebiscite has usually been blamed for their overwhelming vote against the Act, by a margin of nearly 8–1.[29] Exultantly the *BMJ* hailed this result as proving that the ordinary doctors were behind their leaders and 'how ill-timed, inept and untrue were his [Bevan's] vicious remarks about raucous-voiced and politically poisoned people'.[30] More astute, however, was the SMA leader, Dr Aleck Bourne, who wrote, exactly as Bevan had told the Cabinet, that the plebiscite was 'worthless' as an indicator of what individual doctors would do on 5 July.[31] A truer barometer was the poor response to the BMA's appeal for a 'fighting fund' to finance the continuation of their campaign.

Neither Bevan nor Hawton, John Pater has written, 'was in any doubt that in the end the profession would join the service, as it had done in 1912, but both recognized that at the right tactical moment some concessions would have to be made to encourage them to do so'.[32] That moment came at the beginning of April. Bevan had always said that the months after the plebiscite would be the hardest time for the BMA leaders to keep their men solid. Now, by arrangement with Moran, he unveiled his last compromise. In an open letter to Bevan, the Presidents of the three Royal Colleges proposed an

Amending Bill to allay the doctors' last fears of full-time salary by providing that no such change in the conditions of their employment could be introduced by regulation under the 1946 Act, but only by new legislation. Bevan's immediate acceptance of this suggestion is clear evidence of collusion; throughout the dispute with the BMA, his relations with the Royal Colleges had remained excellent. Although Dr Guy Dain of the BMA promptly denied that such a concession would be enough to meet the doctors' case, this was in fact the beginning of the end. A second plebiscite in May showed insufficient support to keep up the fight. Though the leaders declared themselves deeply disappointed, the *BMJ* gave the game away by congratulating the profession on the series of gains that it claimed had been wrung from successive Ministers.[33] Most of these were in fact imaginary, but that had been the BMA's strategy all along: to cry 'wolf' when there was no wolf there in order to repel a small number of mice. It was quite consistent now to pretend that the wolf had been seen off. The BMA at least avoided a repetition of 1912, when the leaders had been left high and dry by their members' decision to join the NHI scheme: this time, as individual doctors flocked to join up, the BMA declared itself content and on the 'Appointed Day' attempted to take for itself as much as possible of the credit for the new Service.

Paradoxically, of course, it was entitled to do so: for it was arguably more responsible than any other body for the final shape and limitations of the NHS. It was, after all, the doctors' rejection of the Ministry of Health's original ideas, based on local authority health centres linked to local authority hospitals, which had created by 1945 the deadlock from which Bevan escaped by nationalising the hospitals while leaving the general practitioner service, as the general practitioners wanted, essentially undisturbed. All the most fundamental criticisms, made at the time and since, of the structure of the NHS as set up in 1948 can be traced back to the decision not to base the service on the local authorities. The various medical services, it is argued, were *fragmented* instead of unified, and the gulf between the GPs and the hospitals widened instead of closed; there was no provision for *preventive* medicine, only treatment; there was inadequate *financial* discipline, and no *democratic* control below the power ultimately vested in the Minister. All these things are true. In retrospect the case for the local authorities can be made to look formidable, the decision to dispossess them a fateful mistake by a Minister ideologically disposed to centralisation and seduced by the claims of professional expertise. But the fact is that the local authority option was not a practical possibility in 1945. There was, for one thing, great force in Bevan's insistence that without local government reorganisation, which was on the Government's agenda but well down the list, the existing structure of local authorities, unevenly distributed between rich and poor areas, town and country, offered too haphazard and patchy a network on which to base an equitable national service. More important, however, it was politically a non-starter because the doctors would not have it: the GPs would not accept

177

local authority health centres and the top consultants would not accept local authority hospitals. The verbal skirmish Bevan had with the BMA was as nothing to the battle he would have had with both branches of the profession had he tried to impose the full SMA-model Health Service. That he chose not to try stands to his credit as political realism. He chose instead to make a virtue of his relative impotence and to stress the positive aspect of what he could deliver, which was a lot: a comprehensive, universal and above all free service which, for all its faults and subsequent difficulties, became a source of pride to all parties for the next thirty years.

Bevan's primary achievement, which no amount of criticism can take away from him, is that he was the Minister who set the Service up; after years of talking, it fell to him to take the key decisions, draft and carry the Bill through Parliament and administer the immense job of creating the machinery and appointing all the necessary Boards and committees to run it. This, as a new Minister with no previous experience, he did with remarkable efficiency and flair. He delivered the new Service to the nation. His secondary achievement, however, was to contrive the appearance of a political triumph for his party when in fact he had enacted virtually none of the cherished nostrums of those in the Labour Party who had cared about health. 'His outstanding success', one of his critics wryly noted, 'was the way he applied the anaesthetic to supporters on his own side, making them believe in things they had opposed almost all their lives.'[34] To do this it can be argued that he *needed* the public row with the BMA. Bevan was much criticised at the time for his handling of the BMA: it was alleged that his initial refusal to negotiate, his unnecessarily abrasive manner and his insistence on retaining some element of basic salary antagonised the doctors where a more emollient Minister would have brought them along with no trouble. Given the BMA's record of resistance to previous Ministers and the essential spuriousness of their violent opposition to Bevan, this must be very doubtful; nothing he could have said or done would have pleased them. At the same time it was politically useful to Bevan that they did make such a fuss: his supporters would have been a great deal more restive if they had not, and his glory as the architect of Labour's crowning achievement much less if the Tories had not felt obliged by the BMA to oppose it. This was something from which he was determined to make as much party capital as possible. When Attlee proposed to make a statesmanlike broadcast describing the Health Service and the other provisions of the Welfare State as national achievements to which all parties had contributed, Bevan protested strongly. 'The Conservatives voted against the National Health Act not only on the Second but on the Third Reading', he wrote. 'I do not see why we should forget this.'[35] The evening before the Service finally came into operation he deliberately punctured Attlee's atmosphere of mutual congratulation by making his notorious, never-to-be-forgiven speech at Manchester characterising the Tories as 'lower than vermin'.[36] It seems clear that Bevan privately welcomed, if he did not positively encourage, the BMA's help in making the NHS appear a more socialist measure than it really was.

For the most part the leaders of the SMA fell in with the general mood, swallowed their criticisms and hailed the NHS as their own. But the one idea that in 1948 they still hoped had been saved from the wreck of their original vision was the concept of the health centre. Throughout the passage of the legislation, both in the wording of the Bill and in his exposition of it, Bevan had laid great stress on the importance attached to health centres; their provision would be a *duty* on the local authorities, and though of course no doctor would be obliged to work in them, their development would be 'encouraged in every possible way'.[37] In time, it was still possible for the SMA to believe, the health centres would be the means of reforming the GP service, keeping alive the possibility of group practice and salaries, and overcoming the fragmentation of the NHS as a whole. In practice, however, as Bevan wearing his other hat as Minister of Housing knew only too well, there were no resources available for building centres; and in fact none were built until the 1960s. That is not the end of the matter, though; for it seems that lack of resources was only the cover for a reversal of departmental thinking which even in Bevan's time resulted in local authorities being *discouraged* from even planning centres. Harry Eckstein in his 1958 book on the NHS shows that Bevan in his capacity as Minister of Housing took no steps to reserve sites for health centres on new housing estates, even when pressed to do so; and quotes Bevan telling him that 'while he had always been in favour of group practice, he had never really believed Health Centres to be required'.[38] No one could have guessed that from his speeches in 1946, but it is probably true. The determining factor was that the Ministry, recognising that the profession would never willingly accept centres, had gone cold on them by 1948; in practice, too, centres seemed likely to be less convenient to the public than the local surgery. This was the most serious disappointment that Bevan inflicted on his Labour supporters, some of whom like Dr Stark Murray of the SMA never really forgave him.[39] It was here, they believed, in his failure to develop even a few health centres as a model for the future, rather than in the necessary compromises of 1946–8, that the possibility of a truly socialist health service slipped through his fingers.

But Bevan had never been committed to the doctrinaire SMA prescription. His idea of socialised medicine centred rather on the two principles of universality and free treatment – the extension on a national scale of the rights offered by the Tredegar Medical Aid Society in his youth. How the treatment was delivered he was content to regard as a matter of administration which he was not prepared to make a point of principle. In 1948 he had secured most of what he wanted from a national health service. Though the NHS became for him the symbol of the Government's commitment to socialism, he was actually much less doctrinaire on health than he was on housing.

*

5 July 1948 marked the end of Bevan's creative period at the Ministry of Health. Now his real problems began. For the coming into operation of the NHS immediately exposed a miscalculation so fundamental that it virtually negated the central assumptions on which the Service had been set up. With hindsight it is so obvious that it is difficult to reconstruct the frame of mind that made it possible. Yet the fact is that the planners of the Health Service – not merely Bevan but, more extraordinarily, all the officials of the Ministry who had been responsible for working out the different administrative models over the past six years – comprehensively underestimated what it was going to cost. They simply projected forward the amounts estimated to have been spent on health care before the war: indeed they actually expected that the cost of the Service would grow *less* as the population got healthier. They not only left out of account the vast amount of illness and disability that had gone untreated before and during the war (though meeting that need was a large part of the point of the new Service); they entirely failed to foresee that, far from declining, the demand for treatment, once freed from financial constraint, would prove literally infinite, and the capacity of the medical profession to devise expensive new treatments scarcely less. Inconceivable though it seems, even the Treasury failed to spot the fact that it was being asked to underwrite an open-ended commitment. Neither did the Opposition: the financing of the Service was not an issue at any stage of the debate over Bevan's Bill. Yet within a few months the Service was plunged into a crisis which seemed to threaten the very conception of the NHS as all parties had hitherto understood and accepted it. For the remaining two and a half years of his tenure of the office, Bevan found himself thrown on to the defensive, obliged to keep coming back to the Cabinet for supplementary estimates at a time of severe financial stringency when every other Department was facing cuts, fighting his colleagues to defend his 'baby' and eventually fighting for his political life for what had not previously been a matter of controversy. From 1948 salaries, private practice and health centres were forgotten issues. With startling suddenness the principle of preserving a free health service became the touchstone of the Government's commitment to socialism.

As early as 13 December 1948 Bevan had to tell the Cabinet that the estimate for the first nine months of the new Service – £176 million – was going to be exceeded by nearly £50 million. He presented this, legitimately, as the price of success. 'The start has been quick and good,' he claimed. Ninety-five per cent of the population had already enrolled, as well as 18,000 doctors, 8,750 dentists, 14,000 chemists and 6,500 opticians. People were seeking dental treatment at a rate of eight and a half million in a full year, and glasses at a rate of eight million a year. 'The rush for spectacles, as for dental treatment', he confessed, 'has exceeded all expectations. ... Part of what has happened has been a natural first flush of the new scheme, with the feeling that everything is free now and it does not matter what is charged up to the

Exchequer.' But he was at pains to play this down. 'There is also, without doubt, a sheer increase due to people getting things they need but could not afford before, and this the scheme intended.' The biggest single reason for the underestimate was the £150 million paid to medical personnel: the dentists, specialists and nurses had all received large increases, and the dentists in particular were being overpaid due to a miscalculation of how long they would need to treat each patient.[40]

In February 1949 the Conservatives tried to make capital out of the Government's embarrassment. Churchill solemnly alleged mismanagement of the national finances 'without precedent in time of peace'.[41] But Bevan was not embarrassed; in the Commons he trounced the Opposition (Churchill did not even attend) by daring them to vote against the extra £50 million. 'Is it the arithmetic that they quarrel about', he demanded, 'or the policy?' The estimates for the first year could only be a guess: the error was a reflection of success, due to more doctors and dentists than expected joining from the start. 'If they had not come in,' Bevan claimed, 'I would not have had a deficit: I would have had a surplus, and I would then be praised by the Opposition for being a financial success and a failure as Minister of Health.' The Tories, he taunted, should stop being so sour. 'Pale and miserable lot, instead of welcoming every increase in the health of the nation ... they groan at it. They hate it because they think it spells electoral defeat.'[42] As he had done before, he was determined to saddle them with their opposition to the NHS itself. When the vote was called at the end of the debate the Government supporters happily roared 'Aye'; but there was no answering 'No' from the Tories, just a second's silence before the Labour benches exploded in derision. Collapse of Opposition; first round to Bevan.

Only three months later, however, he was having to warn the Cabinet that he would be needing a supplementary estimate for 1949–50 as well. He claimed that the first rush of pent-up demand for false teeth and spectacles was tailing off, but insisted that 'the genuine need for these services was, and is, much greater than anyone knew'. The Cabinet had to face the fact 'that unless we are to deprive people of services they genuinely require we cannot expect the cost of the service to be as low as we had hoped'.[43] In the beleaguered economic climate of 1949 the Cabinet was reluctant to accept any such thing. Bevan emphasised that his Department was trying in every possible way to restrain costs, and in particular was placing a limit on dentists' earnings. He insisted that administration took only 2.1 per cent of the cost of the Service; but this was the trouble. The major expenditure was outside the Department's control: the initiative lay with the patients who sought treatment and the doctors who, in their untrammelled professional judgement, prescribed it, whether by hospitalisation or by drugs. Moreover, as Morrison had warned at the outset, the Regional Hospital Boards and Hospital Management Committees were subject to no clear financial discipline: Bevan's 'new developments in the techniques of government' had not yet materialised. Nevertheless Bevan had at this stage a sympathetic ally in the Chancellor of the Exchequer, his old mentor Cripps (who had succeeded Dalton in 1947'. While asserting that supplementary estimates 'should not yet be accepted in principle' while the search for economies went on, Cripps agreed that there should be no question of cutting services.[44]

The obvious alternative was to maintain the services by making them to some small degree self-supporting; in other words by making charges, either for prescriptions or for the 'hotel' cost of staying in hospital. From the moment the possibility was first raised, Bevan set his face against it. 'The imposition of a charge', he told the Cabinet in May 1949, 'would greatly reduce the prestige of the service, and the need to waive it in necessitous cases would introduce many complications and an expensive administration.'[45] The latter was indeed a serious consideration: the sums that could be recovered by a charge were always going to be small. But the first reason, Bevan's characteristic concern for the 'prestige' of the Service, shows that he already saw the argument as a matter of socialist symbolism rather than of figures. He was continually holding up the NHS as a model which he liked to imagine that the socialist parties of the world were watching with admiration and bated breath. He was also convinced, of course, that it was a vote-winner for Labour at home. Conversely, however, those of his colleagues, headed by Morrison, who believed that NHS spending was out of control feared that the impression of extravagance was a vote-loser and came to believe that it would never be brought under control until charges were imposed. To them, too, the figures were secondary. Charges became a symbol for both parties.

The issue came to a head in October, following a serious sterling crisis over the summer culminating in devaluation. In order to take advantage of devaluation and restore the balance of payments, Cripps needed yet another swingeing package of expenditure cuts from all Departments, and though he was still remarkably accommodating to Bevan, the Health Service could not expect to escape completely. Bevan did his best, in public as well as in private, to deflect the Chancellor's axe. At a party rally in Staffordshire in September, the week after devaluation, he announced defiantly: 'I have made up my mind that the health service is not going to be touched, and there is no disposition by the Government to touch it. The Government have made up their mind to solve their problems without raiding the social services, and the health service is sacrosanct.'[46] This was, in the literal sense he plainly intended, quite untrue; moreover such a shameless attempt by a spending Minister to pre-empt Cabinet decisions was bound to infuriate his colleagues. After heated arguments in the Economic Policy Committee of the Cabinet Bevan was compelled to back down: his threats to resign rather than accept charges cut no ice with a Chancellor who was adamant that he must have the cuts he demanded or resign himself.[47] For Bevan, this was no moment for a useless gesture. Accordingly Attlee, recommending Cripps's package to the Cabinet on 20 October, could put into his mouth words that were far from his real feelings:

> In the case of drug prescriptions, the Minister of Health is of opinion that it would be beneficial to the efficiency of the scheme if a flat rate charge were imposed which would have substantial effect in eliminating unnecessary resort to prescriptions and the Committee recommend that a charge of one shilling should be made for each prescription.

This was expected to yield £10 million a year.[48]

Bevan's acceptance of prescription charges at the hands of Cripps in 1949 was widely remembered against him two years later when he did resign rather than accept the charges on false teeth and spectacles imposed by Hugh Gaitskell. So how did he square his conscience on this occasion? Of course the difference in his relationship with the two Chancellors – his long-standing respect for Cripps and his contempt for Gaitskell – was an important factor: in 1949 he still retained a faith in the efficacy of the Government as an instrument for advancing socialism which he had largely lost by 1951. More narrowly than this, though, Bevan was persuaded to agree to this breach of the principle of free treatment in 1949 on two significant conditions – or rather one explicit condition and one understanding. The condition, accepted by the Cabinet on 21 October, was that old age pensioners would be exempt from charges.[49] This, Bevan calculated, would take £4 million from the anticipated £10 million saving straight away: he undoubtedly hoped that the expense of administering this and possibly other exemptions (for instance for the chronic sick, or diabetics) would convince the Chancellor that the damage to the symbol of a free service would not be worth the candle-ends that would be collected. The understanding was intended, by Bevan at least, to have the same result. Charges were to be presented as a response to abuse, that is to *protect* the Service, not as a revenue-raising exercise intended to undermine the principle of the free Service by making patients pay. This was the line taken both by Attlee, announcing the shilling charge in the Commons on 24 October, and by Bevan himself. 'The purpose', Attlee declared, 'is to reduce excessive and in some cases unnecessary resort to doctors and chemists, of which there is evidence which has for some time troubled my right hon. friend the Minister of Health. ... The resultant saving will contribute about £10 million, *although this is not the primary purpose of the charge.*'[50] The importance of this qualification for Bevan cannot be exaggerated. Once he had settled on this for him rather surprising theme – echoing and thereby confirming the alarmist stories of the Tory press – Bevan warmed to it in characteristically vivid language. 'Now that we have got the National Health Service based on free prescriptions,' he told Indian students in London in a phrase that was to be picked up and quoted against him, 'I shudder to think of the cascade of medicine which is pouring down British throats at the present time. I wish I could believe that its efficiency was equal to the credulity with which it is being swallowed.'[51] Undoubtedly, as part of his effort to control NHS spending, he was anxious to reduce the drugs bill; but he thought more in terms of controlling the drug companies and requiring doctors to prescribe generic instead of proprietary drugs than of charging patients. Here again his calculation was that charges would be unnecessary as well as administratively unworkable. He agreed to the inclusion of a power to impose charges in the National Health Service (Amendment) Bill – the Bill promised to the doctors in 1948 – in the expectation that it would never have to be used. He was at pains to present it as a reserve power, the very threat of which should be sufficient to discourage abuse.

By the time he came to defend the new clause in the House of Commons on 9 December he had practically talked it out of existence. 'It is quite incorrect to say that it was the purely financial aspect of this matter that weighed most with me when I accepted this tentative proposal.' Had it been a revenue-raising measure, he argued, the Government would have imposed charges over the whole of the Health Service. He claimed that the proposed charge would not really breach the principle of a free health service at all, since the patient would only pay the first shilling and it would be free after that! The lack of outcry at the announcement showed that there was public recognition of an abuse needing to be curbed. There was no need to worry, he assured his supporters, 'because I am as deeply concerned with maintaining the Socialist approach to this service as anyone on this side of the House'.

> Therefore, as far as I am concerned, this is put forward only for the purpose of temporary easement, if it be practicable, and there will then be a residual financial advantage, the extent of which no one knows, because we do not yet know what the exemptions will be. What is practically certain is that the figure of £10 million was based on the assumption that there would be no exemptions, and that any exemptions will reduce that amount.

'What we are considering', he concluded, the threat becoming more and more remote with every word, 'is not a considerable retreat from the position we have taken up, but merely a mitigation of the burden which has fallen on the general practitioner service at the present time. . . . I am convinced that, as the Service develops, there will be a growing sense of responsibility, and that discipline of this sort will not be necessary in the service as a whole.' Did this mean, he was asked, that if it proved unnecessary he would not introduce the charge at all? 'Certainly,' he replied. 'As I have said, I am not anxious to burden myself with a complicated administrative machine if I can achieve the same results by other means.'[52] So successfully did he appease his possible critics that only one Labour Member voted with the Liberals and a handful of Independents against the clause: ten future Bevanites, including Jennie Lee and Ian Mikardo, voted for it.

Quite accurately, the Tory who followed Bevan accused him of 'wriggling out' of Attlee's initially firm commitment to save £10 million.[53] In the short term it was undoubtedly a brilliant political performance. Prescription charges might be on the statute book, but Bevan believed that he had ensured that they would never actually be imposed. If necessary, he lived to fight another day; but he probably thought that he had won. One of his primary purposes had been to ensure that there should be no dilution of the Health Service before the General Election (which he would have liked to have seen held that autumn). Once Labour was safely returned, as he had no doubt it would be, its socialist vigour would be renewed and the Health Service would be assured of another five years to settle down and prove itself with no more of these niggling threats. He himself publicly anticipated removal to another Department (it was 'practically certain', he told a medical dinner in November, 'that my period in office at the Ministry of Health is almost ended')[54] and did not appear to fear for the safety of the NHS in other hands. It was a profound miscalculation on all three levels. Labour was returned in February 1950 only by a whisker; he himself was not moved from the Ministry of Health; and the most serious threats to the free Health Service were yet to come.

Chapter 13

Bevan in the Attlee Cabinet

Bevan was always something of an outsider in the 1945 Cabinet. Of course he had been in the Labour Party all his life, had known most of his colleagues intimately in the House of Commons for the past fifteen years and now deserved his chance in government as much as any of them. But he had deliberately cast himself as a rebel in the thirties and still more so during the war, when all the senior figures in the party, even including Cripps, had been in the Government while he assailed them mercilessly from below the gangway. They were now experienced, hardened Ministers, he an irresponsible tyro. Bevan, of course, had never lacked confidence either in himself or in his class and the socialist ideas he felt he stood for. He had strong views about everything and could never be prevented from arguing them. He was, from the outset, one of the most talkative members of the Cabinet, aware of being one of only two or three left-wingers with a responsibility to put the left-wing view. Nevertheless his role in the first years after 1945 was not in any respect a disruptive one. He recognised that he was the most junior member of the Cabinet, despite the political importance of his office, and he had no complaint about that. Though he put his oar in freely, he was too fully occupied in his own double department to have much time for sustained involvement in the wider issues facing the Government. Above all, he was perfectly content with the general conduct and direction of the Government which was doing all, certainly at home and to a great extent abroad, that he could have hoped a Labour Government would do in its first years. The dawn, in 1945–7, was still bright, even though the economic weather was already rough.

The Government was overwhelmingly dominated by its five leading figures, three of whom – Bevin, Morrison and Dalton – had been for years Bevan's avowed political opponents, only one – Cripps – his friend. The fifth was the Prime Minister, the apparently insignificant little man who amazed everyone by the skill with which he handled his powerful and mettlesome colleagues. Bevan had acquired a certain respect for Attlee during the thirties and had almost certainly voted for him over Morrison in 1935. Even so in

1945 he was one of those, with Cripps, who thought him too meek a personality to lead Labour in government and surprisingly supported Morrison's brief, vain attempt to reopen the leadership question before Attlee went to the Palace.[1] (Attlee, backed by Bevin, showed his steel by simply ignoring Morrison.) Thereafter Bevan's respect for Attlee grew again, as Attlee first gave him office, then backed him on several critical occasions in Cabinet against Morrison (most notably on his hospital scheme which he could never have carried without the Prime Minister's quiet support, but also at several points on housing) and, more generally, showed himself punctilious in implementing Labour's socialist programme. 'Dear Clem,' he was moved to write after Attlee had attempted to explain Labour to the two Houses of the US Congress in November 1945, 'That was a noble speech. I felt very proud.'[2] Over the next six years his view of Attlee veered between exasperation and respect. For his part Attlee is said to have looked on Bevan as a wayward pupil of great promise who might make a brilliant leader if he could only control himself;[3] against this it has to be said that if this were so, he did not do all he might have over the next few years to bring him on.

Attlee's favour did, however, serve to shield Bevan from Morrison and Bevin. These two, fortunately for Bevan, loathed one another even more than they loathed him, so there was little danger of their combining against him, especially since Attlee had so constructed his Government as to keep them effectively apart, Bevin at the Foreign Office, Morrison overlord of the home front.* With Bevin, after their bruising encounters before and during the war, Bevan had surprisingly few quarrels between 1945 and 1951. He differed at a number of points from Bevin's foreign policy, most seriously over Palestine: but he did not dissent from the central thrust of Bevin's policy towards the USSR nor from the foundation of NATO. Of course he derided Bevin's heavyweight style on occasion: 'He's a big bumble bee caught in a web and he thinks he's the spider,' he once told Dalton.[4] Nevertheless he respected the massive strength of Bevin's personality, and he could not but take some pleasure in the spectacle of this rough working man ruling the Foreign Office and speaking for Britain before the world. Bevin's might not be a 'socialist' foreign policy but he was the living proof that the working class had taken power. Bevin, meanwhile, had acquired an increased regard for his 'namesake' and seems to have taken some care not to provoke him.[5]

With Morrison Bevan could not help but clash throughout the life of the Government, with mounting bitterness and ultimately catastrophic result. As Deputy Prime Minister, Lord President and Leader of the House of Commons, Morrison was given a complete overview of domestic policy. He

---

* There are conflicting accounts of whether it was of Bevan or Morrison that Bevin made his famous retort, when someone remarked that one of them – whichever it was – was his own worst enemy, 'Not while I'm alive he ain't.' But surely it must have been Bevan. No one would ever have described Morrison as his own worst enemy, whereas it was constantly being said of Bevan. But the remark probably dated from before 1945.

was by nature a wirepuller who liked to know everything that was going on; he was also intensely jealous of Attlee, ambitious for himself, saw intrigues everywhere and loathed intellectuals who thought fancy ideas a substitute for organisation and hard work. Bevan he regarded as the epitome of this type: at the same time – the pot calling the kettle black – he believed him to be consumed with personal ambition. He used to carry around in his wallet a cutting of the wartime speech in which Bevan had jokingly described himself pursuing the coat-tails of power from the Town Council to the County Council to Parliament, and would show it to anyone at a moment's notice.[6] There was a deep feud here, fully though less obsessively reciprocated by Bevan, which makes it remarkable that Bevan was briefly prepared to prefer Morrison to Attlee as Prime Minister. The reason can only be that he at least recognised Morrison as an energetic executive, which he doubted that Attlee was. Once the Government was formed, however, it soon seemed that over the whole field of policy Morrison stood in Bevan's way. On hospital re-organisation Morrison, as the champion of local government, was almost bound to oppose Bevan; but it was the same on housing where the same consideration might have been expected to range the Lord President on Bevan's side. Later they collided over steel nationalisation and increasingly over the whole future direction and purpose of the Government. Bevan came to see Morrison as a brake on progress towards socialism and Morrison to perceive Bevan first as an electoral liability, then as his most dangerous rival for Attlee's succession.

Dalton was an old opponent from the thirties, too: the principal proponent of the rearmament which Bevan had so strenuously denounced. But here the antagonism had not been so personal, and in Government Bevan and Dalton quickly formed a good working relationship. As Chancellor of the Exchequer, Dalton might have been expected to be an obstacle to a Minister of Health with an ambitious social programme; in fact the cost of the NHS did not become a problem until after Dalton had left the Treasury, nor was money the problem on the housing side. In the early days of the Government Dalton was Bevan's staunchest ally, happy to take over the whole funding of the hospitals, willing to hold down council house rents, proud to be the Chancellor who financed the Welfare State.[7] In May 1946 Dalton recorded in his diary an exchange which clearly set the seal on a new understanding. After a shouting match across the Cabinet table which Attlee had to intervene to stop, 'We both looked thunder at each other for about thirty seconds, and then grins broke through and I passed him a note saying "As half a real Welshman [Glamorgan] to a real half Welshman [Monmouth], we must allow for these poor Saxons' lack of understanding of our high-spirited natures"'. Bevan wrote back '"As one bastard to another I accept your apology."'[8] Thereafter, as Dalton's diary shows, they remained on good terms and in general agreement until near the end of the Government's life.

With Cripps, his old leader in the days of the Unity Campaign and the

Popular Front, Bevan's relations between 1945 and 1950 went rather the other way, though there remained a special bond of sympathy between them. Whereas Dalton moved somewhat to the left after the war, Cripps – while retaining his puritanical fervour – moved sharply to the right. Whereas Dalton was under the circumstances an astonishingly open-handed Chancellor, Cripps after 1947 became a byword for iron austerity – at just the moment when the true cost of the National Health Service was becoming apparent. Cripps was in fact more understanding towards Bevan's difficulties than probably any other Chancellor would have been – their old association still counted for a lot; even so he was obliged by 1949–50 to enforce strict limits on Bevan's spending on both health and housing, even to the extent of requiring Bevan to take power to impose prescription charges. Bevan felt betrayed by Cripps's determination on this score; nevertheless he accepted from his old mentor what he would not have taken from anyone else, and was certainly not prepared to take from Hugh Gaitskell. Cripps was still the only figure in the Labour leadership to whom Bevan looked up, the only one whose socialist convictions he could not impugn even when he was imposing a financial strait-jacket which squeezed the life out of socialist ambitions. Cripps was the one colleague who could restrain Bevan when he began to get restive around 1950; in this view it was no coincidence that Bevan finally kicked over the traces six months after Cripps retired.

With other members of the Cabinet Bevan had as little to do as possible. For the older trade union members like George Isaacs (Labour), Tom Williams (Agriculture) and George Tomlinson (Works, later Education) he had no time at all. As in the war, he was often bracketed with Manny Shinwell (initially Fuel and Power) as a troublesome left-winger, and the two of them were indeed frequently in the same corner – against the American Loan, in favour of an incomes policy, against Bevin's Palestine policy – until Shinwell was demoted to the War Office in 1947 and changed rapidly into a crusty right-winger. (He was already over sixty in 1945.) But even as rebels they had never had much in common. Two of his oldest friends, John Strachey and George Strauss, held important positions outside the Cabinet, Strachey as Minister of Food, Strauss (from 1947) as Minister of Supply; but both were now respectable middle-of-the-roaders and no longer his political allies. In truth Bevan had no political allies unless one counts the support he received from Cripps, Dalton and Attlee among the leadership and towards the end of the Government from the young Harold Wilson. Bevan was an outsider, who continued to choose his friends from outside the Government and to a considerable extent from outside politics altogether. He remained close to Michael Foot and his other old colleagues on *Tribune*, which continued to give him loyal support; but *Tribune* at this period was firmly loyal to the Government as a whole, and he was for the most part strict in giving them no privy information.* As a Cabinet Minister Bevan was always exceptionally jealous of constitutional proprieties:[9] although several of them were his personal friends he had no organised contact during the years of the Labour Government with the Keep Left group who became the nucleus of the later Bevanites. Even Jennie was left to pursue her own line as a sometimes dissident backbencher with little more guidance or counter-pressure from Nye than the rest of them. Away from government, Bevan really preferred to get away from politics entirely. At Cliveden Place he and Jennie continued to entertain a varied gallery of artists and actresses, writers and foreign journalists, while she jealously guarded his privacy from the intrusions of the press. No one ever took politics more seriously than Bevan: at the same time no one knew better that politics was merely one facet of a full life.

From the outset, then, Bevan was always a rather special Minister. Though junior, he did not confine his interventions to his own brief; admire, resent or loathe him, his colleagues could not ignore him or fail to recognise him as an exceptional personality in their midst. At forty-seven he was almost the only obviously coming man in that first elderly Cabinet that met in 1945: 'I feel pretty sure he will be Prime Minister one day,' wrote the leader of the generation behind, Hugh Gaitskell, who did not join the Cabinet until 1950.[10] For this reason, despite his initial juniority, his heavy departmental load and the hostility of Morrison, he was within a couple of years increasingly drawn into the Cabinet's inner circle. After 1947, when the economic planning machinery of the Government was restructured under Cripps, Bevan became a member both of the Economic Policy Committee and of the Production Committee where, in the words of Douglas Jay (now a Treasury Minister), 'the real work was done'.[11] From the middle of 1949, when Attlee began to consult his colleagues about the timing of the General Election, the group he chose to confide in comprised the Big Five plus the Chief Whip and Bevan.[12] Bevan was also centrally involved in considering the programme on which the election should be fought – another opportunity for conflict with Morrison. He owed this position, of course, to the fact that he regularly topped the constituencies' poll for the National Executive, by substantial margins over Morrison, Dalton and Jim Griffiths. As well as Minister of Health, Bevan was also quite self-consciously the principal representative in the Government of the Labour Party in the country.

This did not, however, at first, put him at odds with the Government. Right up to 1950 the Government continued to enjoy the enthusiastic support of the constituencies to an extent unknown in later Labour history; and Bevan broadly shared their satisfaction. On the home front particularly, as it pressed on immediately with its nationalisation programme, beginning with

* Foot became joint editor of *Tribune* in 1948.

the coal mines, it was fulfilling the central aspiration which had brought him into politics in the first place. Despite his long-held belief in direct parliamentary control, he made no recorded difficulty about the Morrisonian structure of nationalisation under an autonomous National Coal Board, nor did he object to the choice of a Welsh coal owner, Lord Hyndley, to head it; his only objection to the high level of compensation – criticised by some on the left – was that it should not be presented in such a way that the miners felt they were still working for the owners after all.[13] He was greatly impressed by the boost to production which he believed resulted from the miners' knowledge that they were no longer working for the owners but for the nation. 'The spiritual change among the miners themselves', he told the 1948 Party Conference, 'has already saved British industry.'[14] He had no patience with those in the party who immediately started finding fault with what had been achieved, such as railway workers who complained after nationalisation that nothing had changed. In 1949 and 1950 he insisted that nationalisation was only a start but nonetheless a tremendous start in which Labour should take pride. 'I speak as a trade unionist who has been fighting for this all my life, and I do not want to see it spoiled now because there are some people who cannot see the wood for the trees.'[15] The same fierce pride in the Labour Government led Bevan to take as strong a line as any right-winger towards dockers who struck against Cripps's wage freeze in 1948. 'It would be prudent to have wide powers to deal with any trouble that might arise if relations between troops and strikers become strained,' he urged the Cabinet's Emergencies Committee.[16] It was a matter of loyalty. With Labour's own Government in trouble he had no qualms about using troops against wreckers. With Shinwell, Bevan had consistently advocated an incomes policy on socialist grounds, believing planned wages to be a necessary part of a planned economy, long before the crisis of 1947 forced the unions reluctantly to accept control.[17] Indeed on socialist grounds he positively gloried in even the most unpopular aspects of the Government's egalitarianism, arguing for instance in July 1946 that bread rationing had 'raised the moral stature of the UK throughout the world'.[18] By such exalted criteria, Bevan had no doubt that Labour's Government was indeed a Socialist Government.

His attitude to the Government's foreign policy was somewhat more critical, but only at the margins. As much as Bevin, he took it for granted that Britain was and should remain a great power – not for power's sake, of course, but as an example to the world of the success of democratic socialism. Instinctively, it is true, he was better-disposed towards the Soviet Union and more suspicious of the United States than Bevin. On the one hand he had always been prepared to make allowances for the first workers' state and had made a big emotional commitment to Russia's claims as an ally during the war; on the other his ideological dislike of American capitalism was enhanced by a strong aesthetic prejudice derived from his revered Rodo.

Bevan would have dearly liked to see Britain charting an independent third course between the Superpowers – particularly taking the lead in fostering the growth of democracy in countries like Spain, Greece and Yugoslavia where the onset of the Cold War tended on the contrary to stifle it. But he clearly recognised the economic constraints on Britain's independence, was quickly cured of his lingering illusions about the Soviet Union by Stalin's brutality in Eastern Europe, and was soon convinced of the rightness and necessity of basing the defence of Western Europe in the Atlantic Alliance.

At the very beginning of the Government's life, Britain's financial dependence on the United States was sharply underlined when Congress voted to end Lend–Lease immediately and the new Government – regarded with the deepest ideological suspicion in Washington – was obliged to negotiate under unfavourable conditions a large loan to carry the country through the next few years. For several weeks the Cabinet agonised before swallowing this bitter pill, but Bevin, Dalton and Cripps insisted that there was no alternative and only Bevan and Shinwell ultimately held out for rejecting the American terms. These included the dismantling of tariffs and the early restoration of full convertibility between the pound and the dollar, which Shinwell and Bevan regarded as 'incompatible with the successful operation of a planned economy in this country'.[19] Bevan's wider concern was that the US was trying to draw Britain into supporting a world economic order based on nineteenth-century financial liberalism which the USSR would be unable to accept.[20] At this stage it was still the Americans whom he suspected of disrupting the wartime harmony of the Allies and from whom he was anxious for Britain to guard her independence. For this, he maintained later, the British people would in 1945 have been ready to make 'heroic sacrifices'.[21] Heroic they would have had to be: none of the Government's welfare programme would have been conceivable for many years. In the event, ironically, the Welfare State and Bevan's own National Health Service were made possible by an American loan which he had opposed. He may in truth have done so only for the record, knowing that the loan would be approved but anxious to make his protest (immediately leaked) against the grip of American capitalism. Thereafter he continued to urge greater economic independence of the US: for instance during the 1947 balance-of-payments crisis which followed the short-lived return to convertibility he argued in Cabinet that Britain should not approach the Americans as a suppliant but confront them with the fact that Britain's need to defend sterling against the dominance of the dollar restricted world trade and thus damaged the American economy too.[22] Always he was for expansion. But after December 1945 he accepted that Britain had not the economic strength to go it alone: in 1947 he recognised that 'heroic sacrifices' were not an option.

He was ungrudgingly grateful, therefore, for Marshall Aid, without which, he told the 1948 Conference, Britain would have had one and a half million people unemployed.[23] But of course he wanted to be independent of the need for such aid as quickly as possible, to which end he treated Conference to a tremendous oration on the need for higher production ('the Bridge to Socialism'). On the military front he seemed – until the Korean War began to get out of hand in 1950 – to have fewer doubts about the Americans than on the purely economic. This is an area on which he naturally said little in public; but he offered no opposition in Cabinet to the formation of NATO and there is no reason to think that he had any more reservations about it than any other member of the Government. *Tribune* itself in those days, after all, supported NATO warmly. Bevan had never been any sort of pacifist or neutralist; he abhorred the brutal empire into which the Soviet system had degenerated and had no sympathy with the fellow-travellers in the Parliamentary Labour Party who made excuses for it. (In 1949 he fully supported the expulsion of Konni Zilliacus and others from the party; he intervened on the NEC, characteristically, to second a procedural objection that Zilliacus should not be expelled without a hearing – doubtless he recalled his own expulsion in 1939 – but he did not dispute the sentence.)[24] After initial scepticism in 1946 ('Fears with regard to Russia seemed to be exaggerated. ... We must not allow Russian intransigence to drive us into an untenable position in foreign policy'),[25] he appeared to accept as readily as did practically everyone in all parties in the later 1940s the reality of a Soviet military threat to Western Europe: the second of three responsibilities which he laid on the Labour Party in 1950 (following building socialism at home and helping the underdeveloped world) was 'to protect our way of life against the possibility of armed attack'.[26] He had always argued strongly against the policy of trying to keep Germany divided and weak, believing it to be both impractical and politically mistaken. ('The attempt to prevent the creation of a central government in Germany would break down within a few years and would have provided meanwhile an effective stimulus to the growth of a neo-Fascist movement');[27] but by late 1948 he was urging a further reason for building Germany up as much as possible: 'They were a better barrier against Communism than the French.'[28] The West certainly felt the need of a barrier in 1948. In February the Russians engineered a coup in Czechoslovakia; in April there was a real fear, which Bevan shared, of the Communists gaining power in Italy;[29] and in June the Russians blockaded Berlin. Confronted with this latter challenge, no one was more hawkish than Bevan. Before the bold decision was taken to relieve the city by airlift, Bevan argued strongly for sending in tanks across the Soviet-occupied zone of Germany: a direct military response – the response also favoured by the American Commander in Europe, General Clay – which would have compelled the Russians to resist and could easily have led to war.[30] It was to offer a solid front against further Soviet adventurism that NATO was formed the following year, with the Americans – Bevin's great achievement – accepting a full share in the defence of Europe.

Bevan, then, though he began to distance himself from it after 1951, fully supported at the time the central anti-Soviet and pro-American thrust of Bevin's foreign policy. Had he been Foreign Secretary he might have given it a more socialist colouring at the edges; for instance, he would certainly have made more explicit his support for anti-colonial liberation movements in the Empire for which Bevin had little sympathy. He also strongly supported Dalton's attempts in 1947 to reduce Britain's overseas military commitments in order to reduce the burden of defence expenditure and protect domestic spending – attempts that were roughly vetoed by Bevin, with Attlee's support.[31] But he quarrelled seriously with Bevin in one area only: Palestine.

In Palestine Britain faced the intractable problem of extricating itself honourably from its League of Nations (now United Nations) mandate, of trying somehow to honour the 1917 Balfour Declaration and Labour's long-standing promises to the Jews without antagonising the Arabs. In 1946–7 Bevan, along with Shinwell, Strachey, Dalton and others in the Government and a large and vocal pressure group in the parliamentary party led by Richard Crossman, took up a strongly pro-Zionist position against Bevin's resolutely even-handed policy whose only effect was to antagonise both sides. Believing Bevin to have been subverted by the traditionally pro-Arab sympathies of the Foreign Office, they urged increased Jewish immigration and open support for a socialist, democratic State of Israel. For a time feelings on both sides ran very high. In February 1947 Bevan was talking of resignation unless Palestine were partitioned at once.[32] (He never threatened resignation on any other foreign policy matter.) By September, however, after months of Jewish terrorism, even he merely wanted to be rid of the whole problem, as Bevin was obliged to admit failure to achieve any sort of compromise.[33] The mandate was accordingly surrendered the following year, and the Jews were left to create their Zionist State by force of arms. Bevan always considered Bevin's policy wrongly conceived. 'He had always been doubtful', he told the Cabinet in 1949, whether Britain's position in the Middle East (whose strategic importance he did not question) 'should be maintained through support of the unstable and reactionary Governments of the Arab states. ... We should have done better to base our position in the Middle East on the friendship of the Jews who, if we had pursued a different policy, would have been glad to give us all the facilities we needed to establish strong military bases in Palestine.'[34]

Such a view reflected a generous admiration of the Jews, partly ideological, partly humanitarian following the revelation of the holocaust, which was widespread on the left after the war and indeed for thirty years thereafter. From the hard-headed strategic standpoint on which Bevan tried to argue it, however, it suffered from two glaring weaknesses. First, it entirely overlooked the importance to Britain of Arab oil: the Foreign Office had some reason for not wanting to quarrel with the sheiks. Second, in its one-sided sympathy for the Jewish desire for their national home, the Zionist view chose to disregard the claims of the Palestinian Arab population to the same territory. Bevin's attempted even-handedness seemed to many, perhaps most, members of the Labour Party in 1947 pig-headed, callous, reactionary – even anti-Semitic. Admittedly it achieved no settlement and led only to ignominious withdrawal, leaving the protagonists to fight it out. Nevertheless from the perspective of the 1980s Bevin's policy looks to have been based on a much shrewder appreciation of the realities on the ground than Bevan's.

There is one last matter to be mentioned in connection with the Labour Government's foreign policy, though here again it is a question of a dog that did not bark. It is practically certain that Bevan knew nothing of the decision taken in 1946 to go ahead and manufacture a British atom bomb: the decision was taken by a very small group of Ministers of whom he was not one.[35] It is possible that he learned of it some time over the next few years before it became public knowledge in 1952; certainly that is the implication, for what it is worth, of the 1962 recollections of George Strauss, who as Minister of Supply was in the secret from 1947. But there is no reason to think that Bevan would have raised any objection, either moral or military, if he had known; it is striking that he never made any retrospective protest even on constitutional grounds. On the major point, Strauss's account is quite consistent with Bevan's view of Britain's role in the world: even in later years when he was tempted to renounce the Bomb he remained liable to contradictory assertions that Britain must have it.

> Nye always held the view that Britain ought to be effectively armed. He always held the view in Government, when we were discussing the development of the atomic bomb, that Britain should have and must have the atomic bomb. As long as America had it, we must develop it too ... to be effectively independent, because his fear of being subservient to America was always in his mind. He wanted us to have a bomb too, to enable us to play a more useful part in world affairs.[36]

This was Bevin's view. It was Attlee's view. There is no reason to think that it was not, and every reason to think that it was, also Bevan's view.

5

The Promise Fades, 1947–1951

Chapter 14

First Doubts: 'Consolidation' and the 1950 Election

The issue over which Bevan's confidence in the Government began to crack was the proposed nationalisation of iron and steel. This had been included in Labour's programme as a result of the Mikardo resolution carried at Conference in 1944; but Herbert Morrison had been deeply opposed to it at the time, and several other Ministers, including Attlee, were unenthusiastic. So, not unimportantly, were the iron and steel trade unions. There was a general recognition that the industry was in need of reorganisation, probably Government-assisted; but nationalisation raised some sharp questions which had not arisen with the other industries on the Government's shopping list. Steel was the first manufacturing industry that the Government proposed to touch: the others had all been monopoly utility or extractive industries. Moreover it was one around which no neat boundary could be drawn: it involved many processes and impinged on numerous other industries (engineering, machine tools, etc.). This, for the advocates of nationalisation, was the whole point. As Dalton characteristically expressed it, 'We weren't really beginning our Socialist programme until we had gone past all the utility junk – such as transport and electricity – which were publicly owned in every capitalist country in the world. Practical Socialism ... only really began with Coal and Iron and Steel, and there was a strong political argument for breaking the power of a most dangerous body of capitalists.'[1] This was Bevan's view precisely. He had direct experience of the inadequacy of private enterprise in the chequered history of the Ebbw Vale steelworks in his own constituency. More important, he believed quite simply that steel was power and that if Labour was serious about taking the economic power of the country into public control steel must be in the front of the programme.[2] Of course the Tories and the industry would protest: that only showed that Labour was on the right track. Steel was the test of the Government's socialist intentions. He was shocked that there should be any question of backsliding.

In Cabinet Bevan was the most impassioned proponent of immediate nationalisation; but he did not have to fight this battle alone. Dalton and Cripps were with him, and probably a majority of Ministers, including

Bevin, recognised in principle that Labour had a manifesto commitment which it was bound to honour. Disagreement arose first over timing and then over whether it might be possible to take power to control the industry without going to the length of full public ownership. On timing, Dalton and Bevan won an early victory in April 1947 when, in Morrison's absence, the Cabinet determined to press on with steel, ahead of gas, in the 1947–8 session.[3] The draft Bill which the Minister of Supply, John Wilmot, produced, however, was a compromise measure which left the structure of the industry virtually intact. At the same time the mounting balance-of-payments crisis convinced Attlee and Bevin that it was not the moment to disrupt a key productive industry. Morrison, returned from illness, took over the task of patching up with the steel masters a formula which should give the Government the appearance of public control with little of the reality. Battle was now joined in earnest. In Cabinet on 24 July Bevan was 'strongly opposed to the compromise proposals' under which 'the real power would continue to reside in the [Iron and Steel Trades] Federation'. Not to proceed with full nationalisation in 1947–8, he argued, 'would dishearten and divide Government supporters'.

> He did not accept the view that the Government's programme of nationalisation should be brought to a standstill because the economic situation was difficult and he believed that if the Government, instead of strengthening the hands of the Iron and Steel Trades Federation by indicating that they might be prepared to compromise, were to press on with legislation to implement the scheme which they had already approved, the output of steel would not suffer.[4]

A week later he repeated this argument, maintaining that 'to attempt to justify a departure from the Cabinet's earlier decision on the ground that the economic conditions rendered it inopportune was a negation of the principles of the Party and was tantamount to an indefinite postponement of any real measure of socialisation'.[5] Moreover, Dalton recorded, 'he threatened to resign if we did not have the big Bill next Session'.[6]

Cripps thought this a mistake. 'One should not threaten resignation openly in the Cabinet,' he told Dalton, 'as this caused others also to harden their positions.'[6] But Bevan was 'playing a very individual hand on this'.[7] In uncompromising speeches at Blaenau Ffestiniog and Morpeth he took the issue to the country, 'nailing his trousers to the mast' as Dalton put it. He or those whom Dalton called his 'stooges' – evidence that on this issue he was, or at least was seen to be, making use of the Keep Left group – were also active in the parliamentary party, spreading the rumour of his resignation if the Cabinet weakened.[8] The result of a highly charged few days was in fact a compromise, but not Morrison's compromise, which was firmly rejected. While only Bevan, Strachey and Tomlinson stood out for immediate nationalisation, Dalton and Cripps rallied a majority of the Cabinet around a third option, reaffirming the Government's commitment to nationalisation but postponing it, in view of the economic situation, to 1948–9. This Bevan accepted, on condition that there should also be a Parliament Bill to curtail the power of the House of Lords to prevent it reaching the statute book before the General Election.[9]

This was a victory of principle, at least; but to Bevan it was a dismayingly hard battle over a point that should not have had to be fought over at all. In several ways it marked a watershed in his attitude to and role within the Government. Steel was the first issue outside his own Department on which he had taken the lead in Cabinet and gone out on a limb beyond his senior allies, Dalton and Cripps. It had firmly identified Morrison in his mind not merely as an interfering busybody but as a serious drag on the Government's advance towards socialism. At the same time he had given a glimpse, for the first time since joining the Government, of his own potential for causing trouble. 'It is clear that Bevan had hoped to bring something off and failed,' Hugh Gaitskell wrote in his dairy, quoting his patron Dalton to the effect that in the last week 'Bevan's head had swollen enormously.' Ignoring the fact that he had been substantially successful in reasserting the Government's commitment to nationalisation, Gaitskell believed that the failure of Bevan's attempt to 'stab his colleagues' would weaken his position in the Government: his bluff about resignation had been called and the Big Five 'can afford to be less frightened of him. This weakening is important,' Gaitskell wrote, 'because it will strengthen the hands of those who know that we must cut building and prob- ably housing if we are to get our exports up.'[10] Here the battle lines of the future are ominously foreshadowed.

But in fact it is far from clear that Gaitskell accurately reflected Dalton's view of the affair. For the Big Five were by no means as united as the somewhat green Parliamentary Secretary to the Ministry of Fuel and Power imagined, and certainly not united against Bevan. Dalton and Cripps, on the contrary, had come to the conclusion as a result of the coal and convertibility crises of 1947 that Attlee was after all too weak and lacking in leadership to continue as Prime Minister and should be replaced by Bevin. Bevan was not a prime mover in their plot, but he was very much a part of their calculations. It is not of much signifi- cance that as long ago as February he had spoken 'very contemptuously' of Attlee to Dalton;[11] but on the substantial grounds of their dissatisfaction with Attlee's direction of the Government – first their anxiety to reduce overseas defence commitments rather than social spending to make room for increased exports, and second, their disillusion with the Government's virtually non- existent economic planning machinery (Morrison's special responsibility) – the three of them were in complete agreement. Over steel, too, Cripps's only worry was that Bevan was getting out of line: there was no point in his resigning on his own. Cripps, Dalton noted on 8 August, 'was clearly thinking in terms of some new combination in which he and I and AB would be together'.[12] The particular post which Cripps had in mind for Bevan was Minister of Supply, with the specific job of pressing on with the nationalisation of steel.[13]

Cripps's and Dalton's purpose, then, despite proposing to make Bevin Prime Minister, was to move the Government sharply to the left. To stand any chance of success, however, they needed the support of Morrison; and not only was Morrison far from sharing Cripps's and Dalton's policy objectives, he had no intention of helping to depose Attlee in order to put Bevin in his place. He was all in favour – as in 1945 – of deposing Attlee but still saw himself as the obvious successor. Bevin, on the other hand, remained staunchly loyal to Attlee. The proposed putsch therefore fell to the ground. When Cripps, never short of courage, confronted Attlee alone on 9 September the Prime Minister coolly disarmed him by offering him the new post of Minister of Economic Affairs, taking over most of Morrison's planning functions. This outcome, at least, Bevan warmly welcomed, though unfortunately the experiment of a planning Ministry separate from the Exchequer ended after less than two months when Dalton was obliged to resign after leaking a Budget secret and Cripps reunited both functions under the Treasury. In the meantime Morrison remained Deputy Prime Minister, in which capacity Attlee consulted him by letter in mid-September about possible further changes in the Government.

One of the moves he proposed was to shift Bevan to the Ministry of Supply – as suggested by Cripps.[14] Morrison, predictably, stamped hard on this idea. 'I am doubtful about your proposal', he wrote, 'as I am abt the political judgement (at times) of the source from which it probably came.'

> It is I suggest important not even to appear to reward intrigue and disloyalty or to appear to manifest fear. I am not sure this job is up his street, able and brilliant as in many ways he is. Private industry has got to be brought along over the wide field concerned & – whatever happens – the iron and steel people have to be handled with decision *and* care if we are to get the output which is vital. In any case I think it is vital that the socialisation shd not go forward next Session. ... I earnestly trust you will be firm about this. ... For myself I wd have done the forward deal with industry & I think it's a tragedy we didn't. But if you put the colleague you mention there *and* his policy, it will be a smack in the eye for you, me and the TUC who have been helpful & wd have been more helpful if my hands in advocacy had not been tied. I wd still urge [the Ministry of] Labour for him instead of Supply.[15]

'I note your points about Aneurin,' Attlee replied. 'I am seeing him today to get a clear position about Iron and Steel.' Evidently he did not favour Morrison's idea of sending him to Labour. 'It might be better for him to go to the Board of Trade,' he wrote, adding darkly *'but I think he needs a change of office.'*[16] This is a fairly startling remark. Today it seems extraordinary that the Prime Minister should have considered moving Bevan from the Ministry of Health before the National Health Service by which his name is remembered had even been inaugurated. Attlee's intention may reflect concern at Bevan's embittered relations with the BMA and a feeling that he was not the best man to see his own legislation into effect; more probably it is a reflection of the relative lack of public attention paid to health compared with housing, where Bevan was in 1947 under heavy criticism for having failed so far to build the houses Labour had promised. On neither count, however, is confidence in Attlee's judgement increased by his proposal to Morrison to replace Bevan with his former Parliamentary Secretary (just promoted to be Minister of Works) Charles Key, a worthy trade unionist whom it is hard to see either charming the doctors or galvanising the building industry.[17] More positively it is just possible that Attlee thought Bevan was ready for promotion. The Board of Trade – the job Cripps had just left – would certainly have been that; but the same cannot be said for Supply, even though Bevan would have retained his seat in the Cabinet and would have had the chance to push through the full nationalisation of steel without delay. But then why should Attlee, who was not keen on steel nationalisation, have offered him that job? Morrison had reason to be alarmed. The whole picture is obscure. In the end it seems that Attlee did offer Bevan the choice of Trade or Supply, 'but in such a way that he turned it down and was going to stay on at the Ministry of Health'.[18] Clearly Attlee did not press, still less require him to move. Having declined, however, Bevan then saw Cripps, who tried to change his mind. 'After our talk,' Cripps wrote to Dalton, 'he rang up Clem and said he would like to see him again and I hope this means he will accept.'[19]

It did not. If Bevan did see Attlee again, he may well have found that the offer was not repeated. It seems most likely that it was not one that Attlee ever intended him to accept: it was rather another way of calling his bluff. Having refused to take responsibility for nationalising steel himself, he was then poorly placed to criticise others for dragging their feet. The upshot was that Bevan stayed at Health – which it is hard to believe was not what he preferred all along – in order to see the Health Service into operation and some results from his efforts on housing. George Strauss became Minister of Supply – nominally a left-winger but very cautious in practice – and Harold Wilson, aged only thirty-one, became President of the Board of Trade. Shinwell was demoted from the Cabinet to the War Office and replaced as Minister of Fuel and Power (outside the Cabinet) by Gaitskell. Ellen Wilkinson had died earlier in the year; in November Dalton was obliged to leave the Government. Cripps became Chancellor in his place and inaugurated his regime of iron austerity. Thus the Cripps–Dalton–Bevan alliance that had been beginning to form was broken up, and Bevan found himself the only left-wing voice in the Cabinet, more isolated just as he was becoming more self-assertive and more concerned about the Government's fading socialist purpose.

What mattered to Bevan more than the detail of any particular item of legislation was that the Government should retain its sense of movement towards the eventual socialisation of British society. It was most important, as Labour ticked off its 1945 agenda, that it should not be able to be represented, in the

203

run-up to the 1950 election, as having completed its task. Still less should the Tory press be allowed to denigrate what had been achieved. This was Bevan's insistent theme in 1948–9, to counter the sense of exhaustion that was beginning to overtake the battered Government and recapture the historic purpose of replacing moribund capitalism with a new order of society which it had begun, but only begun, to realise. 'Our enemies are trying to surround us with a cocoon of defeatism,' he told the 1948 Conference.[20] The papers – 'the most prostituted press in the world' – highlighted shortages, rationing and queues in the shops. But shortages, Bevan insisted, were better than the pre-war situation when there was plenty in the shops but millions had no money with which to buy. He positively rejoiced in rationing, the planned direction of resources and the socialist philosophy of 'fair shares for all'. It was the same with nationalisation: of course there was some disappointment and growing argument about how the nationalised industries should be most effectively and democratically run, but this in itself was a triumph of public accountability. There were no such arguments before the war.[21] There could be, he declared in a favourite phrase, 'no immaculate conception of socialism'.[22] Labour was trying to change a society moulded by capitalist psychology, 'hag-ridden by memories of the past'. The party was engaged in an historic experiment, not merely to change the mode of production but to transform the attitudes and social relationships that capitalism engendered. 'We know that unless the workers can divest themselves of that psychology, we shall fail.' Without 'spiritual dedication', he warned in 1949, Labour would fail to finish what it had begun.[23]

Likewise it was necessary to keep on hitting the Tories. Just because Labour was now winning there was no reason to let up on the class war. The Tories must not be allowed to get away with pretending that they had changed their spots. He was determined not to let them share any of the credit for the National Health Service by pretending that they had not voted against it at every stage. It was precisely to sabotage Attlee's generous non-party broadcast on the inauguration of the Health Service that Bevan made on 4 July 1948 the most notorious speech of his career.[24] Speaking at Belle Vue, Manchester, he recalled the unemployment and destitution, mitigated by pitiful measures of relief, that had been visited on the industrial districts after the last war, and told again his own searing memory of having to live off his sister and being advised to emigrate.

> That is why no amount of cajolery, and no attempts at ethical or social seduction, can eradicate from my heart a deep burning hatred for the Tory Party that inflicted those bitter experiences on me. So far as I am concerned they are lower than vermin.
>
> They condemned millions of first-class people to semi-starvation. I warn young men and women, do not listen to what they are saying now. ... They have not changed – if they have, they are slightly worse than they were.[25]

Lifted out of its context, the single word 'vermin' was taken up by the 'prostituted' press and never forgotten or forgiven as long as Bevan lived. There are Tories who have not forgiven it to this day. He had monstrously insulted, it was said, eight million people, dragged the language of politics into the gutter and revealed a depth of hatred in his own soul that disqualified him from political respect. Churchill seized with both hands the opportunity to dub his old *bête noire* 'the Minister of Disease – for is not morbid hatred a form of mental disease?'[26] Attlee, whose own broadcast had been undercut, felt obliged to rebuke his colleague, though it must be said more paternally than sternly. (His letter ended: 'Please, be a bit more careful in your own interest. Yours ever, Clem'.[27] Later, as the extent of the propaganda gift to the Tories became clearer – some of the sillier Young Conservatives even formed a 'Vermin Club' and took to wearing rodent badges – he became less forgiving. The offending phrase was probably not premeditated and – as the *Economist* pointed out in its obituary of Bevan in 1960 – looked in cold print and sounded when repeated in the accents of outraged colonels a great deal more extreme than it probably did to those who heard it: 'Sing it in the lilt of St David ... and the phrase becomes more of a term of belittlement, less an expression of unquenchable bile.'[28] Nevertheless Bevan undoubtedly meant what he said about not forgiving or trusting the Tories and was not greatly troubled by the fuss over his characteristically vivid expression. He had made his attitude clear the previous year in connection with steel nationalisation, when he had taken pleasure in the howls of protest from the Opposition. 'Democracy means that if you hurt people they have the right to squeal. But when you hear the squeals you must carefully find out who is squealing. If the right people are squealing then we are doing the job properly.'[29] Bevan was disturbed at the Government's apparent readiness to draw back at the first objection; Tory 'squeals' were the only reassurance to the Government's supporters that it was not letting them down. 'We need twenty years of power', he asserted in a truculent defence of his 'vermin' speech at the Durham Miners' Gala, 'to transfer the citadels of capitalism from the hands of a few people to the control of the nation. Only after twenty years can we afford to be polite. Then maybe I won't have enough energy to be rude, but while we have the energy, let us be rude to the right people.'[30]

Anxious though he was in principle to keep up the momentum, however, Bevan was realist enough to be quite pragmatic about where and when to seek the next advance. In his own departmental field he resisted strongly the repeated calls at Conference that he should nationalise the building industry: this, he insisted, would not help to build a single extra house, while the attempt to compensate every jobbing builder would be a nightmare. In this case he was content merely 'to interpose a piece of Socialist planning and sanity into the jungle of private enterprise'.[31] By requiring them to build for the local authorities, instead of for sale, he claimed, 'the building employers are slowly being disciplined ... to serve a social purpose'.[32] Nationalisation was not the only way. Conference's darling though he was, Bevan was as ready as anyone to defy its resolutions when he thought them ill timed. Twice, in 1947 and again in 1948, he suffered defeats over his refusal to bring in immediate legislation to abolish tied cottages, and lectured Conference sternly on the limits of its authority. 'There is such a thing as Parliamentary tactics. . . . Leave it to us to see when we can do it.'[33] Not that as a Minister he had much time for the parliamentary party either. He was as high-handed as Bevin in ignoring the Liaison Committees set up by Morrison to involve backbenchers in the work of the departments; in 1946 he was the subject of a formal complaint on this score.[34] In office, Bevan took the clear view that it was the responsibility of the Government to govern.

Again, despite his general predisposition in favour of nationalisation, Bevan took a surprisingly cautious view of what specific industries should be included on Labour's shopping list for 1950. In discussions between the Government and the NEC in 1948–9 he markedly failed to support the Keep Left group's call, once again formulated by Ian Mikardo, for the nationalisation of shipbuilding, aircraft construction, machine tools, parts of the motor industry and the High Street banks. The one item that he, along with Jim Griffiths, made a strong fight for was industrial assurance; but this proposal was eventually watered down to 'mutualisation' after a rare alliance of Morrison, Cripps and Dalton had combined to reject nationalisation on electoral grounds.[35] In the end the only candidates for public ownership to be included in the 1950 manifesto were sugar, cement, meat wholesaling and water supplies – a curiously peripheral ragbag which scarcely threatened the 'commanding heights' of the economy. One can only conclude that Bevan's attention was concentrated on the symbolic case of steel. At the Blackpool Conference in June 1949 he won the applause of the whole party with a resounding but ambiguous disquisition on the proper balance between public and private ownership. What the speech really amounted to was a confession that even he, the tribune of the left, did not know where to go next.

After celebrating the achievement so far, Bevan admitted that Labour was now moving into uncharted waters. 'We have to exercise our imaginations', he told delegates, 'as to what we can do further. Indeed, we have to restate the relationship between the public and the private sector.' He took for granted that the public should predominate. The major industries in the country, he asserted, had no more to do with what H.G.Wells had called 'private economic adventure' than the atom bomb had with the bow and arrow. There had to be planned use of national resources. At the same time private enterprise still had its part to play in less vital areas. There followed a crucial admission:

> Therefore the kind of society which we envisage and which we shall have to live in will be a mixed society, a mixed economy, in which all the essential instruments of planning are in the hands of the State, in which the characteristic form of employment will be by the Community in one form or another but

206

eurin Bevan and Jennie Lee on their wedding day, 25 October 1934.

Bevan speaking at a May Day rally at Hyde Park Corner, 1936.

litor of *Tribune*: Bevan defends the freedom of the press in wartime at a meeting of the ational Council for Civil Liberties, April 1942.

The new Minister of Health at his desk.

Best foot forward: Bevan on his way to his first Cabinet meeting, August 1945.

The Labour Cabinet, 1945. Bevan, the youngest member of an elderly team, stands slightly apart at the end of the second row. The front row is (*left to right*) Addison, Jowitt, Cripps, Greenwood, Bevin, Attlee, Morrison, Dalton, Alexander, Ede and Ellen Wilkinson. Shinwell stands behind Alexander.

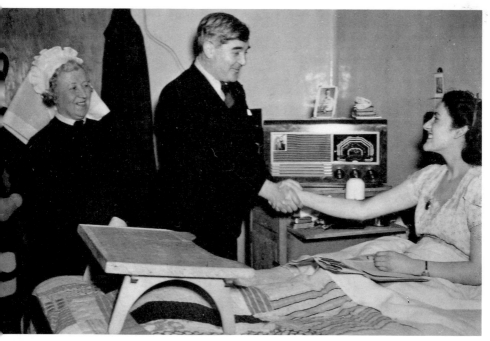

...van visiting the tuberculosis centre at Papworth Hospital shortly before it was taken over by ... National Health Service in July 1948.

...aring his other hat, Bevan opening a new housing estate at Elstree, Hertfordshire, March ...9.

Colleagues in office:
Bevan with Dalton,
Morrison and (head in
hand) Attlee at the
Labour Party
Conference, Blackpool,
June 1949.

Colleagues out of office: Bevan with Harold Wilson, Ian Mikardo, Tom Driberg and
Barbara Castle at the Scarborough Conference just before the October 1951 General
Election. A year later all five, plus Richard Crossman, were elected to the National Executive

Weaving a spell of words: Bevan indoors and out. At Conference 1950 (*top*), 1951 (*middle right*) and 1955 (*middle left*); and in Trafalgar Square denouncing Suez, November 1956 (*bottom left*) and H-Bomb tests, April 1958 (*bottom right*).

Nye and Jennie by the Black Sea during their visit to the Soviet Union to talk to Khrushchev, September 1957.

Outward reconciliation: the Gaitskell-Bevan axis (with Barbara Castle). A Labour election poster, October 1959.

where we shall have for a very long time the light cavalry of private, competitive industry.[36]

In terms of specific action, this could mean as much or as little as anyone wished to read into it: in this sense it was a skilful pre-election fudge in the interest of unity. Ian Mikardo commented in *Tribune* that what sounded right-wing in Cripps's mouth sounded left-wing when Bevan said it.[37] More seriously one might see it as a recognition on Bevan's part that further nationalisation, while desirable in theory, was in practice fraught with more difficulties than he had foreseen. The truth was that Labour was approaching a crossroads. While fiercely contemptuous of those like Morrison who wanted merely to 'consolidate' what had already been achieved, Bevan could see the way ahead, after steel, only in generalities. In the latter part of his speech he fell back on the spiritual benefits of socialism, rebuking those like Richard Acland who felt that in emphasising the need for more production the Government was losing sight of the religious impulse. This was the context of his famous formulation: 'The language of priorities is the religion of socialism.' National planning, he asserted, involved making 'ethical choices on a national scale. ... Every attempt to choose between alternative choices of conduct is a moral choice.' Labour had chosen to make women, children and the old the first claim on the national product. 'What is that except using economic planning in order to serve a moral purpose?' Finally he left the awkward details of shopping lists far behind:

> Therefore I say that this great movement, so far from having to go down with its head bowed, as though it had its eyes fixed on the mud, should, on the contrary, raise its head high and look at the stars. We have become so preoccupied with documents and papers that we sometimes fail to realise where we are going. These are merely the prosaic instruments of a masterly design. These are merely the bits and pieces we are fitting into the great structure, and I am convinced that, given another period of office, we shall not only materially improve the well-being of Great Britain but we shall have established a British society of which Britons everywhere can be proud and which will be an example to the rest of mankind.[38]

Bevan was happy so long as he thought the *direction* was right and was satisfied that socialist *principles* were still intact. Hence the debate within the party over the next two years – of which he was increasingly the storm centre – revolved less around issues in their own right than around issues as symbols: symbols of priorities. Steel, after a fight, had been won: George Strauss's nationalisation Bill was forced through Parliament, against much greater Tory opposition than any previous measure had aroused, during 1948–9 (though a deal was done with the Lords whereby vesting day was postponed until 1951). Now attention shifted to the defence of social welfare spending and in particular, for Bevan, the NHS and housing. He was deeply disturbed by Cripps's determination to control health spending even at the expense of imposing prescription charges. He fought hard for the symbol of a free service, but he knew that Cripps was not an opponent against whom he could hope to prevail in open Cabinet; instead he reluctantly accepted a 1/- reserve charge, did his best to talk it out of existence and determined for his own part that it should never be imposed.[39] In the short term his 'manoeuvre', as he later called it, worked. On the housing side he was less successful. Following devaluation in September 1949, his budget was cut by £35 million and his building programme, just as he had got the rate of completions up to 200,000 houses a year, was cut back to 170,000 for 1950.[40] Defeated in the Economic Policy Committee, he characteristically tried to reopen the issue by appealing direct to Attlee, claiming that he had accepted his share only on the understanding that 'the already gorged and swollen defence estimates' would be cut back commensurately, which he now discovered not to be the case, and arguing that housing made 'its own peculiar and essential contribution to national revival' and should therefore not be cut.[41] Bevan could always make out a dazzling case that his own Department should be immune from whatever disciplines were being imposed on others. This was one of the characteristics which, while it delighted his civil servants, most infuriated his colleagues and earned him a damaging reputation as a bad 'team' player, leaving him dangerously short of allies when he needed them. On this occasion Attlee wrote him in his own hand a stern rebuke to the effect that reopening what had already been agreed would be unfair to other Ministers, adding that 'It really does not advance matters to talk about gorged and swollen defence estimates any more than it does to talk about grossly extravagant Health services. These adjectives in either case are not based on knowledge.'[42] The even-handedness of the last sentence, at a time when Gaitskell and Morrison were increasingly making an emotive issue of the extravagance of the Health Service, might have been some encouragement to Bevan to think that there at least he would have the Prime Minister's quiet backing. Nevertheless the housing cuts went through.

The September devaluation had been a shock to the Government, not least to Cripps, who resisted it as long as possible. It was effectively engineered, in his absence through ill-health, by a trio of younger Ministers – Gaitskell, Douglas Jay and Harold Wilson. Bevan, after initial doubts, 'was won over without great difficulty'[43] in the hope, vain as it turned out, that it might obviate the need for spending cuts. The necessity was due, ironically, not to any indigenous British crisis, but to a sudden downturn in the American economy with a consequent heavy fall in Britain's dollar earnings and hence in the balance of payments. Naturally, however, the Tories seized on it as a condemnation of the Government's economic management. Parliament was recalled and Churchill took the chance to make a superb, rollicking electioneering speech, roaming freely from devaluation over the whole field of socialist iniquity.[44] With one of his rare strokes of imagination, Attlee chose Bevan to reply. For almost the whole life of the 1945 Parliament, Members had been waiting for Bevan and Churchill to resume their wartime duel. It was becoming a matter for comment that Churchill seemed careful to avoid a confrontation. In February he had denounced Bevan's supplementary health estimates, but then shied away from pressing his motion of censure in the Commons. 'Churchill in the country', the Keep Left MP J.P.W.Mallalieu noted in *Tribune*, 'has been a roaring lion but in the House, with Bevan on the opposite bench, he has merely pulled faces.'[45] Now, for the first time, Attlee risked unleashing Bevan, beyond the confines of his own Department, in a general economic debate to confront Churchill on the high ground of his own choosing.

The result was one of Bevan's greatest parliamentary performances. Freed by Churchill's own speech from any necessity to keep strictly to devaluation, he took the chance to deliver a stinging condemnation of the Opposition's persistent denigration of Britain's economic achievement since the war. 'I welcome this opportunity', Bevan began, 'of pricking the bloated bladder of lies with the poniard of truth.' He stammered slightly on the word 'poniard' and from that moment had the House in the palm of his hand. He went on to demonstrate, citing one economic indicator after another, that contrary to Churchill's 'flatulent generalities' and 'vicious misrepresentation', Britain had since 1945 achieved the most remarkable economic recovery of any European nation, with exports in particular more than 30 per cent above their pre-war level. Bitterly he contrasted Labour's proud record with the Tories' sour criticism which had helped, by 'talking down' the pound, to make devaluation necessary; at the same time he repeatedly pricked the old warrior on the bench opposite with impudent gibes which recalled not so much his wartime attacks as his very first mockery of the great man in his maiden speech more than twenty years before. The reason why Churchill moved so gracefully across the pages of history, he suggested, was 'because he carries a light weight of fact'. He recalled that it was Churchill who had put Britain back on the gold standard as Chancellor of the Exchequer in 1926, and brought the House down by quoting Robert Boothby's description of him then as reluctantly 'shackled to reality'. Finally, and most tellingly, he portrayed Churchill not as the leader of the Conservative Party at all but as the 'decoy' of the very 'crowd of mediocrities' who had kept him out of office before the war. Did he not remember that 'it was the Labour Party that virtually made him Prime Minister?' The men whom Churchill hoped to lead back to power in 1950, Bevan concluded with a long quotation from one of his most majestic indictments of appeasement, were none other than the 'guilty men' of 1940.[46]

'I almost believed at that moment', wrote Mallalieu in *Tribune*, 'that Winston was going to abstain on his own amendment.' No one who saw and heard it, Mallalieu exulted, would ever forget Bevan's speech. 'It hauled down Winston's election flag and trampled on it. It cut the already shaky ground from under Winston's feet. And as for his followers ... Bevan not merely pressed their noses to the brimstone but hurled them over the abyss into the everlasting bonfire.'[47] It was by general acclaim a parliamentary triumph: nothing to do with devaluation, but a *tour de force* of destructive debating which left Labour Members wondering why they had kept their heaviest artillery under wraps, confined to health and housing matters, for so long. Even those of his colleagues who found Bevan's conduct in Cabinet most aggravating could not deny his power. The following week his growing public impact was confirmed by a readers' poll in the *Sunday Pictorial* which showed Bevan by far and away the most popular choice for Prime Minister, easily beating Attlee, Cripps and Morrison.[48] Even as he came into increasing conflict with his colleagues over programmes and expenditure, Bevan was emerging as the freshest and most forceful personality in a tiring Government.

Ever since May he had been pressing for an early election, rather than hang on till 1950. This he believed was the answer to the Government's loss of momentum. 'Our Party in the House', he told Dalton, 'will be getting nervous and demoralised, and there will be no more really interesting legislation. We shall be marking time, and lose our power of manoeuvre.'[49] Dalton agreed, and so as the devaluation crisis threatened did Cripps, who was determined not to introduce another Budget in the present Parliament. For the past year the Chancellor had been holding regular informal dinners of selected economic Ministers – Bevan, Strauss, Strachey, Gaitskell, Jay and Wilson ('I could not help feeling', Gaitskell noted in April 1948, 'that Stafford was surveying his future Cabinet');[50] by September 1949 all except Jay, who had changed his mind, favoured an early election.[51] They all feared another hard winter, further shortages and power cuts. Bevan's concern was still more with party morale and his sense that the Government had run out of steam. An election would offer an escape from his collision course with Cripps over economies. A renewed mandate – he never doubted that Labour would win – would reinvigorate the Government, sweep away the doubts and confusions and restore its socialist purpose. He believed that the Government's difficulties stemmed partly from its civil service advisers, who had been happy to serve it when its authority was fresh, beginning psychologically to hedge against the possibility of a Tory Government. An early election, he argued, could not be called running away when the Tories themselves were demanding one: Labour should call their bluff.[52] It is difficult to believe that he was not right. But Attlee was afraid of seeming opportunist. He dismissed the Cripps group as 'all the intellectuals', believing that Labour voters expected the Government to serve out its term;[53] and Bevin and Morrison for different reasons agreed with him. So the Government missed the legitimate opportunity that undoubtedly existed after devaluation, and staggered on with a strong sense of anti-climax, cutting its cherished programmes, until December, by which time Cripps was advising that 'he couldn't hold sterling beyond February' and only Morrison of the inner group of Ministers still wanted to hold on till June. So, by default, the date was set for 23 February.[54]

Even so, few Ministers contemplated the possibility of defeat. 'Most of my colleagues', Gaitskell recorded, 'expect us to have a majority of 70 to 100.' He himself was more doubtful; but Bevan was one of the optimists. At an austere New Year party given by Cripps, the whole company wrote down their forecasts. When Gaitskell's guess – a majority of thirty – was read out, 'Nye said "I would rather not be in power at all."' 'That may well be,' replied Gaitskell, 'but I think you are all too optimistic.'[55] Bevan was not only optimistic, he was scornful – as in 1945 – of those who were not, equating doubt with weakness of will. 'I am not interested in the election of another Labour Government,' he characteristically told the journalist Leslie Hunter, a confidant of Morrison. 'I am interested in the election of a Government which will make Britain a socialist country.'[56] To try to restore the party's fading vision he contributed to *Tribune* at the beginning of the campaign a remarkable reassertion of his own faith in the socialist direction of history.

It was remarkable for its remoteness from the hurly-burly of the hustings. 'Judged by long-term values,' he wrote, 'the chief danger in a general election lies in the loss of perspective. The foreground of the political stage is too crowded by personalities, colourful and otherwise, the air is thick with incidental noises, and subordinate themes obtrude themselves to the exclusion of the grand motif that historical reflection will eventually winnow from the ruck of contemporary irrelevances.' It was his task to recover 'long-term values' and restate history's 'grand motif' by reminding the party of first principles. In the past few years it had been 'so absorbed in busy every-day affairs that theoretical thinking has been neglected. More than ever we need lamps for our feet or we shall stumble in the way.' He set out to offer 'a restatement of the relations between the individual and society'.

Bevan's argument was his old belief, newly formulated, that modern society tended inevitably towards socialism. 'The technics [sic] of modern industrial civilisation call for an educated, trained population which in its turn demands full political status. . . . The machine educates the man and the educated man demands political enfranchisement. This is a law of modern society.' Hitler, Bevan maintained, had tried to defy that law and failed; likewise, he believed, it was 'the yeast that is fermenting internal relations in the Soviet Union. . . . A totalitarian state or a one-party state is a persistent contradiction with the needs of a thriving industrial community.' But, Bevan went on, 'if political dictatorship is uncongenial to a community trained and educated by the techniques of modern civilisation so equally is economic anarchy'. The worker, accustomed to discipline and co-ordination at work, 'cannot understand why there should be [a] plan inside the factory and planlessness outside. It does not make sense to him that planned operations in his work should be described as efficiency while chaos everywhere else should be called freedom. . . . It seems to him that if men are made to fit inside the factory so should factories be made to fit each other.' At last Bevan touched on the issue, or non-issue, of the election:

It is here that the concept of the common ownership of the basic instrument of production fits into his outlook. It means for him not only the removal of the private owner but also a way of rationalising the relation between industry and industry. The owners fight each other. Industries belong to each other. They are not hostile. They are complementary. They should be made to fit together and their separate ownership by predatory interests ... seen as a barrier to their efficient co-ordination.

From this Bevan moved to an explicit assertion that Keynesianism was not enough. Even the Tories now admitted the duty of government to maintain full employment. What they had not begun to see, he believed, were the implications of their admission.

An insistence on the maintenance of full employment means constant intervention by government in the main agencies and streams of industrial and financial activity. Those who believe that the end can be achieved by injecting, or withdrawing, purchasing power from the financial system from time to time are pipe-dreaming. ... The truth is that such large sums are involved in the heavy long-term investments of the basic industries that the saliva of private greed does not flow long enough to digest them into the economic system.

Hence again the need for public ownership of the major industries. 'The main economic structure must be planned, purposive and reasonably predictable.'

Finally Bevan returned to the fact that by accepting the responsibility of planning the economy, socialists accepted the duty of determining priorities, and ended with a typically sweeping historical excursion to demonstrate the moral superiority of socialism over earlier stages of social development:

Before the Industrial Revolution the order of priorities in society was decided by tradition, rank, usage and the edicts of princes, kings and potentates. With the Industrial Revolution the burden of deciding was abandoned to the higgling of the market and the compulsions of greed. Now the people, through their representative institutions, must choose between a number of competing claims, and when that happens we have left the lower levels of economic planning and are treading the uplands of moral decision. This is the complete answer to those who think Socialism is merely a matter of appetite. On the contrary, it is the first time in human history that mankind will have accepted the obligation of free collective moral choice as the ultimate arbiter in social affairs. This, in truth, is the People's Coming of Age.[57]

It is a wonderfully plausible theory; but of course it begs more questions than it answers. It does not begin to propose the mechanisms or the criteria by which the people's representatives in their objective wisdom shall exercise their moral choice between competing priorities nor suggest why their deliberations should be free of the 'compulsions of greed' redefined as sectional or regional interest. The implication is that politics will cease when 'the People' make the decisions. The prospect is as unconvincing in the long term as it was unhelpful in the electoral short term. Once again the most striking quality of Bevan's socialism when he tries – very ingeniously – to restate first principles for modern conditions is its extreme vagueness, revealing behind the confident neo-Marxism a disappointingly naive idealism which is in sharp, even tragic contrast to the robust practical politician Bevan was when he was not trying to theorise. By 1950 his anger and his intellect were coming apart. It was a painful process, not only for himself but for the party.

In the election campaign Bevan, though he spoke to packed meetings all round the country, was firmly kept out of the limelight. Despite opinion polls evidencing his popularity with faithful Labour voters, he was regarded by the party managers as a liability with the middle-class electorate which Morrison's 'consolidation' strategy was designed to reassure. The Tories – particularly Beaverbrook's *Daily Express* – made him their bogeyman and continued to make great capital of his 'vermin' speech, representing him as the bacillus of class hatred and spite which poisoned the Labour Party.[58] A significantly prominent part was played by Bevan's old antagonist Dr Hill of the BMA, now a Conservative candidate, who skilfully exploited his popularity as the former 'Radio Doctor' in a highly effective election broadcast which did not neglect to mention 'vermin', disparaged the Minister of Health's responsibility for the nation's healthier children ('Bevan's Bonny Babies' were really Lord Woolton's), and denied him any achievement at all in housing. 'In many towns', Hill claimed, 'there are much bigger waiting lists than in 1945. ... No wonder Mr Aneurin Bevan isn't broadcasting'.[59] While Labour continued to play Bevan down, its opponents continued to play him up as an issue in himself. In a fence-sitting final editorial, the still-Liberal *Manchester Guardian* found itself unable to support either the Tories '(even led by Mr Churchill with all his virtues)' or Labour '(with such an encumbrance as Mr Bevan)'.[60] Before the polls had even closed, Bevan was being set up as the scapegoat for Labour's poor result.

Chapter 15

Rumbling Volcano: Rearmament and Other Discontents

The General Election result was a crushing disappointment to Labour. It was not that the party lost votes: it actually increased its poll from just under twelve million votes to over thirteen million. But on a higher turnout than in 1945 the Conservatives gained more, rising from under ten million to twelve and a half million – 43 per cent of the vote against Labour's 46 per cent. More important than percentages, however, the Tories captured eighty seats and reduced Labour's majority in the House of Commons to a bare five. The disappointing size of the electoral swing apart, this was the worst possible result for the immediate future. As Dalton wrote in his diary, with ten more seats Labour would have had a working majority, with ten less it would have had a chance to regroup in Opposition while letting the Tories try to form a precarious Government. 'As it is we have office without authority or power and it is difficult to see how we can improve our position.'[1] Another election could not be long delayed, but in the meantime events could only move further against a tired Government which had clearly failed to win a vote of confidence. Labour, though not beaten, was emasculated.

The right was quick to blame Bevan for having frightened the middling voter. Competing estimates – by their nature mere guesses – circulated to the effect that his 'vermin' speech had cost Labour two, or even three, million votes.[2] Even Attlee now lent himself to this explanation of the result, citing not only the 'vermin' speech but another in which Bevan was reported to have said that the middle classes only wanted servants in order to have someone to order about.[3] Gaitskell naturally agreed and noted in his diary that the result 'seemed to suggest that the Morrison policy of going slow and retrenchment – a move to the right rather than to the left – would have been appropriate'.[4] Bevan, equally naturally, took the opposite view. He too felt vindicated by the drop in enthusiasm for Labour, which he believed reflected the party's own loss of momentum and faith. On this analysis Morrisonianism – in which admittedly he had acquiesced in the preparation of Labour's cautious programme – had met the response it deserved. The right course now was for the Government to press on boldly with implementing the measures of socialisation it had promised. On the contrary, at its first post-election meeting on 25 February the Cabinet agreed that 'there could be no question of attempting to carry through any of the controversial legislation which had been promised in the Party's Election Manifesto'.[5] Bevan was unable to attend this meeting: he was reported to be skulking in his tent, but actually was unwell. At the next meeting, on 2 March, however, he strongly opposed the suggestion that the Government should present an anodyne King's Speech shorn of all socialist measures. 'He would deprecate any reference, in the Speech or in the debate, to the difficulties of the Parliamentary situation. He saw no reason why the Government should limit in any way their discretion to choose suitable issues on which to contest the next General Election, whenever it came.'[6] In particular he thought the Government's small majority no reason to halt the implementation of the nationalisation of steel. On this one item, the Government felt committed to press ahead; but there was nothing else of significance in the King's Speech. The Government simply waited for something to turn up.

It actually survived eighteen months, though what turned up was the Korean War. But the psychological background to Bevan's restlessness over the next year, and his eventual resignation, is his belief that the Government no longer existed for the purpose of doing anything: it merely existed. In these circumstances, he warned directly at Conference in October, divisions in the party were bound to open up. From 1945 to 1950, he claimed, Labour had achieved 'a greater degree of unity' than he had ever known. 'And the reason why we achieved that unity was that we achieved it in activity. We are always better when we are getting on with the job. As the Prime Minister said yesterday, negation is the Tory policy.'[7] The trouble was it was also the Government's policy. Thus while Bevan had had his differences with his colleagues between 1945 and 1950 he had been kept fundamentally loyal by his sense that the Government was, at its own pace, introducing socialism and his confidence that it was moving in the right historical direction. In 1950–1, conversely, he had no such confidence and his fundamental loyalty came under increasing strain.

It had been generally expected that Attlee would shift him to another department. Bevan himself had told a medical dinner in November that he would soon be leaving the Ministry of Health.[8] After the election, though, Attlee's idea was – belatedly – to split up the Ministry of Health, merging housing with Town and Country Planning under Dalton but leaving Bevan 'to clear up the mess he has made' on the health side.[9] This, however, would have been a sharp demotion for Bevan. He had himself been urging for some time that health and housing should be split;[10] nevertheless he was understandably not prepared to stay on himself to preside over a truncated department and declined to do so. Dalton, for his part, was unwilling to take over housing if Bevan was still to be the Minister of Health with whom he would have to effect the transfer and suggested that Attlee send Bevan to the Colonial Office: 'Nye, I am told, would like the Colonies very much.'[11] He probably would have: he was becoming keenly interested in the relations between the developed and the underdeveloped world, which he went so far the following year as to call the 'central issue' of the 1951 election.[12] But Attlee considered him too colour-prejudiced – 'pro-black and anti-white' – for the Colonial Office and preferred to leave him at Health, even at the cost of postponing the division of the department.[13] Once again, no one was happy – not Bevan, who after five years was ready for a new job and thought he deserved promotion, not the threat of having his present job halved; nor Dalton, who would have liked the housing job; nor Cripps, who would have welcomed a more pliable Minister of Health; nor Gaitskell, who thought the only result of sending Bevan back 'to clear up the mess he has created' would be that 'the mess will not be cleared up'. 'How much better it would have been', Gaitskell reflected, 'if he had gone to the Colonies where he would have been out of the public eye at home and Jim Griffiths had gone to Health.'[14]

Returning to Health, Bevan had little to do except resume his rearguard action against prescription charges. This was not the sort of new challenge that was likely either to engage his enthusiasm, as the Colonies might have done, or to commit him actively to the support of the Government. Leaving him at Health was a serious mistake on Attlee's part, not for the reason Gaitskell believed, but because it left Bevan restless and underoccupied, while confirming the general sense of a Government of old men staggering on without initiative or imagination. Part of Bevan's danger, Gaitskell noted in March, was that he was 'so much the best debater, so much the most effective speaker on the Front Bench, indeed in the House' that he could always raise his prestige in the party by a good speech or two.[15] Attlee would have been well advised to bind that prestige into the very heart of his Government instead of, as he appeared to do, keeping it at arm's length. Even before the promotion of Gaitskell to the Exchequer in October, Bevan had good reason to feel that he was not being accorded the position of influence in the new Government that his seniority and ability deserved. He was already said to be 'disturbed' by Gaitskell's appointment after the election as deputy to the ailing Cripps.[16]

One effect of Gaitskell's appointment was to stiffen Cripps on the critical question of the cost of the National Health Service. For no sooner was the election over than Bevan submitted another large supplementary estimate of £90 million for 1949–50, with a long paper repeating his opposition to the introduction of charges on either appliances or prescriptions, and maintaining bluntly that 'Allowing for all sensible administrative measures to prevent waste, the plain fact is that the cost of the hospital service not only will, but ought to, increase.' 'To slash the health service now', he argued, 'by curtailing benefit or by importing the principle of charges to patients could scarcely be justified at this very early stage of the evolution of the service.' The inevitable early abuses were already levelling out: savings on the drugs bill – which amounted to £31.7 million in 1949–50 – could better be made by restricting the prescription of proprietary brands than by imposing charges with all the administrative complication of allowing exemptions and the consequent objectionable return to a means test. 'If the course of the service can be held steady at this stage,' he concluded, 'there seems every chance that there will be much calmer water ahead, and an ambitious social venture will be found to have been amply justified. It is, in short, too early to panic; nor is there any good cause to do so.'[17]

To the Treasury, and to other spending Departments whose own budgets were under attack to accommodate the swelling Health Service, this seemed hopelessly complacent. In fact, Bevan can now be seen to have been right: health spending *was* levelling out and by the following year was steady. But understandably, with the final cost every year so far exceeding the previous year by about £100 million, it did not seem so at the time, and the way Bevan talked did not encourage the impression that he even wanted to control expenditure. This was where Gaitskell became involved. He had scarcely arrived at the Treasury before, in his own words, 'I begged Stafford to insist on two things. First, Treasury control should be established as effectively as it is over other Government expenditure and secondly there should be a definite limit placed on the total National Health Service expenditure.' He explicitly hoped that this ceiling would be fixed below the estimate 'so that we should be quietly committed up to the hilt to finding the rest of the money ... by making charges of some kind'. This entry is the clearest evidence that, over the battles of the next year, Gaitskell positively *wanted* to impose charges. According to his own account, it took forty-eight hours to bring Cripps up to the mark. 'As usual, there was a policy compromise because of the threat of Bevan's resignation and the unwillingness of the Cabinet to accept the principle of charging just yet.'[18] Nevertheless Gaitskell thought he had got most of what he wanted. At Cabinet on 13 March, in return for agreeing to the £90 million supplementary estimate and defending it, despite his previous assurances that it would not happen again, in the House of Commons, Cripps secured Bevan's agreement to a fixed ceiling of £392 million for 1950–1 which should definitely not be exceeded; there would also be stricter Treasury control of the hospital service immediately, without waiting for the Departmental enquiry which Bevan had set up under Sir Cyril Jones.[19] This Bevan accepted, thinking that was the end of the matter. 'I do hope', he wrote to Attlee, 'that I can have a little peace to get on with my proper work without this continual nibbling.'[20]

But a fortnight later Cripps returned to the attack. He had come to the conclusion, he informed the Cabinet, first that the £392 million allocation for 1950–1 was 'already making an unfairly large claim on our resources, having regard to the other claims to be met' and, second, that even this ceiling would prove inadequate to contain growing demand. The Government had the choice, therefore, of limiting the growth of the Service or finding a new source of income from charges. It would be 'politically unrealistic' to freeze the development of the Service: 'I have therefore reached the conclusion that we should be prepared to impose charges.' He proposed to announce in his Budget on 18 April the introduction of charges to reduce the estimate for 1951–2 to £350 million.[21]

Once again Bevan leapt to the defence of his baby. In a written reply to Cripps's written proposal, and again in Cabinet on 3 April, he rehearsed again the technical and administrative arguments, as well as the arguments of principle, against charges. To raise £32 million from the dental and optical services and from prescriptions – the other £10 million was earmarked to come from 'hotel' charges for staying in hospital – would mean recovering from patients *one-third* of their total cost.[22] 'The Government's abandonment of a free and comprehensive health service would be a shock to their supporters in this country and' – Bevan always believed that the eyes of the world were on his great experiment – 'a grave disappointment to Socialist opinion throughout the world.'[23] Surprisingly, perhaps, he carried the day. Morrison, who had reason to feel that his original warnings of lack of financial control of the hospital service had been vindicated, urged strongly that the repeated supplementary estimates were 'intolerable' and went so far as to argue that 'in seeking to provide a comprehensive health service for all, the Government had been trying to do too much too quickly'.[24] But when discussion resumed on 4 April the general gut-feeling of the Cabinet was still strongly against hospital charges and prescription charges; although it was agreed in principle to accept charges on false teeth and spectacles, it was also agreed that it would look weak to announce them only in principle, so it was resolved merely to work out a scheme for possible charges and hold it in reserve to introduce if necessary. Meanwhile, Attlee summed up, the Government would pursue economies in the Health Service by other means.[25] This constituted another remarkable victory over an apparently determined Chancellor, who was persuaded to withdraw a clear proposal he had made only five days before. As its price, however, Bevan was obliged to accept the establishment of a high-powered Cabinet Committee chaired by Attlee himself – rather like the one set up four years earlier to overcome housing delays – to keep health spending under continuous surveillance.

'That night', according to Michael Foot, 'he came home white with passion.'[26] The special Cabinet Committee to oversee the spending of his department was certainly an indignity for a senior Minister; and its meetings were often stormy. They brought Bevan for the first time into open conflict with Gaitskell, whose role on the committee was, in his own words, 'to act as Treasury prosecutor against the Minister of Health'.[27] Once Bevan walked out, until brought back and pacified by Attlee. The next day, 29 June, he also ceased attending Cripps's Thursday dinners, needled by what he regarded as the Treasury Ministers' continued harping on the need for charges when he wanted to believe the matter had been decided. 'I have made it clear to you, the Prime Minister and Gaitskell', he wrote to Cripps, 'that I consider the imposition of charges on any part of the Health Service raises issues of such seriousness and importance that I could never agree to it. If it were decided by the Government to impose them, my resignation would immediately follow. Despite this,' he complained, 'spokesmen of the Treasury and you have not hesitated to press this so-called solution upon the Government. But surely it must be apparent to you that it can hardly create friendly relations if, in spite of the knowledge of how seriously I regard this question, you continue to press it. I am not such a hypocrite that I can pretend to have amiable discourses with people who are indifferent to my most strongly held opinions'.[28]

It is clear that the Cripps dinners were becoming highly charged occasions. John Stachey recalled Bevan lashing Gaitskell 'with the fury of his tongue' while Gaitskell 'would sit rather silent under it, occasionally replying with a dry factual contradiction'.[29] On the other hand, Gaitskell's own diary, at least earlier in the summer, records some perfectly amicable evenings: 'The thing I like about [Bevan] is that one can have a terrific row with him in a Cabinet Committee and yet remain on quite cordial terms, with a good deal of friendly backchat.'[30] But this friendliness may have been more on Gaitskell's side, rather nervous of Bevan as he clearly was, than on Bevan's. Strachey once asked Bevan, after one of his tongue-lashings of Gaitskell, why he seemed to be going out of his way to make a rift between himself and one of the most considerable men in the Government. '"Considerable!" Aneurin replied. "But he's nothing, nothing, nothing."'[31] This undoubtedly expressed Bevan's determined view, the more bitterly held the more it became clear that Gaitskell's position in the Government was indeed considerable.

Whatever happened at Cripps's dinners, however, it turned out that Attlee's committee actually served Bevan's purpose, rather than his critics'. Either it was singularly effective in controlling expenditure, or it simply reflected the fact that expenditure was slowing down anyway under the impact of the Department's own efforts; possibly a combination of the two. At any rate, by the end of the year its monthly reports to the Cabinet showed that the cost of the hospital service – which, despite all the marginal sound and fury about prescription charges, represented overwhelmingly the lion's share of the cost of the Health Service as a whole – was essentially stable.[32] Subsequent studies, beginning with the Guillebaud Committee in 1955, have confirmed that this was so.[33] The committee to which Bevan took such exception thus actually supported his argument. In doing so it took most of the urgency out of the impending crisis. Had political perceptions had time to catch up with economic reality; had the Korean War not changed the arithmetic; had Cripps remained Chancellor, instead of giving way to a successor who believed in health charges in principle and was ready to make an issue of them; had political factors, in short, not combined to keep the issue alive, Health Service charges might well have been forgotten by 1951. Certainly by the autumn of 1950 it seemed that Bevan had once again, with the support of the majority of the Cabinet and the acquiescence of the Chancellor, beaten off the threat, perhaps finally.

The external event which transformed the whole outlook and overshadowed the final year of the Labour Government's life was the North Korean invasion of South Korea on 25 June. At first, the response of the whole Cabinet was unanimous. Britain was quick to give moral, and then military, support to the Americans' determination to resist the Communist aggressor in the name of the United Nations. Dalton recorded on 27 June that Bevan was 'rather excited by lack of consultation' on the Americans' part;[34] he always disliked the sight of London appearing slavishly to follow Washington. Nevertheless he 'unhesitatingly' told Kenneth Younger, the 42-year-old Minister of State at the Foreign Office thrust into sudden prominence by Bevin's illness, that Britain had no choice: 'When you are in a world-wide alliance, you can't retreat from it on a single issue.'[35] All but the very farthest fringe of the Labour Party agreed: only two fellow-travellers voted against Britain's participation while *Tribune*, with Michael Foot to the fore, was categoric in contrasting the UN's resolution approvingly with the record of appeasement in the thirties. Bevan began to have doubts, however, when what he had already called, the previous autumn, the 'gorged and swollen defence estimates' were suddenly swelled further to pay for Britain's military commitment. Whereas the previous year's defence budget had totalled £740 million, the Cabinet was asked on 1 August to sanction annual expenditure for the next three years of £950 million. The threat to the social services budget, particularly to his housing programme and the Health Service, was obvious. Bevan entered a formal protest, deploying for the first time a sophisticated 'guns or butter' argument that was to become his consistent line over the coming year. 'Our foreign policy', he claimed, with doubtful authority,

> has hitherto been based on the view that the best method of defence against Russian imperialism was to improve the social and economic conditions of the countries now threatened by Communist encroachment. The United States Government seemed now to be abandoning this social and political defence in favour of a military defence. He believed that this change of policy was misjudged and that we should be ill-advised to follow it.[36]

For the moment, as a minority of one in the Cabinet, he swallowed his dissent: in November he issued a statement publicly endorsing the rearmament programme, now increased to £3600 million in three years.[37] Cost apart, however, the war was becoming harder to support on political grounds as General MacArthur, not content with beating the North Koreans back to the 38th parallel, refused to stop but pursued them deep into North Korea and right up to the borders of China, threatening to go further and carry the war into China itself, until on 26 November the Chinese retaliated and drove MacArthur in turn back in disarray. In common with most Labour feeling, Bevan's sympathies were all with the Chinese: one of his cardinal axioms was that the West had made an enemy of the Soviet Union (and turned the Bolshevik Revolution tragically in on itself) by its clumsy intervention in 1918–20, and he was concerned that the Allies should not make the same mistake with China, driving her into the arms of Russia. Attlee and Bevin held the same view scarcely less strongly: Britain had recognised Communist China in January 1950, within months of Mao's conquest of power, and Bevin was firm in giving no support to Chiang Kai-shek's Formosa. In December, after reports that the Americans were considering using the atomic bomb in Korea, Attlee made a celebrated flight to Washington to convey to President Truman British alarm at the direction the war was taking. Bevan, according to Dalton, had been one of the first to propose the trip.[38] What it achieved is a matter for debate. Certainly MacArthur's megalomania was restrained, and in April he was sacked. On the other hand Attlee returned having committed Britain more firmly than ever to the conventional defence of South Korea and to a still heavier burden of defence expenditure. The Americans were now pressing for a three-year programme of £6000 million. The whole Cabinet agreed on 18 December that this was impossible. But almost the whole Cabinet, from Attlee downwards, accepted the obligation to step up spending still further.[39]

Gaitskell was now Chancellor of the Exchequer. In the middle of October Cripps had finally been forced by ill health to resign. There is some evidence that Attlee seriously considered Bevan as his successor: it is said that Cripps wanted him, even a story that Bevan thought he had been promised the job.[40] In fact, though, neither Bevin nor Morrison would have stood for Bevan's appointment, while Dalton was lobbying hard for Gaitskell, who had already been virtual acting Chancellor for months. Politics and personality apart, it could hardly be claimed that finance was Bevan's *forte*; his appointment would have horrified the City. Junior though he was, Gaitskell was really the obvious choice. But Bevan was furious. It was not primarily that he wanted the job for himself; nor solely that he despised and distrusted Gaitskell, though of course this personal animosity gave the edge to his anger. It was rather that he believed in principle that the leading positions in the Government should go to senior figures in the party, with roots in the party, who represented the party in a way that an inexperienced Old Wykehamist like Gaitskell did not. 'I feel bound to tell you for my part', he wrote uncompromisingly to Attlee, 'I think the appointment of Gaitskell to be a great mistake. I should have thought it was essential to find out whether the holder of this great office would commend himself to the main elements and currents of opinion in the Party. After all the policies which he will have to propound and carry out are bound to have the most profound and important repercussions throughout the movement'.[41]

There was a good deal of substance in the argument about Gaitskell's lack of roots, and Bevan was not the only person to be surprised by the elevation of so junior a technocrat to the fourth position in the Government. In addition, he was quite justified in feeling that the new Chancellor was not fundamentally a socialist in his meaning of the word, as Cripps, for all his recent austerity, unquestionably was. More specifically, he had good reason to fear that Gaitskell's appointment spelled a new attack on the Health Service. (In fact, unknown to Bevan, on his very first day in office Gaitskell wrote to Attlee reopening the question of charges.)[42] On all these grounds Bevan was entitled to be disturbed. Where he was unwise was in letting his anger show so bitterly. Douglas Jay was shocked when two days later Bevan descended on him behind the Speaker's chair, in full hearing of anyone who was passing, and 'began to pour forth with uncontrolled passion a torrent of vitriolic abuse on the head of Attlee for daring to make such an appointment'.[43] And Dalton recorded that he had heard, even from Bevan's supporters like John Freeman, that 'Nye is being very difficult and behaving very badly and alienating many friends and supporters.'[44] The fact is that Bevan, already unhappy with the direction of the Government, took Gaitskell's promotion as a personal affront, a slap in the face for himself personally and everything he believed in. Gaitskell himself was near the mark when he wrote in his diary: 'I suspect that Nye is not so much jealous but humiliated at my being put over him.'[45] It was not that he wanted to be Chancellor; but he thought he deserved better than to be passed over for such a newcomer as Gaitskell – particularly one with a fixation about charges in the Health Service.

At the same time that he promoted Gaitskell, Attlee offered Bevan the Ministry of Labour. This was not a promotion. Nevertheless Bevan was about to take it when he heard about Gaitskell; then, in Dalton's words, he 'turned up his nose at it'.[46] The job he would still have preferred was Colonies, but that was not on offer. So during the autumn he hung on at Health, to the mounting irritation of his old enemy Morrison and his new rival Gaitskell, who were determined that he should be moved, and Dalton who was waiting to take over housing. 'HM said he couldn't make out why the PM was apparently afraid of him,' Dalton noted at the end of October. 'He ought to tell him to take Labour.' The Chief Whip, William Whiteley, also claimed to have told Attlee bluntly 'that he should say to Nye "Labour or out", that then he'd take Labour; if he resigned, it wouldn't do anyone but himself much harm'.[47] But Attlee, though he did not trust Bevan enough to promote him, was equally reluctant to risk his resignation and would not force him. Not until January was Bevan finally persuaded to move to Labour, with the assurance that he would be given an increased role on the economic side of the Government. Why at such a moment did he agree to go, leaving the Ministry of Health to be split up and the Health Service unrepresented in the Cabinet? According to Michael Foot, he agonised about possible resignation on the rearmament issue but decided that it was not the moment.[48] He claimed later that he had only agreed on condition that there should be no new attack on the Health Service.[49] Maybe he thought that the evidence that health spending was now under control was incontrovertible. Probably he was just worn down. However he allowed himself to be satisfied, it is hard to believe that Attlee gave him any explicit assurance. Attlee knew Gaitskell's mind. For his part Gaitskell greeted the news of Bevan's acceptance with undisguised relief. 'There now at least seems to be some possibility', he wrote, 'that AB may be moved from the Ministry of Health to the Ministry of Labour. That might make a lot of difference to my financial policy. It is too early to speak but it may be the removal of the obstacle in the way of general economy in public expenditure not only in the Ministry of Health but in other fields as well, which in turn may make possible various other ideas.'[50] Gaitskell certainly knew of no assurance to Bevan which should bind his hands.

Bevan moved to the Ministry of Labour on 17 January 1951. He resigned on 23 April, just thirteen weeks later. So he was not in the office long enough to make any significant impact on the Department. In those thirteen weeks, however, he was faced with more than his share of sensitive problems, problems of a kind which were not up his street and which undoubtedly contributed to his general state of personal dissatisfaction. The Ministry of Labour was in truth just about the most unsuitable job that could have been found for him. Its primary function involved dealing with the trade union leaders, with whom his relations had always been bad, and enforcing a wages policy which the unions had accepted since 1948 but which was now beginning to break down under pressure from a variety of quarters. It is difficult to see why Gaitskell and others were so keen that Bevan should go there, except that they thought it would be good for him, after taking all the credit for the Health Service, to have to take responsibility for the harder side of government. On the other hand the move was generally well received as a shrewd instance of setting a thief to catch thieves, and the loyal Mallalieu in *Tribune* hailed it as a positive promotion from one tough job to another that in the new circumstances of rearmament was even tougher.[51] This was the key point. For the full title of the Department was the Ministry of Labour *and National Service* and by going there Bevan was taking responsibility not only for industrial relations but for the whole manpower side of the rearmament programme. 'The greater energy and drive of Nye Bevan are needed in the new job,' Mallalieu asserted. Politically it was also a clever way of locking the chief Cabinet critic of the rearmament programme into its detailed administration.

The trickiest problem on the industrial relations side was what to do about Order 1305, a wartime order originally passed in 1940 but renewed in 1945 and still in force in 1950, referring disputes to compulsory arbitration with a

223

twenty-one-day cooling-off period during which industrial action was prohibited on pain of prison. In the immediate post-war years it had been accepted with little protest, but by late 1950, when the Attorney-General Sir Hartley Shawcross used it to prosecute ten striking gas workers, the Ministry of Labour was receiving an avalanche of demands from trade unions and other labour bodies for its repeal.[52] At its last meeting before Bevan's switch of jobs the Cabinet agreed to a recommendation by Shawcross and the retiring Minister of Labour, George Isaacs, that the order should be retained but modified to substitute fines for imprisonment.[53] So the essential decision was taken before Bevan came to the Department: he had the awkward job of selling it to the unions and employers. This he began to do at a meeting with both sides on 24 January; but almost immediately Shawcross proceeded to prosecute seven London dockers, who received fines. This provoked another wave of party protest, and Bevan determined to repeal the order after all. But he had left office before he could do so.

In February Bevan achieved his first – and, as it turned out, only – tangible success in his new job by helping to avert a threatened national rail strike. It was a familiar scenario. After years of restraint during which their pay had slipped behind that of other workers the NUR was demanding a rise of $7\frac{1}{2}$ per cent. The British Railways Board insisted that it could only afford 5 per cent. Had the Government been true to its own crumbling incomes policy it would have put its weight firmly behind the Board, as Alfred Barnes, the Minister of Transport, wanted. Bevan, however, formerly an advocate of planned incomes, now thought the Government's policy too inflexible and believed that more money could be found to satisfy the railwaymen: while the Cabinet as a whole was alarmed by the 'crippling economic effects' of a rail stoppage, 'far outweighing in consequence the amounts which now appeared to be at issue between the Railway Executive and the unions'. Coal stocks at the power stations were low: a strike would bring 'immediate industrial paralysis' at a moment when the rearmament programme called for accelerated industrial output. The Cabinet accordingly instructed Barnes to convey to the Board the 'serious view' which the Government took of the consequences of a strike. The next day the men got their $7\frac{1}{2}$ per cent.[54] Bevan was widely praised; but it is difficult to see what he had done but to back one side, under the threat of a damaging strike, against the other, blowing another big hole in the Government's effort to restrain inflation. He had taken a tougher line over pay when he had been at the Ministry of Health and large settlements threatened his budget. At the Ministry of Labour he was determined not to be cast as the man responsible for screwing down the workers' wages.

But the overriding issue at the beginning of 1951 was the rearmament programme. After the general acceptance in December that it would have to be stepped up, the Cabinet returned to the subject at two long meetings on 15 and 25 January. In view of later suggestions, at the time of his resignation, that he had not opposed the enlarged programme at the time, it is important to stress that Bevan actually made his reservations very clear.[55] At the first meeting on 15 January he intervened immediately and at length to question Attlee's intention of making a speech explaining the Soviet threat and the need to accelerate defence preparations before the Cabinet had seen detailed proposals and considered their economic consequences. It was a mistake, he argued, to talk generally of increased rearmament before the Government knew what the impact would be on the civil economy and what sacrifices would be asked of the public. The Cabinet, he insisted, had not yet accepted that rearmament should entail any cutbacks in existing social services and the Prime Minister should not now make any statement which pre-empted future Cabinet decisions. 'He was not', he warned, 'at present disposed to accept any reduction in the National Health Service.'

He carefully did not rule out such reduction if it was shown to be necessary. But he did not believe it was. He believed on the contrary that unnecessary rearmament served Russia's purpose rather than Britain's. The conventional military wisdom was that the Soviet Union, using Korea as a decoy, was poised to strike at any moment against Western Europe. Against this professional wisdom Bevan felt no diffidence about setting his own belief that the USSR had no such intention or capacity. Military advisers, he maintained, always exaggerate the strength of a potential enemy. The Cabinet Secretary recorded the development of his argument at unusual length.

> He did not believe that Russia's steel production was sufficient to enable her to maintain and support military forces on the scale which was being assumed by the intelligence experts. His information was that the Soviet bureaucracy had failed to organise Russia's industrial potential. He did not believe that the Soviet Government were relying on a military coup. If this was their policy, they would have taken military action before now: he did not believe that they had been deterred from this merely by fear of atomic attack. In his view their main strategy was to force the Western democracies to rearm on a scale which would impair their economy and embitter their peoples. He therefore thought it would be folly for the democracies to adopt vast defence programmes which would put such a strain on their economies, and impose such delays on their attempts to promote economic development in the underdeveloped territories, as to give the Soviet Government the opportunity which they sought. Russia had not sufficient economic strength to win a long war against the democracies. It followed that the democracies need only rearm to the extent necessary to ensure that they could not be overrun in the first few months of a war.

'Rearmament', Bevan concluded, 'should therefore be approached with restraint, not enthusiasm.'[56]

In so far as it was agreed that Attlee should wait a few more days before making any public statement, Bevan could be said to have won this round. But when the Cabinet came to consider the detailed programme ten days later it was clear that his argument had cut no ice. An early Soviet attack, it was stated, presumably by Attlee, 'would rapidly overrun the Continent. While Russia might not possess the industrial potential for waging a long war against the democracies, she would in an early war be able to make formidable gains.' The suggestion that Russia was motivated only by self-defence was swept aside: 'In fact ... the moves she had made suggested an aggressive intent'. The reality of the danger having been thus authoritatively reasserted, Gaitskell proceeded to spell out the economic cost, and the practical difficulties, of an enlarged programme to meet it. The target was now to spend £4700 million over three years – a 30 per cent increase over the £3600 million agreed in the autumn, though still below the £6000 million the Americans were pressing for. Bevan did not participate so prominently in the argument over this figure. He did not have to; for Gaitskell himself, before urging the Cabinet to accept it, drew a devastating picture of the consequences of diverting some 600,000 workers from other industries into defence production. Exports and investments, the housebuilding programme and consumer spending would all suffer. Yet there was no certainty, with a shortage of dollars and the Americans themselves stockpiling for their own defence programme, that Britain would be able to obtain the additional raw materials or the machine tools necessary to achieve this target. In view of the scarcity of key materials, Gaitskell admitted, 'there was a danger that the increased defence programme might, in practice, yield less and not more production within the next two years'.[57] This was to be the critical point of contention over the next three months. Could all the money being diverted into defence actually be spent? And if it was, would this expenditure – even on its own terms, conceding the military desirability of increased defence – be cost-effective? Gaitskell had acknowledged on 25 January that the answer to both questions might very well be 'no'.

Nevertheless the programme was agreed, with Bevan and other Ministers who felt misgivings consoling themselves that – like prescription charges – it would never actually be carried out. The reason why the now-dominant triumvirate of Attlee, Morrison and Gaitskell – backed by a dying Bevan – believed it essential to set the £4700 million target was political. It was necessary to satisfy the Americans. As Attlee had put it on 18 December, 'One could not ignore the risk ... that the United States might lose interest in the defence of Europe, if her allies in the North Atlantic Treaty Organisation failed to play their proper part.' Moreover Britain was not just one of the allies: the wartime partnership of Britain and America must remain the 'mainspring' of Atlantic defence.[58] Britain, they believed, must be prepared to make any domestic sacrifice in the vain attempt to match American power and maintain the illusion of equality of status. And yet, paradoxically, this quest for equality precluded any difference from the Americans, since this would only have demonstrated Britain's impotence. This was the background to a heated little crisis which blew up over the Americans' desire to carry at the United Nations a resolution branding China as an aggressor in Korea. Most of the British Cabinet, including Attlee, were alarmed at the apparent eagerness of some Americans to widen the conflict into a full-scale war with China and strongly opposed any such provocative action. For some days the Cabinet hesitated while Gladwyn Jebb at the UN tried to soften the US resolution. Then on 25 January, in the absence of Bevin, it decided to vote against it.[59] The Minister most outraged by this dangerous irresponsibility was Gaitskell, who flexed his muscles for the first time, threatened resignation and succeeded by furious lobbying of the Foreign Office, the Chiefs of Staff and other military top brass in persuading the Cabinet the next day to reverse itself and instruct Jebb after all to vote for the American resolution, with some cosmetic amendments.[60] For Gaitskell, the issue was simple. 'After all', he told Dalton, 'the Americans were, in the last resort, our friends and the Russians weren't.'[61] When it was put so starkly most of the Cabinet agreed. But this storm in a teacup opened another ground of antagonism between Gaitskell and Bevan, who was naturally one of the strongest opponents of the American resolution and thought it 'disgraceful' that the Cabinet should have its decision overturned by a 'backstairs intrigue'. The episode hardened Bevan's suspicion of American-led rearmament and, once again, of the man who was pushing it. 'Gaitskell', Kenneth Younger recalled in 1961, 'was very pro-American which automatically made Nye anti-American.'[62] His contempt for a Chancellor who was 'nothing, nothing, nothing' was now taking on a more serious form as the issues of health charges at home and the Cold War abroad came together in the rearmament programme, and he increasingly recognised in Gaitskell the most determined and formidable opponent of everything he believed the Labour Party stood for.

And yet he still remained loyal. His loyalty, and his value to the Government were strikingly demonstrated in a brilliant reply to an Opposition censure motion in the House of Commons on 15 February. With typical opportunism Churchill had led the assault, alleging that the Government had been 'dilatory, inefficient and irresolute' in its response to the need for rearmament and had neglected the security of the country. Once again – it was now becoming a habit on major occasions – Bevan was put up to answer him. This time, as Minister of Labour responsible for the diversion of manpower, he had a Departmental pretext for doing so: this was the dividend for the Government of getting him directly involved. If he was not going to resign, he had no choice but to defend the agreed programme. At the very conclusion of his speech, Bevan did so, in words which were often quoted against him after he had resigned. Yet this single sentence was no more than a loyal nod towards collective Cabinet responsibility. The whole argument of his speech was a public reiteration of his belief that rearmament was not the way to counter the Russians. They would be beaten in the field of ideas, by the superiority of the Western example, by democracy. He repeated the simple view he had argued privately in Cabinet that the Soviet Union, producing only 25 million tons of steel a year, had not the industrial capacity to take on the 140 million tons a year produced by NATO. In seeking security in armaments, he jeered, the Tories were as old-fashioned as the Communists: 'The Soviet thinking has not adjusted itself to the fact that the most revolutionary power in the world is political democracy.' 'I am convinced' – he repeated another favourite formula – 'that the only kind of political system which is consistent with a modern artisan population is political representative democracy.' Western democracy, he asserted, had nothing to fear from Soviet dictatorship, but on the basis of 'armed preparedness' should seek 'not appeasement but the pacification of the tensions of the world'.

This would not be achieved by over-rapid rearmament. 'If we turn over the complicated machinery of modern industry to war preparation too quickly, or try to do it too quickly, we shall do so in a campaign of hate, in a campaign of hysteria, which may make it very difficult to control that machine when it has been created.... We have seen in other places' – he meant America – 'that a campaign for increased arms production is accompanied by a campaign of intolerance and hatred and witch-hunting. ... We in this country are not at all anxious to imitate what has been done in other places.'

His message, therefore, barely coded, was: slow down. Only his last sentence gave any comfort to those in his own party and the party opposite who wanted to press on faster, and even then he qualified the commitment with his own distinctive gloss: 'We shall carry it out', he promised, referring to the £4700 million programme; 'we shall fulfil our obligation to our friends and Allies; and at the same time we shall try to prevent an exacerbation of the world atmosphere as makes it impossible for nations to come together in peace and harmony and give mankind another breathing space.'[63] Though he was winding up for the Government it was from first to last entirely Bevan's own speech, delivered – after some Departmental details at the beginning – without notes and expressing his own philosophy. And yet it was another parliamentary triumph, acclaimed on all sides of the House. Churchill himself praised it warmly; Gaitskell praised it ('One of the most brilliant performances I have ever heard him give') and found nothing in it to object to.[64] Once again Mallalieu in *Tribune* recorded a wider than merely Bevanite view:

> There was in Bevan's speech a sense of a philosophy, a sense of moving purposefully towards a known, desirable and attainable object. For that, both sides of the House have long been hungry. They devoured it when it was offered.
> As we left the Chamber after the Division, a friendly opponent said to me: "Tonight is the first time I have wanted to vote for your— Government!" That might also have gone for some members of the Labour Party in recent weeks.
> The hungry sheep looked up and, for once, were fed.[65]

But it did Bevan little good.

Three weeks later, on 9 March, Attlee finally, reluctantly – and, in the end, clumsily – retired Ernest Bevin from the Foreign Office. There was no obvious successor. Dalton would have been the best-qualified choice but he insisted that, having missed the job in 1945, he 'didn't want soiled bedclothes & only for an hour'.[66] Instead he recorded in his diary several conversations with Attlee in which they considered the alternatives. One option was to follow the precedent of raising Gaitskell to the Exchequer and promote one of the younger Ministers with Foreign Office experience, Kenneth Younger or Hector McNeil; but Attlee thought the Foreign Office needed a senior figure. Another candidate mentioned but quickly dismissed was the Attorney-General, Sir Hartley Shawcross. Alternatively, the Prime Minister could play safe with Chuter Ede or Jim Griffiths; Attlee liked the idea of another trade unionist to follow Bevin and led Dalton to believe that he had made up his mind on Griffiths.[67] In the end, possibly influenced by Gaitskell, he gave the job to Herbert Morrison – an appointment which turned out to be disastrously unsuitable. The one name strikingly absent from these discussions is that of Bevan. A senior Minister, with a keen interest in foreign affairs, evidently unsettled where he was and in view both of his following in the party and of his effectiveness in Parliament deserving a senior job – in retrospect the case for Bevan appears strong. But the case against him was strong too: at a time when close co-operation with the Americans was paramount, Bevan's appointment would have been regarded in Washington as an affront, signalling a reversal or at least a modification of the policy of Anglo-American partnership followed by Bevin and Attlee since 1945. If this consideration by itself were not enough to rule him out, Bevan's impetuous temperament, undiplomatic tongue and reputation as an extreme left-winger combined to make the Foreign Office seem the last place a prudent Prime Minister would think of putting him at any time. His 'vermin' speech still resounded: the imagination shuddered at a repetition of that on the international stage. It is likely also that Attlee had not forgotten Bevan's enthusiasm for sending tanks to Berlin in 1948.

It is very easy to play with the idea that Attlee should have taken his courage in both hands and appointed Bevan. This was Dalton's view in retrospect,[68] and also that of Kenneth Younger, looking back in 1961:

> The only really interesting point would have been if Clem had been prepared to consider Nye. In point of fact, I think it would have been the best policy. I think there were many reasons why it was difficult for Clem to do this, but I think if he had done it, it would only have needed about one visit to Washington and the Americans would have been eating out of his hand. He would in fact have proved to be rather right-wing, very solidly anti-Communist. ... I always thought this is what he would be like, when he got near to responsibility.[69]

This may very well be true. Attlee's failure even to consider Bevan can justly be criticised as unimaginative and consistent with his generally inept and distrustful handling of his most brilliant but difficult Minister after his one bold stroke of appointing him to the Ministry of Health in 1945. From the purely domestic political point of view Attlee would certainly have been well advised, for the sake of the balance, the vigour and the survival of the Government to have taken the chance to promote Bevan, having already passed him over for the Treasury six months earlier. Even from the foreign affairs point of view Morrison – ignorant, insular and jingoistic – was such a bad appointment that it might have been worth taking the risk with Bevan after all. Even Bevin, who loathed being succeeded by his oldest enemy and would have preferred Griffiths, told Francis Williams: 'I'd sooner have Nye than 'Erbert. He might have turned out quite good.'[70] One is inclined to feel that the confident Attlee of 1945, with a big majority behind him, might have risked Bevan, but that by 1951 the tired Prime Minister of a precarious Government could only make the tired and cautious choice. It was not the moment to upset the Americans, even temporarily. Morrison was Deputy Prime Minister, and the last of the old Big Five still fully active; if he wanted the job – as it seems he did, against his friends' advice, in order as he thought to complete his credentials for the Premiership – then Attlee was prepared, with few illusions, to let him have it.[71] Morrison would certainly have been dead against giving it to Bevan. In the circumstances of 1951, then, the notion of Bevan becoming Foreign Secretary was never a realistic possibility. Nevertheless the fact that he was not even seriously considered for the job was another blow to the pride of an already discontented Minister whom it might have been wise to flatter a little, and yet one more reason for him to feel that remaining in the Government afforded him little influence now or in the future.

In later years Attlee claimed that he thought that Bevan did not want the job.[72] But Bevan certainly did want it. The appointment of Morrison to the Foreign Office was in this respect quite different from that of Gaitskell to the Treasury. Strongly as he had objected on party grounds to Gaitskell, Bevan knew quite well that he himself was not well suited to be Chancellor. But he did fancy himself as Foreign Secretary and he particularly believed, with good reason, that he knew a great deal more about foreign affairs than Morrison. Morrison's appointment was therefore a triple blow. First, he would have liked the job himself. Second, being passed over for a major office for the second time in six months was confirmation that Attlee was never likely to give him any position of real responsibility. And third, the appointment further strengthened the already dominating influence in the Government of his two most bitter personal and political opponents. The balance of the Government seemed to be being tilted ever further to the right. All in all a proud man, with a conviction both of his own worth and of the importance of the conception of socialism which he stood for and which he considered to be under deliberate attack, had a good deal to feel sore about in the spring of 1951. A lot of highly combustible material was getting very dry. Then, only two weeks after this latest rebuff, Gaitskell – knowing very well what he was doing – applied the match.

Chapter 16

Eruption: Bevan *versus* Gaitskell

It was in the Cabinet Social Services Committee on 15 March that Bevan first learned that Gaitskell had secured from his successor at the Ministry of Health, Hilary Marquand, agreement to the health charges which he had so strongly resisted. Gaitskell's aim was to hold the NHS in 1951–2 to the same ceiling as in 1950–1 – £393 million, which, for the first time since the inauguration of the Service, had not been exceeded. Marquand's original estimate had been for £423 million, but he thought that £10 million could be squeezed from the hospitals and another £20 million found by charges on false teeth and spectacles (about which he raised no difficulty) and (more reluctantly) on prescriptions, to bring the figure back to £393 million. Bevan questioned the need for charges, repeating his doubt that the full £1,250 million now allocated to to defence could actually be spent, but held his main fire for the full Cabinet.[1] His hope of support there, however, was crucially reduced by a compromise achieved in the meantime on the initiative of Bevin, still in the Cabinet as Lord Privy Seal and making his last significant contribution before his death on 10 April. Uneasiness about the Chancellor's package centred on the resurrection of prescription charges. Bevin suggested raising the ceiling to £400 million, which would allow the prescription charge to be abandoned; and Gaitskell agreed.[2] Thus when the Cabinet met on 22 March (under the chairmanship of Morrison, Attlee having gone into hospital the previous day with an ulcer) he was able to propose an increased ceiling and only £13 million to be raised from charges on teeth and spectacles, cleverly balanced by an extra £20 million for increased old age pensions. Few Ministers felt that the charges on teeth and spectacles could be regarded as a serious infringement of the principle of a free service ('Those who required them', Marquand explained, 'were normally at work and in a good state of general health. It was a different matter to impose charges on people who were sick'); and faced with the choice of free dentures or higher pensions most opted for the latter. When he insisted on treating free teeth and spectacles as a matter of principle, therefore, Bevan found himself practically alone.

He used three arguments. First, he thought the sum to be saved a 'paltry' one to justify departure from what he regarded as a central principle of Labour policy; for £100 million, he suggested, it might be understandable, but not for £23 million. Second, 'he found it difficult to believe that the reasons for the proposal were entirely financial in character, since suggestions for a scheme of charges had been put forward persistently for the last three years'.[3] He repeated his claim, which Attlee was not present to confirm or deny, that he had only consented to move from the Ministry of Health on the assurance that the matter would not be reopened.[4] Third, he denied that the choice lay between a free health service and higher pensions. 'The real cost was the cost of the increased defence programme; and if the Chancellor of the Exchequer was not prepared to accept a tolerance of a few millions in his budgeting, he should meet his difficulties by reducing defence expenditure. Shortages of raw materials would in any event make it impossible to spend wisely the amount now allocated for defence.' Finally he predicted that the Government would not be able to get health charges through the House of Commons except by an embarrassing dependence on Tory votes.

But only two Ministers shared Bevan's view that charges breached the principle of a free service – Jim Griffiths and Harold Wilson; and of these Griffiths reluctantly accepted them. Wilson followed Bevan's line that the abandonment of the symbol of the Welfare State would make headlines in the United States and also believed – with some authority as President of the Board of Trade – that the sums allocated to defence would not easily be spent, concluding that he too would prefer a cut in defence expenditure to health charges.[5] But Wilson, despite his office, carried little weight. Dalton dismissed him contemptuously as 'Nye's dog',[6] and he was widely regarded as more calculating than sincere. After Shinwell, as Minister of Defence, had come in hard to say that the rearmament expenditure was essential and an entirely free health service a pipedream the Cabinet regretfully endorsed Gaitskell's package. At this Bevan declared that he must reserve his position, nearly walked out of the Cabinet there and then, but was 'reasoned with sweetly & asked to think again, reminded that none of this will be public till Budget Day three weeks hence'. If this carried the hint of possible compromise, Gaitskell quickly dashed it, saying that '*he* couldn't go on, unless he got Cabinet support on [the] point raised today'. 'Nye looked very evil this morning,' Dalton wrote. But Dalton did not think he would resign.[7]

Easter then intervened. A few days later Bevan, as he had done in 1949, went public in what looked like a calculated attempt in invoke constituency feeling against his colleagues. In fact what he said may well have been unpremeditated. At a rowdy meeting in Bermondsey, facing a crowd of angry dockers calling for the repeal of Order 1305, he replied to one heckler: 'I will not be a member of a Government which imposes charges on the patient.'[8] When this remark, intended or unintended, was picked up by the press, the possibility of Bevan's resignation suddenly became serious. If he had meant

to put pressure on the Cabinet, he only succeeded in hardening their atti-
tude and particularly that of Gaitskell, who told Dalton angrily that 'we
couldn't always be blackmailed & give way. If we didn't stand up to him,
Nye would do to our Party what L[loyd] G[eorge] had done to the Liberals.
It would ... do us good in the country to make a stand on this.' When
Dalton said he was afraid Bevan was not bluffing any more, and that
Strachey and Wilson might resign as well, Gaitskell 'said we'd be well rid
of the three of them'.[9] At the same time Bevan had boxed himself into a
corner: he was now publicly committed to resign if he did not get his way.

Dalton, as Gaitskell's mentor, and committed to Gaitskell, but also until
recently a good friend of Bevan, tried to intercede, telling Gaitskell on 5
April that he 'thought too little of the Party and too much, relatively, of the
general body of the electorate';[10] and describing graphically to Bevan on 6
April the electoral smash he would bring on the party if he resigned. But at
this talk Bevan was bitter, against Gaitskell and 'to a less extent' against
Morrison and Attlee for appointing him. Gaitskell, he said, was 'a second
Snowden ... trying to please his friends in the Treasury'. He had 'blindly
accepted an impossible Rearmament programme. He was wildly pro-
American and anti-Russian. He had tried a year ago to get Nye to agree to
charges. ... He had always been against the Health Service.' Bevan, Dalton
concluded, 'clearly feels an attempt is being made to drive him out'. If the
party was split and defeated, he insisted, 'it wouldn't be his fault'. Unless at
the pre-Budget Cabinet the following Monday the charges were withdrawn,
'my resignation will be in the Press at the same time as the report of the
Budget speech'.[11]

The argument actually stretched over two meetings on the Monday (9
April) – three hours in the morning and another two and a half in the
evening. In the morning Bevan repeated his contention that the health
charges were 'not financially necessary'. 'In a Budget of over £4,000 million
it should not be difficult to find so small a sum as £13 million in some other
way which would not breach the principle of a free Health Service.' The
Chancellor was being unrealistically, vindictively, precise. 'The Defence
Estimates for the coming financial year totalled £1,250 million; and of this
the estimated cost of defence production amounted to £510 million. These
were large figures and must be subject to a substantial margin of error.' He
repeated that 'If the Cabinet reaffirmed their decision that these charges
should be imposed, he would be obliged to resign from the Government.'

Gaitskell replied that the Budget was a carefully balanced package which
he could not tinker with now, and that the defence estimates were as accurate as possible. According to the Cabinet minutes, 'A long discussion
ensued.' Bevan and Wilson, with some support from Chuter Ede, pressed
their argument that the parliamentary party would not accept charges; but
the majority felt that if the Cabinet did not split neither would the party.
Bevan suggested finding the extra £13 million by increasing the National

234

Insurance contribution to the NHS, or reducing the Budget surplus; but Gaitskell dismissed both devices as inflationary and for good measure stated that he was 'by no means satisfied that, even within the social services, the Health Service had the first claim on any additional money that might be available'.[12] 'If he had £23 million to spare, he wouldn't use [it] to keep false teeth and spectacles free. He would rather spend it on improved family allowances, or on more old age pensions, or on [a] smaller income tax increase'[13] – anything, it appeared, rather than appease Bevan. Finally Bevan was deluged with appeals to him not to plunge the party into electoral disaster. This Gaitskell thought 'a mistake because it really flattered his own self-importance. One Member after another said that it would be disastrous, catastrophic etc., and this led him to say "If it is going to be all these things why does not the Chancellor give way?"' According to Dalton he actually asked, '"Aren't I worth £23 millions?" He became very irritated at constant appeals to *him*. Why not appeal to others?'[14]

Bevan had now worked himself up into a state of angry self-justification in which the actual issue had got lost in his conviction of righteous martyrdom at the hands of pygmies. This was the very worst way to impress his colleagues and only lost him sympathy. 'Who are they?' he demanded of Dalton during the afternoon recess. 'I didn't choose them. The PM chooses them. They are either old men or rootless men, like Gaitskell and Gordon Walker. They are dismantling the Welfare State.'[15] This was wild talk. By behaving in this manner, Bevan made it easier for Gaitskell than it need have been.

By the time the Cabinet reassembled at 6.30, Morrison had visited Attlee in hospital and returned with a typically headmasterly ruling effectively telling Bevan to pull himself together – 'Must think of the Movement, not himself. ... Crisis at the moment sheer stark folly'[16] – which, glossed by Morrison, spelled out plainly that if Labour were defeated 'the responsibility for bringing it about would rest with any Ministers who resigned from the Government at the present juncture'. Bevan, however, brushed this aside:

> This was, for him, a question of principle. He had given three years to building up the Health Service; he had proclaimed it on many public platforms as one of the outstanding achievements of the Labour Party in office: he had, in particular, upheld the conception of a free Service as an embodiment of Socialist principles. It was too much now to ask him to go into the division lobby in support of a measure authorising the imposition of charges for dentures and spectacles provided under this Service.

He recognised the possible consequences of his resigning, but refused to accept responsibility for them. 'A Minister', he argued, 'must be free to resign if he felt that he could not conscientiously share collective responsibility for decisions which his colleagues wished to take.' In the past five years he had accepted many decisions with which he had disagreed. 'But, latterly, he had come to feel that he could bring more influence to bear on Government policy from outside the Cabinet than he could ever hope to exercise within it; and, when a Minister reached that position, it was time for him to go.'[17]

Doubtless the official minute makes his statement sound more measured than it really was. Bevan was clearly threatening that if he was forced to resign he would carry the attack to his former colleagues over a broad front. By contrast Gaitskell, again insisting quietly that he would have to resign if the Cabinet did not back him, shrewdly promised that if this were their judgement he would 'make no trouble whatever and would always support the Party'. This, Dalton observed, was 'a high moral attitude compared with Nye'.[18] Nevertheless the threat to the Government's survival was sufficiently serious to prolong the meeting until 9.15, while Ministers searched desperately for a formula to avert it. One quite sensible suggestion was that charges might be postponed for six months while it was seen whether the defence allocation could all be spent.[19] Another – 'the most dangerous proposal from my own point of view', Gaitskell called it – would have fixed the NHS ceiling at £400 million but left open the means by which health spending would be kept within it, as had been done in 1950. This, Gaitskell objected, was 'dishonest' – or, if the charges were eventually to be evaded, 'dangerous'.[20] The most ingenious proposal was to scrap the charges on teeth and spectacles and go back to prescription charges instead, which Bevan had accepted in 1949. But this was quite unrealistic: not even Bevan would have accepted them now. So, eventually, Morrison collected the voices; but not before Bevan had once again explicitly given the lie to the charge that he had widened the issue of his resignation only after the event:

> In the course of further discussion the Minister of Labour indicated that, if he resigned from the Government, he would feel obliged to make it clear that his differences with his colleagues had not been restricted to this question of charges under the National Health Service. He was also gravely concerned about the economic consequences of the increased defence programme. While he supported the policy of rebuilding the armed strength of the western democracies, he was concerned about the pace and volume of their rearmament programmes. He believed that, by trying to do too much too quickly in response to United States pressure, the western democracies were in grave danger of undermining their economic strength. The United Kingdom Government would in his view make a double mistake if they allowed the increased defence programme, not only to disrupt the national economy, but to do this at the expense of the social services.

In the end, however, only Wilson and George Tomlinson, who (to the disgust of Dalton and Gaitskell) frankly thought that Bevan *was* worth £13 million, supported him. Bevan immediately announced that he would resign the next day.[21]

But he did not. If he was going to resign, it is now clear that this was the moment when he should have done so, with very much greater dignity and effect than he achieved two weeks later. Instead he came under immense pressure from all sections of the parliamentary party – the left as much as the right – not to do it, and he yielded. That evening he and Wilson saw Attlee in hospital, and Attlee indicated that he would try to persuade Gaitskell to be 'more reasonable'.[22] Surely, Bevan must have thought, Gaitskell would bow to the authority of the Prime Minister. Then the next morning Richard Crossman 'sent Mikardo, rather unwilling, to breakfast with Nye ... to dissuade him from resigning'. According to Dalton, this breakfast had to be kept secret from Michael Foot, who was 'passionately in favour of Nye resigning. He is almost the only one.'[23] For the moment Bevan was dissuaded. Meanwhile Gaitskell saw Attlee, who did his best, as he had promised, to find a compromise. But Gaitskell was unbending. 'I had made up my mind that I would announce the charges and I refused to give way. ... We sat there talking quietly for, I suppose, half to three quarters of an hour, he urging that after all anything might happen within the next few weeks' – he evidently meant an early election – 'and implying that there would be a lot of opposition to the charges, and I simply saying that my position was impossible unless this went through.' Gaitskell offered his own resignation, but it was out of the question for Attlee to have accepted his Chancellor's resignation on Budget Day. Confronted with Gaitskell's absolute refusal to budge, Attlee had no choice but to concede: 'Very well, they [meaning Bevan and Wilson] will have to go.'[24]

At the very last minute even Morrison put pressure on Gaitskell, and to him Gaitskell made a tiny concession. He struck out the sentence in his speech announcing that the charges would come into force retrospectively on 12 April. Morrison thought this 'might just make the difference'.[25] In fact, of course, such a detail was beside the point. In the Chamber, however, the Budget was received surprisingly well. It was well delivered, its general shape impressed the party, the pension increases were popular and the cost of rearmament was seen to be placed mainly on the better-off. It was immediately clear that the health charges did not stir the Labour anger Bevan – and Attlee – had anticipated. Bevan did not take his usual place on the Front Bench to hear the speech, but only came into the House towards the end, when he stood with Jennie behind the Speaker's chair. 'It was a great shock to him', Dalton thought, 'that there was no outcry when the charges were announced – hardly an audible reaction on either side of the House. Only Jennie, standing with him, said "Shame!" just above her breath. Then he strode out into the passage.'[26] It was evident that he had much less support than he had expected. Gaitskell was universally judged to have brought off a triumph.

That evening Bevan was deluged with further appeals from friends and colleagues of every shade of opinion in the party that he do nothing rash but wait for the party meeting the next day. A typical representation came from a group of five junior Ministers led by Jim Callaghan simply urging him not to split the party.[27] A more significant one, however, came from John Freeman, Under-Secretary at the Ministry of Supply, who had promised to resign with Bevan if he went, but who now told him that in view of the popularity of the Budget there would be 'amazement as well as anger' if he went on that. Freeman's concern was with the bigger issue of rearmament, not with health charges. If Bevan stayed his hand, he urged alluringly, a much broader prospect would soon arise:

> If you could find some way of not making your resignation public at this moment and on this issue, you would not lack the opportunities in coming weeks – perhaps even days – to go out on an issue to which millions of Labour supporters would rally enthusiastically – the drive towards war, the absence of any coherent foreign policy, the inflationary and anti-working class character of our rearmament economies. The split on all this would be just as big; we should still probably lose the election, though not by so much; but three-quarters of the Labour movement would rally to you, and you would hold the initiative and have a good chance of capturing the machine. I beg you to think long and earnestly before you throw away this tremendous opportunity which I believe to be close at hand.[28]

Faced with this barrage of assorted advice – he also saw Attlee again – Bevan was persuaded that this was not the moment. 'He will now wait for tomorrow's Party meeting,' Dalton noted with relief.[29] Apart from Foot, and possibly Wilson, only one voice urged him to go at once. 'Ni Darling,' wrote Jennie, '. . . On reflection the Party meeting would certainly come down against you. . . . It is better if you made your decision known before then.'[30] But Bevan decided to attend the party meeting, where he made what was seen as a conciliatory speech saying that he and his friends would not take 'a certain step', but that there was still time for 'further consideration'. Party unity should not be imposed on one side only. Dalton recognised the continuing threat in this, but thought that 'Every hour makes it more difficult for the resigners now.'[31] Certainly the press assumed that the crisis was over. 'Bevan Gives Way On Health Charges', announced the *Daily Telegraph*.[32] 'There will be no resignations', the *Daily Herald* asserted.[33] 'The rumours about the resignation of Aneurin Bevan remain rumours after all,' the *New Statesman* concluded with relief. 'Right-wing dogma clashed with Left-wing dogma, and the results were very nearly fatal.'[34] But the press was writing the crisis off too soon.

Before Cabinet on 12 April Bevan 'rather gleefully' told Dalton, 'It's not finished yet.'[35] His new ploy, of which Dalton had had wind the previous evening, was to delay the introduction of the health charges by playing up Attlee's hint of an early election. If there was to be an election in June, he argued, there was no point, or indeed possibility, of passing the necessary Bill before it. Why then split the party for nothing? The Cabinet, however – 'apart from the Dog [Wilson] who monotonously affirms that he agrees with his master' – was not convinced.[36] Morrison denied any idea of a June election and insisted that any delay would give the impression that the Government was wavering. It was agreed to introduce the charges Bill in five days' time on 17 April and hold the Second Reading on the 23rd.[37] Bevan's response was simply to say that he would not be able to vote for it. 'That's all,' Dalton wrote. 'No threat of further resignation.' Dalton thought Bevan had missed the boat – again.[38] But over the weekend, in what Michael Foot calls 'interminable days and nights at Cliveden Place', Foot himself and Jennie pushed him back towards the brink: as Foot puts it, 'his own determination was backed by the few who knew him most intimately. ... During that weekend, also, Archie Lush arrived from Tredegar to stress how strongly opinion there backed Bevan's Bermondsey declaration and its near-inevitable consequences.'[39] A few days later Bevan was claiming ominously at the House to have 'much more support in the constituency parties than he thought'.[40] By the time the Cabinet met again on 19 April – the last Cabinet he ever attended – he was once more screwed up to a high pitch of personal grievance and paranoia. 'Why should I have to put up with all these absurdities?', he demanded, glaring at Gaitskell.[41] Now he declared that he would not vote for the charges on Second Reading and would resign if the Bill was carried on to Third Reading.[42] Dalton reflected the Cabinet's mounting impatience with 'this continued nerve war – first he threatened to resign before the Budget, then on Budget day, then if the charges were brought in, then he wouldn't vote [on] second reading, and now this!'[43]

Yet there was still some inclination to find a formula which would satisfy Bevan. Shinwell, of all people, proposed making the health charges temporary. Bevan seized on this: 'Ah! That might make all the difference,' and passed across the table to Wilson a note, which he unwisely allowed his neighbour Chuter Ede to read, saying 'We've got them on the run!'[44] Ede was then charged with holding further talks to see if a form of words could be found. Gaitskell would not agree to Shinwell's blunt 'should not be permanent', but agreed to 'need not necessarily be permanent'. This was, at last, a substantial concession which, had Bevan still been seriously looking for concessions, could have got him off the hook. When it was put to him, however, he 'tossed it aside contemptuously, calling it "a bromide". He then went on to say that he would not be satisfied with anything except an agreement which left it open as to whether the charges ever came into force at all. He followed this up with a long and rather excited statement that the arms programme could not be carried out, and that it was all nonsense and that we were really wasting our time over this sort of thing.'[45] Ede and Whiteley, the Chief Whip, who was also present, now concluded that Bevan was no longer interested in anything short of total surrender to his views. They resolved, with Gaitskell and Morrison, that the time had come when the Prime Minister would have to tell Bevan that 'he must either play with the team or go'.[46] He arranged to see Attlee the next day.

But the decisive push was given the same evening. So far – apart from Bevan's Bermondsey retort – the controversy had been carried on behind closed doors. Now *Tribune* threw them open with a violent frontal assault on the Budget, repeating out loud everything that Bevan had been saying privately about Gaitskell for months. Specifically, it likened him to the turncoat Philip Snowden, cuttingly juxtaposing Neville Chamberlain's deadly praise of Snowden's 1931 Budget with the praises of the City and the Tory press for Gaitskell's twenty years on. 'Mr Gaitskell', *The Times* had written approvingly, 'seems to have resisted most of the temptations which beset a Socialist Chancellor of the Exchequer.' *Tribune* denied that Gaitskell *was* a socialist Chancellor of the Exchequer, attacked him for financing rearmament out of teeth and spectacles and accused him bitterly of having delivered Labour's free Health Service over to a future Tory Chancellor with an open invitation to raid it as he liked; and all unnecessarily, since the rearmament estimates were unrealistic anyway.[47] *Tribune* was now controlled by Michael Foot and Jennie Lee and financed, mischievously, by Bevan's old friend Beaverbrook.[48] The lead editorial on 20 April (which was followed by similar articles by Mikardo and Mallalieu) was clearly written by Foot; but the arguments were all Bevan's, and Foot would not have published them without Bevan's knowledge and approval. This 'most wicked publication', as Dalton called it,[49] marked Foot's and Jennie's victory over the cooler counsels which had contended for Bevan's ear. Now there could be no going back. War had been declared. 'Bevanism' was out in the open and the Labour Party was publicly split.

The next day, with Ede, Morrison, Gaitskell and Whiteley around his bed, Attlee wrote Bevan an 'ultimatum' telling him firmly that he must accept collective responsibility or leave the Government. 'I shall be glad to know today that you are prepared to carry out loyally the decisions of the Government,' the letter ended.[50] But there was no possibility that Bevan could withdraw now. *Tribune* had burned his boats. His resignation was in Attlee's hands the following (Saturday) afternoon.

> The Budget, in my view, is wrongly conceived in that it fails to apportion fairly the burdens of expenditure as between different social classes. It is wrong because it is based upon a scale of military expenditure, in the coming year, which is physically unattainable, without grave extravagance in its spending.
>
> It is wrong because it envisages rising prices as a means of reducing civilian consumption, with all the consequences of industrial disturbance involved.
>
> It is wrong because it is the beginning of the destruction of those social services in which Labour has taken a special pride and which were giving Britain the moral leadership of the world.
>
> I am sure you will agree that it is always better that policies should be carried out by those who believe in them. It would be dishonourable of me to allow my name to be associated in the carrying out of policies which are repugnant to my conscience and contrary to my expressed opinion.

I am sorry that I feel it necessary to take this step after so many years of co-operation in a Government which has done so much for the cause of Labour and the progress of mankind.

I need hardly say that my adherence to the cause of Labour and Socialism is stronger than ever and that I believe that renewed efforts by all of us will result in another thrust towards the goal of our hopes.[51]

In his prompt and characteristically terse reply, Attlee noted that 'you have extended the area of disagreement with your colleagues a long way beyond the specific matter to which as I understood you had taken objection. I had certainly gathered that if the proposal for imposing charges on dentures and spectacles were dropped, you would have been satisfied.'[52] This only shows how out of touch with the situation Attlee was. It may well be that if the charges had been dropped, Bevan would not have resigned. That was the point of principle, and personal grievance, on which he stuck. But it is also the case that he had consistently objected to the scale of the increased re-armament programme ever since it was first mooted before Christmas, and had stated quite specifically at the pre-Budget Cabinet on 9 April that 'if he resigned from the Government, he would feel obliged to make it clear that his differences with his colleagues had not been restricted to [the] question of charges under the National Health Service'.[53] If Attlee did not know this, it can only be because he had not read the minutes and Morrison had failed to tell him. Similarly, it had always been known that if Wilson, Freeman and any others resigned with Bevan, their principal ground would be rearmament. Health charges, which had a special emotional significance for Bevan, were the sticking point; but the significance of that emotive symbol arose only in the context of a much wider political objection to the Government's priorities. Criticism of Bevan on the ground that he widened the issue only after he resigned is therefore misplaced.

But the reception he encountered in the House of Commons when he made his resignation statement on the Monday afternoon (23 April) showed how little sympathy his action commanded in the Parliamentary Labour Party. 'No cheer when he entered, in the middle of questions', Dalton wrote, 'nor when he rose at the end of questions, hardly any cheers while he was speaking, nor when he sat down'.[54] Not even the Tories taunted him. He spoke in silence to a hostile House; and for once – as even Jennie Lee admits[55] – he spoke badly. Most of the speech reads well enough today; but in delivery it was too bitter, too egotistical, too self-righteous to be effective. It did nothing to persuade even his friends and potential supporters that he was not plunging the party into turmoil and electoral disaster for inadequate and essentially personal reasons of frustration and pique.

The beginning of the speech was devoted to the folly of the rearmament programme, which he now declared was not only unrealisable but 'already known by the Chancellor of the Exchequer to be unrealisable'. 'I begged over and over again', he claimed, 'that we should not put figures in the Budget on account of defence expenditure which would not be realised.' The Cabinet minutes bear out the second contention and show that there was more than a grain of truth in the first. Moreover, in so far as the programme was realised, Bevan maintained as he had always done that it was money wasted. Quoting the warnings he had given in his misinterpreted speech in February, he asserted that they had been fully vindicated: the worldwide inflation unleashed by the American programme constituted a greater economic threat to the West than the military threat it was intended to contain. 'The fact is that the Western world has embarked upon a campaign of arms production upon a scale, so quickly and of such an extent that the foundations of political liberty and Parliamentary democracy will not be able to sustain the shock.' He enlarged again on his attractive, but to military strategists dangerously unprovable, theory of how to beat the Russians:

> It has always been clear that the weapons of the totalitarian states are, first, social and economic, and only next military; and if in attempting to meet the military effect of these totalitarian machines, the energies of the Western world are dissipated and the standard of life is lowered or industrial disturbances are created, then Soviet Communism establishes a whole series of Trojan horses in every Western economy.

Following this characteristic but somewhat academic opening, however, the mood of the speech changed abruptly. Suddenly Bevan was echoing, quite precisely, *Tribune*'s criticism of Gaitskell for a Budget which 'ran away' from socialism and was 'hailed with pleasure in the City'. 'It was a remarkable Budget. It united the City, satisfied the Opposition and disunited the Labour Party – all this', he alleged in a phrase that became one of the texts of Bevanism over the next few years, 'because we have allowed ourselves to be dragged too far behind the wheels of American diplomacy.' Britain, he claimed, 'has a message for the world which is distinct from that of America or that of the Soviet Union. Ever since 1945 we have been engaged in this country on the most remarkable piece of social reconstruction the world has ever seen.' By 1950 Britain had attained 'the moral leadership of the world'. 'There is only one hope for mankind', he declared, 'and that hope still remains in this little island.' What his colleagues – former colleagues – had done since 1950, however, was to dissipate this moral leadership by pursuing an impossible armaments programme, trying to put 'too large a programme on too narrow a base'. 'We have to adjust our paper figures to physical realities, and that is what the Treasury has not done.'

Gaitskell would certainly have retorted that that was just what he was trying to with the Health Service. At any rate the spectacle of Bevan lecturing Gaitskell on financial management was a strange one. Undeterred, however, Bevan went on to 'give a word of advice' to the Government – another prescription which was to become an axiom of Bevanism until it was finally tried, with disappointing results, by Harold Wilson in 1964:

Take economic planning away from the Treasury. They know nothing about it. The great difficulty with the Treasury is that they think they move men about when they move pieces of paper about. .... It has been perfectly obvious on several occasions that there are too many economists advising the Treasury, and now we have the added misfortune of an economist in the Chancellor of the Exchequer himself.

(He was forgetting, perhaps, that Dalton, the Chancellor who first financed the Health Service, was just as much a professional economist as Gaitskell.)

I therefore seriously suggest to the Government that they should set up a production department and put the Chancellor of the Exchequer in the position where he ought to be now, under modern planning, that is, with the function of making an annual statement of accounts. Then we should have some realism in the Budget. We should not be pushing out figures when the facts are in the opposite direction.

Now that he had Gaitskell firmly in his sights, Bevan at last reached the Health Service. Again he raised the spectre of 1931. He was accused, he said, of 'quarrelling about a triviality – spectacles and dentures'. 'You may call it a triviality,' he retorted. 'I remember the triviality that started the avalanche in 1931.' Gaitskell's triviality was to take £13 million out of a Budget of £4,000.

If he finds it necessary to mutilate, or begin to mutilate, the Health Service for £13 million out of £4,000 million, what will he do next year? Or are you next year going to take your stand on the upper denture? The lower half apparently does not matter, but the top half is sacroscanct? Is that right? ... The Health Service is squeezed between the artificial figure and rising prices. What is to be squeezed out next year? Is it the upper half? When that has been squeezed out and the same principle holds good, what do you squeeze out the year after? Prescriptions? Hospital charges? Where do you stop?

'After all', he continued, 'the National Health Service was something of which we were all very proud, and even the Opposition was beginning to be proud of it. It had only to last a few more years to become part of our traditions, and traditionalists would have claimed the credit for all of it. Why should we throw it away?' The answer, he implied, was the malice of a Chancellor who in his Budget speech had 'not one word of commendation for the Health Service'. It was 'the arithmetic of Bedlam' for Gaitskell to say, with a surplus of £39 million, that he had to have the £13 million. 'He cannot say that his arithmetic is so precise ... when last year the Treasury was £247 million out. ... What is the cause of it?' he demanded. 'Why has it been done?'

Just before he finished, Bevan turned aside to answer, in what turned out to be the most controversial section of the whole speech, the charge that he had himself agreed to prescription charges in 1949. 'The prescription charge', he countered, 'I knew would never be made, because it was impracticable.' The

243

House erupted. 'Well', Bevan insisted above the clamour, 'it was never made'.

> I will tell my hon. Friends something else too. There was another policy – there was a proposed reduction of 25,000 on the housing programme, was there not? It was never made. It was necessary for me at that time to use what everybody always said were bad tactics upon my part – I had to manoeuvre and I did manoeuvre and saved the 25,000 houses and the prescription charge.

While the House caught its breath at this astonishing confession, or rather boast, by a Cabinet Minister that he had knowingly deceived his colleagues, Bevan moved to his conclusion, calling on the Labour Party to stay true to its principles:

> There is only one hope for mankind – and that is democratic Socialism. There is only one Party in Great Britain which can do it – and that is the Labour Party. But I ask them carefully to consider how far they are polluting the stream. We have gone a long way – a very long way – against great difficulties. Do not let us change direction now. Let us make it clear, quite clear, to the rest of the world that we stand where we stood, that we are not going to allow ourselves to be diverted from our path by the exigencies of the immediate situation. We shall do what is necessary to defend ourselves – defend ourselves by arms and not only with arms but with the spiritual resources of our people.[56]

There was a good deal of nonsense in this tirade, as well as some sense; but the latter was no more welcome than the former to a parliamentary party which was in no mood to be lectured by an egotistical renegade the only practical result of whose principles seemed likely to be the early return of a Tory Government. 'It was an extraordinary performance,' Gaitskell wrote, 'totally lacking in any understanding of what people expected, and turned people even more sharply against him.'[57] Dalton agreed: 'His attack on Hugh, and his confession of having tricked his colleagues by his manoeuvres on prescription charges & [the] housing programme, were not liked.' It was 'a most vicious speech, most quotable by the Tories'.[58] More significantly, even John Freeman, who still felt bound by his promise to resign with Bevan, and did so the same day, wrote regretfully to Dalton: 'Nothing could have done more to influence me the other way than Nye's outburst this afternoon.'[59] The newspapers had a field day. Bevan's flop in the House seemed to set the seal on a spectacularly bungled resignation.

But still the worst was yet to come. The final act of the resignation drama took place the next morning (Tuesday 24th) at a special meeting of the PLP. Gaitskell made 'a very good and calm defence' of his Budget and the rearmament programme, for which he received what Douglas Jay thought was 'the biggest applause he had ever heard at a Party meeting'.[60] By contrast, when it was his turn to speak, Bevan immediately launched into another appalling display of bad temper which made his performance in the House seem quite statesmanlike. 'He was sweating & shouting & seemed on the edge of a nervous breakdown,' Dalton wrote.[61] Gaitskell gives a similar picture.

He almost screamed at the platform. At one point he said 'I won't have it. I won't have it.' And this, of course, was greeted with derision. '*You* won't have it?' called other Members of the Party. Of course in the Cabinet we have had this on a number of times but they had not seen it before.[62]

At another point he spoke of '*my* Health Service' and claimed wildly that without it Gaitskell would never have been Chancellor (presumably because Labour would have lost in 1950).[63]

Once again he raised the ghosts of 1931. 'He had been a young man in 1931, when Snowden was Chancellor & in this very room he had been howled down when he warned the Party where it was going.' But this time the past was devastatingly invoked against Bevan himself. Only one name stank in Labour nostrils more than Snowden's. 'This is Mosley speaking,' Dalton whispered loudly to Morrison, beside him on the platform. Ede, summing up, hinted at the same comparison. Jennie Lee jumped to her feet to protest. 'I mention no names,' replied Ede, 'but the cap seems to fit.' A moment later he did mention that one of the speakers that morning had reminded him of Mosley. 'Now you've said it,' shouted Bevan furiously. The meeting broke up in angry recrimination.[64] In the vote, only a handful of loyal friends supported the three resigners. In this mood of shattered fraternity, the whole party trooped across the road to Westminster Abbey to attend the memorial service for Ernest Bevin: also perhaps, many of them must have felt, for the Labour Government itself of which he had been the ballast.

Bevan's resignation qualifies as a true political tragedy. So many of the classic elements are present. First there was the long rumbling build-up leading to a false climax and the protracted, unheroic conclusion after the crisis had apparently been passed. Then there is the sense of remorseless inevitability working itself out through a combination of quite minor historical accidents. At the heart of the matter was a real clash of political philosophies; but it found expression in a petty argument over budgetary priorities, based upon assumptions which were afterwards shown to be unfounded. Above all there was the rivalry of two contrasting personalities, with the turbulent hero finally brought down by his antagonist's cool exploitation of one fatal defect of character: in this respect Bevan's is a personal tragedy to compare with Antony's or Othello's. Finally there is the consequence: the Labour Party riven in two, doomed to waste itself in fractious opposition for half a generation, until both the principal protagonists were dead. Bevan's defeat was scarcely Gaitskell's victory. Between them they practically destroyed the thing that in their different ways they loved. Which then, or neither, was most to blame?

On the fundamental question of the rearmament programme, it was Bevan who was quickly proved to have been right. Or at least, if that is too downright, it can be said that Bevan's contention that the £4,700 million programme was economically impossible and militarily unnecessary turned out to be well grounded. Ironically it was the Tories, returning to office in October 1951 after having denounced Labour's programme as recently as February as inadequate, who announced in December a scaling down of Labour's intentions.[65] It was partly that the necessary raw materials and machine tools were not available; partly that where they were available their costs had soared and the expense of buying them, at the same time as directing domestic production out of exports into military equipment, ran the country into balance-of-payments difficulties (which were then worsened by the Persian oil crisis). Whether or not Bevan, Wilson and Freeman were right in detail, they were broadly vindicated. In November 1952 it was announced that defence expenditure in 1951–2, instead of the £1,250 million projected, had been only £1,129 million. The three-year estimate of £4,700 million for 1951–4 was revised down to £4279 million, and in fact the total spent was only £3,878 million.[66] Churchill now spoke benignly of the lessening of international tension which allowed these reductions to be made without risk.

It can still be maintained, of course, in defence of Gaitskell, that it was politically necessary in April 1951 to please the Americans by announcing as big an arms programme as possible, even though it was known to be unrealistic. On this argument it has been suggested that Bevan and his co-resigners should have recognised that the full programme would never actually be carried out and therefore have let it go without a fuss. Gaitskell, it can be argued, was merely 'manoeuvring', as Bevan himself had done on prescription charges.[67] The difficulty with this, however, is that if the rearmament target was privately acknowledged to be unreal, the consequent health charges were not, but were to be introduced immediately. From the point of view of preventing health charges, it was the Chancellor's budgeting for the full £4,700 million, not the actual expenditure, which mattered.

So far as Gaitskell's personal role is concerned, it is fair to recognise that he was an unusually junior and inexperienced Chancellor, while it takes a strong Chancellor at the best of times to resist the unanimous demands of the Service chiefs for what they regard as militarily essential. In this case, with British troops in action in Korea and the threat of a Soviet invasion of Western Europe regarded very seriously, Gaitskell had little option but to give them what they wanted; nor was there any inclination among his senior colleagues or the majority of the Cabinet to do otherwise. Nevertheless the fact remains that on this question Gaitskell and the majority of the Cabinet were wrong and Bevan, Wilson and Freeman were right. The suggestion that Bevan, for his part, only took up Wilson's arguments when he needed to widen the issue after resigning on health charges holds little water. He had been making his opposition to excessive rearmament known to his colleagues for months. It has been suggested that he would have done better to resign earlier, over the big issue, instead of waiting for the minor one.[68] But it is hard to see how he could plausibly have done so. The scale of rearmament was a matter of judgement. It became a question of principle only when it involved unacceptable costs.

On the immediate question of health charges, the balance is more even. Gaitskell, backed by Morrison and others, thought he had an irrefutable case that spending on the National Health Service was too high and continually rising and needed to be checked, in the interest not only of rearmament but of the other social services. The fact that his predecessor, Cripps, had been driven to the same view is adduced as evidence that he was moved by no animus against the free service as such. There are two answers to this. The first is that health spending was in fact under control by 1951: the sharply rising cost in the first three years had been an inevitable feature of a new service which had greatly underestimated the scale of pent-up demand; to the chagrin of both Tories and Gaitskellites, the Guillebaud Committee in 1955 authoritatively acquitted the Service in this period of the sort of inherent extravagance of which it was widely accused. Therefore there was no need for Gaitskell to resurrect in 1951 the sort of charges which Cripps had been obliged to consider in 1949. Secondly, even if it were granted that the Health Service was too expensive, charges on the patient for teeth and spectacles were a trifling and essentially irrelevant response, raising an insignificant amount of revenue at maximum public irritation and political cost. By far the greatest expense of the NHS was the hospital service: it was in the area of hospital administration that financial control of the Service was, at the outset, weakest. Charges on the patient for teeth and spectacles were a mean and merely marginal response to this problem, which was in fact by 1951 well on the way to being solved.

Nevertheless Bevan was wrong to make charges a point of principle. For one thing, he was on weak ground politically, having accepted prescription charges in 1949, however much he claimed that they would never have been introduced. For another, there were already a number of minor services within the NHS for which patients were charged, such as regular transport to hospital in rural areas:[69] it was perfectly possible to regard false teeth and spectacles as similarly ancillary services, not central to the concept of free treatment. Prescription charges were much more problematic; and it is significant that Cabinet pressure forced Gaitskell to drop these in 1951 while hardly a single Minister apart from Bevan and Wilson, and no more than a handful of Labour MPs, regarded teeth and spectacles as breaching the principle. Charges may have been irrelevant or unnecessary; but by taking quite so absolutist a view of their iniquity, Bevan seemed to his colleagues to get the whole matter out of proportion, thus weakening and personalising his case. And that was where he began to go wrong.

Bevan had some reason to feel personally aggrieved. He had been passed over twice for the highest offices, and he had no faith that those who had been preferred to him believed in the sort of socialism that he believed in. More specifically, he had every reason to regard Gaitskell as a determined opponent who was using health charges as a means of driving him out of the Government. As early as June 1950, at the time he ceased attending Cripps's dinners, he had let it be known categorically that he regarded charges as a resigning matter. That Gaitskell, knowing this, had continued to press them, when they could not plausibly be represented as unavoidable, could only appear to him as a calculated challenge which he was bound to take up. It is true that Gaitskell's diaries give no support to such an interpretation of his motive. On the other hand it is difficult to see why he was quite so determined on health charges, even before the Korean War and doubly so afterwards. Once into the argument, Gaitskell undoubtedly felt it essential, both for his own political credibility and for the Government's, that he should win it. Once into the argument, he felt that it would be an intolerable situation for the whole of the rest of the Cabinet to be forced to give in to the threats of two of its members. This explains his quite exceptional stubbornness in the face of suggestions, even from the Prime Minister, that he bend a little. Once into the argument, once he had drawn up his Budget and presented it to Cabinet, it may be that he was right. It is still difficult to see why he was so determined on health charges, except to provoke Bevan. If this was his intention, he succeeded beyond any reasonable expectations.

For from this point on, Bevan behaved abominably. If he was going to resign he should have done so promptly and with dignity on the clear matter of principle on 10 April. It is perhaps to his credit that he allowed himself to be persuaded to think of the damage to the party and agreed to stay on. But having so agreed, he should have stuck to it. It was intolerable to keep the threat of his resignation hanging over the party for the next fortnight. Three influences combined to change his mind. The first was his own pride. He stayed his resignation on Budget Day in the expectation that his conciliatory gesture would be answered by some comparable concession by Gaitskell, under pressure from the Cabinet if necessary; having hoped to get his way by threatening to resign, he now expected to get it by withdrawing his threat. He was hurt and angry when his magnanimity was rebuffed. 'Aren't I worth £13 million?' It was a bitter shock to discover that in the estimation of his colleagues – 'either old men or rootless men' – he was not. In this mood he gave way to childish tantrums of envy, self-pity, paranoia and ultimately hysteria.

Secondly, his injured pride was worked on by his wife and favourite political disciple, Michael Foot. Practically all the future Bevanites, who supported him once he had resigned, were opposed to him doing so at that time on that issue, for the reasons set out in Freeman's letter of 10 April. But more than any of them it was the faithful Foot, playing the role of Iago, and

Jennie – above all Jennie – who had his ear. Jennie's influence on Bevan's political career generally was not great. He normally knew his own mind and went his own way without reference to her, just as she pursued her own career, at a lower level, independently of him. Their marriage was in that respect remarkably equal – two politicians of similar sympathies living together and providing one another with companionship and a private refuge from public storms, but not normally operating as a political duo. Only at moments of perplexity did Jennie's influence weigh with Nye; in the view of most of their colleagues it was usually a bad influence. She remained all her life the fiery rebel who had got into Parliament at twenty-three and followed Maxton out of the Labour Party in 1932. Bevan had been a rebel too, and the strain of rebellion was always strong within him; but it contended with an equally strong practical desire to win and use power. Jennie's Nye was the romantic rebel, not the responsible Minister, and her influence was usually directed at persuading him to kick over the traces. 'Jennie', Freeman told Dalton on 17 April, 'is opposition-minded & doesn't like Nye being in Government & has a guilt-complex about a Cabinet Minister's salary.'[70] If his pride was wounded, she was the last person to advise him to turn the other cheek.* Summing up her influence years later, Attlee remarked pithily: 'He needed a sedative. He got an irritant.'[71]

But it was not only Bevan's ego that Jennie and Foot flattered. They were also able to play on his genuine and legitimate feeling that the Government had lost its sense of direction and was drifting inexorably to the right; that the left needed a leader; and that he, as that leader, would have more influence outside the Government than inside it and should come out now while there was still time to restore the party's commitment to socialism before the next election. He did believe, with good reason, that he could lead and educate the electorate to embrace socialism better than anyone else. On several occasions since 1948 he had felt that he might be better employed in that educational role than sitting gagged in Cabinet. Now, when pride and principle were urging him to go, this was another argument against holding back.

It is an argument which underlines the peculiar political circumstances against which the whole drama was played out. For the Government, as the crisis loomed, was leaderless. Two or three years earlier, the conflict between Bevan and Gaitskell could have been contained and defused by the combined authority of the Big Five. But in April 1951 Bevin was dead, Cripps retired, Dalton discredited and Attlee temporarily on the sidelines. This left the whole onus of responsibility for averting the crisis on Morrison, who as Foreign Secretary, a long-standing critic of the Health Service and

---

* George Thomas, then a left-winger who regarded himself as a supporter of Bevan, was shaken by Jennie's reaction when he urged her to use her influence to persuade Nye not to resign. 'You yellow-livered cur,' she told him. 'You're just like all the rest! You're another MacDonald or Snowden. Go away from me!' 'I could hardly believe my ears.' (George Thomas, *Mr Speaker: The Memoirs of Viscount Tonypandy* [Century 1985], pp. 69–70.)

an old enemy of Bevan was strongly predisposed towards Gaitskell. Morrison made one half-hearted effort to suggest a compromise, but he did not – perhaps he did not feel he had the authority – take the situation in hand and impose a compromise as a fit Attlee, with a good deal more instinctive sympathy for Bevan's case, just might have done. Attlee much later blamed Morrison for having 'lost' Bevan and Wilson;[72] he inclined to believe that he could have found a way to keep them, and it is possible that he could. It is equally arguable that even from his hospital bed he should have asserted himself much more strongly. In the end, whether one blames Attlee or Morrison or simply the fact that there was a vacuum at the top, the absence of leadership, resulting in the two rivals being left to confront one another without the restraining influence that Cripps on the one hand and Bevin on the other might have exerted, was a critical factor in bringing a dangerous situation to a disastrous conclusion.

Finally then, what is the verdict? There can be no simple apportionment of blame. Attlee and Morrison must take their share of it, and even between the two principals there was right and wrong on both sides. But it comes down to this: that on the economic merits of the argument, both about rearmament and the financing of the Health Service, Bevan was broadly right and Gaitskell wrong; that by insisting on pressing health charges Gaitskell knowingly and unnecessarily provoked the crisis; but that when it came to the point, by getting the matter out of perspective, by overplaying his hand so self-indulgently, by losing his temper and abusing his colleagues, and ultimately in allowing himself to be persuaded to resign, against the better judgement of his cooler friends, Bevan was wrong, catastrophically wrong. By his resignation he opened a split in the Labour Party which helped to ensure electoral defeat six months later and which then, back in opposition, widened inexorably into a bitter feud which kept the party out of power for thirteen years. It did not, if that was his calculation, enable him to recapture the party for true socialism: on the contrary, by acting the part of a disloyal and power-crazed wrecker, Bevan disqualified himself in these few weeks from any prospect of ever winning the leadership, and his ideas from receiving serious consideration. On the other hand, Gaitskell's victory was pyrrhic. If his purpose was, as his diary suggests, to demonstrate to the country Labour's capacity to govern responsibly, it was achieved at the cost of denying the party the chance to govern again at all in his lifetime. His high-mindedness did not reap the electoral reward he thought it deserved. 'It is really a fight for the soul of the Labour Party,' he told Dalton at the height of the crisis: if Bevan were to win it, 'I am afraid . . . we shall be out of power for years and years.'[73] Bevan did not win it, but the fight itself kept Labour out of power for years and years. Perhaps Bevan, with all his faults, was worth £13 million after all.

6

Kicking Against the Pricks, 1951–1955

Chapter 17

The Beginnings of Bevanism: the 1951 Election and After

Bevan's resignation opened a new chapter in the history of the Labour Party. Some would say it was the beginning of the end of the Labour Party. For whereas in Government he had been an isolated figure supported by only one or two cronies to whom he was scrupulous about not divulging details of the battles he was waging in Cabinet, the moment he resigned he found himself immediately at the head of a substantial dissatisfied minority within the party which had hitherto lacked either a leader or legitimacy. Until he resigned the mainstream left, excluding only a few extreme pacifists and fellow-travellers (who had mostly been expelled in 1948–9), were safely included within the fold and basically loyal, despite numerous grouses, to what they still regarded as 'their' Labour Government. Bevan's resignation opened a Pandora's box of grievances, mutual suspicion and genuine differences of political philosophy which, once released, proved impossible to put back into the box again but, on the contrary, took wing and multiplied to create a deep division in the party which has never healed. This is why Bevan's action, however justified on grounds of policy, was politically so ill judged. It marked a fatal watershed from which Labour's once steady upward progress – admittedly already showing signs of faltering – went into steep and prolonged decline.

The left in the 1945 Parliament had been activated by most of the same concerns which later characterised the Bevanites – the more vigorous pursuit of socialism at home, naturally, but more particularly a 'socialist' foreign policy less dependent on the United States and less wedded to the Cold War. There was, moreover, an obvious continuity of personnel between the Keep Left group, formed in November 1946, and the Bevanite group of 1951–5: the original pamphlet *Keep Left* was written by Michael Foot, Ian Mikardo and Richard Crossman and signed by a dozen more MPs including Geoffrey Bing, Donald Bruce, Harold Davies, Leslie Hale, J.P.W.Mallalieu and Stephen Swingler – all prominent Bevanites. Nevertheless the moderation of *Keep Left*'s criticism of the Government is striking. After Bevin complained furiously at the 1947 Conference that he had been stabbed in the back by backbench criticism while he had been battling for Britain's interests abroad, they virtually disappeared from view for two years. So far were they from being rebels that in 1948 Crossman and Mikardo actually claimed that most of what *Keep Left* had proposed was now Government policy.[1] A second pamphlet, *Keeping Left*, published in January 1950 and endorsed by a significantly different group of signatories, including Barbara Castle, was still less subversive: in the shocked aftermath of the Berlin crisis and the Prague coup, *Keeping Left* explicitly accepted the necessity of the American alliance to contain Communism in Europe. *Tribune* too at this time strongly supported NATO and, at its outbreak, the Korean War. The proto-Bevanites, as they may be called before 1951, were unquestionably a group – meeting regularly at the House, taking minutes, issuing papers and from July 1950, on Mikardo's initiative, holding 'Brains Trusts' around the country, very much as they were to do after 1951. But they were a group of no great importance, numbering no more than a dozen regulars, displaying no public rancour and posing no threat to party unity.[2]

This harmonious picture was already beginning to change in early 1951 under the impact of rearmament, which gave the group for the first time an issue of first-class importance round which it could cohere and grow. The economists Thomas Balogh and Dudley Seers contributed papers on how to pay for rearmament, and discreet contact was established with those Ministers – Wilson, Freeman, Strauss and, contrary to his previous practice, Bevan himself – who were known to be unhappy about the Government's commitment and the means the Chancellor proposed of paying for it.[3] The ground was therefore to some extent prepared before Bevan's resignation. Even so, it was his act of resignation which transformed the situation. Augmented by the adherence of the three resigning Ministers, the old Keep Left group was an immeasurably stronger political force; by the same token Bevan, by the acquisition of an organised following, was converted for the first time in his life from an isolated malcontent into the leader of a faction. More important than these formal dispositions, however, was the bitterness which the resignation crisis engendered; it was this which ensured that what might have been no more than a disagreement over budgetary priorities exploded so violently into a left–right feud, polarised around the personalities of Bevan and Gaitskell, with the partisans of both vowing vengeance on the other. It was Bevan's publicising of the breach, his open attacks on Gaitskell, his displays of temper at party meetings, that created the atmosphere of recrimination which made the comradely resolution of differences impossible. In this respect, despite his sincere belief that it was socialism, not personalities, which concerned him, his genuine ambivalence about leading a faction and his eloquent calls for unity, the dispute is rightly called the Bevanite split. From the moment of his resignation he, Bevan, the rightness or wrongness of his resignation and the threat or challenge which he was seen to pose to the future of the Labour Party were the issues to which all other issues were inescapably subordinated.

Tribune did its best to keep the pot boiling. 'Now that the first shock of the resignations is passed', it wrote excitedly on 4 May, 'the Labour Movement is lustily enjoying its new freedom. ... The dynamism of free discussion is already carrying us forward to new positions of Socialist strength and Socialist unity.'[4] In the spirit of free discussion it gave space to Anthony Crosland to rebut Bevan's criticism of the Budget, then roundly ridiculed his arguments as Tory nonsense.[5] It lost no opportunity over the summer to insist that Bevan had been right and in September, when Gaitskell on a visit to America was forced to admit the difficulty of meeting the planned level of rearmament, demanded gleefully in a front-page headline that was not calculated to mend fences, 'Has Gaitskell Joined the Bevanites?'[6] The *New Statesman*, much of it written by Crossman and Freeman, took the same line that the resignations, far from damaging the party, had revitalised it.[7] As a matter of fact there is something to be said for this view. Party membership was increasing;[8] in July the *Tribune* pamphlet *One Way Only*, with an introduction by Bevan, Wilson and Freeman, quickly sold 100,000 copies; and most surprisingly the Gallup poll, which had shown Labour trailing the Tories by eleven points in March, showed the deficit reduced to only six points in June. It was the right who feared an autumn Conference at which they might be humiliatingly rejected by a Bevanite rank and file, and believed that the very existence of a vocal left wing must inevitably hurt Labour at the election, whenever it came. From the diaries of Gaitskell and Dalton, and the recorded comments of Morrison, it is perfectly clear that the right, over-reacting in the conviction that Bevanism was a cancer which needed to be cut out of the party, contributed at least as much as the left to ensuring that the passions of April were not allowed to die away.[9] 'Herbert and I', Gaitskell noted in August, 'think that the PM has taken a very weak line about Bevan.'[10]

Bevan himself, meanwhile, adopted a studiously high-minded line, denying the existence of any party split and insisting, in a notable speech in Glasgow on May Day, on the moral priority of aid to the underdeveloped world. Despite all the resources of modern civilisation, he charged, millions were still dying of famine in India, adding, in a phrase which still rings hauntingly in 1987: 'We shall find people starving to death by the side of television sets if we are not careful.'[11] This was in fact the central theme of *One Way Only*: that the resources being poured into armaments to meet a grossly exaggerated threat from the Soviet Union should be diverted to building up the backward nations and supporting, not opposing, the 'social revolution in Asia, Africa and the Middle East' which should be recognised as 'the dominant fact of the twentieth century'.[12] *One Way Only*, and Bevan's speeches in these months, were a clear and commendable attempt to lift the level of debate from the mundane details of teeth and spectacles to face the worldwide implications of rearmament, Korea and the Cold War. By its tone of reasoned argument, *One Way Only* disappointed and rather bewildered the press, which was primed to expect a written distillation of Bevanite spleen.

In Parliament, after the explosion of his resignation speech, Bevan was equally conciliatory. He intervened a couple of times on the Health Charges Bill only to attack the Tories, not Gaitskell (though in July he did allow himself another mild dig at the Treasury's methods of book-keeping).[13] The point must be stressed that in the months immediately after April Bevan gave little sign of leading a revolt against the Labour leadership. Released from the provocations of office, his basic loyalty to the survival of a Labour Government – struggling on with a majority of six – reasserted itself and he personally did nothing to rock the boat.

In August he and Jennie visited Yugoslavia, where they were deeply impressed by Tito and Milovan Djilas, heroic resistance leaders whom they romantically embraced as comrades in socialism. Henceforward Yugoslavia was for Bevan the model of a small backward country struggling to establish its own form of socialism in defiance equally of the Soviet Union and the USA. In Yugoslavia too he found time, with Jennie's help, to write, or rather collate, the book he had been planning since before the war, a book which was to set out the fundamentals of a humane British parliamentary socialism as he saw them: his personal creed. But *In Place Of Fear* was not yet finished when Bevan returned in September to face the General Election which Attlee, against the advice of many of his colleagues, had rather wearily decided to call for 25 October.

First came the party Conference – the heat largely taken out of it by the imminent election. The Bevanites demonstrated their strength in the constituencies by taking four of the seven places on the NEC, with Barbara Castle coming second behind Bevan, Tom Driberg and Mikardo third and sixth, and Shinwell, the Minister departmentally responsible for rearmament, humiliatingly pushed off. Gaitskell thought the results 'pretty grim' and privately put them down to 'some pretty shameful canvassing' by the Bevanites to concentrate their vote.[14] At the Conference itself, however, all was unity. 'The argument we were going to have', Bevan told the annual *Tribune* rally, 'has now been replaced by a bigger argument. When the Prime Minister announced the General Election, from that moment I made up my mind that our argument must wait until the other argument is over.'[15] Replying to the main debate in the Conference proper, on Labour's manifesto, he devoted most of his speech to the specifically Bevanite concern of how Britain could aid the poor countries of the world without provoking inflation at home.

> It is not going to be possible to prevent those hundreds of millions of populations over-running Western civilisation or bringing it down unless we can bring to them assistance from our own resources, and that assistance cannot come from capitalism, because those areas are no longer possible areas of profitable investment. This is as I see it the central issue of the election.

The only answer was socialist planning of resources between home consumption, rearmament (to which he did not deny a necessary role) and aid. The possibility of a return to Tory government in the present state of the world, he proclaimed, substituting Churchillian 'rodomontades' for 'the quiet, moderate, balanced approach of Clem Attlee', was frightening: it was Churchill and the Tories, he alleged, who by their clumsy intervention in 1918–20 had distorted the course of the Russian Revolution and prepared the way for the 'malignancy' of Stalin. 'That is why, now that the Orient is in the same kind of ferment, we do not want China, we do not want Indonesia and we do not want the Middle East to be driven into the same form of totalitarian tyranny that the Tories drove the Soviet revolution into after 1917.'

Despite this boldly individual view of the priorities facing the party, however, Bevan ended with a rousing warning against disunity. Complimenting an earlier speaker who had reminded Conference that her generation of Labour voters had not been worried about high electricity bills – they simply had no light – he rejoiced in the revolution accomplished since 1945:

> That is the reason why, no matter what our differences, we must never allow the British Labour Movement to become schismatic. We must avoid at all costs a repetition here of what has happened to continental socialist movements. That is why we must never carry doctrinaire differences to the point of schism; that is why our movement is based primarily on the industrial masses. It is not based so much upon ideologies as upon social experience and we work out the ideologies in terms of the social experience. That is why when the election was decided upon my friends and myself had no hesitation at all in saying that nothing must prevent us from uniting our forces to destroy the challenge now made to the Socialist Movement, because our lives would have been intolerable if we had done anything at all that made it possible for a Conservative majority to get back at Westminster.[16]

To Gaitskell, Morrison and Dalton this was brazen hypocrisy. To them Bevan was the schismatic, Bevan the doctrinaire. And so he was, up to a point. Yet this passage perfectly embodies what was at bottom the most deeply held tenet of his socialism: that it was based, as he said, not on Marx but on the social experience of the industrial masses. Marx explained that social experience, but doctrine came second to class; his fundamental doctrine was still the class struggle, now to be peacefully accomplished through Parliament. That was what to him the Bevanite quarrel was all about. That is why it was so profound: it cut deeper than matters of mere doctrine. His objection was to Labour becoming dominated by people whose socialism was not founded on the experience of the industrial masses. His objection to Gaitskell was less a personal than a symbolic one.

But commitment to the Labour Party itself was his supreme value, so that he had no difficulty at election time in closing ranks. 'Therefore,' he concluded his rallying speech at Scarborough, 'let us go into the fight joyously. It is a good thing to have a fight – with the right people. ... I think we shall win. I really believe that.' The electorate would remember 1918, 1933, the destruction of Spain, the Tories' record of international treachery, and send

257

Labour back to power, 'because in Labour and in Labour only resides the hope of future peace for mankind'.[17]

Maybe the electorate did remember. The 1951 election was certainly fought to an unusual degree on foreign affairs. British interests were under threat in both Persia (where Dr Moussadeq had nationalised the oilfields) and Suez (where the Egyptian Government unilaterally abrogated the treaty securing British control of the canal). The Tories accused Labour of weakness. Morrison – who had in fact been eager to send troops himself to both trouble-spots – responded angrily by branding Churchill a warmonger. The *Daily Mirror* took up Bevan's contrast between Churchill and Attlee with its famous scare headline 'Whose Finger On The Trigger?' Churchill, with a heavy-handed attempt at rhyme, tried to make the three issues of the campaign 'Sud*an*, Abad*an*, Bev*an*'; but all the evidence suggests that, contrary to the expectations of the Gaitskellites, the Bevan bogey raised very little alarm. Left-wing candidates did no better or worse than right-wing ones. At home, Labour stood proudly on its record of social welfare and full employment, with no specific commitments to further nationalisation, and in the event did remarkably well, polling nearly fourteen million votes, more than ever before or since and 200,000 more than the Conservatives. After six years of Labour Government this was a moral victory. But the Tories won more seats – 321 to 295, an overall majority of seven. The difference was that the Liberals, their funds exhausted by the 1950 contest, could afford to put up only 109 candidates; in several critical seats, straight fights benefited the Tories.[18] So Churchill sneaked back. But Labour had no sense of defeat. Dalton thought the results 'wonderful'. No one dreamed that Labour would be out for thirteen years. *Tribune* thought it 'a tragedy that Labour's period of Government has been interrupted' and two months later was still writing complacently of Churchill's 'stopgap administration'. Attlee told Dalton that he expected to be Prime Minister again before the end of 1953. Unusually, then, after a defeat, there was no need of a post-mortem. The Bevanites could not after all be blamed for a débâcle, while members of the Government themselves admitted that they were tired and needed a break from office. Had the party now pulled together, regrouped and recouped its energies in opposition, all might still have been well. But the genie was out of the bottle and, with defeat, the last restraints were now off. To some on both sides of the party, opposition provided an opportunity for settling the argument once and for all, while 'regrouping' meant the extermination of the other.

The first thing the Bevanites had to decide when the new Parliament met was whether to stand for the Shadow Cabinet. Bevan, who was the only one of them who might have got elected, was determined not to; so that was that. 'What was the good of resigning in order to be free to speak', he argued at a group meeting at Crossman's house attended by twenty-four of a possible thirty-two members, 'if he at once surrenders that freedom by joining the Committee?'[19] The point was partly that he wanted to be able to speak over the whole spectrum of policy, but more particularly that he wanted to be able to attack the Tories' anticipated acquiescence in American attitudes in Korea and the Far East (which he feared were leading 'straight towards war' with China)[20] without being inhibited, as Attlee and his colleagues were, by Labour's commitments in this area. It was a reasonable position, but it had the effect of emphasising at the very start of the session that the Bevanites intended to hold themselves apart from the rest of the party, thus confirming the loyalists' worst suspicions. It was true that the Bevanites did continue to meet and organise themselves as a separate group; yet already Richard Crossman's diaries were beginning to repeat the refrain which re-echoes with increasing frustration over the next three years, that they were a group without a leader or a coherent strategy. Whatever some of the others wanted – the three keenest to create an effective dissenting bloc were probably Crossman, Mikardo and Wilson – Bevan himself really only wanted a group of compliant followers to amplify his own concerns. He was torn, as so often in his career, between the instinct to rebel and the powerful contrary pull of loyalty to the movement. 'He is an extraordinary mixture of withdrawnness and boldness,' Crossman wrote on 26 November, 'and he is always advising Ian Mikardo against rushing into action. ... He cannot stand the idea of uniting with Morrison and Gaitskell. Yet, on the other hand, when it comes to the point, he jibs at each fighting action as you propose it.'[21] 'So far from being a great strategist and organiser of cabals,' Crossman concluded in December, 'Nye is an individualist who, however, is an extraordinarily pleasant member of a group. But the last thing he does is to lead it. He dominates its discussions simply because he is fertile in ideas, but leadership and organisation are things he instinctively shrinks away from.'[22]

During the autumn Bevan was, as Gaitskell noted suspiciously, 'very quiescent',[23] working to finish *In Place Of Fear*. He did not make his first speech in the new House until 4 December, when he weighed in to deride Harold Macmillan's vaunted housing programme. Churchill had promised at the election to build 300,000 houses a year. At the expense of what, Bevan asked: 'Schools? Factories? Hospitals? Power stations?' Defending his own record in much more difficult circumstances, he put his finger unerringly on the secret of Macmillan's numbers trick: 'If we reduce the size of houses to rabbit hutches, of course we can build more.'[24] Crossman recorded that the Labour benches were relieved to have him back. 'Somehow they all felt better and safer, hearing him attacking Tory housing policy, although that policy is largely a continuation of ours.'*[25]

Two days later Churchill mischievously stirred up Labour's quarrel by

---

* Dalton, as Minister of Housing from January to October 1951, had already cut the size of Bevan's houses.

admitting that the new Government would not be able to spend the full rearmament allocation provided for by Labour, back-handedly complimenting 'the right hon. Gentleman the Member for Ebbw Vale ... for having, it appears by accident, perhaps not for the best of motives, happened to be right'.[26] Bevan was furious at the graceless manner of Churchill's admission. But *Tribune* exulted, gleefully quoting back all the solemn warnings of only a few months before that the £4,700 million programme was 'essential to our survival', 'the *minimum* required to deter aggression' and could be fulfilled 'without too great strain'. 'A main item in the Bevanite thesis', Foot crowed, 'is proved to the hilt.' It was proved 'as irrefragably as anything can be proved in politics' that the free Health Service was sacrificed 'on the basis of figures about which Mr Gaitskell happened to be wrong as surely as Aneurin Bevan, in Churchill's phrase, "happened to be right"'.[27] Thus vindicated, and with his book finished, Bevan began in the New Year to emerge on to the offensive, both against the Government and implicitly against his former colleagues.

On 31 January, in an economic debate, he made his first big parliamentary speech since April – 'a major event', delivered to 'packed and wildly enthusiastic Labour benches',[28] brilliantly pulling together all the themes with which he had been playing since his resignation. First he attacked the Treasury, highlighting the tension between its 'hysterical attempts to put the balance sheet right, leaving the underlying economic facts alone' and the Labour Government's socialist efforts at rational planning. Successive Chancellors of the Exchequer, he mocked, were 'bound to get the figures right even if the facts are wrong'.

> In this country we have an annual Budget. Every year the figures are totted up and every year they have to balance. Why? Because we are still carrying on, in an industrial community, the conventions of a pastoral society. Just because the harvest occurs every year in an agricultural community, we must have an annual Budget, although in a modern industrial society the annual crops are an insignificant proportion of total production, and no balance sheet today corresponds with the actual facts.
>
> That is the reason why my right hon. Friend [Gaitskell] – I do not blame him for this: he was the inheritor of the convention, although he followed it with conspicuous enthusiasm – tried to push into one annual statement of accounts for 1951–52 machine tools which will not arrive before 1953. That is a fact, because the statement of accounts bears no relationship at all to the rhythm of industrial production.

What was required, he asserted, reviving the principal proposal of the abortive Cripps putsch against Attlee in 1947, was a Minister of Economic Planning – to initiate, among other things, the search for raw materials which could not be left to private enterprise.

Then, with a devastating debating ploy, he trapped Churchill into endorsing his Chancellor's proposal, for book-keeping reasons, to run down industrial stocks at a time when, in his capacity as Minister of Defence, he

260

was warning of the imminent risk of war. 'The right hon. Gentleman', he charged, 'is not fit for his Office.' Churchill could only counter that Bevan was trying to repay him for calling him a 'squalid nuisance' during the war. 'I must say', Bevan retorted, 'that I thought I had repaid that account pretty often.'

When Bevan was on song the House did not want to let him stop. Three times in this fifty-minute speech he suggested that he had spoken too long, and three times he was urged to 'Go on'. He ended with an attack on the Tories for perpetuating and extending – as he had warned Labour that they would – Gaitskell's health charges, not only on teeth and spectacles but now on prescriptions and hearing aids as well, with provision for exemptions. 'That means more staff, more interrogation, more humiliation and more means tests everywhere. . . . We get more and more overheads, and less and less service to the patient.' In his wider concerns since then, he had not forgotten the issue of principle on which he actually resigned; in a further vindication of his stand then, Labour in opposition was now united around repealing the Tory charges. 'There are certain disciplines, certain sacrifices,' he concluded, 'that the country is prepared to make until the economy is put on a wholesome basis, but these charges are cruel, unnecessary, mean and unjust, and there is no mandate for them. They ought to be withdrawn.'[29]

With this speech, Bevan reasserted his pre-eminence, whether in the Shadow Cabinet or out of it, as Labour's most compelling champion. 'When he speaks in the House,' Dalton noted, 'he exercises a hypnotic influence over many of our people. It's pathetic and dangerous to watch their eyes fixed on him.'[30] In February he made another significant intervention in a foreign affairs debate, coming to the rescue, ironically, of Morrison, who had been floored by Churchill unscrupulously revealing his willingness, as Foreign Secretary, to agree to the United States bombing China. Bevan rebuked Churchill's constitutional impropriety and counter-attacked effectively, challenging Churchill to disown a broadcast by John Foster Dulles to the effect that America 'would not stand idly by' while any Far Eastern country remained under Communism.

> On this side of the House we are afraid that the activities now going on in Korea are being slowly converted into a world-wide attack on Communism, and we believe that, if it is allowed to continue much further, it will mean the end of independence in British foreign policy and it may mean the end of civilisation.

The Americans, Bevan insisted, misunderstood what was happening in Asia. The spread of Communism was not due to the machinations of the Soviet Union, but to poverty.

> It is the consequence of a revolution which will go on for the rest of this century and will not be contained by the military arms of the United States of America, Great Britain or Western Europe all together. That is why we think that a very great deal of energy, of material wealth, is being thrown away in fighting the

261

wrong sort of war. The war that we want fought is a war against those despairing social conditions that give rise to war.*[31]

Following this speech, Chuter Ede noted growing concern on the right of the party that Bevan was being allowed to make so much of the parliamentary running.[32] Morrison's ineptitude in foreign affairs was becoming an embarrassment even to his friends, while admiration for Bevan was reviving. Gaitskell now began organising some of his younger friends – Tony Crosland, Roy Jenkins, Christopher Mayhew, Woodrow Wyatt – to make sure that the right's case was properly put.[33] On the NEC, Bevan continued to bicker angrily with Morrison: on one occasion they had a stand-up row over which of them had won or lost Labour more votes at the last election.[34] But these rows were hidden from the party at large. Dalton was alarmed to find that Crosland and Maurice Edelman considered that Bevan had not put a foot wrong since the election and might yet be Attlee's successor.[35] The sense that Bevan's stock was rising was the background to the crisis which broke over the Tory Government's Defence White Paper on 5 March.

A clash was, as Crossman wrote afterwards, practically unavoidable on this issue. 'After all, the three Ministers who resigned in '51 could not have been expected to change their minds over the last twelve months, any more than those who had not resigned could be expected to do so.'[36] The Labour leadership was in a difficulty, wanting to oppose the Government but feeling debarred from criticising an armaments programme which was smaller than they had budgeted for themselves, and anxious not to repeat the party's mistake in the thirties by being seen to vote against the defence estimates. Prompted by Gaitskell, they refused to consider a Bevanite proposal that the party unite on the recognition that circumstances had changed since 1951.[37] Instead they put up what *Tribune* rightly called a 'sham amendment'[38] supporting the Government's programme but doubting its capacity to carry it out, with a three-line whip instructing members to support the amendment and abstain on the Government's motion. In the division, however, fifty-seven Labour members, by no means all of them paid-up Bevanites, abstained on the amendment and voted against the Government.

Such ostentatious indiscipline on the part of a quarter of the parliamentary party created, as Gaitskell flatly put it, 'great indignation',[39] and the Shadow Cabinet immediately proposed strong action against the rebels. At once Bevan, without consulting his colleagues, raised the temperature further by announcing in his constituency that he would not sign any undertaking to toe the line in future; he seemed positively to ask to be expelled and for a wild moment even to contemplate setting up a rival party.[40] But the indignation was not all directed against the Bevanites. It soon became clear that there was a large central body of the party which was equally critical of the leadership

---

* It was soon after this that the Third World aid organisation War on Want was founded, with Harold Wilson taking a prominent role among its patrons.

for getting it into such a mess, and a compromise resolution initiated by George Strauss and John Strachey quickly gathered signatures. Gaitskell – whom Ede blamed for having forced the 'showdown'[41] – was contemptuous of the fainthearts who were 'frightened at the prospect of Bevan and some of the others having to go out of the Party altogether'. Such a possibility did not worry Gaitskell. 'I was naturally quite prepared for this to happen,' he confided to his diary, 'and indeed there would have been some advantage for it would have left us much freer to attack him.'

'However', he continued, 'as it turned out, that was not the view of the majority'.[42] On the contrary, at a party meeting on 10 March the Strauss/ Strachey compromise was carried – despite another violent diatribe by Bevan at his most provocative – by 162 votes to 73. Instead of accepting it, Attlee unwisely insisted on his own tougher motion and was humiliatingly rebuffed by a similar margin. Although even under the compromise Standing Orders – suspended in 1945 – were restored, forbidding members in future to vote against majority decisions and allowing abstention only on grounds of 'conscience', this was a significant victory for the Bevanites. Those on the right who had wanted to crack the whip in the hope that the Bevanites would expel themselves were soundly defeated by the solid centre of the party; for once the majority's urge for unity was exerted in favour of the left. 'The fact is', Crossman reflected, 'that, without Bevin to advise him, Attlee has completely misjudged the attitude of the unions, which realistically assess the strength of Bevanism in the rank and file. In this meeting Attlee's support was almost exclusively middle class.'[43]

Chapter 18

The Manifesto That Wasn't:
In Place of Fear

Three weeks later, with perfect timing, *In Place of Fear* was published. 'The creed of the most talked-about figure in British politics', boasted the publishers' advertisements. 'A plan for the future which NOBODY can ignore'.[1] Had it really been a plan for the future, Bevan could have dictated the agenda of British politics for the next ten years. The Labour Party, its hold on the majority of the electorate still intact despite the loss of office, was just beginning the search for a fresh definition of practical socialism to recapture the inspiration of 1945 and build on its historic achievements up to 1950. Of course, Morrison and Gaitskell would not have tamely swallowed a Bevanite programme; but such a programme in the spring of 1952 would have given the Bevanites an initiative which they were at that moment well positioned to exploit. Unfortunately for such hopes, Bevan's book was not a programme at all; even as a creed it was disappointingly woolly and backward-looking. He cannot be blamed, of course, for his publishers' hype: *In Place of Fear* was never intended as a Bevanite manifesto. Had he been the determined leader of an extremist faction that his enemies in the party and in the press assumed him to be, perhaps it would have been. Characteristically, on the contrary, the book is a highly personal, utterly unstructured, mish-mash of autobiography and sub-Marxist philosophy, questionable assertions and idealistic hopes; illumined by many striking phrases and seductive ideas, but pervaded by a dismaying sense of muddle and irrelevance. It must be one of the most disillusioning books ever written by a prophet to whom so many ardent followers looked for a way forward.

The glimpses of autobiography – many of them quoted earlier – are the most interesting part of the book. Ostensibly Bevan despised the 'nonsense' of romantic biography (p. 21).[2] Yet his description of his own formative experiences in South Wales graphically illustrates the belief he had expressed at Scarborough that ideology should be based on the social experience of the industrial masses. Above all it illustrates his belief that his own experience in Tredegar between 1910 and 1930 represented the authentic formative experience of the labour movement itself, the experience which made Labour a socialist party but which the modern Labour Party was in danger of growing away from. ('A political party which begins to pick its personnel from un-representative types', he warns in a characteristic aside, 'is in for trouble' [p. 35]; the allusion is unmistakable.) The description of his early grounding in socialist literature, from Jack London to Marx, is immensely revealing. At the same time it lends support to the damaging impression that he had not read very much since. 'You never see him reading a book, and you never hear him say "I don't know",' a Labour Member remarked significantly to Dalton in 1954.[3] Bevan as a boy had been a voracious reader; as a young MP in the 1929 Parliament he could still hold his own with John Strachey. But by the fifties his pretensions to intellectualism tended to consist of readings to friends of selected passages from his favourite Rodo. The *Times* review of *In Place of Fear* was harsh, but surely accurate, in putting its finger on this limitation of his thinking. 'The self-educating', Bevan writes in explanation of his discovery of Marx, 'naturally seize on the knowledge which makes their own experience intelligible' (p. 38). They equally prefer, the reviewer shrewdly suggested, 'the knowledge which their own experience makes intelligible. The close relationship between thought and experience, which an academic education seeks to break down, is obviously important, for it is the symbols of Mr Bevan's past experience which still remain the most formative influence on his thought.'[4]

Patronising, perhaps, but hard to deny. The central shortcoming of *In Place of Fear* is that its political analysis is no more than a tired rehash of the ideas Bevan had developed in *Tribune* in the thirties. Then they had seemed fresh, ingenious and plausible; capitalism had indeed seemed to many people on the verge of collapse and Bevan offered a cleverly argued hope that the transition to a social order less wasteful of human talent could be achieved painlessly and democratically. To propose the same analysis in 1952, however, taking no account of the intervening impact of the war and six years of Labour Government, was an admission that his historical theorising had failed to keep up with the progress of history. His favourite formulation was still that society was a battleground between three forces – property, poverty and democracy. 'Either poverty will use democracy to win the struggle against property, or property, in fear of poverty, will destroy democracy' (p. 23). The neat logic of this had always been questionable: democracy is not a 'force' in the same sense that property and poverty are. But more important in 1952, the crude black and white division of society into property and poverty, if it ever had been true outside South Wales, was now patently out of date. Quite apart from the innumerable complex gradations of the class structure and the steady expansion of the middle class, full employment, Labour's Welfare State and Bevan's own Health Service had made nonsense of any such simple dichotomy. Then again, still true to Marx – whose primacy in socialist theory he specifically acknowledged (pp. 37–8) – Bevan saw only two possible forms of society: capitalism and socialism.* He still simply assumed the overthrow of the former and its replacement by the latter, because he believed that this was the way society was evolving and must evolve. Capitalism was anarchy; socialism applied science. Capitalism's irremediable inefficiency Bevan still demonstrated by the example of the steel industry in the thirties and specifically by the closure of Ebbw Vale (pp. 92–4). There was great force in Bevan's pre-war criticism of the closing of old factories and the siting of new ones strictly according to market forces, ignoring the social costs to blighted communities. But both the wartime Coalition Government and the post-war Labour Government had shown that much could be done to direct industry to the depressed areas by regional policy stopping well short of the overthrow of capitalism. Bevan's fundamentalist formulas prevented him from seeing that the range of possible alternatives to free-market capitalism was now much broader than an overnight transition to socialism.

'The student of politics', Bevan himself warns at one point, 'must ... seek neither universality nor immortality for his ideas. ... He must also be on his guard against the old words, for the words persist when the reality that lay behind them has changed. ... From that point on, our ideas degenerate into a kind of folklore' (p. 34). Wise words: Bevan was in so many respects a wise man, capable of great practical insight and considerable self-awareness. But he was intellectually incapable of acting on his own advice, because he was not willing, by the fifties, to do the hard thinking necessary to adapt his ideas to a new reality. Thus they did degenerate, and folklore was precisely what he ended up with.

Of course there are some interesting practical proposals thrown out at various points in the book. For instance, Bevan now shared what by 1950 had become the orthodox criticism on the left of the Morrisonian structure of the existing nationalised industries. Accepting his share of the blame, he called for a greater degree of industrial democracy and – what he had always advocated – direct parliamentary control (p. 127). Condemning the narrow attitude of trade union leaders who were quite content with the existing corporate structure, he proposed to get away from the free-for-all of the annual wages round by linking wages to the cost of living. This would allow the proper planning of relative incomes (p. 137). In one particularly significant passage, however, Bevan argued that people do not object to inequality as such, but only to *unmerited* inequality (pp. 84–5). This was a touchy point, since the ideal of equality was increasingly, as they placed less and less emphasis on nationalisation, the principal objective which the Gaitskellites were choosing to place at the centre of their redefinition of socialism. Of course, Bevan's contention is true up to a point: the sense of fairness is a

---

* Actually he saw three: the competitive (or capitalist), the democratic socialist and the monolithic (or communist). But in the British context, where Bevan believed that Marx had underestimated the vitality of democracy, he thought the third model could effectively be ruled out (p. 64).

cherished characteristic of British society. At the same time the British public also thrives on the dream of unmerited inequality held out by the football pools. This was the sort of human weakness which Bevan was never able to acknowledge. But it goes to the heart of the public's resistance to socialism. Most people in all classes, however irrationally, prefer to trust their fate to chance and fortune rather than have it settled over their heads by all-wise bureaucrats. Rationing, tolerated with good humour during and for some time after the war, soon became unpopular; the public has a sceptical awareness that bureaucrats are occupationally liable to create anomalies which are less bearable than injustices of fate precisely for being man-made. Against this scepticism the orderly aspirations of fundamentalists and revisionists, Bevanites and Gaitskellites alike, have persistently beaten in vain.

Order rather than equality lay at the heart of Bevan's socialism. *In Place of Fear* offers rare, revealing glimpses of his idea of a socialist society in action. By the flickering light of his unstated assumptions it is possible to piece together the vision of an ordered hierarchy headed by a well-rewarded meritocratic elite – the planners. Throughout the book these planners are assumed, but they are never described. Who are they? What is to be their training? And what is to be their relationship with the sovereign Parliament? These are vital questions, for on them falls the whole responsibility for the rational ordering of the socialist society. In a full-employment economy it is the planners who are to make all the choices as to the use of resources, and they who determine the allocation of rewards and benefits. They are to do this not merely as economic planners, but by assuming a Platonic role as moral Guardians, enforcing 'common values'. 'From this point on', Bevan writes, 'moral considerations take precedence over economic motives; and this is because the choice between the worthwhileness of different forms of consumption implies an order of values' (p. 183). The creation of wealth is barely touched upon. 'A free Health Service', Bevan asserts characteristically, 'is pure socialism'; yet there is not a word in his chapter on the subject of how to pay for it. It is of course a standard criticism of socialists that they are concerned exclusively with how to share out the cake, not with how to expand it; but it is absolutely true of *In Place of Fear*. At one point Bevan allows that competition and acquisitiveness played a necessary part in creating modern industrial affluence (p. 59). But he considers that society has now evolved beyond the need for such base incentives and can henceforth do without them. Ever-increasing prosperity, to be achieved by the application of 'science', is taken for granted.

Most important from the point of view of current debate within the Labour Party, Bevan still had no time at all for Keynesian economics. Demand management admittedly was better than leaving the unemployed to rot. *But it was not socialism*. Recalling his thorough condemnation of the historic Full Employment White Paper of 1944, *In Place of Fear* reveals that

267

eight years and the experience of government had not changed Bevan's fund-amentalist view that the Keynesian 'revolution' was 'wholly opposed to Socialism'. 'To the Socialist', he still insisted, 'parliamentary power is to be used progressively until the main streams of economic activity are brought under public direction' – in other words until the economy was predominantly in public ownership. Then, he believed, with a wonderful faith in the om-nipotence of planners, deflationary crises would be not merely ameliorated but *eliminated* (pp. 50–1). This passage strikingly illustrates something Crossman noted in December 1951, that Bevan was not really interested in the detailed mechanics of economic management but only with 'achieving Power, with a very big and very vague P'.[5] Once that was done, he believed, everything else would fall into place.

The political lesson for Labour, therefore, was clear and simple. All it had to do was to recover its faith in socialism. MacDonald had failed in 1929 because he had no solid grounding in socialist theory (p. 45). The 1945 Government, by contrast, knew exactly what it wanted to accomplish. 'We were intellectually and spiritually armed for our task' (p. 125). Since then, Bevan believed, the party had lost its way, trimming for the middle ground and afraid of being thought 'doctrinaire'. Without naming him, Bevan unmistakably indicated Morrison: 'It has always been to me a painful spectacle when some Labour spokesman tries to justify a piece of Socialist legislation on exclusively "prac-tical" grounds' (p. 125). 'Consolidation at this stage' he explicitly dismissed as 'foolish' (p. 144). 'Whenever the Labour Party has made a mistake, it has not been in consequence of pursuing its principles too roughly or too far, but by making too many concessions to conventional opinion.' Labour must be a truly socialist party or it was no different from the Tories. 'We are not there yet, but there is a danger that we shall get there if recent tendencies are not corrected' (p. 126). This is the closest *In Place of Fear* comes to being a factional manifesto.

Of much greater relevance, and more lasting interest, than this doctrinal fundamentalism is the book's second theme: Bevan's growing conviction that the really important question confronting the world in 1952 was the rela-tionship between the rich and the poor countries. Here he was reacting to current events and having to adapt his old thinking to a reality not dreamed of in Tredegar in 1910. The Cold War, he insisted, as he had been insisting since 1950, was a diversion. 'It is a profound mistake to look upon our relations with backward peoples simply as one aspect of the struggle with the Soviet Union. If the Soviet system did not exist the problem would still be there' (p. 163). The West greatly exaggerated the military threat posed by the Soviet Union, which had neither the desire nor the capacity to engage in a major war. He had no illusions about the USSR.* 'Russian peace propaganda is a sham, and a

---

* Not many illusions anyway. But he clung to his belief that Soviet society must inevitably become more free as it became a more complex and prosperous industrial society: 'Economic importance combined with political nullity', he asserted confidently, 'cannot last' (p. 168).

cynical sham at that' (p. 160). Nevertheless his view was that the Russians were trying to alarm the West into a destabilising arms race, by which they hoped to gain their ends without a shot being fired. And the West was playing into their hands. 'We have allowed the Russians to divert us from the one policy that might help to pacify the world. The answer to social upheaval is social amelioration, not bombing planes and guns' (p. 163). In attempting to meet Communism with force, the West had 'mistaken the nature of the menace, and so it not only prescribes the wrong remedy, but the remedy itself feeds the danger' (p. 153).

The right remedy was aid. Bevan's argument was most pithily summarised by the *Listener*:

> The way to deal with a Chinese Communist is not to point a gun at him but to offer him a tractor. The West can offer tractors, but Russia cannot. The West, however, is destroying its own power to offer tractors by the size of its rearmament programmes. In this way it has thrown away its main advantage and contributes ... to those economic tensions on which Russia relies far more than she does on any aggressive plans of her own.[6]

So Bevan produced the one novel and constructive proposal in his book: a suggestion to beat swords into ploughshares by persuading both the Eastern and Western alliances, under the auspices of the UN, to undertake balanced disarmament by committing themselves by a specified date to divert a certain proportion of their arms spending into development aid. Today this seems a hopelessly naive proposition. But Bevan was writing only six years after the end of the war when the memory of the wartime anti-fascist alliance was still fresh, when Marshall Aid had shown what could be done, and the Cold War had not yet frozen into an entrenched system of 'mutually assured destruction'; when it was still possible to believe that a gesture of imaginative goodwill could yet break the circle of mutual suspicion. And it remains a far-sighted and thoroughly sensible aspiration, whose relevance, if it were only practicable, has become even more urgent in the famine-ravaged 1980s than it was in 1952. Bevan's humane concern with the interdependence of the whole planet, his realisation that letting the hungry nations starve while the West grew fat on their resources 'is not only manifestly unjust. It is also exceedingly unsafe for us' (p. 165) essentially anticipates the Brandt Report of 1980. It is to Bevan's great credit that long before there was much understanding or interest in the West in the problems of the underdeveloped world he tried to make it a priority issue of domestic politics. This was not a cause which would have been taken up with such emphasis by a politician merely ambitious to seize the leadership of his party.

Doubts arise, however, over his faith in the United Nations as the instrument not only for channelling aid but, more positively, for directing the use of the world's resources 'in accordance with some carefully worked out plan of priorities' (p. 193). The delusion that the UN was an autonomous agency in its own right rather than simply a public forum for airing the grievances of its component States was common right across the political spectrum in the fifties. But Bevan's deludedness was greater than most in that he seemed to see the UN as the germ of a world government, the 'controlling brain' of a world socialist State. Towards the end of *In Place of Fear* his comfortable view of British society evolving from competitive selfishness to planned altruism is projected, with still less credibility, on to the whole world. Different countries' different stages of development; the existence of real conflicts of national economic interest; the growing – not diminishing – force of nationalism, all aspects of the real world of which Bevan was at other times perfectly well aware are lost sight of in a fog of what can only be called idealistic waffle. His familiar dialectical trick, which one can see at work throughout the book, is to slide from prescription to prediction. From urging that in order to save the world from hunger, anarchy and physical annihilation the nations *must* co-operate it is an easy step to assert that therefore they WILL co-operate. Evolution towards the light becomes a law of history. Bevan's constructive proposal ends in facile optimism.

In Place of Fear ends in bathos. The final hymn to democratic socialism, astonishingly described by Michael Foot as 'the most apt and memorable ever written',[7] reads like a secular parody of the thirteenth chapter of Corinthians ('Charity is not puffed up'):

> The philosophy of Democratic Socialism is essentially cool in temper. It sees society in its context with nature and is conscious of the limitations imposed by physical conditions. It sees the individual in his context with society and is therefore compassionate and tolerant. Because it knows that all political action must be a choice between a number of possible alternatives it eschews all absolute proscriptions and final decisions. Consequently it is not able to offer the thrill of the complete abandonment of private judgement, which is the allure of modern Soviet Communism and of Fascism, its running mate. Nor can it escape the burden of social choice so attractively suggested by those who believe in *laissez-faire* principles and in the automatism of the price system. It accepts the obligation to choose among different kinds of social action and in so doing to bear the pains of rejecting what is not practicable or less desirable.
>
> Democratic Socialism is the child of modern society and so of relativist philosophy. It seeks the truth in any given situation, knowing all the time that if this be pushed too far it falls into error. It struggles against the evils that flow from private property, yet realizes that all forms of private property are not necessarily evil. Its chief enemy is vacillation, for it must achieve passion in action in the pursuit of qualified judgements. It must know how to enjoy the struggle, while recognizing that progress is not the elimination of struggle but rather a change in its terms. (pp. 201–2)

This was supposed to be the credo of the most forthright and uncompromising British socialist of his generation. It is instead a sad confession of political bankruptcy. On this evidence Bevanism, if it was dependent on Bevan himself for inspiration, was a road that led nowhere. Socialism was still the shining city on a hill; the emerging compromise of welfare capitalism was a sell-out; but Bevan could offer no route forward from one to the other, only an appeal to faith. For all its humanity and good intentions, *In Place of Fear* is the wordy last gasp of a dying political tradition, not the herald of its rebirth. The very flaccidity of the book's conclusion suggests that Bevan in his heart knew it as well as anyone.

In the short term *In Place of Fear* created a considerable stir. Helped by 'tremendous publicity'[8] and published simultaneously in hardback (10/6d) and paperback (6/-), it quickly sold 37,000 copies.[9] It did not matter that the reviewers were mainly critical – that was to be expected – nor even that they criticised it as much for its tedious verbosity as for the views it attempted to expound. (Dalton thought it 'very dull'.)[10] The fact is that any book by Bevan that spring would have made a stir. The loyal Mallalieu in *Tribune*, making the best of a tricky assignment, argued that *In Place of Fear*, though not a programme, aimed to 'set a mood', as William Morris had once set a mood, 'in which the Labour movement can do its thinking and feeling'.[11] In fact it did not so much set a mood as chime with an existing mood. The left was already making the running in the party. The publication of *In Place of Fear* contributed to that mood and stoked the row over the activities of the Bevanites which climaxed at the Morecambe Conference in October. Nevertheless the book itself, as a book, added very little to Bevanism as it already existed in March. On the one hand a group of maverick individuals, on the other a set of half-formed attitudes: holding them loosely together a dominating, exasperating, charismatic figurehead. When the mood of 1952 began to ebb, Bevanism was no closer to having acquired a body of doctrine or philosophy than it had been before. The opportunity to stake out the agenda for the next Labour Government had been missed: the initiative had been handed back to the right. In due course Tony Crosland, for the Gaitskellites, filled the gap which Bevan had left. *The Future of Socialism* was everything that *In Place of Fear* was not. It became the bible of the revisionists, and captured the mind of the party for the next twenty years. *In Place of Fear* signally failed to become the bible even of the fundamentalists, let alone capture the party.

Chapter 19

'A Party Within a Party'?

Despite the bathos of *In Place of Fear*, it was nevertheless in the spring and summer of 1952 the Bevanites who seemed to hold the initiative. In Parliament Bevan himself was in fighting form – leading the attack on the Tories' NHS charges,[1] deriding Macmillan's housing programme,[2] pleading for a relaxation of the Cold War ('If only we could get some co-operation, if we could only build a bridge, however slender, that very thing might itself be a watershed in history').[3] Other Bevanites – Crossman, Wilson, Geoffrey Bing – were almost equally effective. In the country, Bevan drew enormous audiences wherever he spoke; *Tribune*, after a precarious two years appearing only fortnightly, was successfully relaunched as a weekly, with a rising circulation and a new emphasis on industry; and the *Tribune* Brains Trusts went from strength to strength, with constituency parties queuing up to hold one in their own locality.[4] And party membership continued to grow: individual membership increased in 1952 by 15 per cent over the previous year.[5] To the right, all this activity was alarming. They felt, with some reason, that their position was being undermined among the rank and file, sometimes in their own constituencies. There was particular resentment of the Brains Trusts; the battered *Tribune* van or Gavin Faringdon's Rolls-Royce would descend on a chosen constituency with a panel of four or five Bevanite MPs – a typical panel might be Crossman, Barbara Castle, Leslie Hale and Stephen Swingler, with Mikardo in the chair – without inviting the local MP or prospective candidate to participate.[6] This bred allegations of exclusiveness. So did the impression that the Bevanites met secretly at Westminster to plan tactics, concert their line and agree speakers before every important Commons debate and party meeting.

It was of course perfectly true that they did all these things. The argument that developed was over whether it was proper for them to organise in this way and, behind that, why they were doing it. The right had no doubt why. Gaitskell believed that Bevan 'just wants to lead the Party, and that is all the Bevanites want'.[7] This view was luridly reflected practically daily in the press: with a unanimity which stretched from *The Times* and the *Express* on the right through the Liberal *News Chronicle* and *Manchester Guardian* – no paper was more violently anti-Bevan than the *Guardian* – to Labour's own *Daily Herald*, Bevan was portrayed as a power-crazed hate-merchant concerned only to 'grab the Socialist leadership',[8] his followers as a shady clique of stooges. Little effort was made to understand what they were trying to say, or why the constituency parties were so keen to hear them. The allegation crystallised in August that the Bevanites constituted 'a party within a party'. First used by the *News Chronicle*,[9] the phrase was taken up by the Labour right in a concerted attack, with Patrick Gordon Walker, Frank Pakenham (both former Cabinet Ministers), George Brown and Richard Stokes leading the hunt. Foot and Freeman endeavoured to reply. All this was preliminary to the autumn Conference, which was launched with the screaming front-page headline in the *Sunday Pictorial* END THE BEVAN MYTH[10] and a demand from Arthur Deakin, Bevin's successor as General Secretary of the TGWU – rapidly established as the bluntest and most rightwing of the big trade union leaders – that the Bevanites 'get rid of their whips, dismiss their business managers and conform to the party Constitution'.[11]

Such a demand supposed that the Bevanites' organisation was a great deal more sophisticated than it was. Despite their 'secret' meetings at the House of Commons, their private circulation of policy papers, their Brains Trusts and their perfectly open polemics in *Tribune*, the Bevanites were in reality still not much more than a group of congenial friends who had got to know one another as under-employed backbenchers in the 1945 Parliament, on whom the role of the organised left had been thrust somewhat accidentally by Bevan's resignation. It was often remarked that they were mainly middle-class intellectuals, lawyers and journalists; but the real point is that they were all good talkers and heavy drinkers who enjoyed one another's company: not so much 'a party within a party', as Tom Driberg remarked, as 'The Smoking Room within the Smoking Room'.[12] (The class divide in the PLP was clear: the trade union members congregated in the Tea Room.) Those who were less naturally convivial, like Wilson and Freeman, were emotionally not part of the inner group, though as ex-Ministers they lent it political weight. Plenty of other prominent left-wingers, for instance S.O.Davies and Fenner Brockway, normally voted with the group and even attended group meetings, but were still less part of the inner coterie. The Bevanites were really more socially than politically exclusive: less a coherent faction than an awkward squad. Mikardo, the sinister wire-puller of the right's imagination, did his best, but most of the individuals involved were temperamentally averse to being organised. Likewise Crossman was always hankering for a clearly worked-out left-wing policy; but the members of the group were much too argumentative a lot to take their line from Crossman or anyone else, Bevan included. The 'left' position on a particular issue was usually fairly clear. Out of general discussion an attitude might emerge which Crossman or Mikardo would cobble into a resolution for which most of the group and a floating number of sympathisers would vote. But there were no whips.

Nor was there a plot, in any but the most general sense, to make Bevan leader. Bevan himself might talk in one of his moods of 'capturing' the constituency parties and so putting a 'squeeze' on the parliamentary party by threatening right-wingers with deselection;[13] but there was no attempt to organise the sort of pressure the more ruthless Bennites applied in the 1970s, and Bevan in another mood would have been the first to condemn it if there had been. Altogether, as Crossman noted, he was 'a somewhat reluctant Bevanite'.[14] His whole upbringing and philosophy made him acutely sensitive to the charge of sectarianism. Instinctively he disapproved of the group and he was the most irregular attender at its meetings. 'Nye has never liked the cliquiness of a close-knit group, such as Ian Mikardo delights in organizing. . . . On the other hand he wants support.'[15] This was a dilemma he never satisfactorily resolved. He needed the Bevanites because they were the only supporters he had. He was incapable of seeking support in the Tea Room, with whose solid habitués his relations had always been characterised by mutual incomprehension bordering on contempt. But he knew, with his belief in 'representative types', that Foot and Crossman, Driberg, Mallalieu, Bing and their like – public schoolboys all – were not the Labour Party. His solution was always to argue for throwing the group open as much as possible so that all sympathetic Members could attend – thus making it less of a conspiracy than ever – while concentrating on what he called 'socialist education' in the country. He valued the group – and *Tribune* in particular – primarily as a sounding board to amplify and project his personal battle to prevent Morrison and Gaitskell reneging on Labour's commitment to old-time socialism. (In June he delivered in *Tribune* another strong attack on the 'Fresh Thinkers . . . who want to substitute novel remedies for the struggle for power in the State. . . . Now that we are engaged once again in policy-making it is essential that we should keep before us that one of the central principles of Socialism is the substitution of public for private ownership. There is no way around this.')[16] Of course he would have liked the leadership. But he wanted – perhaps even expected – it to come to him by the reconversion of the Labour Party to the true socialism for which he stood, not through any sort of secret plotting which was as foreign to his nature as to his view of history. He knew, they all knew – Crossman certainly knew and Wilson soon realised it – that the Bevanites were not a platform on which could be based a bid for personal power.

Thus the claim that the Bevanites represented 'a party within a party' was exaggerated; it was also, so far as 'conforming to the party Constitution' was concerned, beside the point. Historically the ILP had existed for years as a separately organised party within the Labour Party; less controversially, the Co-operative Party survives to this day as a party within the Labour Party, electing its own representative to Labour's NEC. The Bevanites were not structurally, nor ideologically, nor financially as separate as either of these. The constitutional arguments were no more than the rationalisation of a power struggle. The only reason there was a row over the Bevanites' very amateurish organisation was because they gave parliamentary leadership to a genuine grass-roots threat to the right's control of the party. Following the loss of momentum since 1950, the April 1951 resignations and the loss of office in October, a tired and ageing leadership seemed reluctant to distance itself sufficiently from the Tory Government, particularly in foreign affairs, to please the party activists. At Morecambe the activists had their revenge.

Morecambe was in Michael Foot's words 'rowdy, convulsive, vulgar, splenetic';[17] in Dalton's 'the worst [Labour Party] Conference, for bad temper & general hatred, since 1926';[18] in the view of most of those who were there the worst ever, unsurpassed even in 1980. For the first time at a Labour Conference the normal fraternal courtesies were overborne by an ugly mood of bigoted intolerance. Right-wing speakers, notably Deakin when he attacked the Bevanites, were booed and jeered. Not only that. Motions of a distinctively Bevanite colour were carried reaffirming the principle of a free health service and instructing the NEC to draw up a list of 'key and major industries' to be taken into public ownership. Another calling for a review of rearmament attracted 2.2 million votes (against 3.6 million); and a fourth advocating political strikes to bring down the Government drew 1.7 million (against 4 million). It was the last, going well beyond anything that Bevan or any of his immediate associates would have approved, which gave rise to allegations of Communist influence in the Conference, feeding off the Bevanites' successes. What these results clearly showed was that the left was in the ascendant, not only in the constituency parties but in some unions too. But the most dramatic happening at Morecambe, which concentrated attention, perhaps misleadingly, on the parliamentary Bevanites, was the result of the voting for the seven constituency places on the NEC. By means of some fairly elementary 'plumping' for their six candidates, the left succeeded in taking six of the seven positions: Bevan, Barbara Castle, Tom Driberg and Ian Mikardo were joined by Wilson and Crossman, while Dalton and Morrison were defeated. Only Jim Griffiths of the old guard survived; Gaitskell, whom Dalton had expected to be elected, came tenth with barely half the vote of the lowest Bevanite. The unpredicted imbalance of this result (attributed by Dalton to 'half vague emotion, half Mikardo's cunning organisation')[19] constituted a great victory for the Bevanites; yet a somewhat pyrrhic one. The constituency parties had clearly demonstrated their impatience for a more full-blooded socialism, and had given the left a solid base on the NEC which it has never subsequently lost. At the same time the slap in the face for Morrison and the howls of delight with which it was greeted in the galleries gave wide offence and shocked many in the centre of the party into joining with the right to make a stand against what suddenly seemed a serious threat to Labour's traditional values. The Bevanites in the House were a tolerable nuisance; 'Bevanism' as it manifested itself at Morecambe was a threat to the very survival of Labour as a party of government.

Two days after the Conference ended Gaitskell made the right's reply in a famous speech at Stalybridge. Alleging that 'about one-sixth of the Constituency Party delegates appeared to be Communists or Communist-inspired' and asserting that the 'stream of grossly misleading propaganda ... poisonous innuendoes and malicious attacks' poured out by *Tribune* made unity impossible, he declared that it was 'time to end the attempt at mob rule by a group of frustrated journalists and restore the authority and leadership of the solid sound sensible majority of the movement'.[20] The first allegation was unsubstantiated and created great resentment; the second was exaggerated and oversensitive; but the phrase 'mob rule' seemed to many an accurate description of what they had seen at Morecambe, while 'frustrated journalists' cut the middle-class Bevanites neatly down to size: besides Foot and Mikardo in *Tribune*, Crossman and Freeman wrote for the *New Statesman*, Crossman also had a column in the *Sunday Pictorial*, Driberg one in *Reynold's News* and others of the group wrote regularly in other papers. The Bevanites' first reaction was that Gaitskell's attack would misfire.[21] The bellweather John Strachey rebuked Gaitskell for giving ammunition to the Tories.[22] In fact the effect of the speech was finally to persuade Attlee – hitherto, to the exasperation of Gaitskell and Morrison, inscrutable above the storm which raged around him – that he must come off the fence and assert his leadership, against the Bevanites. At the Festival Hall on 11 October he declared 'quite intolerable ... the existence of a party within a party with separate leadership, separate meetings, supported by its own press. ... I say ... "Work with the team. Turn your guns on the enemy, not your own friends."'[23]

Bevan realised immediately that such an appeal was not one which the Bevanites could resist. Nor did he believe that they needed to resist it. He regarded the resolutions carried at Morecambe – all of which Gaitskell at Stalybridge had explicitly accepted – as providing the basis on which the party could be reunited. Now that the left had shown that it could not be ignored, and the issues which had led to his resignation from the Government in 1951 had been resolved in his favour, he was ready to re-enter the mainstream of the party and rejoin the Shadow Cabinet. Characteristically, he sat down to write an article for *Tribune* to this effect without consulting his friends.[24] When Crossman and Mikardo argued that the morrow of victory was not the moment to capitulate, Crossman wrote, 'Nye got very angry with me.'

'To continue the Group now is to perpetuate schism,' he said. 'If you were to continue the Group in these conditions and I were the Leader, I would have you expelled. The Group is intolerable.' I then asked, 'Then why hasn't it been intolerable for the past six months?' 'Well of course it's been intolerable,' he said. 'We've got away with it. And we needed it then. We don't need it now. That's the point of Morecambe. We're in a strong enough position not to need protection and if we go on with it we shall alienate the people we are trying to win in the Parliamentary Party and we shall lose the support of nearly half the constituencies within twelve months because they will be able to pillory us as a sectarian conspiracy.'[25]

But Bevan's idea was not exactly to disband the Bevanite group: rather to throw it open, as he had argued before, to the whole party. In fact, in his *Tribune* article he denied that there had ever been anything secret about it. And he strongly defended *Tribune* itself and the Brains Trusts, comparing them with the Left Book Club before the war which had done so much to prepare the ground for 1945:

> We want to build Labour unity. We will do our utmost to carry out the decisions arrived at at the Morecambe Conference. We invite all members of the Parliamentary Labour Party to find out for themselves what our activities are. But one thing we will not do. We will not abandon our right to carry on Socialist education in Great Britain, in order to provide an enlightened Socialist movement behind a Socialist majority in the next Parliament.[26]

Bevan, now supported by Crossman and Wilson, had a tricky time getting the rest of the group to 'agree' this line without telling them that his article for *Tribune* was already in print – a good example of the reality of group democracy. ('Diddling forty colleagues', Crossman called it.)[27] Still it was not enough to satisfy Attlee, who was now determined that all groups be outlawed altogether. At the first party meeting of the new session, he brushed aside the constitutional precedents: 'You can argue a lot about groups, but they're like the elephant. I may not be able to define one but I know one when I see one. Groups are all right for special purposes but what I disapprove of is an omnicompetent Group like the ILP used to be. . . . The proposal to throw the Group open to other members of the Party is not good enough, since it would only create a rival Party meeting.'[28] This time refusing to allow any compromise to be moved, he forced an immediate vote and won it by 188 to 51. The Bevanites had no choice but to accept defeat.

Under protest, they agreed formally to disband (though naturally, as Crossman wrote, 'we should have to concert ways and means of continuing to keep in contact').[29] After some hesitation, Bevan decided to hold to his intention that he and Wilson should stand for election to the Shadow Cabinet, though in order to show that they had not tamely submitted to the party's 'ultimatum' he insisted that he should first stand against Morrison for the Deputy Leadership.[30] No one expected him to win; but he attracted 82 votes to Morrison's 194 – considerably more than either Crossman or Dalton anticipated, evidence of a renewed desire in the centre of the party to heal the rift. The Shadow Cabinet elections, however, told a different story. Bevan was narrowly elected in twelfth place, but Wilson was thirteenth and the other Bevanites nowhere. *Tribune* angrily called the result 'Morecambe in Reverse', which was perfectly fair.[31] 'Here is the Parliamentary Party voting for all the old guard who were voted down at Morecambe,' wrote Crossman – the elected twelve still included elderly troupers like Ede (aged seventy), Shinwell (sixty-eight), Glenvil Hall (sixty-five) and indeed Dalton (sixty-five) – 'and voting down the Bevanites systematically'.[32] (With characteristic indiscretion, 'Dear Dr Dalton' told him of the list of candidates to be backed 'by all right-minded persons'.)[33] By agreeing to disband the group, only to see Bevan alone voted into a Shadow Cabinet in which he would be permanently one against eleven (fourteen including Attlee, Morrison and the Chief Whip), the Bevanites felt they had been duped. Without their weekly meetings, the group 'rapidly disintegrated', while Bevan himself, bound by collective responsibility, was a prisoner of the right. Crossman did not think Bevan minded much about the group;[34] but it could only be a matter of time before he revolted again against his solitary confinement.

Chapter 20

The Disintegration of the Bevanites

During the whole of 1953, Bevan made a conscientious effort to play the part of the loyal frontbencher. He made his debut in this role before the end of 1952, when his colleagues (overruling Gaitskell, who was 'violently against')[1] entrusted him with winding up a Censure debate against the Government. He responded with a good (though backward-looking) party speech accusing the Tories of restoring the balance of payments only by reducing imports (which was temporarily true) and increasing unemployment (which was not), just as they had done in the thirties. 'The apotheosis of Winston Churchill', he jeered, 'is to be like Stanley Baldwin.' It was a fixed tenet of his socialist faith that unemployment must go up under the Tories, whether it actually did or not. He derided Macmillan's house-building boom as 'the only small figleaf with which hon. Gentlemen opposite are covering their nakedness'.[2] Thereafter he was largely confined to 'shadowing' the functions he had held in Government, housing and health.

On both subjects he was principally concerned to vindicate his own record. On the surface Macmillan's 300,000 house-building target was a rebuke to Labour's failure to complete in any one year more than 240,000. Bevan in his own defence pointed out that Macmillan was achieving his figure first by building smaller houses (therefore actually building fewer bedrooms) than Labour; second, by diverting resources away from the repair of existing houses, which had formed a large part of Labour's programme; and third, by starving other forms of building, like schools and factories. Now that the materials shortages with which he had wrestled were forgotten, he maintained, any fool could build houses. The allocation of resources was simply a planning decision. 'All one needs to say is what one is not going to do.'[3] Bevan believed that Macmillan's programme was a public relations exercise. To a great extent he was quite right. But it was a highly successful one.

Bevan also attacked Macmillan's reliance on private enterprise rather than the local authorities, which meant that the houses got built where they were profitable, not where they were needed; and similarly dismissed his Housing Repairs and Rents Bill (which raised controlled rents in order to enable landlords to carry out necessary repairs) as a typical Tory measure designed to put money in the pockets of landlords while having no effect on the condition of their property: 'the maximum of demagogy with the minimum of practical results'.[4] 'We must acknowledge the fact', he argued, going some way beyond existing Labour policy, 'that not only slum clearance and reconditioning must be carried out by local authorities, but that all rent-controlled houses must eventually become the property of local authorities.'[5] Bevan had always seen housing as a social service, to be publicly provided like the Health Service. Bringing the private rented sector into municipal ownership now became a key item to be included in Labour's next instalment of nationalisation. In 1954 he succeeded in getting a commitment to muni-cipalisation carried through Conference – 'I challenge any of my comrades who think that Socialism is now an outworn principle to tell me how they would solve the problem of rented houses in any other way but by building more rented houses, and keeping in a proper state of repair the millions of rented houses already there'.[6] Despite doubts about its practicability, a some-what vague nod in this direction was duly included in Labour's programme for the 1955 election.

With Macmillan's housing policy Bevan had a genuine quarrel. He got even angrier about the Tory Government's treatment of the National Health Service; but this was very largely a phoney war. From the moment the Tories returned to power – indeed before – Bevan had accused them of wanting to 'dismantle' the free Health Service. His complaint against Gaitskell was that he had made it easy for them by taking the first step. In March 1952 he had furiously denounced the Treasury ('once more the little men were adding up their silly sums') for 'pulling down ... something of which everybody, including the Conservatives, were beginning to be proud' and solemnly claimed to see in Harry Crookshank's extension of Gaitskell's charges 'the beginnings of the end of British Parliamentary Government'.[7] This ludi-crous reversion to his apocalyptic predictions of the thirties brought forth a famous parliamentary riposte. The Tory backbencher who had the luck to follow him was Iain Macleod. 'I want to deal closely and with relish', he began, 'with the vulgar, crude and intemperate speech to which the House of Commons has just listened.' Macleod's reply was in the great tradition of ambitious young men making their names overnight by a direct assault on the biggest figure on the other side: Lloyd George on Joseph Chamberlain; F.E.Smith and in 1930 Bevan himself on Lloyd George. Bevan, Macleod jeered, had 'made a great reputation in the previous two Parliaments by always speaking at the end of health debates and never answering any points. He is much less effective when he comes down into the arena.' With detailed figures and skilfully quoting him against himself, Macleod took Bevan's wilder allegations apart.[8] It happened that Churchill had been in the Cham-ber to hear Bevan. Less than six weeks later he appointed Macleod Minister of Health.

Bevan professed himself flattered that the way for a Tory to win promotion should be to attack him; but for the next three years he continually asserted that Macleod had been appointed because he had shown himself in this speech 'an avowed enemy' of the Health Service and therefore just the man Churchill was looking for to destroy it.[9] In fact neither Macleod nor the Tories had any intention of destroying the Service. This was another example of Bevan's preconception that Tories must always behave like the Tories of his youth. Nevertheless the Government was still worried by the apparently bottomless cost of health care and keen to make savings and political capital by eliminating alleged extravagance. So in April 1953 Macleod set up a Departmental enquiry chaired by a Cambridge don, Claude Guillebaud, 'to suggest means, whether by modifications in organisation or otherwise, of ensuring the most effective use of such Exchequer funds as may be made available'.[10] To Bevan this review was an obvious preliminary to dismantling the Service. Characteristically he tried to present it as a constitutional outrage: like his predecessors in the thirties Macleod was trying to take a sensitive issue out of the control of Parliament by devolving it to an 'expert' committee. There was already in the Health Service itself provision for keeping it under continuous review. The Guillebaud Committee reminded him painfully of the May Committee whose report had precipitated the crisis of 1931.[11] In reality Guillebaud, when he reported in 1955, broadly endorsed the existing structure of financial control, retrospectively vindicated Bevan's administration of the early years of the Service, refuted the impression of extravagance and pronounced the NHS excellent value for money. Although the charges imposed by Gaitskell and Crookshank in 1951–2 remained in force until the Wilson Government, in a short-lived flourish of Bevanite piety, abolished them in 1964 (only to restore them in 1968), the Health Service was henceforth recognised by both parties as a sacred cow.

In the meantime, however, it was the alleged extravagance of the Service, not its success, which the Tories continued most unfairly to stick on Bevan. 'I know perfectly well', Macleod mocked typically in 1953, 'that ... the House will give the fullest value to the views of a Minister of Health who never got his Estimates within £100 million of the right figure.'[12] For his own part, Bevan stoutly defended his record, except in one particular: he increasingly blamed himself for allowing the doctors such scope to exploit pay beds, which he feared in 1953 were becoming 'a very evil racket indeed' as whole wards in public hospitals became private and beds were kept empty despite waiting lists for admission. In Parliament and at Conference he blamed the doctors and hospital administrators for abusing the compact agreed in 1948. 'There is no single piece of social machinery in Great Britain where the profession handling it has more self-government than in the National Health Service.' Regrettably, however, 'there are members of the medical profession who have not proved themselves worthy of the responsibility with which they were entrusted.'[13] From a socialist point of view, medical syndicalism had let him down. Nevertheless, unlike Barbara Castle twenty years later, he did not advocate abolishing pay beds, merely that they should be 'a diminishing quantity' and 'strictly curtailed', according to medical, not financial criteria.[14] He still recognised his side of the compact if the doctors held to theirs.

During 1953 Labour produced its first new general policy statement since leaving office. During the months of its preparation Bevan and his five allies on the NEC did their best to influence it their way, pressing for a new shopping list of industries to be nationalised, including chemicals, aircraft production, heavy engineering and machine tools – all argued in terms of a 'five-year plan for viability', to close the dollar gap by a planned expansion of national production and exports. Bevan was also very keen on land nationalisation, intended to reduce food imports. With Mikardo, Crossman and Wilson doing the hard work (advised by Balogh and Dudley Seers), the Bevanites were beginning to put together a coherent programme, relevant to the actualities of the moment, of a sort that had been entirely absent from *In Place of Fear*.[15] But of course they were still a minority on the NEC; and though they managed to get chemicals and the renationalisation of steel and road transport included, their amendments were generally voted down 14–6 by the trade union majority controlled by Deakin. Faced with this solid obstacle Bevan veered between the impulse to resign, leading to occasional angry outbursts, and what Crossman called 'spasms of compromise' when he became 'sweet as a cooing dove'.[16] Neither approach had any noticeable effect on the arithmetic. When the final statement, entitled *Challenge to Britain*, was published he was still 'in two minds whether we should resign in protest against an outrageous document or stay on the Executive and claim a triumph. There are no half measures with Nye.' He decided to claim a triumph: 'If we admit we've been defeated it will be hopeless.'[17] *Tribune* accordingly announced its verdict: 'GOOD! But it can be a whole lot better,' listing eight measures still required to make a truly Bevanite programme: the nationalisation of rented land (1) and industrial assurance (2), with the nationalised industries directly accountable to Parliament (3), a National Investment Board (4) and direct physical controls on the use of resources (5); plus a Capital Gains Tax (6), reduced arms sales (7) and equal pay (8).[18] Bevan remained dissatisfied, but was still – despite continuing rows and niggles with Gaitskell in the Shadow Cabinet – committed to trying to work within the leadership, not against it.

Stalemated on further nationalisation – not to say bored with detailed arguments about the machine-tools industry in which he really was not interested (he was much happier on familiar ground lambasting the Tories for denationalising steel: 'They know which side their bread is buttered. ... The steel magnates go after the boodle ... with the greatest cynicism and rapacity ... The whole affair is a naked example of the uses to which the Tories put political power')[19] – Bevan was increasingly turning his attention to foreign affairs. Like many others in the West he was hopeful that the death of Stalin in March 1953 offered an historic opportunity to relax international tension. In a series of rather inflated *Tribune* articles in July and August entitled 'In Place of the Cold War' he enlarged on his theory of an inevitable liberalisation of Soviet society, his conviction that the Soviet Union was suffering from 'acute social indigestion' as a result of having pushed too far West at the end of the war into more advanced economies which it could not hope to control indefinitely, and his belief that the Russians' overpowering fear of another war must make them amenable to peace feelers if the West would only take the initiative.[20] Like so much of his thinking, all this was little more than pretentious rationalisation of what he wanted to believe. More than ever he thought it was up to the British and the Americans to show goodwill to tempt the Russians out of their isolation. Above all he blamed the Americans for their insistence on rearming Western Germany as part of NATO, instead of seeking agreement with the Russians for a unified, neutral Germany. In 1953–4 this blew up into the latest issue to split the Labour Party down the middle.

The divide this time was not a simple one between left and right: Dalton for one, fiercely anti-German since 1914–18, was embarrassed to find himself on this issue aligned with the Bevanites, while the Atlanticists, led by Morrison and Gaitskell, who loyally followed the American line to which Morrison had committed the party in the dying days of the Labour Government, found the majority sentiment of the party for once against them. The argument was supposed to be about how to treat with the Russians and how best to secure peace in Europe, by confrontation or by partnership. But it was not always conducted at such a statesmanlike level. Michael Foot in his biography of Bevan understandably conceals the extent to which the left at the time exploited the most virulent anti-German prejudice. *Tribune* explicitly saw the victory of the Christian Democrat Konrad Adenauer in the Federal Republic's first post-war elections as 'the resurgence of German nationalism', hailed by 'the same people who were content to lick the jackboots of the Nazis',[21] and almost weekly carried stories under headlines like 'Now Dr Adenauer Finds His Dr Goebbels' and 'The Rebirth of the German Reichswehr'.[22] 'Once more', Foot alleged, 'a German Chancellor holds the key to European politics.'[23]

Bevan implicitly sanctioned this sort of lurid scaremongering and indulged in a good deal of it himself. In April 1954 he blamed the Americans for having 'financed into existence … a reactionary Government … in Western Germany' and claimed that 'all the evidence available points to a revival of Nazism'.[23] The *Tribune* pamphlet *It Need Not Happen*, signed by Bevan, Castle, Crossman, Driberg, Mikardo and Wilson, dismissed as worthless the safeguards under which twelve German divisions were to be created under the umbrella of a combined European Defence Community: 'The twelve divisions will be Nazi-led and Nazi-trained. … The European

Defence Community in fact is not an alternative to a German national army, but merely the first step towards its creation.'[24] The serious purpose of this alarmism was to try to revive the spirit of the wartime alliance with the Soviet Union by breathing new life into the common enemy. American policy seemed designed to perpetuate the Cold War by drawing the front line between East and West permanently through the middle of Germany. Then, according to *It Need Not Happen*, 'World War III becomes inevitable.'[25] The Bevanite alternative was to try to reach an accommodation with the Russians by recognising their fear of German 'revanchism' and joining with them to keep Germany united but neutral, disarmed and, it was fondly hoped, democratic. This involved a degree of trust in Soviet intentions which, even after the death of Stalin, Western Governments were unable to entertain. It also overlooked the reality that the Russians, behind their opportunistic democratic assurances, were perfectly content with a status quo that kept Germany divided and themselves in control of half of it. It is difficult today to see what all the alarm was about. German rearmament was really a side-issue, rendered irrelevant when the French Assembly vetoed the EDC in August 1954. Subsequently West Germany was quietly rearmed within NATO without any of the dire consequences predicted by the Bevanites.

Disregarding the emotive spectre of resurgent Hitlerism, all that the Bevanites were asking in 1954 was that the West should refrain from institutionalising the Cold War in Europe until the possibilities of peace talks had been exhausted. The Government and the Labour right believed in 'negotiating from strength'; the left believed that the West commanded more than enough strength already and could safely afford a gesture of restraint that might thaw the atmosphere. The wider importance of the row inside the Labour Party, however, was that it underlined the gulf of attitude between those who broadly accepted the American view of international politics as a holy war against world Communism, controlled from Moscow, and those who, following Bevan's analysis, rejected the crudity of such a view and demanded a more independent and enlightened British policy which should recognise, and support, the role of healthy anti-colonialism in much of what the Americans mistook for Communism, particularly in Asia. The belief that Britain was still being dragged too tamely at the wheels of American diplomacy and that Labour at least should be distancing itself from this subservience was the ground of Bevan's next, unpremeditated but long simmering, revolt against the party line.

It was born out of a mixture of frustration and growing disenchantment with the claustrophobic world of Westminster. Now fifty-six, Bevan was suddenly at an age, and a stage in his career, when he could no longer be bothered with the daily grind of parliamentary life when it did not seem to be getting him anywhere. Increasingly he looked to the world stage to raise his horizons, developing a taste for foreign travel which both flattered his bruised pride and accorded with his conviction that the real problems of modern politics were global problems. During 1953 he was abroad almost as much as he was at home. In February/March he visited India, Burma and Pakistan, taking in Israel on the way; in June he visited Italy; in August he and Jennie went again to Yugoslavia; and in December they went to Egypt. From every trip he returned fired with a new enthusiasm which made wrangling with Morrison and Gaitskell in the Shadow Cabinet more tedious than ever. ('He has a wonderful instinct for Italian politics,' Crossman recorded after that visit, 'which are the sort of romantic, personal politics he completely understands.'[26] He knew exactly what the Italian socialist leader Pietro Nenni should be doing to outbid the Communists – and had doubtless told him.) For Jawaharlal Nehru in particular Bevan acquired an admiration similar to his veneration of Tito. Newly independent India, like defiant Yugoslavia, offered a model of non-alignment, pointing the possibility of a third force in the world between the Superpower blocs. Nehru was the acknowledged leader of that spirit of enlightened anti-imperialism on which Bevan pinned his hopes of progress towards a democratic socialist world community. Back in the House of Commons in December he had to defend himself against furious Tory condemnation of a series of syndicated articles he had written for Indian and Egyptian newspapers asserting that 'the great struggle in the world today is not a struggle between two or three imperialisms; it is a struggle between the national idea and the imperial idea'.

> We shall not be able to adjust the policies of this country to the necessities of the world unless we can put ourselves abreast of those movements of ordinary people everywhere who are trying not only to raise their material standards but also to throw from their shoulders an imperial yoke which has been there too long.[27]

Bevan now saw the whole world as his constituency. He found it correspondingly difficult to maintain any sustained concentration on domestic politics.

The Bevanites languished while he was away. 'In Nye's absence, no one else seems to have the dynamic to do anything,' lamented Crossman;[28] while Dalton recorded thankfully that Bevanism had now been proved to be 'a One Man Band'.[29] But it was not much different when he was there. Since its formal disbandment, the old parliamentary group of forty-odd had dwindled to the inner core of a dozen or so who still lunched together on Tuesdays at Crossman's house in Vincent Square.* In the autumn, after a dull Conference, there were moves led by Freeman, Crossman and Barbara Castle to reactivate the larger group. 'Very bold words were used by many people,'

---

* That was at Westminster. But there was also an active 'Second XI' of candidates and others outside Parliament who carried on propaganda work in the country; and the *Tribune* Brains Trusts continued. 'Bevanism' retained more vitality in the constituencies and the unions than in the House of Commons. (See Mark Jenkins, *Bevanism: Labour's High Tide* (Spokesman 1979), pp. 168–71.)

Freeman reported to Crossman, who was away: but 'much disgruntlement [was] expressed when Nye, at the end, urged caution and slowness'.[30] By January, Crossman wrote, even the inner group was disintegrating. 'Nye failed to turn up on Tuesdays, asked for our lunch to be changed to Thursdays and then didn't turn up on two successive Thursdays. As usual he had excellent excuses but really he was evading pressure from Ian Mikardo to start the Friends of *Tribune* as a cover for reorganizing the groups. Nye reacted against this instinctively, though he wasn't prepared to say so.'[31]

While giving little encouragement to his friends, however, Bevan still could not help feuding with his opponents. In the Shadow Cabinet Dalton recorded him 'fratching at great length [at] everyone outside his circle',[32] 'increasingly unfit to hold high office in [the] Party; much too full of egoism and bile and getting worse'.[33] In July he was 'very rude and truculent' when criticised for having abstained on a minor NHS matter on which he was personally committed and refused to discuss it. 'But *we* are going to discuss it,' Attlee insisted. 'N[ye] then says "Then I shall leave the C[ommittee]" in high tantrum, picks up his papers and sweeps from the room.'[34] Such rows were a regular feature of both the Shadow Cabinet and the NEC. Crossman explained Bevan's behaviour to Dalton by saying that in these committees he felt an 'inferiority complex, beaten before he starts'.[35] His growing disillusion was made even clearer to Crossman when they travelled together to Conference at Margate:

> Nye spent a good deal of the time saying how futile the sort of life he was having was and that he would never address any more public meetings. [His huge audiences of the past two years were slipping – though he boasted the contrary to Dalton.][36] He was supposed to attend a compositing meeting but after a pleasant journey we quietly arrived two hours late and retired to Nye's bedroom for drinks, after which we dined alone.
>
> Nye was due to make his big speech at the Sunday demonstration and at dinner Jennie said that he would go upstairs early to prepare it. At half-past one I left him still drinking and he didn't wake up till midday on Sunday.[37]

When Parliament reassembled, Bevan stood again against Morrison for the Deputy Leadership. Both lost votes compared with the year before – the result was 181 to 76 – which Dalton thought was fair comment.[38] It was clear that neither was ever likely to command sufficient confidence in the party to succeed Attlee. Bevan, Crossman recorded, was 'deeply disturbed by his lack of success in the election for the deputy leadership and feels that he is in a dead end. Should he go on leading a Group which seems to repel everybody else from supporting him? But if the Group is disbanded, doesn't he lose his position on the Left and wouldn't he be a prisoner once again, as he was in the Cabinet? All this makes him needful of self-confidence and so very self-assertive and volatile.'[39]

In the new Shadow Cabinet elections, Bevan moved up from twelfth place to ninth, but nothing else changed. Wilson was still thirteenth; Bevan was still a prisoner. He complained openly that he could not speak when he wanted 'to put a slightly different point of view', and grumbled that it was 'a very doubtful advantage being a member'.[40] Jennie was reported as saying that 'she didn't think that Nye would be able to stay on the ... Committee for a whole year'.[41] If he was looking for a pretext to resign he nearly found one the very next week when the Committee censured Mallalieu for pointing out, very mildly, in *Tribune* that some members of the PLP clearly talked left in their constituencies but voted right at Westminster.[42] Told firmly by Attlee that he must learn to listen as well as talk, he was once again, according to Dalton, 'quite out of control', accusing the right of wanting to suppress *Tribune* because it was the only paper that supported him, fixing Gaitskell with 'a glare of concentrated hatred' while telling him that he was 'too young in the Movement to know what he was talking about' and again walking out, declaring that 'whatever you agree to in your present mood, I am against it'.[43]

In view of all this it is only surprising that Bevan lasted on the Committee for another five months. The fact that he did so is the clearest indication that he was not actively looking for an excuse to resign. During the early part of 1954 he withdrew very much into his shell, spoke only twice in the House of Commons, visited Israel again and managed to avoid any further rows. When he did suddenly resign, the bolt fell out of a clear blue sky. Things were just beginning to look up for Labour. In a debate on 5 April, following the news that the Americans had successfully exploded an H-Bomb in the Pacific, Attlee had made one of the most effective speeches of his life, calling for immediate three-power talks and a ban on further tests, while Churchill had made one of his worst. Two Scottish by-elections showed a swing against the Government. 'Labour, in fact', as Mallalieu subsequently wrote in *Tribune*, 'had just begun to bask in the unaccustomed and unexpected luxury of unity, to profit from the mistakes of its opponents, to assume once again the leadership of Britain.'[44] Then on 13 April, Eden made a statement in the House about the situation in Indo-China, where the Chinese were supporting Ho Chi-minh's already seven-year-old war against the French. The Americans were pressing Britain to join in concerted action against the Communists. Eden spoke cautiously of being ready to examine the possibility of some form of collective defence in the area, under the United Nations. Attlee gave even more cautious support, so long as the purpose was clearly and solely anti-Communist and not intended to shore up 'obsolete colonialism'. 'Immediately', wrote Crossman, 'Nye rose, pushed his way along the Table, stood literally on Attlee's toes and denounced the whole idea, lock, stock and barrel, in a way that made him seem to be repudiating Attlee's leadership.'[45] Was Eden aware, he asked, that his statement would be 'deeply resented by the majority of people in Great Britain?' That it would be 'universally regarded as a surrender to American pressure?' That it would be taken as giving British support to 'establishing a NATO in South-East Asia for the purpose of imposing European colonial rule upon certain people in that area?' And that if the course were persisted in, 'it will estrange the Commonwealth members in that part of the world?'[46] Eden answered mildly. The whole House knew that by his extraordinary upstaging of his leader Bevan had thrown the Labour Party back into turmoil.

The next day at the Shadow Cabinet there was inevitably another row ('Back in the shit', groaned Dalton characteristically).[47] Again Bevan walked out, saying that he had had to listen to a lot of 'impudent' speeches and that he could not stand the nervous strain. 'Of course, if it is your nerves that are wrong,' Attlee told him acidly, 'I can't do anything about it.'[48] But still he had not actually resigned. He ran into Crossman in the corridor and merely said that he had 'told the buggers that it was quite likely he wouldn't be returning to them after the Recess'.[49] It was April 1951 all over again. Even now Bevan could not bring himself to make the decisive break, but seemed to be expecting the party to beg him to stay on his own terms. Instead he allowed his opponents to force his hand. At the Party meeting the same evening Attlee delivered an 'extremely sharp criticism' of his conduct, which gave Bevan – who had taken his place on the platform as usual – little choice but to announce that he had resigned.[50]

Why did he do it? His intervention in the House was clearly quite unplanned. It happened that it occurred immediately after the weekly Bevanite lunch at Crossman's where they had 'spent most of the time discussing Indo-China and steaming Nye up to the need for a strong Party line'.[51] But they had no idea at lunchtime that Eden was to make a statement that afternoon. Bevan was, as Mallalieu wrote, 'moved more by instinct than by calculation'.[52] No doubt a good lunch also played its part. Attlee's response to Eden's statement seemed inadequately to express Labour's suspicion of American intentions. So, impetuously, Bevan plunged in. Having done so he was bound, as in 1951, to widen the issue to the whole trend of Labour policy. 'I had already profoundly disagreed with the committee on their decision to persuade the Labour Party to support the immediate rearmament of Germany,' he declared in a hastily dictated resignation statement. 'I was deeply shocked at the failure of the parliamentary leadership to repudiate Mr Eden's acceptance of the American initiative, which is tantamount to the diplomatic and military encirclement of republican China.'[53] In a *Tribune* lead article headlined 'AMERICA MUST BE TOLD: YOU GO IT ALONE' he rehearsed the whole history of British acceptance of American leadership since 1945 and asserted that this was the moment to call a halt. Britain must insist on peace in Indo-China on the basis of recognition of China and independence for the Indo-Chinese. 'There are no qualifications to this. If the Indo-Chinese elect to go Communist, they should be allowed to do so.'

The demand that we should join an alliance for the containment of Communism in South-East Asia is not sought as an instrument for the prevention of war but rather as an extension, into the international field, of the defence of American social, political and economic values.

But America had got used to taking British support for granted.

The answer is quite simply that we shall never be able to make America understand our attitude and adjust herself to it until we are prepared to break with her unless she does.

The Alliance with America was forged in the hope of preventing war. It was not intended as opposition to Communism as such. If America wishes this, then the Alliance is distorted beyond its original purpose.

We should tell America so in the plainest possible terms. If after that she persists, she must do so alone.[54]

The trouble with this was that it was very much what Eden, more diplomatically, was doing. The British Government had no wish at all to get involved in a war in Vietnam; Eden did successfully oppose Dulles's demands for joint military action, and went on to chair the Geneva Conference that May, in alternation with the Russians, to a temporarily satisfactory conclusion, resulting in the division of Vietnam into North and South. It may be claimed that strong expressions of British refusal to go to war strengthened Eden's hand; but there was very little difference between Government and Opposition on this issue, and still less ground for a split in the Labour Party. This was why the whole party was so angry with Bevan for appearing gratuitously to create one. Even his friends were angry. He had acted impetuously, without consultation, and now expected them to back him up. It turned out that he had provoked a split not so much in the Labour Party as among the Bevanites.

The result of the last Shadow Cabinet elections suddenly became crucial. Bevan's resignation created a vacancy, which would normally be filled by the runner-up. But the runner-up on this occasion was Harold Wilson, who was immediately placed in an impossible position. 'If he automatically said no to Nye's place, he would just look like Nye's poodle. If he accepted, he would look as if he were breaking up the Bevanite Group.'[55] Bevan himself, Mikardo and most of the rest of the group took it for granted that Wilson could not think of accepting. Wilson, however, supported by Crossman, felt that Bevan's failure to consult had released his followers from any obligation to him. As an ambitious politician he had never made much secret of the fact that his association with the Bevanites was shrewdly calculated to serve his own career. Ever since 1951 he had suffered the gibe that he was no more than 'Nye's dog'. If he now tamely stayed out of the Shadow Cabinet at Bevan's bidding in support of an ill-judged outburst of which he had had no warning, he would never establish his personal credibility. He was determined to take Bevan's place on the Committee. Crossman tried to persuade Bevan that if Wilson were to go on with his blessing, there need not be a split. But Bevan would not have this. Having once resigned, he felt compelled to justify himself by widening the breach: he now talked wildly of exposing the 'futility and weakness' of Attlee and overthrowing the whole of the parliamentary leadership by 'rousing the constituencies' against them. ('Of course,' Crossman commented, 'this is a view which, when Nye is in a different mood, he can annihilate just as easily, and often has.') Crossman thought that to attack Attlee was 'absolutely insane': the left still depended on Attlee as a restraint on Morrison and Gaitskell. But Crossman and Wilson found the whole group against them. 'I don't think anyone there, including Nye, really believed that he hadn't made a grave mistake in resigning,' wrote Crossman (to whom Mikardo admitted privately that he thought Bevan's action had been 'disastrous').[56] Nevertheless, right or wrong, he had to be supported, to keep the group together. Instead, amid bitter allegations of 'MacDonaldism', the group began to break up as Wilson slid inscrutably into Bevan's vacated place. The weathervane Crossman, exasperated with Bevan and looking for a new leader, began equally imperceptibly to move towards an accommodation with the centre.

Bevan's own next move was to announce, on the death of Arthur Greenwood in June, his candidacy for the post of party Treasurer. Instead of 'rousing the constituencies' he was proposing to take the fight into the trade unions. The Treasurer was elected by Conference – in other words by the bloc votes of the big unions. Even before Greenwood died, the 'Big Three' right-wing leaders – Deakin of the TGWU, William Lawther of the Miners and Tom Williamson of the General and Municipal Workers – had already got the vote effectively sewn up for Gaitskell. Bevan was thus inviting certain defeat. His strategy was nevertheless courageous and principled. It was the unions, by their money and their majority on the NEC, who controlled the Labour Party. If the right's domination of the party was ever to be broken it was in the unions that its grip must first be loosened. For years *Tribune* and the Bevanites had been raging against the union bosses' cynical use of their block votes to crush the left, against the wishes, they firmly believed, of the mass of their members. Bevan did not imagine that he would win the treasurership in 1954. But he did believe that by standing he would 'split every trade union and expose Deakin and Tom Williamson by making them prefer an intellectual like Gaitskell to a miner like me'.[57] He brushed aside the objection that by standing for Treasurer he would not be able to stand as well for the constituency section and would lose his seat on the NEC. The Bevanites had already shown that they controlled the constituencies. The battle was now for the unions. By appealing over the heads of the leaders to the rank and file Bevan was aiming to win in two or three years' time.

The strategy was right. To control the party, the left did indeed need to win the unions, to capture for themselves the power to wield the block votes as ruthlessly as the right wielded them now. In due course, beginning with the accession of Frank Cousins to the leadership of the TGWU in 1956, this happened; then the right suddenly became loud in denunciation of the denial of democracy. Bevan's apparently hopeless challenge in 1954 pointed the way to a reversal of roles whose full impact on the party he did not live to see. Nevertheless his decision, as the price of this quixotic gesture, to give up his seat on the NEC (and hence the party chairmanship which by the normal operation of Buggins' Turn would have fallen to him in 1957) dismayed many of his supporters; and Crossman was surely right to diagnose in it a symptom of psychological semi-retirement.[58] That summer he and Jennie sold Cliveden Place and bought a fifty-acre farm in Buckinghamshire – the outward and visible expression of an inner retreat from the tumult of daily politics into the greater privacy and comfort of middle-aged rural domesticity. With increasing frequency Crossman began to notice his reluctance to come up to town for Bevanite lunches, party meetings and other engagements.[59] In November he found Bevan totally out of touch with events, 'since he has no newspapers in the country'.[60] In this mood, to be off the NEC as well as the parliamentary Committee was a release.

Bevan threw himself into farming with all the extravagant enthusiasm which was his most irrepressible characteristic. Believing himself a countryman, full of impractical plans and wonderful theories, enjoying the role of the natural aristocrat while determined not to exploit anyone (Jennie actually ran the business) he found at Asheridge the escape and relaxation and creative fulfilment outside politics that by 1954 he badly needed.[61] The home that Jennie and her still formidable mother made for him there was not as elegant as Cliveden Place, but it was at once simple and spacious – the farmhouse was Tudor, surrounded by a cluster of barns and outbuildings – and comfortable, welcoming and homely. It had the cosiness of Lane End Cottage recreated on a larger scale. Nye and Jennie had a genius for making houses their own.*

Scarcely had they moved to Asheridge, however, at the beginning of the summer recess than Bevan left for five weeks with an official Labour delegation to the Soviet Union and China. It was an incongruous party, including Attlee, the party secretary Morgan Phillips, two or three trade unionists and one of the most implacable of all his opponents on the NEC, Edith Summerskill. Only a strong desire to meet the new Soviet and Chinese leaders could have induced Bevan to travel in such uncongenial company. There is no record, unfortunately, of the personal relations of the trip. But Bevan was greatly encouraged by the personal contact he was able to make with the post-Stalin collective leadership in Moscow – particularly with Malenkov, generally reckoned to be the central figure, with whom he was able to have a two-hour talk, interrupted only by Edith Summerskill who 'kept barging in'.[62] Malenkov, he reported solemnly in *Tribune*, expressed precisely the

---

* A shadow was cast over the move to Asheridge by the discovery that Ma Lee had cancer and could not be expected to live very long. In fact she lived another eight years – longer than Nye.

alarm at the resurgence of Nazism in Western Germany which the Bevanites had been sounding. More generally he found gratifying confirmation of his theory of the inevitable liberalisation of Soviet society and his belief in the possibility of *détente*:

> I hope I am not so ingenuous as to imagine that the pleasant atmosphere of after-dinner conversation is of itself sufficient evidence that the outstanding conflicts with the Soviet Union can easily be settled. But the present self-confidence of Russian leaders is a great improvement on the nervous rigidity of the past. It creates a more hopeful atmosphere for negotiation.
>
> It has always been my view that the Soviet leaders were difficult to deal with after the war, not because they were strong, but because of their overwhelming consciousness of weakness.
>
> I left the Soviet Union with the impression that its leaders are for the first time beginning to feel on top of their domestic situation, and so can face the world with the knowledge that any agreements they might make in external issues will not be accounted to them as weakness. At least that is an advance in the right direction.[63]

Bevan was less impressed with Khrushchev than with Malenkov, and thought that his appointment as General Secretary of the Communist Party meant that the party was 'destined to play a declining role' in Soviet government.[64] Unfortunately for these predictions it was Malenkov who was demoted the following year to Minister of Electric Power Stations and Khrushchev who went on to supreme power, initiating a liberalisation which proved to be extremely limited.

Sympathetic as he was with China, on the other hand, Bevan was repelled by the narrow dogmatism the delegation encountered there. There were no books to be seen except the works of Marx, Lenin and Stalin. He was impressed by the outgoing cosmopolitanism of Chou En-lai but chilled by Mao, who seemed too doctrinaire to accept the modern methods that would be needed to feed, and to contain, China's exploding population. He clung to the hope that Mao had an instinctive, Tito-like understanding of his people. But 'in the new phase on which China is embarked, I put a serious question mark against his judgement'.[65] He was right. He may have misread the signs in Russia, but Bevan when he was not deceiving himself could be very shrewd. He disliked above all being told what to think. Meeting Mao dented his enthusiasm for 'Republican China' quite severely.

From this trip, Bevan returned to face a dismal autumn. He lost the election for the party treasurership by more than 2–1 – 4.3 million votes to 2 million – which was worse than he or anyone else expected. The result concealed two specific body blows. First, his own union, the miners, repudiated him, also by a rank-and-file vote of more than 2–1. Second, it was clear that Gaitskell had won nearly half the votes of the constituency parties, which were supposed to be the Bevanites' particular preserve.[66] Admittedly the Bevanites held their six places on the NEC, with Anthony Greenwood filling Bevan's seat; but both Crossman and Wilson improved their positions and Wilson was rewarded for his opportunism in April by coming first. It was perhaps a good thing that Bevan had disqualified himself from standing for the NEC or he might actually have suffered the humiliation of being eclipsed by his former 'dog'. In the Conference itself the left was cheated of victory on German rearmament when the small woodworkers' union was induced to switch its vote. Attlee opened this debate with a judicious speech warning against 'emotionalism' in foreign affairs.[67] Bevan, unable as a member of the NEC (for a few more days) to reply, was reduced to shouting angrily at Deakin from the floor. The following evening at the annual *Tribune* rally, free now from any collective restraints, he laid into the trade union leaders uninhibitedly, naming names and denouncing the unsocialist bureaucracy which was strangling the party. He also, remembering Attlee's warning against 'emotionalism', spoke bitterly of the sort of politics the present leadership seemed to admire:

> I know now that the right kind of leader for the Labour Party is a desiccated calculating machine who must not in any way permit himself to be swayed by indignation. If he sees suffering, privation or injustice he must not allow it to move him, for that would be evidence of lack of proper education or of absence of self-control. He must speak in calm and objective accents and talk about a dying child in the same way as he would about the pieces inside an internal combustion engine.[68]

It was immediately assumed that this was an attack on Gaitskell; the phrase 'desiccated calculating machine' has indeed stuck to him ever since. In fact it is clear that it was Attlee, if anybody, whom Bevan had in mind and the phrase really described the sort of bloodless puppet that Attlee had seemed to propose as the ideal. Gaitskell was in his own buttoned-up way as emotional as Bevan, which is why their antagonism in these years was so intense. Whatever he intended, however, the speech was seen as another abusive personal attack on the leadership.[69] It did Bevan no good, even among his friends, who were once again dismayed by his capacity to put everyone against him. When Parliament met he was again conspicuous by his significant absences.[70] When the formation of SEATO was debated on 8 November, for instance – the very issue on which he had resigned from the Shadow Cabinet – he did not even bother to attend.[71] So far as the Bevanities were concerned, he was back on a cautious tack urging that nothing should be done which might risk expulsion. Jennie explained that 'after all Parliament and the Executive don't matter now, since everything depends on Nye's trade union campaign'. 'He just isn't leading and doesn't want to,' Crossman wrote, 'and the Left gets weaker day by day.'[72] The Bevanites' last whimper came, appropriately, on German rearmament. Though the EDC was dead, Eden had secured French agreement to arming the Federal Republic within the framework of the Western European Union, with a well-timed promise of a British military commitment, hitherto resisted. The Bevanites were at first determined to vote against this,[73] till Bevan rather shamefacedly changed his mind. Then the Shadow Cabinet, fearing a shambles, switched its three-line whip from supporting the Government to abstention. Ingloriously but self-righteously, the bulk of both left and right duly abstained, each accusing the other of cowardice. Only six pacifists (and one supporter of German rearmament) went into the lobby and were deprived of the whip. Bevan made one of his best speeches for some time – Crossman thought it 'a brilliant tactical oration ... which certainly restored his parliamentary position' – calling once more for talks with the Russians before the new treaty was ratified.[74] But Foot remembered it as 'one of his rare flops';[75] and the reason is clear. The occasion was a flop. After months and years of passionate controversy, the Bevanites had on this issue accepted defeat, toed the party line and failed to back their convictions with their votes. This can be seen as the moment when the Bevanites, as an organised parliamentary challenge to the elected leadership, finally ceased to matter.

Yet there was still one more eruption of what came to be called Bevan's 'spring fever'. Since his original resignation from the Cabinet in April 1951 there had been the major Bevanite revolt on the Defence White Paper in March 1952, then Bevan's resignation from the Shadow Cabinet in April 1954. Now in March 1955 he gave those who wanted to expel him from the party another chance which they very nearly took. Once again the ground of the dispute was the international situation. Once again the row was not so much over what Bevan stood for – which differed only marginally from the official line – as the unacceptable way he presented his demands. As on previous occasions the state of barely suppressed antagonism between the tribal factions required only the spark of Bevan's personality to ignite a crisis. Once again the considerable merits of his case were obscured by his presentation of it and by his opponents' violent over-reaction.

Bevan was trying to seize for Labour the initiative in pressing for four-power talks – a summit conference – to discuss the threat of the H-Bomb in the light of mounting international tension over Germany and the latest trouble-spot, Formosa. This had been Attlee's policy a year before; it was also widely known to have been Churchill's desire before he was incapacitated by a stroke in July 1953. In March 1954 Attlee's call for talks had been endorsed by the whole House of Commons. Now Bevan wanted to revive it and to unite Labour in condemnation of the Government for failing to bring them about. (In Moscow, to the increased alarm of the West, Malenkov was at just this moment replaced by Bulganin and Khrushchev.) Attlee was sympathetic; but he allowed himself to be overridden by Morrison and Gaitskell, who were suspicious of any stratagem that might be used by Bevan to reopen the question of German rearmament.[76] On 9 February a thinly attended PLP rejected Bevan's motion by 93–70. Bevan, however, quickly collected 104 signatures, from well beyond the left, in support of an unofficial motion. This was defiance of a party decision; but it was well-supported defiance and it could reasonably be represented as being in accordance with the party's previously declared policy which the Shadow Cabinet was now repudiating. At the next party meeting on 24 February Bevan offered to withdraw his motion if the party would take over a similar proposal by Fred Peart. Again Attlee, left to himself, would have agreed; but Morrison would not have it and Bevan was formally censured for his presumption by 132 votes to 72.[77]

At this moment the Government announced that Britain was going to manufacture its own H-Bomb. This immediately divided the Labour Party; more specifically, it once again divided the Bevanites. Mikardo, Driberg, Barbara Castle and others took the clear moral line, which later became the unilateralist line, that Labour should have nothing to do with the new weapon.[78] Bevan, however, was not against the British Bomb. He had not been against Britain developing the A-Bomb, and he refused to pretend that there was a difference of principle between the two. 'They are both weapons of imprecision,' he maintained, no different from saturation bombing of civilians by 'conventional' means. 'They are all immoral.'[79] Nevertheless he was 'emphatic' that Labour should not oppose the manufacture of the H-Bomb, since 'the British people were not prepared to see themselves deprived of a modern weapon. . . . Not the H-Bomb but our strategy and foreign policy were the real issues.'[80] The point was to prevent the Bomb being used. Only substantive discussions between the great powers could bargain it away. Britain's independent possession of the Bomb was on this argument essential to enable her to take part in this process. Crossman, who had initially been inclined the other way, quickly took up this argument and developed it into what became the centre position in the nuclear disputes of the next few years: that the only logical options were complete neutrality 'à la Nehru' or accepting a nuclear strategy which would allow substantial savings in conventional forces.[81] Here, however, Bevan parted company from him.

The critical debate took place on 1–2 March. The crux of the matter was the question of 'first use' of nuclear weapons. The Government's White Paper explicitly accepted that deterrence depended on the threat of nuclear retaliation even against conventional attack. The Opposition's amendment – approved at a party meeting on 24 February which Bevan had not attended – confined itself to minor details of cost; it did not criticise the decision to manufacture the Bomb and implicitly endorsed the strategy of nuclear retaliation.[82] It was deliberately intended to blur the issue. Bevan was torn two ways. Crossman, Wilson, Freeman and others thought the official amendment perfectly acceptable; believing that he agreed with them in not opposing British manufacture, they expected him to support it. But Jennie, Foot and Barbara Castle – the unilateralists – wanted to stage a moral protest, and since Bevan would not oppose British manufacture they worked on him instead to make an issue of 'first use'. On the evening of 1 March Crossman thought he had persuaded him his way. But the next day 'Jennie . . . had changed his mind again'; at lunch he was 'fairly determined to lead a new split'. Then George Wigg met him at the House and 'swung him back again'. As they went into the

Chamber together Bevan told Crossman, 'I'm still completely in two minds what I should do.'[83]

Thus, as in 1954, what he did do was not the considered result of rational calculation but the instinct of the moment. Once on his feet, he did what Crossman called 'a magnificent job exposing Churchill and demanding negotiations',[84] drawing from him the important admission that he had been hoping to go to Moscow to meet Malenkov before his stroke in 1953. Since then, Bevan was able to suggest without contradiction, he had been overruled by Eisenhower and Eden.

> That is a sombre thing to say, and a wicked thing to believe – that we have now reached a situation where Great Britain can, in a few short years, run the risk of extinction of its civilisation, and we cannot reach the potential enemy in an attempt to arrive at an accommodation with him because we are now at the mercy of the United States.

Then, however, he turned to the question of 'first use' and bluntly dismissed Labour's official amendment as 'a monstrous evasion'.

> I want my hon. Friends the Leaders of the Opposition to answer me. Do they mean by that language what the Government mean by the White Paper? Do they mean that nuclear weapons will be used with the support of the British Labour movement against any sort of aggression? I want to know the answer. If my right hon. Friend the Leader of the Opposition says that that is the inter-pretation of the Amendment, then I do not propose to vote for it this evening.

This, he maintained, was a policy of suicide. The only alternative was to talk, and since the West was going to have to talk eventually, why not now? He pleaded with Churchill to 'do deeds to match his great words; not attempt to delude the country by the majesty of his language, but inspire it by the dedication of his behaviour. That is what we want from him.' Then he turned again towards the Labour Front Bench: 'We want from my right hon. Friends the Leaders of the Opposition an assurance that the language of their Amendment, moved on our behalf, does not align the Labour movement behind that recklessness; because if we cannot have a lead from *them*, let us give the lead ourselves.'[85]

This seemed another breathtaking challenge to Attlee's leadership. A furious argument immediately blew up over whether by 'them' Bevan had meant the Government or his own Front Bench, and whether by 'ourselves' he had meant the Labour Party as a whole or just the Bevanites. It all de-pended on the interpretation of the sweeping arm gesture with which he had accompanied his words.[86] Either way, in fact, it was a contemptuous rejection of the Shadow Cabinet's carefully imprecise formula. Moreover, having made his point he would not let it rest there. When at the end of the debate Attlee wound up for Labour he deliberately ignored Bevan's question. So Bevan got up and asked it again. 'What we want to know is whether the use of the words to which I have referred in our Amendment associates us with the statement that we should use thermo-nuclear weapons in circumstances of hostilities, although they were not used against us?' Yet again Attlee obfuscated, merely insisting on the 'general thesis, with which I think my right hon. Friend agrees, that deterrents, by the possession of thermo-nuclear weapons, are the best way of preventing another war'.[87] In the subsequent vote no fewer than sixty-two Labour Members abstained with Bevan: numerically a significant revolt. But at least eight former Bevanites, including not only Crossman and Wilson but Freeman, Swingler, Hugh Delargy and Leslie Hale, voted with the leadership.[88] What Bevan had succeeded in doing was to put himself at the head of the unilateralist faction with whom he did not fundamentally agree, while appearing to signal once and for all that he was not interested in working constructively for unity.

Right or wrong – and of course the official amendment *was* an evasion – he had seemed to go out of his way to wreck Attlee's carefully worded formula, and on an issue on which he was not fundamentally at odds with the leadership. The possession of the Bomb might involve a moral absolute. The argument whether or not effective deterrence depended upon Soviet uncertainty as to Western intentions, on the other hand, was finely balanced and hypothetical and afforded no sensible ground for breaking up the party. Bevan's action could not have been more provocatively calculated to humiliate Attlee. He had not raised any objection to the proposed amendment at the party meeting on 24 February; he had not taken the trouble to attend. He had not spoken to Attlee privately. Instead he had challenged him publicly on the floor of the House of Commons, pressing him repeatedly to answer a question he evidently had no intention of answering. This, to say the least, is not what party leaders expect of their backbenchers. There was a strong feeling in the parliamentary party that this time Bevan had gone too far. Even his friends, even *Tribune*, admitted that he had behaved badly.[89] Those who had long believed that the party would never regain the confidence of the electorate until it had rid itself of his disruptive presence thought that the moment for drastic surgery had come. Bevan could be expelled and no one could reasonably object that he had not asked for it. The trouble was that Attlee did not agree. With characteristic modesty he was less worried by the insult to his personal dignity than determined, as he had been steadily and inscrutably for the past twenty years, to maintain his delicate balancing act between left and right. He had no intention of lending his authority to the right's desire for a conclusive showdown.[90] In these circumstances, though it was his authority that had been challenged, the right found itself in the awkward position of appearing more loyalist than the leader.

It is a matter of dispute between Attlee's biographer and Gaitskell's whether Attlee's handling of this crisis was skilful or weak.[91] The best answer is that his political judgement was correct, but his execution, as so often since 1951, culpably remote. His priority was to limit the damage to the party.

Much as he had suffered from Bevan's restlessness and tantrums over the past five years, Attlee still recognised him as representing an authentic strand in Labour's composition. He actually claimed more than once that he had hoped Bevan would be his successor. 'Nye had the leadership on a plate,' he told Crossman. 'I always wanted him to have it. But you know he wants to be two things simultaneously, a rebel and an official leader, and you can't be both.'[92] If he really saw Bevan as his heir, Attlee had shown a curious way of grooming him since 1947: his efforts had seemed rather directed to keeping the left in the party, but firmly in its place. Nevertheless he at least acknowledged that the left had a place in the party. Bevan might not be leadership material, but even after his latest escapade Attlee judged that expelling him would create more outrage and demoralisation among the activists in the constituency parties than would be caused at Westminster by playing the incident down. With an election likely very soon, Labour needed the full-hearted commitment of its activists more than ever. Attlee was shocked at the zeal of Deakin, Morrison and Gaitskell to anathematise the leader of the left at such a time.

To do him justice Gaitskell, though he still had no doubt that 'sooner or later Bevan would have to go', also thought initially that this was not the right moment.[93] At the Shadow Cabinet on 7 March, however, a clear majority – articulated on this occasion by Chuter Ede and Jim Callaghan – was strongly for recommending the PLP to withdraw the whip, leading to possible expulsion; so Gaitskell acquiesced. Attlee said little or nothing.[94] Only when Gaitskell and the others were committed did he make clear, first to the PLP and then at the NEC, his distaste for extreme measures, thus showing up the right as vindictively bent on expulsion against his will. In the end Attlee achieved the result he wanted: Bevan was not expelled and Labour went into the General Election at least formally united. Nevertheless the party suffered the maximum disruption and recrimination over several weeks when the issue hung in the balance. Much of this could have been avoided if Attlee had given a clear lead against expulsion from the beginning.

For his part Bevan did not make it easy for Attlee. As always when he had climbed out on a limb, he refused to climb down and expected his supporters to back him. At its meeting on 7 March the Shadow Cabinet actually met his main policy point by agreeing to press for four-power talks, as he had demanded in his original motion. Again, a lot of trouble might have been avoided if they had done this earlier. But all that was needed now was for Bevan to apologise to Attlee for his behaviour in the House and he would have cut most of the ground from under his opponents' feet. On the contrary, when Crossman and Barbara Castle visited him at his farm, where he had retired to bed with 'flu, they found him 'sitting up, wonderfully obstreperous, in bed. ... When Barbara said he ought to apologize ... Nye shouted, like a petulant child, "I won't, I won't".'[95] He wanted the six Bevanites on the NEC to announce that they would all resign if he was expelled. This Crossman and

Wilson, Greenwood and Castle – like Wilson the year before – were extremely reluctant to do. Fortunately Bevan's timely indisposition caused the postponement for a week of the party meeting called to consider his case. In the interval MPs were bombarded with resolutions from the constituencies against expulsion. It was also anticipated that Churchill was finally about to retire and that Eden would call an immediate election to capitalise on Labour's disunity. Under this double pressure the PLP when it eventually met on 16 March delivered a verdict far more ambiguous than would have been the case a week before. An amendment merely censuring Bevan's conduct was defeated by only 138 votes to 124. Then the Shadow Cabinet's motion to withdraw the whip, which Attlee pointedly refused to present as an issue of confidence in himself, was carried by only 141–112.[96] This was not much of a mandate for the NEC to proceed with expulsion.

Gaitskell and the right, however, were now fully committed, the more so because they felt let down by Attlee's weakness. They recognised that expulsion would cause, as Dalton put it, 'a hell of a stink in the constituencies. But heavy trouble can't be avoided whatever we do.'[97] Once embarked on disciplinary action, Gaitskell was characteristically determined to see it through, to the extent that three of his normally loyal supporters, Tony Crosland, Roy Jenkins and Woodrow Wyatt, wrote to warn him that he was getting out of touch with feeling in the party.[98] On 22 March he had a secret conversation with Crossman in which he insisted that it was too late for compromise, revealing with rare frankness the depth of paranoia which had fuelled the right's fear of Bevan over the past four years.

'Bevanism', he said, 'is and only is a conspiracy to seize the leadership for Aneurin Bevan. It is a conspiracy because it has three essentials of conspiracy, a leader in Bevan, an organization run by Mikardo and a newspaper run by Foot.' I laughed and said, 'You really believe in this talk about the Bevanite organization of Mikardo?' Gaitskell said, 'Certainly. It's widespread in the constituencies.'* I said, 'How can you take the *Tribune* seriously, with a genuine circulation of not more than 18,000?' He said, 'It's read everywhere in the constituencies. It's the single most important factor which our people on the Right complain of.'

I tried to suggest that Bevanism was also a protest against the totally inadequate leadership of Morrison and himself. I said that in my view Nye was only half wanting to be Leader and that certainly there had been no serious conspiracy to replace Attlee with Nye. Gaitskell then repeated his whole speech at length and said, 'It's got to be cleaned up. There are extraordinary parallels between Nye and Adolf Hitler. They are demagogues of exactly the same sort.'

I remarked mildly that I thought Nye showed a really genuine interest in

* In his own diary Gaitskell admitted that 'unfortunately we have very little detailed knowledge' of the Bevanite organisation, 'but ... most of us are convinced [it] does exist' (Gaitskell diary, 2 April 1955, p. 400). He also noted of this conversation with Crossman: 'Naturally I was very much on my guard.' One wonders what he would have said if he had talked freely! (Ibid., 23 March 1955, p. 392.)

parliamentary liberty. 'Oh,' Gaitskell said, 'there are minor differences but what's striking is the resemblance.'

'If Nye were out of the Party', Gaitskell concluded, 'the main Tory propaganda for the next Election would be killed, whereas, if the Executive failed to carry his expulsion, the Tories would assert that Bevan is indispensable and the main master of the Party.'[99] At the Executive next day, however, Gaitskell and Morrison found Attlee now openly against them. The PLP vote, he argued, had been too narrow to justify expulsion, at least until Bevan had been given another chance to apologise and pledge his loyalty for the future. Normally the Leader's view would have prevailed without much difficulty; but on this occasion Morrison and Gaitskell fought it to a vote and lost only by 14–13 when the strongly anti-Bevanite Glaswegian Jean Mann unexpectedly voted, not against expulsion, but in favour of going through all the motions of requiring guarantees of good behaviour first.[100] It was widely assumed that Bevan would refuse to give such assurances and would thus be seen to expel himself. As usual he was subject to conflicting influences, with Jennie, Foot and Mallalieu urging him not to 'grovel'. In that mood he was still truculent, striking heroic poses, appealing to 'the hundreds of thousands of people in the country who support my stand' and seeming actually to want to be expelled.[101] But this time he was persuaded that he could not refuse the olive branch which Attlee, at some risk to his own position, was holding out to him. He was summoned to appear before a sub-committee of the NEC on 29 March. For once he defended himself with great skill. Gaitskell and his allies were anxious to question him on a wide range of past misdemeanours and to commit him not only to accept majority decisions but to refrain from attacks on the trade unions and disband the imagined Bevanite organisation. Bevan, however, saw Attlee in advance and concerted with him a prepared statement in which he denied ever having intended to cause Attlee any embarrassment, apologised handsomely 'for any pain I may have caused him' and pledged that 'I ask for nothing more than the opportunity to serve our Party under his leadership'.[102] Before the investigating sub-committee he then blandly refused to be drawn on the wider questions. His enemies were stymied. They considered Bevan's assurances worthless, but the moment when expulsion might have been possible had passed. At the full NEC the next day Attlee seconded a resolution moved by Jim Griffiths welcoming Bevan's apology and proposing to restore the whip, withdrawn only two weeks before. All the hardliners could do was to carry, by fifteen votes to ten *against* Attlee, an amendment stiffening his motion – it now merely 'noted' Bevan's apology – and promising 'drastic action against any future violations of Party discipline'.[103] Thus Bevan escaped again, and Labour was saved the foolishness of expelling one of its most prominent leaders a matter of weeks before a general election. Seven days later Eden succeeded Churchill as Prime Minister. Almost immediately he called the election for 26 May.

Chapter 21

The Leadership Resolved: Gaitskell Victorious

There was never much doubt that the Government would win the 1955 election. The Tories went to the country with a new and popular Prime Minister and a 4 per cent lead in the opinion polls. Labour set its divisions aside and rallied loyally around Attlee and a studiously moderate manifesto emphasising peace and welfare rather than further nationalisation. (The free Health Service was to be restored; but only the renationalisation of steel and road haulage and the nationalisation of 'sections of the chemical and machine tool industries' survived from the shopping list agreed in 1953.) The Tories and some of the newspapers did their best to suggest that Bevan would be the dominating force in a Labour Government. The *Daily Sketch* claimed to 'rock the nation' with the revelation that Bevan would be Prime Minister if Labour won;[1] while Cummings in the *Daily Express* drew Bevan lurking menacingly behind a reassuring cardboard mask of Attlee.[2] But the Bevan bogey did not really run. A more plausible explanation of Labour's defeat lay in the electorate's perception of the party, after all the squabbles of the past four years – continuing right up to the announcement of the election – as deeply divided. For this the right was quick to blame the Bevanites.[3] On the other hand the party as a whole under Attlee (now seventy-two) and Morrison (sixty-seven), with people like Ede (seventy-three) and Shinwell (seventy-one) still in the Shadow Cabinet, did not present an inspiring alternative to a Government now led by Eden, Macmillan and Butler which had had the good fortune to preside over the end of austerity and rationing and the beginnings of affluence. This was of course the crucial factor. 'For the first time within living memory', Bevan wrote in *Tribune*, 'a Tory Government managed to exist for more than three years without inflicting mass unemployment on the country.' On this analysis, 'Labour was the victim of its own success.'[4] Equally it could be said to be the victim of its failure since 1951 to work out where it should be going next. The Bevanite rows were, as Crossman suggested to Gaitskell, as much a symptom of this deeper failure as the direct cause of its defeat at the polls.

For the first time since 1931 Labour failed to increase its total vote; on a

301

significantly reduced turnout it actually fell by one and a half million, giving the Tories, whose vote fell much less, an extra twenty-three seats and an overall majority of fifty-eight.[5] Dissension immediately broke out again within the party over why the missing voters had stayed at home. The opposing diagnoses were as clear as ever. For Bevan the reason, in addition to the Government's good luck with the economy, was Labour's 'inability to distinguish itself sufficiently from many of the Government's own policies, particularly in the field of foreign affairs. In the absence of any domestic issue of comparable importance this proved decisive.'[6] Labour's commitment to a bipartisan, slavishly pro-American foreign policy had muted its distinctively socialist alternative. Gaitskell on the other hand dismissed such an interpretation with contempt:

> Can anyone honestly say that if the Labour Party had chosen a policy which reflected more or less the line of the Communist Party we should have achieved a larger vote? Do we really believe that the marginal voters who failed to go to the polls were skulking at home because the Labour Party is not revolutionary enough? I do not believe for a moment that anyone could be led into believing any such thing.[7]

Shorn of its emotive language – 'Communist', 'revolutionary' – this was precisely what Bevan did believe. He had in fact predicted Labour's failure the previous December when commenting on a disappointing by-election result.

> What is the common factor which Labour people share and which sharply distinguishes us from Tories? It is Socialism. If it is not that, then there is nothing, at least nothing worth bothering about. The more we play it down, the less we differ from our opponents and the less reason there is for people to vote for us to get the others out. If we blunt the edge of the socialist case so as to capture the elusive 'floating voter' we produce apathy, for that is nothing more than the recognition of the absence of any real difference between the parties. The fight for socialism unites and excites the party. To mute the fight is to disunite and deflate it.[8]

Labour in the summer of 1955 was undoubtedly deflated. In so far as both left and right felt themselves vindicated by the party's defeat, it also remained fundamentally disunited. Nevertheless there was a strong desire on both sides to try to pull together. Wilson, Crossman and Castle were now clearly distancing themselves from Bevan and emerging as a new centre–left grouping, prepared to co-operate with the right; at the same time Gaitskell's supporters, chastened by their failure to expel Bevan in March as well as by the election result, began to see the need for their man to distance himself similarly from Morrison and move towards the centre.[9] The choice of Attlee's successor could not be postponed much longer. He had already stayed on as leader longer than he should have done or probably wanted, largely in order to keep out Morrison. (It was principally to save the party from Morrison that he may have hoped that Bevan would develop into a possible alternative.) For a time there had been a move, encouraged by Dalton, to promote Jim Griffiths as a centre candidate acceptable to all; but Griffiths – his Marxist training with Bevan at the Central Labour College long forgotten – was too soft-hearted and sentimental an old socialist to be credible.[10] So Attlee lingered on. Now he must go soon. But Gaitskell still seemed to most people, including himself, too young and inexperienced, as well as too divisive, to succeed just yet. There seemed no alternative to Morrison. In these circumstances Bevan was more than usually uncertain what to do.

Should he stand again against Morrison for the Deputy Leadership, or wait for Attlee to go and then stand for Leader? He did not expect to beat Morrison. But 'the only possible salvation for the Party', he suggested to Crossman, Wilson and Strachey on 7 June, 'would be for Morrison to be Leader and me to be Deputy Leader. If Morrison and Gaitskell are elected, the Party won't split; it will disintegrate and never recover.'[11] Bitterly as he disliked Morrison, Bevan was prepared to accept him as a stopgap who at least had roots in the party: the important thing was to prevent the succession of Gaitskell, who he still believed had none. It was just possible, Crossman reckoned, that if Bevan was re-elected to 'a new rejuvenated Shadow Cabinet, where he played along with the team throughout the summer', the 100-odd floating votes in the centre of the party might give him the Deputy Leadership. 'He seemed suddenly aware that the Parliamentary Party, which he has always dismissed as irrelevant, really does matter. I think he has begun to realize that, if Attlee resigns and he is not made Deputy Leader in October, his fate is virtually sealed.' Privately Crossman thought that when Attlee resigned there was 'no chance whatsoever' of avoiding either a Morrison/ Gaitskell ticket or Gaitskell becoming Leader with someone else, perhaps Wilson, as Deputy. 'I simply don't see the Parliamentary Party ever giving Nye a majority. But the main thing is to make him try to win some support by being sensible.'[12]

Still he was pulled the other way by those closest to him who encouraged him to play the romantic rebel. Jennie wanted him to stand for the Deputy Leadership but not for the Shadow Cabinet. 'I like to see people like Harold on the Parliamentary Committee while Nye keeps himself free outside.' When Crossman told him firmly that he must play with the team if he was ever to have a chance of being leader, he replied with a characteristic rationalisation of his behaviour over the last four years: 'I'm not sure I really want to be under these conditions. I'm not a proletarian or an intellectual. I am an aristocrat, with a real distaste for that kind of politics.' He was really, he was beginning to tell himself, too good for the Labour Party. 'Aristocrats are no good in the Labour Party', Crossman rebuked him. 'If you want to be taken seriously, you had better stick on the Parliamentary Committee and not get off it, as you did last time.' 'But the truth is that Nye is three-quarters finished now and three-quarters knows it. ... Jennie's escapism is carrying him back to his farm, which he discussed with me at great length for an hour, showing real enthusiasm.'[13]

In the end when Attlee, yielding to pressure to postpone the issue, announced that he would carry on until the autumn of 1956 Bevan – so often in the past contemptuous of his feeble leadership – stood up in the PLP and begged him not to put any date on his depature. In reality, the longer Attlee delayed the more certain it was that Gaitskell, not Morrison, would succeed him; but Bevan had now belatedly recognised Attlee as the dam holding back the triumph of the right and wanted only to put off the day of his retirement as long as possible. He announced at the same time, to cheers of relief, that he would not be standing for the Deputy Leadership.[14] 'On this occasion', wrote Crossman, '(compared with the episode of the H-Bomb) Nye havered and hovered and then, while on his feet, fell off them but on the right side of the fence.'[15]

Bevan was duly re-elected to a Shadow Cabinet from which most of the old guard had been pressured by the example of Dalton into standing down. He came seventh, evidence of a desire to heal wounds. Wilson, however, came fifth – proof that the old Bevanite left had been overtaken by the new centre–left. Wilson – 'very impressed by the unpopularity of nationalization'[16] – was actually moving rapidly to the centre but still contrived to retain the loyalty of his former associates on the left. If anyone wearing a 'left' ticket was ever going to draw enough support from the centre to make a serious challenge for the leadership, it was henceforth going to be Wilson, not Bevan. Thus Bevan, back in the Shadow Cabinet, was once again isolated. At Wilson's suggestion, the twelve members were all for the first time given shadow portfolios: Bevan got Labour, thus taking him back to 1951. (Foreign Affairs went to Alf Robens, who had taken his place at the Ministry of Labour when he had resigned.) He spoke only once or twice on employment questions over the summer and autumn.[17] Crossman felt that he was merely going through the motions, bored and disillusioned. When he met five of the six Bevanite members of the NEC in September to concert tactics for Conference, Crossman sensed the end of an epoch.

> It was not simply that Nye was out of it through not knowing about the Executive or being more interested in pigs. It was a feeling that somehow a wave of history on which he had risen seemed to be falling, that he was still as brilliant as ever but didn't count so much. There was also a sense that he himself was bored with the evening and would have preferred to have had a dinner without politics.

'What you will have to seriously consider, Barbara,' he said at one point, 'is whether this Labour Party is worth working for at all.'[18]

It was in this resigned spirit that he stood again for Treasurer. Unless he was going to retire altogether, he still had to fight his corner. The fundamental issue was still the undemocratic and anti-socialist domination of the party by the block votes of the big trade unions. In the pre-Conference edition of *Tribune* he argued again that Labour had lost in May because it did not offer a sufficiently distinctive alternative to the Tories. Had working people voted Tory because Labour between 1945 and 1950 had removed their worst grievances and they were now content? 'If that were true,' he contended, 'the answer should be another period of Socialist education, not a muting of the Socialist challenge.' There was no point in Labour simply aping the Tories.

> But is it the case that the Socialist pulse beats more feebly than it did among the mass of Labour members? That is not my experience, and I have spent as much time going around the country as most.
>
> I have been convinced for a long time that the great bulk of the membership of the trade unions as well as in the divisional parties is ready for a new forward thrust. The truth is that this thrust has failed to find expression in the upper reaches of the party.

The block-vote system he condemned as 'a travesty of democracy'. 'The concentration of power in a few hands is always bad, and even if the political policies of the general unions were progressive, their ascendancy within the Labour Party would not be justified.' This, of course, was a proposition to which the left no longer subscribed when in due course it controlled the major unions, any more than it worried Gaitskell and Morrison now. Nevertheless Bevan was perfectly correct in predicting that if the left ever did control the block votes the press would be full of righteous condemnation, whereas now it winked at the unions' crushing of Labour's socialist aspiration. The Treasurership, Bevan argued, with a clear reference to Gaitskell, was used by the unions to place on the NEC those whom the constituency parties had rejected. He explained his decision to stand the previous year.

> It seemed to me that here was an opportunity to challenge the assumption that what the general unions desired must be accepted by the party. So I accepted nomination for the Treasurership knowing that when I did so I would be inviting implacable hostility from the most powerful persons in the party.
>
> Before and since I have been accused of unbounded ambition. It is a curious charge. I would have thought that ambition consisted in coming to terms with the powerful and not in challenging them in the very centre of their power.
>
> I knew that, at least for some years, my defeat was practically certain. But it seemed to me then as it seems to me now that the party will never regain its health until the stranglehold of bureaucracy is broken.

Bevan recognised the party's deep desire for unity; but he still insisted that 'unity must be achieved on the basis of policies which will inspire the party to fight, and not by slurring over the issues which divide us'.

The Labour Party must have as its aim the establishment of a Socialist society. Otherwise it will have no significance in the future life of the nation.

It is in that faith that I have fought and will continue to fight so long as I have the strength to do so.[19]

He lost again, however, even more crushingly than in 1954, by 5.4 million votes to 1.2 million. There was no shaking the right's control of Conference until the present generation of union leaders could be replaced; Bevan's supporters in the unions were working on that, but it would take some years yet. Meanwhile he went back to his farm, coming to London as little as possible. Since he had gone to Asheridge, Crossman noted in November, 'his health, both physical and mental, has improved . . . partly, no doubt, because Jennie is also happier out there'.*[20] The question of the leadership, however, would not go away. Despite his stated intention to go on for another year, the press continued to speculate ever more urgently about when Attlee would go and who would succeed him. Crossman, who had moved in August from the *New Statesman* to the *Daily Mirror*, led the hunt, making clear his defection to Gaitskell. 'You've got to understand', he apologised to Bevan, 'that many of us know all the drawbacks of Gaitskell but accept him as inevitable because you've ruled yourself out.' 'You can't force the Party to accept Gaitskell,' Bevan retorted, 'and I must warn you that, if he is Leader, I might not be able to co-operate.' He had no alternative, but still hoped that something might turn up. 'There are times when no decision is best. The right thing to do now is to wait . . . . Gaitskell might be more acceptable in nine months' time than now.'[21]

Just three weeks later, however, on 7 December, Attlee decided that the state of uncertainty could not be allowed to drag on and abruptly resigned. Bevan in *Tribune* deplored the 'unworthy conspiracy' that had forced him out. 'The Labour Party will come to rue the day it permitted the least reputable among newspapers to fill the role of kingmaker.' Belatedly reconciled to Attlee by the events of the past year, he went on to pay handsome tribute to the retiring leader, emphasising his physical stamina and his impeccable intuition which had enabled him to read correctly the mind of the party. (The implication, once again, was clear.) He only regretted that Attlee had seen fit to boost the fading prestige of the House of Lords by accepting an earldom.[22] Immediately, however, the PLP was plunged into the Byzantine manoeuvrings of a three-cornered election. Morrison and Gaitskell both stood. Morrison rejected the advice of many of his friends that he should bow to the party's desire for a younger leader and withdraw with dignity.[23] Conversely Gaitskell was persuaded by his backers that Morrison was now so discredited that he would risk letting in Bevan if he did not stand.[24] On the other side

---

* 'His hair has suddenly gone quite white,' Dalton noted, 'and his bushy eyebrows too. And his face the colour of beetroot. This may be the fresh air of the farm or it may be drink' (Dalton diary, 6 July 1955).

Bevan was bound to stand again as the standard-bearer of the left. Unwisely, however, he allowed himself to be talked into a discreditable manoeuvre whereby he and Gaitskell should agree to stand down to give Morrison an unopposed succession. This was madness. Morrison was patently no longer up to the job, and the party desperately needed to settle the issue of the leadership, not postpone it. It made some sense for Morrison's stalwarts, most prominently Shinwell and Richard Stokes, to try to throw him what Michael Foot calls 'a lifebelt'.[25] But it made no sense at all for Bevan to stoop to such an unholy alliance with his lifelong enemy; not merely was it unacceptably cynical, but there was no possibility of Gaitskell agreeing. Crossman, Castle and the centre–left were furious; Wilson announced that he would stand himself if Gaitskell were to stand down.[26] Nevertheless Bevan and Morrison had dinner together and patched up a deal whereby Bevan would be rewarded with the Deputy Leadership and, if Labour ever came to power, the Foreign Office.[27] The next day Bevan put out a disingenuous statement offering to accept the proposal of ten respected backbenchers (mostly, as Gaitskell's biographer puts it, 'ageing advocates of seniority') and withdraw from the contest if Gaitskell would do the same.[28] The episode only did him harm: hitherto he had at least been thought incorruptible in his left-wing purity. So far as the election was concerned such a desperate ploy merely served to make Gaitskell seem unstoppable. In fact he won an absolute majority on the first ballot, with 157 votes. Bevan was second with a solid left-wing vote of seventy, neither more nor less than could have been expected. Morrison was humiliated with only forty. It was the end of a long and bitter chapter. The last of the Big Five of 1945 had finally been pushed into the wings; and the man, nine years younger than himself, whom Bevan had dismissed only five years before as 'nothing, nothing, nothing' was leader of the party, with probably twenty years ahead of him. Bevan would now either have to come to terms, spend the rest of his life in futile rows or go out of politics altogether.

He chose pretty quickly to come to terms. He was as sick of rows as anyone, and his Bevanite group had broken up; while for all the attractions of the third course, he had been in politics too long to give up completely. The day after the result was declared, Crossman heard that he was already sounding out his chances of being elected Gaitskell's Deputy.[29] There had to be a new beginning.

7

The Troubled Conscience of the Left, 1955–1960

Chapter 22

Doubtful Rapprochement: Shadow Colonial Secretary and Suez

Gaitskell's election as Labour leader was a watershed for Bevan. Though it could certainly not be said that over the previous four years he had conducted himself like a candidate for the succession, his wayward behaviour had clearly been influenced by the knowledge that the future direction of the party, uncertain for so long, must shortly be resolved. Ever since 1951 an internal power struggle had been in progress, exacerbating every difference of policy and fanning every flame of personal antagonism and injured pride. Now the power struggle was decisively concluded. However unwelcome the result, Bevan recognised that he had to live with it. So, perhaps more important, did his supporters. *Tribune* remained deeply suspicious of Gaitskell and never ceased to lecture him on the meaning of socialism;[1] but it too accepted that for better or worse he was leader and was going to remain so into the next General Election and beyond. Any idea of Bevan superseding him had realistically to be abandoned. Though old grievances still smouldered beneath the surface, the edge was thus taken off the intra-party battle. The next four years, in consequence, turned out quite different from the last four. The greatest difference was that the longer the 1955 Parliament lasted – at least up to 1958 – the more confident Labour felt of winning next time: much more confident than it had ever felt in the distracted years 1952–5. The prospect of office was a powerful incentive to keep on pulling together, from which Bevan himself, once he had the promise of a job worth having, was not immune. With startling suddenness, not much more than a year after nearly being expelled from the party, he was transformed from Labour's *enfant terrible* into its elder statesman.

This transformation was not achieved, however, without some initial hesitation. As so often before, Bevan could not make up his mind whether to signal his acceptance of the new regime by standing for Deputy Leader. Gaitskell gave him no encouragement: rather than hold out the hand of reconciliation he waited to see what Bevan would do. 'If he joins in, so much the better,' he wrote on 9 January, 'if not, well, it just can't be helped.'[2] In the end he stood and won an unexpectedly big vote – 111 against 141 for the safe candidacy of Jim Griffiths, a widely respected senior figure intended to balance the abrasive young leader. The size of Bevan's vote showed a strong impulse in the centre of the party to admit him fully into the new leadership. Bevan, however, reacted gracelessly to the announcement of the result; he declined to congratulate Griffiths, sat muttering for some minutes and then walked out of the meeting. '"There'll soon be trouble," I thought,' Dalton wrote gloomily in his diary, 'and sure enough there was when he spoke two days later in Manchester.'³

It was at a *Tribune* rally that Bevan unburdened himself of his pent-up frustration, asserting that he was 'fed up' with being told that he must 'play with the team' when he had only contempt for the game the rest of the team was playing.

> Play inside the team, indeed! When you join a team in the expectation that you are going to play Rugger, you cannot expect to be enthusiastic if you are asked to play tiddlywinks. Whether you are inside the team or not depends upon the game you are asked to play.

He went on to pour scorn on the 'fresh thinkers' who thought that socialism needed to be reinvented.

> This movement did not start yesterday. It is a very old one in its thinking. We do not need to go into conference to find out why we are here at all. You would have thought some of these people had only just arrived in the socialist movement. You would have thought that the history of the socialist movement began when they came into it. The history of the socialist movement looks as though it is beginning to end when they came into it.

'Do we now burn the books?' he demanded. 'Don't we need to bother with William Morris, or Karl Marx, or Keir Hardie?' He repeated that if Labour was not a socialist party, dedicated to transforming the property relations of society, 'I am not interested in it.' Finally he attacked once again the system of closed voting at party meetings whereby Labour Members were instructed how to speak and vote in the Chamber. 'Is that democracy? It is conspiracy. If it goes on it will be the end of Parliamentary institutions.'⁴

This outburst appeared to be a new gauntlet flung down at Gaitskell's feet to which he was bound to respond. 'During the course of the weekend,' Gaitskell wrote a few days later, 'Mr B made a vitriolic speech attacking me and everybody else, and of course the papers were all speculating as to what we should do about it.'⁵ In fact Gaitskell sensibly decided to ignore it. He had already determined against giving Bevan one of 'the big jobs' in the Shadow Cabinet,⁶ but Griffiths's elevation to Deputy Leader left the colonial affairs spokesmanship vacant, and he had decided to offer him that. He now held to that intention, describing the interview – 'rather a funny scene' – in his diary:

> He came in, evidently expecting that we [that is Gaitskell and Griffiths] were going to put him on the mat about his weekend speech – swaggering in in a sort of defensive way. So I said very sweetly, 'Come along, Nye, come and sit down,'

and went on, 'Allocation of jobs'. He was quite startled, and quite obviously surprised at this development. Then I said, 'We would like you to take the Colonies'. He then proceeded to talk in a more sensible and rational manner than I have heard him do for a long time. He said, 'I would have liked Foreign Affairs.' I ignored that, and then he went on, 'The only difficulty about the Colonies is that I really know so little about them.' This is a very rare admission from Mr B! I said, 'Well, you'll have to learn a lot – it's a job with a lot of work attached to it. But it's something to get your teeth into. You didn't really have much scope when you were doing the Ministry of Labour.' He agreed with all this, and then said he would like to go and visit the Colonies. We said, 'Certainly,' and we would help him. Finally, he said, 'All right, I'll take it.'

Gaitskell evidently felt that he was giving Bevan enough rope to hang himself.

> We are giving him every possible chance. We are giving him a job which is an interesting one, with plenty of Parliamentary scope, with travelling, with something, as I said, that he can really get his teeth into. If despite this, he refuses to work in the team, and goes on behaving as he has been doing recently, sooner or later he will simply get himself out of the Party. But whether he will do that, or whether after all he will settle down, we cannot yet say. I am bound to admit that in the light of what has happened so far, I have the feeling that his pride will always make it very difficult for him to work in a team under my leadership, or indeed under anybody else's who is now on the scene.[7]

Within days of his appointment, as if to show that he could not be bought off so easily, Bevan followed his Manchester *démarche* with two more vigorously anti-establishment speeches, at Cardiff on 10 February ('The Labour movement still exists to make trouble')[8] and at Merthyr on the 12th, where he shared a platform with Jim Griffiths to celebrate the Labour Party's Jubilee. Griffiths recalled that in the early days it was 'not quite polite' to be a socialist. Now, Bevan countered, 'we have almost reached the position where we have to be polite to remain a socialist.'[9] Griffiths thought his speech on this occasion 'the worst form of demagoguery ... what was particularly shocking about it was the tremendously egotistical tone'.[10] Yet this turned out to be almost the last flourish of the old Nye. He continued to write in *Tribune* of the importance of not blurring the ideological line between the parties: Labour was continually being urged to be 'practical', he pointed out on 24 February; but no one could be more doctrinaire than the Tories when it came to denationalising steel.[11] And he continued to campaign for party democracy, announcing at the beginning of March that he would be standing again for the Treasurership: 'Unless we give the membership of the party a greater sense of participation in the formulation of the policies of the party, we shall go into decline.'[12] In addition there were a few more squabbles in the Shadow Cabinet and an incident at a party meeting when Bevan was angry at not being allowed to take his own line on the Budget. ('He really is pretty impossible,' Gaitskell noted.)[13] But from the moment on 29 February that he asked his first Colonial Office questions in the House, followed by a well-received speech on Cyprus on 14 March,[14] Bevan began to buckle down to playing in Gaitskell's team.

It took some time for Gaitskell to begin to credit that this was so. Irritated in March by what he considered Bevan's 'fellow-travelling attitude' on the Middle East ('He was all for discussing the whole thing with the Russians'), Gaitskell wrote sharply in his diary that 'you cannot ... really trust him on these occasions since he has so clear an interest in the speech to be made [i.e. Gaitskell's speech] not being successful'.[15] In the same spirit Gaitskell was closely involved in discussion with trade union leaders to ensure that Bevan should not win the Treasurership. 'I have to be very careful about all this,' he confided, 'and I only hope that nothing about this meeting leaks out.' The problem was to find a right-wing candidate who would retain the wide support that Gaitskell himself had commanded in the last two contests. The Yorkshire miners had already come out for Bevan, so there was a likelihood that the NUM would this time switch its vote. After long discussion on 4 April Frank Cousins, the new leader of the TGWU, not yet a Bevan supporter, nominated George Brown, and other key leaders, including the left-wing leader of the NUR, Jimmy Campbell, fell into line. 'Alf [Robens] said he thought he could swing the USDAW vote in favour of George, and even Ernest Jones thought there was just a possibility the miners might come round.'[16] On 1 May Gaitskell still felt confident that Brown could be elected.[17] Bevanite activity in the unions over the past three years, however, was beginning to bear fruit; in addition there was a growing understanding beyond Gaitskell's immediate circle that Bevan's election would make for a stronger, because more balanced, leadership. In June the NUR Executive voted, against its General Secretary, 13–12 for Bevan and shortly afterwards USDAW followed suit.[18] Even so the issue hung in the balance right up until Blackpool in October.

In the meantime Bevan was 'getting his teeth into' the colonies. The Colonial Office was of course a job he had wanted back in 1950. Though his actual knowledge was, as he admitted to Gaitskell, slight, he had a strong theoretical sympathy for colonial peoples struggling to be free. With the Government facing nationalist disorder all around the world – in Cyprus and Aden and Kenya and even Singapore – the job of Shadow spokesman offered limitless opportunities to contrast Labour's enlightened commitment to democratic progress with the Tories' uncomprehending resort to crude repression. He believed that colonial freedom was not only right but inevitable and thought the policy of trying to resist it not merely futile in the long run but stupid even in the short run, since the history of Ireland and India showed that the colonial power was obliged in the end to talk to those leaders it initially locked up. By opposing the tide of history Britain dissipated the influence it could exert for democracy in the developing world, driving its former colonies instead towards Communism. Writing in *Tribune* in 1957

Bevan gave this familiar liberal argument a characteristically socialist twist. Capitalism, he asserted, was not an option for the newly independent countries as they shook off the imperialist yoke: they could develop their economies rapidly only by strong government action, hence their only choice lay between Communism and democratic socialism.[19] It was Britain's duty as well as her interest to help them to the latter, first by conceding their independence willingly, without their having to fight for it, and second by giving as much economic aid as possible to shore up the infant democracies it left behind; for, as he was fond of affirming, 'political liberty ... is rooted in economic surplus'.[20] Britain herself had not been a democracy during the early stages of her industrialisation. Identifying strongly with the nationalist leaders of vast impoverished new nations like India, Pakistan and Egypt, Bevan had no time for self-righteous British Tories (nor American Republicans) who lectured them about democracy.

Characteristically too, as soon as he began to interest himself in the colonies, Bevan discovered that the democratic channels through which colonial grievances could be properly aired were inadequate. So long as Britain denied to any territory its independence, he maintained, the House of Commons had a duty to take on itself the responsibility of representing the colonial population and controlling the colonial government a great deal more closely than it did at present. 'I seriously suggest', he argued in the course of a debate on the Mau-Mau troubles in Kenya in June 1956, 'that a situation has developed in the colonial dependencies which is getting out of hand.' As violence erupted in one colony after another, the Commons was repeatedly caught unawares. 'If we do not hear of anything untoward happening, no one pays any attention. If there is trouble we are told to shut up till it is all over, and when it is all over we are told to shut up because it is all over.' Questions to the Colonial Secretary every six weeks, and an occasional debate, were no way to ensure the good government of seventy million people. In order to bring the Colonial Office under continuous scrutiny, Bevan suggested that it was time to make 'one of those constitutional adaptations for which our constitution is famous'.[21] Unfortunately he did not offer any detailed proposals. In one respect, his sudden concern with the institutions of Empire simply reflects the egotistic belief he had shown in government that his own Department should take priority over all others. At the same time, however, the lack of parliamentary accountability to which he drew attention was a real deficiency. In each successive crisis the Colonial Office simply backed the Governor on the spot and time and time again the House of Commons was faced with a *fait accompli*.

This was precisely what happened in Cyprus with the deportation of Archbishop Makarios, which was announced retrospectively to Parliament on 12 March 1956 and debated two days later. The physical removal from the island of the leader with whom the Government would eventually have to treat was just the sort of stupidity that Bevan thought typical of the Tories – an

315

act of 'pure fascism', worthy of Hitler or Mussolini.[22] On the wider issue of the future of Cyprus, Bevan argued that the Government had got itself into a muddle. It denied the possibility of independence because Britain needed the island as a military base, having had to shift the headquarters of Mediterranean Command from Egypt as a result of Egyptian nationalist hostility in 1954. But the same reason that had forced the withdrawal from Egypt applied equally in Cyprus. Britain must sooner or later face the truth – in Aden and Singapore and Malta and Gibraltar too – that it was no use having a military base that required continually to be defended against a hostile population. Britain's worldwide defence commitments could not be maintained on such a fragile basis. On the other hand, if Britain would be satisfied with retaining a base on the island then that could be negotiated quite amicably with an independent Cyprus. What Bevan continually attacked was the Tories' obsolete belief – part of what he called their 'truculent nostalgia' – that Britain could still get her way by bullying rather than by civilised agreement between free peoples.[23]

As for the Greek Cypriot demand for *enosis* with Greece, Bevan believed – correctly, as the event showed – that this could be traded for the promise of independence as soon as the British Government changed its rigid posture and started to talk. Labour's suspicion, which he continued to voice even after he had ceased to be specifically responsible for colonial affairs, was that the Government would play the old game of divide and rule by exploiting Turkish demands for partition. When agreement was eventually reached on independence for a united Cyprus in 1959 Bevan welcomed it with reservations: he could not entirely suppress a spirit of 'I told you so', blaming the Government for the number of British servicemen who had had to lose their lives before it took Labour's advice and criticising the failure to set up any institutions through which the two Cypriot communities – each provided under the constitution with its own electoral roll and guaranteed status – could be encouraged to grow together.[24] It was perhaps idealistic to hope that they could ever do so. On the other hand subsequent events, culminating in the Turkish invasion and partition of the island in 1974, showed that the 1960 constitution had indeed failed to solve the problem.

Bevan discharged his duties as Shadow Colonial Secretary for the most part responsibly and well. He ruffled a few feathers, as when he told a meeting of the Movement for Colonial Freedom, 'My advice is, give us as much trouble as possible,' and was loudly heckled by the League of Empire Loyalists.[25] But in August Gaitskell was impressed by his cogency and force when they went together to see the Colonial Secretary, Alan Lennox-Boyd, over the Cyprus crisis;[26] and earlier, in April, he behaved, in Gaitskell's view, 'admirably' at the famous National Executive dinner for the visiting Soviet leaders, Bulganin and Khrushchev, when George Brown got into a violent argument with Khrushchev.[27] Bevan neither joined seriously in the argument – though Brown remembered him advancing on the top table 'wagging his finger and saying in that Welsh lilt of his, "But this is ridiculous, Mr Khrushchev, this is ridiculous"'[28] – nor made capital out of Brown's behaviour afterwards. On the other hand Gaitskell still found him a difficult colleague on defence matters – 'always obstreperous, always arguing, always talking too much and generally, though not always, arguing the wrong way', that is for cuts and less emphasis on NATO.[29] 'It certainly makes things very much easier when he stays away,' Gaitskell noted in July.[30]

Both Gaitskell and Crossman suspected over the summer that Bevan's attention was increasingly concentrated on the contest for the Treasurership. 'Nye still somehow feels', wrote Crossman, 'that, if he is elected Treasurer, this will mean a shift in the balance of power in the Party. But of course', he continued cheerfully, 'it will mean no such thing. Whichever wins will win by a negligible majority and, once Nye is back on the Executive, as I hope he will be, very little will be altered.'[31] Gaitskell still thought it would be 'awkward' if he came back;[32] but the general mood of the party as it gathered at the beginning of October was that Bevan had worked his passage back and that the party needed him. What had started as another left–right battle had become the opportunity for an act of reconciliation. It was always going to be desperately close. The two big general unions, the TGWU and the GMW, with over two million votes between them, were for Brown (a TGWU member); the AEUW was pledged to its own man, Charles Pannell; and Bevan's three biggest backers, the NUM, the NUR and USDAW totalled only 1,380,000 votes. Morgan Phillips reckoned that Bevan would need over 90 per cent of the constituency votes 'and even then couldn't win by more than 50,000 or 60,000'.[33] But by the Sunday Crossman sensed that 'there was virtually nobody left who wanted George Brown to win. ... Everybody realized that the Conference would split wide open at the *Tribune* meeting on Wednesday night if Nye was not elected [and] everybody, whatever their motives, wanted the old boy back on the Executive.'

'I'm sure this explains the explosion of noise which greeted the announcement that Nye had been elected by a larger majority than anyone thought possible. It was ecstasy for most of the constituencies and real relief for everybody else, including most of his enemies.'[34] Bevan won by 3,029,000 votes to Brown's 2,755,000. Immediately, as Crossman had anticipated, he hailed the result as a fresh beginning for the party. 'The central direction of the party', he declared, 'has shifted to the left – and it was time – because the shift of opinion inside the party corresponds, in my view, with the shift of opinion to the left throughout the country. ... I am delighted to be able to believe this evening that we have now set our feet upon a broader road than we have been travelling over the last four or five years.'[35] *Tribune*'s joy was unconfined. Under the front-page headline 'Oh! What A Beautiful Morning!' Michael Foot celebrated not merely 'the most significant shift in British politics since 1951' but 'the happiest political occasion I can remember' since 1945. Taken together with Cousins' emergence as a left-wing leader of the

317

TGWU, Bevan's election was a guarantee that the next Labour Government 'will not be used for trivial purposes' but to secure 'a big extension of public ownership, a genuine enlargement of human freedom, a dramatic change in our relations with the peoples of Asia and Africa ... and a much more imaginative effort to end the stupidities and sterilities of the cold war'.[36] Bevan himself was rather more cautious, acknowledging that 'we shall have our differences and our controversies as we have had them in the past' – he knew that the arithmetic in the Shadow Cabinet would not change – but pledged himself to work 'in the heartiest and most intimate co-operation' with everyone in the party.[37]

Only Gaitskell did not yet appreciate that Bevan's return to the fold was the best thing that could have happened to his leadership. The last diary entry he ever wrote found him pondering, without enthusiasm, 'the problem of Nye'. 'Of course it was to be expected that he would very likely get the Treasurership and there is really nothing new in that. On the other hand, it has pushed him forward, not only in the Executive, but also in the Parliamentary Party.' The problem was sharpened by the fact that Alf Robens had conspicuously failed to measure up as Shadow Foreign Secretary, so that 'everyone is wondering whether we are going to offer [Nye] foreign affairs' – the job he had specifically asked for in February. 'If it were not for Alf's failure I wouldn't think of it myself. But we have to think of it. I do not know what we shall do, and I am inclined to wait a moment and see what opinion in the Party is like.'[38]

The event which made up Gaitskell's mind for him was the Suez crisis, from which Bevan emerged with an enhanced reputation and Gaitskell – quite unfairly – a somewhat reduced one. During the crisis Gaitskell was surprised to find himself co-operating in perfect accord with a colleague who was suddenly winning golden opinions for his 'statesmanship'. By the time Eden's attempted invasion of Egypt had been humiliatingly aborted and Eden himself obliged to resign, the Government's stock had fallen so low that it seemed impossible that it could long survive; while it would no longer have been realistic to attempt to deny Bevan second place – almost co-equal status – in the Labour Government that was now confidently expected to succeed it. It was not, as it turned out, winning the Treasurership but Suez a few weeks later which marked Bevan's metamorphosis into a responsible pillar of the Labour leadership.

Bevan and Gaitskell did not often see eye to eye on any issue of foreign policy. Gaitskell's view of the world was as resolutely bilateral and pro-American as Bevan's was optimistically multilateral and non-aligned. But it happened that while he naturally included Egypt in his category of under-developed ex-colonies that deserved the West's fullest sympathy and aid, Bevan never regarded Colonel Nasser as anything but a military dictator.

When they had met in Cairo in 1952 he had thought Nasser no more than a nationalist – anti-British but with no understanding of the need for social revolution and therefore (in Bevan's view of history) unlikely to last long. Having driven the British out of the Canal Zone in 1954 he had become drunk 'with the heady wine of nationalist success' and was now seeking 'more and more drafts [sic] of the same stimulant' by setting himself up as the leader of pan-Arab unity against Israel. His unilateral nationalisation of the canal on 26 July 1956 was part of this pattern of self-assertion.[39] Of course Bevan did not object to nationalisation. But as he protested in a famous phrase some time after the event, 'if the sending of one's police and soldiers into the darkness of the night to seize somebody else's property is nationalisation, Ali Baba used the wrong terminology.'[40] Bevan had no more hesitation than Eden or Gaitskell in naming Nasser in the same breath as Mussolini and Hitler.[41]

This blunt condemnation of the dictator had brought Bevan into open conflict with his friends on *Tribune*, whose line on 3 August was strongly pro-Nasser and characteristically critical of Gaitskell, who, the paper claimed, 'outdid the Tories in suggesting ways of putting pressure on Egypt'. On an inside page, in sharp contrast, Bevan, while conceding that Egypt was 'legalistically' entitled to nationalise a commercial asset situated in its territory, asserted that the 'socialist reply' was to '*internationalise* all these waterways through which the commerce of the world is articulated':

> If Nasser's action has brought this on to the world agenda, it is all to the good. ... In the meantime Nasser and all Egypt should realise that they have done great damage to the cause of aid to underdeveloped countries, including their own. ...
> Egypt has a right to come into her own, but not into someone else's.[42]

The following week's issue widened the gap, both explicitly and implicitly. While Foot repeated that 'Egypt has an absolute right in law and morality to nationalise the canal. ... She has also the right to devote the profits ... to combating the poverty of her people' – repudiating Bevan's criticism that Nasser intended 'treating the canal like a mediaeval caravan route, and levying tolls for right of way'[43] – Bevan responded, under the headline 'It Must Not Be All "Take", Colonel Nasser', with a further acknowledgement of Egypt's right to assert her nationhood against the exploitation of the former imperialist powers, tempered by a warning that Egypt's rights were not the end of the matter: 'Having conceded the Egyptian case, it is necessary to examine the claims of the world over and above Egyptian sovereign rights. In my view these are equally incontestable.' Characteristically Bevan widened the issue of the control of the canal into a paradigm of the world's progressive evolution from national competition (i.e. capitalism) towards international co-operation (i.e. socialism).

> An absolute assertion of nationalistic values is not consistent with the belief that the better-off nations should help the worse-off. There must be reciprocity. . . . All nations must be prepared to accept some diminution of their sovereign rights if the world is to become friendlier and more closely knit.

At the same time Bevan did not shrink from spelling out to Nasser that Europe's dependence on Middle Eastern oil meant that she could not allow her supply to be conditional on his goodwill. If he denied international control of the canal, the European nations would be bound to find an alternative to the canal by building tankers capable of going round the Cape. 'Egypt's ascendancy,' he warned, 'should she insist on it, is therefore likely to be short-lived.'[44]

Apart from its continued hostility to Nasser, the unspoken significance of this article was that in calling for international control of Suez, Bevan quietly dropped his earlier suggestion that *all* such waterways be internationalised. He took the same line, to Gaitskell's 'particular astonishment', in the Shadow Cabinet. 'He did not of course say he agreed with me,' Gaitskell noted, 'but . . . he was in no doubt about Nasser being a thug and in no doubt about the need for international control' – *without* requiring similar control of Panama. 'You will be surprised to hear this from me,' he announced, 'but I think it would be a great mistake to say anything at the moment which would embarrass the Americans.'[45] The Shadow Cabinet's agreed policy, therefore, was to refer the question of Suez to the United Nations while warning the Government in the strongest terms, both in public and in private, against any thought of using force against Egypt.[46]

One of the legends of Suez is that Gaitskell was slow to rule out the use of force; that his initial reaction to the seizure of the canal was as bellicose as Eden's and that he only came round to an internationalist line under backbench party pressure. There was a good deal of criticism on the left that Bevan's instinctive response was no better than Gaitskell's, until 'a storm among his supporters . . . forced him to veer round . . . into a more anti-war line'.[47] This really is not true of either of them. Gaitskell warned the Government explicitly against the use of force in his very first speech on 2 August and repeatedly thereafter; if these warnings did not initially attract very much attention it was partly because they were balanced by his more strongly worded condemnation of Nasser, partly also perhaps because he never seriously believed that the Government would be so foolish as to attempt it. Neither did Bevan, who imagined that even Tories had now accepted that the use of military force to gain diplomatic ends was obsolete. In this crisis, Kenneth Younger wrote in September, 'Nye & Hugh saw exactly alike, Nye being if anything tougher against Nasser.'[48] But there was no question that either of them, because they were critical of Nasser, was anything other than 'anti-war'. Nevertheless the left felt let down by Bevan, suspecting – with some reason in view of his retreat over Panama – that his advocacy of international control was little more than a high-sounding formula which hid the onset of creeping 'responsibility'. In *Tribune* on 24 August the historian A.J.P.Taylor ('Now Kick Labour's Leaders Back In Line') went for him with typical acerbity:

> We ought to be saying that the Suez Canal is Egyptian in exactly the same way that British Railways or the Port of London are British.
>
> If we want to practice internationalism, we should do it with our own property, not with that of others. Gibraltar, Cyprus and Singapore as international bases would do as a start.
>
> If Nye Bevan had been more persistent in putting this general argument instead of over Suez, I should take his enthusiasm for International Socialism more seriously.
>
> Let us begin by giving up what is ours. Then, after a generation or so, we can exhort others to give up what is theirs.[49]

As tension persisted between Britain and Egypt, Crossman noted on 28 September that Bevan 'certainly doesn't feel at home in this Suez crisis and is just as statesmanlike as Hugh Gaitskell'.[50] The word 'statesmanlike' was clearly not intended as a compliment.

Gaitskell and Bevan still thought it inconceivable that Eden would go to war, in defiance of not only Labour but American warnings and of world opinion. But on 31 October, under the transparent pretence of 'separating the combatants' – having themselves encouraged the Israelis to invade Egypt – French and British planes began to bomb Egyptian airfields; and on 5 November British paratroops successfully occupied Port Said. The scenes in the House of Commons were the most bitter since 1911. On 1 November the House had to be suspended for half an hour after Eden, under strong pressure from Gaitskell, was unable to explain whether or not Britain was legally at war. At the end of a stormy debate Bevan – not Robens – wound up for Labour. At once, with typical perversity, he struck a quite different note, reflective and philosophical. 'It would be a very great mistake for us,' he suggested, 'even on this side of the House, to indict the existing Government as though they bore the exclusive responsibility for the existing state of affairs.'

'The fact of the matter is', he went on, 'that mankind is faced with an entirely novel situation.' First, 'The advent of the hydrogen bomb has stalemated power among the great Powers. ... The tragedy of the world has been that the statesmen of the world have not adjusted themselves to that reality. ... The statesmen of the world have not got together to attempt to solve those problems which formerly were attempted to be solved by war. The Middle East is a characteristic example.' Secondly, 'Not only does the use of force become utterly inadmissible in determining quarrels between nations without running the risk of universal destruction, but the use of force in domestic affairs is now demonstrably failing. ... The Soviet Union itself', he believed, 'is recognising that it cannot hold down whole populations merely by terror and police action. ... I find that an infinitely encouraging fact.' But all countries and all parties were confused by the new situation. 'I am not one, therefore, who is going to say that the British Government are themselves reacting with complete guilt towards this situation.'[51]

These were typical Bevanisms, but of doubtful relevance, though the Government seized on them gratefully. The Labour benches, on the other hand, as Crossman recorded, 'were so warmed up to cries of "warmonger!", "murderer!" etc., and to moral appeals to save the United Nations, that Nye's reflective style was hardly to their taste'.[52] After this opening, however, Bevan became more critical. He expressed astonishment at Eden's 'amateurishness' ('It was perfectly obvious from what he said that he had not thought out at all the implications of the actions of the Government'); could find no difference between the language of the Anglo-French ultimatum to Egypt and that of the German ultimata to Belgium in 1914 and Norway in 1940 ('Quite honestly, this is the language of the bully'); and deplored the Government's defiance of the United Nations ('We are perfectly prepared to admit that the institutions of the United Nations are not by any means as effective as we should like them to be. But ... it is our duty to build them up to a strength at which they can be relied upon. It is not enough to say they are weak and therefore we destroy them'). By the end he was back in harmony with the mainstream of Labour feeling, declaring that Britain was 'dishonoured' by Eden's action.

> We say that Britain has always stood for civilised principles, and for humanity and justice. How do we answer now, when we drop bombs on helpless people?
> ... A nation more powerful than us may drop even worse bombs on British cities. How answer that? With bombs? Bombs with bombs? That is the bankruptcy of statesmanship.

Like every other Labour speaker Bevan ended with an appeal that the Government, even now, stop and retrace their steps. 'Unless the Government are able to say that, in the name of mankind let them, for God's sake, get out.'[53]

That continued to be his line in the succeeding days. On 4 November, at a great Labour demonstration in Trafalgar Square attended by some 20,000 people carrying placards proclaiming 'Law, Not War' and chanting 'Eden Must Go' Bevan – the main speaker, with Tony Greenwood, Edith Summerskill and Harry Nicholas of the TGWU – concentrated on the shame the Government had inflicted on Britain by resorting to force. Eden claimed to have acted to preserve the peace and to protect free passage of the canal. (In fact Nasser's first response had been to block the canal.) 'If Sir Anthony is sincere in what he says', Bevan jeered, '– and he may be – then he is too *stupid* to be Prime Minister. He is either a knave or a fool, and in either capacity we don't want him. The Government have besmirched the name of Britain, they have offended against every sense of decency.' He still went out of his way to stress that because Eden was wrong he was not saying that Nasser was right. 'I am not saying for a single moment that the Israelis did not have the utmost provocation. What we are saying is that it is not possible to create peace in the Middle East by jeopardising the peace of the world'.[54]

The same day the Soviet Union moved to crush the Hungarian revolution. This brutal exercise of force, more swift, ruthless and effective than Eden's, instantly threw Suez into a wider and darker perspective. Since Khrushchev's dramatic denunciation of Stalin in February, which had seemed to confirm all his predictions of the inevitable liberalisation of Soviet society, Bevan, like others in the West, had been watching the process of destalinisation, first in Poland, then in Hungary, with mounting excitement. In a *Tribune* article as recently as 26 October, optimistically headlined 'Gomulka Holds the Aces', he had explained why the Poles were bound to take the lead in throwing off Soviet control and concluded that the Russians would not be so foolish as to use force.[55] One week later the Nagy Government in Hungary had gone further, in terms of a multi-party system and withdrawal from the Warsaw Pact, than Gomulka had dreamed of; at just this moment the British and French invaded Suez, and it seemed obvious to Labour and most anti-Government opinion in Britain that the Russians had deliberately seized the moment, when the attention of the world was distracted and the morality of the West compromised, to send in their tanks. Bevan made much of this line in the House of Commons on 8 November. 'I do not believe that it is possible to separate the events in Hungary from the events in Egypt,' he asserted. 'I have been looking at the timetable of these events and they have a most macabre appearance.' He believed that the Soviet Government was very evenly divided between moderates and hard-liners. 'Even after the invasion of Egypt by Israel, even after the ultimatum sent by Her Majesty's Government to Egypt, the Soviet Prime Minister was still speaking about the withdrawal of Soviet troops from Hungary.' Instead, he claimed, the Anglo-French action had served to weaken the moderate elements in the Kremlin and give a green light to the hard men. From that moment, Bevan persuaded himself, 'a new brutality asserted itself in the Soviet Union. The tragedy in Hungary is the first result.'[56]

It is now clear that the notion that Hungary was in some direct way a consequence of Suez – that the Soviet leaders felt free after 31 October to take action in Hungary that they were not about to take anyway – is nonsense.[57] Bevan's belief in it is characteristic of his tendency to pass off wishful thinking about the Soviet Union as informed analysis. Nevertheless events in Hungary did provide a legitimate new stick with which to beat the Government. If Suez did not 'cause' Hungary, it certainly prohibited the West from condemning the Russian action, reducing Britain and France to the same level in the eyes of the world, professedly democratic powers willing to use force to impose their will where they thought they could get away with it. The difference was, of course, that the Russians did get away with it, whereas Britain and France, under pressure from the Americans, were obliged ignominiously to withdraw, leaving the field after all to the United Nations.

This result Bevan strove heroically to interpret as confirmation of his view that force was becoming obsolete in world affairs. It was not a question of giving the UN 'teeth'.

> The little band of men who have landed on the troubled frontiers in the Middle East should not be seen as the forerunners of the mightiest war machine ever assembled by man, but as the exact opposite. They are the physical manifestation of a moral idea, and if they do not succeed in that capacity then they will fail in every other. ....
> The main idea behind the United Nations is the abandonment of armed force as a means of settling disputes between nations.

Not only, Bevan argued, should the UN keep the peace; it should become the agency for sharing the world's wealth. The Arabs would never respect a UN force which simply enforced the old imperialist 'spheres of influence'.

> If, on the other hand, the UNO Police are seen to be a body armed not only with guns but with the means to develop the resources of the Middle East, to irrigate the desert, plough back the revenues from oil into the countries from which they are taken, help to put the technical knowledge of the Western nations at the disposal of the Arab people; *if all this is done and done by and with the authority of the United Nations, then nothing more would be required to keep the peace in the Middle East.*[58]

Bevan even managed to apply the same wildly optimistic conclusion to Hungary. 'Khrushchev', he declared at Birmingham, 'is as stupid as Anthony Eden is.'

> Khrushchev thinks he can hold down Hungary by using physical force against the Hungarians and he can't. As long as they won't co-operate, Khrushchev is as helpless against the Hungarians as Eden is against the Egyptians, just because the ancient objectives of war are no longer attainable by war.[59]

It was not only Conservatives, unfortunately, who suffered from illusions in foreign affairs. Whether it was his mellowing into 'responsible' statemanship which made him see the world through rose-tinted glasses, or the rose-tinted glasses which caused him to mellow, Bevan around 1956 was beginning, in important respects, to lose contact with the reality of power politics.

Nevertheless, evidence of responsibility was what the PLP was looking for; and during the Suez/Hungary crisis Bevan was judged to have passed the test. The Shadow Cabinet elections on 21 November gave him thirty more votes than in 1955, pushing him up into third place, only one vote behind Robens (Wilson was top). Robens had already offered Gaitskell his resignation and Gaitskell duly appointed Bevan Shadow Foreign Secretary in his place, a promotion which even Dalton now recognised as inevitable.[60] Bevan made his first Commons appearance in this role on 5 December. The occasion was a post-mortem debate, raking over the still warm ashes of the Suez affair. Bevan rose to it with one of the most brilliant debating perform-ances of his life. It was certainly one of the funniest. His condemnation of the Government's débâcle was now couched more in terms of pity and ridicule than of anger. Unanswerably, he mocked the Government's successive and shifting justifications for the attack on Egypt. To 'separate the combatants'? ' One does not fire in order merely to have a ceasefire. One would have thought that the ceasefire was consequent upon having fired in the first place. It could have been accomplished without firing.' To ensure free passage of the canal? 'So wonderfully well organised was this expedition ... that long after we had delivered our ultimatum and bombed Port Said, our ships were still ploughing through the Mediterranean.'

> Did we really believe that Nasser was going to wait for us to arrive? He did what anybody would have thought he would do, and if the Government did not think he would do it, on that account alone they ought to resign. He sank ships in the Canal, the wicked man. What did hon. Gentlemen opposite expect him to do? The result is that, in fact, the first objective realised was the opposite of the one we set out to achieve; the Canal was blocked, and it is still blocked.

The next ground Eden had offered was 'to ensure that Israeli forces withdrew from Egyptian territory'. Or to put it another way: 'We went into Egyptian territory in order to establish our moral right to make the Israelis clear out of Egyptian territory. That is a remarkable war aim, is it not? In order that we get the Israelis out, we went in. ... Unfortunately we had to bomb the Egyptians first.' Finally Eden had claimed to have gone in to prepare the way for the United Nations. Bevan's dismissal of this pretext was withering:

> It is, of course, exactly the same claim which might have been made, if they had thought about it in time, by Mussolini and Hitler, that they made war on the world in order to call the United Nations into being. If it were possible for bacteria to argue with each other they would be able to say that of course their chief justification was the advancement of medical science.

Then, damningly but still wittily, Bevan rehearsed the mounting evidence of Anglo-French collusion with the Israelis in the preparation of the Israeli attack which they went into Egypt ostensibly to stop. Now we know the truth of these suspicions. Then, in the face of Eden's and Selwyn Lloyd's categoric denials, Bevan could only speculate.

> What happened? Did Marianne take John Bull to an unknown rendezvous? Did Marianne say to John Bull that there was a forest fire going to start, and did John Bull then say, 'We ought to put it out', but Marianne said, 'No, let us

warm our hands by it. It is a nice fire'? Did Marianne deceive John Bull or seduce him?

What ultimately offended Labour about the whole fiasco, Bevan concluded, was that Nasser's wrongs had been 'covered by the bigger blunders of the British Government'. Nasser could perfectly well, he believed, have been brought to a civilised agreement about the control of the canal by 'the arts of diplomacy'. True or not, his conclusion is surely incontestable: 'Even if we had occupied Egypt by armed force we could not have secured the freedom of passage through the Canal. ... Why on earth did we imagine that the objective could be realised in that way in the middle of the twentieth century?' The Government themselves, he suggested, did not really believe it could: hence their feebleness throughout the crisis.

> All through this unhappy period Ministers – all of them – have spoken and argued and debated well below their proper form – because they have been synthetic villains. They are not really villains. They have only set off on a villainous course, and they cannot even use the language of villainy.[61]

Thus, when it was all over, Bevan – who had been slow to condemn the Government at the start – almost appeared to forgive the Tories' folly; for, like children playing at soldiers, they knew not what they did. Although on public platforms, and particularly in the 1959 election, he continued to denounce Suez as a crime against an emerging world order, the issue never seemed to stir him to the depths of his soul, as it did Gaitskell. Gaitskell felt personally betrayed by Eden, whose honour he had trusted. Suez excited in him a moral fervour he had not previously revealed. For the first time Gaitskell seemed the emotional one, Bevan the wiser, more reflective statesman. It was a difference – of tone only, not of argument – which the Tories did their utmost to exploit. Suddenly, absurdly, they were decrying Gaitskell as an anti-British traitor while mischievously building up his rival. Macmillan, following Bevan's 5 December speech, contrasted his 'more statesmanlike and philosophic approach' with Gaitskell's 'pure hysteria'; and Butler, winding up the debate, cleverly parodied a popular song of the moment:

> Anything Hugh can do, Nye can do better
> Nye can do anything better than Hugh.[62]

Crossman, returning on the 15th from a visit to Israel, was astonished to fly into an 'extraordinary press campaign which is suggesting that Bevan is the only man fit to lead the Labour Party. ... Curiously enough', he commented shrewdly, 'it actually ... compels Nye to be loyal to Hugh.'[63] The new 'Gaitskell–Bevan axis' he judged at the end of 1956 to be 'pretty firm'.

Chapter 23

The Gaitskell–Bevan Axis: Brighton 1957

The Gaitskell–Bevan axis was consolidated in the course of 1957 on two fronts. The most dramatic demonstration of their new fraternity came over the H-Bomb. But Bevan's famous speech at the Brighton Conference in October only set the public seal on a process which had been going on all year in the policy committees of the NEC on the even more central and symbolic issue of public ownership. The primacy of a clear commitment by the next Labour Government to further extensive nationalisation was the single principle on which Bevan in the battles of the last few years had most specifically insisted. This was what he had meant by playing rugger and not tiddlywinks; at the very least a renewed struggle for such a commitment was what the 'significant shift to the left' he had detected on winning the Treasurership was universally expected to portend. Bevan's tame acquiescence during 1957 in a policy document which was at best a fudge, in reality an abandonment of any intention of further nationalisation, is therefore the measure of his acceptance both of the fact and of the direction of Gaitskell's leadership.

Gaitskell's difficulties after Suez should, it might be thought, have given Bevan the opportunity to impose his increased authority. Gaitskell's reputation was, in Crossman's words, 'sagging in comparison with Nye's';[1] for a time he feared that he would never get a hearing in the House of Commons again.[2] But, as Crossman had predicted, this Tory campaign actually forced Bevan to be loyal. Moreover, after a brief rally to the Government while hostilities were in progress, the Gallup poll soon swung back sharply in favour of Labour. During 1957 Labour's lead never fell below five points; in March it touched ten and in September thirteen. The expectation was not merely that Labour would form the next Government in two or three years' time, but that the Tories might somehow be brought down at any moment. Crossman wrote that in February 'it was touch and go whether they would throw their hand in and have the kind of General Election which Attlee had in October 1951'.[3] Even Bevan, who should have known better, allowed himself to believe that the Government was 'drifting helplessly to political eclipse'.[4] Perhaps he simply hoped the prophecy would be self-fulfilling. In

327

any event it was no time for disunity. The beckoning electoral prospect is one explanation of Bevan's unwonted quiescence during 1957.

Others are laziness, a sense of advancing age, preoccupation with foreign affairs and sheer boredom with the endless round of party committees re-fighting the same old battles. He had been off the NEC for two years and happy to be so. He still much preferred chewing the fat over a drink in the Smoking Room with a few old cronies, or escaping from politics altogether to his farm, to putting in detailed work on future policies. He had always been sceptical of the value of programme-making in Opposition, preferring to believe that if the party's basic commitment to socialism was undimmed a Labour Government would know what to do with power when it got it. If, as he claimed, despite Gaitskell, the party and country were now moving to the left again after the interval of 'consolidation' and discredited Toryism, then it did less harm to let Gaitskell and his friends win their paper battles in the policy committees than to risk splitting the party again over shadows. The return of a Labour Government was too important to the world to be risked for domestic considerations. That, it would seem from an accumulation of hints in his articles and reported remarks, was his rationalisation: a strange, uncertain mixture of optimism and pessimism, amounting almost to fatalism. Accordingly he seems to have made a deliberate decision to discipline himself publicly to the role of loyal subordinate, concentrating on his foreign affairs brief and taking almost no part in the deliberations of the NEC sub-committee on public ownership.

In private he nursed the deepest misgivings. In April he made a four-week tour of Asia, without Jennie – one of the very few times in their married life when he had occasion to write to her. Distance did not lend enchantment to his view of British politics.

> The more I reflect on Gaitskell the more gloomy I become and the more I dread the ordeal before me if ever he becomes Prime Minister. With that power and authority in his possession it will be difficult to brake his reactionary impulses and compel him to make concessions early enough. Even the thought of the effort needed to influence him to the right courses makes my spirit sink.

'It is true', he added over-optimistically, 'that Gaitskell will give in in the last resort but only after the Party suffers damage and leaving the leaders ex-hausted by wholly unnecessary private exertions.'[5]

Over public ownership he was not prepared to make this effort. He attended only rarely the NEC sub-committee, chaired by Jim Griffiths, which drafted the document *Industry and Society*; and without a lead from him the other left-wingers on the committee, Ian Mikardo and Barbara Castle, went along readily enough with a formulation carefully designed to give some encouragement to all points of view while committing the next Government to very little beyond the renationalisation of steel and road haulage. Other industries would be liable to a 'thorough enquiry' if they were thought to be 'failing the nation'; but there was no shopping list of candidates for takeover, nor any detailed criteria by which further nationalisation might be decided on. Instead the idea was floated that the State should buy shares in private companies as a means of controlling investment short of actual ownership. In June the NEC approved the document unanimously. Commending it to the TUC, Bevan spoke 'enthusiastically and strongly in support' of it.[6] Enthusiastic he certainly was not; the fact that he managed to appear so is evidence of his determination to achieve an agreed policy in the interest of unity. Privately he thought it 'a lousy document but one can't spend all one's time fighting'.[7]

Tribune, however, felt no such inhibition. The previous October Will Camp had reviewed the bible of the 'fresh thinkers', Anthony Crosland's *The Future of Socialism* under the outraged headline 'Socialism? How Dare He Use the Word?'[8] On 19 July the paper belatedly discovered that *Industry and Society* was a clever smokescreen for a further betrayal of the true faith. The opening analysis of managerial capitalism it thought admirable. 'The job could not have been better done by a Committee composed of Karl Marx, Keir Hardie and William Morris.' The 'age-long battle against MacDonaldism, Morrisonism, Deakinism and Butskellism' – a splendidly inclusive list of *Tribune*'s enemies – seemed at this point almost to have been won. Thereafter, however, 'Instead of a bold declaration of Labour's resolve to extend public ownership to root out the evils so scathingly exposed, the grand objective becomes lost in a maze of qualifying clauses and timorous inhibitions.'[9] *Tribune*'s line in the weeks before Conference – backed by Mikardo and Mrs Castle who now repented of their earlier acquiescence, and by Jennie who ringingly denounced it as 'Too Pink, Too Blue and Too Yellow'[10] – was that *Industry and Society* would do as a starting-point so long as Conference insisted on putting the right interpretation on it. The touchstone was whether the new Croslandite device of share-buying was seen as a supplement to full-scale nationalisation or as a substitute for it. Mikardo strongly criticised Gaitskell, Wilson and Crossman for implying the latter, claiming that if whole-heartedly enacted the agreed document gave a mandate for the immediate nationalisation, through buying up their equity, of 600 major companies.[11] Bevan, writing in the *News of the World*, lent his voice cautiously to the *Tribune* view: 'It is probably a mistake to anticipate that [share-buying] will even be the main way in which public ownership will be increased.'[12] But he took no further part in the debate. He is said to have obtained an assurance from Gaitskell that the purpose was not to bury public ownership – Gaitskell himself privately favoured the nationalisation of chemicals and aircraft[13] – and with that he forced himself to be content.[14] Only one outburst in the NEC, just before Conference, revealed what an effort his restraint had cost him:

> Nye weighed in and said that he had remained silent during the whole controversy, though he had been unbearably attacked and provoked. Someone had even written suggesting that he had reached an agreement with Gaitskell about nationalization, although in fact he had not discussed the matter with Gaitskell

even for five minutes. ... If this sort of thing went on, he would be forced to register his protests and disagreements in writing.[15]

Crossman thought that Bevan could not bear 'having to sit down under the imputation of agreeing with Gaitskell about nationalization'. What he wanted was the credit for not rocking the boat, not to be thought to have sold his principles. But Crossman judged that this outburst was 'much more an attempt to get out of responsibility and retire to the country than an attempt to achieve supreme power in the Party, which is the last thing he wants'. On this basis Crossman now feared that 'the Bevan–Gaitskell co-existence is extremely fragile'.[16] Here he was wrong, as Brighton showed. In fact his own account confirms the impression that Bevan's desire was to remain the semi-detached philosopher–statesman, without being forced to take too direct a responsibility for compromises to which he gave his reluctant blessing. Bevan wished it to be known that he had come to an accommodation with Gaitskell, not an identity of view.

To the public, however, he simply appeared to have surrendered his most cherished beliefs. 'New Labour Axis Wins' ran the *News Chronicle*'s head-line after Conference had approved *Industry and Society* by a majority of 4–1. 'No Fresh Nationalisation Is Likely for Years Ahead'.[17] The impression was heightened by Jennie speaking and voting with the minority who favoured sending the document back to the NEC for clarification. 'This is the most astonishing Labour Conference I have ever attended,' she declared. 'I am beginning to feel like Alice in Wonderland.'[18] The press could not fail to point up this family split; Jennie was widely assumed to represent her husband's real views. *Tribune* the next day ('We'll Keep the Red Flag Flying Here!')[19] and Jennie the week after ('We Can Still Win the Fight for MORE NATIONALISATION ')[20] continued to assert that the new policy could still be a springboard for real socialism. But the reality was plain to all. Gaitskell had succeeded, with overwhelming support, in keeping the hands of the next Labour Government free of any doctrinaire commitments. By 1959, predictably, the manifesto on which the party fought the General Election was less specific even than *Industry and Society*. Labour, with Bevan's acquiescence, was virtually silent on what he had always insisted was the most distinctive element in its appeal.

The real drama at Brighton, however, came not on the Wednesday with the debate on *Industry and Society* but on the Thursday, in the defence debate. Nationalisation was a stale controversy, which most delegates were happy to see shelved. What to do about the H-Bomb was a new and urgent one, on which feelings ran much higher. It was the most important question for the future not only of Britain but of the world; to many delegates, impatient of the technicalities, it was a simple moral question. The Bomb was evil. It should be renounced. If the Americans and the Russians would not renounce it, then Britain should do so unilaterally, giving a moral lead. If the Superpowers did not follow, then at least Britain's hands would be clean. By 1957, stimulated by the announcement that Britain was about to begin a new series of nuclear tests, unilateralism was a growing force within the Labour Party and among the largely apolitical but leftish young intelligentsia of the post-war generation. The need to harness this sentiment – to embody it, to express and channel it but at the same time to educate it – presented both an oppor-tunity and a challenge to the Labour Party, which was soon profoundly split between a broadly unilateralist left and a right-and-centre leadership com-mitted to nuclear defence until all powers agreed simultaneously to renounce it. For many members of the party at all levels the Bomb posed an agonising dilemma between heart and head, emotional revulsion from the destructive capacity of nuclear weapons on the one hand, realistic assessment of the possibilities of safely negotiating them out of existence on the other. No one was more painfully or publicly racked by this dilemma than Bevan.

For it was to Bevan that the left, still including most of the former Bevanites, naturally looked for leadership. For years he had spoken more powerfully than anyone about the horror of nuclear weapons and the insanity of a defence policy based on mutual suicide, scorning the sinister eu-phemisms of the strategists. 'Of course we are afraid,' he had retorted in reply to a Tory taunt back in 1952. 'We are all afraid. Only a fool is not afraid.'[21] The last time he had nearly been expelled from the party, in March 1955, was when he deliberately blew open Attlee's calculated obfuscation and challenged him directly to renounce a strategy based on the first use of nuclear weapons. On these and other occasions he had spoken the language of unilateralism. Yet he had never been a unilateralist. He had been a member of the Government which had manufactured the British atom bomb and he had never subsequently criticised that decision. He was not opposed to Britain manufacturing the hydrogen bomb. He was neither a pacifist nor a fellow-traveller, nor a Little Englander: on the contrary, his position, when he was discussing the matter seriously, was always that Britain must have whatever modern weapons were necessary to remain a major power, able to exercise an independent influence in the world, not a mere satellite of the United States. His argument in 1955 was against a strategy that relied upon the use of nuclear weapons at an early stage in any crisis. His hope was always that by relaxing the rigidities of the Cold War it would be possible to reach an agreement with the Russians that would enable all powers to dispense with nuclear weapons. In other words he was, in practice, an orthodox multilateralist.

It was in his nature, however, that on any issue on which he was torn two ways he often – particularly on the public platform – seemed to contradict himself. He usually spoke impromptu; his method was to argue with himself and with his audience, trying out ideas as he went along. Inevitably much of what he could be quoted, accurately, as having said, did not represent his considered final view. This was true of Bevan's speeches on any subject, throughout his career; but it is particularly true on the subject of nuclear weapons in the middle fifties. Not only was he searching restlessly for an answer to an insoluble problem. As a responsible Labour spokesman, his words were reported and studied as they had not been when he was an irresponsible left-wing rebel. Hence in the early part of 1957 he gave several hostages to fortune in the form of statements which appeared to line him up with the unilateralists. 'I wish to heaven', he declared in New Delhi during his Indian tour in March, 'that Britain would rise to her moral stature by surrendering her hydrogen bomb experiment. I can see no good purpose at all in Britain also arming herself with that useless weapon.'[22] What was this if not unilateralism? Similarly, at Reading on 5 May he asserted: 'If Britain had the moral stature she could say: "We can make the H-Bomb, but we are not going to make it. We believe that what the human race needs is leadership in the opposite direction away from making the bomb and we are going to give it." '[23]

Bevan was always keen on the idea of moral leadership. When establishing the National Health Service he had believed that the eyes of the world were on Britain and that the cause of socialism worldwide depended on the success of Britain's Labour Government. This sense of Britain's continuing leadership can be criticised as a sort of cultural imperialism, a consoling illusion still cherished particularly on the left long after the political reality of Empire had disappeared. Bevan gave the most explicit expression to this illusion in one of his post-Suez speeches in the House of Commons at the end of 1956:

> Hon. Members opposite have inclined to be very defeatist these last few weeks. They think that they have come to the end of their glory. They say 'England is now a second-class nation. We have demonstrated to the world, by the futility of our conduct in Egypt, that the flame has passed from us and been taken up by someone else, but now we have to consider ourselves as a second-class Power and shelter under a higher wall than our own.
>
> I do not take that view. I do not take the view that Great Britain is a second-class Power. On the contrary, I take the view that this country is a depository of probably more concentrated experience and skill than any other country in the world. I may be wrong ... but I do not see that what is called the extinction of the British Empire is necessarily followed by the rise of another empire, that we are a second-class Power and now have to defer to first-class Powers, because the fact is there are no great Powers – there are only frustrated Powers.
>
> We are not in a situation where great empires are quarrelling about spoil and inheriting the corpses of those they have extinguished. It is not true. It is not correct. The great Powers of the world today, as they look at the armaments they have built up, find themselves hopelessly frustrated. If that be the case, what is the use of speaking about first-class, second-class and third-class Powers? That is surely the wrong language to use. It does not comply with contemporary reality. What we have to seek are new ways of being great,

new modes of pioneering, new fashions of thought, new means of inspiring and igniting the minds of mankind. We can do so.[24]

This is a most revealing passage. Bevan's determination not to concede the leadership of the Western democracies to the Americans was never more clearly expressed. By arguing that possession of the H-Bomb affords only frustration he is able to reassure himself that Britain is still, after all, the equal of the USA. And if all powers are equally powerless, he seems to conclude, Britain, with her 'concentrated experience and skill', still has the possibility of moral leadership ('new ways of being great'). This sort of talk, with the implication that the world was just waiting for Britain's example, betrays in Bevan a depth of wishful thinking very close to that of the avowed unilateralists. It is not surprising that they were led to believe that he was at heart one too.

During the summer he certainly appeared to be moving their way. On 24 May the front page of *Tribune* was devoted to the stirring call: 'DESTROY THE BOMBS BEFORE THEY DESTROY US! by Aneurin Bevan'.[25] A week later Bevan upstaged Gaitskell in the House with the demand that Britain suspend nuclear testing immediately.[26] Macmillan parried the assault, but was evidently shaken by its violence. 'It's clear to me', he wrote in his diary, 'that [Bevan] thinks the H-Bomb can be an electoral winner for the Socialists. ... I fear that he is right.'[27] Macmillan believed that Bevan had sensed an upsurge of old-fashioned radical/nonconformist/anti-militarist sentiment in the electorate – precisely the sentiment which would find expression the following year in the formation of CND – and was going to tap it for all it was worth, in order to embarrass Gaitskell. But Bevan had not actually gone beyond the party line. The illogical compromise imposed by Attlee in 1955 and still uncomfortably maintained by Gaitskell had left the party facing both ways at once: supporting manufacture of the Bomb but opposed to testing it. Gaitskell too had opposed the British tests on 4 June, though less emotionally than Bevan.[28] Their positions were essentially the same: the difference was that Bevan talked and wrote as though he believed that nuclear weapons could and must be abolished multilaterally, whereas Gaitskell more cautiously stressed the difficulties in the way of agreement.

In July they travelled together to a meeting of the Socialist International in Vienna where they agreed to a joint declaration proposing nuclear disarmament by stages, beginning with a test ban treaty which it was hoped would lead on to halting production and the destruction of existing stocks, all with provision for international inspection but without the precondition, on which the West had hitherto insisted, that there must be political agreement over Germany and other matters before disarmament could be considered.[29] This policy, which had the benefit of not requiring the immediate cessation of manufacture, was approved by the PLP on 10 July. In September Bevan, with Jennie, visited the Soviet Union and talked with Khrushchev, on holiday by the Black Sea. He was more impressed than he had been the previous year in London. Jennie wrote a glowing account for *Tribune*, describing Khrushchev as 'the opposite of everything we mean by stuffed shirt'.[30] For his part, Bevan was confirmed in his conviction that it was possible to talk sensibly to the Russians if Western leaders would only try. But what particularly impressed him was Khrushchev's contemptuous indifference to the suggestion that Britain might disarm unilaterally. Not only would the Russians not be moved to follow suit; Khrushchev hinted that they might actually feel more threatened by a 'Washington–Bonn axis' unrestrained by Britain.[31] Bevan came back from the Crimea, just before the party Conference, full of the idea that a future Labour Foreign Secretary – himself – could deal with the Russians, but only if he had an independent hand to play *vis-à-vis* both them and the Americans.

That was the line he eventually took in the debate at Brighton. But still there was a hiccup before his mind was quite made up. On the Wednesday before Conference the NEC seemed to be about to adopt, at Bevan's suggestion, the Vienna resolution committing Britain to suspend nuclear tests but leaving unstated the likely corollary that this would lead to stopping manufacture, when Barbara Castle and Sydney Silverman began to 'needle' him that this evaded the main point, and Bevan suddenly proposed a 'footnote' making it explicit.

> At this point Sam Watson [the respected leader of the Durham miners] asked Nye whether he really meant that, at this forthcoming Party Conference, the Executive should commit the Party to this complete reversal of policy on the British H-Bomb. Nye said that he had thought about this matter more than any other political problem in his whole life and had come to the conclusion that this was what he meant; that, if he were to speak for the Executive, this is what he must say; and that, if he could not say it, he must decline to speak. He put it forward, not on grounds of military security, such as Ian Mikardo had mentioned, which seemed to him opportunist, but on moral grounds, because the weapons were evil.[32]

Suddenly it seemed that Bevan was about to bust open the party again. Gaitskell stated curtly that he could not agree to an explicit renunciation of the British weapon. The meeting was adjourned, though not before Bevan had fired off his second outburst about not being prepared to be thought to have agreed with Gaitskell over *Industry and Society*. Yet the next day they had a perfectly amicable and constructive talk. Bevan seemed 'not in the least inclined for a row' over either issue.[33] He was simply worried about how he was going to argue for stopping tests without being allowed to say that logically this must lead to stopping manufacture. They agreed that the two of them should prepare a paper for the NEC on Sunday. In fact no such paper ever materialised. Instead Gaitskell shrewdly left it to Sam Watson to persuade Bevan where his duty lay. Watson later told Crossman that he had taken to Bevan's hotel room in Brighton 'a bottle of whisky and ten little bottles, five of tonic and five of soda, and that by the end of the evening Nye wasn't noticing whether it was tonic or soda. They had really talked for two whole evenings and Sam had gradually got Nye round to the mood of the next Foreign Secretary and the representative of the world's mineworkers.'[34] He was still in that exalted mood on the Sunday afternoon when, according to Crossman's account, he 'proceeded, without turning a hair, to repudiate everything he had said on Thursday morning in the guise of answering Edith [Summerskill] and Sydney [Silverman], the chief independent advocates of nuclear renunciation'.

> Nye started by saying that we could not consider nuclear weapons in the abstract. Composite 24, if properly considered, involved the whole of our foreign policy, since the repudiation of nuclear weapons by Britain would affect every relation we had with every other country all over the world. How, for instance, could we do this without consulting the members of the Commonwealth? How could we do it without ending our alliance with America? How could we do it without jeopardizing the Baghdad Pact? ...
>
> The passing of this resolution, Nye said, would come as a terrible blow, not least in Moscow, where the Russians regarded us as a moderating influence and would be appalled if we suddenly abdicated. On the other hand, it was perfectly proper to propose the suspension of tests as a contribution to breaking the disarmament deadlock. And, if we proposed the suspension of tests, we would have to be realistic and admit that this might in fact involve holding up the production of nuclear weapons since, for all we knew, Britain might be unable to produce weapons without further tests. But, if this holding up of production did in fact take place as a result of suspending tests, the motive for it would not be moralistic, like Edith's and Sydney's, but purely practical. Nye concluded with the words, 'Surely it would be a mistake to take all the cards out of the hand of Labour's next Foreign Secretary.'

'I think this was the first occasion', Crossman commented, 'on which a majority of those present had heard one of Nye's intellectual emotional somersaults.' Gaitskell said that 'he agreed with every word Nye had said and only wished he could have said it as well.'[35] The unilateralists – Silverman, Summerskill, Castle, Mikardo and Greenwood – were staggered. Over the next three days they and Foot and Jennie tried their best, as they had done successfully in 1951, 1954 and 1955, to turn him round again. But this time Bevan's mind was made up. Morally, he told the journalist Geoffrey Goodman as he rehearsed his speech up and down the promenade for nearly an hour on the Tuesday morning, he accepted 'almost without demur' the case for a unilateral British lead. But he was 'wholly convinced ... that for the Labour Party to have committed itself to unilateralism would have been to make a declaration of impotence'.[36] By the evening Foot knew that 'his choice was irrevocable'.[37] At the *Tribune* rally, usually the exhilarating highspot of the Bevanite year, Bevan was responsible as never before, 'truisms and platitudes ... curling round his lips in a very serene way'[38] as he described his talks with Khrushchev and told his audience of his 'deep conviction that we have not very much time left'.[39] This was unmistakably, as the press noted, the speech of a future Foreign Secretary. His speech in the defence debate the next morning should not therefore have come to his supporters as such a terrible shock. And yet it did.

It was not so much what he said as the way that he said it. This could not be a statesmanlike speech. Screwed up to make what he knew many in the hall would regard as an act of betrayal, he spoke badly until he was heckled and then got angry and confronted his accusers more baldly, more offensively than he need have done with his rejection of their passionately held views. It was a tense debate from the start, rhetorically dominated by the unilateralists. The allegedly Trotskyist mover of the unilateralist resolution, Vivienne Mendelson, specifically reminded Bevan that only months before, at the Welsh Miners' Gala, he had urged the Labour Party to 'call the people out on to the streets against the Bomb'. The seconder, full of Welsh *hwyl*, was one of his closest friends among the old Bevanites, Harold Davies. John Strachey and the veteran peace campaigner Philip Noel-Baker appealed for the multi-lateralist approach, Strachey declaring that unilateral renunciation would leave Britain 'a wholly dependent satellite of the United States'. But Frank Cousins unashamedly raised the temperature again, asserting that on this issue he was 'proud to be emotional. . . . I have a six-year-old daughter, and I will not compromise with anybody on the future of that child.' The West Indian Dr David Pitt spoke in similarly emotive vein.[40] Then Bevan rose to reply for the Executive; in the gallery Michael Foot 'still hoped against hope that a miracle was possible'.[41]

'As a speech,' Crossman wrote, 'Nye's performance was far the worst I have ever heard him make. . . . He rasped off about the H-Bomb straightaway . . . got the audience up against him and then just floundered round and round in circles, trying to say to Conference what he had said to us privately last Sunday but failing to find the words or the arguments.'[42] Protesting that he was as much against the Bomb as anyone, he based his case on the somewhat pedantic objection that the Norwood resolution did not say what it really meant.

> You may decide in this country unilaterally that you will have nothing to do with experiments, nor with manufacture, nor with use. With none of these sentiments do I disagree, none of them at all. But you can't, can you, if you don't want to be guilty, appear to be benefiting by the products of someone else's guilt? . . . What this Conference ought not to do, and I beg them not to do it now, is to decide upon the dismantling of the whole fabric of British inter-national relationships without putting anything in its place, as a by-product of a resolution in which that was never stated at all.[43]

'And yet it was immensely impressive directly they started heckling him,' Crossman continued, 'for at this point the old bull turned. I was sitting at the far end and I could see that vast, blue-suited figure and bright red face and the iron grey hair – angry (and he's terrific when he's angry), mortally offended and repudiating with violent indignation the suggestion that he was grooming himself as Foreign Secretary. It was this suggestion that really brought out his best replies.'[44] 'I saw in the newspapers the other day,' he said, 'that some of my actions could be explained only on the basis that I was anxious to become Foreign Secretary. I am bound to say that it is a pretty bitter one to say to me. ... Is it necessary to recall to those who said "Hear, hear" that I myself threw up office a few years ago? And I will not take office under any circumstances to do anything that I do not believe I should do.' Then, provoked, he launched into the central, unpremeditated section of his speech after which his relations with the left would never be the same again:

> If you carry this resolution and follow out all its implications and do not run away from it you will send a Foreign Secretary, whoever he may be, naked into the conference chamber. Able to preach sermons, of course; he could make good sermons. But action of that sort is not necessarily the way in which you can take away the menace of this bomb from the world.

It might be, he suggested, that the option of unilateral action could be kept in reserve to be considered if collective diplomatic efforts produced no result. 'Do it now!' the hecklers urged him.

> 'Do it now,' you say. This is the answer I give from the platform. Do it now as a Labour Party Conference? You cannot do it now. It is not in your hands to do it. All you can do is pass a resolution. What you are saying is ... that a British Foreign Secretary gets up in the United Nations without consultation ... without telling any members of the Commonwealth, without concerting with them, that the British Labour movement decides unilaterally that this country contracts out of all its commitments and obligations entered into with other countries and members of the Commonwealth – without consultation at all. And you call that statesmanship. I call it an emotional spasm.[45]

'At these words', wrote James Cameron in the *News Chronicle*, 'something like an emotional spasm did indeed go through that stark, crowded arena.'[46] These were the words that never would be forgotten or forgiven. Bevan had rubbed the nose of Conference in its own impotence. Their own Nye had dismissed the righteous aspirations of the left as so much hot air. 'If many had not been nearer to tears,' wrote Michael Foot, 'the whole place might have broken into uproar.'[47] As it was, the last five minutes of Bevan's speech was, as *Tribune* reported it, 'practically a dialogue between floor and platform' as Bevan, committed now to open confrontation, strove to educate his audience in the facts of diplomatic life.

> The decision to use the Bomb, said Bevan, 'won't be taken by Parliaments; it may not be taken by Cabinets; it may be taken by one man.'
> 'Don't give it to him!' was the reply.
> 'But he's got it.'
> 'Then take it away from him!'

Bevan expostulated: 'We can't. I'm speaking of the other man's bomb.'[48]

'Do you think I'm afraid?' he challenged at one point. 'I shall say what I believe, and I will give the guidance that I think is the true guidance, and I do not care what happens. But I will tell you this, that, in my opinion, in carrying out resolution 24 ... you will do more to precipitate incidents that could easily lead to a third world war ...' – the rest of this sentence was lost in angry shouts of disagreement. 'I know that you are deeply convinced', he concluded,

> that the action you suggest is the most effective way of influencing the course of international affairs. I am deeply convinced that you are wrong. It is therefore not a question of who is in favour of the hydrogen bomb and who is against the hydrogen bomb; but a question of what is the most effective way of getting the damn thing destroyed. ... I have reached my conclusion after a lot of agonised thinking, and I am convinced deeply of this, that if resolution 24 is adopted with all the implications I have pointed out, it will very greatly embarrass a Socialist Government and may have disastrous consequences throughout the world.[49]

'At noon today', wrote James Cameron 'the star of Aneurin Bevan skipped in its course, the new man took over formally from the old, and at least one aspect of politics can never be the same again.' He went on wryly to describe the scene:

> Aneurin Bevan insisting on the hydrogen bomb; Aneurin Bevan writhing on the twin hooks of conscience and expediency, passionately defending the American alliance; Aneurin Bevan, his face vermilion, hearing for the first time the jeers of the Left, producing what one had not expected from Bevan: Casuistry. And, of course, triumphantly, if that is what triumph is.[50]

One immediate measure of Bevan's impact was that Cousins, despite his own speech, was unable to carry his TGWU delegation which, during the lunch adjournment, voted by the narrowest of margins against the Norwood resolution, ensuring that its rejection was overwhelming – 5,836,000 to 781,000. But more important than the vote was the symbolism. By this speech – coming on top of his acquiescence in *Industry and Society* the previous day – Bevan had bound himself irrevocably to Gaitskell. If it was a triumph, it was a bitter triumph and Bevan knew it. Crossman found him, immediately afterwards, 'flustered and flurried, but when Barbara and Ian attacked him ... he did not concede to them in any way'.[51] His pride was now involved in the stand he had taken. By the force of his personality he had been able to face down the hecklers in the hall; Foot and Mikardo and Barbara Castle, though dismayed, could not but respect his integrity. He could do nothing, however, but suffer in silence the gleeful congratulations of the Tories ('Bevan into Bevin' crowed the *Daily Telegraph*)[52] and the angry, incredulous reproaches that filled the columns of *Tribune*. 'I never thought it possible for anyone calling himself a Socialist to support in any form whatever the testing or use or storage of the H-Bomb,' ran one letter. 'The tender, compassionate heart of our Socialism has been torn out and replaced with a desiccated calculating machine. ... In the sacred name of Unity, who has made a monkey out of our Nye?'[53] The repeated charge was that after all his talk of morality, when it came to the point he had embraced, like any Tory, the crudest power politics.

Bevan stood by what he had said, but he thought what he had said had been misrepresented. Not sending a British Foreign Secretary 'naked into the conference chamber' did not mean, as orthodox deterrence theory had it, that because the Russians had the Bomb Britain must have one too. Every country in the world, he had frequently pointed out, could use that argument, and France, China and others already were using it. In context, what he had been arguing was that Britain would have more possibility of inducing others to give up their nuclear weapons if Britain had something to give up too. The British Bomb was a bargaining counter which should be surrendered only as a means of getting others to follow suit. The purpose was disarmament rather than deterrence.[54] This was, and still is, a thoroughly rational position. In practice, however, as the subsequent thirty years have shown, it makes no difference whether the nuclear balance is maintained for purposes of negotiation or of threatened retaliation. There was thus some substance to the charge of casuistry. Moreover the argument that all Conference could do was pass a resolution cut both ways: there would be no overnight sundering of alliances if the unilateralist resolution were carried. Labour was after all only the Opposition, not the Government.

There was also substance in the charge that Bevan wanted to be Foreign Secretary. But why not? Though he spent only six years of his life in office he believed, above everything, in obtaining and using power. He genuinely believed, perhaps naively, but not dishonourably, that as Foreign Secretary he could take the decisive initiative which might bring the powers together and help to lift the threat of nuclear destruction from the world. He did not believe that any Western statesmen yet, locked into their Cold War attitudes, had seriously tried. (The one possible exception was Churchill, when he was too ill to do anything about it.) But with Labour currently thirteen points ahead in the Gallup poll he was confident that he would get his chance in two or three years, if the party just held together and did not tear itself apart over hypotheses. Why then did he not, as one *Tribune* reader suggested, 'simply state that international relations were so fluid and delicate that we should not cling to any one method of getting rid of the H-Bomb? "Give me a free hand and trust me to take the best road, when the time comes," he should have said. And the delegates would have given him a free hand.'[55] This is a fair criticism, or would be if Bevan had been a more calculating sort of politician. By working his Conference magic, by massaging a few sensibilities, he could almost certainly have got the Norwood resolution defeated without flaying its supporters – his supporters – as he did. But Bevan was a politician of instinct. Throughout his life, in his greatest speeches and his worst, he thought on his feet and reacted to the promptings of the moment. On this occasion he knew what he had to say but not exactly how he was going to say it. By allowing himself to be provoked, by responding as he did with talk of 'emotional spasms', he got his free hand; but at the cost of bitterly antagonising the left and widening the unilateralist/multilateralist division in the party which he, had he been able to play it differently, might have been the man to bridge.

Brighton 1957, the *New Statesman* solemnly recorded, marked 'The End of Bevanism'.[56] In reality, in the sense of a distinct group within the parliamentary party and on the NEC personally associated with Bevan, it had been dead for some years, killed by the defection first of Wilson and Crossman, then of Bevan himself, to co-operation with Gaitskell. The following which Bevan had built up, however, in the constituency parties and the unions since 1952 remained; indeed 'Bevanites' in this wider sense were increasingly moving into positions of influence, as the swelling support for unilateralism within the party showed. What happened in 1957 was that this growing element in the party was suddenly and rudely deprived of the leader to whom it had hitherto looked up. One immediate consequence was the foundation of the unilateralist Campaign for Nuclear Disarmament – outside the Labour Party, but predominantly composed of Labour sympathisers – only four months later. The climax of this development was reached only after Bevan's death when the party – with Frank Cousins now swinging several of the big union block votes to the left – was briefly captured for unilateralism. The point is that 'Bevanism' was revealed to have very little to do with Bevan. After 1957, the left in the constituencies – the 'New Left', reinforced by disillusioned defectors from the Communist Party after Hungary, followed in the 1970s by the Bennite 'hard left' – increasingly diverged from the Bevanite 'old left', the dwindling group of parliamentarians still, if only sentimentally, attached to Bevan. To the New Left, Brighton showed that Bevan, like other parliamentarians before him, had finally sold out to the system. He had talked of party and union democracy; but his belief that he, as Foreign Secretary, could do a deal with his friend Khrushchev reflected the inherent elitism of his new statesmanlike role. He had put his trust in leaders, no longer in peoples, from whom alone real change could come. The left's task was to go back to the people and begin again mobilising the working class for peace and socialism through the unions, in the universities and through CND. Leaders, the moral was, always let you down; and Bevan had turned out to be just another leader.[57]

Chapter 24

The Confusions of a Shadow Foreign Secretary

Brighton set Bevan's course for the last two years of his political life. It was a somewhat solitary course on which he now embarked, and not a very happy final period. In binding himself in unbreakable alliance with Gaitskell he ruptured his relations with old friends on the left but forged no compensating links of comradeship on the right. Twice in the first few weeks he and Gaitskell lunched together, occasions which Crossman (with some exaggeration) considered 'really decisive events in the lives of these two men, who had never before had a drink with each other, far less a meal'.[1] But if Crossman thought that this signalled a new intimacy in their relationship he was wrong. Personally there was no advance beyond the uneasy accommodation already achieved. Bevan remained publicly supportive but privately critical of Gaitskell's performance as leader: he entertained no illusions that Gaitskell would lead the sort of Labour Government he hoped to see. Gaitskell for his part was grateful for Bevan's loyalty but remained on his guard: Bevan as Shadow Foreign Secretary was an unpredictable and always potentially dangerous senior colleague whom he had to carry for the sake of unity, never a trusted member of his team. Gaitskell in fact handled Bevan reasonably tactfully. But the two men still moved in different social circles and thought within entirely different frames of political reference. The only Gaitskellite with whom Bevan developed any sort of understanding was George Brown, who was significantly and self-consciously not a member of Gaitskell's much resented 'Hampstead set' of Oxford-educated economists.

On the other side Bevan was deeply hurt by the bitterness of his former supporters who could not understand why he felt he had to take the stand he did at Brighton. 'The sheer malignity of some of the remarks hurled at him and the poison letters sent to him', Jennie wrote many years later, 'darkened his life.'[2] The breach with Michael Foot was particularly painful. Bevan was very upset that Foot, as editor, swung *Tribune* – which he had some reason to regard after twenty years as *his* paper – uncompromisingly behind the unilateralist line. To his credit, he did not try to stop Foot or replace him, though Jennie was one of the three directors. More weeks than not he continued to contribute an article, usually on foreign affairs. But their relations deteriorated badly. By June 1959 Foot could tell Crossman that he and Bevan had 'had no political contact for over a year'.[3] Jennie was never such a support to Nye as at this time. Though a convinced unilateralist herself, she wrote a loyal article two weeks after Brighton explaining his thinking and urging the left to remember all the other foreign policy positions on which the right had given ground since 1951.[4] Perhaps alone, Jennie saw how severely wounded Bevan had been by the trauma of Brighton.

One of the press comments which he most resented was the suggestion in the *New Statesman* that he had 'sold himself too cheap'. 'Unity has been achieved entirely on Mr Gaitskell's terms and Mr Bevan has surrendered unconditionally. ... The method of his reunion with Mr Gaitskell had robbed him of his only source of power. He enters the Cabinet Room naked, a complete prisoner of his former opponents.'[5] In narrow policy terms that may have been so; over both public ownership and the H-Bomb Bevan had accepted positions which he could not now disown without making himself ridiculous. In a broader sense, however, the political advantage was a good deal more finely balanced. For by trouncing the unilateralists at Brighton, Bevan had put Gaitskell heavily in his debt. Far from having delivered himself 'naked' to his former opponents, he had actually earned the right to be left to conduct Labour's foreign policy – except where it involved specific and controversial commitments – largely in accordance with his own ideas. How the relationship would have worked out in office it is impossible to tell. It is inconceivable that Gaitskell, who had his own strong views, would have allowed Bevan the latitude that Bevin had enjoyed under Attlee. In the very much looser circumstances of opposition, however, the unspoken price of Brighton and of Bevan's acquiescence in Gaitskell's 'revisionist' domestic policy was that Bevan should have his head abroad. Gaitskell did not always like this very much. He was particularly exercised by Bevan's frequently incautious articles in *Tribune* (syndicated in several countries round the world), which he thought 'very undesirable in a future Foreign Secretary'.[6] To take two examples, in May/June 1958 Bevan roundly described de Gaulle on his return to power in France as a dictator, making explicit comparison with Hitler;[7] while the previous year, long before Gaitskell or the party as a whole had got round officially to determining Labour's attitude to the European Common Market, Bevan had damned it from his own fundamentalist viewpoint as an anti-democratic return to the capitalist jungle.[8] It was a measure of Bevan's substantial independence that he could not easily be rebuked for such unauthorised pronouncements.

On the more central questions of international politics, too, the views which Bevan preached – it is the right word – not only in *Tribune* but in his speeches in foreign affairs debates in the House of Commons, were very much his own, characterised by his distinctive mixture of insight, homespun philosophy and wishful thinking. Their starting-point was his unshakeable conviction that the Soviet Union was evolving, and was bound to evolve, towards a more democratic form of society. He spoke and wrote frequently of the 'profound changes' which he believed were at work within Soviet society and which it was the duty of the West to encourage by relaxing, not increasing, the military pressure on Russia.[9] The barbarity of the Soviet regime hitherto he explained as being due not to its Communism but to its 'Byzantinism',[10] which he confidently expected to disappear with Stalin. Welcoming Khrushchev's denunciation of Stalin as confirming this analysis, he was ready (in 1956) to predict quite specific measures of liberalisation such as an independent judiciary, open courts and a right of appeal, and even the emergence of competing parties, which he thought the theoreticians, bowing to necessity, would have no difficulty in reconciling with Marxist doctrine.[11] Professing (in 1957) to see the Supreme Soviet asserting a greater independence of the Politbureau, he optimistically compared Stalin with Charles I and portrayed Khrushchev as a sort of Hanoverian who would not be able to disregard Parliament so easily![12] Having previously expressed his confidence in the reality of the new collective leadership, Bevan was momentarily nonplussed by Khrushchev's increasing assertion of his own personality cult.[13] But this did not deflect his certainty that rising living standards would rapidly bring the Soviet people 'into line with what we call the free peoples of the West'.[14] Impressed by his visit to the Soviet Union in 1957, and particularly with Soviet technical education, he was sure that living standards were rising. In the very week of Labour's Brighton Conference, the Russians successfully launched their *sputnik*. In the next issue of *Tribune* Bevan wrote glowingly – in terms, indeed, that might almost have been dictated by Tass – of the onward march of Soviet man which this achievement represented: 'An ever-moving conveyor belt, carrying ever-increasing numbers of artisans, doctors, lawyers, professors, technicians, scientists, artists, the whole kaleidoscope which makes up a modern society, keeps surging forward.'[15] ('What about the workers?', the loyal *Tribune* reader might have asked.) Of course Bevan was not blind to the present reality of Soviet life. 'Speaking for myself', he wrote in 1959 with somewhat exaggerated caution, 'I still think the weight of the argument lies with the defenders of Western democracy.' But it was 'inevitable', he thought, 'for doubts to arise about the possible lines of future advance'. Soviet achievements in space, taking place 'against a background of industrial stagnation and even of economic recession among the capitalist nations of the West', appeared to Bevan proof of what he had always held as an article of faith, the superior efficiency of the planned economy. The Soviet leaders, commanding 'an instrument for expanding production and stimulating the industrial arts with apparently rising momentum', had 'thrown down the gauntlet' to the West.[16] Of course we now know that this was fantasy. Bevan was taken in by Khrushchev's boastful bluster and his own preconceptions. This gross misjudgement of the fundamental nature of the Soviet Union nevertheless underlay all his other foreign policy attitudes.

It underlay the confidence he had expressed ever since 1950 that the Soviet Union had no intention of launching a military attack on Western Europe. On the contrary, he believed that the Russians would be willing to withdraw their armies from Eastern Europe if only NATO would make a reciprocal withdrawal. 'In 1944 and 1945', he told the House of Commons after the invasion of Hungary, 'the Red Army went beyond its sociological frontiers. Where it conquered it stopped; but what it conquered it could not hold. It has always been clear ... that the time would come when the Russians would find that these areas were socially indigestible.'[17] The same ferment that was at work in Russia he believed to be still more advanced in Poland and Hungary and Czechoslovakia (as in Yugoslavia), with the added ingredient of a powerful nationalism. 'The Russian rulers themselves', he wrote in *Tribune*, 'are well aware that some alternative must be found in place of the repression that they are using in Hungary.'[18] 'The *cordon sanitaire* that Stalin created around himself becomes increasingly irrelevant when one considers modern weapons'.[19] That being so, Bevan persuaded himself, the Russians' only wish was to be helped to retreat from an occupation which brought them only embarrassment and expense.

Bevan believed that the Russians were serious about peace talks; or if they were not, that it was up to the West to expose them by treating their proposals seriously. As it was, he held that Khrushchev and Bulganin, by making a series of offers which were never properly explored, were winning the propaganda war. The Russians at least appeared in the eyes of the world to be willing to discuss disarmament while the West dragged its feet, making preconditions which the Russians could not possibly be expected to accept. It was one of Bevan's most consistent themes that by insisting that a satisfactory political settlement, specifically of the German problem, must precede any measures of disarmament, Western leaders – Eisenhower and Dulles, Macmillan and Selwyn Lloyd – were putting the cart before the horse and effectively blocking any hope of progress. Repeatedly in these years he urged them to take up the latest Soviet offer; repeatedly he accused them of paying only lip-service to the desire to negotiate.[20] Particularly, of course, he blamed the Americans for perpetuating the Cold War mentality, castigating Dulles's 'adolescent values'[21] and condemning his violent language towards the Soviet Union ('this materialistic, atheistic despotism, aimed at dominating the world') as 'the language of religious war'.[22] The Americans' 'obsession' with Communism, he argued, had diverted NATO from its original purpose as a security pact into an ideological crusade which endangered the very survival of the planet.[23] Another recurring theme, therefore, was the need for Britain and France to 'get off the escalator', not to leave NATO (Gaitskell would never have allowed him to suggest that) but to assert their independence within NATO and be prepared to open talks directly with the

Russians to break the deadlock.[24] Too often, on the contrary, he thought Macmillan and Lloyd, like Bevin and Eden before them, tamely followed the US lead.

Bevan's world view, unlike Gaitskell's, remained resolutely multilateral. He was convinced not only that the rigid polarisation of the Cold War was a bad thing but that the post-war structure of alliances was now breaking down. NATO, he believed, was becoming irrelevant; SEATO and the Baghdad Pact were doomed attempts to reimpose an old world order on new nations which would not stand for it.[25] The future lay with the growing number of non-aligned nations, with India and the new Commonwealth, with China and with the UN. Bevan was particularly critical of the refusal of the Americans to admit Communist China to the UN, while they absurdly persisted in regarding Chiang Kai-shek's Formosa as the 'real' China. 'It is a monstrous offence', he raged in *Tribune*,

> that the most populous nation on earth should be cut off from communication with so many other nations, merely because the vision of the leaders of the United States falls so lamentably short of the material power they command. ... If Mr Foster Dulles was a secret Communist agent he could not be more successful. ... If they persist in their present policies, then the smaller powers should concert themselves to defy a leadership so myopic, so smugly self-satisfied, so dangerous and so unequal to the imperious needs of the time.[26]

Gaitskell would not have expressed it so strongly; but even he thought the Americans' support for Chiang Kai-shek – even to the brink of war in 1958 over Quemoy and Matsu – dangerously misconceived. In 1959 Bevan blamed the West's policy of non-recognition for provoking the contempt for world opinion displayed by Mao's brutal invasion of Tibet.[27]

He also deplored the Americans' Cold War attitudes in the Middle East, embodied in the 'Eisenhower doctrine' which offered support to any country in the area opposed to Communism. This he regarded as neo-colonialism, the Americans simply moving in to fill the vacuum left by Britain's humiliation at Suez.[28] He had long urged that there could be no settlement in the Middle East unless the Russians were invited to share in it – an attitude which Gaitskell in 1956 dismissed sharply as 'fellow-travelling', but which he later came to accept.[29] Besides objecting to the Americans in Lebanon and the British in Jordan intervening to prop up unpopular client regimes,[30] Bevan had a grand scheme of his own, which he expounded in the House of Commons in March 1957, for pacifying the whole of the Middle East by means of a collective aid programme, to be administered by the United Nations, to return to the area the benefit of the oil revenues extracted from it, sharing out the wealth between oil-producing and non-oil-producing countries alike, 'without any of the taints of imperialism against which they are now revolting'.[31] If this was too idealistic to be practical, it was typical of Bevan's desire to use the UN in a

345

far more positive role than mere peace-keeping. By making it the channel for worldwide aid from the developed to the under-developed nations, he hoped to make it the instrument of a sort of world socialism, in contradistinction to the heavy-handed 'dollar diplomacy' – aid with strings – practised by the Americans in defence of capitalism.[32] Bevan wanted the UN also to assert its political authority, specifically in the Middle East by insisting, after Suez, that Nasser should now honour his obligation to the organisation which had halted Israel's invasion by withdrawing his embargo on Israeli ships using the canal.[33] None of this came to pass, of course, nor is it easy to believe that Bevan, had he ever become Foreign Secretary, would have made much difference. Yet however optimistic some of its premises, his was an honourable vision of a world less divided by ideology, race and money than that we have learned, with increasing resignation, to live with over the past forty years. Bevan would at least have brought some generous aspirations to the Foreign Office to flavour, if no more, the conduct of British policy.

How very different, though, these frankly idealistic aspirations are from the deterministic Marxism which Bevan had preached before the war. Then, right up to 1939, he had seen international politics simply but clearly in terms of monopoly capital and the power relations of competing empires. Now it was all so much more complicated. One of the competing empires was the flawed workers' state, the Soviet Union. At the same time nuclear weapons made the prospect of war between the rival imperialisms too frightening to contemplate. Like any other liberal, old-fashioned radical or sentimental socialist, therefore, Bevan was reduced to high-minded appeals to morality and goodwill, mutual interdependence and the virtues of negotiation in the overriding interest of preserving peace. He derided – no one more scathingly – the American and occasional Tory idiocy 'Better dead than Red'.[34] Conversely, however, it was equally true that to be Red was now less important than staying alive. 'After all, the primary condition for arguing about different social systems is that one should be alive to argue about them.'[35] Exactly as it had in domestic politics, therefore, the intellectual certainty which had sustained him through the thirties, the confidence that the laws of history were working themselves out towards a socialist conclusion, had dissolved in a fog of uncertainty and disillusion. As a statesman in the late fifties, all Bevan had left to steer by were his aspirations, cruelly tempered by reality. When it came to practical policy-making he veered unpredictably and unhappily between the two.

On one issue he was strikingly successful in winning the party to his view: this was the policy of 'disengagement' in central Europe. At the time of the great row over German rearmament in 1954, the Bevanites' alternative had been to negotiate with the Russians the creation of a unified, neutral disarmed Germany; the right had backed the Eisenhower–Eden policy of rearming West Germany as a member of NATO. Now, after Hungary, building on his belief that the Russians would welcome a way to withdraw from Eastern Europe, Bevan widened the proposal to include Poland, Hungary and Czechoslovakia as well as both parts of Germany, in a demilitarised nuclear-free zone, open to inspection by both sides.[36] By 1957, as part of the party's generally leftward compromise on nuclear matters – virtually anything short of unilateral renunciation – this had become official Labour policy and was known, ironically, as the 'Gaitskell plan'. In 1958 a somewhat more limited proposal for nuclear withdrawal (the Rapacki plan) was put forward by the Russians through the agency of the Polish Foreign Minister. One problem, which ensured its rapid rejection by the West, was that the Russians would have been left with a heavy preponderance of conventional forces. Another was that the West was now thoroughly committed to supporting the Federal Republic. This was the factor which most alarmed Bevan, who was still luridly convinced that West Germany was 'coming more and more under the same economic and financial influences which helped to create the Germany of Hitler'[37] and held that Adenauer was being given a veto on the most hopeful possibility of progress towards disarmament. 'It suits Dr Adenauer and his friends,' he wrote in August 1957, 'as it suited Hitler, to delude the people of the West until the military revival of Germany once more makes her the arbiter of European destinies.'[38] West Germany was growing stronger all the time, he argued in the House of Commons in December 1958 (*Tribune* backed him with pictures of new Heinkels and Messerschmitts for the new *Luftwaffe*):[39] the West should agree to disengagement now while it was still possible.[40] He insisted, on the basis of a brief visit to Bonn in 1957, that the great majority of Germans would welcome demilitarisation as the price of reunification and peace.[41] But the whole idea was a non-starter. The Russians were never going to give up East Germany: the NATO view was that their offers were simply a renewed diplomatic offensive against West Berlin, which accordingly became again, as in 1949, a symbol of resistance to Communism. The Cold War in Europe was a real confrontation of powers whose opposed ideologies occupied real territories on either side of the Iron Curtain. It was not merely a chilly atmosphere that could be warmed up by a willingness to talk. 'Disengagement' united the Labour Party but did not achieve much else.

On the really difficult question of nuclear weapons the party remained bitterly divided and its leaders thoroughly confused as they tried to make moral and practical sense of Bevan's Brighton policy of retaining the British deterrent in order to negotiate it away. At the heart of the confusion was Bevan himself. During 1958–9, on every issue of detail that would have given substance to the Brighton formula – the suspension of tests, the question of American bases in Britain, the possibility of first use and finally the 'non-nuclear club' – he contradicted himself practically from day to day. Crossman's diary records him swinging violently between 'realistic' and 'patriotic' right-wing attitudes and emotional left-wing ones. For instance, on American rocket bases: on 17 December 1957 he told Crossman that he was opposed to having them in Britain or indeed in Europe;[42] three days later in the House of Commons he argued the party line that they should be under British control;[43] then in January he tore into Peggy Herbison at the NEC who objected to bases being sited in Scotland: 'You people who have been supporting NATO have got to swallow these bases because they are merely a logical extension of our atomic defences and Peggy Herbison has no right, therefore, to bleat about them.'[44] On first use, in March 1958, Bevan first backed Cousins at a joint NEC/TUC meeting, asserting that he 'would rather see a Russian conventional army occupying Britain than make the world a charnel house by using nuclear weapons first. . . . It was totally impossible for any rational man to make up his mind to use nuclear weapons to ward off a conventional attack';[45] then was persuaded by George Brown, John Strachey and Denis Healey that there was a whole spectrum of nuclear weapons ranging from 'atomic tactical' to 'uncontrollable thermo-nuclear'. 'We've got to get it across to the Russians', he now declared, 'that, if they attack us, we shall create a belt of destruction behind the Russian armies right across the satellite countries.' 'This', Crossman commented, 'from the man who, only ten days ago, was saying that he would rather see Britain occupied by Russia than use a nuclear weapon!' Crossman 'came to the conclusion that Nye had been squared by an agreement under which, if he will become a supporter of nuclear tactical weapons, the others might agree to a declaration against the use of thermo-nuclear weapons first'.[46]

The question of first use was actually omitted from the agreed policy statement which emerged from these intricate discussions. The emphasis was on the pledge that a Labour Government would suspend nuclear tests immediately – though this was something which Bevan on American television the previous November had specifically ruled out[47] – in the hope that the Russians and Americans would be encouraged to follow suit. (The same month the Russians announced that they were suspending tests; but since they had just completed a series of tests the Americans were not impressed.) On 13 April Gaitskell and Bevan spoke together to a Labour rally in Trafalgar Square intended to seal the party's unity on this policy. Bevan, faced with unilateralist placards proclaiming 'A vote for Bevan is a vote for the H-Bomb' and 'No H-Bombs – not even Nye's', endorsed the step-by-step approach and pleaded for the party to 'close ranks and accomplish what can be done in the immediate circumstances facing us' instead of dissipating their energies on distant goals that only spread division.[48] Two weeks later he addressed the London Labour Conference and was heckled continuously. It was Brighton over again, as he rounded angrily on those who questioned the integrity of anyone who disagreed with them:

> There you are! There are the moralists. There are the pure saints. You see how these comrades like to polarise the movement. ... Do not let us destroy the movement by charges of insincerity from one side or the other.

Unilateral renunciation of the British bomb, he insisted again, was irrelevant. The question was: 'How can we so concert our policies as to get rid not only of our own hydrogen bomb but all the other hydrogen bombs as well?' That could only be done by Britain standing with her allies. Bevan then denounced the unilateralists in the strongest terms a Labour leader can use:

> Those who desire that Great Britain should have no allies, and only Russia should have allies, are enemies of Great Britain and, not only that, they are enemies of the working class movement.[49]

The final plank of Labour's unifying platform on nuclear weapons was put in place in June 1959: this was the 'non-nuclear club' proposal whereby Britain would promise to stop production if all other countries, except the United States and the Soviet Union, agreed to do the same. This was a transparently improbable supposition: France and China, the next two countries close to acquiring a nuclear capability were most unlikely to agree. Moreover Britain would be left entirely dependent on the United States and the polarisation of the world between states protected by the American umbrella and those protected by the Russians would be sharpened. Both Bevan and Gaitskell saw these objections perfectly clearly.[50] But CND was gaining ground in the country and in the unions: the second Aldermaston march had taken place at Easter and on 5 June the quintessentially moderate GMW voted unexpectedly against the British Bomb. In these circumstances Gaitskell was quicker than Bevan to recognise the possibilities of a conditional offer to give it up in circumstances which were never likely to be realised. The uncompromising unilateralists like Cousins were not deceived; and on 3 June Bevan told Crossman that 'he and Frank Cousins saw eye to eye on the matter. . . . Nye said it was diplomatically impossible and raised every kind of objection'.[51] Only a few days later, however, at the International Sub-Committee of the NEC, he expounded the proposal with complete conviction 'as though he had just thought of it'.[52] Cousins was understandably furious. At the joint NEC/TUC meeting called on 23 June to approve the new policy he protested that the non-nuclear club was nothing but 'a tricky manoeuvre, when any fool could see that China would anyway refuse to join'.

> There followed a long, animated altercation between Nye and Cousins, until Nye, timing it nicely, burst out that trade unions have useful functions but were a poor place for making serious political decisions. He would rather get out than be told by the trade unions what to do in the Foreign Office. Anyway, the way union delegates voted at their conferences bore no relation to the way their members voted at the Elections. The history of our Movement was the story of unions striking revolutionary postures at Conferences and then failing to carry them out. Moreover, the fact was that we were just before an Election and, if Frank Cousins carried this division further, he would make defeat certain. 'I have led more controversies and rebellions than anyone else here, but whenever Elections approach I call for unity against the common foe.'[53]

Here once again was Bevan, determined that unity was the overriding priority, using all his authority on Gaitskell's behalf to crush the right of dissent. Ernie Bevin would have approved. He brushed aside Cousins' awkward questions about first use and the difference between 'stopping', 'suspending' or 'refraining from' nuclear tests as 'mere questions of nomenclature, on which there was no serious controversy'. Yet only the week before he and Gaitskell had had a sharp confrontation on this very point, Gaitskell insisting on the open-ended 'suspend', Bevan preferring the slightly stronger 'refrain from':

> Finally Nye blew up. 'My dear Hugh', he said quietly, 'if you believe I am going to cross every *t* and dot every *i* of the drafts you write, you are sadly mistaken. I am just not going to.' After which he muttered to me *sotto voce*, 'Now you know how he broke up the Labour Government in 1951, digging his toes in for £11 million in a £3,000 million rearmament scheme.'[54]

He was still angry several hours later.

Bevan had experienced other such moments of exasperation with Gaitskell, which only underline the heroic effort he was making to remain loyal. Over dinner with Crossman in December 1958 he had unburdened himself at revealing length about Gaitskell's shortcomings and about others who would be his colleagues in a Gaitskell Government. 'Straightaway he began to discuss the hopelessness of Gaitskell's leadership, his lack of instinct, his tendency to look over his shoulder and hold up his finger to see which way the wind was blowing.'

> 'He simply isn't a Leader,' Nye said. 'Baldwin, Chamberlain, Attlee were not leaders like Churchill but at least they had an instinct and at least they knew when to stop talking. This man is hopeless from the start.'

'Then do you think we are doomed to defeat?' Crossman asked. (The polls had quite suddenly tipped the Tories' way.)

> 'No, I think we shall win the Election and the trouble will come very soon afterwards. Gaitskell's an honest man, a man of integrity. Gaitskell's an intelligent man. He's not an intellectual, by the way, like you, but he is an intelligent man who hates ideas, and that's why he always distrusts you and me and consorts with dreary people like Roy Jenkins and Patrick Gordon Walker. They're the ones who are always advising him to hedge and to avoid dangerous debates. They are the ones who will advise him when he is Prime Minister, and there is a crisis, to go National. And of course there's Harold Wilson. He's much more dangerous than Gaitskell because he isn't honest and he isn't a man of principle but a sheer, absolute careerist, out for himself alone.'

Crossman asked why Bevan could not 'take over the real spiritual leadership', let Gaitskell be the formal leader 'and just advise him and push him'.

> 'Because he isn't a man you can advise. He's too brittle for that. If he disagrees with you, that's that, and you can't influence him. He isn't a man who is impressed or influenced. He is just scared or runs away. Gaitskell's piddling

all the time for fear of losing the Election. That's the basic trouble. He thinks of nothing else except the Election and every single principle is sacrificed. It's no good asking me to change that.'

The only essential difference between Labour and Conservative, Bevan still repeated, was public ownership. 'Once you abandon that, you betray Socialism.' Yet Crossman found him 'astonishingly resigned to the whole thing, without fury or anger as he used to be. ... I did not myself feel any particular sense of destiny about the Foreign Office or anything else.'[55]

Others had noticed the same thing. Bevan had not only mellowed with responsibility. He seemed to have lost his vital spark. In place of his old challenging optimism, his speeches seemed increasingly depressed, as if he was beginning to despair of the possibility of ever settling the world's problems. He spoke of events having the inevitability of Greek tragedy and harped frequently on the idea that time was running out. Privately he talked about his age. His health was beginning to fail: he suffered from congestion of the lungs – Jennie feared latent pneumoconiosis – and at Scarborough for the 1958 Conference he developed a painful swelling in the neck.[56] Crossman's diary that autumn repeatedly refers to 'poor soft Nye' or 'old Nye': 'What an irony', he wrote in November, 'that just now, when Nye is really soft and has lost all leadership, he should head the [Shadow Cabinet] poll.'[57] He had always been lazy, relying on talk and intuition rather than reading to brief himself. His frequent reversals of position over nuclear weapons revealed that on questions of such novelty and complexity this was no longer enough. 'I've given up the old man, he's absolutely hopeless,' Denis Healey confided cruelly in January 1958. 'He doesn't understand any of these subjects.'[58] 'If Mr Bevan complains of the number of boring committees he has to sit through when he is in Opposition,' Crossman wondered, 'what will he feel like as Foreign Secretary, with six committees a day in the Foreign Office?'[59]

The Times carried a perceptive article on these lines in December 1958. 'Mr Bevan', it noted, 'has become the bleakest Job's comforter in the Commons. ... Since he became the Shadow Foreign Secretary, he has lost the resilience, the buoyancy, the superabundant vitality that for so long marked his every political action.'

> Some observers are beginning to ... speculate whether the Foreign Secretaryship ... may not be pre-eminently the political role for which Mr Bevan's singular gifts of intellect and eloquence are least happily suited. It is a role which must hedge him about with taboos and we know that Mr Bevan must be as nature intended him. ...
>
> It is a role where the persuasive orator will not by right enjoy an advantage over the dull, persevering expert, as he normally does in Parliament. It is a role where there is only the certainty of hard, patient toil and little or nothing to show at the end of it. When you have passed 60, as Mr Bevan himself has said, to be Foreign Secretary is not much of a prospect, the world being what it is.

But the Labour Party play out their own inevitable Greek drama. . . . If Labour wins office at the next election Mr Bevan, as he knows and all the party knows, will have to be Foreign Secretary whether he wants the office or not. He is the one man of stature in the party who has the personal power to reconcile the right and the left wings, as they were never wholly reconciled under the leadership of Ernest Bevin, on a foreign policy that in practice can never be fundamentally distinctive from Conservative foreign policy.

So Mr Bevan is on a personal escalator (to use one of his own images) and the party cannot allow him to get off.[60]

The fact was that Bevan was increasingly going through the motions as Shadow Foreign Secretary, rather than preparing seriously for power. The gleaming prospect of becoming Foreign Secretary on which Sam Watson had played to stiffen his resolve at Brighton quickly tarnished. It remained his duty to the party, to Britain and the world; if anyone could stop the arms race he probably still believed it was himself. But by 1959 he was sounding less and less hopeful. Foreign affairs, even so, remained by far the best portfolio for him, if only because it kept him away from domestic politics, with which he was still more disillusioned; with the world as his parish he got under Gaitskell's feet less than anyone would have predicted. He was actually abroad a good deal of the time, which suited both of them. Bevan enjoyed travel, and doors were opened to Britain's Shadow Foreign Secretary wherever he went. During 1957 alone he visited Italy in February; India, Pakistan, Persia, Turkey, Iraq, Israel and Malta in April; France in June; Vienna for the Socialist International in July; the USSR and Poland in September; the United States in November; and West Germany in December. Generally he was concerned to establish his credentials as a world statesman. But several of these trips excited controversy of one sort or another.

In India he addressed both Houses of the Indian Parliament at a time of severe strain in Anglo-Indian relations, following Suez and British criticism of Indian policy in Kashmir, when there was talk of India leaving the Commonwealth; in one of the supreme speeches of his life, invoking a broader ideal of a Commonwealth in which nations could differ but not part, he helped to turn the tide of Indian opinion.[61] In France, conversely, Bevan attended the conference of the French Socialist Party in Toulouse and was 'distressed and . . . shocked' by the 'note of strident chauvinism' with which the delegates rejected his fraternal criticism of Suez and French policy in Algeria. The persistence of colonialist attitudes even on the left, he wrote in *Tribune*, 'seemed to be evidence of a morbid psychology in France. False conceptions of past greatness, and a host of recollections of past glory, are leading France to dangerous and false conclusions.'[62] (One year later General de Gaulle came to power with the support, to Bevan's disgust, of much of the Socialist Party.) In the United States he had brief talks with Eisenhower and Dulles but spent most of his two-week visit touring the country preaching the need for *détente* with the Russians, trying to overcome the American fear of Communism by expounding his own optimistic view of the evolution of Soviet society. He was better received by students than by business audiences, who reacted angrily when he suggested that the emergence of Communist China was no more irregular than the birth of the United States, or told them that, yes, Khrushchev was a ruthless man but probably no more so than many of those whose hands he had just shaken! Bevan returned home discouraged by direct exposure to American attitudes to the Cold War and depressed by American society generally, which he pronounced more conformist, more complacent and less vigorous than he had found it in 1934.[63]

The trip which attracted the greatest attention, however, was Bevan's visit, in company with Crossman and Morgan Phillips, to the conference of the Italian Socialist Party in Venice in February 1957 – a jaunt subsequently referred to among his friends as 'the Venetian blind'. Bevan undoubtedly had a good time. Crossman sketched a memorable picture of him enjoying himself:

> Bland, ebullient, impeccably dressed in his beautiful new suit, fresh white linen with his handkerchief falling out of his breast pocket, pretentiously discussing the qualities of Italian wine, pretending to knowledge of Venetian architecture, laying down the law about Italian politics with vitality and charm, and occasionally with the wildest irresponsibility![64]

Politically, in fact, Bevan scored a considerable success. Undeterred by charges that he was interfering in Italian domestic politics, he threw his weight into encouraging the left-wing Socialist Party (led by Pietro Nenni), hitherto boycotted by the British Labour Party, to break with the Communists and be ready to merge with the Social Democratic Party (led by Giuseppe Saragat). This they eventually voted to do – a result seen as a serious setback for the Communists and a victory for democratic socialism. The politics of the Bevan–Phillips–Crossman visit were soon overshadowed, however, by an article in the *Spectator* which was taken to suggest that the three British delegates (Crossman actually attended as a journalist) had been drunk for much of the conference.[65] They determined to sue for libel.

This was a highly dangerous proceeding, because there is no question that they did drink a good deal. Certainly Phillips did. According to Crossman's diary, 'he drank steadily – I think mainly to avoid conversation – with the result that he got tiddly by midday and soaked by dinner time'.[66] But Phillips was an inexperienced traveller who hated 'abroad'. Crossman's description is directly contrasted with the picture of Bevan already quoted. Bevan had no wish to avoid conversation, was much more likely (as Michael Foot points out)[67] to drink wine than the whisky the *Spectator* article alleged and, though never abstemious, was well able to hold what he drank. The risk of going to court, however, was – in Crossman's own word – 'appalling'.[68] Degrees of drunkenness are notoriously subjective, sobriety very difficult to prove. Bevan seems to have thought that, after years of slander by the press, the opportunity to win some damages was too good to miss. In the end, thanks to a sympathetic judge – the eighty-year-old Lord Chief Justice Goddard – and a poor showing by the thirty-year-old editor of the *Spectator*, Sir Ian Gilmour, all three were awarded £2,500.[69] Ever since, there have been repeated allegations that they committed perjury.[70] Crossman is said to have boasted fifteen years later that he and Bevan had been 'pissed as newts'.[71] But this is hearsay. His diary at the time of the trial, on the other hand, admits that Phillips had been 'dead drunk for most of the conference'.[72] Since all three litigants sued together and received the same damages this is pretty damning. The charge against a public figure of Bevan's standing is a serious one. Michael Foot has denied it vigorously and at length;[73] but in all but legal terms Bevan's innocence is as unproven as his guilt. Since it is not denied that all of them had been drinking, though doubtless varying amounts, it was at best over-sensitive, rash and irresponsible – not to mention vindictive towards the young journalist, Jenny Nicholson, whose career was ended by the affair – to go to court. For the words complained of were not very terrible:

> Messrs Bevan, Morgan Phillips and Richard Crossman ... puzzled the Italians by their capacity to fill themselves like tanks with whisky and coffee, while they (because of their livers and also because they are abstemious by nature) were keeping going on mineral water and an occasional coffee. Although the Italians were never sure if the British delegation was sober, they always attributed to them an immense political acumen.[74]

Rather a compliment than a libel, one might have thought.

Bevan's last foreign trip was with Gaitskell, Denis Healey and their wives to the Soviet Union on the eve of the 1959 election. The visit was very obviously arranged to try to match Macmillan's success a few months earlier (this was the occasion of his famous white fur hat) by demonstrating that Labour's leaders too could tread the world stage. It was not a great success, either politically – the Russians were not very interested in talking to an opposition party that now looked unlikely to win the election – or personally. Their enforced proximity over a week of discussions and entertainments raised all sorts of tensions and misunderstandings between Gaitskell and Bevan and their even more antagonistic and protective wives – of most of which Gaitskell appeared to remain blithely unaware. After Bevan's death he recalled warmly that 'Nye was in tremendous form throughout those ten days. Ebullient, gay, full of enthusiasm. ...'[75] In fact Bevan, having been to Russia before in his own right, was bored and irritated at having to undergo the same formal round of hospitality as Gaitskell's deputy.[76] It was in some ways a microcosm of their whole relationship since 1955. The British Ambassador noticed that Bevan was very subdued by comparison with 1957.[77] He was in truth already a sick man. While they were in Moscow, however, the news came through that Macmillan had called the General Election for 8 October. Missing out a projected visit to Poland, the party flew straight back to London. Wearily Bevan dragged himself into his last electoral fight.

Chapter 25

Labour in the Affluent Society: the Nemesis of Gaitskellism

Two years earlier, it had seemed that Labour had only to wait for the Tories' time to run out before sweeping them from power on a wave of revulsion from the fiasco of Suez. But during 1958 the tide had turned. Suez turned out not to be so unpopular after all. If there was any sense of national humiliation, public anger was directed not at the Government but at Labour for wallowing in it. By a virtuoso combination of unflappability and flair, Macmillan contrived to dispel his party's mood of defeatism, projecting in its place an irresistible aura of success, based on a visibly rising standard of living. 'Most of our people', he proclaimed famously in July 1957, 'have never had it so good'.[1] Labour was forced to fight on the Tories' terms, protesting that the Government was really presiding over a stagnant economy and asserting unconvincingly that they had the secret of still faster growth. By the time Macmillan called the election Gallup gave the Conservatives a five-point lead.

Bevan was deeply depressed by this turnaround, not simply for the obvious reason that Labour seemed after all to be heading for a third defeat, but because it confirmed his gloomiest forebodings about the direction in which the party, and British politics, were evolving. He had always insisted on the need to emphasise the unbridgeable difference in philosophy and principle between the parties. The purposeless amorality of the Tory Government, clinging to office after Suez in what he had come to call 'the squalid Parliament', disgusted him.[2] Macmillan he regarded as a fraudulent poseur – 'posturing', as he told the Durham Miners' Gala in July, 'like an incandescent aspidistra'.[3] 'I have watched him carefully for years', he told a Manchester audience in March. 'Behind that Edwardian countenance there is nothing.'[4] But he had never expected anything of the Tories. Toryism had always been 'organised spivvery', a confidence trick on the public, ruling-class interest artfully disguised by one charade or another to persuade the poor to sustain the privileges of the rich. What really sickened him in 1959 was that instead of exposing the Tory fraud and boldly appealing to the public on an entirely different platform, Labour was allowing them to get away with it by playing the same cynical, shallow game itself. In the rare *Tribune* articles which he devoted to domestic politics Bevan still vainly asserted the inevitable demise of capitalism, ridiculing the system of 'private economic adventure – miscalled "private enterprise"' as being dependent on 'the deliberate cultivation of unpredictability' and therefore 'wholly opposed to the scientific spirit of the age', which demanded planning.[5] But no one else in the party leadership now talked this way. Very occasionally – for instance at the *Tribune* rally at the very bland Scarborough Conference in 1958 – he delivered a coded warning that electoral victory would be 'dead ashes' unless accompanied by a renewed dedication to socialism.[6] But he knew that the pass had been sold and that he himself, by agreeing to make unity the single overriding value, had helped to sell it. Thus he went into the election with a sinking heart.

Geoffrey Goodman, the Industrial Correspondent of the *Daily Herald*, accompanied Bevan on his campaign tour and kept a diary which vividly documents his mood. The most telling insight is Bevan's fear of letting his real feelings show. 'One is bound to be frightened of what one might say,' he told Goodman before a meeting in Coventry. 'A large meeting has its dangers. You are sometimes tempted to say things you shouldn't say.' He explained that he had been 'forcing himself to exercise tremendous restraint in his meetings so far', concentrating on foreign affairs and going on about Suez in order to avoid having to talk about domestic matters. 'Obviously he would have liked to have had a great outburst on Socialist policies. ... But he knows that if he let off the brakes he would do immense damage and might lose the election.'[7] Clearly nothing could be more disillusioning for a politician of Bevan's inspirational style than the knowledge that if he said what he really believed he would condemn his party to defeat.

It is not certain from Goodman's diary how seriously Bevan expected to win, nor how seriously – when he thought about what lay ahead of him if Labour did win – he even wanted to win. Of course any politician engaged in an election must believe in victory, and the polls did show Labour narrowing the gap during the campaign. At least once, thinking of disarmament, Bevan affirmed, 'We must win this election, it is vital. A great deal hangs on it.' He talked characteristically of cutting out all the Foreign Office protocol, the dinners and receptions and attending on the Queen; of seeking a wider Commonwealth bloc to amplify Britain's influence; and he still clung to the British Bomb 'as a buoy', insisting that to throw it away in advance would be 'an act of sheer folly'. More often, however, 'he became defeatist about the immensity of the task and the complexity of the problem'. He doubted whether he would be able to stand the job for more than a year, regarding Gaitskell as 'a great obstacle', likely to be 'constantly interfering'. At other times he assumed defeat and was equally gloomy about what would happen then. Goodman suggested that the party would swing left, but Bevan saw little hope of that unless the parliamentary party ('rotten through and through; corrupt; full of patronage, and seeking after

357

patronage; unprincipled') could be made more responsive and accountable to the party outside. He saw little chance of a revolt against what he called significantly – Harold Wilson was originally a statistician – 'the clique of statisticians'. 'If we lose there will be a rallying around and a protection society will be formed round Gaitskell.' Even if he were to stand against Gaitskell, the PLP would think him at sixty-two – sixty-seven by the time of the next election – too old to elect in his place. By the eve of polling day, however, Bevan was more resolute: 'There will have to be a showdown. I will quarrel with Gaitskell straight away. I refuse to belong to a Party unless that Party is the vehicle of principles in which I believe – Socialist principles.'[8]

Astonishingly, Bevan succeeded in letting none of this bitterness show. Despite both physical exhaustion and weariness of spirit, he fought a loyal and – apart from one bout of influenza – energetic campaign. Though 'frequently anxious and querulous both before and after meetings', Goodman noted, 'he still has amazing vitality on the platform ... vigorous, effective, passionate, alive'.[9] By contrast he loathed television, believing that it turned politicians into 'pure salesmen – like American politicians', and had never taken the trouble to master its techniques.* Yet in a rare appearance in a party broadcast with Gaitskell on 28 September he exuded 'sweet reasonableness'.[10] He seemed 'extremely nice', wrote Crossman after the recording, 'and we all felt wonderful'.[11] Ironically it was Gaitskell who upset the applecart with an ill-judged pledge, agreed only with Wilson, that Labour – despite offering increased social benefits, including higher pensions and the abolition of the health charges imposed by Gaitskell himself in 1951 – would not increase income tax. At a stroke, this apparently unconsidered commitment undercut Gaitskell's carefully cultivated image of financial rectitude and left him open to delighted charges from the Tories that he was conducting a cynical auction. Bevan's instant reaction was widely shared. Turning to Geoffrey Goodman 'with anger in his eyes, he said, "He's thrown it away. He's lost the election."'[12] Though in view of the eventual margin the effect of a single incident should not be exaggerated, Gaitskell's blunder has been regarded ever since as the turning-point of the campaign; from this moment Labour, not the Government, was forced on to the defensive. Bevan's criticism, however, was characteristically not simply tactical but principled; his objection was not merely to the electoral consequences but to the pledge itself. Telephoning Crossman 'in righteous indignation', he pointed out that 'this would tie the hands of the next Labour Government. ... When he was told that Hugh had consulted Harold Wilson before saying it, his anger was hardly appeased. Indeed, this convinced Nye that there was a real conspiracy going on to strangle the last traces of Socialism.'[13]

Whatever the impact of Gaitskell's gaffe, no one predicted the scale of

* There was an additional personal reason for his dislike of television: unaccustomed nervousness due to his unfamiliarity with the medium tended to bring out his latent but never entirely forgotten stammer.

Labour's defeat. *The Times* on polling day, echoing Bevan's criticism of 'a poor campaign' in which the parties had competed merely in appealing to the electorate's 'cupidity and envy, jealousy and fear',[14] thought the election 'could easily produce a result as close as the general elections of 1950 and 1951'.[15] The polls were still very close. Gaitskell was hopeful right up to the end. In fact the Tories won another 21 seats to increase their overall majority to exactly 100. Statistically their share of an enlarged poll actually fell slightly to 49.4 per cent; but that represented an increase of half a million votes, while Labour's vote actually declined for the second time running by 12.2 per cent (43.8 per cent). The difference was made up by the Liberals, whose previously negligible share more than doubled to nearly 6 per cent – a fact open to differing interpretations by analysts seeking to explain Labour's failure. The post-mortem began immediately. The alternative explanations within the party were the same as in 1955: the party had offered either too much socialism or too little. Gaitskell's friends – most prominently Douglas Jay and Roy Jenkins – were quickly off the mark with suggestions that Labour had become too closely identified with a shrinking working class and was still lumbered in the public mind with an unpopular commitment to old-fashioned nationalisation. Jay actually proposed that the party should change its name. Gaitskell was careful to say nothing in public, but he was universally assumed to be sympathetic to these ideas, especially when word got out of a secret conclave at his Hampstead home on the Sunday after the election.[16]

Bevan was actually even quicker off the mark in the opposite sense. That same Sunday he had an article in the *News of the World* refuting Tory claims that the result spelled the end of socialism: socialism had not been defeated because the Labour Party had not, in his view, fought the election on socialism at all, but on a programme better described as 'pre-1914 Liberalism brought up to date'. Though the inquest had hardly yet begun, he accused those in the party who wanted to 'find out why a majority of the electorate voted Conservative and then adjust our policies accordingly' of being 'engaged in a subtle and persistent effort to convert the Labour movement into a faceless nonentity'.[17] To the left it seemed monstrous that the right, having dominated the party since 1951 and fought the election on its own terms, should now maintain that defeat called for a further shift in their favour. On the contrary, Bevan believed that the right had received the nemesis it deserved: the electorate had rightly rejected a party that had not the courage of its own principles, but would respond with relief to a clear socialist lead. *Tribune* on 16 October voiced precisely his distaste for the so-called 'affluent society' – more correctly 'the unjust society, the casino society, the ugly society'. 'Over a considerable period', it charged, 'and in its fundamentals, the unjust society has not been challenged by the Labour Party. That is the root cause of the Tory victory.'[18] Gaitskell's income tax pledge epitomised a party which promised all sorts of good things but did not want to change the basis of society. The decks were being cleared for another open left–right split, with Bevan apparently preparing to resume the leadership of the left's revolt.

But as so often before he was pulled two ways. This time, however, the pull of unity was strongly reinforced by physical exhaustion. Bevan simply had not the strength to lead a new revolt. If he had won, if he had toppled Gaitskell and become leader, he knew he had not the reserves of energy, patience and enthusiasm to unite and lead the party in the direction he would have wanted to go. The most he could do was to make clear his opposition to any dilution of Labour's traditional aims, using the authority he had built up by his loyalty over the past four years to give him an effective veto over constitutional or other changes. Accordingly when Gaitskell came to lunch with him at Asheridge on 12 October he indicated his wish to take over the Deputy Leadership from Jim Griffiths – he was elected unopposed at the beginning of the new parliamentary session in November – but was otherwise quite amenable, showing 'no sign whatsoever of wanting to lead a Left attack on moderate policies'.[19] Ten days later, when he and Gaitskell met trade union leaders to discuss the future, Frank Cousins noted that they drew diametrically opposed conclusions from the election; but once again there was no row.[20] In the corner of the Smoking Room, Bevan would still sound off to old Bevanite cronies about Gaitskell's 'outrageous intrigues'; but Crossman found him 'deeply injured' rather than 'explosive' – 'all the more formidable because he was relatively quiet'.[21] He was reassured by the strong reaction against the Jay/Jenkins proposals in the PLP on 21 October. When Mikardo the next day tried to interest him in a revived Bevanite group he would have nothing to do with it, saying that the Hampstead group had been 'routed' and 'everything was all right'.[22] He had finally learned the lesson from 1952–5 that he had more authority as an admired individual than as the leader of a factious group.

Labour had missed its regular Conference in the autumn because of the election. Instead a special weekend conference was arranged at Blackpool at the end of November. This was where the collision should have come if Bevan had been determined on a stand-up fight. The scene was set, the battle lines drawn. Gaitskell was to open the debate, Bevan to wind it up. In fact it was a conference dominated by three speeches. Barbara Castle seized the opportunity as that year's party Chairman to launch the proceedings with a rousing *Tribune*/Bevanite defence of old-style socialism. Opening the afternoon session, Gaitskell then broke his seven-week silence with a considered attack, not on public ownership as such but on the impression enshrined in Clause IV of the party constitution that Labour's purpose was to nationalise the entire economy. Bevan, the next day, was left with a sort of casting vote. He could have used it to endorse Barbara Castle and repudiate Gaitskell.

Instead he made what turned out to be his last appearance at a Labour Conference in the role of peacemaker.

Gaitskell in his speech was careful not to repudiate nationalisation altogether. Indeed he still favoured more public ownership than the Labour Governments of the 1960s and 1970s ever contemplated: 'public competitive enterprises, State factories in development areas, a greater share of total trading going to the co-operative movement. . . . I cannot agree that we have reached the frontier of public ownership as a whole.'[23] Nevertheless in insisting that public ownership was a means and not an end, and in warning the party that Clause IV left it open to endless misrepresentation, he was striking at the very symbol of the party's commitment to socialism. And Bevan was, if anyone, the guardian of the party's symbols. Michael Foot on that Saturday, like Barbara Castle before him, received an ovation for a passionate defence of pure Clause IV fundamentalism. Nor was it only the left to whom the symbol mattered. It turned out in the following few months that the party as a whole, including even the most conservative trade unionists, however unenthusiastic for socialism in practice, was deeply wedded to the symbol. Gaitskell was obliged to modify his attempt to rewrite the party constitution; he was allowed to add a new gloss, but not to touch Clause IV itself. Bevan played a major part in enforcing this retreat; yet he did it not by open confrontation but by a virtuoso fudge.

It was a close-run thing. He was under strong pressure from his old friends to take the bold course, to stand up as a defender of the constitution and tell Conference exactly what he thought of Gaitskell, his 'clique of statisticians' and their milk-and-water socialism. Although he had been shown a copy of Gaitskell's speech on Friday night and was understood by Gaitskell's aides to have approved it, when he heard it he was 'absolutely livid'. At dinner that Saturday evening 'he was still wondering whether to blow the whole thing wide open. . . . he was not in much of a mood to be talked out of it.'[24] Instead, by the time he wound up on the Sunday he was in benign, philosophical mood, binding the party's wounds and restoring its self-belief in one of the cleverest, most effective and yet at the same time most heartfelt speeches of his life.

With mellow humour, first of all, he disposed of the suggestion that Gaitskell's and Mrs Castle's speeches had been fundamentally opposed. 'The speech of Hugh Gaitskell yesterday and the speech of Barbara before', he claimed, 'did in fact contain a very important ingredient of unity.'

> I used to be taught as a boy . . . one of Euclid's deductions: if two things are equal to a third thing, they are equal to each other. Yesterday Barbara quoted from a speech I made some years ago, and she said that I believed that Socialism in the context of modern society meant the conquest of the commanding heights of the economy.* Hugh Gaitskell quoted the same thing. So Barbara and Hugh quoted

* The phrase was not in fact Bevan's own. Though it had come to be specifically associated with him in the past eight years, it had already been current in Labour debate in the thirties and actually originated with Lenin.

me. If Euclid's deduction is correct they are both equal to me and therefore must be equal to each other.

So, he concluded, 'we have a kind of trinity' – though he declined to say whether he regarded himself as the father, the son or the holy ghost.

Having thus thrown the mantle of his endorsement over Gaitskell, he went on, in the most conciliatory way possible, to reassert his own, and by extension the party's, continuing fidelity to its traditional beliefs. He dismissed the suggestion that the electorate had voted against Labour because they did not like nationalisation. If it was true, then the obverse was that twelve million people had voted *for* Labour because they *did* want it. 'That is the biggest single vote ever given for public ownership in any country in the whole world. Then why the hell this defeatism?' Was it suggested that the party should change its principles just because the electorate had not voted for it? They might as well have reacted to defeat in 1935 by coming out in favour of unemployment. The lesson was that Labour had not yet succeeded in getting its message through to the people.

> The problem is one of education, not of surrender! The so-called affluent society is an ugly society still. It is a vulgar society. It is a meretricious society. It is a society in which priorities have gone all wrong. I once said ... that the language of priorities is the religion of Socialism ... but you can only get your priorities right if you have the power to put them right, and the argument, comrades, is about power in society. ... The argument is about power and only about power, because only by the possession of power can you get the priorities correct.

The job was not to tailor Labour's policies to the electorate but, he argued – 'I agree with Barbara, I agree with Hugh and I agree with myself' – to improve the presentation of existing policies.

Then, with brilliant rhetorical daring, Bevan lifted the eyes of the Conference beyond mere tactics, switching the attack to the Tories and revealing that his fundamental identification of socialism with progress had not changed in forty years.

> I am not despondent. It is the Tories who are in trouble, not us. ... We may have lost, but they have not won. ...
>
> The fact of the matter is: modern capitalism has not succeeded; it has failed. Even from its own mouth it has failed. We are asked in 1959 to believe that if we are only patient, if we only work hard, we will double the standard of living in twenty-five years. That is the same rate of progress as before the war. With all the techniques of modern production, with electronics, with all the new industrial techniques, the capitalists of Great Britain can promise us exactly the same rate of progress as before the war.

'The challenge which is going to take place in the next ten years is not going to come from Harold Macmillan,' Bevan scoffed. 'He cannot challenge anything.' The challenge Britain would face came not from the

United States, nor from Germany nor France. 'The challenge is going to come from Russia'.

> The challenge is going to come from those nations who, however wrong they may be – and I think they are wrong in many fundamental respects – nevertheless are at long last being able to reap the material fruits of economic planning and of public ownership. That is where the challenge is coming from, and I want to meet it, because I am not a Communist, I am a Social Democrat. I believe that it is possible for a modern intelligent community to organise its economic life rationally, with decent orders of priority, and it is not necessary to resort to dictatorship in order to do it.

As always, Bevan believed that the eyes of the world were on Britain. 'What are we going to say, comrades?' he demanded finally. 'Are we going to accept the defeat? ... What are we going to say to the rest of the world? Are we going to send a message from this great Labour movement, which is the father and mother of modern democracy and modern Socialism, that we in Blackpool in 1959 have turned our backs on our principles because of a temporary unpopularity in a temporarily affluent society? ...'

> I have enough faith in my fellow creatures in Great Britain to believe that when they have got over the delirium of the television, when they realise that their new homes that they have been put into are mortgaged to the hilt, when they realise that the moneylender has been elevated to the highest position in the land, when they realise that the refinements for which they should look are not there, that it is a vulgar society of which no decent person could be proud, when they realise all those things, when the years go by and they see the challenge of modern society not being met by the Tories who can consolidate their political powers only on the basis of national mediocrity, who are unable to exploit the resources of their scientists because they are prevented by the greed of their capitalism from doing so, when they realise that the flower of our youth goes abroad today because they are not being given opportunities of using their skill and their knowledge properly at home, when they realise that all the tides of history are flowing in our direction, that we are not beaten, that we represent the future: then, when we say it and mean it, then we shall lead our people to where they deserve to be led.[25]

In this, his last great speech, one of his last public statements of any sort, Bevan appeared at last to have the whole Labour Party eating out of his hand. He was not merely the elder statesman any more; quoting himself, and quoting Gaitskell and Barbara Castle quoting himself, he actually seemed to be rehearsing the posthumous role which his ghost would play at all subsequent Labour Conferences, the guardian of the party's conscience. The speech was a political *tour de force* by which he had contrived at the end to assert his authority over the upstart Gaitskell in the very act of securing his leadership. 'Bevan Challenges Gaitskell Policy', ran the *News Chronicle*'s headline.[26] 'Mr Bevan Saves Mr Gaitskell', countered the *Daily Telegraph* the same day.[27] Both were right, as *Tribune* was delighted to observe: 'For the big event that happened there is now ... apparent. Mr Bevan restored the chance of substantial unity which Mr Gaitskell appeared to have imperilled.'[28] With one speech he had effectively torpedoed Gaitskell's attempt to rewrite the party constitution and restored the basis of unity *on his own terms*. It was Vicky in the *Evening Standard* who best captured the essence of what had happened: his cartoon at the end of the Conference showed the Leader and Deputy Leader riding together into Blackpool on a tandem – and riding out again with their positions reversed, Bevan now in front.[29]

There are conflicting views of what Bevan would have done with his moral victory, had he lived. After Blackpool he made a number of characteristically wild statements to Crossman, Wilson and others suggesting that he would now overthrow Gaitskell and take over the leadership.[30] Ian Mikardo for one remains convinced that he could have done it: that in the wake of the General Election débâcle many trade union MPs of the centre and right were sufficiently disillusioned with Gaitskell's leadership and affronted by his attack on Clause IV to be ready to ditch him and elevate the once-hated Bevan in his place.[31] It is possible, but seems inherently unlikely, even had Bevan had the energy or the will to make a serious attempt. The truth is surely that he had not. He had never been primarily interested in the leadership as such, but in protecting and promoting his views within the party. By December 1959 he had achieved at last a position of secure authority, in some ways greater as Deputy than it would have been as Leader. Weakened by defeat, Gaitskell could no longer afford to be at odds with Bevan. Bevan had established an effective veto over too much – or at any rate too overt – revisionism in domestic policy; Gaitskell also needed Bevan's protection of his left flank in the defence controversy which was about to blow up again. As Leader, it would have been Bevan who would have had to propitiate the right; and the nuclear issue would have exposed his confusions more cruelly than ever. Politically, as well as personally, he was better off at this stage of his career as the keeper of the party's conscience; and he surely knew it.

For the still glowing faith which had illuminated his peroration at Blackpool now represented only one part of his mind. It showed that his belief in what should be was unchanged; but the last ten years had severely dented his certainty that the future would be as he had always so confidently asserted. Though he denied despondency at Blackpool, his angry denunciations of Macmillan's 'meretricious society' were inspired by the bitter, inadmissible fear that the Tories *had* won. He greatly feared that the British working class on whom he had pinned his hopes had been seduced by their televisions and consumer goods from the path of socialism and that it might now be impossible to get them back to it. 'History gave them their chance – and they didn't take it,' he told Geoffrey Goodman during the election. 'Now it is probably too late.'[32] The words might stand as the epitaph of Bevan's career.

He had been brooding on this failure of British democracy to evolve as he had been convinced it should; and the result was a remarkable, thoughtful speech delivered in the House of Commons during the debate on the Address on 3 November (some three weeks before his assertion of faith undimmed at Blackpool). This was one of only two speeches he lived to make in the new House. (The second, a month later, was a heavily ironic welcome for the Government's resumption of relations with Egypt.)*[33] If his rhetorical triumph at Blackpool was a fitting finale to his tempestuous relations with his party, this last major speech in the Commons was an equally appropriate summation of the high seriousness with which he had always treated Parliament. His theme was nothing less than the central problem of democratic government, as it had been revealed by the experience of both Labour and Conservative Governments since the war. The last twenty-five years have only gone to show how penetrating Bevan's analysis was.

'I would describe the central problem falling upon representative government in the Western world', he began, 'as how to persuade the people to forgo immediate satisfactions in order to build up the economic resources of the country. ... that is the problem and it has not been solved yet.'

> We failed to solve it. We frankly admit that. In the years immediately after the war we made very great efforts to build up fixed capital equipment and sacrificed our Parliamentary majority. Our name became identified with greyness and dullness, frugalities, shortages. ... We spent five years in doing what we thought was right, holding back present consumption, holding back immediate satisfaction, holding down the standard of living, to canalise and divert resources into building up the economy.
>
> Hon. Members may not agree at all about how it was done, but I think that there is no one on that side of the House who would deny that it was necessary to do that somehow. ... It was absolutely essential that personal consumption at that time should hold back so that we could try to build up the resources of the nation.
>
> So the problem for us today ... is to try to reconcile popular representative government with setting aside sufficient of the national income in order to expand productive resources. I say at once that the party opposite has failed as signally as we failed because its Parliamentary majority has been consistent with industrial stagnation. It has solved half the problem. It retained political popularity at the expense of the industrial resources of the nation.

In other words, Bevan suggested, overriding Conservative protests, the Tories had ridden back to power on a wave of shallow 'affluence' bought at the expense of the future.

No less a witness than 'Rab' Butler admitted many years later that Bevan's charge was essentially true.[34] But Bevan was not principally concerned to make party points. He went on to widen the argument, pointing out that the

---

* Appropriately, his very last intervention in the House was an argument with the new Speaker on a Point of Order (House of Commons, 2 December 1959, *Hansard*, vol. 614, cols 1186–9).

problem was especially difficult for the new democracies in less developed parts of the world.

> As a result of attempting to solve it, democratic government in Pakistan has collapsed, and democratic government in India, faced with exactly the same difficulties, is assailed by enemies from without and from within. It is, therefore, a very, very cruel dilemma that representative institutions have to face, especially in backward parts of the world.

Part of the solution, in Britain at least, Bevan suggested, lay in 'democratic education'. And here he drew a somewhat extraordinary but characteristic comparison with the Soviet Union.

> Whatever its defects – and there are many – there are very few citizens in the Soviet Union who are not aware of the relationship between personal and public consumption and who do not realise, grimly and oppressively, that it is necessary, if the economic foundations of society are to be expanded, that the basic industries must first have their share of the national income before personal consumption can rise very much.
>
> That process of education has not gone very far in this country, and in the last few years I am afraid that it has not proceeded to any extent at all. Indeed, there has been recently a disposition on the part of the people as a whole to take the cash in hand and waive the rest.

In a democracy, Bevan had always believed, democratic education was the job of Parliament. But now there was 'a considerable gulf growing between this House and the nation. ... We are not reaching the country to the extent that we did. ... The fact is that Parliamentary reporting has become a sheer travesty.' As a result, 'there do not exist at present in Britain the normal processes of democratic education that make the people aware of the problems which lie ahead of us, and of their own responsibilities'. To meet this situation he offered to an astonished House the heretical suggestion – surprising above all from one who so abhorred the medium – that Parliament should be televised. ('Oh no, Nye!' exclaimed one old Tory.)

> I know that hon. Members shake their heads, but why should they be so shy? Would it not be an excellent thing if, instead of speeches being made in comparative obscurity, and, in fact, never heard at all except by the few Members who assemble here to hear them, they were heard by their constituents? ... In these days when all the apparatus of mass suggestion are against democratic education, we should seriously consider re-establishing intelligent communication between the House of Commons and the electorate as a whole. That, surely, is a democratic process.

Has the case ever been more simply put? Yet twenty-seven years later, though the press reporting of Parliament has further declined to an extent that Bevan would not have believed possible, and the coverage of politics has become more and more trivialised, the House of Commons still continues to vote against the cameras. As a result, as he predicted, it has become more and

366

more remote from the life of the nation. Bevan's concern that Parliament should reflect the nation as closely as possible, that nothing should be hidden from it and that the House of Commons, rather than the streets, should be the forum in which the conflicts of society should be aired and resolved, had been a consistent theme of his career right back to the thirties, when he had raged at the National Government for shuffling off unemployment assistance to a non-elected board, and during the war, when he had insisted on bringing into the open all the doubts and fears, grudges and grievances which Churchill and the Coalition would rather have suppressed. Belief in the centrality of Parliament was at the very heart of his faith in democracy. He spoke on this occasion solely for himself, and attracted little support for a proposal which was too far ahead of its time to be greeted with anything but horror and derision. Nevertheless it was a far-sighted and appropriate swansong, in his last major parliamentary speech, that he should have called for the opening up to the public of the historic chamber which he had not merely adorned, but vitalised, for the previous thirty years.*

In the remainder of the speech Bevan poked some easy fun at Macmillan's incongruous appointment of Lord Hailsham as Minister of Science ('I am quite certain that when Mr Khrushchev heard that Lord Hailsham had been made responsible for the British answer to the Russian scientific challenge, a chill went right through the Kremlin. ... The Prime Minister has an absolute genius for putting flamboyant labels on empty luggage'), then returned to his main theme of how democratic Britain was going to meet the imagined challenge from Soviet planning. After the perceptiveness of his earlier remarks, his conclusion illustrates his unparalleled capacity throughout his career to combine great penetration with utter wrongheadedness. The difficulty of economic planning in a democracy, subject to a five-year electoral cycle, has proved a real problem, not only for socialists (though particularly, for some deep-seated reason, in Britain). But it was a fantasy to imagine that it was much easier, or that 'planning' was the recipe for guaranteed prosperity, in a dictatorship. It is an extraordinary thing, and a tribute to the power of the dogma which had formed his mind from an early age, that Bevan went to his grave believing in Khrushchev's boasts that Soviet economic growth was poised to leave the capitalist West struggling in its wake.

> Unless we plan our resources purposefully, unless we are prepared to accept the disciplines that are necessary, we shall not be able to meet the challenge of the Communist world. As the years go by, and the people see us languishing

---

* One of Bevan's strongest objections to the non-televising of Parliament was that it gave to the broadcasters the power of deciding which politicians should be invited to appear on television and radio. It was, he complained, 'a most humiliating state of affairs' that 'Members of the House are picked out to take part in television broadcasts at the *ipse dixit* of the bureaucracy at Broadcasting House.... In my opinion, there is something essentially squalid ... in Members of Parliament beginning increasingly to rely upon fees provided by bureaucrats in the BBC.' This criticism is as valid today.

behind, trying to prevent the evils of inflation by industrial stagnation, trying all the time to catch up with things because we have not acted soon enough – when they see the Communist world, planned, organised, publicly owned and flaunting its achievements to the rest of the world – they will come to be educated by what they will experience, they will realise that Western democracy is falling behind in the race because it is not prepared to read intelligently the lessons of the twentieth century.[35]

The picture of the British economy stagnating through the sixties and seventies is depressingly accurate; but, contrary to Bevan's assumption, it is emphatically not the Soviet Union that has been the international pacesetter but the capitalist economies, particularly of the Far East. The last prophecy which he left the House of Commons could hardly have been more comprehensively, but characteristically, flawed. For all the wonderful vigour of his mind; for all the seductive plausibility of his theorising; for all the democratic inspiration with which he humanised and sophisticated the crude Marxism which he imbibed in the South Wales of his youth, sadly it cannot be said that Bevan read correctly the lessons of the twentieth century.

Just after Christmas Bevan went into the Royal Free Hospital for an abdominal operation. It revealed a malignant cancer. The truth was kept from him, and he lived for another six months in the illusion that he would recover. In February he was able to return to Asheridge; in March he was able to give an interview to reporters, to whom he strenuously denied that he was writing his memoirs: 'I strongly disapprove of people in active public life writing their memoirs.'[36] He was still planning to be fit for the party Conference in October. Gaitskell's leadership was increasingly under attack: there were still those in the party who looked to Bevan to come back in the guise of saviour.[37] But it was not to be. After Easter he went into a decline; and on 6 July 1960 he died.

Epilogue: The Mantle of Nye

For a man who had been so violently abused for most of his life, almost as much by colleagues in his own party as by his political opponents, Bevan's death released an extraordinary outburst of national mourning. In the Tory press the memory that he had once called Conservatives 'lower than vermin' was forgiven, if not quite forgotten; the popular papers which had attacked him relentlessly as a dangerous extremist warped by ambition and class hatred now outbid one another with sorrowing headlines, picture spreads recalling his humble beginnings and stormy life, and sentimental articles. ('Farewell, Bright Spirit', wrote William Barklay in the *Daily Express*; 'Unmanageable, Incalculable, Adored – and Hated ... Bevan *was* the history of Socialism'.)[1] The *Daily Mirror* lost no time in setting up an Aneurin Bevan Memorial Fund. With some reason, Tom Driberg in *Reynolds' News* protested his 'disgust' at the sickly tributes to Nye's genius 'by journalists and politicians who, with a few exceptions, hated his guts, vilified and abused him throughout his career and, if of his own party, intrigued or voted for his expulsion from it'.[2] Driberg, however, was ungenerous. As the *Observer* remarked the same Sunday, 'The nation – and the Press – surprised itself by the extent of its real sorrow and sense of loss'.[3] It was suddenly recognised that Bevan's death was not merely 'a grievous loss to the Labour Party',[4] which left the Opposition 'immeasurably poorer' (*The Times*);[5] it was 'one of the biggest political tragedies of our times' (*Daily Mail*).[6] 'This man of leaping wit and towering personality was unquestionably one of Britain's great men' (*Daily Herald*).[7] The papers unexpectedly discovered that, with Churchill retired, 'the death of Nye Bevan deprives British politics of its greatest practising parliamentarian' (*News Chronicle*).[8]

'It is strange to think that he was once so hated,' the *Daily Express* reflected.[9] Now Bevan was celebrated as a brilliant orator, as a true democrat, as a much loved British character – even by Henry Fairlie in the *Daily Mail* as one of the last great patriots ('Why I Class Him with Winston Churchill').[10] In an effort to explain this posthumous canonisation of a man previously so reviled, much was made of his transformation in the last few years from the wrecker into the potential saviour of the Labour Party. 'The roistering, excitable crusader who more than once split the party had become the great unifying force,' wrote Walter Terry in the *Mail*. 'Where once he fought and argued, he latterly built up and strengthened'.[11] In the *Express*'s view, 'the passionate partisan had emerged as a shrewd, perceptive statesman. He had become a political genius who understood the art of the possible. The public sensed the change.' As a result, 'the bitterness which his name once provoked had given way to admiration and respect. ... The real tragedy of Aneurin Bevan is that he could have done so much more for Britain.'[12]

'It is a bitter irony', the *Guardian* suggested, 'for Labour to have lost Mr Bevan, so often the rebel, at just the moment when he might have been its best hope of preserving unity.'[13] There was a general consensus, inconceivable a few years before, that Bevan's death was a heavy blow to Gaitskell. At the same time the *Guardian* was one of the few papers to recall that 'for all his vitality and power as a politician, in the years since the war Mr Bevan was the despair more often than he was the hope of the Labour Party'.[14] The least forgiving of his persistent critics was the *News Chronicle*, which struck a discordant note amid the general acclaim by pointing out bluntly that Bevan 'was far from being the complete statesman. His judgement was bad and he lacked originality of thought – although never of phrase.'[15] A cool assessment in the same paper by Laurence Thompson concluded that 'the seeds of bitterness and emotional unbalance planted in him by his early experiences made him sometimes a little man when he was potentially a great one'.[16]

The tendency of all these comments, both the critical and the uncritical, was to present the mellow, statesmanlike Bevan of the past few years as the real man while diverting attention as tactfully as possible from the rest of his career – playing down his history of rebellion, expulsion and near-expulsion from the party either by romanticising it as the product of a poor background and a warm heart or by regretting it as youthful folly, happily cast aside in his maturity. No paper, except *Tribune*, even hinted at the alternative view that the first fifty-eight years of Bevan's life might have represented the true Bevan and the last four merely the tired aberration of a man who had lost his way. In this way his life was emptied of its meaning. The view was practically universal that the anger which had fired him was now obsolete, for the social transformation he had striven for had been accomplished. Laurence Thompson saw him as 'the last of a great line of British working-class intellectuals', citing Lansbury, Fred Jowett and Maxton as other examples; their successors in Macmillan's Britain now went via grammar school to university and into the professions.[17] In the London *Evening News* the Tory MP Charles Curran saw him likewise as 'the last of the demagogues': 'In the coalfield from which he came, Marx and Engels have been supplanted by Marks and Spencer; and the sound of class war is drowned by the hum of the spin dryer.' He concluded: 'There will be no more Aneurin Bevans.'[18]

This was true. But the assumption that Bevan would have seen this as success, or regarded the spin dryer in every kitchen as the victory of socialism, was profoundly untrue. On the contrary he regarded the hire-purchase society as the negation of socialism: a squalid bribe by which the working class had been tricked by the cunning Tories – shamefully abetted by an emasculated Labour Party and the short-sightedness of the unions – into surrendering their historic birthright. Bevan was indeed the last of a line; but that did not mean that the cause he fought for had been won. On the contrary it had been lost. He was a socialist of an old-fashioned sort, at once moralistic and mechanistic, which was outdated in the cynical and opportunist climate of the 1950s. Although relatively young, Bevan had learned his socialism at such an early age, before 1914, that he was effectively of the same generation as Attlee and Morrison, and similarly bemused by the consumer society into which their welfare socialism had unexpectedly evolved. They were all, in their rather different ways, products of the late Victorian age of earnest social optimism, imbued with a high-minded belief in the possibility of making men better – not merely better off – by social engineering. Attlee and Morrison were able to retire, their work done, before the consumer society got into its stride. But Bevan had the misfortune to be overtaken by forces he did not understand while still in his fifties and in active politics. He died, still only sixty-two but thoroughly out of sympathy with the age into which he had survived, with the bitter knowledge that all he had struggled for and believed inevitable had not, and now almost certainly would not, come to pass. Yet no sense of Bevan's disillusion with the direction society had taken since 1950 comes through his obituaries. In celebrating the man, Fleet Street preferred to forget what he had stood for. Thus in the moment of his death was born a conspiracy to strip his legacy of its uncomfortable content of fundamentalist Socialism, a process gratefully continued by those in the Labour Party who called themselves his heirs.

Very quickly the Mantle of Nye became the essential attribute to which any aspiring Labour leader must lay claim. It became *de rigueur* at Labour Conferences in the sixties to quote Bevan as it was at Tory ones to quote Churchill. No one was more skilful at wrapping himself in these borrowed clothes than Harold Wilson. Many former Bevanites suspected in retrospect that this had been his game ever since 1951, when his resignation with Nye had seemed to owe more to calculation of his personal advantage, stimulated by jealousy of Gaitskell, than to conviction; in so far as it was genuine it was based on technical doubts as to the economic practicality of rearmament rather than any principled objection to Health Service charges. Certainly the author of the famous 'bonfire of controls' was never a doctrinaire socialist. But he succeeded in milking his resignation for all it was worth, becoming chairman of the Bevanite group between 1951 and 1953, securing election to the National Executive on the Bevanite ticket in 1952 and allowing himself to be associated with the left on relatively minor issues like German rearmament, trade with Eastern Europe and aid for the under-developed world while hedging his position on nationalisation and defence. Above all he had made friends and built up loyalties on the left which he somehow managed to retain even after he stepped into Bevan's place in the Shadow Cabinet in April 1954 and moved more and more openly towards the centre. When Bevan died, Wilson had already so positioned himself that he had the leadership of the left virtually tied up. In the debate on Clause IV of the party constitution he defended the status quo, not on fundamentalist grounds but on the ground of not needlessly offending the fundamentalists; in the still more bitter row over nuclear weapons he took up a similarly fudged position against the 'divisiveness' of Gaitskell's stand. He was thus able to stand against Gaitskell for the party leadership in November 1960, drawing on his Bevanite associations from 1951 to secure the left's vote while simultaneously invoking Bevan's 1959 appeal to unity to attract the centre. He did not win, but he put down the marker that enabled him to beat George Brown and Jim Callaghan when Gaitskell unexpectedly died in 1963.[19]

Crossman's diary vividly records the sense of a new dawn which Wilson's election aroused in his old associates who still liked to think of themselves as Bevanites.[20] Of course Crossman had for some time been no more of a genuine left-winger than Wilson himself. But the *Tribune* loyalists were hardly less excited. For the 1964 General Election Michael Foot wrote a campaign biography of Wilson so crassly eulogistic that subsequently, when disillusion followed, he excluded it from his entry in *Who's Who*.[21] Given that Foot had succeeded to Bevan's Ebbw Vale seat in 1960 and had already published in 1962 the first volume of his biography of Bevan he could scarcely have invested Wilson more explicitly or more formally with the Mantle. Though Wilson was careful in forming his Government to keep a balance between left and right – former Bevanites and former Gaitskellites – it is clear, from Crossman's diary and Barbara Castle's, that he knew who his friends were. His rooted suspicion of senior Ministers like Brown, Roy Jenkins and Tony Crosland who had been Gaitskellites was so extreme as to cripple any sense of comradeship. At moments of crisis the Prime Minister's trust was placed exclusively in his old cronies from Bevanite days – Crossman and Castle, Thomas Balogh – and younger adherents like Peter Shore.[22] The 1951 divide continued to run right down the middle of the 1964–70 Government. Yet it was not a policy divide. Wilson and his 'Bevanite' allies did not press any recognisably Bevanite policies against the opposition of their 'Gaitskellite' colleagues.

He was adept, certainly, at making symbolic gestures. Prescription charges were immediately abolished (only to be restored in 1968). Barbara Castle was made Minister for Overseas Development, and Jennie Lee Minister for the Arts; both were significant new departures, but neither went to the heart of economic policy or did much to advance socialism. The Department of Economic Affairs appeared to be created to do that, implementing Bevan's old hankering to take economic planning away from the Treasury; but it was given no real powers and after George Brown's departure in 1966 retained only a shadowy existence until it was quietly wound up in 1969. The only measure of nationalisation promised in 1964 or undertaken in office was the renationalisation of steel. Of any intention of creating a socialist Britain in any sense in which Bevan would have understood the word, the 1964 Government was entirely innocent.

The Bevan legacy was now reduced to a sense of lost fire, represented by Foot fulminating from the back benches against Wilson's failed technocracy, wage restraint and support for the Americans in Vietnam. (Characteristically Wilson responded to the latter by sending an amiable old Bevanite, Harold Davies, to Hanoi to try to patch up peace.) Of the former Bevanites in the Cabinet, only Barbara Castle still gave off any glow of radicalism; but in 1968 she too compromised her credentials with the left by her attempted trade union legislation (to which, characteristically again, she gave the spuriously Bevanite title *In Place of Strife*). The old left's disillusion was well expressed by the former business manager of *Tribune* and veteran of countless protest marches, Peggy Duff, in her memoirs *Left, Left, Left*, published in 1971:

> The Gaitskells, those who opposed Nye and, later, many of those who stood with him, saw Labour achieving power and retaining it only through a more efficient, technological management of a capitalist society. A little more gentle to the poor, a little less racist to the coloured people, a little more compliant to the United States, a little more capable of raising the GNP. No fire this time or next time. Fire died with Aneurin.[23]

But what did fire mean? Very little. What use was fire in the belly without a coherent analysis of what was wrong with welfare capitalism and a clear programme to set Labour back on the road to socialism? When Labour returned to office in 1974 and Michael Foot joined the Government to symbolise that the rift of 1964–70 had been healed, his contribution turned out to be finding out what the leaders of the biggest trade unions wanted and giving it to them. Anything further from Bevan's understanding of socialism it would be hard to imagine. But by now the sentimental old Bevanites of the *Tribune* left had been outflanked by the hard men of a new left, disingenuously led by the born-again Tony Benn, intent not only on putting socialism back on the agenda for the first time since 1945, but on imposing it on the party and the country by organised 'entryism' and an intolerant form of democratic centralism.

The dominance of the new left after 1979 led Labour to schism in 1981 and electoral disaster in 1983, under the now sadly bedraggled leadership of Michael Foot. From that low point its fortunes have been partially revived by a new leader once more draping himself in the Mantle of Nye. As a matter of fact Neil Kinnock has a strong geographical claim to the mantle; he is not merely Welsh but was actually brought up in Tredegar – in Bevan's birthplace, in Bevan's constituency, in a council bungalow built by Bevan as Minister of Health. He can still remember copies of *In Place of Fear* piled up in shop windows and selling like hot cakes. As long ago as 1978 he was asked to write a preface to a paperback reissue; and for years he has been contracted to another publisher for an anthology of Bevanisms to be entitled *What Nye Said*.[24] Yet once again the descent he seeks to claim from Bevan is largely spurious. As leader he is trying to recreate that vague sense of generous humanity which is the attribute most fondly associated with Bevan's memory. And he is trying to restore Labour's battered credentials as a democratic party. But he is doing this at the expense of its commitment to socialism. His overriding concern, quite candidly, is to be elected, and he is well aware that in the present political climate socialism is a liability. More explicitly even than Gaitskell or Wilson in 1959 or 1964, he is out to recapture the middle ground now occupied by the SDP/Liberal Alliance. To do this he is employing all the resources of slick public relations to promote Labour once again as the sensible, moderate, caring party by contrast with the callous Tories, and he is willing to stamp as hard as necessary on the left to keep socialism off the party's banner. This is the opposite response to Bevan's repeated calls in the late 1950s, during a similar period of Conservative ascendancy, to go back to fundamentals and rekindle the electorate's understanding of Labour's distinctive vision by 'socialist education'. Far from wishing to encourage the restatement of socialist aims for the 1990s, Kinnock wishes only that the ideologues should pipe down and stop rocking the boat. Socialism in any meaningful form whatever is once more firmly shelved. The one issue on which Kinnock seems determined not to compromise is, ironically, the one on which Bevan did disappoint the left: nuclear disarmament.

This may or may not be good politics. Labour may win the next election or it may not; Kinnock may discover a clear sense of direction in office, or he may flounder. But what his leadership has most starkly highlighted is the steep decline over the last thirty years in the serious content of political debate. Perhaps Macmillan started it; Bevan early recognised him for a shallow political conjuror and loathed him for it. But Wilson was Macmillan's apt pupil, and the slide into mere image politics gathered pace in the sixties. Margaret Thatcher, though no intellectual, has been a partial exception, at least marshalling her expensive public relations to project a clear view of the alternative society she would like to offer. But Labour – whether out of confusion or electoral calculation – has failed abjectly to take up the challenge; and democracy has suffered. Here, even more than in his failure to make Britain a socialist society or Labour a socialist party, was where Bevan's life was really lived in vain. Even above socialism he believed passionately in democracy, and he believed that the vitality of democracy depended upon the serious discussion by an informed electorate of opposed philosophies and a real choice between rival visions of the future. Even in his own day he considered the newspapers to be filled with pornography and royalty, thought the level of reporting of Parliament a disgrace and feared for democracy's survival in a climate of such desperate triviality. What he would have thought of the popular press of the 1980s, of the abdication even by the 'quality' papers of the job of parliamentary reporting, of the instant politics of the television studio and the universal obsession with the latest opinion poll beggars the imagination. Of all his obituarists, as they weighed up his qualities and his faults, only Henry Fairlie seized on this particular aspect of Bevan's contribution to his time:

> The overwhelming impression that remains is of a man of size, a man whose intellect was capacious, lively and illuminating, a man whose emotions were strong and human, a man who believed greatly in his country and who believed also, which is rare in these days, in the power of ideas, a man who strove to retain the predominance of politics over economics or mass-psychology.

For this, in the end, is what we owe to politicians like him.

A democracy cannot survive healthily without the example of individual leaders who dare all as individuals and leave, long after their failures are forgotten, the imprint of a great human being.[25]

Whether Nye Bevan actually left such an imprint on posterity as his contemporaries imagined it has been the argument of this book to doubt. The Mantle of Nye is today a pretty threadbare garment. In his life, Bevan proved to be mistaken in his confident anticipation of the course of history. He was unable to persuade his fellow-countrymen, even in his own party, to share his vision of the right way forward for Britain and the world. In death his memory has been more honoured, but at the same time more subtly traduced, than he ever was in life. Yet Fairlie was surely right. As well as a rare humanity and gaiety, intelligence, anger and wit, Bevan brought to the life of politics a passionate seriousness which no one who has come after him has begun to match. If to be irreplaceable is to be great, Bevan was a great man after all.

Notes

Introduction

1 Michael Foot, *Aneurin Bevan, 1945–1960* (Davis Poynter 1973), Paladin edition (1975) p. 625.
2 *Labour Party Annual Conference Report, 1949*, 169–72.

Chapter One: The Education of a Socialist

1 Aneurin Bevan, *In Place of Fear* (MacGibbon & Kee 1952), Quartet edition (1978), p. 22.
2 D.J.Davies, *Ninety Years of Endeavour: The Tredegar Workmen's Hall, 1861–1951*.
3 House of Commons, 7 April 1937 (*Hansard*, vol. 322, cols 252–7).
4 Jack London, *The Iron Heel* (1907), (Journeyman Press 1984), p. 20.
5 Ibid., p. 121.
6 Ibid., p. 63.
7 House of Commons, 21 January 1954 (*Hansard*, vol. 522, cols 1219–20).
8 *Daily Express*, n.d. 1932, quoted in Michael Foot, *Aneurin Bevan, 1897–1945* (MacGibbon & Kee 1962), Paladin edition (1975) p. 23.
9 House of Commons, 21 January 1954 (*Hansard*, vol. 522, cols 1219–20).
10 Foot, op. cit., p. 37.
11 *The Miners' Next Step*, quoted in Bob Holton, *British Syndicalism, 1900–1914: Myths and Realities* (Pluto Press 1976), p. 86.
12 Bevan, op. cit., p. 40.
13 Richard Jones, quoted in Foot, op. cit. (1975 edition only), pp. 34–6.
14 Harold Finch, *Memoirs of a Bedwellty MP* (Sterling Press, Risca, Newport, Monmouthshire 1972), p. 21.
15 W.W.Craik, *The Central Labour College, 1909–24* (Lawrence & Wishart 1964), pp. 123–4.
16 George Phippen, quoted in Foot, op. cit. (1975 edition only), p. 40n.
17 *Plebs*, January 1921, pp. 19–21.

Chapter Two: The Miners' Struggle

1 Hywel Francis and David Smith, *The Fed: A History of the South Wales Miners in the Twentieth Century* (Lawrence & Wishart 1980), pp. 31–2, 48.

Notes

2 'Celticus' (Aneurin Bevan MP), *Why Not Trust The Tories?* (Fanfare Press, 1944), pp. 22–3.
3 Aneurin Bevan, *In Place of Fear* (MacGibbon & Kee 1952), Quartet edition (1978), pp. 40–1.
4 Ibid.
5 House of Commons, n.d. 1947 (quoted in *Daily Mail*, 21 August 1947).
6 Bevan, *In Place of Fear*, p. 45.
7 House of Commons, (*Hansard*, vol. 307, cols 1828–32).
8 *South Wales Weekly Argus*, 8 April 1922.
9 Quoted in Michael Foot, *Aneurin Bevan, 1897–1945* (MacGibbon & Kee 1962), Paladin edition (1975), p. 56.
10 *South Wales Weekly Argus*, n.d. 1925 (quoted in Foot, op. cit., p. 58).
11 D.J.Davies, *Ninety Years of Endeavour: The Tredegar Workmen's Hall, 1861–1951.*
12 *Daily News*, 19 March 1930.
13 Harold Finch, *Memoirs of a Bedwellty MP* (Sterling Press, Risca, Newport, Monmouthshire, 1972), pp. 33–5.
14 Bevan, *In Place of Fear*, pp. 45–6.
15 Francis and Smith, op. cit., pp. 55–7.
16 Foot, op. cit., pp. 74–5.
17 MFGB Delegate Conference, London, 30 July 1926 (p. 38).
18 Ibid., 16 August 1926 (pp. 40–1).
19 Ibid., 7 October 1926 (pp. 37–8).
20 Ibid., 4 November 1926 (pp. 27–8).
21 Ibid., 13 November 1926 (pp. 84–5).
22 Ibid., 19 November 1926 (pp. 24–5).
23 Francis and Smith, op. cit., p. 76.
24 Bevan, *In Place of Fear*, p. 46.
25 Davies, op. cit.
26 Sian Rhiannon Williams, 'The Bedwellty Board of Guardians and the Default Act of 1927', *Llafur*, vol. 2, no. 4 (1979).
27 Foot, op. cit., p. 84.
28 *South Wales Weekly Argus*, 22 March 1924 (quoted in Foot, op. cit., p. 69).
29 Finch, op. cit., p. 54.
30 W.W.Craik, *Bryn Roberts and the N.U.P.E.* (Allen & Unwin 1955), p. 5.
31 Foot, op. cit., p. 70.
32 *Western Mail*, 12 March 1928.
33 Foot, op. cit., p. 86.
34 *Western Mail*, 12 March 1928.
35 House of Commons, 15 December 1943 (*Hansard*, vol. 395, cols 1616–17).
36 Gordon Lang (Monmouth ILP) to E.T.John, 28 November 1923, quoted in J.GrahamJones, 'Evan Davies and Ebbw Vale: A Note', *Llafur*, vol. 3, no. 3 (1982).
37 Archie Lush interview, quoted in Jones, op. cit.
38 *Western Mail*, 18 March 1929.
39 *South Wales Weekly Argus*, 30 March 1929.
40 Foot, op. cit., p. 97.
41 *The Times*, 1 June 1929.
42 James Griffiths, quoted in Jones, op. cit.
43 *Daily Herald*, 21 June 1929.

Chapter Three: MacDonald, Mosley and the Débâcle of 1931

1 House of Commons, 10 July 1929 (*Hansard*, vol. 229, cols 874–5).
2 Ibid., 16 July 1929 (vol. 230, cols 338–43).
3 Ibid., 23 July 1929 (vol. 230, cols 1191–6).
4 Ibid., 13 November 1929 (vol. 231, cols 2125–38).
5 Ibid., 27 February 1930 (vol. 235, cols 2462–8).
6 Ibid., 5 December 1929 (vol. 232, cols 2693–7).
7 Bevan recalled this episode in the House of Commons on 23 July 1953 (vol. 518, cols 598–611).
8 Jennie Lee, *My Life With Nye* (Jonathan Cape 1980), Penguin edition (1981), p. 82.
9 Hugh Thomas, *John Strachey* (Eyre Methuen 1973), p. 89.
10 Robert Skidelsky, *Oswald Mosley* (Macmillan 1975), p. 162.
11 Ibid.
12 Ibid., p. 173.
13 Ibid., p. 174.
14 Ibid., p. 136.
15 Ibid., pp. 192–4.
16 House of Commons, 4 November 1930 (*Hansard*, vol. 244, cols 754–62).
17 Ibid.
18 Skidelsky, op. cit., p. 237.
19 Ibid.
20 *Manchester Guardian*, 10 December 1930.
21 *Daily Herald*, 8 December 1930.
22 Skidelsky, op. cit., p. 241.
23 Jennie Lee, *Tomorrow Is a New Day* (Cresset Press 1939), p. 151.
24 House of Commons, 15 July 1931 (*Hansard*, vol. 255, cols 531–9).
25 Ibid., 24 May 1932 (vol. 266, cols 221–7).
26 Thomas, op. cit., pp. 107–8.
27 House of Commons, 18 September 1931 (*Hansard*, vol. 256, cols 1214–21).
28 Ibid., 21 September 1931 (vol. 256, cols 1332–9).

Chapter Four: The Aftermath of 1931

1 House of Commons, 4 December 1933 (*Hansard*, vol. 283, cols 1309–24).
2 Aneurin Bevan, *In Place of Fear* (MacGibbon & Kee 1952), Quartet edition (1978), p. 23.
3 Michael Foot, *Aneurin Bevan 1897–1945* (MacGibbon & Kee 1962), Paladin edition (1975), pp. 152–5.
4 Robert Rhodes James (ed.), *Chips: The Diaries of Sir Henry Channon* (Weidenfeld & Nicolson 1967), p. 120 (22–3 April 1937).
5 House of Commons, 10 December 1931 (*Hansard*, vol. 260, cols 2150–9).
6 Ibid., 3 December 1934 (vol. 295, cols 1303–14).
7 Ibid.
8 Ibid., 6 December 1934 (vol. 295, cols 1942–6).
9 Ibid., 14 November 1932 (vol. 270, cols 830–9).

10 Ibid., 2 May 1934 (vol. 289, cols 404–12).
11 Ibid., 5 April 1932 (vol. 264, cols 63–72).
12 Ibid., 22 July 1936 (vol. 315, cols 595).
13 Ibid., 9 November 1932 (vol. 270, cols 398–411).
14 Ibid., 14 November 1932 (vol. 270, cols 830–9).
15 Ibid., 26 November 1931 (vol. 260, cols 624–33).
16 Ibid., 5 April 1932 (vol. 264, cols 63–72).
17 Ibid., 23 November 1931 (vol. 260, cols 106–10).
18 Ibid., 13 March 1933 (vol. 275, cols 1674–84).
19 Ibid., 7 February 1933 (vol. 274, cols 88–95).
20 Ibid., 11 March 1936 (vol. 309, cols 2180–6).
21 Ibid., 8 June 1934 (vol. 290, cols 1271–9).
22 Ibid., 19 June 1935 (vol. 303, cols 458–64).
23 Ibid., 23 July 1935 (vol. 304, cols 1756–68).
24 Ibid., 11 March 1936 (vol. 309, cols 2180–6).
25 Ibid., 8 December 1936 (vol. 318, cols 1912–21).
26 Ibid., 23 May 1932 (vol. 266, cols 37–45).
27 Ibid., 18 April 1934 (vol. 288, cols 1074–81).
28 Ibid., 10 July 1933 (vol. 280, cols 810–20).
29 Ibid., 9 November 1932 (vol. 270, cols 398–411).
30 Ibid., 12 April 1933 (vol. 276, cols 2692–8).
31 Ibid., 22 June 1936 (vol. 313, cols 1531–8).
32 Ibid., 27 April 1933 (vol. 277, cols 309–23).
33 Ibid., 5 April 1933 (vol. 276, cols 1837–48).
34 Ibid., 27 April 1933 (vol. 277, cols 309–23).
35 Ibid., 26 March 1934 (vol. 287, cols 1742–7).
36 Ibid., 4 December 1933 (vol. 283, cols 1309–24).
37 Ibid., 11 December 1933 (vol. 284, cols 139–49).
38 Ibid., 9 June 1932 (vol. 266, cols 2151–5).
39 Ibid., 15 July 1931 (vol. 255, cols 531–9).
40 Ibid., 28 April 1936 (vol. 311, cols 779–82).
41 Ibid., 22 April 1937 (vol. 322, cols 2122–4).
42 Ibid., 7 February 1933 (vol. 274, col. 91).
43 Ibid., 22 March 1936 (vol. 310, cols 921–5).
44 *The Times*, 8 September 1933.
45 Foot, op. cit., p. 172.
46 *Socialist*, November 1936 (quoted in Ben Pimlott, *Labour and the Left in the 1930s* (Cambridge 1977), p. 93).
47 *The Times*, 9 November 1936.
48 Jennie Lee, *Tomorrow Is a New Day* (Cresset Press 1939), p. 151.
49 Foot, op. cit., p. 156.
50 *Labour Party Annual Conference Report, 1934*, pp. 138–9.
51 Ibid., pp. 140–1.

Chapter Five: 'Bollinger Bolshevik, Lounge-Lizard Lenin'

1 W.E.D.Allen to Bevan, quoted in Michael Foot, *Aneurin Bevan, 1897–1945* (MacGibbon & Kee 1962), Paladin edition (1975), p. 187n.

2 Tom Clarke, *My Lloyd George Diary* (Methuen 1939), p. 164.
3 *Evening Standard*, 8 August 1958.
4 Foot, op. cit., p. 185.
5 Bevan to Beaverbrook, 11 March 1932 (Beaverbrook papers C/37).
6 Bevan to Beaverbrook, 14 May 1935 (loc. cit.).
7 Jennie Lee, *My Life With Nye* (Jonathan Cape 1980), Penguin edition (1981), p. 117.
8 Ibid., p. 120.
9 *Daily Express*, 26 October 1934.
10 *Sunday Chronicle*, 27 December 1936.
11 José Enrique Rodo, *Ariel* (Houghton Mifflin 1922), pp. 26–7, 33–4.
12 Ibid., pp. 68–9.
13 Ibid., p. 80.
14 Ibid., pp. 112–13.
15 Ibid., p. 117.
16 Ibid., p. 131.
17 'Watchman', *Right Honourable Gentlemen* (Right Book Club 1940), pp. 213–14.

Chapter Six: Fascism and the Approach of War

1 House of Commons, 28 November 1934 (*Hansard*, vol. 295, cols 933–9).
2 *Labour Party Annual Conference Report, 1936*, pp. 177–8.
3 *Tribune*, 1 January 1937.
4 Ibid., 29 January 1937.
5 Ibid., 5 February 1937.
6 Ibid., 12 February 1937.
7 Ibid., 19 February 1937.
8 Ibid., 19 March 1937.
9 *Labour Party Annual Conference Report, 1937*, pp. 208–9.
10 Ibid., p. 211.
11 *Tribune*, 29 October 1937.
12 Ibid., 19 November 1937.
13 Ibid., 5 November 1937.
14 House of Commons, 22 July 1936 (*Hansard*, vol. 315, cols 865–79).
15 *Tribune*, 12 March 1937.
16 Ibid., 18 June 1937.
17 Ibid., 9 July 1937.
18 Ibid., 23 December 1937.
19 Ibid., 18 March 1938.
20 Speech at Pontypool, 1 May 1938; quoted in Michael Foot, *Aneurin Bevan, 1897–1945* (MacGibbon & Kee 1962), Paladin edition (1975), p. 280.
21 *Tribune*, 12 November 1937.
22 Ibid., 25 February 1938.
23 House of Commons, 4 May 1939 (*Hansard*, vol. 346, cols 2131–40).
24 *Tribune*, 4 February 1938.
25 Ibid., 8 April 1938.

Notes

26 Ibid., 7 October 1938.
27 Ibid., 25 November 1938.
28 Ibid., 16 December 1938.
29 Ibid., 9 December 1938.
30 House of Commons, 20 December 1938 (*Hansard*, vol. 342, cols 2759–66).
31 Speech at the Queen's Hall, 25 January 1939, quoted in Foot, op. cit., p. 289.
32 *Tribune*, 10 March 1939.
33 Speech at Welwyn Garden City, 5 March 1939 (*The Times*, 6 March 1939).
34 *Tribune*, 6 April 1939.
35 Ibid., 26 May 1939.
36 *The Times*, 31 May 1939.
37 *Tribune*, 3 March 1939.
38 House of Commons, 4 May 1939 (*Hansard*, vol. 346, cols 2131–40).
39 Ibid., 2 August 1939 (vol. 350, cols 2454–7).
40 Ibid., 24 August 1939 (vol. 351, cols 55–9).
41 *Tribune*, 8 September 1939.

Chapter Seven: Backs to the Wall

1 See T.D.Burridge, *British Labour and Hitler's War* (Deutsch 1976), pp. 25–36.
2 *Tribune*, 24 November 1939.
3 Ibid., 1 December 1939.
4 Ibid., 17 and 24 November 1939, 5 January 1940.
5 House of Commons, 24 October 1939 (*Hansard*, vol. 352, cols 1286–91); *Tribune*, 5 April 1940.
6 *Tribune*, 5 January 1940.
7 Ibid., 3 November 1939.
8 Ibid., 2 February 1940.
9 Ibid., 26 January 1940.
10 House of Commons, 25 April 1940 (*Hansard*, vol. 360, cols 460–8).
11 Sonia Orwell and Ian Angus (eds), *The Collected Essays, Journalism and Letters of George Orwell* (Secker & Warburg 1968), Penguin edition (1970) vol. 2, p. 351, and vol. 4, p. 277.
12 *Tribune*, 17 May 1940.
13 Ibid., 21 June 1940.
14 Ibid.
15 Ibid., 21 and 28 June, 5 July 1940.
16 Ibid., 17 May 1940.
17 Ibid., 21 and 28 June, 5 July 1940.
18 Ibid., 21 June 1940.
19 Ibid., 24 May 1940.
20 House of Commons, 23 July 1940 (*Hansard*, vol. 363, cols 727–34).
21 Ibid., 8 October 1940 (vol. 365, cols 345–50).
22 Ibid., 15 August 1940 (vol. 364, col. 964).
23 *Tribune*, 30 August 1940.
24 Michael Foot, *Aneurin Bevan, 1897–1945* (MacGibbon & Kee 1962), Paladin edition (1975), p. 302n.

25 House of Commons, 8 October 1940 (vol. 365, cols 345–50).
26 *Tribune*, 30 August 1940.
27 Ibid., 18 October 1940.
28 Ibid., 14 February 1941.
29 House of Commons, 5 November 1940 (*Hansard*, vol. 365, cols 1297–1303).
30 *Tribune*, 13 September 1940.
31 House of Commons, 28 January 1941 (*Hansard*, vol. 368, cols 463–79).
32 *Tribune*, 4 and 25 October, 13 December 1940, 3 January 1941.
33 Ibid., 4 and 11 October 1940.
34 Ibid., 11 October 1940.
35 Ibid., 3 January 1941.
36 Ibid., 8 November 1940.
37 House of Commons, 13 February 1941 (*Hansard*, vol. 368, cols 1598–1605).
38 *Tribune*, 7 February 1941.
39 Ibid., 6 June 1941.
40 Sir John Wheeler-Bennett (ed.), *Action This Day: Working with Churchill* (Macmillan 1968), p. 69.
41 *Tribune*, 27 June 1941.
42 Ibid., 18 July 1941.
43 Ibid., 27 June 1941.
44 Ibid., 18 July 1941.
45 Ibid., 18 July 1941.
46 Winston S.Churchill, *War Speeches* (Cassell 1951), vol. I, pp. 452–4.
47 House of Commons, 24 June 1941 (*Hansard*, vol. 372, cols 992–4).
48 *Tribune*, 4 July 1941.
49 Ibid., 5 September 1941.
50 Ibid.
51 Ibid., 10 October 1941.
52 Ibid., 1 August 1941.
53 House of Commons, 5 August 1941 (*Hansard*, vol. 373, cols 1838–44).
54 Ibid., 23 October 1941 (vol. 374, cols 1972–82).
55 *Tribune*, 21 March 1941.
56 House of Commons, 23 October 1941 (vol. 374, cols 1972–82).
57 Ibid., 12 November 1942 (vol. 385, cols 130–9).
58 Ibid., 18 December 1941 (vol. 376, cols 2202–6).

Chapter Eight: Bevan at War

1 *Tribune*, 5 December 1941.
2 Sonia Orwell and Ian Angus (eds), *The Collected Essays, Journalism and Letters of George Orwell* (Secker & Warburg 1968), Penguin edition (1970) vol. 3, p. 409.
3 *Tribune*, 31 January 1947; Orwell and Angus, op. cit., vol. 4, pp. 276–80.
4 Orwell and Angus, op. cit., vol. 3, pp. 206–7; see also Bernard Crick, *George Orwell: A Life* (Secker & Warburg 1980), Penguin edition (1982), p. 481.
5 T.R.Fyvel, *George Orwell: A Personal Memoir* (Weidenfeld & Nicolson 1982), p. 140.

6 Ibid., p. 125.
7 Hugh Dalton diary, 11 June 1941.
8 Ibid., 5 February 1942; *Tribune*, 27 February 1942.
9 *Tribune*, 24 July 1942; Nigel Nicolson (ed.), *Harold Nicolson: Diaries and Letters, 1939–45* (Collins 1967), Fontana edition (1970), p. 276 (28 January 1943).
10 Nicolson, op. cit., p. 242 (26 September 1942).
11 Ibid., p. 192 (4 December 1941).
12 Lord Butler, *The Art of Memory* (Hodder & Stoughton 1982), p. 79.
13 Jean Nicol, *Meet Me at the Savoy* (Museum Press 1955), p. 68.
14 Michael Foot, *Aneurin Bevan, 1897–1945* (MacGibbon & Kee 1962), Paladin edition (1975), p. 463.
15 Michael Foot, *Aneurin Bevan, 1945–1960* (Davis Poynter 1973), Paladin edition (1975), p. 43.
16 Ibid.

Chapter Nine: 'Squalid Nuisance'

1 *Tribune*, 30 January 1942.
2 Ibid., 6 March 1942.
3 Ibid., 13 March 1942.
4 Ibid., 10 October 1941.
5 Ibid., 13 March 1942.
6 See Paul Addison, *The Road To 1945* (Jonathan Cape 1975), pp. 156–9.
7 *Tribune*, 8 May 1942.
8 *Labour Party Annual Conference Report, 1942*, pp. 147–9.
9 *Tribune*, 1 and 8 May 1942.
10 Ibid., 15 May 1942.
11 Ibid.
12 House of Commons, 1 July 1942 (*Hansard*, vol. 381, cols 224–37, 237–48).
13 Ibid., 2 July 1942 (vol. 382, cols 527–40).
14 Ibid., 2 July 1942 (vol. 382, cols 540–1, 550).
15 Nigel Nicolson (ed.), *Harold Nicolson: Diaries and Letters, 1939–1945* (Collins 1967), Fontana edition (1970), pp. 229–30 (2 July 1942).
16 House of Commons, 2 July 1942 (*Hansard*, vol. 382, cols 583–610).
17 Nicolson, op. cit., pp. 229–30.
18 Lord Butler, *The Art of Memory* (Hodder & Stoughton 1982), p. 85.
19 *Tribune*, 7 August 1942.
20 Ibid., 17 July 1942.
21 Ibid., 23 October 1942.
22 House of Commons, 9 September 1942 (*Hansard*, vol. 383, cols 240–9).
23 *Tribune*, 24 June 1942.
24 A.J.P. Taylor, *Beaverbrook* (Hamish Hamilton 1972), Penguin edition (1974), p. 680.
25 House of Commons, 12 November 1942 (*Hansard*, vol. 385, cols 130–9).
26 *The Times*, 10 November 1943.
27 House of Commons, 12 November 1942 (*Hansard*, vol. 385, cols 130–9).

28 Ibid.
29 *Tribune*, 13 November 1942.
30 Ibid., 11 December 1942.
31 Ibid., 1 January 1943.
32 Ibid., 21 May 1943.
33 Ibid., 15 May 1943.
34 House of Commons, 15 December 1943 (*Hansard*, vol. 395, cols 1615–27).
35 Ibid., 3 August 1943 (vol. 391, cols 2201–13).
36 *Tribune*, 20 August 1943.
37 Ibid., 3 September 1943.
38 Ibid., 21 May 1943.
39 House of Commons, 18 July 1944 (*Hansard*, vol. 402, cols 68–80).
40 Ibid., 29 September 1944 (vol. 403, cols 627–36).
41 *Tribune*, 29 September 1944.
42 Ibid., 20 April 1945.
43 Ibid., 12 January 1945.
44 House of Commons, 15 December 1943 (*Hansard*, vol. 395, cols 1615–27).
45 *Tribune*, 7 April 1944.
46 Ibid., 2 February 1945.
47 Ibid., 8 December 1944, 7 April 1944.
48 Ibid., 2 February 1945.
49 Ibid., 7 April 1944.
50 House of Commons, 2 August 1944 (*Hansard*, vol. 402, cols 1436–9).
51 Ibid., 18 July 1944 (vol. 402, cols 68–80).
52 *Tribune*, 20 August 1943.

Chapter Ten: Labour's Reckoning

 1 *Tribune*, 11 December 1942.
 2 Ibid., 30 October 1942.
 3 Ibid., 4 December 1942.
 4 Ibid., 15 January 1943.
 5 Paul Addison, *The Road to 1945* (Jonathan Cape 1975), pp. 226–8.
 6 *Tribune*, 11 June 1943.
 7 Ibid., 18 June 1943.
 8 Ibid., 17 December 1943.
 9 The phrase is Arthur Marwick's: see Arthur Marwick, *Britain in the Century of Total War* (Bodley Head 1968), Penguin edition (1970), p. 313.
10 *Tribune*, 11 February 1944.
11 House of Commons, 23 June 1944 (*Hansard*, vol. 401, cols 525–32).
12 *Tribune*, 25 October 1940.
13 *Plan For Britain: A Collection of Essays Prepared for the Fabian Society* (Routledge 1943), pp. 34–50.
14 House of Commons, 22 September 1944 (*Hansard*, vol. 403, cols 627–36).
15 Ibid., 28 April 1944 (vol. 399, cols 1061–74).
16 Ibid. (vol. 399, cols 1118–19).

17 *The Times*, 3 May 1944.
18 Michael Foot, *Aneurin Bevan, 1897–1945* (MacGibbon & Kee 1962), Paladin edition (1975), pp. 456–7.
19 *Tribune*, 5 May 1944.
20 Foot, op. cit., p. 460.
21 House of Commons, 20 December 1944 (*Hansard*, vol. 406, cols 1873–82).
22 Ibid.
23 *Labour Party Annual Conference Report, 1944*, pp. 148–9.
24 House of Commons, 19 January 1945 (*Hansard*, vol. 407, cols 569–80).
25 See *Labour Party Annual Conference Reports, 1944* and *1945*; and Addison, op. cit., p. 255.
26 *Tribune*, 19 January 1945.
27 Ibid., 20 April 1945.
28 Ibid., 2 October 1942.
29 Ibid., 19 January 1945.
30 Ibid., 30 March 1945.
31 'Celticus' (Aneurin Bevan MP), *Why Not Trust the Tories?* (Fanfare Press 1944), p. 13.
32 Ibid., p. 46.
33 Ibid., p. 55.
34 Ibid., p. 78.
35 Ibid., p. 25.
36 Ibid., pp. 81–2.
37 Ibid., pp. 82–3.
38 Ibid., pp. 88–9.
39 *Tribune*, 25 May 1945.
40 *Labour Party Annual Conference Report, 1945*, pp. 130–2.
41 *Tribune*, 27 April 1945.
42 Chuter Ede diary, 23 July 1945 (Add. Mss. 59701).
43 House of Commons, 14 June 1945 (*Hansard*, vol. 411, cols 1783–9).
44 *Tribune*, 6 July 1945.
45 Ibid., 13 July 1945.
46 House of Commons, 6 December 1945 (*Hansard*, vol. 416, col. 2544).
47 See John Colville, *Footprints in Time* (Collins 1976), p. 244.
48 Reference mislaid.

Chapter Eleven: Minister of Health: the Housing Crisis

1 Jennie Lee, *My Life With Nye* (Jonathan Cape 1980), Penguin edition (1981), p. 182.
2 C.R.Attlee, *As It Happened* (Heinemann 1954), p. 154.
3 Francis Williams, *The Triple Challenge: The Future of Socialist Britain* (Heinemann 1948), pp. 137–8.
4 Ibid., p. 135.
5 Michael Foot, *Aneurin Bevan, 1945–1960* (Davis Poynter 1973), Paladin edition (1975), p. 39.
6 Interview, John Pater.

7 See Roger Eatwell, *The 1945–1951 Labour Governments* (Batsford 1979), p. 41.
8 Alan Sked and Chris Cook, *Post-War Britain: A Political History* (Penguin 1979), p. 51.
9 'Celticus' (Aneurin Bevan MP), *Why Not Trust the Tories?* (Fanfare Press 1944), pp. 76–7.
10 Foot, op. cit., p. 58.
11 Stephen Merrett, *State Housing in Britain* (Routledge & Kegan Paul 1979), pp. 236–7; Fred Berry, *Housing: The Great British Failure* (Charles Knight 1974), pp. 47–8; Sked and Cook, op. cit., p. 51.
12 CAB 129/1, CP (45)118 (16 August 1945).
13 Sked and Cook, op. cit., p. 51.
14 Jennie Lee, op. cit., p. 184; Hugh Dalton diary, 30 October 1950.
15 Jennie Lee, op. cit., p. 184.
16 CAB 128/1 *passim*.
17 CAB 129/3, CP (45)208.
18 *Labour Party Annual Conference Report, 1947*, pp. 191–4.
19 Hugh Dalton, *High Tide and After* (Muller 1962), p. 358.
20 CAB 124/450 (8 August 1945).
21 House of Commons, 17 October 1945 (*Hansard*, vol. 414, cols 1217–33).
22 Ibid., 13 March 1950 (vol. 472, cols 861–70).
23 CAB 128/1, CM 39(45) (9 October 1945).
24 PREM 8/228 (11 October 1945).
25 Ibid.
26 CAB 128/1, CM 41(45) (15 October 1945).
27 House of Commons, 17 October 1945 (*Hansard*, vol. 414, cols 1217–33).
28 PREM 8/228 (15 October, 3 December 1945).
29 CAB 129/3, CP (45)225 (13 October 1945).
30 PREM 8/228 (15 October, 3 December 1945).
31 PREM 8/228 (2 November 1945).
32 PREM 8/228 (Bridges to Attlee, 8 November 1945).
33 CAB 129/4, CP (45)274 (8 November 1945).
34 PREM 8/228 (7 and 10 December 1945).
35 PREM 8/228 (14 December 1945).
36 CAB 134/320 (11 December 1945).
37 PREM 8/232 (Bevan, Buchanan, Tomlinson and Wilmot to Attlee, 11 April 1946).
38 CAB 134/320 (23 January, 13 February, 13 March, 28 March 1946).
39 Francis Williams, op. cit., p. 136.
40 CAB 129/6, CP (46)50 (11 February 1946).
41 Merrett, op. cit., pp. 239, 242–3.
42 PREM 8/228 (Tomlinson to Bevan, 26 July 1946; Bevan to Tomlinson, 2 August 1946).
43 CAB 134/320, HG (46)7 (10 November 1946).
44 CAB 124/452 (9 January 1946).
45 CAB 134/320 (12 December 1946).
46 CAB 128/6, CM 68(46) (15 July 1946).
47 See Ron Bailey, *The Squatters* (Penguin 1973); Paul Addison, *Now the War Is Over* (BBC/Jonathan Cape 1985), pp. 65–70.

48 CAB 128/6, CM 78(46), CM 80(46), CM 81(46), CM 82(46) (14 August, 9, 12 and 17 September 1946).
49 CAB 124/451 (12 November 1946).
50 CAB 128/9, CM 9(47) (17 January 1947).
51 CAB 128/6, CM 73(46) (25 July 1946).
52 CAB 128/9, CM 69(47), CM 74(47), CM 76(47), CM 81(47), CM 95(47) (5 and 25 August, 20 September, 20 October, 15 December 1947).
53 Merrett, op. cit., p. 239. (These are Great Britain figures.)
54 House of Commons, 18 December 1947 (*Hansard*, vol. 445, cols 2001–12).
55 Ibid., 14 July 1948 (vol. 453, cols 1313–22).
56 CAB 124/453 (3 November 1948).
57 CAB 128/12, CM 15(48) (19 February 1948).
58 CAB 128/12, CM 16(48) (23 February 1948).
59 Cmnd 7552 (2 November 1948).
60 *Labour Party Annual Conference Report, 1949*, pp. 216–18.
61 Merrett, op. cit., p. 239.
62 Bevan to Attlee, 21 October 1949 (Attlee papers, dep. 89, ff. 282–4).
63 CAB 128/17, CM 21(50) (17 April 1950).
64 CAB 128/18, CM 86(50) (14 December 1950).
65 House of Commons, 17 October 1945 (*Hansard*, vol. 414, cols 1217–33).

Chapter Twelve: Minister of Health: the Creation of the NHS

1 The Labour Party, *A National Service for Health* (1943), p. 18.
2 John E.Pater, *The Making of the National Health Service* (King Edward's Hospital Fund 1981), p. 104.
3 Rudolf Klein, *The Politics of the National Health Service* (Longman 1983), p. 7.
4 Pater, op. cit., p. 178.
5 Brian Abel-Smith, *The Hospitals, 1800–1948* (Heinemann 1964), p. 480.
6 CAB 129/3, CP (45)205 (5 October 1945).
7 CAB 129/3, CP (45)227 (12 October 1945).
8 CAB 129/3, CP (45)231 (16 October 1945).
9 CAB 128/1, CM 43(45) (18 October 1945).
10 CAB 128/2, CM 65(45) (20 December 1945); CAB 128/5, CM 3(46) (8 January 1946), CM 22(46) (8 March 1946).
11 Pater, op. cit., p. 122.
12 Ibid., p. 93; Lord Hill of Luton, *Both Sides of the Hill* (Heinemann 1964), p. 85.
13 CAB 129/7, CP (46)86 (1 March 1946).
14 See Pater, op. cit., p. 107; Harry Eckstein, *The English Health Service* (Harvard 1958), p. 159.
15 Eckstein, op. cit., p. 160n.
16 Quoted in Harry Eckstein, *Pressure Group Politics: The Case of the BMA* (Allen & Unwin 1960), p. 94.
17 House of Commons, 30 April 1946 (*Hansard*, vol. 422, cols 63–81).
18 Ibid.
19 Ibid., 2 May 1946 (vol. 422, col. 392).

20 CAB 128/2, CM 65(45) (20 December 1945).
21 House of Commons, 9 February 1948 (*Hansard*, vol. 447, cols 35–50).
22 See Eckstein, *Pressure Group Politics*, p. 99.
23 Pater, op. cit., p. 153.
24 CAB 129/23, CP (48)23 (19 January 1948).
25 Ibid.
26 House of Commons, 9 February 1948 (*Hansard*, vol. 447, cols 35–50).
27 Ibid. (cols 50–62).
28 *Lancet*, 14 February 1948, quoted in Pater, op. cit., p. 157.
29 E.g. Eckstein, *The English Health Service*, p. 161.
30 *British Medical Journal*, 13 March 1948.
31 Ibid., 6 March 1948.
32 Pater, op. cit., p. 179.
33 *BMJ*, 15 May 1948.
34 Michael Foot, *Aneurin Bevan, 1945–1960* (Davis Poynter 1973), Paladin edition (1975), p. 155.
35 Bevan to Attlee, 2 July 1948 (Attlee papers, dep. 72, ff. 13–14).
36 Speech at Manchester, 4 July 1948 (*The Times*, 5 July 1948).
37 House of Commons, 30 April 1946 (*Hansard*, vol. 422, cols 63–81).
38 Eckstein, *The English Health Service*, p. 252.
39 See D.Stark Murray in *Aneurin Bevan: An Appreciation of His Services to the Health of the People* (Socialist Medical Association 1962).
40 CAB 129/31, CP (48)302 (13 December 1948).
41 *The Times*, 13 February 1949.
42 House of Commons, 17 February 1949 (*Hansard*, vol. 461, cols 1448–61).
43 CAB 129/34, CP (49)105 (6 May 1949).
44 CAB 128/15, CM 37(49) (23 May 1949).
45 As previous.
46 Speech at Hednesford, Staffordshire, 25 September 1949 (*The Times*, 26 September 1949).
47 CAB 134/220 (14 and 20 October 1949); Philip Williams (ed.), *The Diary of Hugh Gaitskell* (Jonathan Cape 1983), p. 155 (26 October 1949).
48 CAB 129/37, CP (49)205 (20 October 1949).
49 CAB 128/16, CM 61(49) (21 October 1949).
50 House of Commons, 24 October 1949 (*Hansard*, vol. 468, col. 1019).
51 Speech at University College, London, 15 November 1949 (*The Times*, 16 November 1949).
52 House of Commons, 9 December 1949 (*Hansard*, vol. 470, cols 2258–65).
53 Ibid.
54 Speech to Medical Officers of Health, 24 November 1949 (*The Times*, 25 November 1949).

Chapter Thirteen: Bevan in the Attlee Cabinet

1 Bernard Donoghue and George Jones, *Herbert Morrison: Portrait of a Politician* (Weidenfeld & Nicolson 1973), p. 340.

Notes

2 Bevan to Attlee, 13 November 1945 (Attlee papers, dep. 26, f. 228).
3 See Kenneth Harris, *Attlee* (Weidenfeld & Nicolson 1982), pp. 449–50.
4 Hugh Dalton diary, 20 May 1946.
5 Alan Bullock, *Ernest Bevin: Foreign Secretary, 1945–51* (Heinemann 1983), p. 77.
6 Leslie Hunter, *The Road to Brighton Pier* (Arthur Barker 1959), p. 24.
7 Kenneth O.Morgan, *Labour in Power, 1945–1951* (Oxford 1984), pp. 164, 180; Michael Foot, *Aneurin Bevan, 1945–1960* (Davis Poynter 1973), Paladin edition (1975), pp. 72–3, 137; Ben Pimlott, *Hugh Dalton* (Jonathan Cape 1985), pp. 491, 495.
8 Dalton diary, 20 May 1946.
9 Even in April 1951 – see Dalton diary, 11 April 1951; but see also 8 and 12 August 1947.
10 Philip Williams (ed.), *The Diary of Hugh Gaitskell* (Jonathan Cape 1983), p. 72 (18 June 1948).
11 Douglas Jay, *Change and Fortune: A Political Record* (Hutchinson 1980), p. 174.
12 Dalton diary, 19 July, 29 September, 7 December 1949.
13 CAB 128/2, CM 62(45). He was beginning to object to the semi-autonomous boards by 1948 – see *Gaitskell Diary*, p. 72 (18 June 1948).
14 *Labour Party Annual Conference Report, 1948*, pp. 138–40.
15 *Labour Party Annual Conference Report, 1949*, pp. 169–72.
16 CAB 134/175 (28 June 1948).
17 CAB 128/10, CM 62(47) (17 July 1947); CAB 128/12, CM 9(48) (2 February 1948); Morgan, op. cit., pp. 80, 132.
18 CAB 128/8, CM 70(46) (21 July 1946).
19 CAB 128/4, CM 57(45) (29 November 1945).
20 CAB 128/4, CM 50(45) (6 November 1945).
21 CAB 128/10, CM 52(47) (5 June 1947).
22 CAB 128/10, CM 69(47) (5 August 1947).
23 *Labour Party Annual Conference Report, 1948*, pp. 138–40.
24 Morgan, op. cit., pp. 58, 72.
25 CAB 128/5, CM 14(46) (February 1946), quoted in Alan Bullock, op. cit., p. 222.
26 *Labour Party Annual Conference Report, 1950*, pp.130–3.
27 CAB 128/9, CM 25(47) (27 February 1947).
28 Dalton diary, 'end of 1948'.
29 Bullock, op. cit., p. 544.
30 Foot, op. cit., pp. 227–8; Morgan, op. cit., p. 389.
31 CAB 128/10, CM 65(47) (29 July 1947).
32 Dalton diary, 5 February 1947.
33 CAB 128/10, CM 76(47) (20 September 1947).
34 CAB 128/15, CM 3(49) (17 January 1949).
35 Morgan, op. cit., pp. 283, 433.
36 George Strauss interview, 19 January 1962 (Nuffield Oral History Project).

Chapter Fourteen: First Doubts

1 Hugh Dalton diary, 12 April 1946.

2 E.g. speech in Glasgow, 2 October 1949 (*The Times*, 3 October 1949).
3 CAB 128/9, CM 37(47) (17 April 1947).
4 CAB 128/10, CM 64(47) (24 July 1947).
5 CAB 128/10, CM 66(47) (31 July 1947).
6 Dalton diary, 31 July 1947.
7 Ibid., 8 August 1947.
8 Ibid.
9 CAB 128/10, CM 70(47) (7 August 1947).
10 Philip Williams (ed.), *The Diary of Hugh Gaitskell* (Jonathan Cape 1983), p. 24 (12 August 1947).
11 Dalton diary, 5 February 1947.
12 Ibid., 8 August 1947.
13 Ibid., 5 September 1947.
14 Attlee to Morrison, 15 September 1947 (Morrison papers 39).
15 Morrison to Attlee, 19 September 1947 (ibid., 40).
16 Attlee to Morrison, 23 September 1947 (ibid., 41).
17 Attlee to Morrison, 15 September 1947 (ibid., 39).
18 Cripps to Dalton, 24 September 1947 (Dalton papers IIC, 9/3).
19 Ibid.
20 *Labour Party Annual Conference Report, 1948*, pp. 138–40.
21 *Labour Party Annual Conference Report, 1949*, pp. 169–72.
22 *Labour Party Annual Conference Report, 1950*, pp. 130–3.
23 *Labour Party Annual Conference Report, 1949*, pp. 169–72.
24 See Bevan to Attlee, 2 July 1948 (Attlee papers, dep. 72, ff. 13–14).
25 Speech at Manchester, 4 July 1948 (*The Times*, 5 July 1948).
26 Michael Foot, *Aneurin Bevan, 1945–1960* (Davis Poynter 1973), Paladin edition (1975), pp. 239–40.
27 Ibid., p. 238.
28 *Economist*, 9 July 1960
29 Foot, op. cit., p. 221.
30 Ibid., p. 241.
31 *Labour Party Annual Conference Report, 1950*, pp. 130–3.
32 *Labour Party Annual Conference Report, 1947*, pp. 191–4.
33 Ibid., pp. 126–7.
34 Bernard Donoghue and George Jones, *Herbert Morrison: Portrait of a Politician* (Weidenfeld & Nicolson 1973), p. 369.
35 Dalton diary, 11 October, 23 November 1949; Kenneth O.Morgan, *Labour in Power, 1945–51* (Oxford 1984), pp. 124–6.
36 *Labour Party Annual Conference Report, 1949*, pp. 169–72.
37 *Tribune*, 17 June 1949.
38 *Labour Party Annual Conference Report, 1949*, pp. 169–72.
39 CAB 129/37, CP (49)205 (20 October 1949); House of Commons, 9 December 1949 (*Hansard*, vol. 470, cols 2258–65).
40 CAB 128/16, CM 61(49) (21 October 1949).
41 Bevan to Attlee, 21 October 1949 (Attlee papers, dep. 89, ff. 282–4).
42 Attlee to Bevan, n.d. [22 October 1949?] (ibid., ff. 285–7).
43 *Gaitskell Diary*, p. 131 (3 August 1949).
44 House of Commons, 28 September 1949 (*Hansard*, vol. 468, cols 157–76).

45 *Tribune*, 30 September 1949.
46 House of Commons, 29 September 1949 (*Hansard*, vol. 468, cols 309–25).
47 *Tribune*, 7 October 1949.
48 Dalton diary, 11 October 1949.
49 Ibid., 24 May 1949.
50 *Gaitskell Diary*, p. 62 (23 April 1948).
51 Dalton diary, October 1949.
52 Ibid., 19 July, 29 September, 11 October 1949.
53 Ibid., 5 October 1949.
54 Ibid., 7 December 1949.
55 *Gaitskell Diary*, pp. 161–2 (27 January 1950).
56 Leslie Hunter, *The Road to Brighton Pier* (Arthur Barker 1959), p. 22.
57 *Tribune*, 3 February 1950.
58 See H.G.Nicholas, *The British General Election of 1950* (Macmillan 1951), pp. 124, 179.
59 Lord Hill of Luton, *The Other Side of the Hill* (Heinemann 1964), p. 131.
60 *Manchester Guardian*, 21 February 1950.

Chapter Fifteen: Rumbling Volcano

1 Hugh Dalton diary, 25 February 1950.
2 Michael Foot, *Aneurin Bevan, 1945–1960* (Davis Poynter 1973), Paladin edition (1975), p. 247.
3 Dalton diary, 27 February 1950.
4 Philip Williams (ed.), *The Diary of Hugh Gaitskell* (Jonathan Cape 1983), p. 167 (21 March 1950).
5 CAB 128/17, CM 5(50) (25 February 1950).
6 CAB 128/17, CM 6(50) (2 March 1950).
7 *Labour Party Annual Conference Report, 1950*, p. 130.
8 *The Times*, 25 November 1949.
9 Dalton diary, 27 February 1950.
10 Ibid., 11 October 1949.
11 Ibid., 28 February 1950.
12 *Labour Party Annual Conference Report, 1951*, p. 122.
13 Dalton diary, 30 October 1950.
14 *Gaitskell Diary*, p. 174 (21 March 1950).
15 Ibid.
16 Kenneth Harris, *Attlee* (Weidenfeld & Nicolson 1982), p. 447.
17 CAB 129/38, CP (50)31 (10 March 1950).
18 *Gaitskell Diary*, p. 174 (21 March 1950).
19 CAB 128/17, CM 10(50) (13 March 1950).
20 Foot, op. cit., p. 289.
21 CAB 129/38, CP(50)53 (29 March 1950).
22 CAB 129/38, CP (50)56 (30 March 1950).
23 CAB 128/17, CM 17(50) (3 April 1950).
24 Ibid.

25 CAB 128/18, CM 18(50) (4 April 1950).
26 Foot, op. cit., p. 291.
27 *Gaitskell Diary*, p. 193 (11 August 1950).
28 Foot, op. cit., pp. 293–4.
29 Philip Williams, *Hugh Gaitskell* (Jonathan Cape 1979), p. 215.
30 *Gaitskell Diary*, p. 188 (26 May 1950).
31 Williams, op. cit., p. 215.
32 CAB 134/518 (monthly reports 15 July, 21 September, 13 October and 16 November 1950).
33 Cmnd 9663 (November 1955); John E. Pater, *The Making of the National Health Service* (King Edward's Hospital Fund 1981), pp. 180–9; Almont Lindsay, *Socialised Medicine in England and Wales* (University of North Carolina Press 1962), pp. 118–20.
34 Dalton diary, 27 June 1950.
35 Kenneth Younger interview, 27 December 1961 (Nuffield Oral History Project).
36 CAB 128/18, CM 52(50) (1 August 1950).
37 *News Chronicle*, 23 November 1950.
38 Dalton diary, 30 November 1950.
39 CAB 128/18, CM 87(50).
40 Hugh Dalton, *High Tide and After* (Muller 1962), p. 358; Harris, op. cit., p. 447; Younger interview.
41 Foot, op. cit., p. 297.
42 Gaitskell to Attlee, 4 October 1950 (quoted in Kenneth O. Morgan, *Labour in Power, 1945–1951* [Oxford 1984], pp. 445–6).
43 Douglas Jay, *Change and Fortune: A Political Record* (Hutchinson 1980), p. 202.
44 Dalton diary, 30 October 1950.
45 *Gaitskell Diary*, p. 216 (3 November 1950).
46 Dalton diary, 30 October 1950.
47 Ibid.
48 Foot, op. cit., pp. 308–9.
49 Dalton diary, 22 March, 6 April 1950.
50 *Gaitskell Diary*, pp. 226–7 (10 January 1951).
51 *Tribune*, 26 January 1951.
52 LAB 10/994.
53 CAB 128/19, CM 3(51) (15 January 1951).
54 CAB 128/19, CM 13(51) (12 February 1951).
55 E.g. Attlee to Bevan, 21 April 1951 (*The Times*, 23 April 1951); Dalton diary, 11 April 1951; George Strauss interview, 19 January 1962 (Nuffield Oral History Project); Williams, op. cit., pp. 247–8.
56 CAB 128/19, CM 3(51) (15 January 1951).
57 CAB 128/19, CM 7(51) (25 January 1951).
58 CAB 128/18, CM 87(50) (18 December 1950).
59 CAB 128/19, CM 8(51) (25 January 1951).
60 CAB 128/19, CM 9(51) (26 January 1951).
61 Dalton diary, 9 February 1951.
62 Younger interview.
63 House of Commons, 15 February 1951 (*Hansard*, vol. 484, cols 728–40).

64 *Gaitskell Diary*, p. 237 (16 February 1951).
65 *Tribune*, 23 February 1951.
66 Dalton diary, 28 January 1951.
67 Ibid., 9, 19 and 20 February 1951.
68 Dalton, op. cit., p. 362.
69 Younger interview.
70 Alan Bullock, *Ernest Bevin: Foreign Secretary, 1945–1951* (Heinemann 1984), p. 834.
71 Dalton diary, 12 March 1951; Bernard Donoghue and George Jones, *Herbert Morrison: Portrait of a Politician* (Weidenfeld & Nicolson 1973), pp. 467–8.
72 Harris, op. cit., p. 472.

Chapter Sixteen: Eruption

1 CAB 130/66 (15 March 1951).
2 Philip Williams (ed.), *The Diary of Hugh Gaitskell* (Jonathan Cape 1983), p. 242 (30 April 1951).
3 CAB 128/19, CM 22(51) (22 March 1951).
4 Hugh Dalton diary, 22 March 1951.
5 CAB 128/19, CM 22(51) (22 March 1951).
6 Dalton diary, 9 April 1951.
7 Ibid., 22 March 1951.
8 *The Times*, 4 April 1951; *Gaitskell Diary*, p. 243 (30 April 1951).
9 Dalton diary, 5 April 1951.
10 Ibid.
11 Ibid., 6 April 1951.
12 CAB 128/19, CM 25(51) (9 April 1951).
13 Dalton diary, 9 April 1951.
14 Ibid.
15 Ibid.
16 Morrison papers, 50.
17 CAB 128/19, CM 26(51) (9 April 1951).
18 Dalton diary, 9 April 1951.
19 CAB 128/19, CM 26(51) (9 April 1951).
20 *Gaitskell Diary*, p. 244 (30 April 1951).
21 CAB 128/19, CM 26(51) (9 April 1951).
22 Kenneth Harris, *Attlee* (Weidenfeld & Nicolson 1982), p. 475.
23 Dalton diary, 10 April 1951.
24 *Gaitskell Diary*, p. 245 (30 April 1951); Harris, op. cit., p. 475.
25 *Gaitskell Diary*, p. 247 (30 April 1951).
26 Dalton diary, 10 April 1951.
27 Michael Foot, *Aneurin Bevan, 1945–1960* (Davis Poynter 1973), Paladin edition (1975), p. 322. This letter was signed by Callaghan, Alf Robens, Michael Stewart, Arthur Blenkinsop and Fred Lee.
28 Ibid., pp. 323–4.
29 Dalton diary, 10 April 1951.

30 Foot, op. cit., p. 324.
31 Dalton diary, 11 April 1951.
32 *Daily Telegraph*, 12 April 1951.
33 *Daily Herald*, 12 April 1951.
34 *New Statesman*, 14 April 1951.
35 Dalton diary, 12 April 1951.
36 Ibid.
37 CAB 128/19, CM 27(51) (12 April 1951).
38 Dalton diary, 12 April 1951.
39 Foot, op. cit., pp. 325–6.
40 Dalton diary, 18 April 1951.
41 Ibid., 19 April 1951.
42 CAB 128/19, CM 29(51) (19 April 1951).
43 Dalton diary, 19 April 1951.
44 Ibid.
45 *Gaitskell Diary*, p. 254 (4 May 1951).
46 Dalton diary, 20 April 1951.
47 *Tribune*, 20 April 1951.
48 A.J.P.Taylor, *Beaverbrook* (Hamish Hamilton 1972), Penguin edition (1974), p. 764; Philip Williams, *Hugh Gaitskell* (Jonathan Cape 1979), p. 257.
49 Dalton diary, 20 April 1951.
50 Foot, op. cit. pp. 327–8; Harris, op. cit., p. 477.
51 Foot, op. cit., pp. 328–9; *The Times*, 23 April 1951.
52 Foot, op. cit., p. 329; Harris, op. cit., p. 477; *The Times*, 23 April 1951.
53 CAB 128/19, CM 25(51) (9 April 1951).
54 Dalton diary, 23 April 1951.
55 Jennie Lee, *My Life With Nye* (Jonathan Cape 1980), Penguin edition (1981), p. 223.
56 House of Commons, 23 April 1951 (*Hansard*, vol. 487, cols 34–43).
57 *Gaitskell Diary*, pp. 255–6 (4 May 1951).
58 Dalton diary, 23 April 1951.
59 Freeman to Dalton, 23 April 1951 (Dalton papers, IIC 9/18); Dalton diary, 23 April 1951.
60 *Gaitskell Diary*, pp. 255–6 (4 May 1951).
61 Dalton diary, 24 April 1951.
62 *Gaitskell Diary*, pp. 255–6 (4 May 1951).
63 Dalton diary, 24 April 1951.
64 Ibid.
65 House of Commons, 6 December 1951 (*Hansard*, vol. 494, cols 2601–3).
66 Kenneth O.Morgan, *Labour in Power, 1945–1951* (Oxford 1984), pp. 459–60.
67 See Leslie Hunter, *The Road to Brighton Pier* (Arthur Barker 1959), pp. 39–40.
68 E.g. by Crossman, in Dalton diary, 11 April 1951.
69 Williams, op. cit., p. 263.
70 Dalton diary, 17 April 1951.
71 Harris, op. cit., p. 450.
72 Bernard Donoghue and George Jones, *Herbert Morrison: Portrait of a Politician* (Weidenfeld & Nicolson 1973), p. 490.
73 *Gaitskell Diary*, p. 257 (4 May 1951).

Chapter Seventeen: The Beginnings of Bevanism

1 *Tribune*, 26 November, 17 December 1948.
2 See Mark Jenkins, *Bevanism: Labour's High Tide* (Spokesman 1979), pp. 147–50.
3 Ibid., pp. 149–52, 174.
4 *Tribune*, 4 May 1951.
5 Ibid.
6 Ibid., 21 September 1951.
7 *New Statesman*, 5 May 1951.
8 Jenkins, op. cit., pp. 119–20.
9 Hugh Dalton diary, 4 June 1951; Philip Williams (ed.), *The Diary of Hugh Gaitskell* (Jonathan Cape 1983), p. 271 (10 August 1951).
10 *Gaitskell Diary*, p. 271 (10 August 1951).
11 Michael Foot, *Aneurin Bevan, 1945–1960* (Davis Poynter 1973), Paladin edition (1975), p. 343.
12 *One Way Only* (Tribune 1951), Introduction.
13 House of Commons, 2 May, 7 May and 2 July 1951 (*Hansard*, vol. 487, cols 1250–4 and 1661–2; vol. 489, cols 1915–18).
14 *Gaitskell Diary*, p. 290 (16 November 1951).
15 *Tribune*, 5 October 1951.
16 *Labour Party Annual Conference Report, 1951*, pp. 120–2.
17 Ibid.
18 See D.E.Butler, *The British General Election of 1951* (Macmillan 1952).
19 Janet Morgan (ed.), *The Backbench Diaries of Richard Crossman* (Hamish Hamilton and Jonathan Cape 1981), p. 27 (30 October 1951).
20 Ibid., p. 63 (21 January 1952).
21 Ibid., pp. 42–3 (26 November 1951).
22 Ibid., p. 53 (17 December 1951).
23 *Gaitskell Diary*, p. 310 (21 March 1952).
24 House of Commons, 4 December 1951 (*Hansard*, vol. 494, cols 2252–63).
25 *Crossman Diary*, p. 47 (4 December 1951).
26 House of Commons, 6 December 1951 (*Hansard*, vol. 494, cols 2601–3).
27 *Tribune*, 14 December 1951.
28 *Crossman Diary*, pp. 67–8 (31 January 1952).
29 House of Commons, 31 January 1951 (*Hansard*, vol. 495, cols 393–406).
30 Dalton diary, 3 February 1952.
31 House of Commons, 26 February 1952 (*Hansard*, vol. 496, cols 982–94).
32 Chuter Ede diary, 2 March 1952 (Add. Mss. 59703).
33 *Gaitskell Diary*, p. 311 (21 March 1952).
34 Dalton diary, 23 January 1952.
35 Ibid., 22 February 1952.
36 *Crossman Diary*, p. 87 (6 March 1952).
37 *Gaitskell Diary*, p. 312 (21 March 1952).
38 *Tribune*, 7 March 1952.
39 *Gaitskell Diary*, p. 312 (21 March 1952).
40 *Crossman Diary*, pp. 90–2 (10 March 1952).
41 Ede diary, 5 March 1952.
42 *Gaitskell Diary*, p. 312 (21 March 1952).

43 *Crossman Diary*, p. 94 (11 March 1952).

Chapter Eighteen: The Manifesto That Wasn't

1 *Tribune*, 4 April 1952.
2 Aneurin Bevan, *In Place of Fear* (MacGibbon & Kee 1952). All page references
   are to the paperback edition published by Quartet in 1978.
3 Hugh Dalton diary, 12 May 1952.
4 *The Times*, 4 April 1952.
5 Janet Morgan (ed.), *The Backbench Diaries of Richard Crossman* (Hamish Hamilton and Jonathan Cape 1981), p. 53 (17 December 1951).
6 *The Listener*, 5 April 1952.
7 Michael Foot, *Aneurin Bevan, 1945–1960* (Davis Poynter 1973), Paladin edition
   (1975), p. 367.
8 Dalton diary, 9 April 1952.
9 Mark Jenkins, *Bevanism: Labour's High Tide* (Spokesman 1979), p. 306.
10 Dalton diary, 9 April 1952.
11 *Tribune*, 4 April 1952.

Chapter Nineteen: 'A Party Within a Party'?

1 House of Commons, 27 March, 8, 9 and 23 April 1952 (*Hansard*, vol. 498, cols
   877–86, 2518–23, 2676–90, 2903–6; vol. 499, cols 466–72).
2 Ibid., 22 April, 30 July 1952 (vol. 499, cols 257–67; vol. 504, cols 1522–36).
3 Ibid., 14 May, 25 June 1952 (vol. 500, cols 1511–20; vol. 502, cols 2264–71).
4 Mark Jenkins, *Bevanism: Labour's High Tide* (Spokesman 1979), pp.170–1.
5 Ibid., pp. 120–1.
6 See Peggy Duff, *Left, Left, Left* (Alison & Busby 1971), p. 44.
7 Hugh Dalton diary, 3 January 1952.
8 *Sunday Express*, 3 February 1952.
9 A.J.Cummings in the *News Chronicle*, 5 August 1952.
10 *Sunday Pictorial*, 28 September 1952.
11 *Labour Party Annual Conference Report, 1952*, p. 127.
12 Janet Morgan (ed.), *The Backbench Diaries of Richard Crossman* (Hamish Hamilton and Jonathan Cape 1981), p. 159 (15 October 1952).
13 Ibid., p. 42 (26 November 1951).
14 Ibid., p. 63 (21 January 1952).
15 Ibid., p. 99 (10 April 1952).
16 *Tribune*, 13 June 1952.
17 Michael Foot, *Aneurin Bevan, 1945–1960* (Davis Poynter 1973), Paladin edition
   (1975), p. 376.
18 Dalton diary, 30 September 1952.
19 Ibid.
20 Philip Williams, *Hugh Gaitskell* (Jonathan Cape 1979), pp. 304–5.

21 *Crossman Diary*, pp. 154–5 (6 October 1952).
22 Ibid., pp. 155–6 (13 October 1952).
23 *The Times*, 13 October 1952.
24 *Crossman Diary*, p. 156 (13 October 1952).
25 Ibid., p. 157 (14 October 1952).
26 *Tribune*, 17 October 1952.
27 *Crossman Diary*, pp. 159–60 (15 October 1952).
28 Ibid., pp. 163–4 (23 October 1952).
29 Ibid., p. 173 (28 October 1952).
30 Ibid., pp. 178–9 (12 November 1952); Dalton diary, 11 November 1952.
31 *Tribune*, 5 December 1952.
32 *Crossman Diary*, p. 182 (19 November 1952).
33 Ibid., p. 184 (26 November 1952).
34 Ibid., p. 196 (20 January 1953).

Chapter Twenty: The Disintegration of the Bevanites

1 Hugh Dalton diary, 2 December 1953.
2 House of Commons, 4 December 1952 (*Hansard*, vol. 508, cols 1870–9).
3 Ibid., 4 November 1953 (vol. 520, cols 226–41).
4 Ibid., 30 November 1953 (vol. 521, cols 812–30).
5 Ibid., 4 November 1953 (vol. 520, cols 226–41).
6 *Labour Party Annual Conference Report, 1954*, pp. 110–11.
7 House of Commons, 27 March 1952 (*Hansard*, vol. 498, cols 877–86).
8 Ibid. (cols 886–95, 961–7).
9 Ibid., 1 April 1953 (vol. 513, cols 1229–33).
10 Ibid., 18 May 1953 (vol. 515, cols 1716–35).
11 Ibid., 1 April and 18 May (vol. 513, cols 1229–33; vol. 515, cols 1716–35).
12 Ibid., 1 April 1953 (vol. 513, col. 1233).
13 Ibid., 29 April 1953 (vol. 514, cols 2291–5).
14 *Labour Party Annual Conference Report, 1953*, pp. 181–3.
15 Janet Morgan (ed.), *The Backbench Diaries of Richard Crossman* (Hamish Hamilton and Jonathan Cape 1981), pp. 188–91 (15 December 1952).
16 Ibid., pp. 224–7, 231–3 (28 April, 19 May 1953).
17 Ibid., p. 244 (18 June 1953).
18 *Tribune*, 19 June 1953.
19 Ibid., 18 June 1954.
20 Ibid., 17, 24, 31 July and 7 August 1953.
21 Ibid., 11 September 1953.
22 Ibid., 8 January 1954.
23 Ibid., 16 April 1954.
24 A.Bevan, B.Castle, R.Crossman, T.Driberg, I.Mikardo and H.Wilson, *It Need Not Happen: The Alternative to German Rearmament* (Tribune 1954), pp. 20–4.
25 Ibid.
26 *Crossman Diary*, p. 244 (18 June 1953).

27 House of Commons, 17 December 1953 (*Hansard*, vol. 522, cols 601–11); *Tribune*, 18 December 1953.
28 *Crossman Diary*, p. 210 (23 March 1953).
29 Dalton diary, 26 March 1953.
30 *Crossman Diary*, p. 271 (12 November 1953).
31 Ibid., p. 290 (3 March 1954).
32 Dalton diary, 17 June 1953.
33 Ibid., 23 June 1953.
34 Ibid., 8 July 1953.
35 Ibid., 23 June 1953.
36 Ibid., 21 July 1953.
37 *Crossman Diary*, p. 266 (2 October 1953).
38 Dalton diary, 29 October 1953.
39 *Crossman Diary*, p. 271 (30 October 1953).
40 Dalton diary, 18 November 1953.
41 Ibid., 17 November 1953.
42 *Tribune*, 13 November 1953.
43 Dalton diary, 25 November 1953.
44 *Tribune*, 23 April 1954.
45 *Crossman Diary*, pp. 311–12 (21 April 1954).
46 House of Commons, 13 April 1954 (*Hansard*, vol. 526, cols 969–75).
47 Dalton diary, 13 April 1954.
48 Ibid., 14 April 1954.
49 *Crossman Diary*, p. 312 (21 April 1954).
50 Ibid.
51 Ibid., p. 310 (21 April 1954).
52 *Tribune*, 23 April 1954.
53 *Annual Register, 1954*, p. 21.
54 *Tribune*, 16 April 1954.
55 *Crossman Diary*, p. 313 (21 April 1954).
56 Ibid., pp. 317–19 (28 April 1954); see also Crossman to Wilson, 22 April 1954, in ibid., p. 316.
57 Ibid., pp. 323–4 (6 May 1954).
58 Ibid., pp. 326–7 (8 July 1954).
59 Ibid., p. 353 (12 October 1954).
60 Ibid., p. 366 (22 November 1954).
61 Michael Foot, *Aneurin Bevan, 1945–1960* (Davis Poynter 1973), Paladin edition (1975), pp. 437–9.
62 Bevan's diary, quoted in ibid., p. 441.
63 *Tribune*, 24 September 1954.
64 Bevan's diary, quoted in Foot, op. cit., p. 441.
65 *Tribune*, 15 October 1954.
66 Philip Williams, *Hugh Gaitskell* (Jonathan Cape 1979), pp. 329, 332; *Crossman Diary*, p. 349 (1 October 1954).
67 Kenneth Harris, *Attlee* (Weidenfeld & Nicolson 1982), p. 522.
68 Foot, op. cit., p. 447.
69 *Crossman Diary*, p. 360 (27 October 1954).
70 Ibid., pp. 364–5 (15 November 1954).

71 Ibid., pp. 355–6 (19 October 1954).
72 Ibid., p. 365 (15 November 1954).
73 Ibid., p. 363 (15 November 1954).
74 Ibid., pp. 365–9 (22 November 1954).
75 Foot, op. cit., p. 448.
76 Harris, op. cit., p. 526.
77 *Crossman Diary*, p. 391 (28 February 1955); Harris, op. cit., p. 527.
78 *Crossman Diary*, pp. 387–8 (22 February 1955).
79 House of Commons, 2 March 1955 (*Hansard*, vol. 537, cols 2109–22).
80 *Crossman Diary*, p. 386 (22 February 1955).
81 Ibid., pp. 387–8 (22 February 1955).
82 Harris, op. cit., p. 527.
83 *Crossman Diary*, p. 393 (3 March 1955).
84 Ibid., p. 394 (3 March 1955).
85 House of Commons, 2 March 1955 (*Hansard*, vol. 537, cols 2109–22).
86 See R.J.Edwards in *Tribune*, 18 March 1955.
87 House of Commons, 2 March 1955 (*Hansard*, vol. 537, col. 2176).
88 Ibid.
89 *Tribune*, 11 March 1955.
90 Harris, op. cit., pp. 529–30.
91 See ibid.; Williams, op. cit., pp. 340–5.
92 *Crossman Diary*, pp. 397, 406 (8 and 16 March 1955).
93 Philip Williams (ed.), *The Diary of Hugh Gaitskell* (Jonathan Cape 1983), p. 368 (19 March 1955).
94 See ibid., p. 369 (19 March 1955); Dalton diary, 7 March 1955; Harris, op. cit., p. 529.
95 *Crossman Diary*, pp. 399–400 (15 March 1955).
96 Ibid., pp. 403–5 (16 March 1955); Dalton diary, 16 March 1955; *Gaitskell Diary*, pp. 372–3 (19 March 1955).
97 Dalton diary, 7 March 1955.
98 Crosland, Jenkins and Wyatt to Gaitskell, 21 March 1955, in *Gaitskell Diary*, pp. 394–5.
99 *Crossman Diary*, pp. 409–10 (24 March 1955).
100 Ibid., pp. 411–12 (24 March 1955); *Gaitskell Diary*, pp. 389–91 (25 March 1955).
101 *Crossman Diary*, pp. 412, 413 (24 and 31 March 1955).
102 Harris, op. cit., p. 531; Foot, op. cit., p. 474n.
103 *Crossman Diary*, p. 413 (31 May 1955); *Gaitskell Diary*, pp. 397–401 (2 April 1955); Harris, op. cit., p. 531.

Chapter Twenty-one: The Leadership Resolved

1 *Daily Sketch*, 24 May 1955.
2 See D.E.Butler, *The British General Election of 1955* (Macmillan 1955), p. 79.
3 Michael Foot, *Aneurin Bevan, 1945–1960* (Davis Poynter 1973), Paladin edition (1975), p. 484; Philip Williams, *Hugh Gaitskell* (Jonathan Cape 1979), p. 354.
4 *Tribune*, 2 June 1955.

5 See Butler, op. cit.
6 *Tribune*, 2 June 1955.
7 Ibid., 24 June 1955.
8 Ibid., 3 December 1954.
9 Williams, op. cit., pp. 345, 347; Philip Williams (ed.), *The Diary of Hugh Gaitskell* (Jonathan Cape 1983), p. 401 (2 April 1955).
10 Hugh Dalton diary, 1952 *passim* and 7 February 1953.
11 Janet Morgan (ed.), *The Backbench Diaries of Richard Crossman* (Hamish Hamilton and Jonathan Cape 1981), pp. 425–7 (7 June 1955).
12 Ibid., pp. 426–7 (7 June 1955).
13 Ibid., p. 429 (9 June 1955).
14 Dalton diary, 9 June 1955.
15 *Crossman Diary*, pp. 430–1 (13 June 1955).
16 Ibid., p. 423 (6 June 1955).
17 House of Commons, 19 July 1955 (*Hansard*, vol. 544, cols 312–19) and 2 November 1955 (vol. 545, cols 1136–45). He also spoke on the Housing Subsidies Bill on 21 November and 1 December 1955 (vol. 546, cols 1061–79 and 2577–85).
18 *Crossman Diary*, p. 444 (29 September 1955).
19 *Tribune*, 7 October 1955.
20 *Crossman Diary*, p. 452 (16 November 1955).
21 *Ibid.*
22 *Tribune*, 16 December 1955.
23 Bernard Donoghue and George Jones, *Herbert Morrison: Portrait of a Politician* (Weidenfeld & Nicolson 1973), pp. 538–9.
24 Williams, op. cit., pp. 361–4.
25 Foot, op. cit., pp. 493–4.
26 *Crossman Diary*, p. 458 (16 December 1955).
27 Donoghue and Jones, op. cit., p. 540; Williams, op. cit., p. 366.
28 Williams, op. cit., p. 366; Foot, op. cit., pp. 493–4.
29 *Crossman Diary*, p. 459 (16 December 1955).

Chapter Twenty-two: Doubtful Rapprochement

1 E.g. *Tribune*, 17 August 1956.
2 Philip Williams (ed.), *The Diary of Hugh Gaitskell* (Jonathan Cape 1983), p. 409 (9 January 1956).
3 Hugh Dalton diary, 2 February 1956; see also *Gaitskell Diary*, p. 436 (3 February 1956).
4 *The Times*, 6 February 1956; *Tribune*, 10 February 1956.
5 *Gaitskell Diary*, pp. 438, 442 (14 February 1956).
6 Ibid., p. 409 (9 January 1956).
7 Ibid., pp. 438, 442 (14 February 1956).
8 *The Times*, 12 March 1956.
9 Michael Foot, *Aneurin Bevan, 1945–1960* (Davis Poynter 1973), Paladin edition (1975), p. 500.
10 *Gaitskell Diary*, pp. 438, 442 (14 February 1956).

11 *Tribune*, 24 February 1956.
12 Ibid., 2 March 1956.
13 *Gaitskell Diary*, p. 495 (20 April 1956).
14 House of Commons, 29 February and 14 March 1956 (*Hansard*, vol. 549, cols 1160, 1174; vol. 550, cols 387–402).
15 *Gaitskell Diary*, p. 464 (9 March 1956).
16 Ibid., pp. 473–7 (5 April 1956).
17 Ibid., p. 518 (4 June 1956).
18 Ibid.
19 *Tribune*, 28 June 1956.
20 Ibid., 5 September, 21 November 1958.
21 House of Commons, 6 June 1956 (*Hansard*, vol. 553, cols 1193–1202).
22 Ibid., 1 August 1956 (vol. 558, col. 1473).
23 Ibid., 14 March, 19 July, 14 September 1956 (vol. 550, cols 387–402; vol. 556, cols 1507–16; vol. 558, cols 432–3).
24 Ibid., 19 March 1959 (vol. 602, cols 650–62); *Tribune*, 6 March 1959.
25 *The Times*, 9 June 1956.
26 *Gaitskell Diary*, p. 591 (3 September 1956).
27 Ibid., p. 513 (28 April 1956).
28 George Brown, *In My Way* (Gollancz 1973), p. 73.
29 *Gaitskell Diary*, p. 556 (26 July 1956).
30 Ibid., p. 540 (14 July 1956).
31 Janet Morgan (ed.), *The Backbench Diaries of Richard Crossman* (Hamish Hamilton and Jonathan Cape 1981), p. 503 (3 July 1956).
32 *Gaitskell Diary*, p. 540 (14 July 1956).
33 *Crossman Diary*, pp. 522–3 (26 October 1956).
34 Ibid.
35 *The Times*, 4 October 1956.
36 *Tribune*, 5 October 1956.
37 *The Times*, 4 October 1956.
38 *Gaitskell Diary*, p. 617 (9 October 1956).
39 *Tribune*, 3 August 1956.
40 House of Commons, 16 May 1957 (*Hansard*, vol. 570, cols 679–89).
41 Ibid., 1 August 1956 (vol. 558, col. 1473.).
42 *Tribune*, 3 August 1956.
43 Ibid.
44 Ibid., 10 August 1956.
45 *Gaitskell Diary*, p. 582 (22 August 1956).
46 See Philip Williams, *Hugh Gaitskell* (Jonathan Cape 1979), pp. 418–37.
47 *Crossman Diary*, p. 508 (5 September 1956).
48 Kenneth Younger diary, 16 September 1956, in Williams, op. cit., p. 426.
49 *Tribune*, 24 August 1956.
50 *Crossman Diary*, p. 519 (28 September 1956).
51 House of Commons, 1 November 1956 (*Hansard*, vol. 558, cols 1707–16).
52 *Crossman Diary*, p. 533 (2 November 1956).
53 House of Commons, 1 November 1956 (*Hansard*, vol. 558, cols 1707–16).
54 *News Chronicle*, 5 November 1956.
55 *Tribune*, 26 October 1956.

56 House of Commons, 8 November 1956 (*Hansard*, vol. 560, cols 383–93).
57 See Strobe Talbott (ed.), *Khrushchev Remembers* (Deutsch 1974), Penguin edition (1977), pp. 445ff.
58 *Tribune*, 16 November 1956.
59 *The Times*, 19 November 1956.
60 Dalton diary, 'end of 1956'.
61 House of Commons, 5 December 1956 (*Hansard*, vol. 561, cols 1268–83).
62 Ibid. (cols 1471, 1570).
63 *Crossman Diary*, pp. 556–7 (18 December 1956).

Chapter Twenty-three: 'The Gaitskell–Bevan Axis'

1 Janet Morgan (ed.), *The Backbench Diaries of Richard Crossman* (Hamish Hamilton and Jonathan Cape 1981), p. 570 (25 January 1957).
2 Philip Williams, *Hugh Gaitskell* (Jonathan Cape 1979), p. 439.
3 *Crossman Diary*, p. 588 (3 May 1957).
4 *Tribune*, 18 January 1957.
5 Michael Foot, *Aneurin Bevan, 1945–1960* (Davis Poynter 1973), Paladin edition (1975) p. 546.
6 TUC Report, 1957, p. 461, quoted in Williams, op. cit., p. 447.
7 Michael Foot to Hugh Massingham, 15 July 1957, quoted in Williams, op. cit., pp. 447–8.
8 *Tribune*, 5 October 1956.
9 Ibid., 19 July 1957.
10 Ibid., 23 August 1957.
11 Ibid., 26 July, 13 September 1957.
12 *News of the World*, 21 July 1957, quoted in *Tribune*, 26 July 1957.
13 Williams, op. cit., p. 449.
14 Geoffrey Goodman, *The Awkward Warrior: Frank Cousins: His Life and Times* (Davis Poynter 1979), p. 148.
15 *Crossman Diary*, p. 609 (26 September 1957).
16 Ibid.
17 *News Chronicle*, 3 October 1957.
18 Ibid.
19 *Tribune*, 4 October 1957.
20 Ibid., 11 October 1957.
21 House of Commons, 14 May 1952 (*Hansard*, vol. 500, cols 1511–20).
22 Speech in New Delhi, 28 March 1957 (Foot, op. cit., p. 550).
23 *The Times*, 6 May 1957.
24 House of Commons, 19 December 1956 (*Hansard*, vol. 562, cols 1398–1407).
25 *Tribune*, 24 May 1957.
26 House of Commons, 4 June 1957 (*Hansard*, vol. 571, cols 1080–2).
27 Harold Macmillan, *Riding The Storm* (Macmillan 1971), p. 298; Macmillan to Charles Hill, 5 June 1957, in Foot, op. cit., pp. 550–1n.
28 House of Commons, 4 June 1957 (*Hansard*, vol. 571, cols 1080–2).
29 Williams, op. cit., p. 455.

30 *Tribune*, 27 September 1957.
31 Jennie Lee in *Tribune*, 18 October 1957.
32 *Crossman Diary*, p. 608 (26 September 1957).
33 Ibid., p. 610 (27 September 1957).
34 Ibid., p. 614 (30 September 1957).
35 Ibid.
36 Goodman, op. cit., p. 158.
37 Foot, op. cit., p. 569.
38 *Crossman Diary*, p. 619 (4 October 1957).
39 *The Times*, 2 October 1957.
40 *Labour Party Annual Conference Report, 1957*, pp. 163–79.
41 Foot, op. cit., p. 571.
42 *Crossman Diary*, p. 619 (4 October 1957).
43 *Labour Party Annual Conference Report, 1957*, pp. 179–83.
44 *Crossman Diary*, p. 619 (4 October 1957).
45 *Labour Party Annual Conference Report, 1957*, pp. 179–83.
46 *News Chronicle*, 4 October 1957.
47 Foot, op. cit., p. 574.
48 *Tribune*, 11 October 1957.
49 *Labour Party Annual Conference Report, 1957*, pp. 179–83.
50 *News Chronicle*, 4 October 1957.
51 *Crossman Diary*, p. 619 (4 October 1957).
52 *Daily Telegraph*, 4 October 1957.
53 *Tribune*, 11 October 1957.
54 E.g. House of Commons, 20 February 1958 (*Hansard*, vol. 582, cols 1405–19).
55 *Tribune*, 11 October 1957.
56 *New Statesman*, 12 October 1957.
57 See Mark Jenkins, *Bevanism: Labour's High Tide* (Spokesman 1979), pp. 260–2.

Chapter Twenty-four: The Confusions of a Shadow Foreign Secretary

1 Janet Morgan (ed.), *The Backbench Diaries of Richard Crossman* (Hamish Hamilton and Jonathan Cape 1981), p. 621 (24 October 1957).
2 Jennie Lee, *My Life With Nye* (Jonathan Cape 1980), Penguin edition (1981) p. 279.
3 *Crossman Diary*, p. 751 (5 June 1959).
4 *Tribune*, 18 October 1957.
5 *New Statesman*, 12 October 1957.
6 Hugh Dalton diary, 18 June 1958.
7 *Tribune*, 23 May, 6 June 1958.
8 Ibid., 30 August 1958.
9 House of Commons, 8 November 1956 (*Hansard*, vol. 560, cols 383–93).
10 Ibid., 19 December 1956 (vol. 562, cols 1398–1407).
11 *Tribune*, 9 March 1956.
12 Ibid., 27 September 1957.
13 Ibid., 9 March 1956, 12 July 1957.

14 *The Times*, 2 October 1957.
15 *Tribune*, 11 October 1957.
16 Ibid., 9 January 1959.
17 House of Commons, 19 December 1956 (*Hansard*, vol. 562, cols 1398–1407).
18 *Tribune*, 23 November 1956.
19 House of Commons, 19 December 1956 (*Hansard*, vol. 562, cols 1398–1407).
20 E.g. *Tribune*, 17 February, 6 April and 11 May 1956, 21 June 1957, 3 and 17 January, 7 February, 7 March, 11 April and 20 June 1958; House of Commons, 20 February, 10 June and 30 October 1958, and 8 July 1959 (*Hansard*, vol. 582, cols 1405–19; vol. 589, cols 45–62; vol. 594, cols 331–48; vol. 608, cols 1380–98).
21 *Tribune*, 27 January 1956.
22 House of Commons, 20 December 1957 (*Hansard*, vol. 580, cols 750–62).
23 *Tribune*, 14 March 1958.
24 House of Commons, 4 December 1958 (*Hansard*, vol. 596, cols 1381–93).
25 E.g. *Tribune*, 23 November 1956.
26 Ibid., 15 August 1958.
27 Ibid., 8 August 1958.
28 House of Commons, 14 March 1957, 20 February 1958 (*Hansard*, vol. 566, cols 1333–45; vol. 582, cols. 1405–19).
29 Philip Williams (ed.), *The Diary of Hugh Gaitskell* (Jonathan Cape 1983), p. 464 (9 March 1956); *Tribune*, 23 December 1955, 23 August 1957.
30 House of Commons, 16 and 17 July 1958 (*Hansard*, vol. 591, cols 1353–61, 1446–53); *Tribune*, 25 July 1958.
31 House of Commons, 14 March 1957 (*Hansard*, vol. 566, cols 1333–45).
32 *Tribune*, 6 January, 5 and 19 October 1956, 4 and 11 January 1957, 5 September and 21 November 1958.
33 House of Commons, 14 March 1957 (*Hansard*, vol. 566, cols 1333–45); *Tribune*, 1 February, 17 May 1957.
34 E.g. House of Commons, 20 December 1957 (*Hansard*, vol. 580, cols 750–62).
35 Ibid., 23 July 1957 (vol. 574, cols 333–41).
36 Ibid., 19 December 1956 (vol. 562, cols 1398–1407).
37 Speech at *Tribune* rally, Brighton, 1 October 1957 (*The Times*, 2 October 1957).
38 *Tribune*, 2 August 1957.
39 Ibid., 12 December 1958.
40 House of Commons, 4 December 1958 (*Hansard*, vol. 596, cols 1381–93).
41 Ibid., 20 December 1957 (vol. 580, cols 750–62).
42 *Crossman Diary*, p. 642 (18 December 1957).
43 House of Commons, 20 December 1957 (*Hansard*, vol. 580, cols 750–62).
44 *Crossman Diary*, p. 656 (28 January 1958).
45 Ibid., p. 674 (10 March 1958).
46 Ibid., p. 677 (19 March 1958).
47 *The Times*, 4 November 1957.
48 Ibid., 14 April 1958.
49 Speech at London Labour Conference, 27 April 1958 (ibid., 28 April 1958).
50 See Philip Williams, *Hugh Gaitskell* (Jonathan Cape 1979), pp. 496–9.
51 *Crossman Diary*, p. 750 (5 June 1959).
52 Ibid., pp. 753–4 (10 June 1959).

53 Ibid., p. 759 (23 June 1959).
54 Ibid., pp. 755–6 (18 June 1959).
55 Ibid., pp. 726–7 (18 December 1958).
56 Michael Foot, *Aneurin Bevan, 1945–1960* (Davis Poynter 1973), Paladin edition (1975) pp. 611, 614.
57 *Crossman Diary*, p. 723 (14 November 1958).
58 Ibid., p. 657 (28 January 1958).
59 Ibid., p. 662 (29 January 1958).
60 *The Times*, 8 December 1958.
61 Foot, op. cit., pp. 543–4.
62 *Tribune*, 5 July 1957.
63 *The Times*, 30 October, 6, 13 and 14 November 1957.
64 *Crossman Diary*, p. 574 (14 February 1957).
65 Jenny Nicholson, 'Death in Venice', *Spectator*, 1 March 1957.
66 *Crossman Diary*, p. 574 (14 February 1957).
67 Foot, op. cit., p. 536.
68 *Crossman Diary*, p. 632 (22 November 1957).
69 See ibid., pp. 628–32 (22 November 1957); Foot, op. cit., p. 536; Jennie Lee, op. cit., p. 285.
70 See Iain Adamson, *The Old Fox: A Life of Gilbert Beyfus* (Muller 1963), pp. 236–47; and extensive correspondence in *The Times* and *Spectator*, April to September 1978.
71 *Spectator*, 15 April 1978.
72 *Crossman Diary*, p. 631 (22 November 1957).
73 *The Times*, 23 May 1978.
74 *Spectator*, 1 March 1957.
75 *Labour Party Annual Conference Report, 1960*, p. 97.
76 See Williams, op. cit., pp. 519–21; Foot, op. cit., pp. 617–21; Jennie Lee, op. cit., p. 284.
77 Private information (Sir Patrick Reilly).

Chapter Twenty-five: Labour in the Affluent Society

1 Speech at Bedford, 21 July 1957.
2 House of Commons, 28 July 1959 (*Hansard*, vol. 610, cols 420–9).
3 Speech at Durham Miners' Gala, 18 July 1959 (*The Times*, 20 July 1959).
4 Speech at Manchester, 22 March 1959 (ibid., 23 March 1959).
5 *Tribune*, 7 November 1958.
6 *The Times*, 2 October 1958.
7 Michael Foot, *Aneurin Bevan, 1945–1960* (Davis Poynter 1973), Paladin edition (1975) pp. 622–7.
8 Ibid.
9 Ibid.
10 *The Times*, 29 September 1959.
11 Janet Morgan (ed.), *The Backbench Diaries of Richard Crossman* (Hamish Hamilton and Jonathan Cape 1981), p. 782 (30 September 1959).

12 Geoffrey Goodman, *The Awkward Warrior: Frank Cousins: His Life and Times* (Davis Poynter 1979), p. 237.
13 *Crossman Diary*, p. 782 (30 September 1959).
14 *The Times*, 7 October 1959.
15 Ibid., 8 October 1959.
16 See Philip Williams, *Hugh Gaitskell* (Jonathan Cape 1979), pp. 537–40.
17 *News of the World*, 11 October 1959.
18 *Tribune*, 16 October 1959.
19 *Crossman Diary*, pp. 789–90 (19 October 1959).
20 Goodman, op. cit., p. 244.
21 *Crossman Diary*, pp. 793–4 (21 October 1959).
22 Ibid., p. 796 (23 October 1959).
23 *Labour Party Annual Conference Report, 1959*, pp. 105–14.
24 Williams, op. cit., pp. 551, 556 (citing interviews with Charles Pannell, Douglas Jay, John Harris, Geoffrey Goodman and Anthony Greenwood).
25 *Labour Party Annual Conference Report, 1959*, pp. 151–5.
26 *News Chronicle*, 30 November 1959.
27 *Daily Telegraph*, 30 November 1959.
28 *Tribune*, 4 December 1959.
29 *Evening Standard*, 30 November 1959.
30 Williams, op. cit., p. 558.
31 Interview, Ian Mikardo.
32 Foot, op. cit., p. 625.
33 House of Commons, 1 December 1959 (*Hansard*, vol. 614, cols 1011–13).
34 Lord Butler, *The Art of Memory* (Hodder & Stoughton 1982), p. 93.
35 House of Commons, 3 November 1959 (*Hansard*, vol. 612, cols 860–76).
36 Foot, op. cit., p. 651.
37 *Crossman Diary*, p. 845 (11 May 1960).

Epilogue: The Mantle of Nye

1 *Daily Express*, 7 July 1960.
2 *Reynolds' News*, 10 July 1960.
3 *Observer*, 10 July 1960.
4 *Guardian*, 7 July 1960.
5 *The Times*, 7 July 1960.
6 *Daily Mail*, 7 July 1960.
7 *Daily Herald*, 7 July 1960.
8 *News Chronicle*, 7 July 1960.
9 *Daily Express*, 7 July 1960.
10 *Daily Mail*, 7 July 1960.
11 Ibid.
12 *Daily Express*, 7 July 1960.
13 *Guardian*, 7 July 1960.
14 Ibid.
15 *News Chronicle*, 7 July 1960.

16 Ibid.
17 Ibid.
18 *Evening News*, 7 July 1960.
19 Paul Foot, *The Politics of Harold Wilson* (Penguin 1968).
20 Janet Morgan (ed.), *The Backbench Diaries of Richard Crossman* (Hamish Hamilton and Jonathan Cape 1981), pp. 969–1043 (February–December 1963).
21 Michael Foot, *Harold Wilson – A Pictorial Biography* (Pergamon 1964).
22 Janet Morgan (ed.), *Richard Crossman: The Diaries of a Cabinet Minister* (Hamish Hamilton and Jonathan Cape 1975, 1976, 1977); Barbara Castle, *The Castle Diaries, 1964–70* (Weidenfeld & Nicolson 1984).
23 Peggy Duff, *Left, Left, Left* (Alison & Busby 1971), p. 77.
24 Robert Harris, *The Making of Neil Kinnock* (Faber 1984); G.M.F.Drower, *Neil Kinnock: The Path to Leadership* (Weidenfeld & Nicolson 1984).
25 *Daily Mail*, 7 July 1960; see also Henry Fairlie, *The Life of Politics* (Methuen 1968), pp. 246–7.

Sources and Select Bibliography

Private Papers

Attlee papers (Bodleian Library, Oxford).
Beaverbrook papers (House of Lords Record Office).
Hugh Dalton papers (London School of Economics).
Tom Driberg papers (Christ Church, Oxford).
Chuter Ede diary (British Library).
Herbert Morrison papers (Nuffield College, Oxford).

State Papers

Cabinet Minutes, 1945–51 (CAB 128).
Cabinet Papers, 1945–51 (CAB 124, 129, 130, 134).
Prime Minister's Office Papers, 1945–6 (PREM 8).

Printed Records

Annual Register.
Labour Party Annual Conference Reports, 1926–1960.
Miners' Federation of Great Britain Conference Reports, 1926.
Parliamentary Debates [House of Commons], Fifth Series, vols 229–614 (1929–1959).

Nuffield Oral History Project

George Strauss interview, 19 January 1962 (Anthony King).
Kenneth Younger interview, 27 December 1961 (Richard Rose).

Biographies, Autobiographies and Diaries

Iain Adamson, *The Old Fox: A Life of Gilbert Beyfus* (Muller 1963).
C.R.Attlee, *As It Happened* (Heinemann 1954).
Fred Blackburn, *George Tomlinson* (Heinemann 1954).
Vincent Brome, *Aneurin Bevan* (Longmans 1953).
George Brown, *In My Way: The Political Memoirs of Lord George-Brown* (Gollancz 1973).
W.J.Brown, *So Far* (Allen & Unwin, 1943).
Alan Bullock, *The Life and Times of Ernest Bevin*, vols 1 and 2 (Heinemann 1960, 1967).
Alan Bullock, *Earnest Bevin: Foreign Secretary, 1945–51* (Heinemann 1983).
T.D.Burridge, *Clement Attlee: A Political Biography* (Jonathan Cape 1985).
R.A.Butler, *The Art of the Possible* (Hamish Hamilton 1971).
R.A.Butler, *The Art of Memory* (Hodder & Stoughton 1982).
Churchill By His Contemporaries: An Observer Appreciation (Observer 1965).
Tom Clarke, *My Lloyd George Diary* (Methuen 1939).
Sir John Colville, *Footprints in Time* (Collins 1976).
Sir John Colville, *The Fringes of Power: Downing Street Diaries, 1939–55* (Hodder & Stoughton 1985).
W.W.Craik, *Bryn Roberts and the National Union of Public Employees* (Allen & Unwin 1955).
Bernard Crick, *George Orwell: A Life* (Secker & Warburg 1980).
Hugh Dalton, *Fateful Years: Memoirs 1931–1945* (Muller 1957).
Hugh Dalton, *High Tide and After: Memoirs 1945–1960* (Muller 1962).
Bernard Donoghue and G.W.Jones, *Herbert Morrison: Portrait of a Politician* (Weidenfeld & Nicolson 1973).
G.M.F.Drower, *Neil Kinnock: The Path to Leadership* (Weidenfeld & Nicolson 1984).
Peggy Duff, *Left, Left, Left* (Alison & Busby 1971).
E.Estorick, *Stafford Cripps; A Biography* (Heinemann 1949).
Harold Finch, *Memoirs of a Bedwellty MP* (Sterling Press, Risca, Newport, Monmouthshire 1972).
Nigel Fisher, *Iain Macleod* (Deutsch 1975).
Michael Foot, *Aneurin Bevan, 1897–1945* (MacGibbon & Kee 1962).
Michael Foot, *Aneurin Bevan, 1945–1960* (Davis Poynter 1973).
Michael Foot, *Harold Wilson – A Pictorial Biography* (Pergamon 1964).
Michael Foot, *Debts of Honour* (Davis Poynter 1980).
Michael Foot, *Loyalists and Loners* (Collins 1986).
Paul Foot, *The Politics of Harold Wilson* (Penguin 1968).
T.R.Fyvel, *George Orwell: A Personal Memoir* (Weidenfeld & Nicolson 1982).
Geoffrey Goodman, *The Awkward Warrior: Frank Cousins: His Life and Times* (Davis Poynter 1979).
Neville Goodman, *Wilson Jameson, Architect of National Health* (Allen & Unwin 1970).
James Griffiths, *Pages From Memory* (Dent 1969).
Robert Griffiths, *S.O.Davies: A Socialist Faith* (Gomer Press 1983).
Kenneth Harris, *Attlee* (Weidenfeld & Nicolson 1982).
Robert Harris, *The Making of Neil Kinnock* (Faber 1984).

Lord Hill of Luton, *Both Sides of the Hill* (Heinemann 1964).

Simon Hoggart and David Leigh, *Michael Foot: A Portrait* (Hodder & Stoughton 1981).

Arthur Horner, *Incorrigible Rebel* (MacGibbon & Kee 1960).

Emrys Hughes, *Sydney Silverman, Rebel in Parliament* (Charles Skilton 1969).

Douglas Jay, *Change and Fortune: A Political Record* (Hutchinson 1980).

Mark Krug, *Aneurin Bevan: Cautious Rebel* (T.Yosselof, New York and London 1961).

Jennie Lee, *Tomorrow Is a New Day* (Cresset Press 1939).

Jennie Lee, *This Great Journey* (MacGibbon & Kee 1963).

Jennie Lee, *My Life With Nye* (Jonathan Cape 1980).

Ronald Lewin, *Churchill as Warlord* (Batsford 1973).

C.E.Lysaght, *Brendan Bracken* (Allen Lane 1979).

Geoffrey McDermott, *Leader Lost: A Biography of Hugh Gaitskell* (Leslie Frewin 1972).

Harold Macmillan, *Winds of Change, 1914–39* (Macmillan 1966).

Harold Macmillan, *Riding The Storm, 1956–59* (Macmillan 1971).

David Marquand, *Ramsay Macdonald* (Jonathan Cape 1977).

Kingsley Martin, *Harold Laski, 1893–1950: A Biographical Memoir* (Gollancz 1953).

Keith Middlemas, *The Clydesiders* (Hutchinson 1965).

Janet Morgan (ed.), *The Backbench Diaries of Richard Crossman* (Hamish Hamilton and Jonathan Cape 1981).

Janet Morgan (ed.), *Richard Crossman: The Diaries of a Cabinet Minister* (Hamish Hamilton and Jonathan Cape 1975, 1976, 1977).

Lord Morrison of Lambeth, *Herbert Morrison: An Autobiography* (Odhams 1960).

Oswald Mosley, *My Life* (Nelson 1968).

Jean Nicol, *Meet Me at the Savoy* (Museum Press 1955).

Nigel Nicolson (ed.), *Harold Nicolson: Diaries and Letters, 1939–45* (Collins 1967).

Ben Pimlott, *Hugh Dalton* (Jonathan Cape 1985).

Ben Pimlott (ed.), *The Second World War Diary of Hugh Dalton, 1940–1945* (Jonathan Cape 1986).

Robert Rhodes James (ed.), *Chips: The Diaries of Sir Henry Channon* (Weidenfeld & Nicolson 1967).

W.T.Rodgers (ed.), *Hugh Gaitskell* (Thames & Hudson 1964).

Emanuel Shinwell, *Conflict Without Malice* (Odhams 1955).

Emanuel Shinwell, *I've Lived Through It All* (Gollancz 1973).

Robert Skidelsky, *Oswald Mosley* (Macmillan 1975).

Strobe Talbott (ed.), *Khrushchev Remembers* (Deutsch 1974).

A.J.P.Taylor, *Beaverbrook* (Hamish Hamilton 1972).

George Thomas, *Mr Speaker: The Memoirs of Viscount Tonypandy* (Century 1985).

Hugh Thomas, *John Strachey* (Eyre Methuen 1973).

'Watchman' (Vyvyan Adams), *Right Honourable Gentlemen* (Hamish Hamilton 1939).

Sir John Wheeler-Bennett (ed.), *Action This Day: Working with Churchill* (Macmillan 1968).

Francis Williams, *A Prime Minister Remembers* (Heinemann 1961).

Philip Williams, *Hugh Gaitskell: A Political Biography* (Jonathan Cape 1979).

Philip Williams (ed.), *The Diary of Hugh Gaitskell* (Jonathan Cape 1983).

Woodrow Wyatt, *Confessions of an Optimist* (Collins 1985).

Other Books

Brian Abel-Smith, *The Hospitals, 1800–1948* (Heinemann 1964).
Paul Addison, *The Road to 1945* (Jonathan Cape 1975).
Paul Addison, *Now the War is Over* (BBC/Jonathan Cape 1985).
R.Page Arnot, *The Miners: Years of Struggle: A History of the Miners' Federation of Great Britain (from 1910 onwards)* (Allen & Unwin 1953).
R.Page Arnot, *South Wales Miners: A History of the South Wales Miners' Federation*, vol. 1, 1898–1914 (Allen & Unwin 1967); vol. 2, 1914–1926 (Cymric Federation Press, Cardiff, 1975).
Ron Bailey, *The Squatters* (Penguin 1973).
Fred Berry, *Housing: The Great British Failure* (Charles Knight 1974).
Aneurin Bevan, *In Place of Fear* (MacGibbon & Kee 1952).
Vernon Bogdanor and Robert Skidelsky (eds), *The Age of Affluence, 1951–64* (Macmillan 1970).
Fenner Brockway, *Inside the Left* (Allen & Unwin 1942).
T.D.Burridge, *British Labour and Hitler's War* (Deutsch 1976).
D.E.Butler, *The British General Election of 1951* (Macmillan 1952).
D.E.Butler, *The British General Election of 1955* (Macmillan 1955).
D.E.Butler and Richard Rose, *The British General Election of 1959* (Macmillan 1960).
David Butler and Anne Sloman, *British Political Facts, 1900–1979* (Macmillan 1980).
Alec Cairncross, *Years of Recovery: British Economic Policy, 1945–51* (Methuen 1985).
Angus Calder, *The People's War: Britain 1939–1945* (Jonathan Cape 1969).
'Celticus' (Aneurin Bevan MP), *Why Not Trust the Tories?* (Fanfare Press, 1944).
G.D.H.Cole, *A History of the Labour Party Since 1914* (Routledge & Kegan Paul 1948).
W.W.Craik, *The Central Labour College, 1909–24* (Lawrence & Wishart 1964).
A.J.Cronin, *The Citadel* (Gollancz 1937).
C.A.R.Crosland, *The Future of Socialism* (Jonathan Cape 1956).
D.J.Davies, *Ninety Years of Endeavour: The Tredegar Workmen's Hall, 1861–1951*.
R.E.Dowse, *Left in the Centre: The Independent Labour Party, 1893–1940* (Longman 1966).
H.M.Drucker, *Doctrine and Ethos in the Labour Party* (Allen & Unwin 1979).
Roger Eatwell, *The 1945–1951 Labour Governments* (Batsford 1979).
Harry Eckstein, *The English Health Service* (Harvard 1958).
Harry Eckstein, *Pressure Group Politics: The Case of the BMA* (Allen & Unwin 1960).
Ness Edwards, *The South Wales Miners' Federation* (Lawrence & Wishart 1938).
Henry Fairlie, *The Life of Politics* (Methuen 1968).
Geoffrey Foote, *The Labour Party's Political Thought* (Croom Helm 1985).
Hywel Francis and David Smith, *The Fed: A History of the South Wales Miners in the Twentieth Century* (Lawrence & Wishart 1980).
Pauline Gregg, *The Welfare State* (Harrap 1967).
John Grigg, *1943: The Victory That Never Was* (Eyre Methuen 1980).
William Harrington and Peter Young, *The 1945 Revolution* (Davis Poynter 1978).
Stephen Haseler, *The Gaitskellites: Revisionism in the British Labour Party, 1951–1964* (Macmillan 1969).
Stephen Haseler, *The Tragedy of Labour* (Blackwell 1980).

Douglas Hill, *Tribune 40: The First Forty Years of a Socialist Newspaper* (Quartet 1977).

Bob Holton, *British Syndicalism, 1900–1914; Myths and Realities* (Pluto Press 1976).

Frank Honigsbaum, *The Division in British Medicine* (Kogan Page 1979).

Leslie Hunter, *The Road to Brighton Pier* (Arthur Barker 1959).

Mark Jenkins, *Bevanism: Labour's High Tide* (Spokesman 1979).

Bill Jones, *The Russia Complex: The British Labour Party and the Soviet Union* (Manchester University Press 1977).

Rudolf Klein, *The Politics of the National Health Service* (Longman 1983).

Almont Lindsay, *Socialised Medicine in England and Wales* (University of North Carolina Press 1962).

Jack London, *The Iron Heel* (1907; Journeyman Press 1984).

R.B.McCallum and Alison Readman, *The British General Election of 1945* (Geoffrey Cumberledge/Oxford 1947).

Peter Malpass and Alan Murrie, *Housing Policy and Practice* (Macmillan 1982).

David E.Martin and David Rubinstein (eds), *Ideology and the Labour Movement* (Croom Helm 1979).

Arthur Marwick, *Britain in the Century of Total War* (Bodley Head 1968).

Stephen Merret, *State Housing in Britain* (Routledge & Kegan Paul 1979).

Ralph Miliband, *Parliamentary Socialism* (Allen & Unwin 1961).

Kenneth O.Morgan, *Wales in British Politics, 1868–1922* (Cardiff 1980).

Kenneth O.Morgan, *Labour in Power, 1945–1951* (Oxford 1984).

C.L.Mowat, *Britain Between the Wars, 1918–1940* (Methuen 1955).

H.G.Nicholas, *The British General Election of 1950* (Macmillan 1951).

Sonia Orwell and Ian Angus (eds), *The Collected Essays, Journalism and Letters of George Orwell* (Secker & Warburg 1968).

John E.Pater, *The Making of the National Health Service* (King Edward's Hospital Fund 1981).

Henry Pelling, *A Short History of the Labour Party* (Macmillan 1965).

Henry Pelling, *Britain and the Second World War* (Fontana 1970).

Henry Pelling, *The Labour Governments, 1945–51* (Macmillan 1984).

Ben Pimlott, *Labour and the Left in the 1930s* (Cambridge 1977).

José Enrique Rodo, *Ariel* (Houghton Mifflin 1922).

A.A.Rogow and Peter Shore, *The Labour Government and British Industry, 1945–51* (Blackwell 1955).

Michael Sissons and Philip French (eds), *The Age of Austerity* (Hodder & Stoughton 1963).

Alan Sked and Chris Cook, *Post-War Britain: A Political History* (Penguin 1979).

Robert Skidelsky, *Politicians and the Slump: The Labour Government, 1929–1931* (Macmillan 1967).

David Smith (ed.), *A People and a Proletariat: Essays in the History of Wales, 1780–1980* (Pluto Press).

John Stevenson and Chris Cook, *The Slump: Society and Politics during the Depression* (Jonathan Cape 1977).

A.J.P.Taylor, *English History, 1914–45* (Oxford 1965).

Francis Williams, *The Triple Challenge: The Future of Socialist Britain* (Heinemann 1948).

Pamphlets

A.Bevan, E.J.Strachey and G.Strauss, *What We Saw In Russia* (Hogarth Press 1931).
A.Bevan, B.Castle, R.Crossman, T.Driberg, I.Mikardo and H.Wilson, *It Need Not Happen: The Alternative to German Rearmament* (Tribune 1954).
Aneurin Bevan: An Appreciation of his Services to the Health of the People (Socialist Medical Association 1962).
Going Our Way (Tribune 1951).
Keep Left (New Statesman and Nation 1947).
Keeping Left (New Statesman and Nation 1950).
One Way Only (Tribune 1951).
Plan For Britain: A Collection of Essays Prepared for the Fabian Society (Routledge 1943).

Articles

J.Graham Jones, 'Evan Davies and Ebbw Vale: A Note', *Llafur*, vol. 3, no. 3 (1982).
Philip Williams, 'Foot-Faults in the Gaitskell–Bevan Match', *Political Studies*, vol. XXVII, no. 1 (March 1979).
Sian Rhiannon Williams, 'The Bedwellty Board of Guardians and the Default Act of 1927', *Llafur*, vol. 2, no. 4 (1979).

Newspapers and journals

British Medical Journal
Daily Express
Daily Herald
Daily Mail
Daily Mirror
Daily News
Daily Telegraph
Economist
Evening News
Evening Standard
Lancet
Listener
Llafur
Manchester Guardian
Merthyr Express
News Chronicle
News of the World
New Statesman
Observer
Plebs
Reynolds' News

South Wales Weekly Argus
Spectator
Sunday Chronicle
Sunday Times
The Times
Tribune
Western Mail

Index

Index

Index

Index

Index